INSIDE THE WORLD'S TOUGHEST PRISON

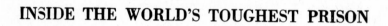

WHEREAS, JOSEPH E. RAGEN, HAS COMPLETED TWENTY YEARS OF SERVICE AS WARDEN OF THE PENITENTIARIES AT JOLIET, ILLINOIS, AND WHEREAS, IN THAT PERIOD OF TIME, HE HAS INAUGURATED AND ESTABLISHED A PROGRAM OF PRISON ADMINISTRATION WHICH HAS BEEN ADOPTED BY MANY PENAL INSTITUTIONS THROUGHOUT THE UNITED STATES, BY ESTABLISHING A PROGRAM OF CUSTODY FIRST, WITH HUMANE DISCIPLINE, REHABILI- TATION, CLASSIFICATION, VOCATIONAL AND ACADEMIC SCHOOLS FOR TRADES AND HIGHER LEARNING, INDUSTRIAL SHOPS AND A FARM PROGRAM TO PRODUCE STATE NEEDS AND EMPLOYMENT, MEDICAL AND MENTAL TREATMENT FOR THOSE IN NEED,

REMODELING THE MEDIEVAL JOLIET BRANCH, THE FARM, NEW BUILDINGS AT STATEVILLE, AND UNIQUE LAND- SCAPING TO FIT HIS PROGRAM, A MERIT SYSTEM FOR EMPLOYEES WHERE QUALITY AND ABILITY IS RECOGNIZED.

WHEREAS, JOSEPH E. RAGEN, HAS BY HIS UNQUESTIONABLE INTEGRITY, BY HIS REFUSAL TO COMPROMISE BETWEEN RIGHT AND WRONG, BY HIS CONSTANT PERSONAL VIGILANCE, BY HIS FAIRNESS AND BY HIS COURAGE, HAS BROUGHT NATIONAL DISTINCTION TO THE STATE OF ILLINOIS, AND THE CITY OF JOLIET, AND HAS RENDERED A SERVICE OF IMMEASURABLE VALUE TO ALL CONCERNED.

NOW THEREFORE BE IT RESOLVED, THAT WE, THE EMPLOYEES OF THIS INSTITUTION AND INTERESTED CITIZENS, CAUSE THIS RESOLUTION TO BE WRITTEN ON A BRONZE PLAQUE AND BE PERMANENTLY FIXED TO THE INSTITUTION AT STATEVILLE, SO THAT IT WILL BE A PERPETUAL TRIBUTE TO AN OUTSTANDING AMERICAN, JOSEPH E. RAGEN, AND THAT IT WILL LIKEWISE SERVE AS A REMINDER TO ALL PUBLIC OFFICIALS AND EMPLOYEES OF THE NECESSITY OF CHARACTER, DEVOTION TO DUTY, FAIRNESS AND COURAGE IN THEIR DAILY WORK, WITH THE HOPE THAT THE HIGH EXAMPLE SET BY JOSEPH E. RAGEN WILL BE AN INSPIRATION TO ALL WHO FOLLOW HIM.

DATED THIS 1ST DAY OF JULY, A.D., 1955

HOW A PRISON Housing Thousands of
Tough Convicts is kept literally free
from riots and escapes.

Inside The World's
Toughest Prison

By

JOSEPH E. RAGEN

Director, Department of Public Safety
State of Illinois
Springfield, Illinois

Formerly, Warden, Joliet-Stateville Prisons
Joliet, Illinois

and

CHARLES FINSTON

Political Editor, Chicago American

CHARLES C THOMAS · PUBLISHER

Springfield · Illinois · U.S.A.

CHARLES C THOMAS • PUBLISHER
BANNERSTONE HOUSE
301-327 East Lawrence Avenue, Springfield, Illinois, U.S.A.

© *1962, by* CHARLES C THOMAS • PUBLISHER
Library of Congress Catalog Card Number: 60-53285

*With THOMAS BOOKS careful attention is given to all details of
manufacturing and design. It is the Publisher's desire to present books
that are satisfactory as to their physical qualities and artistic possibilities
and appropriate for their particular use. THOMAS BOOKS will be true
to those laws of quality that assure a good name and good will.*

Printed in the United States of America

FOREWORD

In this book, I have attempted to put on record much of the information and knowledge I possess concerning the administration of a maximum security penitentiary. It is to be remembered that connected with this maximum security prison is an honor farm to which men are assigned who were maximum security risks when they were received but during their stay in the institution demonstrated they could be trusted, thereby earning assignment to this minimum security division.

Aerial view of Stateville Penitentiary, Joliet, Illinois. In the foreground is the main entrance gate, which is separated from the administration building (rectagular structure which is just outside the Stateville prison wall) by an oval shaped garden. Inside the wall are various circular cell houses and other structures.

The Joliet-Stateville institutions are among the world's largest from the standpoint of physical size, and were the largest in inmate population in 1939. Experts on and students of penology will undoubtedly appreciate the magnitude of the administrative problems involved in running these or any other prisons.

The Joliet, or so-called "Old Prison" (recently completely re-modeled and made modern) has a capacity of some 1,200 inmates. The Stateville prison, which is located some five miles away, has some 3,300 inmates. Most prisons are over-crowded, and it is my opinion that to maintain proper custody and afford better rehabilitation, there should be no more than 1,500 inmates in any institution; 1,000, properly classified and placed in the institution especially designated for their type, would be more practical.

Lines marching from High School to lunch. Stateville, 1959.

Both institutions have been under my jurisdiction as warden since October, 1935, with the exception of an eighteen month period when I was with the U. S. Department of Justice. Prior to 1935, I was warden of the prison at Menard, Illinois.

While I stake no claims to recognition as the top authority on prison administration, I have been summoned to survey and act as consultant and advisor on prison methods, procedures and operations in 20 states as well as in Canada, particularly after disastrous inmates' riots and demonstrations in some of these areas.

We have been fortunate in Joliet to have experienced a minimum of trouble in recent years, even though the great majority of the population is made up of recidivists, long-term men, troublemakers, etc. This is due chiefly to tight security measures; strict, but fair discipline, and loyal, qualified personnel.

Each assignment is charged to a competent employee, who is held responsible for its operation; never placed in the hands of an inmate or group of inmates. Certainly, inmates who have failed in society are not competent to be charged with, or held responsible for, any part of a prison operation, and leading or supervising other failures.

Inmates who have taken advantage of the program offered to better themselves will tell you that prisons have a definite program. Prisons governed by rules that are strict but fair, and supervised by competent personnel are much easier to serve time in than those that are loosely operated.

These measures, on top of classification according to type, a broad work, religious, educational, industrial and recreational program, are designed to contribute to the rehabilitation of criminals.

The contents of this book, if adhered to by other prison officials (although a few do not share my views), would help them to achieve maximum prison security and an orderly administration. I fully realize that what I have written does not embrace all there is to be known about administering a prison. New situations arise daily which challenge the ingenuity of all prison officials, but with loyal, properly trained personnel who know and realize the importance of following practical rules and regulations, the desired end can be accomplished.

Here, I have presented in detail, pertinent data, including rules and regulations that have been compiled after many years of experience; information that has enabled officials at Joliet-Stateville to boast a near-perfect record over a period of years, at least when measured in terms of inmate upheavals, escapes or worse. This does not mean that trouble won't erupt tomorrow, or the next day. We always expect it, look for it and are ready to deal with it. There can never be a let-up. No one should lull himself into the belief that "it can't happen here." There must be definite rules and regulations, and they must be enforced consistently.

It must be remembered that there are never any secrets in a prison. The so-called prison grapevine is a constant channel of information, true or false. However, prison officials must make sure that the grapevine is a two-way street.

The title of this book is based on the fact that the Joliet-Stateville prisons undoubtedly house many of the world's toughest inmates, most of whom come from the Chicago area. They may have made headlines in the news as criminals, but after they are committed here they lose their "big shot" underworld status. Each inmate is treated alike — there are no favorites.

Needless to say, mistakes can be made by prison officials, but one of the watchwords we adhere to closely is that we try not to make the same mistake twice. Every rule, regulation and order which has been issued over a period of years (and I issue them all), is aimed at averting a second mistake which can be disastrous to employees as well as inmates.

One of the basic essentials for an efficient prison administration is that there be no political interference with the activities of the warden or any employee, or any political connivance aimed at benefiting any inmate. This is paramount. We know from experience that political interference of any kind disrupts and disorganizes the serenity of a well operated institution.

There are some people who would have the world believe that prisons are great houses of mystery; that with proper treatment, all confined felons can be transformed into good citizens. Any competent and qualified prison employee will tell you that the people confined in prisons are human beings; some can be re-educated or transformed and will be good citizens after release;

many, if released too soon, will return to crime; others will be problems all of their lives, dangerous if released and should by no means be returned to society but retained in confinement and given proper treatment and care.

I feel everyone is an individual and should be treated accordingly, and in my opinion, a more practical approach is best. There is definitely a place in prison treatment for professional people, but they must take a more practical approach and use less theory. Many professional people have found that theory is not the complete answer, and it has proved very embarrassing to some individuals. Experience has taught me that we must be practical in all phases of prison administration and in releasing felons.

Prison populations in America are increasing each year. In my opinion one of the principal ways to decrease prison populations is to stop the cause — the delinquent child on the street today who will be the prisoner of tomorrow. Children must have proper parental care (a foster home if need be), love, guidance, religion, education, etc. A home, not an institution, is the place to raise good citizens.

Prisons are a tremendous investment of the taxpayers' money, and in reality, in addition to confining felons, are big business. If a windstorm came along today and destroyed the prisons at Joliet, it would cost approximately $150,000,000 to replace the loss.

Readers of this book should realize that I feel there is room for improvement in dealing with violators of all types, juvenile and adult. I am hopeful that my ideas on prison administration, definite and indeterminate sentences, the death penalty, and other controversial and provocative subjects will be accepted in the right spirit. After all, they are based on my experience only.

I would certainly be remiss and unappreciative if I failed to pay tribute to the unswerving loyalty, patience and moral support of my wife, Loretta; my daughter, Jane; and my son, Bill, during my years as a prison official.

It was necessary for me to devote much of my time, day and night, over a long period of years converting a loose, old-fashioned, unworkable, and insecure system of custody, into one that I feel is practical and operating to the advantage of both personnel and inmates and, to the benefit of the public. It was impossible to spend much time with my family. I can only say that without their love and understanding, I could have accomplished little or nothing. Details of those troubles have been narrated vividly in a book called *Warden Ragen of Joliet*, which was authored by Gladys A. Erickson.

It was my good fortune, however, to be able to provide my children with good educations, and watch them grow into model adults. Both are now parents, and I might add that I am now enjoying with my grandchildren some of the things I missed with Jane and Bill as youngsters.

I wish also to stress the unreserved support I received from six governors under whom I have served — Governors Henry Horner, John Stelle, Dwight H. Green, Adlai E. Stevenson, William G. Stratton, and Otto Kerner.

Through the years, each governor has made it possible for me to develop further the improvement program I have nurtured.

I also wish to pay my admiration and respect to all Directors of the Department of Public Safety under whom I served directly — A. L. Bowen, T. P. Sullivan, Donald Walsh, Thomas O'Donnell, Michael F. Seyfrit and Joseph D. Bibb. All understood and sympathized with my goal and gave me unlimited backing.

This, too, is my opportunity to thank publicly, the many associates and employees who have worked at my side through many years. Without their all-out support and complete confidence, many of our accomplishments would have been impossible.

I refer to Assistant Wardens Joseph A. Dort, Lester Acord, Frank J. Pate, Thomas W. Kenny, and Clayton King; captains, lieutenants, sergeants, guards, educational directors and teachers, industrial foremen, maintenance men, clerical aids and a host of others; Dr. Roy G. Barrick, Dr. Arthur V. Huffman and their staff, who developed the department's classification system; and last, but not least, the press, radio, TV and fine citizens of Joliet.

Joseph E. Ragen.

CONTENTS

PART III
ILLINOIS CRIME TRENDS

APPENDICES

INSIDE THE WORLD'S TOUGHEST PRISON

PART I

INCARCERATION OF INMATES

Chapter 1

GENERAL OBSERVATIONS ON CRIME AND PUNISHMENT

It is one of the more specious arguments of the social non-conformist that crime is created by the lawmakers; that without laws there would be no criminals. This, in a certain distorted sense, is quite true, but there remains the far more important truth that so far in their development human beings have not acquired a general intellectual and moral capacity for living harmoniously together in accord with only the material law.

Consequently, divers statutes have been set up, statutes calculated to work for the optimum benefit of the community, the state, and the nation as a whole, and there have been devised penalties to be invoked when said statutes are violated. These penalties vary, of course, according to the gravity of the offense, and it is only at the extreme end of our code that the walls and cross-bars of prison manifest themselves.

Nevertheless, prisons do enter upon the sociological scheme. They are an omnipresent factor in the business of living, and they have some effect upon the daily routine of every citizen in the country. Taxes are collected to build them, and taxes are collected to maintain them. Further, many thousands of persons schedule their lives according to the demands of some penal institution or other. There are the employees, and the relatives of the employees; there are the executives and the workers in the various concerns supplying the institution with food and other commodities; there are the police force, the district attorneys, and the parole agents of the towns and cities adjacent to the

5

prison; there are the men and women at the state capitol whose duties include the administration of public works and welfare.

And there are the inmates themselves . . .

This seems to be the hey-day of propaganda. Newspapers, the radio, television, motion pictures of many types, various periodicals and books — all of these are currently replete with axes in the process of being ground. So proficient have the practitioners of this calling become that it is sometimes impossible to obtain the real facts concerning any given situation until long after the situation has ceased to exist.

Such is the case particularly in connection with prison life. I can recall very few occasions where the unbiased, impartial truth of what constitutes a day "on the inside" has been made available to the public. Newspapers with political policies inimical to the incumbent administration strive to create the impression that penitentiary inmates live in relative luxury. Many magazines of the "sensational" variety publish arcticles and "true life" stories purporting to demonstrate that penal institutions are merely a sort of half-way house at which criminals stop to renew old friendships, form new ones, and perfect plans for a "job" of monstrous criminal magnitude. Motion pictures would have us believe that the average inmate divides his time between suffering the bestial brutality of guards, and plotting the mass escape which will be put down by the authorities — to the accompaniment of many weird and throbbing sound effects — in the last reel.

The fact, of course, is that none of these conditions, however diverting they all may be to the followers of fiction, actually exist in a well-managed penitentiary. Inmates are permitted that degree of personal freedom that is consistent with maximum security; their standard of living is selected for them with the objective of making their forced sojourn as economical as possible to the state and as comfortable as possible for the men themselves, while being afforded no opportunity for large scale scheming.

But if the modern prison is by no means a play-house, neither is it a medieval dungeon. The day is past when it was considered justifiable to leave a man locked in his cell for a long period of years, with only his thoughts and a quantity of oakum to keep him company. Today, many penal administrations are directed

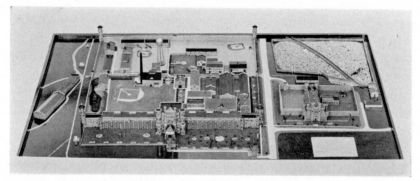

Model of prison at Joliet Branch.

primarily at rehabilitation and reform. Progressive penologists proceed on the assumption that inmates are human, rather than a race apart, and that their life within the walls will be composed of some integers in the human equation as is life "on the outside." There will be humor, pathos, work, play, friendships, enmity — all the multitudinous intangibles that make a mortal tick.

It may be surprising that a warden could attain as great a degree of familiarity with his charges' intimate thoughts and actions. The explanation is quite simple. A warden overhears snatches of conversation; he should receive descriptions — from officers and even from the inmates themselves — of various events in the life of the prison. He reconstructs these fragments into coherent scenes, and thus is able to project himself, as it were, into the characters of many of the men "doing time."

Much has been written and spoken of the "grapevine," that supposedly mysterious agency for the sending and receiving of information. Actually, the "grapevine" is nothing more or less than a word-of-mouth exchange of interesting facts, a gossip train.

And it would be an extremely incapable warden who could not catch an occasional ride on that train. A good warden will make it his business to visit most assignments in his institution daily. No prison can be run well from an armchair in a comfortable office.

For many years it was unfortunate but seemingly true that very few of the really "big time" criminals ever found their way into a penitentiary. Only during the past few years have most of the police forces and courts of this country succeeded in separating themselves from the influence of predatory politicians.

The type of men we see in prisons today, and I particularly refer to Joliet, has changed to a great degree in the past twenty years. They still are received for the same crimes, but there is a difference in the way they violate the law. There is no pattern.

In the "old days" a robber was a robber so-to-speak; a burglar, a burglar; a confidence man, a confidence man, as the name implied. His crime was his "profession" and particularly so if he was a repeater. Many of them were vicious, others had fallen by various means, but there was honor among thieves, so-to-speak.

These people stuck to their "profession" — their word was good to a degree and they were not petty and changeable like a majority of men received today. It is not an unusual thing now to find a man here on his first offense for robbery, second offense, burglary, third for confidence game, etc., or for a combination of crimes. A great percentage are unpredictable. Their word is not good and they go into a tailspin without giving consideration to what the final result may be.

Previously, a prisoner planned his crime, committed it and if he was fortunate, (his way of putting it) he was not arrested. If he was caught, it was chalked up as a loss, an occupational hazard, just as in a poker game, — he took a chance and won or lost as the case might be.

Then too, there were fewer delinquent parents. There was more home life and more character displayed.

We have gone far afield in using too much theory, rather than being practical, and until we become more practical, our crime situation will not decrease, but will increase instead.

In my long experience as a prison administrator, I have come to the conclusion that a great many men can be helped if they are properly classified and given proper supervision during their stay in a prison. I also firmly believe that there are men who should never be released. There are others who should serve long terms and some who can be released in a very short time after being received in prison.

Let's be practical and forget a lot of theory.

Who, then, are the men that fill the prisons? Who are the thousands upon thousands that force society to isolate them for varying periods of time?

They are the casuals and the underprivileged incorrigibles. They are boys whose childhood was insufficiently supervised by their parents, whose earning capacity was never developed by systematic training, whose moral and social faculties were not allowed to expand beyond the stage of self-preservation, and whose native intelligence was insufficient to overcome their other handicaps. Or they are the men who surrender to temptation during an interlude of unaccustomed financial stress.

While it may be reassuring to read headlines exposing the activities of organized criminal groups and announcing the arrest and conviction of the leaders or "syndicate" heads, any feeling that the problem of crime is being solved seems overly optimistic. For every headline concerning the repression of organized criminal groups there are dozens of two-or-three line stories on the inside pages to the effect that yet another unfortunate has been put away for stealing eleven dollars. It is an established fact that concerted action on the part of policing agencies is rapidly diminishing the menace of mobsters. Our major problem revolves around the majority of less notorious and less successful violators who continue to march through the entrance portals of our penitentiaries.

And they will in many cases find conditions far better than they knew when they had their freedom. They will find sanitary surroundings, wholesome food, and an opportunity for subjecting themselves to a much-needed inventory.

But, newspapers to the contrary, they will not find a resort hotel operated for their entertainment. Such latitude is no longer permitted to inmates of Joliet penal institutions. Today, the warden maintains at all times close and personal contact with all phases of prison activity; everything that happens within the walls comes quickly to his attention, and policy is dictated solely by him.

Such a state of affairs, it goes without saying, is a prerequisite of efficient management. The subordinate will almost always reflect the attitude of his superior; slackness on the part of the latter will inevitably produce slackness on the part of the former, and in a prison such laxity is a direct invitation to chaos. As soon as the officers neglect to exercise the proper authority in dealing with the inmates, the inmates will become their own disciplinarians, with disastrous consequences. The keeping of the prisoners is a task entrusted to the warden by the people of the state. To keep them as quiescent as possible during their stay under his jurisdiction is one of the warden's objectives.

The days of personal autonomy should be over for the inmate from the moment he is dressed in until the time he is dressed out, and he must be made to understand this. It is no longer believed that the most effective method of discouraging recidivism is to make prisons so unendurably cruel that no sane man — if a man could leave with all his faculties — would ever do anything to bring about his return to one. Current economic and social factors have made of criminology and penology complex sciences. It is now the specified task of the penitentiary warden to educate the inmates into a conception of behavior consistent with the requirements of civilized progress. Brutal measures benefit no one, and a prison should never be operated as a large torture chamber. But, and this is paramount, adherence to certain rules must be demanded of all inmates at all times. There must be no favoritism exhibited. No man with a number is any better than all other men with numbers. Every effort should be made to provide the men with all possible implements of self-improvement, but there is no room in a penitentiary for pets.

Inmate councils only lead to chaos for the prison administrator who depends upon inmates to help him administer the prison. If we cannot depend upon properly qualified custodial employees, how can we expect law violators to help run a prison?

A prison employee who becomes indebted to a convict for help, other than honorable coöperation in furtherance of the program set up for the well-being of every inmate and employee, is more dangerous than an inmate.

There must be a well-rounded program of maintenance, industries — academic and vocational training — religion, recreation, etc.

There must be discipline for employees, advancement through the ranks, a recreation building, entertainment, etc. when off duty.

Chapter 2

RECEIPT OF NEW INMATES

PROCEDURES

New inmates are received at the diagnostic depot, or receiving station. There are two such depots for the Illinois prison system. One is at Joliet; the other is at Menard.

Since the majority of violators admitted to the penitentiary come from northern portions of the state, the diagnostic depot at Joliet has become the main receiving station as well as the center of professional activity.

When a new inmate is received, his full name and any other necessary identification is checked against the mittimus which accompanied him, in the custody of the sheriff or deputy sheriff. This is done to make sure the inmate's identity corresponds with the necessary admission documents.

The date of delivery of the inmate and the register number (inmate's prison number identification) assigned to him are stamped on the mittimus. The signature of the delivering officer (sheriff or deputy sheriff) is also affixed to the mittimus at this time.

Then the travel voucher is returned to the sheriff or deputy sheriff who completed delivery of the prisoner, and after necessary information has been entered, the voucher is signed by the receiving prison official and the prison seal placed thereon.

The new inmate is then quickly transformed from his civilian status to a prison ward. He is first requested to turn in any money or valuables he may have in his possession. The money

12

is counted in his presence and listed along with other personal valuables.

All personal property is placed in a bag which bears his name. Cash and personal property are forwarded to the chief clerk's office and deposited for safe-keeping. Any property which has no value is considered contraband. The new inmate is requested to sign a release granting authorization for the officer in charge to dispose of contraband items. All personal possessions which are permissible under prison regulations are returned to the inmate.

New inmates are searched thoroughly to be certain every possession on their persons has been accounted for and listed for safe-keeping or disposed of as contraband.

In the next step new inmates are formally enrolled. The "Examination of Prisoner" sheet is filled in. This contains the inmate's committed name; term of court in which he was sentenced; date he was received at the depot; crime for which he was committed; the sentence as directed by the court; racial and other data.

On the reverse side of this sheet is listed again the amount of cash and other valuables inmate carried with him.

The inmate is also asked to read information on the sheet which specifically authorizes institution officials to censor all incoming and outgoing mail. The receiving officer calls this to the inmate's specific attention. The sheet is then signed by the inmate and countersigned by the officer in charge at the depot.

After these preliminaries are completed the inmate is shaved and his hair is trimmed.

He is then put through the institution's Bureau of Identification procedure, which includes being photographed and fingerprinted. Since this is the first precaution against possible escape and the possible need for subsequent detection, the Bureau of Identification document is complete and carries all necessary and pertinent data.

Following this the inmate is sent to the bathroom where all hair on the body is removed after which he is instructed to take a shower. The inmate is then examined thoroughly by a nurse who reports the presence of any contagious disease, vermin or infection which might infect others with whom he comes into contact. He is then ordered to dress in prison garb.

During the next few days the new inmate is subjected to a thorough physical examination by the prison physician and prison dentist. This examination includes a series of typhoid shots, Kahn and undulant fever tests, and vaccination.

Sociologists interviewing new arrival at the Diagnostic Depot, Joliet Branch.

Also, as soon as is possible after his admittance, the new inmate's complete personal history prior to conviction is compiled by the captain at the diagnostic depot. This highlights the inmate's life history, including religious affiliation, marital and family status. At this time, too, the inmate is asked to list relatives and friends with whom he expects to correspond or from whom he expects visits.

The final, and most important, phase of the new inmate admission procedure is the examination given by the Classification Board. This takes from three to six weeks. The board is composed of trained sociologists, psychologists, and psychiatrists. The chief task of this board is to direct the program for the scientific study and classification of prisoners.

The Division of the Criminologist directs and supervises the classification program under which each incoming inmate is microscopically analyzed according to his personality make-up, capacity for improvement and reform, and disposition to respond to correctional treatment.

Inasmuch as the criminologist and his staff do not have any responsibility for the custody, discipline, treatment or training

Protestant minister interviewing inmate, Stateville Penitentiary.

of prisoners, recommendations are outlined in each case concerning the branch of the penitentiary system which may be best

adapted to deal with the inmate's adjustment and training. Broad
suggestions are offered, too, as to the type of cell arrangement
which is best for the new inmate and his aptitude for work,
school and vocational training, health requirements and need for
periodic follow up counseling. These recommendations are advisory only and are submitted for approval, if necessary, of administrative officials in the Illinois Department of Public Safety.

After the extensive examination periods by the Classification
Board are completed, the Captain's office is notified by the institution's mental health department and a transfer order is made
out for the inmate and sent to the Warden for his approval.
Upon receipt of approval from the Warden, the inmate is out-

Father Brinkman interviewing inmate. Stateville Branch, Joliet, Ill.

fitted with regulation state issue clothes and shoes and is transferred to the designated branch.

During the new inmate's stay in the diagnostic depot, one of the basic duties of the captain in charge is to provide him with a copy of the rule book called "Inmate Guidance," provided by the institution. At intervals the assistant warden in charge reviews the rule book and explains in detail each regulation. The inmate is encouraged to ask questions.

Also, during their stay in the diagnostic depot, inmates are interviewed by chaplains of their respective faiths or denominations. They are encouraged to attend a religious service and a majority do.

Chapter 3

CLASSIFICATION OF INMATES

Before new inmates are plunged into the routine of prison life, they undergo one of the most important steps which are aimed at their reform and rehabilitation, and ultimate return to society.

They undergo a thorough examination by the Classification Board, which is part of the Division of the Criminologist.

All classification and diagnostic procedures are conducted under the general direction of the Criminologist. The staff in Illinois numbers five sociologists, two psychiatrists, one psychologist, five stenographers, one clerk and one secretary who are assigned to the Diagnostic Depot at Joliet; two sociologists, one psychologist, and two stenographers at the Pontiac and Dwight institutions; three sociologists, one psychologist, two psychiatrists in the Menard Diagnostic Depot.

When we speak of classification boards and classification of prisoners, what do we mean? By definition, classification is the process of placing things into groups or classes according to some idea or plan.

We have passed far beyond the old method of classifying criminals by physical appearance or merely by type of crime committed. The professional worker in our prisons knows that a prisoner must be understood as an individual before he may be classified. This involves a study in depth of the personality of the criminal who is seriously out of adjustment with himself and the social order.

By personality is meant the whole life of the individual — what he thinks, feels and acts by natural instinct and by habit of social conditioning. The program is based on a study of each prisoner separately, with each of the scientific experts engaged in the study utilizing specialized techniques for the study.

An effective program of rehabilitation must include two main categories. The first is an appraisal of the definite social and vocational deficiencies or lacks in the individual. The second involves planting the seeds of effort which may stimulate the development of socially accepted attitudes to supplant anti-social attitudes or the general haphazard attitude toward life that has nurtured a delinquent behavior.

A number of prisoners come to the institution with varying degrees of economic and social training, but many have never developed their capacities to the point where they are able to compete in our complex society at a level which may be sufficient to sustain themselves or to enable them to assume adult responsibilities in the proper manner.

When these deficiencies arise in combination with delinquent attitudes that are picked up in the environmental process, criminality may result on a situation level.

Of the approximately 5,000 inmates in the Joliet-Stateville institutions, about 80 per cent may be classified, in general, as what we might call normal or sociological offenders. The other 20 per cent of our criminal population might fall into that category in which criminality exists primarily because of deviation of personality.

The first step toward any effective program of rehabilitation is proper segregation in the prison compound. Unfortunately, in Illinois, as in many other states, we do not have available enough institutions to allow for more than general segregation, such as, for example, youthful, improvable offenders; adult, questionably improvable offenders, and adult doubtfully improvable offenders. The ideal setup, of course, would be placement of one man to a cell.

Therefore, recommendations by the Classification Board must include segregation within an institution, if a rehabilitative program is to be at all effective.

These recommendations relate to cell placement, work assignment, and encouragement of the improvable offender to associate with stable inmates who may aid him in a recreation and reformulation of attitudes along acceptable lines; supervision and guidance by qualified personnel.

A thorough knowledge of inter-group relationships within each institution is necessary so that deleterious influences among inmates may be prevented from coming into too close contact with inmates who demonstrate improvable capabilities.

Most of the rehabilitative process in any change in attitude must come from the inmate himself, and only through daily association or contact with the so-called better elements in each prison will he be able to develop a definite and acceptable standard of values, realize some or all of his social mistakes, and begin to formulate new life and social goals which are acceptable outside of prison walls.

The basic philosophy which accompanies removal of offenders from society and their concentration in an institution necessarily makes achievement of a rehabilitative program difficult.

There are many deleterious influences in a prison. Only through careful planning and selected segregation can we hope to keep an inmate from reinforcing the delinquent attitudes which provoked non-conformist behavior prior to his admission to the penitentiary.

The bulk of our inmates are relatively young and immature. Most or all lack a fixed or permanent attitudinal structure. Their records reflect the absence of an established work or employment pattern and they are usually deficient in the area of educational or vocational accomplishment.

It seems to be this group for which there is more hope concerning the probabilities of complete rehabilitation.

Chapter 4

HOW THE CLASSIFICATION BOARD
FUNCTIONS

The development of the classification program came about simultaneously with the study of personality. Early studies cóncentrated on labeling inmates, and not treatment. Personality concepts gradually underwent changing emphasis. Some years ago classification studies were directed toward an interpretation of the criminal act and an evaluation of gross deviations in the personality which were held accountable.

A forward step was achieved when emphasis shifted toward attempting an understanding of the total personality, the aims, the drives, and underlying motivation for the individual's complete behavior pattern, in contrast to a limited appraisal based on the acts for which he was committed.

A later forward step was gained with the realization that an individual's criminal act could only be understood when analyzed and pieced together with his total life adjustment.

Analysis of a criminal's actions is now carried on in a multiple approach, and has been since about 1933. Experts engaged in the analytical work attempt to comprehend the offender's total personality and his social inter-actions with others. It is an integrated approach based on medical-psychiatric, social-sociological and psychological measurements and evaluations.

Individualized studies are carried out by each group of experts. Their impressions and estimates of improvability are coördinated, or synthesized into a succinct, narrative report. This contains an evaluation of criminality, social background, personality assessment, and specific recommendations depending on needs of the inmate being classified.

These reports are distributed to the prison administration, the state Parole and Pardon Board, and the Division of Parole Supervision. The recommendations of the Classification Board are advisory only. The responsibility for implementing these recommendations and administering individualized treatment falls in the sphere of the penal administration.

The State Criminologist, who is the chief administrator of the Diagnostic Depot and supervises activities of the Classification Board, maintains his headquarters at the Joliet Diagnostic Depot. He is also responsible for inmate classification within Pontiac prison; the Menard Prison Diagnostic Depot and the Dwight Reformatory for Women.

The staff has the status of civil servants, governed by Civil Service rules.

It goes without saying that the staff is expected to conduct personal case work in accordance with the principles of progressive corrective practices and the purposes of classification which divide prisoners into specific classes to facilitate their treatment, with a view to their ultimate social rehabilitation.

Particular treatment programs of a psychotherapeutic nature are conducted for inmates placed in detention hospitals and those classified for the Psychiatric division as psychotic, mentally defective, sexually dangerous, or in need of mental treatment.

Reports and relevant documents are compiled at scheduled intervals in connection with parole, pardon and executive clemency hearings, as well as sanity hearings.

CLASSIFICATION CATEGORIES

The following classification categories are in current use within the Illinois State Penitentiary System:

Group   I.   With Psychosis.
Group II.   With intellectual (or mental) deficiency.
          (a) With continuing criminal propensities
          (b) Without continuing criminal propensities,
              i.e. socially improvable.

Group III. Without psychosis or intellectual deficiency.
Group IV. Psychopathic personalities (such as non-conformist, **pathological sexuality, dys-social or anti-social,**
and other specified types.)
Group V. Sexually dangerous persons.

As the classification program is neither rigid nor static, these
categories are considered guideposts. Classification of inmates is
flexible and pertains to the needs of the individual with the long-
range view of his rehabilitation. Generally, youthful first offenders of an improvable type are placed in Pontiac; recidivists are
segregated at Joliet, and questionably improvable first offenders
past the age of twenty-five are sent to Stateville.

Mental defectives (with continuing criminal tendencies), sexually dangerous persons, mentally ill inmates and men in need of
mental treatment are segregated within the Psychiatric Division.
The Menard prison houses generally the ruralite, who is less
sophisticated and less seriously delinquent than those placed at
either Stateville or Joliet. The main objective of the Classification Program as conducted by the Division of the Criminologist
is to render aid in the rehabilitation of offenders and to safeguard
thereby the interests of society.

The Classification Board attempts to place each offender in a
category of relative improvability and to make a prognosis concerning his chances of achieving an accepted adjustment both
within the institution and in the free community. The following
are the categories and definitions used in preparation of the diagnostic studies:

PSYCHOLOGICAL SERVICES

Improvable offender.
Questionably improvable offender.
Doubtfully improvable offender.
Unimprovable offender.

The principle of improvability is the very basis upon which
classifications are to be determined. It is a dynamic and relative,
not a fixed, consideration. Improvability may be defined, arbi-
trarily, as the capacity and disposition of an inmate to improve

himself and to adjust to civilian life, following imprisonment. Capacity and disposition are to be evaluated by the scientific studies of the personality of the individual and by the seasoned judgments of the professional examiners. Whether the subject will be classified as Improvable, Questionably Improvable, Doubtfully Improvable, or Unimprovable, will depend upon the outcome of these desiderata :

The Principle of Prognosis

Favorable prognosis.
Problematical prognosis.
Doubtful prognosis.
Guarded prognosis.
Unfavorable prognosis.

The principal of prognosis is a close analogue of the principle of improvability and has to do with a determination of the degree of improvement the subject has demonstrated or likely can accomplish, and upon his disposition to better himself within the institution and in the free community.

A favorable prognosis suggests both adequate capacity and agreeable disposition toward self-improvement intramurally and extramurally, with a minimum of supervision.

A problematic prognosis indicates either limitation of capacity or fault of disposition in relation to self-betterment and parole adjustment but does not signify serious criminality nor failure on parole.

A doubtful prognosis means that either capacity for self-improvement or disposition to adjust acceptably, or both, are impaired and that failure on parole is likely unless equitable circumstances and adequate supervision can be available.

Guarded prognosis is principally a medical or/and psychiatric term. It is intended, as the word means, to suggest caution or cautiousness as to outcome. Its use in general (not medical) classification prognostics should be revised for those cases which require closest supervision. It serves warning as to potentialities for serious maladjustments.

An unfavorable prognosis means that both capacity and disposition to improve and to adjust are seriously impaired or wanting, and that the subject is not a fit risk for parole.

The Principle of Improvability

The first professional contacts with newly admitted inmates are made by the psychologist. The clinical psychological frame of reference focuses, primarily, attention upon the individual. Within this frame of reference, criminal behavior is viewed as a symptom, the failure of the individual to deal adequately with problems of adjustment. The criminal is one who responds with "acting out" behavior when frustrated. The study of the individual concentrates on his potentialities and shortcomings to arrive at an understanding of the interaction between this personality and the environmental forces exerted upon it. The tools of the psychologist consist of standardized testing procedures through which he attempts to obtain objective data for the final evaluation.

The three main areas of testing are intelligence, vocational interest and personality evaluation. In the first, the three types of test include a literacy test, the Army General Classification Test; a non-verbal groupal test, the Revised Beta Examination; and a more refined intelligence test, the Wechsler-Bellevue Intelligence Scale. The Kuder Preference Record is used to determine an individual's strong inclinations, as well as his dislikes in regard to vocational interests. The third area is explored by tests utilizing projective techniques. These are designed to bring out information about the individual's perception of the environment and his techniques for dealing with it, as well as areas of specific emotional conflict. The three main tests are the Rorschach Method of Personality Diagnosis, the Thematic Apperception Test and the Blacky Pictures.

PSYCHIATRIC SERVICES

Whenever there is any question of mental disorder, or where there appear to be psychiatric implications either within the personality or the offense, the inmate is referred for psychiatric examination. The psychiatrist endeavors to explain criminal behavior in terms of human adjustment, to explain why certain individuals in responding to basic urges and needs resort to anti-social activity. Particular attention is given to the presence of emotional conflicts and repressed painful experiences. The fact that each inmate has failed to adjust in some sense is readily apparent. As only a small proportion of the total number of cases are actually psychotic or pre-psychotic it is necessary for the psychiatrist to have a thorough knowledge of both abnormal and normal personality structures.

If it is determined that the classification is either psychotic or in need of mental treatment, specific recommendations are made for transfer to the Detention Hospital at Stateville for further psychiatric observation. If the need for this placement was merely institutional and transitory, special recommendations are made concerning the special needs of the individual. On the other hand, if the diagnosis is pre-psychotic or with psychosis, classification is made in accordance with the nomenclature recommended by the American Psychiatric Association.

As a functioning member of the Classification Board, the psychiatrist examines and makes suitable treatment recommendation for any inmate whose offense and propensities indicate the possibility of unstable or maladjustive behavior.

SOCIOLOGICAL SERVICES

It is necessary that the sociologist have a thorough knowledge not only of social behavior but of urban areas and processes that take place in delinquent communities that may be factors in the development of a delinquent career. The sociological interview is of utmost importance as community investigations are not feasible. Rapport has to be gained with the classification and specialized techniques of questioning utilized, so that information obtained is valid and reliable.

Prior to sociological interview letters of inquiry about each inmate are sent to persons and institutions, including relatives, employers, clergymen, schools, hospitals, the armed forces, etc., in order to secure information which will show the kind of individual he is and what his former adjustments have been. The purpose of the sociological approach is to understand the individual in relation to his past group experience. It is necessary to make individual case studies in which the individual is the primary object of study. It is necessary that not only facts of inmate's social life are obtained, but also his attitudes, opinions, insight and other essentials which will place him in his social setting.

The data obtained in the interview is then summarized in the initial classification report under three major captions: Offense and Previous Criminal Record, Social Factors, and Personality. In addition to a statement of crime and inmate's version, the sociologist's evaluation as to the type of offender and degree of criminal maturation are included. The second topic presents a summarized life history, emphasizing the degree of socialization and responsibility present at all levels of experience. The concluding portion of the narrative statement sets forth a personality description, incorporating the psychiatric and psychological findings. The conclusion of the report contains an estimate of improvability, prognosis as to further criminal behavior, and recommendations as to segregation and the rehabilitative program.

Chapter 5

TWO NEW INMATES: GEORGE AND TONY

I

What do new inmates talk and think about while they are waiting to be processed for admission by prison officials and oriented for prison life by the Diagnostic Depot?

Cell house interior. Diagnostic Depot. Stateville Branch.

The following conversation between George and Tony, two new inmates, is authentic. It was reproduced some years ago in essence, if not verbatim. George and Tony are actual inmates, disguised, of course, by fictitious names. Both express opinions that may demonstrate an understanding of the problems which institutional authorities face.

Tony was convicted on a charge of armed robbery of a Chicago tavern, in which a brother had been shot and killed. Tony turned to robbery after repeal of the Prohibition act ended his illegal employment as a beer runner for an organized gang. Tony was a court-adjudicated juvenile delinquent at fifteen.

George was sent to prison after being caught trying to pass forged checks in a Chicago currency exchange. He was married and was the father of two children. However, George lacked steady employment and was a heavy drinker, a mixture which compounded his economic plight and upset his family life.

With this background in mind, the following dialogue takes place between George and Tony:

"What's this Diagnostic Depot for?" George asked, after supper on the first day.

"It's a new one on me," Tony confessed. "They didn't have nuttin' like this when I done my other bit here. But from what some of the boys was sayin' today out in the yard, I figure they give you a good goin' over here, see? I don't mean no rough stuff, they just find out what your slant on t'ings is, an' what sort of work you t'ink you can do, an' all like that there."

"Who is 'they'?" George wanted to know.

"Oh, there's the croaker, an' the bug doctor, an'. . . . ."

" 'Bug doctor'? What's a 'bug doctor'?"

"That's one of them 'syko gees.' You know; a doc what can tell if you're bugs or not, an' how soon you're liable to get that way"

"Oh, you mean a psychiatrist."

"That's it. The way I get the dope, he asks you a bunch of questions an' then recommends what oughta be done witcha. Sounds phoney to me. If a guy's gonna blow his top, he can do it just as good wit'out somebody tells him about it in advance."

"Yes," said George, "but maybe if you know about it beforehand you wouldn't do it. I mean, if a doctor told me there was something wrong with me, I'd certainly try to overcome it."

"Maybe so," Tony replied disinterestedly, "me, all I want is that they leave me alone. I shook my time before wit'out none of these here dizzy new methods bein' used on me, an' I can do it again the same way. They won't get no information outa me that I don't t'ink they'd oughta have."

"I don't know," George said doubtfully. "It seems to me that there must be some part of us that isn't working right, or we wouldn't be here. Perhaps if we do what these people think we should, we can find out what the trouble is, and cure ourselves."

Tony looked at him for a moment.

"You ain't gonna make it in here, if you go around givin' off hooey like that," he stated after a time. "Anybody who t'inks a policeman is gonna do him anyt'ing but harm is in line for a lot of grief. Anyone connected wit' a penitentiary is the same as a policeman. He may have on different clothes, but he's a copper in his heart."

"That may be," George insisted, "but I still don't see where there is any percentage in going against them. I couldn't beat them on the outside, so what chance would I have in here, where I can't even lam when things get out of control? Besides, I don't believe that any doctor, whether he's practicing in a penitentiary or his own office, would deliberately do anyone harm."

"Aw, go lay down, jerk," Tony said disgustedly. "You gotta get a lot of them whacky ideas out of your head before you'll be worth a dam'. You come down here with a one-to-ten rap on you, an' you try to tell something to a guy like me, what's got to do from now on. I'll bet you clipped some chump for about seven dollars and a half, so now you're gonna show me how I'd oughta behave."

George rose from the stool on which he had been sitting and stepped over to the side of Tony's bunk.

"Listen, hard guy," he said quietly, "I wouldn't try to tell you anything. In the first place, you're too wise to need any advice, and in the second place, I don't like you well enough to care what happens to you. The fact that you may have to do the rest of your life in here doesn't make my time any easier, and all I'm really interested in is my own little stretch. Furthermore, I can't see that it's any of your business whether I sold somebody the Navy Pier, or clouted three nickles out of a pay telephone. As long as I'm in a cell with you, I'll have to get along with you, but let's not talk about anything except the weather, eh?"

"You petty larceny clowns gimme a pain," Tony said. "You steal a coupla dollars, pick up some twist at a ballroom, an' put on a big act. Then when you get knocked off, some dick bats you on the ear, an' right away you wish you'd never left home. Well, I wish you hadn't. I can't stand a monkey what cries."

"Okay, Big Shot," said George; "okay, you're right, and I'm wrong. Forget I ever mentioned the subject, will you? In fact, keep quiet altogether."

Tony sat up in the bunk, anger very prominent in his dark eyes. He was obviously on the point of issuing an invitation to violence, and George seemed equally willing to cut out the chatter and get down to cases. However, at that moment Whitey stopped at the door again.

"I fixed it for you to get a detail while you're here, Tony," Whitey said. "It's only washing dishes down in the kitchen, but you'll be able to get out of the cell, and you can score for a little extra chunk. Your blood test was all right, so there won't be a hold-up on that account."

"How long will it be before I get shipped over to Stateville, Whitey?" Tony queried.

"Four weeks is the usual time they keep you here."

"Four weeks, eh? I'll have to fill my belly while I got the chance. From what you was tellin' me, it might be a long, hard winter. T'anks for takin' care of me, Whitey. When do I start shampooin' them plates?"

"The captain will probably call you right after breakfast," Whitey said.

"Fine, I'll be ready to go as soon as he gives me the office," Tony said.

When Whitey had resumed his progress along the gallery, Tony turned to George.

"See what it means to have friends?" he said proudly. "It

don't take no time at all for a guy wit' friends to get squared around."

The radio, coming on just then, relieved George of the necessity of a reply.

As Whitey had promised, Tony was called out on a detail after breakfast the following morning, leaving George to lie alone in the cell and meditate on the way of the transgressor. He had stopped cursing himself for a fool and was attempting to consider his position with some degree of rationality, when he heard his number called by the officer in charge of the Depot. He stepped to the door and was summoned to the desk by the wave of a blue-clad arm. Having obeyed the summons, he was directed to the opposite side of the cellhouse, where three officers sat in a row. At the first of these, he was ordered to take off all his clothes, after which one of the institution physicians examined him thoroughly. Next, the condition of his teeth was carefully checked by the dentist, and an inmate clerk questioned him concerning the state of his eyes.

When he again had donned the khaki trousers and jacket that distinguished the "fish," as the new men were called, a stenographer, acting on the guard's instructions, took George into one of the offices.

"I've got to get some routine information from you," the stenographer explained, "so don't think I'm just growing curious all of a sudden."

"Shoot," George invited. "My life is an open book, especially since all you have to do is write to Cook County to find out anything I don't feel like telling you."

"You're showing good sense," the stenographer complimented him. "Some guys try to put on the clam act, and all they do is make it hard on themselves."

Then ensued a quarter-hour devoted to the gathering of vital statistics.

"Date and place of birth," said the stenographer.

"July 11, 1908; Newport, Arkansas."

"Father's name, mother's maiden name, their ages, approximately, father's occupation, their nationalities, their present place of residence."

George told him.

"Education?"

"Two years at university."

"Places of employment, and length of time at each one."

That information was also forthcoming.

"Previous convictions?"

"None."

"Married?"

"Yes."

"Children?"

"Two."

"Wife's place of residence?"

"I don't know," George said. "She came down to the County Jail once and told me that she was moving from our apartment, and that she was going to get a divorce just as soon as they'd give it to her."

The stenographer, with a few final flourishes of his shorthand pencil, closed his notebook and discharged him with an air of efficiency.

"Don't let it get you down, pal," he consoled George. "You're lucky to get it over with in a hurry. Mine waited three years before she gave me the air."

George smiled, although with no great enthusiasm.

"Oh, I'll live, I guess," he said, "but sometimes I can't see much use in the effort."

He went back to his cell and relaxed again on the bunk, relaxed so completely that an inmate had to shout twice to awaken him.

"Hey, buddy; you're wanted at the bug doctor's office."

George rolled out, rubbed his eyes open, and followed the speaker to the far end of the cell block and down a short corridor.

"Go right in; he's waiting for you," said the guide.

George, feeling not quite at ease, entered the office. The psychiatrist was seated at a desk, and his demeanor was reservedly friendly. George's confidence came creeping back home.

"Let's see," said the doctor, glancing at some papers in front of him; "you're George . . . . . . , aren't you?"

"Yes, sir."

"Sit down, George. Have a cigarette? Now, then; tell me all about yourself. Where did you go to school?"

"I finished grade school at Newport, Arkansas, high school at Little Rock, and then I went to university on a scholarship. I completed two years there."

"Why didn't you finish?"

"I got married instead."

"I see. Any children?"

"Yes, sir; two. A boy and a girl."

"How old are they?"

"The boy's six, and the girl's seven."

"Were you and your wife living together at the time of your arrest?"

"Well, technically, I guess we were. You see, the marriage didn't work out very well. It was one of those 'on the bounce' affairs."

"I don't quite understand," the doctor said.

"Well," George elucidated, "there was a girl in St. Louis. I met her while I was going to school, and one thing more or less led to another. Her family didn't approve, though. They have about half the money in Missouri, and I guess they didn't think I was particularly eligible. So I got drunk one night, took a bus to Chicago, met a young lady, and married her. I got a job and didn't bother going back to college. My wife and I got along pretty well, all things considered, for over two years. Then her mother moved to Chicago, and she started spending most of her time at our place. I raised a little hell about it, and the mother-in-law took a couple of rooms at a residential hotel. After that whenever we had a slight difference of opinion, my wife would trot over to dear mother. It went on like this for five years, and finally it got me down. I started hitting the bottle. I was drunk about half the time, and naturally I lost my job. I lost four jobs, to be exact, and after the last one, I didn't bother looking for work any more. I got to know a chap who sold rubber checks, and I began passing them in cigar stores, grocery stores, currency exchanges, wherever I could. And that's about the whole story."

"How many checks did you pass?"

"I was convicted on three counts, with the sentences running concurrently."

"That wasn't my question. I asked how many checks you passed."

"Would you consider it impertinence if I didn't answer that?"

"Not at all." The psychiatrist rubbed his cigarette against the bottom of the ash tray. "It must have taken lots of nerve to walk up and offer a check you knew to be worthless," he suggested.

"No," said George, "it didn't take much nerve. All it took was a couple of stiff hookers of rye."

The psychiatrist again thumbed through the documents bearing on George's case, and as he did so, he disclosed a print of the prison picture for which George had sat immediately upon entrance into the Depot. It was a remarkably misinforming picture. A three-days' growth of beard effectively disguised the natural amiability of the mouth; the rather reddish hair was in disarray; and the blue eyes were rendered almost opaque by fatigue, worry and bad photography.

"I think your best plan," said the doctor to George after some moments of thought, "is to take things as easily as you can. Do whatever work you are assigned to do, and don't worry any more than you have to. At the present time, you seem to be in an excessively nervous condition; this will undoubtedly disappear as the alcohol works its way out of your system. I'll see you again some time within the next year, and I want to see you a greatly improved man."

"I'll do my best, doctor," George promised.

"One other thing," said the doctor, as George rose to leave, "it would be a great disappointment to me if, after investigating your statements, I should find that you haven't been telling me the truth. So many men think they can fool me by lying."

"Everything I've told you is gospel," George said.

"I hope it is. Well, good luck. Here's a friendly tip. Do your own time. Don't let other men talk you into doing anything fool-ish, and don't tell too many people your business."

"I won't," George assured him, and left the office. On the way out, he encountered Tony.

"Well, Boy Scout," said Tony, "do you feel better? I suppose you and the bug doctor talked it over and decided how the joint ought to be run. Or did you just pat him on the back an' tell him you liked his work?"

"Why don't you ask him?" George returned, and passed on.

Tony stalked into the psychiatrist's office.

"Look, Doc," he said, before the other could speak, "you an' me might as well understand each other. What you're tryin' to do might be all right for some of these cons wit' short time, but I ain't interested in your syko. You can get all the facts you need outa my record, an' after that you'll just hafta guess."

The doctor leveled an even gaze upon him.

"All right," he said at last. "If that's the way you want it, that's the way it shall be. You may go......'

Later that day, all the fish, Tony and George included, were assembled in a large room where were arranged twenty or thirty chairs of the schoolroom type — that is, one arm which widened into a flat surface for writing upon.

When all were seated, the psychologist entered and distributed to each man a pencil and a folder. The folder contained several pages of printed questions and on the cover was the heading "Intelligence Test."

"There is a time limit to this test," said the psychologist. "Do not turn a page until I tell you to do so, and do not return to a page after we have passed it. If you don't know the answer to any question, take a guess at it. All ready? Turn to Page One.."

After dinner, the captain who was in charge of the Diagnostic Depot stopped at George's cell.

"Can you press clothes?" he asked George.

"Well, I've put a crease in my own pants once or twice," George answered, "but I don't imagine that makes me an expert."

"I guess you could learn; you look intelligent enough. I'll detail you to the pressing room, and see how you make out."

"I'll do my best," George said.

For the next three weeks, George adjusted himself slowly to his new environment. An hour and a half of every day was spent in the recreation yard, where some exciting softball games took place, and where George got acquainted with a number of the other inmates.

He and Tony arrived at an understanding on the second evening.

"Listen, fellah," said Tony, when they had been locked in for the night, "you an' me might as well try to get along as good as we can. We won't never see t'ings the same way, but that don't mean we can't at least be nice. How about it?"

George extended his hand.

"Suits me," he said heartily. "I never did want to argue with you."

"Aw, I'm kinda hard to figure, sometimes. I get hot too easy. Boy, I'll be glad to go over to Stateville. This Depot is all right, I guess, but it'll be good to see some of the boys again. There's one t'ing I don't never want, though; I don't never want to go to that Old Joint. It must be really tough over there, from what they say. This warden's usin' it as a place to bury the boys that get themselves jammed up, an' the second- and third-time losers." "Say," said Tony in sudden apprehension; "that fits me, don't it? Geeze, I hope they don't ship me inside."

His hopes were ill-founded. Possibly the psychiatrist did not feel that Tony had displayed an amenable attitude, or possibly his previous record counted against him. Whatever the cause, the twenty-second day of their residence at the Diagnostic Depot found Tony and six other "fish" transferred to the Old Prison at Joliet, while the rest, among them George, climbed into the conveyance which would take them to Stateville.

II

The Illinois State Penitentiary has several branches. These are: The Old Prison at Joliet (Joliet has been remodeled completely), the New Prison at Stateville, the Southern Branch at Menard, the Women's Prison at Dwight, the Hospital for Criminally insane at Menard — these two being practically the same institution — the Penal Farm at Vandalia, and the Pontiac Prison.

For many years the Women's Prison was located just across the road from the Joliet Branch but in 1933 the female inmates were removed to Dwight, and the building was remodeled and converted into the Diagnostic Depot.

The purpose of the Diagnostic Depot is exactly what its name implies; it is a place where the ailments of incoming inmates may be diagnosed. These ailments, of course, are many and varied, and demand the attention of persons qualified to deal effectively with them.

The first thing done at the depot is to examine the physical condition of the new arrival. Those afflicted with venereal and other communicable diseases are at once segregated and given the proper treatment. Others whose bodily ills are less virulent but none the less in need of immediate attention are placed in the hospital at the Joliet Branch until cured.

But the infirmities are not all physical. Equally as important are mental defects, which run all the way from minor psychological peculiarities to out-and-out insanity. For the purpose of dealing with their needs, a staff of mental health specialists is maintained. These men have been selected for their positions with great care and are of parallel importance with the medical doctors. Indeed, it may well be that a mental handicap is a greater impediment in the path of reformation than a physical sickness. "As a man thinketh, so is he," and a man entering the penitentiary is apt to think along peculiar lines.

One of the main functions, then, of the Diagnostic Depot, is to determine the individual attitudes of the new inmates. They are interrogated by psychiatrists and sociologists, and their reactions are carefully noted. Then each inmate is classified according to several broad specifications. The test which George and Tony took is patterned after the Army Alpha examination and is designed to reveal the mental age of the subject, with groupings ranging from imbecilic to very superior. The sociologist records data concerning the social stratum to which the inmate belonged before his imprisonment, special mention being made of formal education, financial status, and type of employment. To these are added the opinions of the physicians and the remarks of the district attorney who prosecuted the case. The whole is incorporated into a jacket from which the prison authorities may secure at any time whatever information is desired.

This information also serves as a useful guide when it is to be decided to which branch of the penitentiary the inmate should be sent following his period of quarantine at the depot. Naturally, there are certain generalizations made. For instance, younger first offenders and improvable types are largely sent to Pontiac, the mentally deficient to Menard; but in cases where all other things are equal, the recommendation of the psychiatrist is often the deciding factor. Tony was consigned to Joliet because his outlook was found to be dangerously uncompliant to authority.

There are numerous bare facts which are obtainable with little trouble, such as where the inmate was born, what previous clashes with the law he experienced, and similar matters of record. But there are also the intangibles. How does a man feel about being incarcerated? Is he vengeful? Is he convinced that he has suffered an injustice? Is it his intention to cause the authorities as much inconvenience as he possibly can, or is he willing to abide by the rules of the prison? All of these things must be found out, if they can be, within the first few weeks, so that steps may be taken to administer the necessary treatment.

Perhaps a word should be said here about recidivists. It is held by some penologists that an "old timer," a man who has served two or more penitentiary sentences, is more easily controlled than the one who enters through the big gate for the first time. Others will say that the repeater, being more familiar with prison routine, is more capable of creating a disturbance.

Actually, it is impossible to make a statement covering all instances. A "first timer" is equally as liable to be a trouble-maker as a man serving his fifth term, and, on the other hand, many recidivists conduct themselves with a conscientious regard for the regulations. It all depends upon the man himself.

Consider for a moment the case of Tony. He belongs to that heterogeneous group called "hoodlums." He possesses little intelligence, little physical fear, and an ingrained animosity where the law is concerned. He has little hope of ever again being free, and is accordingly a potentially dangerous man. He must be permitted a minimum of self-rule. Even if he were not under a life sentence, he would offer a difficult problem, for his instincts are all opposed to rehabilitation. When he was "on the outside," he regarded it as part of the game to be periodically arrested, taken to the Detective Bureau for investigation. He looked on life as a constant conflict between the police force and himself, and his incarceration merely substituted the menace of guards for the no longer immediate menace of the police. He is fundamentally generous toward his friends, but he offers his friendship to very few, even those of his own variety. He is almost of a different species from George.

With George, the question is not whether he can be rehabilitated, but how best to offer him assistance in his own efforts to that end. He knows he has been guilty of disrupting the tenor of society and he is anxious to pay for his error. He is definitely not of the substance of which repeaters are made. That conclusion holds true in his particular case and does not imply that all who are serving sentences for similar crimes — confidence game, forgery, etc., do not repeat their offenses after release from prison, as in many instances they do.

There are many men just like George, men whom temporary conditions have led into crime, and whose first trip to the penitentiary will be their last, and there are, unfortunately, quite a few like Tony, in whom incorrigibility is deeply rooted. In between, there are thousands who can be turned in one direction or the other. They are incapable of finding within themselves the material with which to make over their lives, principally because they have never been shown a reason for starting the rebuilding process. They must have guidance.

This guidance is given them from the moment they enter the Diagnostic Depot. They are classified, and they are given work within the prison which is in as great accord as possible with their abilities. They are encouraged to seek self-improvement, and they are shown that, while they will be punished for disobedience, they will also be rewarded for adherence to the rules.

Summarizing, the Diagnostic Depot serves the double function of assisting in the orientation of the new inmate and providing the authorities with information concerning the inmate's proclivities. It irrefutably has proven a long step forward in penology, and its future value is inestimable.

Chapter 6

MANUAL FOR INMATE GUIDANCE

Without rules and regulations for inmates and prison officials, including the warden and his immediate family, jungle rule would prevail in a prison institution.

There could be no safety assured anyone, including inmates. Such a condition once prevailed in the Illinois prison system. This cannot be permitted to happen again, under any conditions.

Since the Joliet-Stateville prisons are maximum security institutions, the primary objective is to see that inmates serve their sentences, as meted out by the courts.

Rules and regulations are promulgated by prison officials to make sure that inmates serve out their time in orderly fashion.

But, while discipline is basic in any prison, inmates must also be prepared for eventual parole or discharge and return to society. Since about 96 per cent of our inmate population is eventually returned to society, it is the incumbent duty of prison officials to pave the way for their reformation and ability to resume their position as self-sustaining and law-abiding members of society.

Toward this end is mapped our rules and regulations. Some may seem to be unduly harsh; others may appear to allow too much latitude.

But let us not forget that we are dealing with human beings, even though they are lawbreakers. Our experience over a long period shows that many inmates, when they leave the institution, do resume their status in society in honorable fashion.

We don't claim that the rules and regulations we have laid down are perfect or all-embracing. From time to time they are altered, tightened or relaxed, as we meet new situations and emergencies. They are designed to upgrade inmates, not belittle them or engender cruel treatment. Yet, strict discipline on a basis of fair treatment for all, without exception, is our watchword.

Each inmate is given a manual of rules and regulations shortly after admission. They are divided into "General Information" and guidance from the warden and specific "do" and "don't" guideposts to cover virtually any situation concerning the inmate.

The rules and regulations follow:

GENERAL INFORMATION

During his first few days in prison, each new inmate is given instructions and an outline of the rules in force in the institution. In view, however, of the mental stress of many men who are spending their first days in prison, they can hardly be expected to grasp and memorize every rule and regulation immediately.

Time does not permit going into certain subjects in which the prisoner may be interested, and concerning which he is entitled to be informed. It is partially to supplement the information given inmates orally and to explain matters which are of interest to them that this booklet is issued. The following pages will answer many questions. The objectives of prison discipline, education, religion, classification, personal conduct, work, health, mental hygiene, good time allowance and parole are all discussed. These are the broad subjects which concern every inmate of a prison.

A comprehensive set of rules governing inmates is also contained in this booklet. There will be orders and rules issued periodically which will apply in the same manner and effect as the rules and regulations herein. They are to be noted carefully when posted on the bulletin board and announced over the public address system.

It will benefit each inmate to read and absorb the contents of this booklet. Only by strict adherence to the rules can he serve his sentence most easily and well, and in taking advantage of the opportunities offered he can profit by his incarceration.

Typical of the advice given to new inmates is the following:

You may have been wondering why you were received at the Diagnostic Depot rather than at the branch of the prison where you will serve your sentence. All prisoners remain at the Depot for a period of time prior to their permanent assignment. This is so that each individual prisoner may be analyzed from the point of view of the psychiatrist, psychologist and sociologist. The State of Illinois has this Classification Board for the purpose of determining in which branch of the Illinois Penitentiary System you are most likely to get along well and accomplish the most.

During your stay at the Diagnostic Depot you are to turn in all personal property to the Captain in charge. Items of value, except clothes, will be mailed to your home upon request if postage is paid. Failure to cooperate in necessary routine, giving needed information for records, the signing of necessary records and coöperation for necessary examination by prison and professional personnel will be cause for disciplinary action and denial of all visits and mail privileges.

Wherever you may be assigned, do the task given you cheerfully and as efficiently as possible. You will be given all the necessary instructions in whatever work you are to do. No unreasonable demands will be made of you. You may ask your officer for information about your work. However, after reasonable instructions it is expected that you turn out the same quantity and quality of work as would be required of you on the outside. Advancements to more desirable positions will depend upon your behavior and the willingness and ability you show.

Perhaps this is the first day you have ever spent in prison. If so you are beginning an entirely new chapter in your life. Your way of living will be completely changed. The sensible approach to your problem is to think things through. Consider the ways necessary to change your daily habits of thought and action so that you may become better adjusted to the new situation in which you find yourself.

The first and most startling difference between life in prison and on the outside is that here you are under the constant supervision and control of others, the prison officials. Where before you could largely come and go as you pleased, it now becomes necessary to adhere to restrictions. You must do certain things at a fixed time and in a certain way.

This may or may not be a completely new experience for you. Probably it will not be a very pleasant one. Among the important things you must remember is to try to understand the reasoning of the officials who enforce the rules. They are not only trying to shape your outlook toward the time you must spend in prison, but also your conduct upon release.

It must be remembered that the prison officials had nothing whatsoever to do with your conviction and commitment to the institution. The officials have no opinion as to your case or your sentence. They are in no sense a court of review. Their first duty under the law is to receive you when you are properly and legally committed, and to keep you safely until such time as you are eligible for release.

While custody is still the first factor in which prison officials are concerned, it is far from all that we are now trying to do. Some years ago prisons were places for punishment in the strictest sense of the word. The very word "penitentiary" meant a place of punishment. Today, we are not primarily interested in punishing offenders. We are more concerned with reforming, rehabilitating and reclaiming them. We are trying to guide and train you so that upon your release you will be better equipped to maintain your place in society.

This is an aim in which the prison administration cannot succeed alone. It requires coöperation on your part. The prison administration may be one-hundred per cent efficient, it may offer a complete and well-rounded program of reform, but if the individual prisoner refuses to do his part, the program cannot fully succeed. We can and will offer you the opportunity to attend religious services, but we cannot make you devout in your worship. We can give you fine schools and even insist that you attend them, but we cannot make you learn unless you are willing. We can point out the ways in which you may better yourself and give you every assistance and encouragement. Whether you actually take advantage of all the opportunities offered is a matter which you, and you alone, can control.

Because we are interested in rehabilitation and reform, we strongly urge you to make full use of your writing and visiting privileges. You may be assured that your visitors will be treated courteously as long as they follow the rules. Write home regularly. Cheerful letters will greatly console those near and dear to you. Keep your difficulties to yourself. Try to keep those already suffering on your account as happy as possible. Complaining can do nothing but make them unhappy.

Do not allow yourself to become associated with any clique or group in prison. You must have acquaintances and must talk to someone, but do not make the mistake of becoming too closely associated with any group. Cliques in prison are not tolerated.

Above all, do your own time. By this we simply mean to look out for your own best interests. Among the inmates of the institution there are some good men, but there are also undesirables. Do not allow them to use you for their selfish purposes. If one should ask you "to do him a favor" which may involve violating the rules of the institution, and if you do him a "favor" and are caught, you will be disciplined and not the man who asked the "favor." If one inmate has a grudge against another, do not let him enlist you in his quarrel. It is no affair of yours. The very fact that he asked you to become involved proves his attempt to use you. "Friends" in prison, generally speaking, are not of much consequence. They can do nothing for you and usually bring you further trouble. Your friends will not ask you to take such chances.

Some offenders, particularly the younger and less experienced, seem to attach some significance to those fellow prisoners considered "gangsters." Men convicted of certain crimes seem to be considered "tough." An association with these individuals is sometimes thought an honor. This is foolish thinking. There are no "big shots" in prison. You are all on equal footing, whether convicted of a widely publicized crime or a lesser one. Hero worship under any circumstances is foolish. It is utterly ridiculous when the "hero" chosen has no other claim to distinction than that his crimes have obtained notoriety for him.

DISCIPLINE

One of the first and most necessary features of a prison is discipline. You will find that there are many rules to guide your conduct, many things you are to do in certain ways, and many things you must not do. Now what is the purpose of these rules? Is it to restrict and repress you as much as possible? Is it to make your life uncomfortable and annoying? Certainly not. The purpose of the strict, but fair, discipline you will find here is threefold:

Marching in lock step in the 1920's. Joliet Branch.

1. Discipline is necessary for the safe operation of the institution. Only by enforcing strict discipline in the institution can the officials guarantee that degree of safety which is their duty to insure.

2. Discipline is necessary for the smooth and efficient operation of the prison. This is not only true of prisons but of any complicated business which employs many men and has many inter-related departments. Our rules in many ways are similar to laws and rules governing society in the free world. There must be authority and respect for authority if it is to function effi-

ciently. A prison is a very complicated unit. There are within it many departments which must work together smoothly.

3. Discipline is in itself one element of reform. Many of you are in prison now because you did not, in boyhood and young

Line marching from the Furniture Factory to lunch. Stateville Branch, 1959

manhood, have enough discipline of the proper kind. To succeed in this world one must learn to discipline himself. The first step in this direction is to learn to take orders cheerfully and obediently from those in authority.

Courtesy will be extended by all employees, and inmates will be expected to do likewise.

During your stay here, you will be under the supervision of employees of different ranks. Each of them has his own duties to perform. It will benefit you to coöperate and follow orders as directed. You will thereby keep your record free from disciplinary reports. Employees' orders are issued by the Department and the Warden of the institution to which they are assigned, some by law and some by rule. Learn to obey and accept orders. If you feel you have a complaint, notify an officer and he will make the proper investigation.

Under no circumstances will rules and regulations be changed unless approved by the Warden in writing.

There is a reason for each of the rules. Even if you are unable to see this, you should at least see clearly the wisdom of obeying all of them. All you can succeed in doing by failing to obey the rules is to lay yourself open to disciplinary action. Whether or not you understand the reason for a certain rule, it will be to your advantage to obey it.

RELIGION

A function worthy of your consideration is religious worship. We do not force anyone to go to church, but we strongly urge that you attend one of the services which we offer. It would be utterly impossible to have a representative of every religious denomination in an institution of this type. We offer eight different religious services: Protestant, Catholic, Episcopal, Christian Science, Lutheran, Baptist, Jewish and Orthodox.

It may be possible that you never felt you had the time to devote to the practice of religion. Certainly this is not true now. Think of the great energy which men have put into religion. Consider the thousands of men who have willingly sacrificed their very lives for it. Certainly a subject which can move so many so strongly should merit your investigation.

Even if you believe that religion has no personal value for you, you should look into it at least to see what has made it so important to others. And surely, no matter what your religious views may be, you will agree that the practice of religion can do you no harm. But the matter is entirely up to you. Merely attending services, no matter how regularly, accounts for very little. If you are to get anything from religion, you must study and believe it whole-heartedly.

Religious services are not all that are offered by way of spiritual help and consolation. You will find the chaplains always ready to talk with you concerning your problems. They will offer you the fruits of their years of experience. They are not, in any sense, disciplinary officers. Their only interest is your spiritual development and well being.

ALCOHOLICS ANONYMOUS

If liquor was the cause of your difficulties, do not overlook the Alcoholics Anonymous Program offered. This is important in the rehabilitation program of the inmate who realizes that liquor was one of the causes which led to his incarceration. It is by the regular attendance at AA meetings that you will be able to learn about and become willing to do something towards freeing yourself of this addiction.

MOVIES AND ENTERTAINMENT

Movies and other entertainment will be provided periodically. You may also participate in the various sports and programs offered. If your name is posted on the bulletin board or flashed on the screen while attending recreational activities in the yard or in the chapel, report to your officer immediately for instructions.

EDUCATION

You will find that special emphasis is placed on education in its broadest sense. Many of you would not be here today had you received a more complete education, either of the academic type or vocational training. You would undoubtedly have been better equipped to obtain employment. While you are here, you will be given every opportunity to further your education, and every encouragement to take advantage of the opportunities offered. If you have not finished grammar school, you may attend regular school classes of grammar school. After completing the eighth grade, you will receive a diploma which does not show that it was earned in prison. If you have finished grade school, we urge you to continue your education by attending high school and taking college subjects by correspondence courses. Any credits gained from these courses will not be identified as having been earned in prison. (College by TV also offered.)

There is one thing concerning education which you must keep constantly in mind. There is no short cut to learning. If you wish to improve yourself, you must make up your mind to work. It is the only way in which you will reach your goal. Many men have a sudden "attack" of ambition and decide to learn a certain subject — perhaps a foreign language. They begin, but in a very short time they decide the effort they must make is too great. So they give up. This, of course, does not build character. Make up your mind that anything worth having will take effort on your part. To persevere is to succeed. All that any school can give you is the opportunity to learn. It can furnish you with expert instructors and the necessary material, but the actual studying you must do yourself. We will do everything possible to help you acquire an education. The benefits from it depend largely upon you.

VOCATIONAL TRAINING

In addition to our academic schools, we offer the opportunity of learning specialized crafts. Our present training facilities offer more than forty varied vocations. Remember that State Laws and educational requirements must be met by both you and the administration before you can qualify for certain vocations. After meeting the requirements, there must be a vacancy in the trade of your choice. Your conduct must be such as to merit such assignment. You must have and keep a definite interest, and must be capable and willing to learn or add to any knowledge you have already.

After your release, the use of the practical knowledge you attained in prison is not the only advantage of studying while here. You will undoubtedly find that you have more time on your hands than ever before. Your problem will be in knowing what to do with this time when not working. Certainly you will find that time passes more quickly and you will be happier if you find something in which you can become interested. The civilian leaders in charge of the various schools will assist you in choosing wisely and make it easier for you to learn. It will serve you well to use some of the time you must spend in your cell for study.

INDUSTRIES

The institution operates a number of industries where various products, equipment and material are manufactured for State use. State use includes State institutions and other State operated agencies, counties, cities, townships, school districts, public libraries and any organization supported by tax monies.

Industrial assignments are gained by satisfactory work and conduct records on other assignments over a period of time. After you have met these requirements, you may request an industrial assignment. At that time your name will be placed on the waiting list until there is a vacancy.

These industries not only offer employment during your confinement in the institution, they offer very good vocational experience as well as pay, which is based on production. It is essential that the items produced be of high quality and skillfully manufactured. Remember that State agencies need not buy from this institution if the products we manufacture are inferior and not up to standard in quality and workmanship. Were it not for our industries and State use law, a great percentage of our inmate population would be unemployed.

Therefore, if you are assigned to one of our industries, it will benefit you to do your best in the production of the respective products.

RECREATION

We stress work because we believe that good working habits are one of the finest assets any man can possess. But we also stress play. Every man in prison is permitted a recreation period each day, weather permitting. We urge you to make the most of it. Take part in games, get some exercise every day and keep physically fit. Not only does play keep you in better health, but it also teaches good sportsmanship, and is a splendid way to work off some of that extra energy we all have. The safest, healthiest and best way to "blow off steam" is in hard physical exercise. In addition, use your radio, attend our movies and athletic events

CLEANLINESS

Cleanliness is of great importance. It is not only next to god-liness, but is a safeguard to health. Teeth kept very clean cause little trouble. This holds true of other parts of the body. Disease has very little chance in a body kept really clean. Self-respect, too, is a part of personal cleanliness. No one feels in top form when in need of a bath or shave. It is easy to fall into slovenly habits in prison. You may justify your reason for doing so the fact that you are not going anywhere and no one will see you. Habits like these once started are hard to break. Don't lose your pride in your personal appearance. It is an essential part of your self-respect.

Cleanliness also applies to your cell and work assignment. Be-cause soap and water are furnished, we expect and demand clean-liness and good housekeeping. Reasons and excuses for lack of these will not be accepted.

MEDICAL AND DENTAL FACILITIES

In each branch of our institution there is a completely equipped hospital, with medical, dental, x-ray facilities, etc. These units are in the charge of skilled doctors, and are maintained entirely for your benefit.

If you are ill, you may be certain you will receive the best pos-sible attention. Do not make the mistake of pretending to be ill for the purpose of shirking your work or to rest. This will not be tolerated. If you are actually sick, do not hesitate to tell your officer. He will arrange for your care. Do not attempt to diagnose your ills or prescribe treatment.

MENTAL WELFARE

Equally important is your mental attitude. We have mentioned some of the things which will help you guard against mental ill-ness. These are study, religion, a vocation in which you can really become interested, and regular exercise. Another suggestion is that you try to keep from forming a habit of brooding over your difficulties. It is easy to slip into the habit of feeling sorry for yourself, sitting for hours staring into space and worrying. This accomplishes absolutely nothing but to make you a likely subject for a nervous breakdown. If you notice yourself beginning to brood, make a determined effort to interest yourself in something. If this fails request an interview with one of the doctors in the Mental Health Department, or supervising prison officials, who will advise and guide you.

Do not try pretending a mental condition to escape reality or accomplish a transfer. Remember, a record is kept by us of every move you make. When you appear before the Parole Board, this record can be, and many times is, detrimental to you.

Try very hard not to hate. Perhaps there are persons toward whom you feel unfriendly, someone you think is trying to do you an injustice. Your hatred will do him no harm, but will definitely affect you. Often he who hates becomes so embittered that he never gets over it, and finally finds no pleasure at all in life.

PERVERSION

The practice of perverted or unnatural sex activities is so disgusting and repulsive it would seem unnecessary to warn anyone against it. There are, unfortunately, some men in prison who resort to such acts. Do not be taken in by the story that since you are deprived of a normal sexual relationship, it is necessary for you to indulge in perversion. This is far from the truth. One can be decent in prison as elsewhere. All that is required is a little self-control. Keep your thoughts clean and you will have no difficulty. Do not allow others to talk to you of such practices, or let your curiosity lead you into trying anything so shameful. Above all, should anyone make such indecent suggestions, simply have nothing further to do with that individual. Sex perversion of every description is strictly prohibited. Anyone found practicing such acts or caught in a compromising position, or in bed with another inmate, will be disciplined by isolation, demotion in grade, statutory time revoked and subjected to prosecution in the local courts.

PAROLE AND DISCHARGE

A subject of universal interest to prisoners is their release on parole and the manner in which the time they must serve is determined. While it does not fall strictly within the field of the

prison authorities, we feel it should be explained as bri\
clearly as possible. There are in Illinois two types of se\
definite and indeterminate. Definite sentences are given f\
crimes of murder, voluntary manslaughter, treason, kidna_ping
and rape. Other crimes carry indeterminate sentences. Each cell
house has booklets entitled "Rules and Statutes Relating to
Parole and Pardons" available for you to read.

GOOD TIME OFF

In the case of inmates received in the Illinois State Penitentiary system to begin service on their sentences on or after February 1, 1952, "good time" with reference to the minimum of a
sentence to be served before an inmate is eligible for parole consideration shall be figured according to the previous rule table.
"Good Time" with reference to the maximum of a sentence shall
be computed so that in no case shall "total good time made"
exceed one-third of the total number of years of sentence in
accordance with the following table:

Number of Years Sentence	Good Time Granted	Total Good Time Made		Time to be Served if Full Time is Made		
1st year	1 month	1 month		11 months		
2nd year	2 months	3 months		1 year &	9 months	
3rd "	3 "	6 "		2 "	6 "	
4th "	4 "	10 "		3 "	2 "	
5th "	5 "	1 year &	3 months	3 "	9 "	
6th "	6 "	1 "	9 "	4 "	3 "	
7th "	6 "	2 "	3 "	4 "	9 "	
8th "	5 "	2 "	8 "	5 "	4 "	
9th "	4 "	3 "	0 "	6 "	0 "	
10th "	4 "	3 "	4 "	6 "	8 "	
11th "	4 "	3 "	8 "	7 "	4 "	
12th "	4 "	4 "	0 "	8 "	0 "	
13th "	4 "	4 "	4 "	8 "	8 "	
14th "	4 "	4 "	8 "	9 "	4 "	
15th "	4 "	5 "	0 "	10 "	0 "	
16th "	4 "	5 "	4 "	10 "	8 "	
17th "	4 "	5 "	8 "	11 "	4 "	
18th "	4 "	6 "	0 "	12 "	0 "	
19th "	4 "	6 "	4 "	12 "	8 "	
20th "	4 "	6 "	8 "	13 "	4 "	
21st "	4 "	7 "	0 "	14 "	0 "	
22nd "	4 "	7 "	4 "	14 "	8 "	
23rd "	4 "	7 "	8 "	15 "	4 "	
24th "	4 "	8 "	0 "	16 "	0 "	
25th "	4 "	8 "	4 "	16 "	8 "	

For each additional year, four months are earned.

FORFEITURE OF GOOD TIME

In case any convict who may become entitled to any lessening of his sentence by these provisions shall be guilty of violating the prison rules or misconduct, or a violation of any law of the State, he may for the first offense, forfeit two days; for the second offense, four days; for the third offense, eight days; for the fourth offense, sixteen days. In addition, whatever number of days, more than one, that he is in punishment may be forfeited. For more than four offenses, the Director of the Department of Public Safety, upon the recommendation of the Warden of the Division of the Penitentiary in which the convict is imprisoned, shall have the power at his discretion to deprive such convict of any portion or all of the good time that the convict may have earned, or may earn in the future.

PROGRESSIVE MERIT SYSTEM

A "Progressive Merit System" for the purpose of encouraging and rewarding good conduct and industry in the Divisions of the Illinois State Penitentiary has been adopted by the Department of Public Safety.

Under this system prisoners serving indeterminate sentences who are denied parole and their cases continued to future dates for further consideration may by good conduct and industry earn "Merit Time" and thus advance the dates of review of their cases.

Under this system, five grades designated as A, B, C, D, and E were established. The rules for promotion from one grade to another are governed by the behavior and industrial efficiency of the prisoner.

On admission the inmate is placed in C, the neutral grade, where "Merit Time" is neither earned nor lost. If his behavior is satisfactory, the inmate is promoted to B in three months' time. After three months in B, if his behavior remains satisfactory, he is promoted to A.

The inmate must be in A grade at least three months ten days and have served his minimum sentence less "Good Time" before he will be eligible for a parole hearing by the Parole Board.

In A grade the inmates earn ten days "Merit Time" per month, and in B grade five days.

A table of the "Merit Time" which may be earned by a prisoner from the period of a continuance under an indeterminate sentence to speed the time when he may again be considered for parole is as follows:

Continuance in Years from Date of Admission	"Merit Time" Earned in Years, Months, Days			Case Reviewed in Years, Months, Days		
2	0	6	15	1	5	15
3	0	10	15	2	1	15
4	1	2	15	2	9	15
5	1	6	15	3	5	15
6	1	10	15	4	1	15
7	2	2	15	4	9	15
8	2	6	15	5	5	15
9	2	10	15	6	1	15
10	3	2	15	6	9	15
11	3	6	15	7	5	15
12	3	10	15	8	1	15
13	4	2	15	8	9	15
14	4	6	15	9	5	15
15	4	10	15	10	1	15
16	5	2	15	10	9	15
17	5	6	15	11	5	15
18	5	10	15	12	1	15
19	6	2	15	12	9	15
20	6	6	15	13	5	15

Remember the time earned under the progressive merit system is something which is not yours by law. It is not a legal right, but something you are given the opportunity to earn. It may be revoked should your conduct warrant it. If your conduct has been such that you have been punished repeatedly, you can hardly expect favorable consideration. Protect it by obeying the rules of the institution.

If an inmate continually violates the institutional rules and warnings, the denial of any or all privileges, such as recreational, commissary, smoking, etc., and other methods of discipline fail to bring about a marked improvement in his conduct record, instead of placing him in Isolation, the disciplinarian will recommend that a specified number of days be taken from the inmate's "Statutory Good Time." The disciplinarian will continue to hold court on each ticket and will advise the inmate that he is recommending that a certain number of days be revoked. These days are recorded and, when thirty (30) days have accumulated by this

method, the inmate is referred to the Merit Staff for final disposition. Of course, this does not mean that thirty days is all that
can be taken. If deserved, all of the inmate's "good time" may
be taken and for serious and continuous violations, Isolation time
may be included.

DEMOTIONS

For violation of prison rules, an inmate may, at the discretion
of the Merit Staff, be demoted in grade. For every grade he is
demoted, he must remain three months in the grade to which he
was demoted. Upon demotion, promotion to the next grade is
as follows:

A to E:	E — 12 Mos.	D — 3	Mos.	C — 7½ Mos.	B — 3 Mos.
A to D:	D — 9 "	C — 4½	"	B — 3	"
A to C:	C — 6 "	B — 3	"		
A to B:	B — 3 "				
B to E:	E — 9 "	D — 3	"	C — 6½ "	B — 3 "
B to D:	D — 6 "	C — 4	"	B — 3	"
B to C:	C — 3 "	B — 3	"		
C to E:	E — 6 "	D — 3	"	C — 5½ "	B — 3 "
C to D:	D — 3 "	C — 3½	"	B — 3	"
D to E:	E — 3 "	D — 3	"	C — 4½ "	B — 3 "

It would be well to remember that if you are demoted to "E"
or "D" grades, you may lose certain privileges, such as movies,
ball games, commissary, smoking, etc. If you are demoted in
grade, and during the period of your demotion, you were scheduled to appear before the Parole Board, you would be ineligible
to appear. Your case would be automatically continued until you
have again made grade.

Whether you think so or not, there always will be prisons, and
men will be confined in them for law violations. You can help decrease their number, if you will do your own time as easily as
possible by coöperating and learning something while you are here.

INSTRUCTIONS FOR FILING PETITION FOR EXECUTIVE CLEMENCY, YOUR PETITION SHOULD CONSIST OF THREE SECTIONS:

1. A brief summary of your life; that is, when and where you
were born; parents' names and addresses, if alive; if not, date of
death; the extent of your education and schools attended; places

of employment until time of your arrest, etc. In other words, a general account of your life from the date of your birth until the time of your arrest.

2. Your version of the crime. The State's version is on file and is therefore known. Give your own account as to just what happened, how, etc. If you claim innocence and for that reason are unable to say how the crime was committed, describe the circumstances surrounding your arrest, conviction, etc.

3. Your plea and reasons you think make you deserving of a definite sentence parole or executive clemency.

Seven copies of your petition either typed or hand printed are to be sent to the Parole Office at least forty-five days before Pardon Day.

For the benefit of inmates granted parole on the current monthly docket, and those being released on discharge, a Parole and Discharge School has been established at this institution. Sessions are conducted by various parole agents, personnel representatives from industries and commerce, and law enforcing officers. All of them offer advice and suggestions concerning employment, and the adjustments to be made in the community where these men will live and work.

Also, for one month before inmates see the Parole Board, and for each month after they have seen the Board and have been granted a parole, fifteen (15) special letters may be given to the Parole Agent. The letters must pertain to employment only, and are to be directed to (1) people who are interested in your welfare and are willing to help you, or (2), people who have employment for men with your qualifications. Do not attempt to obtain employment for which you are not qualified. Surplus and unimportant matters in letters will be cause for rejection. A complete record will be kept of your correspondence. All letters will be carefully censored to see that they pertain to your employment only.

Your relatives and friends will be expected to find employment for you. The parole authorities will help only when all other efforts have failed.

Beware of False Prophets

Advise those near and dear to you that it has been known that persons on the outside will contact relatives and friends of inmates and build up false stories of having connections with State Officials or Members of the Parole Board. They will say that for a consideration, they could get you released on parole, obtain jobs, etc. Under no circumstances should persons interested in your welfare heed the statements of these "good will ambassadors." The law of averages will release a certain percentage of these inmates at every parole meeting. These imposters can very easily inform your relatives or friends that they were instrumental in securing your parole and thereby collect for their so-called services, when in actual fact, they had contacted no one in your behalf and had nothing whatsoever to do with your parole.

Also, beware of the inmate, who upon his release from the institution, because of some ill-feeling he may have had for you during his incarceration, will contact your friends and relatives. Without giving his name he may inform them that you are seriously ill, or convey other than good news, which actually is untrue.

Finally, life in prison, as anywhere, can be complex. You will have to make many adjustments. If you will remember that one of the main aims of the prison administration is directed toward the reformation and rehabilitation of inmates, your task of readjustment depends on your attitude, understanding, and coöperation. Think over what you have read regarding obedience to discipline; attendance at church and at school; the tone of your letters to your relatives; your attitude toward your work; the matter of "gangsters" and "cliques"; sex perversion; play and exercise; cleanliness; brooding and hatred then make your decision. These are the problems which confront most prisoners.

Remember that what this prison experience does for you is very largely up to you. It is never too late to start anew. A great many men make good after their release from prison, mainly by reeducating themselves during their stay in the institution.

There are many again who fail after their release, because

they attempt to learn how better to violate the law. It would be well to remember that nearly all violators come back or go to meet their Maker, thereby ending as complete losses. You cannot hope to gain by violating the law. No one, for any length of time, can cheat society and prosper.

Following is a list of the rules and regulations of the institution. These apply generally and to specific places and activities. They are clear and concise. Study them carefully. Only by the strict adherence to each and every one can you do your time most easily and well, and earn the maximum time off your sentence in accordance with the law. Keep in mind that the inmate who does not coöperate will pay by the loss of good time and/or disciplinary action on the part of the prison authorities, in a court established for that purpose. You can never win by violating the rules. Remember, too, if you violate a law of the State while in prison, you can be indicted and tried in the local courts and the sentence you receive will run consecutively to the sentence you now are serving. Of course, the violation of any State law is also a violation of the prison rules.

It would be well to remember that under the law, men confined in the prisons of the State are to be clothed, fed, housed and given medical care only. All other concessions are privileges granted by the officials of the institution and the Department of Public Safety, and these will be granted only if your conduct warrants them. Therefore, it will pay you dividends to live within the rules.

If you fail to ask questions about the Rules and Regulations during your stay at the Diagnostic Depot or soon after transfer to the Branch of the Institution where you will serve your time, it will be understood by the officials that you have full knowledge of them.

The rules, regulations and instructions listed under each of the following subjects and assignments must be strictly observed. Failure to do so will be considered a violation. Those who violate can expect one or more of the following disciplinary actions — reprimand, denial of privileges, isolation, segregation, reduction in grade, loss of good time, and/or prosecution.

Cell House

All assignments are made by the Senior Captains. If you have good reason for a cell transfer within the assignment, you may contact the Cell House Keeper or a Lieutenant and state your reason. After proper investigation, if he feels a cell transfer is important, the change will be made.

You may write requests to the Warden, Assistant Warden, Captains, Chaplains or Mental Health Department. Deposit these in the box provided for that purpose in each cell house. Give your name, number and assignment. Keep your request brief and to the point.

If your shoes or clothing, cell or any equipment contained therein, are in need of repair, notify your officer immediately. Do not permit anything to deteriorate beyond repair.

On entering or leaving the cell house with your regular line, go in cell formation directly to or from your cell (unless you have special permission to step out of line), stand in front of your cell door and when the signal is given by your officer, open, step in or out of cell, closing the door quietly.

Under no circumstances will the officials of the Institutions be responsible for watches, pens or pencils, or any personal property left in the cell. However, the officials will attempt to keep cells from being pilfered. If you are going to be out of your cell for any of the following reasons, Isolation, Hospital or Writ turn in personal property to Cell House Keeper before leaving cell house. Or have cell partner turn in your property with inventory sheet, or notify the officer in whose custody you are, who will notify the Cell House Keeper, who will pick up your property, but under no circumstances will the officials of the institution be responsible for it.

Not Permitted

1. Talking on the galleries, when marching either to or from the cell in line, or enroute to and from your cell alone.
2. Shouting and motioning.
3. Entering cell other than your own.
4. Depositing any article in cell other than your own.

Cell

You are housed in a cell which is modern. It is equipped with toilet, lavatory and all facilities necessary for your comfort. You are expected to keep this equipment in perfect condition. Under no circumstances is refuse such as large pieces of paper, fruit peelings, rags or debris which may cause clogging to be thrown into the toilet. Water is of great value and must not be wasted. Leaking faucets and toilets are to be reported to your Cell House Keeper, and toilets flushed only when necessary.

On occupying a cell, make certain that no contraband articles are contained in it. You will be held responsible for contraband found in your cell or on your person.

Keep your cell walls, bars, windows, bed, wash basin, toilet, stool, floor and furniture in the cleanest condition possible.

Make up your bed immediately after rising in the morning in a neat and uniform manner. Your officer and Cell House Keeper will instruct you in doing this properly.

In the evening you may talk in a low tone until the bell sounds. At this time you will undress and retire.

Practice on band instruments is permissible in your cell (in the round houses only) from 6:30 to 7:30 P.M.

When the signal is given to stand for a count, immediately stand in the front of your cell, hands on the door. If the signal is given for a recount, go through the same procedure.

Not Permitted

1. More than prescribed furniture.
2. Other than designated number of blankets.
3. Mattresses other than issued by the Cell House Keeper.
4. To scratch or mark the walls and furnishings in your cell. Items such as earphones and personal effects are to be kept in their proper place when not in use.
5. Use of window-sill as shelf.
6. Covering of any type on dresser.
7. Obstruction or darkening of light bulb or having smaller or larger bulb than is issued by the Cell House Keeper.
8. Throwing refuse on the cell floor, the gallery or the cell

house floor. It must be deposited in the waste cans or places provided for that purpose in the cell house.

9. Spitting on the floor, either in your cell or elsewhere in the institution.

10. Authorized medicines to accumulate in your cell. Empty bottles and medicines no longer needed are to be given the cell house keeper for disposal.

11. Books other than those issued by the Library and those marked "Permitted" by the Librarian, Chaplain and the Superintendent of Schools.

12. Accumulation of old newspapers, magazines or other periodic literature. Newspapers may be retained only ten (10) days; weekly magazines thirty (30) days; and monthly magazines ninety (90) days. They may, however, be forwarded to another inmate providing they are first sent to the Cell House Keeper with the name, number and cell number of the inmate to receive same, but must bear no other writing, marks, etc. There need be no limit to the number of inmates who may have a magazine or paper. It may be passed from one to any number within a cellhouse.

13. Singing, whistling, dancing, shouting, talking from one cell to another, booing and all forms of boisterous conduct.

14. Closing cell door with violence or jerking it open. Operate it with firm but gentle motion.

15. Articles other than those listed will be considered contraband (unless special permission is granted).

BASIC NEEDS ALLOWED EACH CELL

Broom
Calendar (Current Year Only)
Cell Mirror (1)
Checker Board, 1 — 18"
Cribbage Board, 1 — 18"
Earphones (must be worn when used and not to be tinkered with. When not in use, radio equipment is to be hung on hooks provided).
Mop Rags (must be kept clean).
Rule Book
Table or chest of drawers.
Thread (small quantity).

BASIC NEEDS ALLOWED EACH MAN

Arch supporters, 1 pair (prescribed by doctor only).

Blankets, as allotted.
Bed sheet, 2
Bible, 1
Belt, 1 — State Issue
Can opener, 1
Checkers, 1 set
Chess, 1 set
Cigar, 12
Chewing Tobacco, 5 plugs, Commissary
Chewing Tobacco, 1, State Issue
Cigarettes, 10 packs, Commissary
Church Card (one denomination)
Coat, 1
Cup, 1
Comb, 1
Denim jacket
Drawing instruments with course (with permit)
Drawing materials with course (with permit)
Dominoes, 1 set
Eye shade, 1
Eye Glasses
Fountain pen, 1 (Maximum value $5.00)
Face cloth, 1
Gloves, State issue, numbered
Heel cushions, 1 pair
Hickory shirt, 3
Handkerchiefs, 6, Commissary
Handkerchiefs, 2, State issue
Hair brush, 1
Ink, 1 bottle
Jewelry, (None)
Library Book, 1, Fiction (Not to be held more than one (1) week).
Library Book, 1, Non-fiction (Not to be held more than two (2) weeks).
Law Books, 6
Mattress, 1
Magazines (Not to accumulate)
Musical instruments (with permit) Broken or parts of musical instruments to be turned in to officer immediately.
Nail Clippers, 1
Newspapers (Not to accumulate)
Pillow, 1
Pillow slip, 1
Pen, Pencil set, 1
Pencil, State issue, 1
Pipes, 2
Pictures (No newspaper or magazine) censored
Pants, 3 pr.
Playing cards, 1 (pinochle)
Playing cards, 1 (Straight)
Paper, 1 ream
Stool, 1
Soap, Commissary, 2 Bars
Soap, State Issue, 1 Bar
Shirts, 3, (except in rare cases where work shirts are properly authorized).
Smoking Tobacco, 10 Sacks, Commissary
Smoking Tobacco, 1 (lb. tin)
Smoking Tobacco, 1, State Issue
School Supplies (Books, Tablets, etc.)

Shoes, 1 pr. State Issue, Numbered
Shoes, 1 pr. Commissary, Numbered
Sox, 3 pr. State Issue
Sox, 2 pr. Commissary
Slippers, 1 pr. Commissary, Numbered
Toilet paper, 1 roll
Typewriter, 1 (with permit)
Tennis Shoes, 1 pr. (To be worn in recreation yard only)
Tennis Ball, Numbered
Tooth Brush, 1
Tooth Paste or Powder, 1 tube or 1 tin
Towels, 2, State Issue
Towels, 2, Commissary, Numbered
Underwear, 3, State Issue, Numbered
Underwear, 3, Commissary, Numbered
Watch, 1 (Registered) (Maximum value $5.00)
All Commissary Items (One Week Supply)

Condemnation order must be presented to purchase shoes. All clothing and personal property must be numbered.

BATHING

Modern shower room. Joliet Branch.

You are required to take a bath and change your clothing as directed unless excused by the doctor.

When your line is taken to bathe, in cell formation, you will line up single file in front of the bath house according to the sequence of your cell. Strip and be prepared to enter the shower upon signal. Follow the man in front of you and take the bath stall immediately next to his. Ample time is given for your bath. Cleanse yourself thoroughly.

At signal from officer step out of shower, dry yourself, dress and be prepared to march out.

Deposit soiled clothing as directed.

Not Permitted

1. Talking.
2. Smoking.
3. Standing on clothing, towels, paper, benches or anything of like nature.
4. Placing shoes on benches.

MARCHING

When your line is being formed, take your place quietly.

At "fall in" order, form a line properly paired, cease all activity and stand at attention.

When ordered to "forward march," step forward with left foot first, maintaining paired up formation. Keep in step with the man in front of you as well as the man beside you and at arm's length behind the man ahead of you.

You are to walk with eyes to the front and be paired with the inmate beside you when marching or when line has stopped.

Remain in line until the order is given to "fall out."

Not Permitted

1. Talking or whistling.
2. Smoking.
3. Crowding, pushing or shoving.
5. Walking with hands in pockets.

FOOD DEPARTMENTS

It is a recognized fact that food is important. Your health and well being stand to gain by its proper handling and preparation.

For your meals, the State purchases good foods in plentiful quantities and varieties. For you to handle these foods in a slipshod manner is much the same as purposely injuring yourself.

Insofar as assignments to particular tasks are concerned, new workers are, in most instances, placed at one of the more menial jobs. This practice is followed even though a particular worker may be skilled, and is not in the least planned as an insult to his skill or his pride. By this method, the supervisor has a fair opportunity for judging his proper permanent placement. At the same time, the worker may progress toward the work most appealing to him. Inmates with a desire to cook or to bake have but to display a willing attitude toward their work to open a wide vista of training along these lines.

Men assigned to the culinary departments do not have the easiest of tasks but their work is important and necessary in the highest degree. They must, before assignment, be examined and given a clean bill of health by a physician, and thereafter, periodically submit to such examinations. They must be scrupulously clean about their clothing, person and their work. Orders, sometimes difficult to understand, must be followed. It is imperative and to the advantage of all that these orders be followed explicitly. Assignments to particular tasks are made by the officer to meet the needs of the department as well as placing the worker where he will be best adapted.

Inmates assigned to the Vegetable Room and other culinary departments may at first think their work is drab and unimportant. This is far from the truth. The skill necessary in preparing vegetables for cooking is fully as important as cooking itself. Poorly prepared vegetables result in unappetizing food to be eaten by both you and your fellow inmates. To throw half the potato away in peeling is to throw your own food away. Remember that vegetables and all foods are produced and purchased for a specified period, and new supplies are not purchased to replace those wasted. You may think there is no art in cleaning, preparing and serving vegetables, and no demand for men trained in this work, but hotels and large restaurants pay good salaries to men trained in this field.

STORE, GENERAL KITCHEN, BAKERY, CANNING PLANT AND DAIRY DEPARTMENT

Assignment to any of these will afford you the opportunity for extensive training and knowledge toward good paying employment upon your release. Good cooks, bakers, canners, butchers and dairy employees are always in demand. Good quality foods are produced and purchased for you in large quantities. Willful waste and spoiling only robs you and fellow inmates of needed food because all food items are produced and purchased in your behalf for a given length of time and cannot be replaced. Further, your relatives and friends pay for your waste in taxes.

Apprentices cannot expect to prepare and turn out an edible product without first learning the fundamentals of such preparation, and without a good groundwork of knowledge and practice. By sincere application and following instructions as given, much may be accomplished. Pot cooking in modern steam kettles, fry cooking on the range, oven cooking, baking, roasting, salad making, short order work, diet cooking, food care and handling, etc. are all included. All departments offer excellent training. When you have mastered one phase of the work, you can proceed to the next. To cook, bake, preserve and prepare food successfully takes will, determination and practice. Wearing a white cap and coat will not make you an expert. Neither the work nor the way of learning is easy, but the results can prove worthwhile.

Orders and instructions are issued for definite reasons, and must be heeded. Be sure you understand an order, for to guess at the meaning may well result in a spoiled or poor tasting food. Concentrate on one thing at a time rather than attempt to learn everything at once. Forget your friends here and there and try to serve better food to everyone.

All meals are served in the dining rooms of each division of the institution. A small percentage because of physical condition are served special meals prepared on the doctor's recommendation at the diet table. A very small minority of inmates are assigned to the employees' mess, as are men assigned to the Administration Building and hospitals and have their food in the employees' kitchen for the convenience of the institution. All others in all assignments throughout the institution are served their food in the inmates' dining rooms and at no time will there be special dishes prepared for anyone or any group. Men assigned to preparing or serving food are entitled to no more or better food than the general population; therefore, the bakery will prepare all bread and bakery products only. All other foods will be prepared according to the menus only, in designated kitchens and served in designated dining rooms only. If at any time other than the above procedure is followed, those who do so will violate an institution rule.

Strict rules of cleanliness must be rigidly observed, both as to the person and equipment in general. Daily showers, frequent shaves, clean hands and fingernails are a must. Hands must be washed every time you leave the lavatory.

Smoking is strictly prohibited while preparing or handling foods or the utensils in which they are prepared.

Particular care must be taken of the tools, knives or utensils issued to you. Losing them will cause you, and everyone concerned, trouble.

DINING ROOM

Generally, the duties of all inmates assigned to the Dining Room revolve about the serving of meals. Assignment to any of the various tasks is made solely by the employee in charge. While all orders and instructions come from the Warden, they are subject to enforcement by his employees. Therefore, if in doubt, consult your superior. You will be instructed as to your duties and expected to perform them properly.

Orders as to the proper apportioning of foods must be strictly observed. To do otherwise would result in the first man receiving more than his share and the last man losing his portion. To be found disregarding such orders could lose you several meals.

Finally, in serving foodstuffs, it might be well to consider how you would like them served to you.

Personal cleanliness, keeping fingernails clean and washing hands before leaving lavatory are a must, as is the proper care and cleanliness of all utensils.

Smoking is not permitted from the time the food trucks are brought out of the kitchen for any meal until all meals are over and the dining room is cleared and all utensils in proper place.

Inmates assigned to dispense food over the stands and waiters in the aisles, are particularly cautioned against arguing or talking with inmates passing the stand or seated at the tables, or while meals are being served.

Discipline here for infraction of the rules may well seem to come quickly and doubly hard. However, such rules are an absolute necessity and actually for your common good. It is hoped that you will observe them for reasons far more helpful to you than fear of punishment.

DINING ROOM BEHAVIOR

You must go to all meals, whether you care to eat or not. Exempt will be men who are receiving Communion on Sunday and Holy Days. Hands and face must be clean, hair combed and clothes as clean as possible.

When signal is given to go to the Dining Room, step out of your cell with cup in hand and proceed to the Dining Room and return in cell formation.

Proceed quietly following the man in front of you. Choose food which will be served to you from the steam table. After being served, continue following the man preceding you, occupying a seat in proper sequence, without commotion or unnecessary noise.

You are, after being seated, permitted to talk in a low tone with the man on either side of you.

Beverages and seconds, excepting meat, will be served you at your table, if requested.

Learn signals for obtaining salt, bread, etc.

When the bell rings, indicating the end of the meal, all talking must stop. Remain seated until the table ahead of you is vacated. Then upon the signal from the officer, you will be instructed to rise and march out.

Have your knife, fork, and spoon in hand and deposit them in the receptacle provided for the purpose as you leave the Dining room..

Not Permitted

1. Talking in line to and from the Dining Room.
2. Stepping to one side and passing other inmates, stopping and allowing other inmates to pass you.
3. Reaching into food containers. You must accept what is given to you by the waiter who is supervised by an officer.
4. Asking for or receiving any special part of the food on the steam table.
5. Taking more food than you feel you can eat. Edibles are not to be left on your plate.
6. Smoking.
7. Loud talking or boisterous behavior.
8. Demanding special servings of food.
9. Arguing with waiters at any time.

THE CHAPEL BUILDING

The principal purpose of the chapel building is for religious services and chaplain activities in general. Secondly, when not used for religious activities, it is open for the showing of movies, for entertainment, and for other programs.

Your conduct at all times in the chapel building must be befitting the dignity of the place.

RELIGIOUS ACTIVITIES

Although not compulsory, everyone is urged to attend one of the eight religious services conducted each week. You may attend the service of your choice, but of one denomination only. The Chaplain will issue a card upon request. Should you lose or misplace your card, you still are permitted to attend the service of your choice one Sunday by informing the cell-house officer and requesting him to notify the Chaplain. The cell-house officer will then issue you a pass and will, within the next day or two, ask the Chaplain to issue you another card.

The Chaplains of the various denominations invite you to consult with them. You are urged to do so by asking them directly or through your officer.

The following rules apply to all church services:

Upon entering the Chapel with your line, remove your cap and go to the seat designated by your officer.

If you are summoned by ticket or pass, present it immediately to the officer and follow his instructions.

Not Permitted

1. Talking.
2. Smoking.
3. "Contacting" or carrying messages.
4. Leaving spot designated by officer without permission.
5. To drop any refuse or debris on the floor, such as paper, etc.

SHOP ASSIGNMENTS

An employee is responsible for the operation of all assignments. He will help you lay out your work if you are in doubt as to the procedure.

No inmate will be placed in charge of an assignment or in supervising fellow inmates. The employees in charge of all assignments will pick qualified inmate leaders to help unskilled men, and teach the various vocations, etc.

You may, while working at your assignment, contact the Warden, Assistant Wardens, Captains, Lieutenants, and Chaplains on matters of personal interest, providing they are not busy or accompanied by visitors.

You are expected to apply yourself as faithfully and diligently as would be required on the outside.

Your shop and place of assignment must be kept neat and ready for inspection.

Take particular care of all tools and instruments used at your assignment. Tools issued to you will be charged to you and must be returned to the officer. Never give your tools to another inmate or let them out of your sight. If a tool or piece of equipment is lost, broken or in need of repair, report it to the officer immediately.

Not Permitted

1. Leaving shop or place of assignment without permission. If ill or unable to work, report to your officer and follow his instructions.

2. Carrying knives, tools or material of any kind from your place of assignment without permission in writing from your officer. Men working on out-of-shop assignments must have needed tools listed on work order when leaving shops and are responsible for their safe return.

3. Possession or manufacture of knife, weapon or contraband of any description.

4. Cleaning or repairing of any machine which is in motion.

5. Willful waste or destruction of State Property.

6. Inferior work or work not up to standard.

SAFETY

Before any piece of equipment is put into motion, be sure that it is safe to operate and during operation use hand rails and all safety devices provided. Gloves should not be worn or rags or waste used while operating any lathes or any moving equipment.

Never attempt to oil, grease, repair or clean any machinery while it is in motion.

You will be expected to use respirators and goggles on any assignment where health or injury may be involved.

No one but a qualified tradesman is to attempt to repair or replace any electrical device or any equipment of any type at any time.

Accidents happen because of carelessness and it is important to use judgment in the handling of all equipment; good house keeping is certainly important at all times. If oil, water, or grease is spilled, it is to be cleaned up immediately, as a slip can cause a serious accident.

There are more injuries in the home, on the recreation yard and during leisure time through carelessness and failure to apply common sense and good sportsmanship than there are during working hours. Use good judgment at all times.

Never take a chance on losing a life or a limb. In short, never trust to the care and exercise of others when your own or a fellow inmate's safety is involved. Safety pays dividends. Ask your civilian supervisor for advice and instructions.

HOSPITAL

If you have need for emergency dental or medical attention, notify your officer immediately and act as he directs. Otherwise report to the hospital on regular sick call. You must at all times conduct yourself in a quiet manner.

When your turn comes to see the Doctor, state your case simply. Do not attempt to diagnose your own case or prescribe treatment. Follow the Doctor's orders.

If you are hospitalized, remain in your room and in bed. Your conduct must be quiet and of the same manner as a patient in an outside hospital.

Diet cards will be issued to those inmates so specified by the doctor or dentist. These cards, if necessary, must be renewed at least every thirty (30) days. It is expected and demanded that men in the diet line live up to the recommendations of the doctor or dentist. If you have a diet card and are found in another line, the card will be revoked.

Men in need of dental work are to ask the officer in charge of the sick line. Because of the great number of men who are in need of dental work and the replacing of dentures, it is impossible to take care of all needs immediately. Your name will be placed on the dental list. You will be provided with the necessary treatment as soon as possible. Every effort will be made to take care of emergencies immediately.

Not Permitted

1. Talking.
2. "Contacting."
3. Pretending illness or injury.
4. Treatment other than prescribed by the Doctor.

5. Drugs or medicines other than issued you at the hospital, nor are they to accumulate or remain in your possession longer than one week from date noted on container.

COMMISSARY

One of the privileges granted inmates in good standing is that of trading weekly at the Commissary. Here you may buy cigars, cigarettes, tobacco, candy, foodstuffs of various kinds, toilet items and other permitted articles. All are sold at prices as near to or below current retail prices as possible. Profits are placed in the Inmates' Benefit Fund which pays for chapel supplies, athletic equipment, library books, schools and educational supplies, motion pictures and other items directly connected with inmate recreation and rehabilitation, both mental and physical.

The Commissary is not the concession of any employee or official. Profits are used only to pay the salary of employees directly connected with its operation, or in behalf of one of the above-mentioned activities.

If you are employed as a clerk in the Commissary, you will be held responsible for money transfers accepted by you from other inmates in payment for merchandise purchased. Know your customer. Do not accept forgeries.

If you wish to trade in the Commissary, obtain order blanks in the cell houses. Have your orders filled out properly before entering Commissary.

Enter the Commissary only if and when designated by your officer.

File past the commissary officer with your order in your hand. After he has placed your balance on the order, put your thumb print on the order in two places and secure your order as instructed by the officer.

Not Permitted

1. To enter Commissary if you do not have funds or have been denied Commissary privileges.

2. Spending more than designated amount each week with the exception of exempted articles indicated on Commissary List.

(Those in hospital or Detention will be limited in their commissary privileges.)

3. Spending more than $2.00 per week if you are confined in Segregation.

4. Purchasing more than 10 packages of cigarettes or 10 sacks of tobacco in one (1) week.

5. More than one (1) week's supply of Commissary purchased items, edibles and tobacco in your cell. (If more than the limited amount of Commissary items is found in your possession, all will be confiscated.)

6. Having others "hold" personal property for you.

7. To have or eat Commissary purchased foodstuffs anywhere other than in your cell.

8. Loud talking, arguing or "contacting."

9. Smoking.

10. Trading or trafficking.

11. Forging or any irregularity in connection with Commissary orders.

12. Exchange of Commissary purchased articles.

13. Commissary items in your possession not purchased by you will be declared contraband and confiscated.

14. After original purchase of a can opener, finger-nail clippers or cards, used items must be turned in before new can be re-purchased.

15. To transfer to other Institutions commissary purchases other than tobacco and toilet articles.

BARBER SHOP

Inmate barbers assigned to the Barber Shops will be issued equipment and tools for their use only, and will be held responsible for all equipment until turned into the officer upon request. Hands must be scrupulously clean and must be washed after using the lavatory. Barbering tools must be kept in a completely sanitary condition at all times. Barbers must practice barbering on assigned chair only, unless directed by the officer, and only regulation hair-cuts and shaves are to be given.

Smoking will not be permitted by barbers while they are barbering.

Inmate barber students are expected to put forth as much effort as possible in learning their trade. Those showing an indifferent attitude can expect to be transferred, as there are others waiting and eager to learn.

Not Permitted

1. Laying down barbering tools where they can be picked up by others.

2. Accepting cigarettes, candy or other payment for barber work.

3. Talking.

4. Smoking.

5. "Contacting."

Inmates entering the waiting room for barber work must enter in single file and be seated by the officer in charge. They are to remain until called for barber work. Then they are to occupy the chair assigned to them. When the barber work is completed, they must return to the waiting room and be seated until further order from the officer.

Not Permitted

1. Requesting special chair or barber work, or giving payment for same. If found to be wearing other than regulation hair style, you will be immediately escorted to Isolation by the Lieutenant and all hair will be clipped.

2. Use of preparation on hair other than that issued at Barber Shop or authorized by Doctor.

3. Talking in Barber Shop or waiting room.

4. "Contacting" in Barber Shop or waiting room.

5. Smoking in Barber Shop or waiting room.

6. Returning to waiting room after trading at Commissary.

LIBRARY

Branch Libraries are located in all cell houses at Stateville, Joliet, the Diagnostic Depot and the Farm. Each is well supplied with books of all types, fiction, non-fiction educational, etc.

These are maintained for your benefit and we encourage their use during your stay in the Institution. A catalog and routine has been set up for the obtaining of books. Any further information you desire concerning the use of the Library can be secured from the Cell House Keeper.

The same care of books is expected here as is demanded by a a library on the outside. Do not write in, ear-mark or otherwise deface books.

All books are to be returned to the Library after one week excepting non-fiction, which may be held two weeks.

Isolation cells, 1959. Stateville Branch.

ISOLATION

It has always been our desire to operate the Institution without Isolation and Segregation, but for some reason, a small percentage of inmates will violate rules and refuse to coöperate by not living within rules. Because denial of privileges and other minor disciplinary action do not seem to be effective, isolation-segregation must be of necessity a part of this Institution.

Men who violate minor rules to an extent where denial of privileges is no longer effective can expect to be placed in Isolation. You will be given Isolation clothing and the required number of blankets. You are expected to handle them so that they are not torn or destroyed. You will be given one meal each day, consisting of food the same as that served in the inmates' dining room. Your stay can be extended beyond the original punishment given you, depending upon your conduct while in Isolation.

Remember that if you are in Isolation at the time you are scheduled to appear before the Parole Board, you cannot appear before the members for hearing. Your case will be continued until such time as is directed by the Parole Board.

Not Permitted

1. Pretending a mental illness or feigning suicide in the hope of escaping punishment.
2. Mail and Visiting privileges.
3. Reading material.
4. Smoking.
5. Loud talking, noise or any unnecessary commotion.
6. Bad conduct of any kind.
7. Unnecessary use of running water and lavatory.
8. Tampering with equipment or building.
9. Damage to walls or contents of cell.

SEGREGATION

There are a few nonconformists and agitators in the Institution who, by the use of other disciplinary measures, cannot be made to understand that this is a prison and we must have discipline. We will not tolerate infringement of the Rules and Regulations of the Institution by permitting these men to continue as agitators and trouble-makers. Therefore, if you have violated the rules to the extent that it is necessary to place you in Segregation, you should know that no time need be set and you may be confined for an indefinite stay.

The mittimus in the hands of the Warden commands that you

be securely confined until your release by due process of law. Neither the mittimus nor court order indicates the type of assignment you are to be given. All that the law requires is that the Warden keep you securely confined, fed, clothed and supplied with medical attention, if necessary. Therefore, men who find their way to Segregation, select their own place of assignment by reason of their behavior and general misconduct.

If you are confined in Segregation, you must comply with all the rules and regulations of the Institution. You will be given one visit each month of thirty (30) minutes duration, on any day except Saturdays, Sundays or Holidays. Your visit will be conducted in the presence of an employee of the Institution. At no time is a foreign language to be spoken by you or your visitors. Those violating this rule can expect expiration of their visit immediately.

Men in grade "A" may spend a maximum of $2.00 per week in the inmates' Commissary.

Not Permitted

1. Damage or destruction of State Property.
2. Lack of cleanliness and good housekeeping (cell).
3. Stopping Warden, or any employee, when accompanied by visitors. You may write a letter requesting an interview with an officer or employee.
4. Other than designated reading material.

OUTSIDE DETAIL AND FARM

Men assigned to the East Side Detail at the Joliet Branch and those assigned to the Outside Detail at Stateville will be given consideration for transfer to the Farm, providing they do not violate the rules and regulations of the Institution, and perform all work assigned to them while serving on these details. In most instances, seniority rules insofar as vacancies on the Farm are concerned, except in cases where it may be necessary to transfer a tradesman.

Farming is healthy, appealing work. There are many opporities for learning worthwhile vocations such as gardening, general farming, dairying, swine and cattle raising, etc.

ing quarters are to be maintained in the same manner
r cell and only permitted items are to be in your room
ent or on your person at any time.

tted

1. Crossing of State Property line or leaving State Property
will be considered an attempt to escape, or an escape, and upon
prosecution and conviction, the sentence is one to ten years.
2. Over-feeding, over-working, mistreating or abusing livestock.
3. Careless maintenance of farm machinery and implements,
or use of broken machinery until properly repaired.
4. Laying down reins unless securely tied.
5. Crossing or driving trucks or vehicles on the public highway without the permission of an employee. Only designated
routes and roads are to be followed.
6. Speed of vehicles must not exceed thirty miles per hour.
7. Smoking or lighting matches in any building where feed,
hay, straw, or animals are housed.

INMATE MAIL

You may correspond with those persons appearing on your
"Approved" writing list, and with attorney and courts.

Sign your full name and register number at the bottom of the
letter and coupon. Instruct your correspondents to include your
register number on incoming mail.

Checks and money orders received without proper name and
number will be returned to the sender.

All grades write each Sunday. Date both letter and coupon.

Grades "D" and "E" are permitted to write each Sunday to
their immediate relatives, courts and lawyers.

Contents of permitted letters must be relative to your welfare
and the welfare of your family, or the actual matters pertaining
to your case.

Letters must be written clearly and legibly and not underlined
or interlined.

Special letters of necessity are granted for emergencies, sickness or death only.

Letters written by other than the sender must have the writer's name and number inserted in the space provided on the coupon.

All letters, incoming and outgoing, within the boundaries of the United States must be written in the English language.

You are permitted to retain fifteen (15) personal letters only (in your cell) with the exception of those from attorneys and courts. For the protection of your relatives, do not let your letters fall into the hands of other inmates.

Not Permitted

1. Discussion of subjects that are controversial.
2. Instructions concerning business.
3. Addressing of letters to General Delivery in large cities.
4. Use of another inmate's name and number.
5. Writing to former inmates of this or any other penal institution, or to any person having a criminal record, excepting relatives by permission.
6. Corresponding with relatives or friends of another inmate.
7. Mention of another inmate's name or number or anything pertaining to another inmate.
8. Discussion of the institution or its personnel.
9. Expressions of a vulgar, profane or malicious nature.
10. Untruths and false accusations.
11. Soliciting funds, reading material, or anything of like nature.
12. Cartoons, sketches or drawings in correspondence. Reading Material and all permitted articles must be ordered through the Chief Clerk's Office.
13. All cash will be refused and returned to the sender. All remittances must be in the form of a check, or money order, bearing inmates number.
14. Packages or merchandise from outside.

It is permissible to receive religious and approved magazines and newspapers from our chaplains, and newspapers on our "permitted list" providing they are purchased through the Chief Clerk's Office only, and come directly from the publisher.

PERMITTED MAGAZINE LIST

Advertising Magazine
Aeroplane Magazine
All Pets Magazine
Argosy
Atlantic Magazine
Automobile Magazine
Baker's Weekly
Barron's
Baseball Publications
Bee & Insect Magazines
Billboard
Bovine Publications
Boxing and Wrestling
Bridge World
Business Education World
Business Week Magazines
Catholic Digest
Chess Publications
Christian Life
Community News Service
Commonwealth
Construction Models
Crossword Puzzles
Current Events
Current History
Display World
Dog Magazines
Domestic Engineering
Ebony
Editor and Publisher
Electrical and Construction Main-
tenance
Electrical World
Esquire
Farm Publications
Football Publications
Forbes
Foreign Affairs
Fortnight
Fortune
Fruit Publications
Future Magazine
Gregg Writer
Science Newsletter
Science of Mind
Science & Mechanics Magazine
Scientific American
Shoe & Leather Reported
Signs of the Times
Stamp Publications
The Minerologist
All Sports Magazine

All State Scenic Magazine
American Magazine
Harper's
Hobbies Magazine
Holiday
Homes and Gardens Magazine
Horse Magazines
Hunting and Fishing Magazines
Ideals
Industrial Marketing
Law Publications
Leatherneck
Life
Look
Magazine Digest
McCall's
Modern Plastics
Moody Monthly
Motion Picture
Motor Boat Magazines
Motorcycle Magazines
Movie Life
Music Publications
National Digest
National Geographic
Newsweek
Omnibook
Opportunity Magazine
Our World
Pathfinder
Photography Magazines
Poetry Magazines
Popular Handicraft
Poultry Magazines
Prairie Farmer
Printer's Ink
Radio Publications
Railroad Magazines
Reader's Digest
Redbook
Refrigerator Publications
Sales Management
Saturday Evening Post
Saturday Review of Literature
Time
True
T.V. Publications
University of Chicago Round Table
War Veterans' Magazine
Welding Magazines
Writer's Digest

Because of the type of institution, and the men who live within its boundaries, the officials reserve the right to reject any merchandise, packages, messages or mail, either incoming or outgoing.

VISITS

During your stay at the Diagnostic Depot, provide the officer, upon request, with a list of those persons from whom you expect visits and mail. Remember that a close investigation will be made as to their relationship with you.

We encourage visits by members of your family. Because our visiting facilities are limited and must of necessity be closely supervised, Rules and Regulations will be strictly enforced. If you violate the visiting rules or permit your visitors to do so, you can expect to have your visits discontinued immediately and further visits denied.

Visitors coming long distances are to make arrangements with the officer at the Information Desk and the Visiting Room for overtime and future visits.

Visits by lawyers will not be charged against your regular family visit. However, attorneys will not be permitted to visit on Sundays or Holidays, and their visits must be confined between the hours of 8:00 A.M. and 3:00 P.M.

There will be no visits for the first thirty (30) days of your incarceration. Thereafter (with the exception of men assigned to the Farm), you will be permitted "approved" visits every two (2) weeks with two (2) adults, and never more than two (2) children (by permission), on any week day except Sundays and Holidays.

Only one (1) adult and a child in arms will be permitted to visit any inmate on Saturday. Time will be regulated according to number of outside visitors.

Generally speaking, most visits will be of one hour duration. On days involving a great number of visitors, it may be necessary to limit visiting time. You will find that on week days other than Saturday, the visiting rooms are less crowded, thereby making it a better and more worthwhile time for your visits. It would be well to advise your visitors of this.

You may embrace your visitor over the table directly in front of the officer. After the embrace, show your hands and mouth to the officer.

Relatives having small children are to be seated at the table holding them in their arms.

Not Permitted

1. Requests that outsiders be placed on your "approved" visiting list. (Unless you can establish some relationship or very good and definite reason.)

2. Visits from persons with a criminal record.

3. Having more than two (2) persons visit with you in the visiting room.

4. Reaching over the glass partition in visiting room. (If any type of document is involved, it is to be given to the officer in charge, who will either approve or forward it to the proper destination for approval.)

5. Misbehavior of children. They must remain seated at table.

If you are assigned to any of the following, your visiting days will be as indicated, and you should so inform your "approved" visitors immediately upon assignment.

Hospital: If you are a patient, you will be permitted your regular visit on any day except Saturday, Sunday and Holidays unless your condition is serious in nature. Then arrangements will be made with relatives when registering at the Information Desk.

Isolation: No visits.

Segregation: One (1) half-hour visit each month on any day except Saturday, Sunday and Holidays, under the supervision of an employee. No foreign language is to be spoken.

Farm Stateville: Sunday only, between the hours of 10:00 a.m. and 2:00 p.m. No more than five (5) members of a family may be present at one time. Families are permitted to bring foodstuffs, but all will be thoroughly inspected. Your visitors must confine their visit to you only. Only designated buildings and park are to be entered by you or visitors.

Outside Detail Stateville: Saturday only, every two (2) weeks.

East Side Detail-Joliet Branch: Saturday only, every two (2) weeks.

Quarry-Joliet Branch: Saturday between 8:00 a.m. and 3:00 p.m. and Wednesday between noon and 3:00 p.m. every two (2) weeks.

GENERAL RULES AND INSTRUCTIONS

Give the administration and prison personnel credit for knowing something about prisoners and the operation of prisons. You may be able to fool a few employees part of the time, but remember someone will notice your movements and behavior. If you are directly or indirectly responsible for the violation of any of the rules of the institution, you will be disciplined by the denial of privileges, being placed in isolation, loss of good time, reduction in grade, or by prosecution in the local courts, or a combination of all if the violation should so warrant.

Never underestimate the knowledge employees have gained in the prison service over a period of years. Nearly all have been tried and are not lacking in the knowledge and movement of inmates who attempt by word of mouth, or by their activities, to violate the rules of the institution.

It will benefit you, therefore, to take particular note of the following:

Any inmate participating either actively or passively in a mutiny, riot or insurrection, destruction of state property, attack upon the person of any civilian, employee, or inmate, will be dealt with severely; and inmates will find that the Warden, and those employees under him, will resist any attempt by an inmate or inmates to participate in the above and they will be dealt with quickly and severely. There will be no compromise under any circumstances; and any inmate who attacks an employee, a civilian, or another inmate, or participates or attempts to participate in the destruction of state property, or attempts to riot or escape can be assured that resistance will be met with all forces available, including firearms; and any inmate who attempts to force his way through any gate will be met with the same resistance and firearms; and for the perpetration of any of the above, you can be punished by being deprived of all statutory good time, special punishment and loss of privileges as is warranted and deemed advisable and prosecution to the fullest extent of the law.

You are subject to a search at any time.

When wearing a coat, you must have at least two buttons buttoned at all times while in line, on the various walks, in the tunnels, etc.

In wearing a shirt without a coat, the top collar button only may remain open but your sleeves may be rolled up except when in line, the dining room or chapel.

Upon entering the chapel, administration building, hospital, isolation office and other specified places, remove your cap and conduct yourself in a quiet and respectful manner.

Employees must always be addressed respectfully, using their title, if known. (If not known, use the title "Mr.") Conversation with employees must be limited.

In asking to see the Warden, Assistant Wardens, Senior Captains, the Chaplains, etc., you must do so through the regular channels. Requests may be placed in the box provided in the cell house. Sign your name, number and assignment. Keep your request brief and to the point.

When the Warden, Assistant Wardens, Supervising Officials or visitors enter your assignment, stand, if you are not occupied at some task.

Generally speaking, most assignments will be given on a seniority basis. There are so many men required for each assignment. When vacancies occur, the man next in line on the list in the hands of the Captains will be given consideration. Remember that those requesting assignments must meet the educational and institutional requirements, and be capable of carrying on the work. Your record will always be considered a factor in all assignments.

If you are assigned to a clerical or other position in the institution, you must follow the rules and regulations issued by the civilian employee in charge. You are to follow his instructions for keeping all records, and all other procedures. If, in the performance of your daily routine, you should discover a discrepancy, you are to notify immediately the civilian in charge. Under no circumstances are you to attempt to change any procedure or correct any record that may not coincide with the rules and instructions given you.

Inmates assigned to any of the various industrial shops of the institution will earn money in the production of finished products. It will be compulsory that you save at least $50.00 from your earnings, an average of at least $5.00 per month until this amount has accumulated. This will be set aside for your release day.

Relatives and friends desiring to send money may do so in the form of a money order, bank draft, cashier's check, etc. bearing inmate's number which will be placed to your credit. Cash will be returned to the sender.

In making transfers of money you may have on deposit at the institution your name and number must be written legibly, and you must specify the relationship and reasons for the transfer, and your signature must be witnessed by an employee of the institution.

Remember, there are persons confined here, who have little or no regard for anyone other than themselves. Therefore, for your own good and the protection of those near and dear to you, it will pay you well to refrain from disclosing their names and addresses. You will then avoid the possibility of their being contacted by unscrupulous persons.

Anything not issued by the institution or purchased in the commissary is considered contraband, with the exception of specially permitted items, such as typewriters, musical instruments, etc. Anyone carrying, holding or having contraband in his possession will be considered the owner.

If you have been transferred to a new cell or new assignment, remember this is a prison and the man who left the premises and previously occupied the cell or assignment may have left contraband. If any is found in your possession, it will be charged to you. It will serve you well to inspect thoroughly the premises in which you live and work.

Money on the person of an inmate is contraband. It will be

confiscated, never returned and placed in the Inmates' Benefit Fund.

Radios, television sets, typewriters and other permitted articles are to be registered and charged to the original purchaser. Under no circumstances can they be transferred from one inmate to another, but you may, on leaving the institution, donate whatever property you have to the institution. Inmates will be granted the use of this property by permission only.

The repairing of all "permitted" articles must be done in the Vocational School only. No one is authorized to make his own repairs. Inmates having musical instruments are charged with their safekeeping, and broken strings and parts must be turned in to the officer immediately.

Library Books, school supplies, drawing instruments, paints, brushes and other permitted articles are to be registered. You will be charged with their safekeeping.

All law and educational books may be sent home after proper censorship. This is to be done only at your regular visit and only upon request. Books are not to be mailed or sent by express. This same procedure applies to typewriters, musical instruments, radios, etc., providing you have a registered permit.

All articles, religious or otherwise, issued or purchased, must be retained as issued. They must be carried in the pocket, worn around the neck or remain in the cell.

All clothing worn by the inmate on the day he is received becomes the property of the state. The institution furnishes all clothes required during your stay here. On the day you are released, you will be furnished a complete outfit of dress clothing, but no work clothes.

Inmates appearing in courts on writ and remanded to the custody of a sheriff pending the disposal of their case must not dispose of the clothing issued to them at the institution. Under no circumstances are they permitted to wear clothing other than was issued to them, nor are they, on their return, to bring other than permitted articles. Clothing worn back to the institution or given to you at the County Jail will become the property of the state.

You are responsible for all state property issued to you. It will also be your responsibility upon your release date to return all such articles, including clothing, etc., to the place designated for the disposal of such property.

Inmates who are being discharged or paroled, or who are being returned to Court on writs and have personal property which they want to take with them upon leaving the institution, may send their property to the mail office for censoring at least ten (10) days in advance of their release day.

Inmates desiring to donate their personal property to the institution, for the use of other inmates may do so ten (10) days prior to their release day. However, it will become state property and not the property of the individual.

Permitted

1. Writing to the Warden, Assistant Wardens, and other supervisory officials requesting necessary information or other requirements. Keep request short and to the point. Sign your name, number, and give your assignment.

2. The preparation of petitions for writs or documents pertaining to your case only, or having an attorney do it for you. Any court papers pertaining to similar cases providing they are received from the various courts or attorneys and are properly stamped with a censor stamp. Your own typewriter or one borrowed by permission. Documents will be mailed to courts and attorneys, Governor, Director, Superintendent of Prisons and Parole Board only. They must be forwarded to the Record Office. In due time you will be called by a member of their staff for notarization of your signature if necessary.

3. To spend the designated amount each week at the Inmates' Commissary on items other than shoes, underwear, and other designated items.

4. Use of your funds for the purchase of government bonds. You may do so by submitting the proper form which may be obtained from your Cell House Keeper. After a period of approximately fifteen (15) days you will receive a receipt from the Chief

Clerk's Office showing the denomination and serial number of the bond purchased. These bonds will not be converted into cash for a period of less than one year from date of purchase. At the expiration of one year, if you desire to do so, you must forward a written request, together with the receipt for the bond you wish converted, to the Chief Clerk's Office. It must be understood that there will be a waiting period pending the arrival of a bank representative. At this time you will be summoned for the purpose of signing the bond or bonds you wish converted. Government Bonds purchased in the Institution will be retained in your personal jacket until your release date. They will under no circumstances be forwarded out of the Institution or be relinquished to anyone other than you personally.

5. The purchase (by permission only) of new typewriters, musical instruments, drawing material and equipment, and in some cases television sets and radios if you are in assignments where they are permissible. All permits are to be issued by the Assistant Wardens or Captains. Those having permisson to purchase television sets, radios and other permitted items must do so through the Chief Clerk's Office. The only exception to this rule would be typewriters or musical instruments. We will endeavor to purchase the name brand you desire providing the quality and price are suitable.

6. All educational books are to be ordered through the school. Religious books and items must be ordered through the Chaplains. They are subject to final approval by the Chief Clerk's Office.

7. Fiction and non-fiction books are to be ordered through the Chief Clerk's Office and will after thirty (30) days become the property of the State.

8. A maximum of six (6) law books may be ordered through the Chief Clerk's Office.

Not Permitted

1. Insolence to either employees or inmates.
2. Agitating, fighting, scufflling or violence of any form.
3. Profane or abusive language.

4. Whistling, catcalls, derisive shouts, etc.

5. Running. (The only exception to this important rule is in the recreation yard.)

6. Staring, motioning or speaking to outside visitors.

7. Stealing or taking State Property or property of others.

8. Defacing or destroying State Property or property of others.

9. Falsifying.

10. Gambling in any form.

11. Smoking when going from one assignment to another. (You are permitted to smoke only in designated places. Ask your officer where and when.

12. Tinted glasses (unless prescribed by doctor). Inmates having permission to wear tinted glasses are to remove them when passing through all gates.

13. Sex perversion, immoral acts, or any sex irregularities.

14. The manufacturing or making of contraband of any type or description.

15. All articles, cigarettes, tobacco, etc. not duly authorized.

16. Hoarding or accumulating chewing or smoking tobacco, or Commissary items.

17. Allowing foodstuffs, either purchased in the Commissary or served in the Dining Room, to set so that they ferment and form a mash of alcoholic content.

18. Trafficking, bartering and trading.

19. Writing notes, letters or "contacting" other inmates.

20. Passing notes or letters or assisting other inmates in "contacting" each other.

21. Visiting the sick bed or attending funeral of relative or friend.

22. To direct any business you may have owned prior to your incarceration, no matter how legitimate it was. (If you were interested in any type of business prior to your commitment, arrange on your first visit for the supervision of your interests for the duration of your sentence.)

23. Attempting to practice law or preparing writs or documents pertaining to the case of another. (Remember all writs

are sworn to. Do not place yourself in the position of being charged with and prosecuted for perjury.

24. The Record Office will notarize documents made up for individuals to be mailed to courts, attorneys, Safety Department heads, etc. However, it will reject documents made up for an inmate by another inmate or witnessed by another inmate.

25. Forwarding money from the Institution to a relative or friend with the idea of having the money returned to you or another inmate. Checks and money orders without proper names and numbers will be returned to the sender.

26. Signing checks or vouchers or receipts for anything that is not your property.

27. To leave your assignment except on an authorized pass, timed and recorded by the officer in the cell house or any assignment. Upon reaching the point of destination shown on the ticket, your time of arrival and departure must be recorded by the officer in charge and the ticket must be given to the officer in the cell house or assignment when you return. You are not to loiter or kill time enroute.

28. Refusal to work or accept assignment. (However, you may give your reason to the Captain or assigning officer. If the assigning officer makes the assignment, you must accept it but are privileged to contact the Warden or Assistant Wardrens later.

29. To mutilate, disfigure or discolor your body in any manner, nor can any mark or tattoo be placed on or be removed from any part of your body.

30. Jewelry of any kind other than "permitted" watch.

31. Pictures pasted in albums. They are to be held by tabs securing the corners.

32. Newspaper clipping and other articles of publication to be a part of any album.

33. Retaining of newspapers for more than ten (10) days, weekly magazines for more than thirty (30) days and monthly magazines for more than ninety (90) days from receiving date.

34. Television sets or radios to be brought in from the outside.

35. Radio in cell house.

36. Crime programs on radios or television sets.

37. Tinkering, nor will any inmate attempt to repair or re-do any piece of equipment, unless he calls a foreman or supervising officer who has the knowledge.

38. Commercializing of all types, painting, writing for any publication or selling any article whatsoever, nor will patents be recorded or forwarded from Institution.

On the whole, most of the inmates who are received here want to do their time in the best possible way, and earn or gain their release either by parole or discharge. Some, because of an erroneous concept, feel that the rules and regulations do not apply to them. They attempt to lay out their own way of operation by agitating, inciting riots, and in some instances, insurrections.

THIS IS TO INFORM YOU THAT IF AT ANY TIME A MASS ASSAULT IS STARTED AND YOU HAVE NO DESIRE TO PARTICIPATE YOU ARE TO GO TO YOUR CELL IN AN ORDERLY MANNER AND REMAIN THERE, WHICH WILL INDICATE THAT YOU HAVE NO DESIRE TO BECOME A PART OF SUCH MASS DISTURBANCE. WE MUST INFORM THOSE WHO DO PARTICIPATE IN SUCH CONDUCT THAT THE INSTITUTION IS AUTHORIZED AND HAS A TRAINED, HEAVILY ARMED RIOT SQUAD WHICH CAN AND WILL MOVE IN IMMEDIATELY WITH THE INTENTION OF TAKING ACTION EVEN BY THE USE OF FIREARMS, AND THOSE WHO TAKE PART OR ENCOURAGE CONDUCT OF THIS TYPE, WILL FIND THEMSELVES DEALT WITH SEVERELY, WITH PERHAPS LOSS OF LIFE AS THE FINAL RESULT. WE WILL NOT COMPROMISE OR ACCEDE TO ANY DEMANDS. IF YOU HAVE A COMPLAINT, YOU WILL BE GIVEN AN INDIVIDUAL HEARING. GROUPS OR COMMITTEES WILL NOT BE RECOGNIZED AT ANY TIME.

If the Courts of the State have seen fit to commit you to this Institution, you can only be released by parole, discharge or court order. Therefore:

ANY INMATE WHO ATTEMPTS TO ESCAPE OR DOES ESCAPE, OR RESISTS AN ORDER BY AN EMPLOYEE, HAS VIOLATED A LAW OF THE STATE OF ILLINOIS, AND IS INDICTED AND TRIED IN THE LOCAL COURTS, AND ANY SENTENCE RECEIVED FOR SUCH VIOLATION WILL RUN CONSECUTIVE TO THE SENTENCE YOU ARE NOW SERVING. ANY INMATE WHO AIDS OR ABETS ANOTHER IN-

MATE IN ESCAPING OR ATTEMPTING TO ESCAPE, WILL BE TRIED
IN THE COURTS, AND IF CONVICTED WILL BE GIVEN THE SEN-
TENCE IMPOSED UPON THE PERSON SO ATTEMPTING OR ACCOM-
PLISHING SUCH ESCAPE, WHICH SENTENCE WILL RUN CONSECU-
TIVE TO THE SENTENCE NOW BEING SERVED.

REMEMBER THAT THE RULES AND REGULATIONS HEREIN SET
FORTH ARE IN SUPPLEMENT, NOT INSTEAD OF THOSE ALREADY
IN FORCE AND EFFECT, AND POSTED ON THE BULLETIN BOARDS
IN THE VARIOUS LOCATIONS AND ASSIGNMENTS THROUGHOUT
THE INSTITUTION.

PAY NO ATTENTION TO RUMORS OR THE PRISON "GRAPEVINE."
ALL NEW RULES AND REGULATIONS AND INFORMATION PER-
TAINING TO THE GENERAL INMATE POPULATION WILL BE READ
OVER THE PUBLIC ADDRESS SYSTEM AND POSTED ON THE BULLE-
TIN BOARDS.

ANY RULES OR REGULATIONS APPEARING IN THIS BOOK, OR
WHICH MAY BE POSTED ON THE BULLETIN BOARDS, OR AN-
NOUNCED OVER THE PUBLIC ADDRESS SYSTEM MAY BE SUPPLE-
MENTED, RESCINDED OR COUNTERMANDED BY THE WARDEN.

Remember, the monies needed for the maintenance and operation of this Institution are derived from the taxes paid by your
relatives and friends. Therefore, that which you waste or destroy is costly to them. The more money needed to operate a
prison, the less that can be spent on delinquency preventatives to
educate and guide the boy or girl of today who may become a
prisoner tomorrow, if society does not take an interest in them.

It would be well for you to keep in mind that by virtue of good
advertising, commercial organizations reap great dividends. If
their product is bad, the very fact that it is found to be so injures
the reputation of that product. Men in prison are a product. In
years past, men having a prison record were frowned upon by
the public and had little opportunity to become successful after
their release. This is not so today. A few years ago, prison administrators and organizations interested in prisons and the men
confined there, began advertising the potential value of these
men if given the opportunity, despite the fact that they had been
in prison.

We have made great strides with the public. Employment today is not too difficult to find. Many industrial organizations will accept you, particularly if you possess the knowledge helpful to the industry they represent.

People in general are prejudiced by publicity surrounding penal institutions and inmates. If it is favorable, it is beneficial to the men who are products of prison. If the publicity is bad, it will injure the cause which prison administrators are trying to bring to the public. For your own welfare, do not become a party to the creation of bad publicity.

Since the public is always interested in the activities behind prison walls, it will pay you dividends to see that the publicity is good. Many people have visited and will visit this Institution. The press is always welcome and there are no secrets insofar as they and the public are concerned. Do not destroy the chances you, and those following you, may have. Many have made a mistake, have paid for it and after their release have become useful citizens. If your neighbor feels he wants bad publicity, let him make his own bad conduct record. The record you make during your stay here will be kept by the officials. If it is bad, it will certainly be of no help to you. To see a man with a bad record in or out of prison, is to see a man who is a failure.

ILLINOIS REVISED STATUTES 1955
CHAPTER 38 — PENITENTIARIES
ESCAPE — PENALTY

228. Whoever conveys into the penitentiary, or into any jail or other place of confinement, any disguise, instrument, tool, weapon or other thing adapted or useful to aid a prisoner in making his escape, with intent to facilitate the escape of any prisoner there lawfully committed or detained, or by any means whatever aids, abets, or assists such prisoner to escape or to attempt to escape from any jail, prison, or any lawful detention whether such escape is effected or attempted or not, or conceals or assists any convict after he had escaped, shall upon conviction thereof be given the same penalty as the prisoner whom he aided or abetted, except that in case the prisoner is sentenced to death,

the penalty for such aid shall be imprisonment for life in the penitentiary.

KIDNAPPING

384. PUNISHMENT. Whoever willfully and without lawful authority forcibly or secretly confines or imprisons any other person within this State against his will, or forcibly carries or sends such person out of the State, or forcibly seizes or confines, or inveigles, or kidnaps any other person, with the intent to cause such person to be secretly confined or imprisoned in this State against his will, or to cause such person to be sent out of the State against his will, shall be imprisoned in the penitentiary for a term of not less than one year and not exceeding five years, or fined not exceeding $1,000, or both.

In case any person being hooded, robed or masked so as to conceal his identity, violates any of the provisions of this section, he shall be fined not less than $500, nor more than $2,000, or imprisoned in the penitentiary not less than five years nor more than fourteen years, or both.

KIDNAPPING FOR RANSOM

386. Be it enacted by the People of the State of Illinois, represented in the General Assembly: That every person who shall willfully, unlawfully and forcibly seize and secretly confine within this state, or take, carry or send, or cause to be taken, carried or sent out of this state, any person against his will or against the will of the parent, guardian or legal custodian of such person, for the purpose of extorting ransom or money or other valuable thing or concession from such person, his parent, guardian or legal custodian; and every person who shall inveigle, decoy or kidnap with intent secretly to confine within this State, or take, carry or send, or cause to be taken, carried or sent out of same, any person against his will or against the will of the parent, guardian or legal custodian of such person, for the purpose of extorting ransom or money or other valuable thing or concession from such person, his parent, guardian or legal custodian, shall, upon conviction, suffer death, or be punished by imprisonment in the peni-

tentiary for life or any term not less than five (5) years. Any person charged with such offense may be tried in any county into which or through which, the person so seized or inveigled, decoyed or kidnapped shall have been taken, carried or brought.

PERJURY AND SUBORNATION

473. PUNISHMENT. Every person, having taken a lawful oath or made affirmation, in any judicial proceeding, or in any other matter where by law an oath or affirmation is required, who shall swear or affirm willfully, corruptly, and falsely, in a matter material to the issue or point in question, or shall suborn any other person to swear or affirm, as aforesaid, shall be deemed guilty of perjury or subornation of perjury (as the case may be), and shall be imprisoned in the penitentiary not less than one year nor more than fourteen years.

476. ATTEMPT TO SUBORN. Whoever endeavors to incite or procure any other person to commit perjury, though no perjury is committed, shall be imprisoned in the penitentiary not less than one nor more than five years or confined in the county jail not exceeding one year, and fined not exceeding $1,000.

INJURIES TO PROPERTY

511. If any persons thus unlawfully and riotously assembled, pull down or begin to pull or destroy any dwelling house, building, ship or vessel, or perpetrate any premeditated injury, not a felony, or any person, such person or persons so offending shall be imprisoned in the penitentiary for a term of not less than one year or more than five years, . . .

ILLINOIS REVISED STATUTES 1955 CHAPTER 38 — PENITENTIARIES ESCAPE — PENALTY

121. Whoever being a prisoner in the Illinois State Penitentiary escapes or attempts to escape therefrom, or escapes or attempts to escape while in the custody of an employee of the Illinois State Penitentiary, is guilty of a felony and, upon conviction thereof, shall be imprisoned in the penitentiary not less than one year and not more than ten; provided, however, that any sentence of imprisonment imposed upon conviction of any prisoner for so es-

caping or attempting to escape shall not commence until the expiration of the term which the prisoner was serving at the time of the escape or attempt to escape.

DISCIPLINE — ESCAPE — KILLING CONVICT

38. Whenever several convicts combined, or any single convict, shall offer violence to any officer or guard of the penitentiary, or to any convict, or do or attempt to do any injury to any building or workshops, or any appurtenances thereof, or shall attempt to escape, or shall disobey or resist any lawful command, the officers of the penitentiary and guards shall use all suitable means to defend themselves, to enforce the observance of discipline, to secure the persons of the offenders, and prevent such attempted violence or escape; and if said officers or guards employed in said penitentiary, or any of them, shall, in the attempt to prevent the escape of any convict, or in attempting to retake any convict who has escaped, or in attempting to prevent or suppress a riot, revolt, mutiny or insurrection, take the life of a convict, such officer or guard shall not be held responsible therefor, unless the same was done unnecessarily or wantonly.

CRIMES COMMITTED IN PENITENTIARY

118. When any crime is committed within any division or part of the penitentiary system by any person confined therein, cognizance thereof shall be taken by any court of that county wherein such division or part is situated having jurisdiction over the particular class of offenses to which such crime belongs. Such court shall try and punish the person charged with such crime in the same manner and subject to the same rules and limitations as are now established by law in relation to other persons charged with crime in such county. But in case of conviction, the sentence of said convict shall not commence to run until the expiration of the sentence under which he is then held in confinement in the penitentiary system. Provided, that in case such convict shall be sentenced to punishment by death, the sentence shall be executed at such time as the court may fix without regard to the sentence under which such convict may be held in the penitentiary; and

provided, further, that all fees and costs arising from the prosecution of convicts for crimes committed within the penitentiary system, which would otherwise be paid by the County, shall be paid by the State.

Chapter 7

EXAMPLES OF IMPROVABLE AND
UNIMPROVABLE CASES

In order to bring into clear focus how the prison's classification report is prepared for each incoming inmate, samples are presented of improvable and unimprovable cases.

These are actual case reports. Of course, the true identity of each inmate is withheld for obvious reasons.

No two cases, as can be deduced, are alike. By the same token, each case is a challenge to those who participate in assessing an inmate's personality.

The same thorough analysis is given to each inmate, regardless of the nature of the crime. The tests do not end after an inmate is received and placed in a cell.

Repeat tests are given periodically in efforts to determine progress or lack of progress on the part of the inmate in adjusting to prison life and in rehabilitating himself.

The first four cases presented are examples of unimprovable cases, as determined by our experts. Then, are given samples of two improvable cases.

The cases follow:

CASE A
STATE OF ILLINOIS
DEPARTMENT OF PUBLIC SAFETY
DIVISION OF THE CRIMINOLOGIST
Joliet Diagnostic Depot UNIT
CLASSIFICATION REPORT

No. 00000   2-25-55

| Name: DOE, John | Age: 24 | Admitted: 2-4-55 |
| Crime: Assault with intent to commit murder | | Sentence: 12-14 yrs. |

OFFENSE: Inmate was admitted February 4, 1955 from Cook County under a sentence of from twelve to fourteen years for assault with intent to commit murder. The official statement tells us that inmate forced his way into the apartment of a couple in Chicago, grabbed the wife, and had his hand over her mouth. As she began to scream the husband began fighting with inmate, who then pulled out a gun and fired at the man, striking him in the right side. Inmate was apprehended as he ran down the stairs trying to get out of the building. Inmate admits his guilt. He stated that he was, "on the lam", from the police, because of his escape from San Quentin, that when the police began looking for him in the building he tried to "duck" into this apartment, believing at the time that it was unoccupied. He claims that he only shot at the wall to frighten off the man, but that the bullet ricocheted off the wall and hit the man.

PREVIOUS RECORD: A term at St. Charles between May 14, 1948 and January 7, 1949 after earlier having been placed on juvenile probation for taking two suits from a tailor shop, and for running away from home on several occasions. On July 20, 1949 he was placed under court supervision for tampering with a motor vehicle. On November 8, of that year he received a thirty day sentence in the House of Correction for auto tampering. On December 23, 1950 he was arrested in Chicago for investigation, and in April 1950 was placed on probation for a period of three years for receiving stolen property. In November 1950 he served ten days in the Cook County jail for carrying a concealed weapon. On January 13, 1950 he was arrested in LaCrosse, Wisconsin, and again charged with carrying a concealed weapon. He was admitted to ISP April 17, 1951 under a year to a year and a day sentence for receiving stolen property. After his arrest in LaCrosse, Wisconsin it was determined that he had in his possession jewelry which had been taken in an earlier burglary. Following his release from ISP, March 19, 1952 inmate stated he went to Chicago where he began living with his brother Loe, who had served an earlier term in Joliet also. On March 25, 1952 he was placed on supervision for contributing to delinquency. Inmate explaining that at that time the brother had a fifteen year old girl in the rooms where they were staying. According to the California summary, inmate and his brother had pulled some stickups in Chicago area to get enough money to go west, and after a short time they departed, taking with them the young girl who the brother later married. They went to Seattle where they remained a short while. While there they were arrested on suspicion of burglary and both brothers escaped from a police officer and then took a bus to California. They were in Los Angeles about six days and during that time reportedly committed about fourteen armed robberies, before their arrest. They were approached after they had been caught in the act of holding up a gas station and during the subsequent chase, inmate was wounded and in return he fired at the police. On August 22, 1952 inmate was sentenced to the state penitentiary at San Quentin for robbery, after he and his brother had been caught in the act of holding up a gas station. "We were both drunk and feeling good." On September 8, 1954 inmate escaped from this prison, stating that he was outside the walls on a special detail, and merely walked away. The California report however, indicates that inmate had broken away from maximum custody but that the authorities do not know just how he effected his escape. There is presently a warrant on file for inmate's return to California jurisdiction.

SOCIAL FACTORS: Inmate was born July 30, 1931 in Chicago, the second of five children born to parents of German-English and Scotch-Irish background. The father was said to have committed suicide in March 1951 after attempting to shoot inmate's mother. Inmate grew up on the near north side of Chicago, living with his parents until he was sixteen years of age, when he entered the Army. Receiving an honorable discharge December 31, 1947, because of minority. It was after this enlistment that he served a term at St. Charles. Inmate attended public schools in Chicago, getting as far as the 9th grade before he terminated at age 16. His early work record was rather brief, he had worked as a machine operator, and at other short term odd employments. After he left the Illinois State Penitentiary he apparently had no work at all, being involved in further difficulty almost immediately, and apparently he made little effort to achieve a legitimate livelihood.

PERSONALITY: Inmate is a twenty-four year old individual of superior academic intellect, rather self-composed in the interview, and definitely attempting at all times to make the most possible favorable impression. He has had a lot of criminal experience for a youth of his years, seems to have definitely identified himself with the antisocial elements of society. He came out of a conflictful home situation in which there was little opportunity for proper training or an appreciation of adequate social standards, and the learning that he has picked up in the streets and in institutions has all been of a deleterious character. He shows an amenability to go along under very strict supervision, but he certainly is an individual who could not be depended upon to not violate a position of trust. The California report indicates that inmate had been suspected of being one of the ringleaders in a plot previous to the time that he took off and that there-after demonstrated a rather hostile attitude towards the custodial authorities there. It is felt that naturation in this case, unfortunately is going forward in a deleterious fashion and that the picture now is more omnious than it was during our earlier contest with this individual.

CLASSIFICATION Group III. Without psychosis or mental deficiency. Egocentric unstable, aggressive personality, very doubtfully improvable. Guarded prognosis. Superior intelligence (Army Alpha 120).

RECOMMENDATION: Stateville Division.
Maximum security is indicated. A routine work assignment would seem sufficient at first, later inmate might be tried out on same training type of assignment.

John Roe, Chairman
Classification Board

Dictated by
V. V. Rooy
Supervising Sociologist/ jb
JOHN DOE —(#) 0 0 0 0 0
ROEY: dd . . . gth
FEBRUARY 4 — 1955

SOCIAL HISTORY DATA:
Inmate states that John Doe is his full & correct name and that he has used the alias "Joe Doe"; that he was born July 30, 1931, in Chicago, Ill., and of married parents; that his father was born in Tenn., and his mother in Ill., the parents living together until death of his father during Year 1951, his mother becoming deceased during Year 1954; that he has one brother: Moe Doe (age unknown) and two sisters: Mae (25) & Elo (18); that he has lived in this state all his life (23 years) and had resided at the New Lawrence Hotel, Lawrence & Kenmore, Chgo., Ill., for about 2 days prior to arrest; that he left home at age of 16 years as a run-away and after enlisting in the U.S. Army Air Force, was Honorably Discharged due to Minority; that he is of German-English descent.

EDUCATION:
Completed 8 grades, leaving school at age of 15 years, and is of no religious faiths.

TRADE:
Has no trade, and due to always being incarcerated has never in his life been gainfully employed.

MARITAL STATUS:
Single and has never been married.

INMATE'S STATEMENT:
"I was trapped in a house when the cops came around on a routine check to see if I was there after my escape. I tried to get into another apartment to hide out and when I broke in a lady started screaming. I grabbed her then had a tussle with her husband. During the scuffle the gun I had went off and he was shot."

PREVIOUS RECORD:
Please see reverse side of this sheet for prior record.

IMMEDIATE FAMILY:
BROTHER: Loe Doe, SP., San Quentine, Calif., #00000; SISTERS: Mae Odoe, 0110 C. Pierce Drive, Philadelphia, Pa., and Elo Coe, 0011 N. Winthrop Ave., Chgo., Ill.

C-O-R-R-E-S-P-O-N- D-E-N-T-S

BROTHER: Lee Doe,	SP. # 00000	San Quentin, Calif.
SISTERS: Mrs. Mae Odoe	0110 N. Winthrop Ave.,	Chgo., Ill.
Mrs. Elo Coe	0011 C. Pierce Drive,	Philadelphia, Pa.

NOTIFY: Sister, Mrs. Elo Coe

Illinois State Penitentiary
EXAMINATION BLANK

Name............JOHN DOE............... Alias.........JOE DOE............... Number....00000....
Received....Feb. 4, 1955...... County....Cook...... Color....White...... Age....23 Yrs.....
Crime........Assault to Commit Murder................. Sentence...........12-14 Yrs.............
Date of Birth....7-30-31.... Nativity....Chicago, Ill..... Father....Tenn.....Mother....Ill.
Citizenship....American........ Father....American.... Nationality....German-English
How long in U.S........Life.................... Naturalized...................... Alien.............
Parents Living......No........... Father Died......1951............ Mother Died......1954.........
Marital State:........Single........ Wife Living................. Number of Children.............
Parents Living Together....Until father died.......... Divorced.......... Separated........
Social Security
Born of Married Parents....Yes........ Religion....Has None........ Number....Unknown
Economic Conditions......Poor........... Associates......None........ Disposition..............
Residence Before 14 Years of Age.......Urban............. After........Urban....................
Loe Doe, San Quentin Pen.,
Relatives Inmates of Penal Institutions....BRO.: Calif., #00000....Asylum....Nome
Age Left
Education....8th Grade............... School....15 yrs................. Dependents....None..........
Bank Account....No......... Real....Estate....No........... Inherit Anything....Nothing......
Occupation........Has None...................... How Long Employed.......Never Worked....
Military Services: Army-Navy Marines-Coast Guard........A.A.F............................
Date Enl. or Drafted........Sept., 1947, at Chgo., Ill., to San Antonio, Tex.; Disch.
(Minority)
Discharge Date....12-31-1947........ Type of Discharge....Honorable - # 00 000 000
Smokes....Yes........ Chews....No........ Drinks....Yes...... Heavy....Yes...... Moderate........
Drug Addict....No........ What Kind........ How Long........ Present Condition.............
Selective Service Board No...................... Address of Board................................
Selective Service Order No......................Classification..............................
Actual Residence: County........Cook...... P.O. Address........Chicago, Ill.................
Time in State Last Residence.......Life.................... Total Time........23 Yrs...............
New Lawrence Hotel,
Address When Arrested....Lawrence & Kenmore........... How Long....2 Days........
Age When First Arrested....10 Yrs...................... What For....Larceny.....................
Age When First Left Home....16 Yrs...................... Why....Ran-Away....................

Date of Crime....October 2, 1954....................... Motive of Crime....P.G.—.................
Working When Arrested....No........ How Long Idle....Life........
                                    Why....Always Incarcerated
Number of Previous Arrests....Numerous.... Number of Previous Convictions....3
Criminal Record....1 Term Prob., Chicago, Inn. (Rec. Stolen Prop.) 1950 — 5
    Yrs.; Volated; ISP, J. #00000 (Rec. Stolen Prop.) 1951 — 1 Yr. to 1 Yr. &
    1 Day; Disch. 1952 SP. San Quentin, Calif. as # 00000 (Robb. armed) 1952
    — 10 Yrs. to Life; ESCAPED Sept., 1954.

PAROLE VIOLATOR
PREVIOUS NUMBER
00011 — PONTIAC

CASE B
STATE OF ILLINOIS
DEPARTMENT OF PUBLIC SAFETY
DIVISION OF THE CRIMINOLOGIST
JOLIET DIAGNOSTIC   UNIT

CLASSIFICATION REPORT

00000   December 28, 1950

Name: DOE, John   Age: 21   ReAdmitted: 12-19-50
Crime: Larceny of a Motor Vehicle   Sentence: 1-20 yrs

RECLASSIFICATION

BEHAVIOR ON PAROLE: Inmate was originally admitted at the Menard
                    Diagnostic Depot March 5, 1947, under a one to
twenty year sentence for auto larceny. He was paroled March 21, 1949, and
returned to the Joliet Diagnostic Depot as a parole violator December 19, 1950.
Inmate was paroled to a farm set-up near Hoopeston, Illinois. He said that,
due to wet weather, there was very little work and, after a few days, he obtained emloyment in town with the Vermillian Malleable Company. He claims
he got along alright the first month on parole, being careful to observe the
various requirements. However, two friends and inmate planned to go to a
dance near Cissna Park and, according to inmate, the friends said they would
furnish the transportation. Later, the three left town in a car and inmate said
he did not know the automobile had been stolen until they were some distance
out of town. Inmate said that he was suspected of stealing the car and, after
that, he left his placement and began evading the authorities. Inmate subsequently stole a car in Danville and was later called by his agent, he said, and
asked to turn himself in so things could be straightened out. Inmate said he
started to do this but did not have the nerve to go through with it and, therefore, left town. Inmate drove this car into Pennsylvania where he wrecked it.
He then stole another car which was loaded with quantity of merchandise.
With this vehicle, inmate traveled about the East Midwest, selling part of the
merchandise and also working now and then to sustain himself. He said he
also maintained some telegraphic communication with his mother and that she,
in turn, would urge to come home. He said he was on his way home with
that car when he was arrested in Indiana and held for the Pennsylvania authorities. He was returned to Pennsylvania and subsequently received a sentence of one and a half years to three years in the Lehigh County Jail, Allen-
town, Pennsylvania, serving between June 10, 1949, and parole December 11,
1950, when he was turned over to the Illinois authorities and admitted here
for consideration as a parole violator.

REVIEW OF ORIGINAL OFFENSE &   Inmate's original commitment oc-
INSTITUTIONAL ADJUSTMENT: curred after he had stolen a car in
Danville, Illinois. While out on bond, inmate stole another car and went to
Chicago, Illinois. He became involved in armed robbery activity and the

theft of another vehicle. He was arrested and subsequently placed on a three year probation, the first six months of which he served in Cook County Jail. He was then turned over to the Danville authorities and sentenced to a term of one to twenty years.

Inmate was classified at the Menard Diagnostic Depot and recommendation was made for segregation at Pontiac. However, he was administratively transferred to Stateville, presumably to make room at Menard. Although inmate was not involved in any serious adjustment difficulties at Stateville, he was transferred to Pontiac July 20, 1948, after reporting that he was disturbed because of annoyances by perversely inclined prisoners. Inmate continued to make a good institutional adjustment at Pontiac.

REVIEW OF PREVIOUS RECORD: Inmate had a number of arrests as a juvenile, spending a short period in the Juvenile Detention Home, Vermilion County. Committed to St. Charles in 1941 with subsequent transfer to Sheridan after making a very poor adjustment record at St. Charles. It is noted that inmate made several attempts to escape and also was reportedly involved in homosexual activity. He was released in 1945.

REVIEW OF SOCIAL FACTORS: Inmate was born February 5, 1929, in Hoopeston, Illinois, the oldest of four children born to parents of English-Irish background. Inmate early began running away from home and by the time he was 12 years old he was making frequent trips to New York City by himself. Inmate's early home life was apparently lacking in adequate parental supervision. It is interesting to note that, at age 13, inmate's sister is already married. Inmate attended public schools in Hoopeston, Illinois, to the 8th grade. He tells us that he also had some high school education while at St. Charles. Inmate's employment record, prior to his original commitment, was very irregular and consisted entirely of shortterm, odd jobs. Following his release on parole in 1949, he continued to follow this pattern of employment. Inmate tells us that he tried to live up to his parole agreement during the first month, being careful to observe the hours rules and other stipulations. However, once he had been accused of stealing the first car, he completely gave up trying to live up to his parole agreement and once more reverted to quite exaggerated recreational pursuits.

PERSONALITY: Inmate is a 21 year old white man of rather dark complexion. He is a youthful appearing personality but of good physical build. He is a decidedly restless, unstable individual who has some insight after the fact. He did not adjust well in the adult institutions previously, making a much better adjustment at Pontiac and it is believed wise, at this time, to return him to that institution. Inmate does not seem predominantly anti-social but high degree of restlessness, which seem predicated upon some inner personality conflict, gives rights to very unpredictable delinquency upon slight provocation. Previous examiners have hoped that, as maturation went forward and his restless tendencies subsided, there would be a more hopeful picture and inmate, today, says he feels, in time, he will be able to outgrow some of his more impulsive, boyish reactions. Inmate is not particularly upset about his return and says he realizes he acted most unwisely and will have to accept the consequences. Just what is in the background of inmate's psychological conflicts is not too well determined, but it has been considered that there is some sibling rivalry and a feeling, on inmate's part, that the younger siblings have been shown preference by the parents. Although his behavior is persistently delinquent, we do not see a picture of organized criminal attitude in this individual.

CLASSIFICATION: Group III. Without psychosis or intellectual defect. Unstable personality. Questionably improvable offender.

Doubtful prognosis. Very superior intelligence (Army Alpha 146). Kahn not reported.

RECOMMENDATION: Joliet Division.
                  Some mechanical trade training might be helpful to
this inmate.

                                        John Roe,
                                        Chairman
                                        Classification Board
NEK: EDO

CASE C
STATE OF ILLINOIS
DEPARTMENT OF PUBLIC SAFETY
DIVISION OF THE CRIMINOLOGIST
MENARD PSYCHIATRIC   UNIT
CLASSIFICATION REPORT

Menard # 00001   July 1, 1952

| Name: DOE, John | Age: 23 | Re-Admitted: 12-19-50 |
| Crime: Auto Larceny | | Sentence: 1-20 yrs. |

RECLASSIFICATION

1. Transfer.
2. Classification
3. Recommendations

1. Stateville Division (Segregation Unit) from the Menard Psychiatric Division.
2. GROUP IV. Psychopathic personality with aggressive, non-conformist attitude. Emotionally immature, unstable, personality with suicidal patterns as attention-getting mechanisms. Questionably improvable offender. Doubtful prognosis.
3. This 23-year-old white male last saw the Board of Pardons and Paroles on the July 1952 docket, so that previous reclassification was not given consideration in order that he could not use this as a technical charge that he was being pushed around. He was originally admitted to the Menard Diagnostic Depot on 3-5-47 under a 1-20 year sentence for larceny. He was paroled on 3-21-49 and returned to the Joliet Diagnostic jail in Pennsylvania. At the present time he is wanted by the authorities at Vermilion County.

His original commitment occurred after he had stolen a car in Danville; while out on bond he stole another car to Chicago where he became involved in an armed robbery and the theft of another vehicle, leading to his admission to the Cook County Jail. He was then turned over to the Danville authorities and admitted under his present sentence. Upon his original admission he was classified for Pontiac, later transferred administratively to Stateville and then transferred back to Pontiac in July 1948.

He was formally reclassified for the Menard General Division from Stateville as an individual who was immature, unstable, inspite of his very superior intelligence, his Army Alpha score being 146, showing that he has never made the most of his opportunities. At the Old Prison he claimed that he was the recipient of homosexual advances, that he had received a number of unsolicited love notes and gifts of cigarettes. These clearly showed the degree of chronic conflict which was existing within that placement and this led to his reclassification.

He was then placed upon #6 gallery unit within the Menard Unit in efforts to stabilize him by giving him hydrotherapy rather than fully reclassifying him for the Psychiatric Division. He was then given opportunity to work within the Psychiatric Division as a clerk. He continued this work until 10-27-51 when he was placed under observation for forging and signing a detail making it possible for him to stay out in the cellhouse until 8 P.M. He spent most of his time with the known passive homosexuals in the Psychiatric Division. He was told that he must break away from this pattern of behavior.

He became acutely disturbed with the result that he was given consideration for shock therapy. In December 1951 he became acutely disturbed, refused to abide by rules and regulations and was finally reclassified for the Psychiatric Division because of his constant refusal to carry out constructive work assignments.

RECLASSIFICATION

1. Transfer.   — 2 —

2. Classification

3. Recommendations

While within the Psychiatric Division he was allowed to work and attend church services. Under the pretext of going to the toilet, while attending church, he went upstairs, climbed among the rafters, remaining there approximately 5 hours at which time he had to be helped down. Throughout this entire period he threatened to jump, stating that he wanted to commit suicide. Upon the promise of the administrative officials that he would not be given shock therapy, he came down. He used this bargaining as a means of getting what he wanted. He was formally reclassified upon the basis of his psychopathic personality and the act was purely an attention-getting mechanism. However, after due consideration by the prison physician, the psychiatrist and the administrative officials, it was felt wisest not to press shock therapy. Upon his promise to do better he was then given an opportunity to work within the Psychiatric Division.

Up to the time of his appearance before the Division of Paroles and Pardons upon the July 1952 docket, he seemingly was making a more satisfactory adjustment. However, basically there was this underlying negativistic attitude. However, recently he has become involved in the obtaining of some $26.00 worth of commissary supplies primarily through an act of forgery, with the result that a disciplinary action is necessary at this time. Whenever interviewed he is quite evasive and attempts to put on a bold front, stating that he is making every attempt to adjust. Fundamentally we are dealing with an individual who is a true psychopathic personality, who knows the difference between right and wrong but clearly disregards everything in order to gain what he feels are his rights. He refuses to profit by previous experience.

He will do anything ,irrespective of the consequences, and it is known that he will carry these to extreme lengths. He has been and is a potential suicide as an attention-getting mechanism, not with the idea that he is depressed or the idea that he is psychotic. He has been classified as potentially psychotic in view of these attention-getting mechanisms and he continues to be a major social problem. We would point out that he has never lived up to his background of very superior intelligence. One feels that he has reached the point where he feels that because of the attention he has received from the administrative officials that he can take advantage of it with immunity. Whenever he is pushed he reacts in an explosive, non-conformist way.

It is, therefore, recommended that he be transferred to the Stateville Segregation Unit, particularly in view of his last disciplinary action.

CLASSIFICATION BOARD

by

Clo C. Clo, M. D. (Member)

Psychiatrist

GBS: Iv

CASE D

STATE OF ILLINOIS

DEPARTMENT OF PUBLIC SAFETY
DIVISION OF THE CRIMINOLOGIST
JOLIET DIAGNOSTIC DEPOT UNIT

CLASSIFICATION REPORT

00000   December 23, 1958

Name: DOE, John	Age: 44
	Admitted: November 21, 1958
	Sentence: 3-6 years

OFFENSE: John Doe was received from DeKalb County on November 21,
          1958 under a sentence of from 3-6 years for burglary. Officially,
on August 18, 1958 our inmate was apprehended during the early hours in a
private DeKalb, Illinois club. He had entered through a window on the 2nd
floor and had broken into a bowling machine and the monies from this machine were found on his person. Doe pled guilty and admits to us that he
perpetrated the burglary, but rationalizes: "I'd came up from West Virginia
and went to Waukegan, Illinois for a few days. I'd been drinking steady for
about 6 weeks and I don't know how I got to DeKalb. I'd been on vodka and
was in a daze: I remember being in the club when I was arrested, but I don't
remember getting there."

PREVIOUS RECORD: The inmate has a long criminal record dating back to
                  June, 1934 when he was arrested and charged in Nor-
wich, Connecticut with burglary. He escaped from police headquarters and
was subsequently apprehended and sentenced in September, 1934 to an indeterminate term in the Connecticut State Prison-Reformatory where he served
18 months and was paroled. In April, 1937 he was sentenced to 2-4 years in
the Colorado State Prison for burglary, but was paroled on August 6, 1938.
He was sentenced to the Indiana State Reformatory under a 2-5 year's sentence in September, 1938 for 2nd degree burglary. During 1940-1941 we note
that he was arrested a number of times for investigation, vagrancy and failure
to register with the Selective Service Board his change of address. The foregoing arrests occurred in Illinois, Virginia, Texas, Wisconsin and Michigan. In
August, 1941 he was sentenced to 5 years in the Iowa State Prison for attempted breaking and entering and was discharged at expiration of sentence.
He was arrested in Chicago for pandering in January, 1945, but disposition is
unshown. Doe was arrested in Des Moines, Iowa in November, 1947, where
he was charged with larceny from building. This charge was later reduced to
petty larceny, for which he was fined $100. and ordered to leave town imme-
diately. In February, 1949 he was charged in Sioux City, Iowa with illegal
possession of narcotics and was fined $400. He was arrested in Casper, Wyom-
ing in May, 1950 on a charge of breaking and entering; however, this charge
was dismissed and he was turned over to federal authorities for auto theft. In
July, 1950 he was sentenced to a 2 years and 6 months term in the United
State Penitentiary, Leavenworth, Kansas, for violation of the Dyer Act. The
inmate was conditionally released on June 22, 1952, but in January, 1953 he
began a 2 years and 4 months term in the Nevada State Prison for grand larceny. He was arrested in Danville, Illinois in December, 1955 for vagrancy,
for which he received a 30 day jail term; in April, 1958 he was arrested in
Boise, Idaho and received a 10 day suspended sentence for a similar offense.

SOCIAL FACTORS: Doe was born on May 25, 1914 in Milwaukee, Wisconsin, an only child. The boy was orphaned at an early age and he reports that his father was killed in World War I and that his mother died during the influenza epidemic of 1919. We are informed that friends of the family became foster-parents to him; that he lived with them until he was 16 years of age. He moved with his foster-parents to Connecticut where he claims to have attended school through the 8th grade. Doe lists his occupation as "painter," but confesses that he has been irregularly employed during periods he was not incarcerated. The inmate advises us that he started drinking at 18 and admits to the excessive use of alcohol during most of his life-time. He explains the vagrancy arrests and rationalizes his burglary offenses as being the result of excessive drinking: "When I wasn't in prison I was drinking and travelling aimlessly. When I needed money I got into trouble. My drinking interfered with my work; I'd lose a job and then wander elsewhere and get another." The inmate declares that he has been employed, off and on during the past 4 years, by a home improvements concern. He worked as an applicator of aluminum siding; this work required considerable traveling. Doe tells us he was married in 1944 and divorced in 1949, stating that both he and his wife were drinking too and that this led to their marital difficulties. Aside from this brief period of marriage, he has had no primary group relationships since his foster-parents died when he was about 20 years of age. He reports that he has had no contact with relatives for many years and claims he knows of only one person whom he can consider a friend. We are advised that a Chicago man had been helping him and has visited him since he came to the ISP. As is indicated above, he has been nomadic during much of his life and currently lists no permanent address. Although he admits to heavy drinking and moderate gambling, he denies that he has ever used narcotics. We note, however, that he was arrested in 1949 for possession of drugs.

PERSONALITY: DOE is a 44 year old white male who is 5′ 8″ in height and weighs 138 pounds. He makes no present physical complaints and the medical report is clear except to mention a superficial puncture in his left chest (auto accident 1948) and to recommend dental attention. We found him to be pleasant on the surface, but impressing us as being "conwise", having served time in 5 state prisons and reformatories and one federal prison before coming here. The inmate was orphaned at an early age and was reared by elderly foster-parents. He has had no primary group contacts since his divorce 8 years ago. This inmate has led a nomadic life while in the free community, has no permanent address and was able to list only one person as a friend. He confesses to a long established pattern of heavy drinking and attributes most of his offenses to his alcoholism. Doe does not appear to be an aggressive offender, but does have a long history of arrests for vagrancy and property crimes in at least 12 states. Reports from prisons, in which he was previously incarcerated, indicated that he adjusts well under supervision and we feel that he will be no problem during his current imprisonment.

PSYCHOLOGICAL: Average Intelligence by AGCT. (41st percentile.)

CLASSIFICATION: Group III. Without psychosis or intellectual defect. Doubtfully improvable. Inadequate personality with a tendency toward nomadism and alcoholism. Guarded prognosis.

RECOMMENDATION: Stateville Division.
He is an experienced painter and would like an assignment of this nature.

John Roe
Classification Board

Administrative Transfer—9-1-44

TRANSFER ORDER NO........000000...............................
................DOE, JOHN J. ....
No........000001....................
Transferred from
Illinois State Penitentiary,
................Menard Diagnostic Depot ....Division
To
Illinois State Penitentiary,
.... Joliet-Stateville Division ....Division
RECEIVED from the Warden of
the Illinois State Penitentiary,
............Menard Diagnostic Depot,............, the body of
................DOE, John J. .... No. ....00000............
This........20........day of........March........, 19....58

....

WARDEN

STATE OF ILLINOIS
DEPARTMENT OF PUBLIC SAFETY

March 6.......1958

TRANSFER ORDER NO........000000.......

In accordance with and pursuant to the power vested in the Department of Public Safety, by virtue of "An Act in relation to the Illinois State Penitentiary, and to repeal certain parts of designated Acts" approved June 30, 1933, as amended,........DOE, JOHN J...
No........00001........an inmate of the Illinois State Penitentiary,........Menard Diagnostic........Division, is hereby ordered transferred to the Illinois State Penitentiary,........Stateville........Division.

Group III. Without Psychosis or mental defect.
Doubtfully improvable offender.
Guarded prognosis.
Recommendations: Stateville Division.
Refer to Classification Report dated February 27, 1958.

Therefore it is ordered that the managing head of the division of said Illinois State Penitentiary, where the above mentioned prisoner is incarcerated, transfer him from said division, at its expense, to the Illinois State Penitentiary,....
....Joliet-Stateville........Division, together with all papers and files including photographs and fingerprints, relating to his case; that the managing head of the division receiving the prisoner, safely incarcerate him there, until legally released, as though said prisoner had been originally committed to said division. This order is issued pursuant to authority given the Superintendent of Prisons to execute said transfer order.

........Gilbert P. Finch ....
SUPERINTENDENT OF PRISONS

Ccy

OF THE DEPARTMENT OF PUBLIC SAFETY

Superintendent of Prisons
Illinois State Penitentiary, ...
Illinois State Penitentiary, ...Joliet-Stateville Division..........
Diagnostic Depot, Joliet
Parole and Padon Board
Criminologist
Statistician

CASE E

STATE OF ILLINOIS
DEPARTMENT OF PUBLIC SAFETY
DIVISION OF THE CRIMINOLOGIST
JOLIET DIAGNOSTIC UNIT
CLASSIFICATION REPORT

No. 00000

| Name: DOE, John | Age: 42 | Admitted: 12-14-53 |
| Crime: MURDER | | Sentence: 14 yrs. |

OFFENSE: John Doe, age 42, was received from Cook County on December 14, 1953, under a sentence of 14 years for murder. According to the official statement of facts, Doe had been separated from his wife for four months and the wife was keeping company with another man. On several occasions, Doe had asked his wife and this man to stop seeing each other. On May 23, 1953, at 7:30 p.m. Doe was walking toward his wife's apartment when he saw his wife and this same man driving away in an automobile. He remained around the neighborhood until shortly after midnight at which time his wife and this man returned. As they attempted to enter the stairway leading to his wife's apartment. Doe stated to the man "I told you to stay away from my wife." He immediately started firing a pistol shooting his wife three times and the other man three times causing the death of both. Doe admits that he intended to shoot the man but claims that the man was attempting to reach into his pocket for a gun at the time he started firing. He states that the shooting of his wife was accidental. Doe tells us he bought this gun about one year prior to the shooting and states that he was raised in the country and was used to keeping a gun around the house.

PREVIOUS RECORD:
There are no prior convictions and Doe tells us that he has no prior records.

SOCIAL FACTORS:
Doe was born in Sibley, Mississippi on December 16, 1911, as the third of three full siblings in a home which remained organized until the mothers' death when Doe was still a small child. There is some discrepancy in regard to the parental family. Doe told our office that he was raised by his mother who was living until 1945. At the Behavior Clinic in Cook County, it was revealed that the mother died when he was small and that he was raised by his father. Perhaps he had a step-mother. At any rate, he lived on a small tenant farm in Mississippi and only attended three years of schooling. His only employment was mostly farm work and working around logging camps. He came to Chicago in 1945 with his wife whom he married in 1940. At the time of the marriage, Doe was 34 years of age and the wife 16. There is reason to believe that the wife was unfaithful to Doe, proven very shortly after they were married. Prior to his offense he worked for almost five years for the Peoples Gas, Light & Coke Co. in Chicago. He worked progressively as a water, gas conveyor man and stoker work. Reports from this company indicates that Doe resigned on May 22, 1953 and this offense occurred on May 23, 1953. Doe claims that he was drinking excessively at the time of this offense. He has no plans for the future.

PERSONALITY:
Physically, Doe is tall in body build and he complains of having bad teeth and a bad stomach. The clinical

impression is that of a dull individual. However, he has had little education and is illiterate. He is capable of aggressive behavior as proven by
this offense. During the interview he was friendly and cooperative and
quite polite. Apparently Doe has been brooding over his wife's relationships with other men for a long time before this offense occurred. Information from the Behavior Clinic indicates that the wife did very little
house keeping and rarely cooked. She worked as a nurses aid and looked
down on Doe and his friends. This Behavior Clinic report also indicated
that Doe laughed foolishly at times but cried if anyone hurt his feelings.
He thought that if he had let anyone down, he would cry for a long time.
He never trusted his wife and was repeatedly complaining to his friends
that everyone was against him. He was described as a man who kept to
himself most of the time, his only interest being in the Bible. While confined he says he is interested in going to school and would like to learn
to read and write.

CLASSIFICATION:
>Group III. Without psychosis or mental deficiency.
>Adult, improvable offender. Dull, normal intelligence.
Bechaler-Bellevue Short Form I.Q. 80. Inadequate personality. Problematic prognosis. Kahn negative.

RECOMMENDATION:
>Stateville Division.
>He tells us that he is interested in learning to
>read and write.
>
>>John Roe,
>>Classification Board.

HGS/jvp

Illinois State Penitentiary
EXAMINATION BLANK

Name.........JOHN DOE............ Alias.........None............ Number 00000............
Received....Dec. 14, 1953.....County......Cook...... Color.........Negro, Age 41 ...
Crime.....Murder...... Sentence 14 yrs........ Date of Birth ....Dec. 16, 1911 ...
Nativity.....Sibley, Miss.......... Father.....Miss........ Mother..... Miss...... Citi-
zenship......American...... Father.....Same...... Nationality.....Afro-American....
How long in U.S.......Life.......... Naturalized......... Alien.......... Parents Liv-
ing.....No.......... Father Died.....1939.......... Mother Died.....1945....... Marital
State....Widower.......... Wife Living....No.......... Number of Children....None ...
Parents Living Together....Until Father died..... Divorced...... Separated.....
Born of Married Parents....Yes........ Religion.....Baptist........ Social Security
Number..... 000 00 0000........ Economic Conditions......Good...... Associates.....
None........ Disposition.......... Residence Before 14 Years of Age.....Rural.......
After.....Urban........ Relatives Inmates of Penal Institutions.......None.........
Asylum............. Education.....3rd........ Age Left School.....12......... Depend-
ents.......... Bank Account.....No.......... Real....... Estate.......No.......... Inherit
Anything.....No.......... Occupation.....Stoker Man.......... How Long Employed
.........3 yrs. at $2.00 a hour........... Military Services: Army-Navy-Marines-
Coast Guard.....None.......... Date Enl. or Drafted......... Discharge Date.......
Type of Discharge......... Smokes.....Yes.......... Chews.......Yes........ Drinks.....
Yes............. Heavy............. Moderate.....Yes............. Drug Addict.....No..........
What Kind............. How Long............. Present Condition............. Selective
Service Board No................. Address of Board.............. Selective Serv-

ice Order No...................... Classification......................... Actual Residence:
County......Cook .... P.O. Address......Chicago, Ill.................. Time
in State Last Residence......7 years........... Total Time......7 years........... Ad-
dress When Arrested......0010 Calumet......... How Long......A few months......
Age When First Arrested......29......... What For....Fighting......... Age When
First Left Home......33......... Why......No Reason......... Date of Crime......May
23, 1953........... Motive of Crime......PNG Jury Trial........... Working When
Arrested......Yes....... How Long Idle......... Why......... Number of Previous
Arrests......1......... Number of Previous Convictions......None......... Criminal
Record......None..........

John Doe — 0 0 0 0 0

ROEY.........DD.........GH

December 14, 1953

SOCIAL HISTORY AND DATA:
Inmate states that his right name is John Doe and that he has never used
a alias; he was born December 16, 1911, at Sibley, Mississippi, of married
parents; both parents were born in Mississippi, and they are both deceased, his father died in 1939 and his mother in 1945, they lived together
until his father's death; he has 2 brothers, Joe and Moe, and no sisters;
he is now 41 years of age and has never served in the armed forces; he has
lived in this state for 7 years and states that he left his home at the age
of 33 years, he just "for no reason"; he has lived at 0010 Calumet, Chicago, Illinois, for a few months; he is of the Afro-American descent.

EDUCATION:
He went to the 3rd grade in school and left school at the age of 12 years;
he is of the Baptist faith.

TRADE:
He worked as a stoker man for 3 years at $2.00 a hour and he was work-
ing at the time of this arrest.

MARITAL STATUS:
He married, Mary Odoe, age 16 years, in 1940, at Natchez, Mississippi and
his wife died in 1953; he states that there were no children from this union.

INMATE'S STATMENT:
He and another guy got into it and a shooting scrape come off and my
wife run in between it and she got shot and killed. Both my wife and the
other guy got killed. It was self defense, my wife got shot accidentally.
The argument was concerning my wife.

PREVIOUS RECORD:
He denies any previous record.

CORRESPONDENTS

Brothers:	Loe Doe	St. Add. Unk.	New Orleans, La.
	Moe Doe	Gen. Del.	Sibley, Miss.
Cousins:	Coe Roe	0110 Michigan	Chicago, Ill.
	Ole Soe	010 East 44th	Same
	Eol Ose	0000 Michigan	Same
Friend:	Noe Looy	00002 Calumet	Same
Cousin	Oney Roo	Gen. Del.	Sibley, Miss.
Half-Bro:	Anyo Doe	Same	Same
Notify:	Brother Loe Doe		

CASE F

STATE OF ILLINOIS
DEPARTMENT OF PUBLIC SAFETY
DIVISION OF THE CRIMINOLOGIST
JOLIET DIAGNOSTIC UNIT
CLASSIFICATION REPORT

No. 00000   8-20-54

| Name: DOE, John | Age: 25 | Admitted: 7-6-54 |
| Crime: MURDER | | Sentence: 18 yrs. |

OFFENSE:

John Doe, age 25, was received from Cook County on 7-6-54 under an 18 year sentence for murder. He pleaded not guilty to the charge. According to the official statement of facts inmate became involved in an argument with the deceased. This occurred in a store. They went out to the sidewalk where they were involved in a fight but the fight was stopped. Inmate then allegedly went next door to a tavern which was owned by his brother and father and he obtained a .45 calibre revolver. He then came out on the street again and after a struggle he fired one shot which ricocheted and struck a man in the foot who was trying to break up the fight. Inmate then broke away and fired two shots at the deceased, one of which hit him in the back of the head. Inmate's version of the offense is entirely different. He claims that this deceased came into inmate's father's store and called his father all kind of names. Inmate states that he told the deceased to have respect for his father. He also told the deceased to leave or he would call the police. Inmate further claims that the deceased ran out to his car and came back with a gun. At this time inmate states he took a revolver from the cash register and shot at the deceased, attempting to frighten him. However, the shot hit the deceased in the head and inmate's father called the police. . . . No previous record.

SOCIAL FACTORS:

Inmate was born in Italy on 8-24-28. He went to school in that country and graduated from grammar school which constitutes only five grades. He then went to High school about seven months. He came to the United States at about the age of 18 and has worked as a laborer and assembler. He probably also worked for his father who owns a liquor store. The most recent employment he reports was with Hotpoint, Inc., between 1951 and 1953 where he was working at the time of his arrest. He expects to return to this employment after he is released. He has never been married.

PERSONALITY:

Physically Doe is about average in body build and he tells us that his health is satisfactory. During the interview he was friendly and cooperative and seems to be rather upset about being in the penitentiary. While in the Diagnostic Depot he developed some kind of toxic skin reaction and was sent to Detention Hospital. He was considered to be an emotionally unstable, inadequate personality. He definitely is not an advanced offender. He would like to go to school while in prison. Reference is made to the Special Progress Report of 7-12-54.

CLASSIFICATION:

Group II., Tentatively, Intellectual (or mental) deficiency. Revised Beta Examination resulting in a

Wechaler-type IQ of 79, indicating borderline intelligence. The clinical appraisal however is low average intelligence. Adult, improvable offender. Inadequate personality. Problematic prognosis. Kahn negative.

RECOMMENDATIONS:

Stateville Division.

He might benefit from academic schooling.

John Roe,
Classification Board.

Dictated by
V. V. Rooy
Sociologist
cm

Illinois State Penitentiary
EXAMINATION BLANK

Name....JOHN DOE.......... Alias...None.......... Number....00000..... Received ... 7-6-54 .... County.....Cook............ Color.....White............ Age.... 25 yrs...... Crime .. Murder.......... Sentence......18 yrs........ Date of Birth..... 8-24-28 ...... Nativity.....Italy.......... Father.....Italy.......... Mother..... Italy.......... Citizenship..... American .... Father.....American.......... Nationality.....Italian............ How long in U.S......7 yrs.......... Naturalized.....Yes.......... Alien.... No .... Parents Living.....Yes.......... Father Died .... Mother Died .... Marital State..... Single.......... Wife Living.......... Number of Children .... Parents Living Together.....Yes.......... Divorced .... Separated .... Born of Married Parents.....Yes.......... Religion.....Catholic .... Social Security Number..... 000 00 0000.......... Economic Conditions.....Good .... Associates..... None.......... Disposition ...... Residence Before 14 years of age.....Rural........ After.....URBAN.......... Relatives Inmates of Penal Institutions .... None........ Alylums...None.......... Education....1 yr. H.S.......... Age Left School ..13 ...... Dependents .... None.......... Bank Account.....None.......... Real.....Estate .... None .... Inherit Anything .... Nothing .... Occupation .... Assembler........ How Long Employed .... 3 yrs. $100. Week .... Military Services: Army-Navy-Marines-Coast Guard.....None.......... Date Enl. or Drafted .... Discharge Date.................. Type of Discharge.............. Smokes..... No .... Chews..... No .... Drinks .... No .... Heavy.......... Moderate .... Drug Addict .... No .... What Kind .... How Long .... Present Condition ...... Selective Service Board No.......... Address of Board ....010 Van Buren St.— 1949 .... Selective Service Order No........... Classification .... Actual Residence: County.....Cook .... P.O. Address .... Chicago, Ill.......... Time in State Last Residence.....7 years .... Total Time ....7 years .... Address When Arrested ... 0010 W. Taylor St.......... How Long ....7 yrs......... Age When First Arrested...25 yrs........ What For........ Current Charge ...... Age When First Left Home .... Never Left............ Why .... Date of Crime .. 11-12-53 .... Motive of Crime.....Plead Not Guilty—Jury .... Working When Arrested.....Yes .... How Long Idle .... Why .... Number of Previous Arrests....None .... Number of Previous Convictions .... Criminal Record.....None...............

JOHN DOE — 0 0 0 0 0

ROEL: . . . DD . . . GM.

JULY 6, 1954

SOCIAL HISTORY DATA:
Inmate tells us that he was born in Italy 8-24-28 into a family of Italian-born parents of Catholic religious background. He says he and his family arrived in the United States in 1947 aboard the U.S.S. Marine Perch, docking at Pier 34 in New York. Inmate has lived since then in Chicago with his parents. At the time of his arrest his address was 0010 W. Taylor Street where he lived seven years. He denies smoking, drinking, and experience with narcotic drugs.

EDUCATION:
He states he completed one year of High School in Italy and that he was attending citizenship school in America.

TRADE:
He worked for three years as an assembler at $100 per week and was employed at the time of his arrest.

MARITAL STATUS:
Inmate states he is single and has never been married.

INMATE'S STATEMENT:
"My father got Liquor store. I come from work and used to help my old man every night. Two guys drop in and have argument with my old man and call my old man bad names and try to beat him up. I was standing working and called the guy over and said, "whatsa matta, you got no respect for my old man.' The guy said, 'I'm not 'fraid of you' and pushed me and the other guy jumped on top me and my old man said 'leave my son alone'. The guy went outside and got a gun in the car and when he come back I got my old man's gun out of a drawer and shot to scare him away and the shot killed him. The guy's friend took the gun off the dead guy and then said dead guy never had a gun." Inmate has no previous record.

CORRESPONDENTS

Mother:	Fran Doe	0010 W. Taylor St.	Chicago, Ill.
Father:	Pot Doe	0010 W. Taylor St.	"
Brother:	Joe Doe	0010 W. Taylor St.	"
Aunt:	Elo Loe	0100 S. Bishop St.	"
Uncle:	Joe Loe	0100 S. Bishop St.	"
God-Fa:	Roc Oal.	0101 S. Halsted St.	'

NOTIFY: PARENTS . . .

PART II

GUARD TRAINING, RULES, EMERGENCY ACTION

Chapter 8

TRAINING MANUAL
FOR
GUARDS AND OFFICERS

The old custom of men reporting for duty as guards at a penal institution with two requisites, brawn and an aptitude for browbeating and aggressiveness, might have sufficed in a day when one idea, custody, was the purpose and design of a prison. Within the minds of the administrators and personnel which made up the organization, not one thought was given to rehabilitation or the preparation of inmates for the inevitable return of a vast percentage to society. Records indicate that more than 95% of all convicted felons are someday released from prison. Cowed and browbeaten as they were during their stay in prison, convicts could not but develop hate and an overpowering desire for vengeance against the world which visited this inhumanity upon them.

Even when an awakened society began to make some provision for a mode of treatment which would do something towards developing a frame of mind in the inmate population which would tend to return them to society as normal and rational human beings, with an urge to adapt themselves to the ordinary plan of living, little thought was given to the selection or training of employees of the institution which were to be the means of developing these desired qualities in those men whose lot it had been to fall within the toils of the law.

When the training of men for this field of work began some years ago, the training period consisted of a short lecture by some official of the institution, followed by a few days' work with another man who, only a few months or years before, had been obliged to work out his own ways and means of handling men.

From this meager training course, the new guard was given an assignment and left pretty well to his own devices in coping with the situations that confront a man engaged in handling the lives and welfare of numbers of his fellows who had fallen astray.

We might draw a parallel to the functioning of another and kindred branch of public service, the police departments. Only a few short years ago, the main qualifications for assignment to police forces were that the individual had the right connections politically, and that he could hold his own in a rough and tumble battle. If he fulfilled these requirements, he was given a badge, outfitted with the usual paraphernalia which custom required of law enforcement agents, and then assigned to a beat, over which he reigned sometimes in fairness and understanding, but too often falling short of the requirements for just administration of his office, so that he built disrespect or fear for the law, rather than the respect and trust which was naturally due. Today, the police departments of our great cities are being filled with highly trained and efficient men, who bring their departments the respect and trust which are rightly theirs. Applicants for police jobs first undergo a lengthy period of training which acquaints them thoroughly with criminal law, traffic regulations, marksmanship, exercise, and the art of self-defense, together with many other instructions in the duties of the police. The results of this training have been immediately reflected in the greater efficiency with which the departments have functioned; in the greater protection resulting to both the police officer and the civilian taxpayer.

The purpose of the guards' school is almost identical with police training. It is the intent of this guards' school to develop and train prospective members of the personnel of the State's penal institutions so that they will possess the qualifications requisite to the leadership of men. Included in the course of instruction, for which this book is to be used both as a textbook for officers in training and as a manual or handbook for all prison officers, will be lectures on the fundamentals of criminology and of prison administration.

Along with the subjects mentioned above, which deal directly with prison work, will be given a course in Leadership. The primary objectives of this course will be to set forth for the consideration of the student officers the principles upon which good leadership must rest. The course will show that a good leader must necessarily lead in the right direction, and that the leader himself must possess qualities which induce others to follow him. What these qualities are, and how they may be made use of to influence others will be the subject matter of the course.

It is intended in writing this combined textbook and handbook to be as general as possible, but, since the school is held at Stateville, frequent reference will be made to prison administration as carried on at the Stateville institution. This, of course, can be done consistently with the ideals of a handbook for prison work in general, due to the fact that all the prisons in the state of Illinois, being operated under one head, are managed very similarly to Stateville.

There is really no necessity for the ordinary prison officer to be master of all or any of the subjects of criminology, penology, sociology, or prison classification, but it is thought well that he should be at least acquainted with the definitions and the general outlines of these subjects. Therefore, it is not the intention of the author of this book to delve very deeply into these subjects, but merely to set forth the ultimate principles upon which such sciences are based, as subject matter for several lectures on each.

Since the matter of prison administration is to be the whole business of a prison officer, this course will cover, thoroughly and completely, the facts pertinent to the running of an institution of this nature. A full and complete course in prison administration can be constructed only on the basis of the duties of the warden, since upon his shoulders rests the entire responsibility for the efficient operation of the institution, from the most major activity to the most minor detail. The outline, therefore, at the beginning of the course in prison administration will be found to be an index to all that is to follow.

It is well known that first impressions are often permanent, and this course is designed to give to each individual a thorough knowledge of the type of work he is to do, so that he will be able to function at once as an active member of the personnel. With the information which new guards will acquire here, they will begin work with a confidence born of a prior knowledge of the subject, and will be able to proceed deliberately, not hesitantly, in the performance of required work. This attitude and aptitude cannot but favorably impress any who might have occasion to view their efforts.

If, for any reason, any officer candidate beginning this course, views this prospectus of the work to be accomplished unfavorably, or even disinterestedly, he should in justice to himself and to the State, make known his attitude to the proper authorities, who will accept his resignation and thereby save him his time and save the State the cost that it would incur in his training.

* * * * * * *

AN OUTLINE OF CRIMINOLOGY

The why and wherefore of human behavior long has been a problem defying the solution of man. The libraries of the world are crowded with books the authors of which have striven to throw light on this problem, and still considerable speculation exists.

The first question in the study of man's behavior must be a consideration of what constitutes correct behavior and what constitutes incorrect behavior . . . that is to say, what is the norm by which man's actions are to be judged good or bad, right or wrong. There are those who claim that right and wrong behavior is merely a matter of conformity with the established customs of the community. If a person conforms to the customs of his community or tribe, he is said to be a good man; if he fails to conform, he is a bad man. Customs are nothing more than the habits of a tribe, a community, or a race. If the opinion described were adhered to, there would be no such thing as a moral act or an immoral act in general. Any idea of unity in morality would be set aside; an act which in the State of Illinois is meritorious, might, in Soviet Russia, be punishable by death.

Viewing the general unity in all nature outside man, it would seem that there is an objective order to which man must conform, regardless of the customs of his state or tribe. Moral right and wrong seem to flow from the nature of things. All creatures and all things have a relationship, and this relationship is objective. It exists without man's consent and often without his knowledge. It is to be remembered in this regard that an error in man's thinking does not change the objective order of things. For many thousands of years all mankind thought the world to be flat, but all mankind's thinking did not alter the actual shape of the world, or its laws. Neither will man's thinking alter the objective relationship that exists between man and nature, between man and nature's God.

Consider, for example, a theory held by some men of great reputation in the field of political science. These men believe that man is the property of the state and is indebted to the state for his existence. Such a concept is, of course, essentially unsound, and all attempts to establish a governmental unit of that nature have gone awry. The state derives its existence from man and is forever subject to man. This is the natural order, and will never be altered by hypotheses and postulates.

Again, according to the very laws of nature, there exists between father and son certain relationships. There are certain things which the father owes the son, and certain things which the son owes the father. The father may fail in his duties toward the son, and likewise the son may fail in his duties toward the father. Both may deny their debt to one another, but the relationship and the mutual debt are there forever. It is above man's power to change the order which exists in nature.

With the promise that there is in nature a certain right order not dependent upon man's knowledge or endorsement, but obtaining forever in spite of either or both, we can define a moral act as one in conformity with that order, and an immoral act as one contrary to that order. The relationship that exists between man and his fellows, between man and nature, between man and nature's Creator, are not all of the same importance. Man's failure, therefore, to comply with the natural order in an unimportant relationship will amount to only a minor offense . .... a large and serious crime, a felony.

An example of this distinction may be seen in the following:

objective order of nature decrees that the land should produce its fruits for the man who labors in the field.

Objective order, again, would possess the laborer with the harvest of the field to meet his needs and the needs of those dependent upon him. Here we have a relationship between a man and a field on the one hand, and between a man and his family on the other. Now, if a neighbor who had not toiled to produce the harvest tried to interfere with this relationship, his attempt would be a violation of the right order of things. The neighbor would be guilty of dishonesty. Such examples could be quoted for one relationship after another, and our conclusions would always be the same: that proper compliance on the part of man with the relationships that exist in the right order in nature constitutes immorality, and that non-compliance constitutes immorality.

Perhaps this very brief sketch has not succeeded in convincing you that there does exist a right order in nature and that man's compliance or non-compliance with this order constitutes the difference between right and wrong behavior. Let us, however, assume such a case to be true, and begin our discussion of the reasons why some men comply and others fail to comply with this order. Here again we enter a field of thought in which there are many conflicting opinions. There are those who hold that man is not responsible for his actions, that he is subject and slave to his internal urges, that he has not the power to say yes or no to a desire that arises within him. Those who hold this opinion are known as determinists. If we accept their opinion of action, there is no use for further study. Under this concept, a man would be an irresponsible creature, subject to no authority except his own personal urges. There would be no moral acts and no immoral acts. There would be no good and evil. To punish a man, if we adhered to this conception of human action, would be to do violence to his personal right, for he could not be held responsible for any of his acts, and therefore he could not be held accountable to society for violations of the laws that society has established.

There are those, again, who hold that man is entirely subject to the laws of biology. The proponents of this doctrine say that if a man is born of a thieving father, he too, almost of necessity, will become a thief. With this theory we cannot agree. We do admit, however, that men inherit certain qualities from their ancestors; that some of these qualities are good and some bad. But we maintain that even though a person has inherited certain weakening qualities from his ancestors, he nevertheless has within him the power to overcome those weaknesses and to make his actions comply with the demands of the right order.

There is also the theory that man's behavior is entirely dependent on his environment. These students believe that the entire behavior of a person is conditioned by the circumstances in which his life is lived. They point to the high delinquency in residential sections. This theory, also, we reject; at least, we do not accept it in its entirety. We admit that environment has a great deal to do with the behavior of man, but we deny that man is incapable of rising above his environmental limitations.

These are but a few of the many theories advanced for the explanation of man's behavior, but in this brief exposition we cannot enter into a discussion of the others. For we must now begin an explanation of our own ideas of man's behavior. Our theory is not a new one, and though many have tried to laugh it to scorn, and are still trying to do so, it nevertheless seems to give the most satisfactory answer to the question of why men do this and why men do that; why some men are decent, respectable and moral, and others despicable, indecent and immoral.

According to our theory there are in man two natures: his spiritual nature and his animal nature. His animal nature contains all the bodily urges of the animal in the field, while his spiritual nature has urges unknown to the animal nature and sometimes diametrically opposed to those urges. The same urge that makes a horse stretch his neck over a wire fence to get an ear of corn exists in man and prompts him to procure, either rightfully or wrongfully, that which his lower nature desires. In man's lower nature there exists, too, the same urge for rest and ease that prompts the horse to hold his head away from the bridle. But over and above these animal urges of men there are urges that come from his spiritual nature; the urge to unravel the mysteries of nature, the urge to know nature's Creator, the urge to possess and to know things true and good and beautiful. We hold, too, that between these two natures of man there exists a relationship — that one is superior to the other, that the urges of the two natures are in constant conflict, and that if right order in accordance with their relationship is to be maintained, the priority of the spiritual urges must prevail.

We argue further that in this spiritual nature of man there are two parts: the intellect and the will. It is the business of the intellect to gather the facts and to present them to the will for adoption or rejection. The will has the power to will what the intellect presents, or not to will it; man can reject any and all urges of his lower nature in deference to an urge of his higher nature. The intellect has the power to recognize right order; the will has the power to choose right order.

Books, many thick books, could be, and have been, written on this subject. What has been said here constitutes but a few bare principles, further explanation of which will be brought forth in the classroom discussions. In conclusion, it may be said that the question of man's behavior, of his doing good or his doing evil, will always be the subject matter of study for the world's most learned minds. The mysteries of the free will of man will probably be just as great mysteries a thousand years from now as they are today.

CRIME AND PUNISHMENT

It may be said that the object and function of law is to maintain an orderly state of society by compelling the individual in close association with other individuals to live in such a way that he pays some regard to the private wills and pleasures of the others, and does not act as if his own interests were everything and theirs nothing. Thus, in one direction the law deprives a man of his powers — his power to assault and rob his neighbors, but in another direction it increases his freedom, for he will in his turn be free from the assault and robbery of his neighbors.

As nearly everyone knows, there are many laws applicable to many different things — civil law, commercial law, international law, parlimentary law, and many others. This chapter will deal with criminal law. All the different branches of jurisprudence have their own codes. There is a criminal code, civil code, etc.

To begin with one must know the definition of a crime. The average layman defines a crime with reference to its consequences as some act for which he may be punished by a criminal court. Any attempt to define a crime with reference to the nature of the act, as distinct from its consequences, is beset with difficulties. The distinction between crimes and civil wrongs is found in every civilized state, but it is not easy to arrive at an exact definition of a crime which will explain the distinction.

At first sight the most obvious practical distinction is that the state takes cognizance of a crime without waiting for the person injured to invoke its aid, whereas, in the case of civil wrongs, it is left to the individual injured to set the law in motion against the person who injured him. For example, if A "holds up" B on the street and robs him of his watch, the state will take proceedings against A to bring about his punishment, even though B does not invoke its aid; if, however, B, having borrowed A's watch, refuses to hand it back when asked to do so, the state will not interfere. A may himself start an action against B for detaining the watch, and if he does so the state will probably order B to return the watch, but unless A brings the matter to the courts the state will not interfere.

This distinction is of value, but there are two objections to it. First, it is always open to a private individual to commence criminal proceedings just as he may commence civil proceedings, although it is still true that the state, if he does not act, may act in criminal proceedings but cannot do so in private proceedings. Secondly, the distinction is not one which relates to the nature of criminal and non-criminal acts, and still leaves to be answered the question of why the state will interfere in certain cases and not in others.

Another distinction that may be suggested is that crimes are wrongful acts which violently offend our moral feelings. This, again, is of value as a rough test, but no more; for a breach of trust, or a breach of contract, which are both mere civil wrongs and not crimes, may be much more offensive morally than many crimes, some of which, e.g., failure to take out a dog license, can scarcely be said to involve any moral turpitude. Again, we cannot say that every act which injures the community is a crime, for the civil wrongs mentioned above may do great injury to the community.

The idea of punishment also helps us to another distinction. When a civil wrong has been committed and the law is invoked by the person injured, the law is not concerned to punish the wrongdoer, but to compensate the injured person. In assessing the damages the court will be concerned, not with the degree of moral guilt involved in the defendant's conduct, but solely with the results of his conduct to the plaintiff. In the case of a crime, however, the object of the court is to inflict on the criminal the punishment deserved by his conduct. If A, while drunk, drives his car at 40 miles per hour down a crowded street and runs into B's car, his acts constitute both the crime of dangerous driving and the civil wrong of causing damage by negligence. Let us assume that for the first of these he is prosecuted by the state and convicted in a criminal court, and for the second, sued and found liable in damages in a civil court. In calculating the punishment to be imposed upon him for the criminal offense the court will consider the speed at which he was driving, the likelihood of injury, the extent of the danger, and also his past record. In calculating the damages which A must pay to B none of these will be relevant; the court will only consider what it will cost B to have his car repaired.

A civil wrong, further, may always be pardoned or settled out of court by the person injured, but it is of itself a crime to agree either not to institute or to withdraw, a criminal prosecution on payment of a sum of money. So if my dog is stolen I should not advertise in the paper and say that if it is returned a reward will be given and "no questions asked." This again illustrates the principle that a crime concerns, not only the criminal and the injured person, but also the state.

We may now conclude that a crime has the following characteristics: (1) It involves a moral wrong; (2) It injures the state; (3) The state will interfere to punish the act; (4) The state in punishing the act is concerned not with the loss caused by the crime to any person, but with the quality of the act done by the criminal.

AN OUTLINE OF PENOLOGY

Penology is the science of punishment by confinement, the management of prisoners and their rehabilitation and reformation. If you step accidentally on a dog, it will probably snap at you. Similarly, in the earliest times, when one man injured another in any way, the offended party extracted punishment on the spot. But, if every member of a community meted out punishment personally for offenses committed against him, the result would be disorder and confusion. Very early in the history of civilization, therefore, the individual members of society delegated to one central authority, the state, the right and the duty to inflict punishment on those who broke the law.

There have been a number of different theories as to why punishment should be inflicted on law breakers. The earliest of these was the embodiment of the idea of personal retaliation — of revenge. The code of Hammurabi, in ancient Babylonia, provided that if a man put out his neighbor's eye, he too, should lose an eye. This sounds strange and barbarous, doesn't it? Yet the Mosaic Law in our own Bible is really based on the idea of an eye for an eye and a tooth for a tooth. And this idea of retaliation has come down through the ages up to very recent times; in fact, it is still practiced in some communities. We may have gotten away from the idea of retribution in exact kind, but until very recently the idea behind most punishment was simply punishment for its own sake.

Much more advanced than this concept, however, is the theory which was universal in the eighteenth and nineteenth centuries, and which still has a large following. Known as the "Deterrence Theory" this doctrine holds that the chief purpose of the punishment of criminals is the effect it will have upon others. In simple words, the proponents of this theory believe that if one man steals from his neighbor, he should be severely punished when caught, since other men, seeing his suffering, will think twice before they commit a similar offense: that the punishment of the offender will frighten others into obeying the laws.

Naturally, if the deterrence theory is correct, the greatest good can be accomplished by punishment only if it is severe, and, above all, if it is public — if it is widely noised about. And so, in England less than a hundred years ago, over one hundred twenty crimes were punishable by death, and the hangings were held on top of a high hill, in full sight of a very large crowd. One of the crimes for which men were being hanged was pocket picking, yet in no place were pickpockets more active than in the crowds assembled to see a pickpocket hanged. It is at least doubtful that the punishment of one criminal does act as a serious deterrent to another.

Only very recently, indeed, within the twentieth century, has there arisen a third great theory on the purpose of punishment. This theory holds that men who commit crimes are punished for two reasons, and for two reasons only. The first is the protection of society by the segregation of the lawbreakers; it is obvious that a murderer cannot kill and a thief cannot steal while he is locked away from the world. But far more important than this merely temporary protection is the second objective of punishment. For holders of the modern theory of punishment believe that its primary purpose is the rehabilitation and reform of the offender himself. Society can be most permanently and securely protected, of course, not by shutting up a criminal for three, or five, or twenty years, but by changing once and for all the attitude of the man who has broken the law, so that he will cease to be dangerous, will cease to be a problem for society. It must be obvious that if it is possible to cure the criminal, this method is far more humane, and far more economical than merely locking him in a cell.

During the course of the world's history many different forms of punishment have been employed. Among the earliest were death and mutilation. In some societies criminals were sold into slavery. Even in Colonial times many forms of punishment which today strike us as cruel and senseless were constantly resorted to. The thief might have his hand cut off, or he might be branded;

men were frequently flogged until they became unconscious; harmless old women, whom some stupid citizen accused of witchcraft, were hanged or burned at the stake; even the women who talked too much were likely to be placed in a pillory, or given a bath on a ducking stool. England, France, and Russia have practiced transportation of criminals on a large scale. The salt mines of Siberia were worked by convicts, and Australia was originally colonized almost entirely by persons transported from England as punishment.

Illinois practices five different kinds of punishment: execution, imprisonment, parole, probation, and punishment by fine. The death penalty is inflicted by electrocution in one of the three electric chairs in the state. One is located in the Cook County Jail and is used for executions in Cook County; one is at Joliet and is used for the execution of persons convicted in the northern section of the state; the third, at Menard, is used for the execution of criminals from the part of the state south of Springfield. The death penalty is prescribed for only two offenses in Illinois: murder and kidnapping for ransom. It has never been used for the latter crime.

There are many moral, religious, and social arguments both in favor of and against capital punishment. These arguments cannot concern us here further than to say that while execution effectively rids society of the offender and hence furnishes complete protection against him, there is, of course, no chance for reform. The death sentence is irrevocable; once it has been inflicted, it is too late to correct mistakes.

Punishment for felonies consists of imprisoning the criminal in a penitentiary. Some crimes, such as murder, rape and kidnapping, carry definite determinate sentences. By far the large majority of crimes ,however, are punishable by imprisonment under indeterminate sentences. Thus, the sentence for armed robbery is for one year to life, that for assault with intent to kill is from one to fourteen years. However, under the indeterminate sentence law, the court may at its discretion set the minimum and maximum number of years to be served by a prisoner at any point within the statutory limits for a particular crime. The use of the indeterminate sentence is a great step forward in penology, and this for two reasons. First, under the indeterminate sentence it is possible to make the sentence fit the criminal, rather than the specific crime he has committed. It is sound sociology and sound penology to release a man just as soon as it is safe to do so; the purpose of punishment in Illinois today is not to get even with the offender, but to reform him. On the other hand, it is equally sound to keep in prison for a very long time those individuals who have proved their inability to make good in free society, even if they may have been apprehended for a comparatively minor offense. The indeterminate sentence makes this possible; for the parole board is empowered to study the individual prisoner and to take into consideration many factors other than the particular crime for which he has been sentenced. Thus, for the good of everyone, all sentences should be from one year to life.

The second great advantage of the indeterminate sentence is that, under it, the prisoner is not released at the expiration of his sentence, scot free and with no further responsibilities. Instead, the convict is released on parole, a limited form of freedom. True, he is permitted to leave the prison and return to his home, but for years he continues to be, legally, a prisoner. During the period of his parole the prisoner must live up to a set of regulations governing his conduct; if he violates them, or if he breaks a law, he can be returned to prison instantly, without the necessity of a trial and conviction in court. The present tendency in penology is to release all men on parole rather than by discharge, and to make all sentences indeterminate.

Parole is a comparatively new procedure, and it has, unfortunately, been made the target of adverse criticism by people who are not well acquainted with the facts. But much work has been done, and is continuing to be done, in learning what men can safely be paroled. The infant science of parole prediction, by which it is possible to tell very accurately in advance the likelihood of a given individual's making good on release, is making great strides.

Probation is the setting aside conditionally of a sentence of imprisonment. If an individual commits a minor infraction of the law, if the infraction is his first, and if the judge believes that under proper supervision the defendant can be made into a law-abiding citizen, he is empowered to pass sentence and then to set aside the sentence and place the defendant on probation for a given period. During this period of probation, the defendant must remain within the jurisdiction of the court, must make reports at regular intervals, and is subject to the supervision of special probation officers. Probation is used almost entirely for youthful, improvable first offenders. It has proven a valuable weapon in reforming many youngsters without placing on them the stigma of imprisonment, and without putting the state to the expense of maintaining them.

Misdemeanors are punishable by imprisonment on the state penal farm at Vandalia, or in the House of Correction in Chicago, or in any County Jail. Sentences are ordinarily for one year or less, and may or may not include a fine. Fines alone are sometimes imposed for the least serious misdemeanors: traffic violations, disorderly conduct, violations of the game laws, gambling, etc.

To sum up, punishment is based on natural law. The right to punish lawbreakers has been assigned by the citizens to the state. The primary purpose of punishment is neither retaliation nor deterrence, but the rehabilitation of the individual offender.

RESPONSIBILITIES OF A PENITENTIARY WARDEN

The duties of a penitentiary warden are too varied and numerous to be categorically listed in this brief chapter. We may, however, sketch the framework of a warden's function and the student's observation will fill in the outline as he gathers experience as a guard. It is well that the employee clearly understand the warden's position as regards his employees and as regards the inmates for whom he is responsible. Again, it is well that he understand the rules the warden makes for the proper administration of a penal institution are not arbitrary rules, that they do not originate from whim or caprice. This section will summarize the genesis of the warden's authority and explain why he is able to make rules and change them as the occasion demands. A good warden, to know and have the feel of the institution, must tour it daily, must make inspections of all assignments and must talk to personnel and inmates. Only in this way will he have its full "pulse," and a knowledge of what is going on.

In the eternal order of things all authority, which is nothing more than the right to make laws and enforce them, comes, in the final analysis, from the Creator.

The first evidence of authority is that of the parent over the child. There is no need for a state or a federal law to assign to parents the authority which is necessary for bringing about the physical and moral protection of their offspring. This authority flows directly from nature and the Creator of nature. The parents, if they see fit to do so, may entrust this authority to others. But this transfer of authority is entirely dependent on the consent of the parents.

Nations may sometimes disregard this authority and usurp the rights of the parents. But this usurpation of authority which is the inherent right of parents will never find justification in a right order of things.

A family consisting of parents and children living in a wilderness and belonging to no constituted community may be considered as a complete unit of government. The parents would have duties towards and rights over the children; the children would have certain duties towards and rights from the parents. In the performance of these duties, the parents need be responsible only to their Creator.

If several families then came into this wilderness, it would be within the power of the parents to transfer to one designated person certain or all of their rights. In this case, then, we should have a legally constituted government for a civilized society. Only through the consent of the people may they be justly governed.

In the latter part of the seventeenth century a few families settled in the territory of what is now the State of Illinois. By mutual consent and majority agreements, these early settlers transferred some of their rights and authority to a chosen few. With the passage of years, families multiplied and a great stream of immigrants flowed into the state. The men who were designated to exercise the rights of the parents increased proportionately. As they were deprived of this authority, or passed on, the torch was transferred to other hands. Thus arose our great State of Illinois. Today the rights and authority of several million parents have been transferred by lawful means into the hands of a small body of men, at the head of which is the governor of the State of Illinois.

Without the consent of at least the majority of these millions of parents, the governor would have no control over them, for authority without consent is tyranny.

The duties of the governor of any large state are too numerous for any one man to shoulder, and it is within his province to delegate much of his authority to able and trustworthy men. We may thus arrive at a full understanding of the origin of a warden's rights and duties. All the authority in the hands of a penitentiary warden derives from the people (from the fathers and mothers of the state) by means of the governor and through the head of the Department of Public Safety. All the authority possessed by the assistant wardens, the captains and the lieutenants, and the other officers of the institution comes from the people, through the warden.

To maintain the proper relationship between one object and all others, there must be certain laws setting forth definitions of these relationships, as well as the sanctions against the breaking down of these same relationships. Between two simple objects the relationship is simple, and the laws governing it need be only simple. Take, for example, two such simple objects as two points. They have neither size, nor weight, nor color. The only attribute of a point is a position, and the only relationship between two points is that of position. A law governing position and nothing else would be adequate in this instance. Going one step further, it will easily be seen that as an object becomes more complex, the more complex will become its relationship to similar objects, and the more complex will become the laws governing this relationship.

The object nearest to the simplicity of a point is a line, for a line has length, direction, and position, and the relationship between one line and another involves these factors. We may thus go from one complex object to another still more complex, until we finally come to the warden of a penitentiary and his relationship to 600 or more employees, to 5,000 or more inmates, and to 10,000,000 or more of his fellow Illinoisans.

With this great multiplicity of laws (written and unwritten) we attempt to maintain these relationships as they should exist in an orderly and just society.

In order to deal scientifically with any wide variety of things, the first step must necessarily be in the direction of classification. In this course dealing with prison administration, it has seemed proper to classify these relationships into four general groups.

Our outline lists them as follows: (1) Duties Toward the State; (2) Duties Toward Inmates; ;(3) Duties Toward Employees; (4) Duties Toward the Neighboring Community.

Further development of these duties of a penitentiary warden will lead us to a complete understanding of the orderly operation of an institution. All those who apply themselves to the task should, at the completion of this course, be well acquainted with the part they are to play and the duties they are to perform when they are entrusted with their appointments as guards in the Illinois State Penitentiary.

COMPLIANCE WITH ORDERS OF THE COURT

The position of the warden makes him legally responsible for the carrying out of certain orders issued by a court of record. One of his duties is the carrying into effect of executions legally ordered by the proper court. In Illinois, the only crimes punishable by death are murder and kidnapping for ransom. The death sentence is carried out by electrocution.

There are many arguments, legal, moral, and sociological, both in favor of and opposed to capital punishment, but these cannot be considered. The point of concern at the moment is that the warden is in no way connected with, nor responsible for, setences of death decreed by the courts, nor with the efforts of the condemned man or his friends to secure pardon or commutation of the sentence. He is charged by law with carrying into effect the order of the court, and this he must do, regardless of his personal views in the matter.

When a prisoner under sentence of death is received at the penitentiary, it is necessary to see that he is confined securely and safely. All medical care which is required must be furnished the condemned man, and constant watch must be kept over him, both to prevent attempts at escape and to forestall suicide. It is for greater ease in safe-keeping that condemned men are usually confined in isolated imprisonment. Men under sentence of death are given certain privileges, such as writing letters, receiving spiritual guidance and assistance, and having visits, under proper precautions, from authorized persons.

The usual time of execution is at one minute after midnight. The warden is present at all executions, and certain officers are detailed to specific posts and tasks connected with it. It is of the highest importance that officers so assigned know thoroughly just what is expected of them, so that the execution may proceed swiftly and smoothly. The law requires the presence of official witnesses at all executions, and certain officials connected with the trial of the condemned man have the privilege of attending. It is important that these witnesses be received, searched, and escorted to their places with as little confusion as possible.

Another important legal duty of the warden is the prompt compliance with those orders of a court known as writs. The term "writ" was first used in English Law and referred originally to orders under the seal of the king. The term is now used to refer to any order or mandatory process under seal, issued in the name of a court or judicial officer. Writs derive their authority either from statutes passed by the state legislature or from common law. Failure to comply with any properly issued writ constitutes contempt of court, which is punishable by imprisonment. Both the warden personally and any officer acting as his agent in the matter are liable.

The writs which are of importance with respect to prisoners are of four kinds. The commonest type of writ is a writ of *habeas corpus*. These words mean "you may have the body," and the writ directs the person who is the custodian of the prisoner named in the writ to produce his body in court. A writ of *habeas corpus* may be issued for any number of reasons; among the commonest is that of compelling the presence of a prisoner in court for the purpose of testifying. This is called a writ of *habeas corpus ad testificandum*. Or the prisoner may be wanted in court for prosecution under an additional charge. A writ issued for this purpose is known as a writ of *habeas corpus ad prosequendun*. Finally, the prisoner may have appealed the sentence under which he is held to a higher court. If this higher court desires to overrule a decision, sentence, or ruling of a lower court, it issues a writ of error or *supersedeas*. Such a writ has the effect of "superseding" the sentence of the lower court, and ordinarily a prisoner is entitled to his temporary liberty under such a writ.

In making a return on a writ and delivering the body of the prisoner named into court, the officer who has charge of the inmate is acting as an agent of the warden. He is at all times the representative of the warden and not of any of the other parties concerned in the proceedings. He must see to it that the prisoner is safely delivered to the place specified and at the time specified in the writ, and he must always and under all circumstances procure a receipt for delivery of the inmate from the court. This is his legal protection. When the proceedings are at an end, the officer must receive some authority from the court either for the return of the prisoner to the institution or for failure to make such return. For example, in a writ of *habeas corpus,* the judge may decide against the prisoner and remand him to the custody of the warden. This means that the officer must return him safely to the prison. The same holds true in the case of a prisoner who has given his testimony under a writ *ad testificandum* and who is no longer required in court. On the other hand, the court may discharge the prisoner. Then, of course, the officer no longer has authority over him, but he must be sure to obtain from the court a valid order for the discharge of the prisoner. Finally, the judge may wish to keep the prisoner available for further court hearings. For this purpose he may remand the prisoner to the custody of the sheriff for safe-keeping in the county jail. Here too the officer's authority is superseded, but he must again be sure to obtain a proper order for turning the prisoner over to the sheriff and a receipt from the latter. He must never think that leaving his prisoner in jail amounts to the same thing as returning him to the penitentiary. He should have proper authority for turning the man over to the sheriff in exactly the same way as if he were letting him go free.

Officers must, of course, be constantly alert when they are taking a prisoner to court or returning him from court on a writ. Some prisoners have seized such opportunities to escape. For example, "Baby Face" Nelson, who later became notorious as a "public enemy," once escaped from a guard who was returning him to prison after a court appearance.

Many sentences are either for definite terms or else carry a definite maximum term. In either case, the prisoner is legally entitled to his discharge when he has served the sentence imposed by the court, and the warden is responsible for discharging the prisoner at the proper time, just as he is for keeping him confined until that time. The crimes of murder, rape, kidnapping, and violation of the habitual criminal act carry definite sentences; most other crimes are punishable by indeterminate sentences, but here too most sentences have a definite maximum.

All prisoners are given by law the opportunity of earning good time allowances from their sentences. Such allowances are granted for good behavior in the institution and may be revoked if the prisoner misbehaves. Authority to grant or withhold such allowances is vested in the Department of Public Safety. Inmates earn one month off the first year of their sentence, two months the second, and so on up to six months. This allowance is given for the sixth year and for every year thereafter. Allowance for good time earned is deducted from the prisoner's maximum sentence in computing the date of his release. If a prisoner were held in prison after the time at which he was entitled to discharge, he would have a suit for damages against the warden.

When eligible for discharge, prisoners have the right to certain items. They must be furnished adequate clothing and railroad fare to the county seat of the county from which they were sentenced. In addition, they must be given any personal belongings which they brought with them when they came to prison and which have been held for them in the vault, and twenty-five to fifty dollars in cash for board and lodging.

Discharge may take place from court. As was explained above, a prisoner who has been returned to court on a writ may be discharged by the judge or by the reversal of the original sentence on the part of a higher court. In addition, inmates who are on parole may be given their discharge, either because the maximum period of their sentence has passed or by order of the Parole Board. Although inmates on parole are, of course, not confined in the penitentiary, they are legally in custody of the warden until they receive their discharges.

The law makes provision for certain visits to which prisoners are entitled. These consist chiefly of visits from legal counsel and of visits from clergymen and spiritual advisers. The bi-monthly visits from relatives and friends, ordinarily permitted inmates in the penitentiary, are privileges and not legal rights.

Some prisoners are released from prison for the purpose of deportation from the country. Deportation is an act of the Federal Government and not of the State. It is employed in cases of illegal entry into the United States by an alien, failure on his part to take out proper citizenship, and the second conviction for a felony. The prisoner is technically discharged by the State, but, instead of being allowed his freedom, he is turned over to the United States marshal.

The warden is also required by law to keep certain legal records with regard to all prisoners. While the warden is charged with this responsibility, the routine work is generally delegated to an official known as the record clerk. The record clerk's duties consist in keeping accurate records of the many kinds required by law and for other purposes and the calculation of the time to be served by each inmate. This is, of course, a tremendous responsibility, and it is therefore necessary that the record clerk be a man of high character, of good education, and that he possess a thorough knowledge of modern filing systems.

As each inmate is received, a complete record is made of the legal details of his case. The record is kept together and filed in a folder bearing the prisoner's name, number, etc. It contains a copy of the prisoner's indictment, of the sentence of the court together with proper commitment papers, and a statement from the judge and from the state's attorney. These papers together form what is called the prisoner's *mittimus* and constitute the legal warrant for holding him in prison. In his "jacket" also are any warrants or other detainers which may be issued against him, his photograph, fingerprints, description, previous record, and vital information concerning himself which he gave upon admittance. Here, too, are filed the authorization which the inmate signs for the censorship of his mail, a record of his personal belongings, the report of the Classification Board, and a record of his punishments in prison. On his jacket is entered also the date when the inmate is eligible for release, whether by parole or discharge. This information is duplicated on a perpetual calendar, which enables the record clerk to know exactly what inmates are entitled to release on any day.

Separate records are kept of all inmates on parole from the institution. This record contains all parole reports, parole card, and notice of violations of parole or of warrants issued. As prisoners are discharged, their records are removed to permanent files, kept in the institutional vault. Here, too, are filed the records of all deceased inmates. Separate files are used for information concerning escaped men and men absent from the institution on writs.

In addition to such legal records, the record clerk keeps a number of general records for current administrative use in the institution. Thus, he has a numerical register of all inmates received, which contains data concerning them; an alphabetical register of the names and known aliases of inmates; a register by nationality, one by religion, one by type of crime, etc. In addition, he keeps the count book, which shows the exact number of inmates and their disposition daily and a number of running records of statistical nature, from which it is possible to obtain information of almost any desired kind with respect to the inmate population.

It must not be thought that the duties mentioned complete the list. The warden, as a citizen, has, of course, the same legal duties as other citizens, but by virtue of his position, he has additional legal duties specifically enumerated.

EMERGENCIES I

In every institution there are rules for the routine operation of the institution, but, over and above these rules, there must be auxiliary rules to guide all action in case of an emergency. In a penitentiary, emergencies are most likely to come about as the result of fire or escape, riot or strike, or unusual weather conditions. In this section will be set forth briefly the general rules that should be followed in case of fire or an escape.

Since no one man is able to do much alone, the first rule in case of fire is to get word of the fire to a superior officer immediately. This can be done by means of the institutional communication system, or by use of a runner. In making a report of the fire, the definite location should be given, as well as other facts such as the nature of the fire and to what extent it is burning. The officer should be sure that the fire department is notified at once. Throughout the institution fire extinguishers have been placed. The officer should do everything in his power to fight the fire and should make use of whatever inmate help is available.

The best qualifications of any officer in an emergency are good judgment and the ability to remain calm and collected. If an officer becomes excited, he will necessarily impart his excitement to those under him. But if he keeps his head and directs the activities calmly, he will find that those working under his direction will also remain calm and carry out his orders effectively. Since a life is worth more than any amount of property, good judgment demands that the officer keep first in mind the safety of all those under him, whether they be inmates or fellow officers. He should bear in mind that in an institution where discipline prevails, men follow orders even at a risk of losing their own lives. Therefore, it is well that the officer consider carefully before giving an order which, in its execution, might endanger a life. When one is in charge and has the lives of other men in his care, he should realize that his first duty is to his charges. His own personal safety should be of secondary importance. A sense of loyalty to duty should be the guiding point in the mind of every officer in any emergency.

The old philosophers have defined courage as the knowledge of when to be afraid. The officer has nothing to fear when he is carrying out the orders of his superior to the best of his ability. But any officer who, through cowardice or disloyalty, fails to carry out the orders of his superior, can bring danger to all and humiliation to the Department of Public Safety and to its administrative officers.

An escape from a prison is not necessarily an emergency in the sense of a disaster, but it is the cause of the temporary breaking up of the routine operation of a penitentiary. The action following the officer's first knowledge of an escape will depend largely on the nature of the escape; that is, from where the escape has been made and the identity of the escapee. The history of the Joliet Prison for the past several years will show that the few escapes that have occurred were made, from the Honor Farm and other trusted assignments outside the walls.

Just as soon as an officer working on the Honor Farm has reason to suspect that an inmate has escaped, he should make a careful check to verify the fact and to ascertain the identity of the escapee. When the escape is known to be an established fact and identification of the escapee has been made, it is the officer's duty to march his remaining men to some secure place as rapidly as possible. It may be difficult to keep the knowledge of the escape from the inmates, but, as far as possible, it should be done. As soon as the officer has his men in a secure place, his duty is to notify the authorities, either by telephone or runner, that an escape has occurred, giving the identity of the escapee and other known facts regarding the circumstances. The officer should then remain with his men to await orders from his superiors.

Other than the inmates assigned to the Honor Farm, the men next most likely to attempt to escape are men on writs. In such cases it is the duty of the officer to notify the institution and local law enforcement agencies in the quickest possible time. After this has been done, the officer should make every effort to follow as closely as possible the trail of the escapee, proceeding with common sense and taking into consideration whatever knowledge he has of the character of the inmate.

While escapes from within the walls are unusual, they sometimes do occur, and in every case someone is to blame, for with every officer carrying out his duty to the letter an escape from within the walls should be an impossibility. In case of an escape from within the walls, almost the same procedure is followed as in escapes from the Honor Farm and escapes from custody away from the institution. The officer first suspecting the escape should make sure that someone is missing and establish his identity by checking his men. When the facts are ascertained and the escape established as a fact, the officer is to make a report to his superior officer, giving the identity of the escapee and whatever clues he has as to the manner of the escape. All other inmates under the officer's charge should be quickly marched to a place of security, and there the officer should await instructions from his superior officers.

For the recapture of men escaping from this institution, a system of quickly blocking all highways has been inaugurated.

INSTITUTIONAL RULES
OFFICERS

Since discipline is one of the most vital factors in the efficient operation of a penitentiary, it is necessary that officers fully comprehend the importance of absolute obedience to the prison rules, not only by the inmates, but also by the officers themselves. There has been prepared in booklet form a complete list of the rules and regulations governing the conduct of employees of the Illinois State Penitentiary. A copy of the booklet is given to every officer, and it is required that all officers study it thoroughly, that they may know at all times exactly what is required of them. In addition, officers should consult the bulletin board daily for new rules.

It is realized, of course, that no officer will voluntarily violate any of the regulations — no conscientious officer, that is — but for the protection of all and to maintain maximum efficiency, it has been necessary to impose penalties upon those officers who, through carelessness, neglect, or willful intent, fail to conduct themselves properly.

These penalties range from a reprimand by a superior officer to summary dismissal, and between these extremes are such lesser punishments as transfer of assignment, demotion and suspension. The penalty will always fit the offense. For instance, personal untidiness might incur a reprimand; inefficiency or inability to handle the alloted work, a change of assignment. Demotion might result from a use of poor judgment in the line of duty, suspension could be caused by failure to report to work on time, and dismissal would follow more serious violations of the regulations.

It should, however, be entirely unnecessary for any officer to bring upon himself any of these penalties. By adhering faithfully to the rules designed to govern his conduct, he can assure himself of the continued approval of his superiors.

DISCIPLINE

Our English word discipline is derived from the Latin word *disciplina,* which, in turn, is formed from the word *discipulus,* which means "pupil" or "disciple." In the Roman world, men with untrained minds were considered but little above the animal kingdom. The only man considered worthy of the name "man" among the Roman people was the man who had been taught by the masters, the man whose mind had been properly ordered for thinking.

The proper English translation for the Latin word *disciplinatus* is "trained" or "cultured." Without some thought, it is difficult to see the relationship between our word "discipline" and our word "culture." But with reflection and observation the similarity in meaning of the two words will be discovered. The cultured mind is a mind that has been trained by rules and laws for orderly and correct thinking. Since proper order is the result of training or disciplining the mind, order is the result of discipline in general.

In a complicated piece of mechanism you will find many little insignificant parts, whose function the untrained man would fail to recognize. But if one of these parts should fail to carry out its assigned duty, the result would be a breakdown in the general purpose of the machine. On the other hand, if every small part does its duty as planned by the designer, the results of the whole mechanism will be the complete fulfillment of the purpose that the designer had in mind. This order in a piece of mechanism is nothing more than a result of discipline.

Discipline, therefore, can be understood as being the book of laws for the proper ordering of the parts that serve the whole.

The perfect order that we see in nature is simply the parts of nature in full obedience to the laws of nature. That water seeks its lowest level, that the stars shine at night, that the earth revolves on its axis, that the sun gives light and heat, and many other such examples, are all the result of nature's laws, and nature's enforcement of the laws. This, indeed, is discipline in the physical world. Students of the animal world and even we who are only casual gazers at the birds and the forest animals recognize the order that exists in the animal kingdom. Birds find their mates and build their nests. When the young arrive, the parents obey nature's laws by protecting them against the dangers of the world to the fullest extent of their powers. Every type of animal we see lives an ordered life. The animal kingdom is a disciplined kingdom.

In the physical world and the animal world, from all appearances, discipline is maintained without any threatening sanction for violating the laws. If the water fails to seek its level, what punishment would it have to anticipate? If the birds fail to build their nests, who would threaten them with punishment? Yet, even without threat of punishment, in both the physical and the animal world we find no attempts to deviate from the proper order of things. In the world of man, however, we find it quite different. The right order of things for man has been properly established, but man oftentimes refuses to comply with the rules by which that order must be maintained. He will deny, when he is found out of order, his knowledge of what that order should have been. Therefore, what he can do and what he cannot do must be written out for him in black and white in the laws of the land. He is rewarded if he obeys, and he is punished if he fails to obey. Discipline among mankind has resulted in the making of rules and laws and enforcing them with sanctions sufficiently stern to force man's compliance with them. Judging from the experience of the past and from our present observations, perfect discipline among man is beyond the realm of hope. It seems quite certain that as long as there are laws and men, men are going to violate the laws. But it will ever be the purpose of those men who have ideas of right order to keep attempting to reach the highest mark of discipline possible.

So far in this discussion, discipline has been treated only in a very general sense, but in the rest of the section it will be treated in a most special and specific sense; that is, discipline in a penitentiary. In a previous chapter on the responsibilities of a penitentiary warden it was shown that with each duty there was an accompanying right which enabled him to discharge his duties. Just as nature, without the right to make laws and enforce them, could accomplish nothing good for nature's world, so would the warden of a penitentiary, without the right to make rules and enforce them, be unable to accomplish anything for the good of the institution as a whole. But nature does have her laws, and they are strictly obeyed. And the order in nature is the duplicate of that order that nature's Creator had in mind for nature. In the mind of a penitentiary warden there is certain order which should prevail throughout the whole institution, from the next highest ranking official to the lowest inmate. With the proper rules and the proper supervision for their complete enforcement, there will and must prevail within the institution that same order which the warden seeks. There would, however, be no purpose in making rules for a penitentiary if there were no sanctions, or punishments behind them to threaten the violators. Man, it seems, will never obey just for the sake of obeying; he obeys because he fears to disobey; he respects rules because he respects the punishment for their violation. No warden worthy of the name takes any personal satisfaction in administering punishment; but, in carrying out his duties, it is necessary that he inflict punishment and that the punishment be severe enough to prevent repeated or further violations.

If the warden's laws and rules for the running of an institution are reasonable and complete and properly enforced, discipline is the inevitable result. Just as in the piece of mechanism which was spoken of before, when every little part performed its duty, the mechanism was a success. There was discipline in all parts and the results produced would necessarily meet with the ideas of the designer. In a penitentiary, with every man doing his duty—that is, obeying the rules the warden has set down—perfect order should prevail throughout the entire institution. If, however, one man fails to comply with the rules, or is neglectful in his duty, and if his failure is not noticed and his compliance forced, the results will be disastrous for the institution as a whole.

EMERGENCIES II

In a preceding section was discussed the proper action for officers in case of fire or escape. It was shown that a cool head, common sense, and obedience to certain definite rules are the prime requirements in such contingencies.

This section will consider the proper procedure for such emergencies as riots, strikes and unusual weather conditions.

Penitentiary strikes and riots are of two kinds: violent and passive. In a violent riot or strike, immediate notification and description of the situation must be made to superiors. This is the first duty of the officer. Again, in making this report, the officer should use the telephone or two way radio as a first means of communication. If possible, the call should be put through to a superior officer in person, rather than to the telephone operator. If it is impossible to reach a telephone or radio, the officer should report the trouble by runner. Failing both of these alternatives, the officer must use his ingenuity, selecting whatever means he may have at his command to make the trouble known to his superiors.

The officer should not lose his nerve or become frightened, both for his sake and for the sake of the institution in general. If he remains calm and cool, he will promote his own safety and the safety of those inmates in his charge who may be non-participants in the disturbance. The officer should not delay making his report until a strike or riot has gained full headway, but should report the situation to his superiors as soon as he has noticed any sign of unrest. Quick action may avert serious trouble at the outset.

Again, as in other emergencies, good judgment becomes a necessary qualification of a good officer. Many things are to be considered, and the time for consideration may be extremely limited, but the officer should do nothing on impulse. He should weigh the facts and then proceed with the utmost caution. Besides his own safety, the officer must consider the safety of non-participating inmates and also the safety of any of his fellow officers who may be involved. It would be foolhardly for one officer alone to expose his own life to a number of angry men armed with deadly weapons. He should guard his own safety by any means possible until help can arrive. He may be sure that assistance will be forthcoming promptly after a report of the trouble has reached those in authority. Upon the arrival of a superior officer, every aid must be given. The officer's duty then is to do as he is ordered, leaving all questions as to "why" and "how" for later consideration.

A few men with proper equipment and by means of concerted action can quell mobs of considerable size. By concerted action is meant complete coöperation between the officers involved; the actions of one should be the actions of all, and that one should be the highest ranking officer present. The superior officer will necessarily be experienced, and will know what orders to give. The officer's part will be to execute all orders given by his superior promptly and unhesitatingly.

Although the work of a penitentiary officer is a comparatively safe occupation, it is possible that there may come a time when he may be obliged to carry out orders involving the risk of personal injury. At such times he must remember that the risk is a part of his job; if he feels that he would hesitate to carry out tasks involving some danger, he should seek employment elsewhere than within penitentiary walls. An officer should never fear the consequences of a superior's order. Cowardice, and cowardice alone, is the thing to be feared.

The second type of riot or strike is the passive type. This takes the form of unresponsiveness on the part of the men to the orders of the officer. Strikes of this nature, if handled properly and in time, can usually be brought quickly under control. It is the duty of every officer, upon gaining knowledge—or even intimation—of such a strike, to notify his superior officer at once. His next move should be to separate the participants from the non-participants. The names and numbers of all the participating inmates should be noted. Non-participating inmates should be conducted to a place of safety—that is, to their cell house or dormitory—as soon as possible. This should be done only after help has arrived and other officers are present to lend assistance. Under no circumstances should the officer in charge leave the participating inmates by themselves. After help has arrived, it is the officer's duty merely to carry out the orders of his superior. Quick action in segregating the participants from the non-participants and in getting the names and numbers of the former is the surest means of bringing the strike to an end.

The proper action for an officer to take in case of unusual weather conditions depends almost entirely upon the post to which the officer is assigned, and on the nature of the weather conditions. Consideration is given here to proper action in case of darkness, fog, or violent storms.

Upon first observing the approach of unusual weather, the officer should keep a constant watch for developments. Too great hesitation in moving towards places of safety could result in death or serious injury during a storm, or escapes during darkness or fog. In making a decision as to the best course of action, the officer should bear in mind two facts. First, if he acts in favor of safety and makes a mistake, no harm will result. Second, if by hesitation he makes a mistake contrary to safety, serious consequences may follow.

Officers in charge of inmates working on the farm detail should never delay in marching their men to a place of safety at the first sign of threatening or unusual weather. If these conditions should change for the better, he can always take his men back to work. If, however, he should be overtaken by darkness or fog and an inmate should escape, the officer should conduct his remaining men to the nearest place of safety. He should never abandon his line to try to recapture an inmate who is escaping.

The proper supervision of inmates and the proper conduct of officers under unusual weather conditions while the inmates are in the cell houses is almost entirely at the discretion of the warden and his captains. In such instances, inmates are to be kept locked in their cells, and the cell house doors are to be kept locked. Officers on the walls and officers patrolling the grounds are to be especially alert and observant. Cell house and institutional counts are made as often as ordered by the captain in charge. No inmates at any time are to be released from the cells or cell houses without the order of the captain in charge. This procedure is followed until, in the opinion of the warden or the captain in charge, the weather has cleared up sufficiently to allow the normal routine of the prison to continue safely. At such time the officer will receive orders from his superiors and will govern himself accordingly.

EMERGENCY ACTION DEPLOYMENT AT STATEVILLE - JOLIET PRISONS

The following plans and instructions have been prepared in order that the most serious and dangerous disaster that can happen in or to a prison may be resisted. Should a riot or man-made fire occur, the chances are 1000 to 1 that someone will lose a life, and it is very possible that several lives will be lost. Without doubt the property loss will be great.

In the opinion of the administration there is no cause for a riot unless some employee weakens. United, the employees of a prison can be compared to a forged chain of security, and a chain is as strong as each link in it. If there is a weak link, it is an employee who is not following the rules—one who is not properly supervising the inmates who are assigned to his division; who is not reporting violations of rules; one who is too weak to speak up, not giving proper application to his job; who is not supervising the use of tools and equipment; who is permitting inmates to connive and organize; and last, but not least, is fraternizing and trafficking with inmates or failing to report an employee who is doing these things.

Failure to report rule violations by employees or inmates to supervising officials can mean the end of an officer's life and can reflect discredit upon his family and loved ones. Every employee's job is: First, custody. Next, the promotion of an educational program, the structure of which has been laid out for all employees to follow. For every rule and regulation of the institution there is a reason, and that reason is sound and will pay dividends to every employee if he will carry out the responsibility that is entrusted to him. There will be little or no trouble in the institution if everyone does his job well, and he can only do his job well if he follows the rules. *Learn Every Rule and the Reason For It. Use Your Head — Think!*

Emergencies such as a severe *storm, Fire, Riot* or *Insurrection* will be signalled by a long blast of the siren, followed by three short blasts of the powerhouse whistle and a few minutes later by three more short blasts of the whistle. Should it become impossible to use these signals, the alert will be passed by word of mouth.

When an emergency is signalled, employees in charge of inmates are, if possible, to move all inmates from their assignments to their respective cell houses and lock them in their cells as soon as possible A definite and positive check of the entire cell house must be made and kept as to the number of inmates and their identity. Only inmates who are *Approved* for the Power House, Kitchen, Wells, Hospital, Master Mechanic Shop and Ice Plant are to remain on their assignments, under the supervision of an employee with full knowledge of the operation of the assignment. As soon as possible, the Chief Guard will assign additional supervisory help to assignments where inmates are held out during an emergency. Employees on these assignments must remain alert and see that no foul play occurs.

Towermen

If an emergency occurs, all towers are to be manned, including all yard towers. Towermen shall be on their feet where they can be seen, guns and ammunition in hand, and ready for action, if necessary. Inmates, except details which are proceeding to an assignment with an officer in orderly manner, are to be stopped from entering any building other than cell houses. Towermen must prevent inmates from firing or destroying buildings or other property, and must, by all means, protect officers and employees if they are being assaulted or crowded. Firearms are to be used if necessary, but with good judgment. Remember that bullets can ricochet. Remain calm and THINK CLEARLY in emergencies.

Men assigned to the dining room tower, as well as those covering the dining room from yard and wall towers, are to protect the Kitchen, Bakery and other assignments within sight so that there is no destruction of equipment or property. However, permit men to leave the dining room and return to cell houses, but hold them to the area leading to the cell houses and see that all of them enter.

It is to be remembered that there are thousands of dollars worth of lumber stored in the lumber yard at the furniture factory at Stateville. Towers Number 3, 4, 5, and 6 have full view of this lumber yard, and no inmate is to be permitted to enter except when accompanied by an officer who is to approve the inmates that accompany him. Towermen are to protect the lumber from being fired.

Armory

At least three qualified men familiar with the Armory are to be assigned if an emergency occurs. Guns, gas, munitions, keys, lights and other equipment are to be issued to officers who report for squad duty. The squad leader (captain or lieutenant) is to remain outside the Armory and approve all property issued. Dog tags or signed slips are to be secured for all property issued. *At Least One Employee is to be Stationed in the Guard Hall at all Times to Deliver Keys, Locks, Lights, and Other Emergency Needs (Except Guns) to Locations Where Needed.*

Keys

The fire watch keys for shops, etc., are to be in the hands of an officer familiar with the key locks, light and water connections, and this officer must be ready to report to the location where needed. He should, if possible, be stationed at or near the Powerhouse.

For Joliet and Stateville

Should an emergency occur at either branch of the institution, the unit having trouble is to notify the others, and all men at each branch of the institution, including the Diagnostic Depot and Farm, are to be locked up. The only exceptions shall be APPROVED inmates needed to man necessary assignments. Employees must remain at their assigned institution, unless called to another unit by the warden or assistant warden, or someone in authority.

Stateville

The laundry gate is a division between the cell house and the educational and industrial area, and should an emergency occur, inmates are to be permitted to return to their cell houses, but not to pass from the cell house area to the back yard. The officer stationed at the laundry gate should always use his post to block movements of inmates in case of trouble, and not permit them in the industrial area.

Emergency Squads

Should an emergency arise, there will be two (2) Emergency Squads for each institution consisting of twelve (12) men each who are trained and understand thoroughly the use of firearms and gas. Names of the Emergency Squads' members will be kept in the Bulletin Book at the guard hall and the Chief Guard will notify each member in writing. All care should be taken so that inmates do not learn the identity of members of the Emergency Squads. Commanding each Emergency Squad will be a captain or lieutenant who is not in charge of the shift on duty. Should an emergency arise all other lieutenants and custodial officers are to report to the captain or lieutenant in charge of custody for their assignment. All members of the Emergency Squads are to report to the guard hall for instructions and details on proper procedure. When instructed and equipped, the squads are to proceed to the emergency scene in formation of four to six abreast, and are never to break formation. United, a few armed men are strong, but divided in pairs or singles they are lost and will fail.

If the insurrection is strong and inmates will not obey and return to their proper cells, tear gas is to be used. Only if the inmates continue to resist, and all other means fail, are munitions to be used. In quelling an insurrection, the objective is not to see how many can be felled to gain command, but how few. Remember, there will be no compromising or bargaining. If inmates persist in violence, they will be put in their place at the sacrifice of life.

We Must Win. We are United and Will be With You. But Use Your Head — Think!

The emergency squad leader can be any captain or lieutenant (except those in charge of a shift on duty), and those men whose names appear on the Bulletin Book, unless assigned to supervise inmates. However, when properly relieved, if supervising inmates, members of the emergency squads are to report to the guard hall as soon as possible, and join their respective squads.

Each member of the squad is to be equipped with one gas mask and one flashlight. Each squad is to be equipped with the following:

1 Microphone
i Gas Kit equipped with 37mm shells
4 Rifles
2 Shotguns
2 Pistols
6 Gas Grenades
1 Machine Gun

2   Bulletproof Vests

A small cart will be available in the vicinity of the Armory and an extra officer will be assigned to carry extra munitions, gas kit, or whatever other paraphernalia is needed.

All Employees

All rules of the institution apply at all times, and when an emergency arises, all employees not on duty are to present themselves for whatever assignment may be in need of help. All employees who are on duty are to remain on their assignments and give proper supervision. They are to protect and refuse admittance to their assignment to anyone other than authorized employees or a unit of inmates under proper supervision. All doors, windows, and entrances must be locked and guarded.

Cell Houses

Cell house keepers must admit all inmates to the cell houses and confine them in their respective cells, if possible, or some cell, immediately at any time when inmates are not properly controlled or supervised by an officer in complete command. If all assigned men are in a cell house, the doors should be locked. The keyman should be between the doors with the keys and no one admitted or released except at the direction of superior officers. Under no circumstances should more than three inmates (clerks, etc.) be released from the cells until approved by the warden, assistant warden, captain or lieutenant, and then only those men approved for various details are to be released. If an emergency occurs, see that all records and the log of the cell house are locked in a cell so that records and cell assignments are not destroyed.

Officers assigned to cell houses are to remain there and patrol the galleries where men are confined, and make reports in writing of any inmate or employee who fails to cooperate or who violates the rules. A key man is to be at each door on the outside of the cell house and no inmate is to be permitted to leave unless approved by a supervising officer. The keys to cell house doors are not to be carried inside the cell house at any time when there is trouble and inmates are out of control.

Tradesmen

Tradesmen—Master Mechanic, Plumber, Electrician, and all Foremen, are to report to the M & M Shop and Power House for duty, and are to supervise and see that water, lights, electricity, steam, etc., are properly provided all points where and when needed, and make themselves available for needed duty. If men are in cell house, shut off water and heat as soon as possible.

Fire Equipment

The fire department, fire chief and assistant fire chief are to report and remain at the fire station with full inmate fire crew to await or answer any fire call and then proceed immediately to the fire.

Sally Port

All employees assigned to the Outside Detail at Stateville are to report and remain at this assignment to give any and all assistance needed when called upon.

At the Joliet Branch at least three employees are to remain at the Sally Port until relieved and are to give assistance when and where needed.

Gatehouse and Gate No. 1

At least three qualified men are to be assigned to each of these posts should an emergency arise, and only employees of the institution are to be admitted. Judgment should be used, and doctors and firemen be admitted if there is an emergency. However, records are to be kept and no one released without approval. Police will not be permitted to enter the institution except on approval of the warden or assistant warden. Instead they should be asked to station themselves on all sides of the wall and be warned not to fraternize or get close to inmates and not to leave guns or munitions or cars unsupervised.

Telephone

At least two employees familiar with outside telephone switchboard are to be available and to call, if a riot occurs, the State

Police, City Police, Sheriff, Joliet and Lockport Fire Departments, all captains, lieutenants, doctors, chaplains and all employees who have phones, asking each to report for duty and, when time permits, the director or assistant director of the Department of Public Safety, giving them whatever information is possessed. The operators on duty shall call for girls to assist in operating the outside and institution switchboards. They shall be courteous to newspapers and advise them the warden or assistant warden will call them as soon as possible.

Each shift is to train at least three employees to operate the institution switchboard efficiently and with speed, and to have a man available on all shifts at all times, if an emergency occurs, to operate the switchboard until the regular operator arrives.

Guard Hall

The officer in charge is to clear the Guard Hall of all inmates and shut off the radio, and work and coöperate in all respects with all employees, using caution at all times. Chief Guard is to assign at least two extra men to the Guard Hall as soon as possible.

Master Mechanic Shop

Inmate tradesmen who are approved are to be held in the M & M Shop for any mechanical emergency.

Power House

Enough approved men are to be held in the Power House to man and operate needed equipment during an emergency.

Kitchens

Enough approved men are to be held for the preparation of food and coffee to be served at the time of the emergency, and men are to be fed in the cell houses at meal time if the serving of food does not weaken control or security.

Hospital

All nurses and first aid men are to be held in the hospital to give needed assistance to doctors.

Ice Plant

The Ice Plant is to be locked and an officer assigned to supervise and see that no unauthorized person enters.

Readiness

All employees are to keep on the alert, be on their feet, and cover their respective assignments, and are never to congregate at any one point. Employees must use their heads, they may have to battle for their lives and those who do not coöperate only encourage non-conformists.

Caution

Under no circumstances are inmates to know the members of the Emergency Squads. The Chief Guard is to see that the quota of the Squad is filled at all times, and the Lieutenant in Charge of Training is to train all men in the use of firearms, gas, etc. Men who are picked and do not measure up are to be replaced. Remember, this may be a fight for our lives — and that we must win.

Training

The Lieutenant in Charge of Training for the Emergency Squad is to train each man on the squad to a degree that he will be proficient with guns and gas equipment of all types, and the Chief Guard is to coöperate in arranging for the squad members to train under the Lieutenant's direction at least two days each week until members have reached a maximum efficiency.

DETECTING SIGNS OF TROUBLE AND UNREST

It has been said that an ounce of prevention is worth a pound of cure, and this maxim is no less applicable to a penitentiary than to any other human situation. Previous sections have been devoted to demonstrating how the officer should conduct himself during times of emergency, but little has been said about forestalling these emergencies.

The routine of a prison is usually uneventful, but trouble sometimes does arise. And this trouble generally is preceded by unmistakable signs in the behavior of that part of the inmate body planning to create the trouble. The "prison-wise" officer will recognize these signs immediately and will take steps to put down whatever disturbance may be planned before any actual outbreak occurs. Since the prevention of trouble in a prison, as anywhere, is preferable, both from the point of efficiency and from the point of expense, than the suppression of trouble, detecting signs of unrest and impending disruption of the prison routine will always be the duty of the good officer. Experience will indicate the many methods of checking the temper and immediate tendencies of the inmate body.

For instance, an officer will notice that, during the recreation periods, the inmates are harmlessly intent on the various games, or are conversing freely and openly with one another as they stroll about the yard. The officer will then be assured that everything is as it should be.

But, on another day, the officer may be aware of a changed atmosphere. There may be no actual disorder, the inmates may seem just as respectful as always—perhaps even more respectful than is customary—but the shouts and laughter which the officer is accustomed to hear may not be in evidence. Groups of inmates may be scattered about the yard, conversing in low tones and gazing furtively about them, and these groups may disperse when the officer approaches to catch a word or two of their conversation.

The officer immediately should confer with his fellow officers and his supervisors, and, if it is felt that conditions among the inmates are not what they should be, a report at once will be made to a superior officer, who will institute an investigation. This investigation may disclose that a hunger strike, or even a riot or wholesale escape was being planned for the future, and, possessing this information, the prison officials will be able to isolate the source of the dissension and prevent the outbreak of trouble.

Such ability and alertness on the part of the officer is invaluable to the prison officials and the state; it also helps the welfare of the inmate body. The history of prison riots, strikes, and escapes indicates plainly that, ultimately the inmates suffer most.

Every officer, therefore, on any assignment, should be able to detect abnormality in the attitude of the inmates, and interpret this abnormality correctly. It should be the constant effort of the officer to maintain an alert and analytical interest in everything taking place within the prison.

OFFICERS' REPORTS AGAINST INMATES

It has been observed that discipline is the fundamental upon which prisons operate. The inmates of a penal institution have no great regard for constituted authority as such, else they would not be inmates. Consequently, it is necessary that certain penalties be exacted of those who fail to obey the rules.

The officer should be thoroughly aware of the seriousness of writing a report. There will be occasions when no other action is feasible, and at such times the officer should discharge his duty without hesitation. He will know from a study of the inmates' rule book exactly what constitutes a violation of those rules, and by looking over reports on file at the Disciplinarian's Office he can learn the technique of making out reports.

It is, however, essential that the officer know when, and when not, to report an inmate. There are many instances when a reprimand will suffice, and in such instances there is little sense in the officer's writing a report. Unjust punishment of an inmate, as well as anyone else, is a thing that must always be avoided. Injustices of any kind within a prison can never find justification. The work of reformation of inmates can be completely broken down by acts of cruelty or injustice.

Of course, there will be occasions when there is no alternative but the writing of a report. Then the officer should have no qualms about the matter. He should ascertain beyond doubt the identity of the offender and make out the report in a clear and concise manner. There should be a lucid and unbiased statement of the offense, including the time and place committed, and the report should be confined to information concerning the circumstances. It is particularly desirable that the officer be guided in these instances by personal observation, rather than by hearsay, otherwise it would be easy for an innocent inmate to be punished, with resultant embarrassment to the officer himself. So that there may be no possibility of misinterpretation by the Discliplinarian, the report should be written legibly and in the simplest language. Accuracy is essential.

Summarizing, the officer should write reports when reports are necessary but, if he exercises a reasonable amount of good judgment, he will find himself able to handle his men in a manner that will reduce this necessity to a bare minimum.

DUTIES OF A WARDEN TO HIS OFFICERS

It has been shown previously that the warden of a penitentiary is responsible to the people of the state for the conduct of employees under him. It also has been demonstrated that, in order to insure the maximum efficiency of his officers, the warden must demand of them adherence to certain rules and regulations. In other words, the officers have definite duties, and in satisfying those duties, they are justifying the faith placed in them by the warden.

It must not be thought, however, that such an arrangement is without reciprocal values. The warden has duties toward his officers as sharply defined as are theirs toward him. He must see to it that their working conditions are in consonance with a progressive administration, and that they are provided with acceptable living quarters. He owes it to his officers to recognize efficiency shown in the line of duty, and the good warden will reward such efficiency, knowing that he thereby will encourage his employees to give their best efforts toward service, and raise the morale of all the officers. A failure on the part of the warden to give credit to his officers where credit is due cannot but result in a lessened interest in their work on the part of the officers, since no man will put forth his best efforts if he sees another man being accorded the same treatment without deserving it. The warden must give rewards with the same impartiality that he exacts penalties. He must realize that dissatisfaction among his officers will inevitably produce a corresponding loss of quality in their work, and that, conversely, a satisfied body of officers will promote the general welfare of the institution. In short, a penitentiary warden must adopt the attitude of a benevolent superior.

As an example of the good a capable warden can accomplish, a summary of the changes effected at Stateville may be given. Not many years ago the officers at Stateville and Joliet were forced to work twelve hours a day. Now the shifts are changed every eight hours. Further there is now in existence a uniform wage scale, by which all officers are paid according to their merited rank, and efforts are made to increase the living allowance of officers who reside outside the institution. This increase is desirable, since an officer supporting a family and maintaining a house will incur more expenses than will a single man who pays only a modest sum for his institutional room and board. Finally, there is this Officers' Training School, inaugurated so that every officer in this penitentiary will know that he can advance in rank and responsibility according to his own capacity for giving satisfaction to his superiors. All advancements are made from the ranks .

From the foregoing, it will be apparent that an enlightened warden will advance the interests of his employees and, having advanced them, keep them on the attained level. He will see that his officers are treated justly with all the consideration they deserve, and it behooves the officers working under such a warden to evidence their appreciation of his efforts by doing their duty to him as well as he has done his to them.

Over and above the duties of a warden toward the institution and the state, there are certain duties toward the neighboring communities that must be fulfilled. These duties involve the conduct of prison employees, the selection of trusties, the coöperation of the prison employees with the law enforcement authorities and friendliness toward neighboring communities.

DUTIES TOWARD NEIGHBORING COMMUNITIES

The conduct of an official or employee in any division of the Department of Public Safety is never his own affair. His actions and behavior, good or bad, will reflect on and be linked with the department or institution at which he is employed. Public confidence in the employees of an institution, and in the manner in which the institution is operated and managed is one of its best assets. There can be no public confidence in it nor in its treatment of inmates when its employees conduct themselves in a manner unbecoming to employees of the state. There can be no confidence in the integrity of its management when propriety and moral standards are flouted with impunity by its employees. Most of the employees conduct themselves as becomes officers and gentlemen, but unfortunately a few cannot be said to do this. Some of the most frequent improprieties are: neglecting to pay just debts, frequenting places of unsavory repute, pretending to have police authority, and general misconduct unbecoming an officer. The law prohibits garnishment of state employees salaries and the only recourse creditors have is through the warden; therefore, employees should avoid making such a procedure necessary. The warden, being interested in protecting the credit of all prison employees, can do this only by seeing that those who are not inclined to pay their debts, do pay them.

Unfortunately some men are unable to have authority without abusing it. Good officers do not display their authority except when they are called upon to exercise that authority for the purpose for which it was given them. A few men, however, on becoming officers and never having been vested with any authority before sometimes become filled with a sense of self-importance and make a display of their authority.

Any unnecessary manifestation of authority is very unbecoming to an officer whether his rank be high or low. The authority that officers have is to be used only when they are on the job. When an officer's work is done he can take home none of the authority he possessed when he was carrying out his day's assignment. When he leaves the institution, except on special assignments, he is just another citizen. A few officers in the past have been known to display their badges as insignia of authority when they were off duty. Such an act is unworthy of a good officer and guilty ones will be subject to discipline. The carrying of firearms or concealed weapons is forbidden to an officer while off duty, as it is to any other citizen, and offenders are subject to punishment under the laws of the State. It is not the intention of the warden to restrain or otherwise hamper the officer while he is off duty. Officers who conduct themselves as gentlemen need never have any fear of criticism or censure of any kind.

For purposes of economy, and as an aid in readjustment, much of the work done outside the walls of the penitentiary is done by prisoners. Such work includes that done on the farm, lawns, etc. Because these prisoners are outside the walls most of the time, more care and much discretion must be used in selecting them. Special consideration must be given to the nature of the crime for which the man was convicted, his prison record, the length of time he has yet to serve, his family connections, prior record as to escapes, etc., and to his personal characteristics and physical capacity for work. It would not be fair to the neighboring communities to literally place in their midst a man of known viciousness, or one with abnormal sex proclivities. These jobs are for the most part given to prisoners who were convicted of the more or less "accidental" type of crime, that is, manslaughter, and crimes committed in the heat of passion, etc. First offenders are also given special consideration for these jobs, as are men who are known to be devoted to their families, men who are of sound mind and have retained an upright frame of mind toward society, and men who are to be released soon from the institution. The men assigned to these jobs are called trusties. They are governed by the same rules that govern the rest of the inmate body. They are confined to the premises of the penitentiary at all times, with the exception of the inmates assigned to the fire truck, who leave the institution on trips only when authorized and accompanied by the proper officials.

It is the duty of the law enforcement authorities to apprehend and bring about the conviction of escaped inmates and to do all in their power to prevent their escape. Coöperation, however, with the law enforcement authorities, makes for a greater degree of security for society. In this way it may be said that the arm of the law is both lengthened and strengthened. Occasionally it is necessary for the prison officials to transport prisoners to different places, such as, to a different prison, or to court on a writ. The State Police then coöperate by furnishing a police escort for the occasion. The State Police are also called upon to aid in the capturing of escaped prisoners. With their efficient and modern radio system they are an indispensable arm in quickly establishing a blockade to effect the capture of escapees. The prison officials can and do coöperate with the law enforcement authorities by offering their services as deputies when they are needed to the police and sheriffs, by complying with writs issued by the courts; by answering court summonses; and by permitting to the authorities access to the prison records. This coöperation is not only maintained between prison officials and state law enforcement agencies, but also between the prison officials and the Federal authorities. This coöperation effects a greater degree of competency and efficiency in the functions of law enforcement.

The Stateville penitentiary is situated in the midst of a group of progressive, coöperative communities, among which are Joliet, Lockport, and Plainfield. The people of these communities have a friendly feeling toward the employees of the institution and it is up to the employees to reciprocate this friendly feeling. Officers and employees living in these communities have many advantages over those living in the outlying areas. They have the advantage of enjoying home and family life, while at the same time being in proximity to the institution and their work. These communities have all the conveniences and facilities that any progressive community has. They are within the metropolitan area of Chicago, and adequate transportation is at hand in the form of rail and bus lines. Educational facilities are not lacking. In addition to the numerous public and parochial schools, several outstanding universities are not far distant. There are also many churches of all denominations, public parks, hospitals, theatres, and many other conveniences.

ASSISTANT WARDEN

During the course of the year, there will be many occasions when it is necessary for the warden to absent himself from the penitentiary. On such occasions, his duties must be assumed and his authority taken over by an assistant.

The assistant warden should have a thorough knowledge of all the component parts of prison life. He must be able to make decisions quickly and justly both in routine matters and in time of emergency. He must command the respect of officers and inmates alike, and be able to act with the assurance born of experience.

Our policy is that an assistant warden be a man who has risen from the ranks, since such a man will be more familiar with the administration of the prison than one would be who has not had previous contact with the institution.

The assistant warden's work is not limited to taking charge of the prison when the warden is away. He has many routine duties, being but one step below the warden in the administrative scale. He is, in fact, the link between the captains and the warden himself, and therefore must take a great deal of the responsibility for the efficient functioning of the institution.

SENIOR CAPTAIN

The Senior Captains, whose offices are in the Isolation Cell block, are not only the prison disciplinarians, at whose discretion lies the punishment of inmates for infractions of the rules, but they are also in charge of assigning inmates to the various divisions, shops, and cell houses. In fact, their duties embrace every phase of inmate life. They are next to the warden and assistant warden and have, therefore, authority in matters pertaining to the daily activity of the inmate body. It follows that their position demands certain exceptional qualifications.

First of all, since they are constantly called upon to pass judgment on prisoners reported for misconduct, they must have a highly developed sense of fair play and justice, innate honesty, impartial outlook, a thorough knowledge of the rules and regulations, and a fundamental firmness. They must be able to make decisions wisely and with finality. And, above all, they must have the faculty for appraising character and personality. Many thousands of men will appear before them in the course of a year, and they must be able to view the case of each on its own merits and with consideration for the individual factors involved. They possess copies of all information and records of all inmates and their assignments, and give personal attention to each individual.

The responsibilities of the Senior Captains are many and varied, and may be roughly divided into three groups: responsibilities to (1) the warden, (2) the officers, (3) the inmates.

In the first group is emphasized the safety of the institution. Agitators and potential trouble makers must be segregated from the rest of the inmate body, and care must be exercised in assigning to important jobs only capable prisoners. It is difficult to decide which of the broad duties of the Senior Captains is the more vital to the welfare of the institution: the punishment of recalcitrant inmates or the dispensing of inmate assignments. Probably they are of equal degree. Certainly a lack of efficiency in either connection would result in disruption of the prison routine.

Next are the responsibilities of the Senior Captains to the officers of the institution, and here, too, their position is of paramount importance. They must consider all reports against inmates and maintain a balance between justice and authority. That is, they must be fair to the inmates and yet support the officers. Further, they must see that there is an equitable distribution of the "problem" inmates, so that no one officer will have in his shop or divisions a disproportionate number of trouble makers. In this connection, the officer must be made to feel that the Senior Captains stand always ready to lend coöperation and advice in the handling of inmates, and that efficient workers will be assigned to those posts calling for them.

Regarding the inmates, the Senior Captains have a great responsibility. In their capacity as Disciplinarian they can, by displaying common sense, and a feeling for justice, keep the morale of the prisoners at a high level. Inmates realize that they must be punished for breaches of discipline, but they have a much higher respect for authority when they know that they will receive impartial justice.

CHIEF GUARD

The Chief Guard is, as the title implies, the Captain in charge of all the custodial officers. The necessary qualifications for this post include a capacity for leadership, an ingrained sense of honesty and impartiality, an understanding of the officers' problems, a firmness in giving orders, and a complete familiarity with the rules and regulations governing the conduct of officers. His responsibility is the efficient behavior of prison officers individually and collectively.

The warden will expect the Chief Guard to be prompt and accurate in making reports, to exercise good judgment in assigning officers to the various posts; to be prompt in the transmission of orders to officers; to insist on the prompt and efficient execution of these orders by the officers; and to be honest in his dealings with both the officers and the warden.

The Chief Guard will exhibit a fairness towards the officers under him, a recognition of merit in their work, and impartiality in recommending officers for promotion according to the merit system, and an equality in the distribution of extra or special duties.

The duties of the Chief Guard as far as the everyday prison routine is concerned are many. He assigns each officer to his post, he presides at roll call, and keeps continuous records of the presence or absence of employees. He submits the payrolls, in keeping with the orders of the warden. He allots vacations and days off. He reports to the warden on the efficiency, or in-efficiency, of the officers. He selects competent officers for key positions. He is responsible for the daily inspection of officers, and sees to it that the appearance and equipment of the officers are satisfactory. He assigns officers to extra and special duties.

In cases of emergency, the Chief Guard has charge and in general supervises the activities of the officers.

LIEUTENANTS

The duties of a lieutenant are diverse. He is the principal link between the officers and the captains, he must be able to follow orders, he must be able to handle any job in an emergency, and he must exercise impartiality in dealing with both officers and inmates.

The lieutenant is principally concerned with maintaining institutional security. He is required to patrol the grounds and buildings at regular intervals, and on these patrols he must be on the watch for possible means of escape, objects that could be used as weapons, and refuse that destroys the cleanliness of the grounds and constitute a fire hazard. He also must be ready to question any suspicious movements he may observe among the inmates and demand an explanation from any inmate found away from the regular assignment. He must investigate and report any disturbance. In such cases, he must make a concise report of the circumstances to the warden and the assistant warden.

The lieutenant will carry out the orders of the warden and the Captains, and will clarify these orders to the officers. He will also observe the actions of officers on duty, and report any violations of orders or laxity in conduct.

With regard to the inmates, the lieutenant will handle minor complaints against a prisoner, forward inmate requests to the proper persons, and pass inmates to the hospital and the dentist.

During general shakedowns, the lieutenant will assign officers to conduct the search of the various assignments, he will observe the thoroughness of the search, he will judge whether questionable articles seized in the search are contraband, and he will issue instructions pertinent to the disposition of contraband and the measures to be taken against the inmates found in possession thereof.

At meal times, the lieutenant will see that all posts in the dining room hall are properly manned by officers ,and that the inmates passing out the food are conducting themselves properly. He will correct situations causing delays in the movement of the various lines and generally supervise the activity in the mess hall.

During emergencies, it will be the duty of the lieutenant to carry out orders from his superiors.

CELL HOUSE KEEPERS

The first prerequisite of a cell house keeper is a thorough knowledge of the rules, regulations, and procedures of the institution. He also must possess considerable intelligence and mental alertness, and ability to judge fairly and wisely and instantaneously.

His foremost duty is to guard against escapes. His precautions in this connection will include periodic testing of the bars in the cell windows and a constant observation of the inmates detailed under him. He must be continuously on guard against disturbances, he must keep his cell house clean and orderly at all times, he must report lack of discipline, and he must keep a constant check on the movements of inmates coming into and going out of the cell house. He must also supervise and assign to their various tasks the officers in his immediate charge.

In emergencies, the cell house keeper must make certain that all inmates in his care are returned to the cells, or that there is proper authorization for their absence. He should make his count as soon as the inmates are in the cell house; then report the count to his superior and await further orders.

The night cell house keeper must take care that no escapes are attempted, and that perversion is not practiced in the cells. It is also his duty to check the count at regular intervals and keep in periodic contact with the front office by telephone.

Cell house keepers are sergeants. Sergeants also occupy the posts at the important gates, the armory, the hospital, and are in charge of the shops. Sergeants are the superiors of the officers and must enforce orders or reprimand any officer.

THE MARKS OF A GOOD OFFICER

It is an army tenet that the terms officer and gentlemen are synonymous. It is no less essential that the same be true, in the broadest sense of the word, of the officer of a penal institution. This all-embracing term indicates the possession of those qualities essential to the leadership by which the good officer will maintain discipline and, in the longer view, contribute, perhaps, the greater part to the rehabilitation of the inmate, for which a more enlightened society now looks to our penal institutions. It is the officer who, by his daily contact with the men in his charge, has the greatest opportunity to influence those men by his example and conduct. It is, therefore, essential that his conduct at all times reflect the good breeding, education, and religious and moral training that the vast majority of the inmate body will be found to lack, and by which lack they have, in a majority of cases, fallen foul of those laws which are but the natural norms of conduct for the more fortunate section of society which the officer represents.

The general term *good breeding* may be said to cover the matters of education and moral training. This breeding will find its expression in his ability to lead by example in the control of his men, their respect for him and all that he represents, rather than by fear of disciplinary action on his part. The better the officer, the less occasion he will have to use disciplinary measures.

One of the most essential products of the above mentioned qualifications is the self-assurance, poise and general demeanor which comes from a thorough knowledge of one's duties and a sense of the capacity for fulfilling them. This knowledge may be obtained (1) by a conscientious study of the general problems peculiar to the work of an officer in a penal institution, and (2) by the constant observation and study of those problems attendant upon his own particular assignment. The officer's knowledge of his job is never complete. He may never say to himself, "I know all there is to know about my work." He constantly improves in his capacity for handling men, or he fails in one of the chief prerequisites of a good officer. In addition, his reputation, both past and present, is of the utmost importance. That his honesty must be unquestioned is, of course, obvious; but that alone is not enough. His personal habits, both within and without the institution, must be above reproach. He must ever bear in mind that he is constantly in the public eye, that he is more than a private individual, and that acts which might pass unnoticed on the part of the average man will become subject for comment when committed by one to whom not only the inmate body but the community as a whole looks for exemplary conduct. He must at all times demonstrate his unequivocal loyalty to the institution and to his superiors and show by word and example his innate respect for properly constituted authority, bearing in mind that it is for lack of these qualities that the majority of these men have become inmates of a penal institution. No one is quicker than the prisoner to note the absence of such loyalty, respect for authority, or the possession of even slightly questionable habits on the part of the officer. The inmate is but human, in that he seeks to justify himself. And one of the easiest ways for him to do this is to note lapses from virtue on the part of those whom the state has given control over him and assigned to the task of fitting him for a better life, consoling himself thereby that his unfortunate position is just a "bad break", that the inherent right or wrong of his acts had nothing to do with his predicament, that his officer is just luckier than he is, etc.

These are the larger qualities, the outstanding characteristics which mark the really good officer, those which are essential to the leadership now substituted for the rule by force and fear which once was the policy of penal institutions. Nor will this leadership serve only the end of the inmate's rehabilitation. The officer will find that the respect and confidence which he thereby establishes will be more conducive to the maintenance of discipline and obedience than would the methods of a bygone day, which inspired fear and wrought hatred, and that the necessary recourse to disciplinary action will be reduced to a minimum.

Matters of physical fitness, such as height, weight, sight, and hearing are, of course, considered before the officer comes to such matters as those already discussed. Any physical abnormality might be enough to bar an otherwise brilliant man from the position, for it is important that the general appearance of an officer should not differ so greatly from the norm as to attract attention. The United States Army requires that no extreme ugliness shall characterize the appearance of an applicant for admission to West Point. In prison work, too, such a handicap would be too great and that the officer might have difficulty in commanding the instantaneous respect and obedience he must have.

Temperament and carriage are two other important qualifications of the good officer. He must at all times be erect and alert, and this condition can be attained only if he is physically and mentally healthy. A listless, slouching attitude on his part quickly affects the men under him and, by reason of the mental apathy thus engendered, makes the larger work of moral uplift impossible.

The physical condition of the officer will also contribute greatly to his temperament. If an officer is slightly ill, or even merely "out of sorts," he is apt, if he does not watch himself closely, to display signs of irritability. He may even be guilty of small acts of injustice which, while not in themselves of any great significance, will go far towards destroying the effect of the good example which he has built up by his deportment over a long period of time, for there is nothing which the inmate body seizes on more avidly in the instinctive campaign for self-justification than injustices imposed upon them by others. It is therefore apparent that an habitually irritable temperament, which would produce acts of petty tyranny, or larger injustices, has no place in the modern scheme of penology. Poise, too, is a matter of utmost importance. Dignity is very essential, that dignity which comes naturally from a realization of the true objects and the importance of the officer's job, a dignity not to be confused with a mere feeling of self importance which might come entirely from the authority delegated to him, but one which springs from a knowledge of the worthwhileness of one's work and his opportunity to contribute to the world's betterment. Calmness in any emergency is naturally a prime essential, but it is in the daily contacts that this calmness is employed to the best advantage. Seldom, if ever, in an officer's career will come an opportunity to show coolness in a really great emergency, but his daily life will be composed of countless small incidents in which he can further the good example by cool and unhurried judgment.

The officer must remember that if he is constantly studying his men, those men are in turn studying him. His personality, his methods in dealing with his charges, his fairness or unfairness, his understanding of their problems, as well as his knowledge of his own duties will be great factors in keeping the men under him satisfied, at least with the strict justice of their lot, and contribute greatly to making him a good officer. Naturally he must be dependable. When given an assignment he is being entrusted with the safe keeping of the men in his immediate charge. This duty is delegated to him by the warden to whom the safekeeping of the entire inmate population has been entrusted by the state.

The word "safekeeping" is not limited entirely in meaning to the keeping of those inmates safely within the physical limits prescribed by the officer's particular assignment. He has duties for their care and protection, and it is important that he be dependable in the discharge of both. He must be observant and ready for whatever action is called for by the particular situation which arises. That he must be courageous is apparent by the very nature of his work, but that courage must be the moral one to be impartial and fair, as well as the physical one to face danger if the need should ever rise. Ambitious? He should be. But he should thoroughly understand his objectives and study the best means of attaining them, realizing that his duty is to contribute to the general plan of penology now in force; that it is his leadership and example which, above all, is required of him; and that only by the advancement of the plan as a whole can he hope to step into a position of even greater responsibility.

A spirit of friendliness will be a big factor in marking him as a good officer. A cheerful, willing, and unquestioning obedience to the orders of his superiors and a friendly courteous attitude toward the public, whether he be on or off duty, are essential; and this attitude of friendliness is not incompatible with his dignity as an officer when dealing with an inmate. It could not be at variance if that dignity is real, if it is the product of the characteristics and qualifications already enumerated, if that dignity springs directly from a realization that he is an important factor in a rebuilding process in which men are the materials used and in which he himself is an extremely important member of the architectural staff.

SELECTION AND PROMOTION OF OFFICERS

It has been mentioned above that penology has made considerable strides during the past fifteen or twenty years. Modern methods make those which prevailed in the comparatively recent past seem almost barbaric, and this progress has affected penitentiary officers almost as much as it has inmates.

For one thing, officers now are chosen on an entirely different basis. Formerly, it was the custom to select only those with a rugged physique. It was felt that the man who could cow the inmates into obedience was the only man capable of holding a job inside the walls. Now, however, the appointment of officers, and the subsequent promotion of those officers, is handled entirely from the point of view of efficiency.

Such being the case, it no longer remains merely a matter of favoritism for an officer to attain a position of trust and authority. Indeed, if a man lacks the attributes which make for increasing efficiency, he will not be employed by the institution in the first place.

It is easily understandable how such an enlightened system of selection and promotion will improve the prison as a whole. Instead of the fear by which the old-time officer was accustomed to control the inmates, the new type commands the respect of the men under him, being infinitely more intelligent and educated than his "strong arm" predecessor. As a result, he encounters much less trouble among the inmates and is in general of so much greater value to society that there really can be no comparison.

The chief characteristics of the present-day prison officer are honesty, common sense, loyalty to the state, a pride in himself and his personal appearance, and an ability to substitute intelligent handling of the inmates for an excessive use of force.

The consequences of the change from politically controlled prisons to prisons operated on an enlightened plane are, without exception, beneficial to everyone—the officer, the inmate, and the state. The state reaps its reward in greater efficiency on the part of the officers; the inmates profit from the sensible attitude of the officer; and the officers themselves have the satisfaction of knowing that they are contributing their share in the modern effort to reform and rehabilitate a prisoner, rather than shove him deeper into degradation and despair.

CONDUCT OF PRISON EMPLOYEES OFF DUTY

It has been noted that there are certain rules and regulations governing the conduct of officers on duty. There are also definite standards of conduct demanded of the officer not on duty, and deviation from these standards is punishable by the same penalties that hold for the institutional rules. A summary of the "off duty" rules will serve to acquaint the prospective officer with what is required of him.

First, the officer must make no pretense of being a policeman while not on penitentiary property. He must not carry firearms, or assume authority that is the right of the city or county police. He must not indulge in braggadocio, interfere in matters not his concern, or attempt inquisition of persons not under his jurisdiction. In other words, he must not exceed his capacity as a private citizen. (This rule, of course, does not apply during manhunts.)

The second rule to be obeyed by officers is not to cause embarrassment to the state. This can best be avoided by exercising discretion while in uniform. The officer should not enter a house of prostitution, gambling house, or disreputable tavern while wearing official garb of the institution. He should not be guilty of drunkenness or of creating any public disturbance whatsoever.

Third, he must keep his own personal affairs in good order. He must not be remiss in supporting those of his family who are dependent on him, and he must be prompt in meeting his obligations. The law prohibits the garnishment of wages of state employees; therefore, creditors of a prison officer must take recourse through the wardren, and the warden, to protect the credit of conscientious employees, must deal severely with delinquent officers.

Another act not countenanced by the authorities is adultery. The state does not care to have the families of its employees broken up, inasmuch as such a condition often makes wards of the state of the wives and children of the offending officer, and generally results in the decreased efficiency of the man concerned.

There are, in addition to the above, a number of civic duties to be assumed by the penitentiary officer. He must vote at the elections, he must take an active interest in the welfare of his community, he must render reasonable assistance to the needy, and he must in all other respects discharge his obligations as a good citizen.

In short, it is required that an officer be guilty of no act, either of commission or omission, which might bring disrespect or criticism to himself, and through him to the Department of Public Safety. He must behave at all times like a gentleman.

ABUSIVE LANGUAGE

It is, of course, admitted that an officer, to maintain control over the inmates in his charge, must exercise his authority at all times, but he must also remember that discretion is a necessary virtue. There will be countless petty offenses committed by the inmates, and the punishment meted out by the officer should be tempered with common sense. After all, a very few of the men incarcerated are basically law-abiding, but all of them are human, and they will be quick to respond to the attitude of their officer.

This being the case, the officer should be careful to keep his relationship with the men on as impersonal a basis as possible. He should not give them the idea that the disciplinary measures he may see fit to resort to arise from his own private feelings. Rather he should foster the impression that he is merely an instrument for the maintaining of order, and that his actions are dictated by his superiors.

Such being the case, the officer must scrupulously refrain from using abusive language when addressing his men. Profanity is, unfortunately, a common means of self-expression, but no one likes to be sworn at. An officer who repeatedly resorts to epithets cannot but provoke ill will among the inmates, and may even arouse some of them to the point where force is necessary to subdue them. It will readily be seen that such a condition is wholly undesirable. An officer's first duty is to keep the inmates as quiet and undemonstrative as possible, and this he cannot do if he incurs their enmity. A good officer will reprimand an inmate when a reprimand is deserved, but he will do so in a manner that will breed no resentment.

There may arise a situation in which it becomes absolutely necessary for an officer to use force, as when two inmates are fighting and will not obey a command to stop, or when an inmate threatens an officer with violence. At such times, the officer will be justified in using such force as necessary and to use any and all means at his disposal to quell the trouble. It is essential that all uprisings among the inmates be put down as speedily and quietly as possible and the officer must use his own discretion as to the best means of attaining that end. It must be borne in mind, however, that the good officer embraces the use of force as a last resort, and that no good will be accomplished by either the threat or the use of force in cases where such action is not warranted. The majority of the inmates are willing to abide by the rules laid down for their conduct and for their sake, as well as for the sake of institutional efficiency, the officer will not use force when other less severe measures will suffice.

SHAKEDOWNS

The term "shakedown," which on the outside means extortion, has a different meaning in a penitentiary. A shakedown in prison argot means a thorough search for contraband. Many prisoners find ways and means to obtain forbidden articles, and shakedowns have to be made periodically to locate and confiscate these articles. There is a lot more to "shaking down" than merely searching cells and prisoners. The officers should have a knowledge of the most likely and *unlikely* places of concealment in cells, shops, or wherever the shakedowns happen to be conducted. Moreover, they should have a knowledge of what constitutes contraband. It would be well for officers to read a list of what is contraband and what is not; there are lists printed for this purpose. Articles of contraband range from "shivs" (knives), guns, to food stolen from the kitchen or store, clothing, intoxicants, and a great many other articles.

At the start of a shakedown, the officers should open the cell door, order the prisoners out, and give them a thorough body search. Then, leaving them out on the gallery, enter the cell and proceed with the shakedown, at the same time keeping a weather eye on the occupants to see that nothing is passed to or from them while they are on the gallery. An important thing to remember while making shakedowns is not to overlook the obvious. For example, if there is a calendar on the wall, examine it and look behind it; don't think that because it is right in front of your face there probably isn't anything hidden behind it or between the pages of the calendar. A few other places of concealment are: between the pages of books, in clothing, between the blankets or bedsheets, in the broom, in a roll of toilet paper. Don't be satisfied merely to look into the drawers of a commode; look behind the drawers, under them, and inside the drawer slides. While the officers are on a shakedown they should not proceed as though they were on a treasure hunt and turn everything upside-down in their efforts to find something, but should go at the job efficiently and intelligently, handling personal articles of the prisoner with care.

Naturally every inmate is not guilty of possessing contraband; so if the officer doesn't find anything of that nature, he should not insist on repeating his efforts in the hope of finding something he missed the first time, unless he has reason to believe that something *is* in the cell. If he has looked carefully and found nothing, the chances are that there is nothing out of the way to be found.

TRAFFICKING

Among the many meanings of the word "traffic" will be found the following: "To engage in illicit sale or purchase; to trade in something not properly for sale." Favors, of whatever nature, are something not properly for sale by the guard to the inmate, and the importance of the rule against such traffic cannot be over-emphasized. The price offered by the inmate for such favors may vary from flattery of the officer to outright offers of money, running the entire gamut of inducements, including promises of favors from the inmate's family or influential friends. The prisoner will not fail to impress the officer with his ability to be close-mouthed. With great patience he will set about building up such a reputation long before making the first tentative advance, and, knowing how highly prized in his own circle is that person who knows how to keep things to himself, he is expert in presenting himself, often by extremely clever indirection.

Prisoners seeking favors are more than clever both in their build-up and final broaching of such a subject to the officer. They are well aware that the new officer is fresh from the "outside" and not yet "prison-smart," that he may be inclined to take the inmate's word as he would that of a person in ordinary life. The first direct approach will probably be a mixture of a request that the officer bring in some harmless article such as a particular brand of tobacco or soap and a well delivered but indirect discourse on the impossibility of the officer being caught. The new officer cannot be too careful against the insidiousness of such an approach. The article desired is harmless, it could not by any stretch of the imagination cause injury to anyone nor even seriously impair the discipline of the institution, there is no chance of being caught — and the officer wants to be a "good fellow," doesn't he?

The records contain the names of otherwise excellent officers who have been discharged for just such harmless favors, just as the penitentiaries are full of men who couldn't see any real harm in "borrowing" just a little of their employer's money, feeling sure, since they fully intended to replace it at some future date, that they never would be caught.

Trafficking can never be justified. Like the borrowing employee who is led on and on to ever greater defalcations, the officer who first permits himself to be so drawn in is led on by the clever inmate through a series of other "harmless" requests to bringing in playing cards, cigarettes, cigarette lighters, etc., until he reaches the point where it is also apparently harmless to bring in money or carry out letters for the prisoner. This may seem a long step, but evidence exists that one thing inevitably leads to another.

The officer who has been brought this far can then be induced, sometimes against his will, to bring in liquor or narcotics, and there have been cases where inmate cleverness has reached a point where an intelligent officer has brought narcotics to an inmate under the impression that he was bringing him a medicine that could not be obtained through the prison hospital. From liquor or narcotics to firearms is but a short step. As far apart as the delivery of a bar of soap may seem from the actual delivery of a pistol to an inmate, and as much as the officer who is tempted to yield in the first instance may scoff at the connection between the two, there is documentary evidence of many actual cases to prove that one thing leads to another. In this very prison a former officer served time from young manhood until his death — a period of more than thirty years. When employed as a foreman at the Pontiac institution, he allowed himself to be prevailed upon to bring a gun to some inmates who attempted to escape. These inmates shot and killed a guard and not only were they hanged, but the ex-foreman was convicted of homicide. He, too, began by bringing into the institution articles which appeared harmless.

This subject of trafficking does not require more lengthy treatment. The rules are clear. It is not the article traffiicked in, but the fact that an officer can be induced to traffic that is important.

GENERAL WELFARE OF INMATES

The broadest and most fundamental objective for the warden concerning inmates is provision for the general welfare of the men in his custody. The courts sentence convicted felons to the care and custoday of the warden in much the same way that a general might entrust the care of a company of men to a captain. Just as the captain must see to the safety, health and general well-being of his soldiers, so must the warden see to it that the general welfare of the inmates is protected and provided for in every possible way.

But "general welfare" is a broad term. Just what, specifically, does it include in this instance? The general welfare of the inmates of a penitentiary may be subdivided into the following five main needs; personal hygiene, health, food, shelter, clothing. Let us consider these headings in order.

For a number of reasons it is essential that the warden make accessible to the inmates certain means of maintaining personal hygiene. First and most important, of course, is the tremendous bearing of hygiene upon health. In a large penitentiary, where thousands of men live in very close quarters, it would be extremely dangerous to the health of the inmate body to permit the standard of hygiene to slump. Filth invites diseases; under penitentiary conditions lack of cleanliness would be an invitation to epidemics. Next is the personal comfort and self-respect of the inmates. Ordinary comfort demands ordinary cleanliness of the person, and it is no part of the sentence meted out to a convict that he be forced to live in squalor and filth. Self respect is one of the most important character traits; it is among the last things to die in a man who is disintegrating; it is absolutely essential to the inmate upon his release if he is to have any chance whatsoever of reclaiming himself. But it is extremely difficult to have any self-respect when one is dirty!

The warden makes provisions for personal hygiene in three major ways: the barber shop, the bath room, and the laundry. The purpose of the institutional barber shop is two-fold: it takes care of the tonsorial needs of the inmates weekly and it aids in the rehabilitation of a number of inmates by giving them instruction and training in a trade by which they will be able to live after their release. Arrangements have been made with the proper state department to make it possible for an inmate to earn his student barber card and his apprentice and master cards in prison. There is a forty-chair barber shop at Stateville. The equipment used is, so far as practical, that which would be found in a well-equipped shop outside: modern barber chairs, electric clippers, etc. The shop is in charge of two officers, the senior of whom is a licensed master barber and empowered by law to give instruction to students.

The bathroom is located centrally with respect to the cell houses and shops. It contains showers, and inmates are given showers each week. The laundry is located in the same building with the bathroom, an arrangement which facilitates the issuing of clean clothes to every inmate at the time of his weekly bath. Here is done all the laundry work for the inmates: shirts, underwear, and pants are laundered weekly for every man.

Ample provision for the health of the inmates is maintained. Housed in, or near, the hospital are not only physicians, surgeons, and a dentist, but also a psychologist, and a sociologist, whose duty it is to look after the mental health of the inmates. The hospital is a light, airy, modern three story building. Each floor contains eight wards, each of which has six beds. The first floor is given over to the care of general medical cases, the second floor to post-operative care of surgical cases, and the third floor is now occupied by a research laboratory, specializing in malariaology, which is managed and staffed jointly by the University of Chicago and the Medical Corps of the United States Army. The hospital is equipped with a thoroughly modern operating-room, x-ray unit, a drug dispensary, a pathological laboratory, and a dressing room, which is on a par with any outside hospital dressing room.

The medical services and hospitals at Joliet-Stateville are operated as one would expect in an average community hospital outside prison walls. The medical staff consists of four civilian physician-surgeons, two at each institution (one a resident on call twenty-four hours a day and the other on a part-time basis); a dentist at each institution; an oculist, a registered pharmacist, and an eye, ear, nose and throat specialist whose services are shared by both institutions.

All incoming inmates must go through a medical, psychiatric, psychological and sociological processing at the Diagnostic Depot before being transferred to one of the state prisons. A prison physician interviews and examines each new inmate, recording medical history and significant findings and defects so that the prison physician of the institution to which the inmate is transferred may take corrective measures. Inmates requiring mental treatment are sent to the psychiatric division at the Menard institution. Active cases of tuberculosis are transferred to the modern tuberculosis hospital at the Pontiac Branch of the Illinois State Penitentiary for treatment, with fine results. All inmates have chest x-rays and routine blood Kahn tests and immunizations are started ,and if possible, completed during their stay at the Diagnostic Depot; otherwise, immunization is completed by the medical department of the institution to which the inmate is transferred. Treatment for venereal disease is given immediately, if indicated. Immunizations against small pox, typhoid fever, tetanus and poliomyelitis are now given routinely.

The prison physician at the institution to which the inmate has been transferred examines each medical jacket accompanying a new inmate and follows through on immunizations, etc., as indicated. Inmates requiring dental work are referred to the prison dentist. Those in need of dental work are taken care of, and if dentures are needed, they are supplied by our own dental labora-

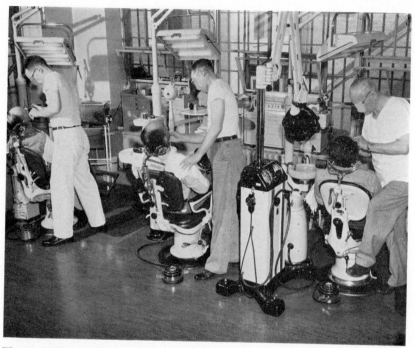

Three chair dentists office supervised by civilian dentist. Stateville Branch.

tory. Men needing spectacles or hearing aids are referred to the eye, ear, nose and throat department where their defects are given attention and corrected if possible.

Annual chest x-rays are taken on all inmates; inmates having a history of arrested pulmonary tuberculosis, syphilis, or infectious hepatitis are routinely barred from food handling assignments.

Formal sick call is held at prescribed times, three days a week; sick inmates are hospitalized. However, anyone becoming ill may be brought to the hospital any time of the day or night.

Practically all of the unusual medical and surgical cases are sent to Stateville from the other branch prisons. Most of the medical treatment and surgery is handled by our own institutional physicians and surgeons. However, when necessary, top specialists in the Joliet and Chicago areas are called in unusual chest, ophthalmologic, orthopedic, neurological, and urological cases. On many occasions, outstanding doctors from our universities are called to examine and perform surgery on inmates. The Chief of Surgery of Billings Hospital, Chicago, Illinois, performed the repair of a femoral aneurysm, (a dilation of communication between major blood vessels). This particular surgical repair included an artery graft. One of Joliet's leading chest surgeons has performed pneumonectomies and lobectomies here, along with the pre-operative work-ups that in some cases included bronchoscopies and biopsies. A Joliet neuro-surgeon has performed delicate brain operations, which were necessary to aspirate a brain tumor in order to save a man's vision.

Considerable plastic surgery has been done by one of Chicago's top plastic surgeons. Included among his cases were the removal of unsightly facial scars, and plastic repair of facial defects that undoubtedly caused the persons involved great psychological damage in the past. Statistics prove that plastic repair of this type has tremendous rehabilitative value.

From a rehabilitation standpoint, the repair of hernias, varicosities, and other functional and organic defects that effect a man's employability are, of course, of prime importance. It is the aim of the medical department to return men to the free community in the best possible physical condition.

One of the real problems that confronts the prison physician is the physical rehabilitation of inmates suffering from crippling effects of gunshot wounds. Particularly difficult are the cases of wounds to the spine. We receive one or two paraplegics each year. They usually require long-term hospitalization with special emphasis on physical therapy. We have, however, had the satisfaction of seeing some paraplegics walk out of the institution unaided, and reasonably capable of holding their own in a competitive world.

Outside of the physicians, pharmacist, and required guard personnel, all other hospital assignments are filled by inmates. Nurses, laboratory technicians, x-ray technicians, dental nurse, dental technicians, and medical record librarians are recruited from the inmate population. There is also an inmate chiropodist. They are trained through an "on-the-job" training program. Most of the inmates are intensely interested and dedicated to their hospital work. Many of them become very proficient and compare favorably in ability with personnel in similar occupations in outside hospitals.

An adjunct of the hospital is the Detention Hospital, in which care is given mentally disturbed inmates. Trained psychiatrists and neurologists staff this department; the attendants are inmates. The Detention Hospital has thirty-two cells given over to the housing of insane and neurotic prisoners. It is equipped for hydrotherapy and has "stripped" cells to accommodate disturbed patients.

The task of maintaining the health level of 3,040 men is a gigantic one, and the hospital and its trained staff, efficient as they are, cannot discharge it without the intelligent coöperation of both the inmates and the officers. An opportunity is given inmates who are ill to go into "sick line" three mornings per week. This is a routine way of handling comparatively non-serious ailments. But sickness is not a respecter of time schedules. It is quite possible for an inmate to be taken sick after the sick line for the day is over. When this occurs, the inmate is instructed to take up the matter with his keeper. Keepers are NOT doctors; they have no business diagnosing an inmate's ailments at any time. The problem of malingering — of pretending to be sick when one is not — is, of course, a big one in a penitentiary. Some inmates will and do complain of being sick when they are not; some inmates constantly suffer from imaginary ills but, let it be repeated, a keeper is not a doctor. When an inmate complains of being sick, it is the duty of the keeper to see to it that the inmate has access to the hospital promptly. A keeper must never risk his judgment against the word of an inmate who professes to be sick. His condition will be diagnosed at the hospital and, if he is malingering, he will be properly handled, but it is no part of the keeper's job to determine whether or not a given inmate is really sick. It is far better to have a hundred men come to the hospital when they are not in urgent need of attention than to let one die because he could not get attention in time. Death comes suddenly in some cases; to permit a man to die for lack of attention amounts to criminal negligence.

The keeper may aid in maintaining the general health of the inmates in other less dramatic ways. Nature, after all, is the great healer, and two of her chief agencies are fresh air and sunlight. The keeper should do all he reasonably can to encourage the men under his care to make the best use possible of these natural aids to health. And, as has been pointed out, cleanliness is a great health aid. It is the clear duty of every keeper to do his utmost to keep the premises under his charge spotlessly clean and to use his influence to the utmost to induce the inmates to keep themselves and their cells clean.

Third among the divisions of the general welfare of the inmates is the matter of housing. Nearly all inmates inside the walls of the institution are housed in cell houses. The Stateville unit has five such cell houses, each housing from six hundred to eleven hundred men. The cell houses are not of the same type: four are circular cell houses of the so-called panopticon type and one is a rectangular cell block. Each of these types has its distinct advantages and disadvantages. In the panopticon cell houses, all the cells are outside; each has a window which can be opened or closed as the inmates of the cell wish. There are four circular tiers of cells, surrounding the circular flag of the cell house. The doors facing inside are entirely of glass. In the center of the flag is an octagonal tower, in which one of the keepers is stationed. This arrangement makes it possible for one keeper to see into all the cells of all the inmates at any time. The word "panopticon" means "all-seeing," and it is from this feature that the name is derived. The ventilation, sanitation, and to a degree, surveillance of the circular cell houses is better in some ways than in the other types; they are on the other hand less compact and economical than the others.

The rectangular cell house contains a five story rectangular tier of cells. Here the cells do not have outside windows, nor is it possible for one keeper to see into all cells from one point.

There are, however, "catwalks" around the outside walls of the cell house, which furnish a vantage point in addition to the regular galleries.

The fourth division of the general welfare of the inmates consists in making provisions for feeding. This department is in charge of a steward, whose duty it is to plan well-balanced meals, to superintend their preparation in the general kitchen, and their serving in the general mess-hall. In addition to the general kitchen and the dining room, the steward has supervision over the butcher shop, the vegetable room, where all the vegetables are cleaned, the bakery, which bakes all the bread and pastries used, and several storage rooms. Perhaps in no department is cleanliness more important than here. Every precaution must be taken to see that food, utensils, and the men who serve them, are clean. Elaborate precautions are taken to see that no inmate with a skin infection, syphilis, tuberculosis, etc., is employed in the handling of food.

Finally, there is the matter of clothing. Inmates are dressed in regulation uniform. New clothes are issued to prisoners on arrival. Thereafter the clothes are kept in repair and, when it becomes necessary, articles of clothing are condemned as no longer usable and are replaced by new ones. All these functions are in the hands of the property officer and his assistants. Routine inspection is made of clothes weekly after they have been washed, and necessary repairs are made at that time. Further, opportunity is given inmates of sending torn clothes or clothes in need of repairs to the clothing room once a week. The articles are either patched or replaced. Similar repair and replacement is made of shoes. A full series record is kept by the property officer, showing the number of articles in the possession of each prisoner and the date of their issue.

PRIVILEGES OF INMATES

Necessarily there are some services to be performed about an institution which could not be assigned to every person. So far as possible, however, it is the purpose of the warden to have the inmates earn their privileges. The most common of these privileges, which may be earned by any and all inmates, are, incoming and outgoing mail, visits, radio and earphones, the use of the commissary, and attendance at and participation in recreation, sports and shows, and library. Although the newly arrived inmate is not actually required to earn these privileges, he is informed that only by continued good behavior may he expect to keep them. Failure to do this can result in the loss of any, or all privileges.

When an inmate is first received at the institution he is required to sign an agreement whereby all mail addressed to him may be opened and censored before being delivered to him. Incoming mail may be in the form of letters, permitted newspapers, and magazines. Letters may be received from relatives and close friends or business acquaintances, with no restriction as to the amount. The Superintendent of Mail has at all times a list of approved magazines and newspapers. Inmates are permitted to subscribe for magazines and newspaper which are included on this list. All subscriptions must be sent direct from the publisher.

Inmates are permitted to write one letter each week, on Sunday, to their friends and relatives. These letters must be respectful and decent in every way, containing no solicitations or remarks derogatory to the institution. Close censorship is maintained over outgoing mail as well as incoming, and accurate records are kept in both instances.

The benefits of this privilege are numerous. Encouragement and constructive criticism from those who are nearest and dearest to him help the inmate in his problems. He is able to keep abreast of the times and the soothing influence of friends' and relatives' letters make for a better behaved person. No matter how monotonous the time may be, most inmates look forward eagerly to writing on Sunday.

Inmates who have not lost the privilege of visits are permitted one visit, of one hour's duration, every two weeks. Here again only relatives and close friends are permitted to visit and only two persons may visit at one time. Visitors coming from a great distance are granted an extended visit. All visits are closely supervised and no visitor under the influence of intoxicants or in possession of contraband articles is allowed to enter the visiting room. Conversation is restricted to the inmate being visited, and boisterous conduct of any kind is not tolerated. Moderate kissing, embracing and hand shaking is permitted at the beginning of the visit. Any display of obscenity results in the immediate termination of the visit.

Though the officer supervising visits must closely adhere to the rules, there are times when he will be called upon to use good judgment in handling a situation. He should remember that some visitors have never been here before and, consequently, are not familiar with the regulations governing visits. Children, especially, are apt to disregard the rules that govern their elders.

Visits are beneficial to both the inmate and the institution. The inmate has a personal association with his friends and relatives that gives him the feeling that he is still very much a part of the outside world. The contact with persons outside the institution is uplifting to him, and here, too, his relatives have a chance to make his burden a little easier. A man who receives visits regularly is, generally, well-behaved. Visits also prove a source of information as to an inmate's family and environment. A visit may provide an outlet for emotion which, if suppressed, might be directed into harmful channels.

The Inmate Commissary was established for the purpose of providing inmates with certain unessential articles not furnished by the institution. The privilege of purchase is limited to inmates who have maintained a good record.

The commissary building is located at a point easily accessible to inmates making their weekly trip to the Barber Shop. Once each week inmates are permitted to visit the commissary and select articles they wish to purchase. The commissary is stocked with goods offered for sale at approximately less than the retail prices. These include foodstuffs, a wide variety of tobacco, candy, toilet articles, and some wearing apparel.

To make a purchase, the inmate must present his order, properly filled out with his name, number, cell, and the articles he wishes to purchase. The order blank is numbered serially and, under the personal supervision of the Officer in Charge the inmate's credit balance is written in and the inmate's fingerprint affixed to the order blank. The order is then given to one of several inmate clerks to be filled. It is the clerk's duty to see that the proper charge is made for the articles purchased and also that the purchase limit is not exceeded. A space is provided at the bottom of the order blank for the inmate's signature, showing receipt of the goods purchased. The order is then initialed by the clerk who filled it. This order is later re-checked by another clerk for correct prices and totals and the amount spent is then deducted from the inmate's balance. Accurate records of purchases and the amount of stock on hand are always available.

The commissary staff is made up of one civilian, the officer in charge, and about a dozen clerks. The officer in charge is selected both for his business ability and capacity to observe closely the daily workings of the commissary. The inmates working in the commissary are selected for clerical ability and their sense of responsibility. They must be speedy and accurate, affable and tactful.

The profits from the commissary are diverted to the Inmates' Benefit Fund. This fund is used to supply all kinds of entertainment for the inmate body. Shows, baseball games, the library books, the purchase of athletic equipment and many school supplies are paid for from the Inmates' Benefit Fund.

The privilege to attend sporting events and shows is one which is valued highly by nearly every inmate. During the summer months a baseball game is scheduled for every Saturday and on some holidays. Great interest is always shown in these games between outside teams and the team made up of inmates. The desire to see fair play is never lacking in either the teams or the spectators. It is the purpose of these games to give the inmates a competitive spirit and to provide periods of relaxation. Besides these games, there are regularly scheduled daily periods of exercise in which softball games are played. These games, played according to a league schedule, provide keen competition among the different teams and their supporters. Volleyball, handball, horseshoes, etc., are also played during these recreation periods.

Perhaps the most cherished privilege is that which gives the inmate the opportunity to attend the movies. For many years this entertainment was sadly lacking at Stateville. But since the erection of the Chapel a few years ago, shows have been given weekly, or oftener, throughout the winter months. By this visual contact with the outside world, the inmate feels more closely connected with the realities of life. The newsreels keep him informed on current events, and the comedies provide the touch of humor that he cannot fail to appreciate.

Censorship is maintained over the shows to see that only the proper type is shown. They must be decent in every respect and interesting. Educational pictures are particularly desirable. The film that glorifies the gangster has no place in the penitentiary program of entertainment and is never shown.

The privileges mentioned are all dependent on the inmate's behavior and the appreciation he shows for them. The warden considers it a part of his duties to extend these privileges to the men in his charge, always provided, of course, that they have been earned.

REHABILITATION AND REFORM

Educational Facilities (School)

The attitude of society towards the inmates of penal institutions has undergone a radical change during the past twenty years. It is now recognized that the punishment of prisoners is no more important than their rehabilitation, and it has been discovered that education is an excellent means to the latter end. Gone from the mind of the general public is the false idea that criminals are possessed of more native intelligence than the ordinary man, and that educating them would only result in an increase in crime. Instead, the trend now is towards preparing the prisoner to take a productive place in society upon his release and education is coming to be looked upon as a very necessary factor in this rehabilitation program.

There are both elementary and high schools at the Stateville penitentiary. The curriculum for each is patterned closely after that which prevails in the public schools of Will County, in which the penitentiary is situated. The teaching staff is recruited from the inmate body, and these teachers are given preliminary courses of instruction to equip them for their duties. Both schools are under the jurisdiction of the Superintendent of Education, who interviews incoming prisoners to determine their educational needs and supervises the operation of the schools. Two additional civilian teachers were added to the staff to assist the Superintendent of Education in his varied duties.

School books and equipment are supplied from the Inmates' Benefit Fund. The schools operate the year around and employ six month terms instead of the customary nine month term of civilian schools. A record is kept of the work done by each student and a report on his progress is made at regular intervals. When a student completes the eighth grade, he receives a diploma from the Will County Superintendent of Schools. High School graduates are accredited by the Lockport Township High School.

Statistics are available to evidence the benefit inmates have derived from attendance at the schools. Another gratifying development in this connection is the change in the attitude of the officers. Formerly, it was considered by them a waste of time to bother teaching the prisoners anything, but most of them have now come to realize that the schools are playing a very important part in the mental growth of the inmates. And this aspect cannot be stressed too heavily. Every officer should encourage the inmates in his charge to take advantage of the educational facilities at their disposal.

Stateville Correspondence School

The Stateville Correspondence School is perhaps the most underrated of any of our departments. This is probably because the work done by correspondence is not readily "seen." The fact is, however, that more inmates are enrolled in correspondence courses than in the three other departments of the academic schools combined. At one time or another in his prison career, almost every inmate takes at least one high school course by correspondence. Each term several inmates complete the requirements for a high school diploma through the medium of correspondence courses. Since these courses can be taken by inmates on any assignment within the institution, it goes without saying that they offer purposeful activity for the many hours each day that nearly every inmate spends in his cell.

It is essential that the officers of the penitentiary appreciate the influence they can exert in promoting activity in the Correspondence School.

TV College

In the autumn of 1956, the Chicago City Junior College began an experiment in which college courses with credit were offered by open circuit television to residents of the City of Chicago.

Flower garden and Vocational School. Stateville Branch.

After nearly two years of negotiations between the warden and the officials of the Chicago City Junior College, a plan was devised whereby inmates of this institution who satisfied the residence and academic entrance requirements of the Chicago system could be enrolled in college credit courses. After an initial trial group of inmates had demonstrated the feasibility of this arrangement, a television classroom was prepared by remodeling the basement of one of the panopticon cell houses and equipping it with television sets, student chairs, and a library.

This program is developing rapidly and is felt to be a real step forward in the rehabilitation program of this institution.

Vocational Training School

As in the case of the grade and correspondence schools, early opposition greeted the efforts to install a vocational school in the

Art class. An artist instructs inmates of the rights and wrongs in the world of art. Stateville Branch.

institution, and to the already mentioned difficulties there were added the lack of building space and the inability to secure trained instructors.

The various obstacles were eventually cleared, building space was converted, equipment was assembled, and courses of instruction were offered. These were naturally rather limited at the start, but as progress was made, others were added, along with new equipment. Finally, a new building was obtained. Now the vocational school does a portion of the department's printing and renders many other services of value not only to this institution but to many other state institutions as well.

Classes are offered in sign and display painting, welding, radio and television repair, body and fender repair, carpentry, masonry, refrigeration, and many other skills, totaling more than forty-two in all.

Libraries

Libraries have made great strides during the past half-century. Working hand-in-hand with publishing houses, printing companies, book binderies, artists, engravers, and authors, they have done much to realize their ambition of a "book for every reader and a reader for every book."

Realizing the therapeutic value of reading, prison administrators should try consistently to improve the facilities and service in their libraries and should abandon the old prison idea that it was sufficient to put a Bible into each cell and hope for the best. However, the Bible in each cell is important.

Joliet-Stateville does have one central library, but we also have many branch libraries and books are always available. It is felt that only a central library in a prison would result in decreased circulation and inferior service. Instead of just one central library, the library holdings are placed in various collections. There are fifteen of these:

(1) Four general collections—one each at the Diagnostic Depot, the Honor Farm, the Joliet Branch and the Stateville Branch.

(2) Two collections of books on philosophy and religion—one at the Joliet Branch and one at Stateville. These are in charge of the full-time chaplains.

(3) One useful arts' collection in the vocational school at Stateville.

(4) One school library housed in the high school at Stateville.

(5) Seven fiction collections. One in each cell house at the Joliet and Stateville Branches. All collections are rotated.

Inmate librarians are in charge of all collections. These men have received some training in the use of the Dewey Decimal classification system and the book of Cutter numbers. There is a comprehensive cataloging system. Author and title cards are kept of the collections.

From the general and fiction collections, distribution is by catalogue. A mimeographed catalogue, arranged according to Dewey headings, is available to all men, and the inmates order their books from the catalogue. Members of the library staff distribute and collect the books on specified days. The men have personal access to the books in the other collections. All library branches are supervised by a civilian.

Reading is by far the most popular pastime at Joliet-Stateville. The circulation figures of the general and fiction collections show an average of five books per man per month. More than one thousand titles are always in circulation from the chaplains' libraries. The schools have many volumes in the hands of their students.

Recently it was decided to add pocket editions to the cell house collections. Through an arrangement with a local news agency, seven copies (one for each cell house) of some forty titles are purchased each month. These books are not classified. They are "put on the route" and pass from cell to cell. Circulation figures are, of course, impossible, but it is safe to say that these books are read and re-read, many, many, times.

Men at Joliet-Stateville read much. Their reading is a hopeful sign for the future.

There is maintained a bookbindery where repair work on the books in the libraries is done. Binding is also performed for other state institutions and public schools.

The value of a library both to the morale of the penitentiary and the individual inmates cannot be overestimated. It serves as an educational medium, and also provides a very necessary form of recreation.

Spiritual Care

The importance of religion is recognized at Joliet-Stateville and I have frequently stated that an officer who does not recognize this importance has no place in a correctional institution. Complete coöperation with the religious program is demanded at Joliet.

Chapel interior. Seven different religious services each week. Stateville Branch.

The basic work of a prison chaplain is identical with the work of every minister, priest, or rabbi on the outside. Just as the minister of religion is an essential part of right living on the outside of a prison, so the prison chaplain is essential for the proper conduct of any prison. Leave religion out of the prison and you might just as well throw away the key on the men confined. No amount of education, vocational training, or physical work will be effective without the practical acknowledgment that this must be animated by character building and religious motivation. In my opinion, the chaplain, if used in other capacities within a prison, lessens his value as a chaplain.

There are two full-time chaplains at the prison, one Protestant and one Catholic. Six part-time ministers are authorized and do conduct the services of their particular denominations each week and are welcome to come in at any time to counsel the members of their flocks, and they do spend much time at the institution. Outside priests, ministers, and rabbis are at all times given preferential treatment in the institution and are permitted and en-

One of six recreation yards. Stateville Branch.

couraged to visit their parishioners. Just as important as the conducting of religious services in a penal institution, is the counseling of individual inmates by the various chaplains.

The institution recognizes that if a man is faithful to his God, he cannot be anything but faithful to his fellow man.

Recreation

The nature of prison life demands that recreational facilities be made available to the inmates. The majority of them are relatively young, and are in constant need of an outlet for their energy. Further, the long hours in the cells tend to promote the storing up of muscular reserve. Lastly, the fact that the yard space is limited makes necessary a certain amout of recreational apparatus.

At Stateville, the inmates play handball, softball, basketball, touch football, and badminton. They may also pitch horseshoes, exercise on the parallel bars or with weight lifting apparatus, etc., or simply walk about the yard.

In the cells they are permitted to read, play cards, checkers and chess, draw or sketch and, with permission, play a musical instrument. For those to whom none of these pastimes appeal, there is the radio, which is turned on in the afternoons and evenings for the various broadcasts of sporting events, news summaries, and network programs.

PERSONALITIES OF INMATES

So far, the men over whom the officer will have jurisdiction have been considered wholly as a large body, or smaller groups thereof. The concern will be with the men as individuals, as human beings possessing separate and distinct personalities.

Equality of treatment and opportunity is a basic principle of democracy. It is also important in the administration of a prison. Justice must be handed down with complete impartiality, and basic distinctions in the handling of the inmate population must be sedulously avoided. Unwarranted discrimination invariably causes dissension.

However, the inmate population is composed, as stated above, of many thousands of individuals, each of whom has a distinct personality and background. For purposes of classification, these individuals are grouped into categories, ranging from the group which requires maximum security to those who need only a minimum of surveillance.

Sometimes a man's moral and intellectual peculiarities may be deduced from the type of crime he commits. For instance, wanton murderers may be assumed, pending further observation, to be fundamentally dangerous. It may also be assumed that in most cases, the farm boy who is incarcerated for raiding his neighbor's hen house is a comparatively harmless lawbreaker.

Naturally, there must be a difference in the methods of handling different offenders, but the sort of crime for which the prisoner has been sentenced is by no means an infallible guide to his personality. Too often major violations of the prison rules are committed by men serving short sentences for minor crimes. On the other hand, "lifers" and other long-term prisoners, convicted on such charges as murder and manslaughter, are often the most tractable of prisoners. This paradox is too common to be considered unusual.

The prison officer who permits his prejudice against a certain type of crime to interfere with the impartial discharge of his duties is guilty of generating resentment and ill-feeling within the walls. Once a man has been received into prison, the crime for which he has been committed becomes, insofar as the prison officer is concerned, of secondary importance. The officer's primary concern is that the prisoner be safely incarcerated and that he obey all the rules of the institution. The prison officer's duties, essentially, are limited to maintaining order within the institution, and what a man was before imprisonment should not enter into the officer's calculations. It is more to be desired that the officer give thought to what the man will be when he leaves prison; the treatment an inmate receives behind the walls to a great extent determines his future conduct.

All this, however, does not alter the fact that inmates are classifiable. We may permit ourselves to make certain generalizations showing the relationship between crimes and the criminal, remembering always that these generalizations should do no more than serve as tentative guides to the treatment of the individual prisoner.

In the first group will be found the untutored rural boy whose mental equipment is inadequate to cope with the complexities of the modern world. The line of demarcation between right and wrong is never clearly defined in his mind, and often he commits transgressions without being aware that he has broken the law. This type of offender comes usually from an emotionally unstable household, where poverty has settled into a chronic condition. Because of his untrained mind, he becomes a flexible tool in the hands of more worldly companions.

Once this type of country youth passes within the gates of an institution, he is usually amenable to the rules and regulations. He has neither desire nor aptitude for becoming a prison "big-shot," and he is therefore excluded from all cliques, which sometimes form within a prison. Since this type of youth offers little, if any, menace, it is not necessary to maintain an inexorable vigilance over him. If his conduct has made him eligible, it is advisable that some sort of trusty work be given him.

The chance offender falls into another category. He is the man whose life has been exemplary till the day when he succumbs to temptation without stopping to visualize the consequences. Usually, he confined himself to crimes growing out of his business affiliations, such as embezzlement, violations of the Blue Sky Law, and illegal speculations. The chance offender ordinarily manages to reach middle age without coming into conflict with the law. In nearly all cases, once he has paid for his crime, the penitentiary will see him no more. His first crime is his last.

Offenders belonging to this group are comparatively of a superior mentality. Because they have not made a habit of crime, their morals are more or less intact. While the educational facilities of the institution are made available to every inmate, it is especially desirable that the chance offender be encouraged to improve his cultural background. He is an exceptionally hopeful prospect for law-abiding society.

In the third group fall the physically and mentally handicapped, including the aged, crippled, and the mentally defective. When assigning them to their places in the prison pattern, care must be taken that the work is not beyond their capacities. If the inmate who is handicapped displays a desire to conform to prison regulations, minor infractions of the rules should call for a reprimand, rather than for isolation confinement.

To the average man, a criminal's life would seem to consist of devoting every hour in every day to anti-social activity. Actually, under the highly organized police systems of today, the criminal is forced to limit his crimes and space his lawless acts at fairly wide intervals. During these intervals the lawbreaker usually conducts himself is much the same quiet manner as his law-abiding neighbor. The few young and inexperienced felons who try to emulate bad men of frontier days soon find out that their criminal careers have ended before they had barely begun.

When the average criminal passes within the walls of a prison, he is quickly made aware that he cannot "get away with anything." The result is that his periods of insurrection against established order become less and less frequent. If the convict is of normal intelligence and has no psychopathic tendencies, the law-abiding intervals between crime become his habitual mode of life.

It must not be forgotten, however, that there are those whose minds cannot comprehend the overwhelming odds against the criminal. Their egotism blinds them to the impossibility of their winning out over the forces of constituted authority. Their minds teem with half-digested schemes, and though they constantly suffer the consequences of their folly, they believe that the next time—always the next time—they will "out-smart" the other fellow and the authorities.

There is little that can be done in the way of reformation for the schemer and gangster until he is made to understand that he can't win. There seems to be but one method of bringing this fact into his consciousness, and that is by keeping his every movement under constant observation. He should not be "hounded," but at the slightest deviation from the course of conduct laid down for him by the prison administration, he should be brought before the Disciplinary Officer.

As his attitude undergoes a change for the better, surveillance should be relaxed gradually to the point where he is no longer the object of special attention. For, after all, there are two influences paramount in the conditioning of man's acts: fear of punishment for transgressions, and hope of reward for virtue.

Summarizing, the officer should realize that while it is extremely unwise to "play" favorites among the inmates, and while all the inmates are subject to the regulations issued by the warden, there nevertheless will be individual cases that demand special consideration. Therefore, it is advisable that the officer study the personalities of his men as closely as possible, that he may judge exceptional circumstances on the basis of the particular inmate involved. Disciplinary measures are a necessary part of prison administration, but discretion should be exercised by the officer invoking these measures.

BUSINESS MANAGEMENT

The fundamental principle of our American form of government is that public monies be expended only by authorization of our legislative body.

The budget together with a summary of anticipated revenue affords the Legislature an opportunity to study the proposed programs and expenditures of all state government obligations and to allot funds in harmony with the tax programs.

The method to employ in preparing the budget should consist of compiling all financial and pertinent data from the accounting system and the various assignments of the institution.

The interpretation of this data serves as a basis for estimating the forthcoming biennial operations in order to achieve the Warden's desired program.

Appropriations form F-1, which is the "Allotment of Appropriations for Current Expenses and Equipment," broken down into quarterly periods, must be completed.

It then becomes necessary to adhere to these figures as closely as possible.

The first requisite in attaining this goal is to have an adequate accounting system and then make certain the system is being employed accurately.

Accounting is the most important tool of Business Management.

Any successful accounting system therefore must consist of an orderly arrangement of each of the elements of every financial transaction in minute detail.

Governmental accounting is both a means of control and a means of reporting managemet.

Good accounting will produce statistical data relating to the activities of all the assignments and serve as a guide for future action. All expenses incurred in the operation of the institution are chargeable to one of the following appropriations from the General Revenue Fund:

Personal Service—Salaries

Contractual Service—Salaries, Gas, Lights, Professional Services, etc.

Postage—

Travel—Employees' Travel Expense

Commodities—Food, Clothing, etc.

Stationery—Printing and Office Supplies

Equipment—

Travel and Allowance—Inmates' Travel Allowances and Gratuities.

These appropriations are not interchangeable. For instance, an equipment item may not be charged to the commodity appropriation or vice versa.

All requirements are requisitioned on either quarterly semi-annual or annual requisitions that emanate from the assignment level.

The requisitions are received in the office of the Business Manager where they are thoroughly checked for correct item numbers, prices, extensions, etc.

The Business Manager's Office maintains an encumbrance control for all appropriations and the current status of each appropriation is shown on all requisitions.

The requisitions are approved by the Warden and submitted to the General Office in Springfield for handling and final approval by the Director of the Department of Public Safety.

The requisitions are then directed to the State Purchasing Agent.

Requisitions from all state agencies are compiled in the purchasing office and bids are sent out to various vendors for competitive bidding.

Awards are made to the low bidder provided the items meet the rigid specifications of the State of Illinois.

In the event the low bidder cannot meet these specifications the lowest bidder complying with the specifications is issued a Purchase Order. A copy of this purchase order is received in our Business Office where it is checked to be sure the items cover the original requisition. Prices and extensions are also carefully checked. After the purchase order has been thoroughly checked copies are made and sent to the receiving department, General Store, and the assignment that instituted the requisitions.

At the request of the assignment head the vendor is notified to deliver all or part of the items covered by the Purchase Order. Upon receipt of the items it is the duty of the receiving officer to inspect the shipment for count and breakage and forward a receiving ticket to the Business Manager's Office immediately.

When the items reach the assignment level they must be inspected to be sure they meet State Specifications as to size, quantity, quality, etc.

In the event any item does not meet specifications, a formal complaint to vendor must be filed immediately and the item is to be held until a proper replacement is received. The State Purchasing Agent authorizes us to act in his behalf when emergency purchases are required.

A blanket authorization to make these purchases is granted by the purchasing agent, provided they do not exceed $50.00 per item. Quotations from various vendors are tabulated and awards are made according to the procedure employed by the purchasing agent.

All invoices covering commodities, equipment, services, etc., must be submitted on State of Illinois Invoice-Voucher Forms FA-13. Upon receipt of invoices they are checked and processed in the office of the Business Manager for transmittal to the General Office in Springfield.

The distribution of invoices as to expenses, improvements, inventories, etc., is also handled in the Business Office.

The books and records maintained in the Business Manager's Office include the following pertinent to the General Revenue Fund:

General Ledger—asset, liability and expense accounts.

—*General Journal*—all special entries for posting to the general ledger.

Stores Inventory Ledgers—perpetual record of each stores inventory item.

Appropriations Control Ledger—balances of unexpended appropriations.

Encumbrance Control Ledger—memorandum record of appropriation encumbrances.

Property Ledger—property balances by location code control.

Property Control Transfer Journal—record of properties transferred to Property Control Section, Department of Finance.

Industries, including a furniture factory, sheet metal shop, textile mill, garment department, shoe factory, bookbindery, mattress shop, etc., are operated by qualified employees, supervisory personnel, and inmate labor.

The funds necessary to operate the industries are appropriated by the Legislature from the "Working Capital Revolving Fund."

All of the products manufactured in the industries are sold only to tax supported bodies of the State of Illinois and the receipts from the sale of these products are deposited in the same "Working Capital Revolving Fund."

The books and records pertinent to the Working Capital Revolving Fund are also maintained in the office of the Business Manager and include the following:

General Ledger—asset, liability and expense accounts.

General Journal—all special entries for posting to the general ledger.

Sales Register—manual record of sales by industry.

Accounts Receivable Ledger—manually posted detail of balances by customer.

Invoice Journal—manual grouping of purchases by account distribution.

Schedule Book—balances of unexpended appropriations.

Property Ledger—property balance by location code control.

Encumbrance Control Ledger—memorandum record of appropriation encumbrances.

The following reports are prepared in the Business Manager's Office:

Monthly Reports:

1. Monthly report of Appropriations, Encumbrances and Balances—Industry and Institution.
2. Summary of Farm Accounts.
3. Accounts Receivable—Statement.
4. Monthly Meal Report.

Quarterly Reports:

1. Quarterly Financial Report to the Governor.
2. Industrial Profit and Loss Statement.
3. Motor Fuel Tax Refund Claim.
4. Status of Standard Accounts.

Annual Reports:

1. Industrial Profit and Loss Statement.
2. Balance Sheet—Industry and Institution.
3. Allotment of Appropriations for one-year period.

Inmate Benefit Fund

The monies necessary to operate this fund are derived from inmate commissary profits and Inmate Trust Fund interest earnings. This fund is used to purchase various supplies and equipment which benefits the entire inmate population such as religious supplies, athletic supplies and equipment, vocational school supplies and equipment, motion picture entertainment, library books, magazines and periodicals.

In effect, all profits that accrue from inmate funds go back to the inmates in the manner just described.

Officers' Amusement Fund

Officers' commissaries are provided for use by the employee personnel and an officers' barber shop is also available. Profits that accrue from these sources are deposited in the officers' amusement fund and are used for the purchase and operation of employee busses, library books, radio and television sets, employees' parties, etc. The balance in this fund has accumulated to the extent that in the near future, we expect to erect a building to be used for the convenience of our employee personnel. The building will contain a gymnasium, a library, bowling alleys, pool tables, and a kitchen where food may be prepared. It will also include a large room where employee dinners and dances may be held.

The institution and industrial payrolls are computed and vouchered in the office of the Business Manager.

The Inmates' and Officers' Trust Funds are the responsibility of the Warden who delegates authority for their handling to the Business Manager and his assistants.

The books and records maintained to provide financial control and administrative information necessary to operate the trust funds include the following books:

General Ledger—asset, liability, and expense accounts.

General Journal—all special entries for posting to general ledger.

Cash Receipts and Disbursements Journal—detail record of cash receipts and disbursements by account classification.

Inmate Trust Account Ledger—detail inmate trust account balances.

Officers' Commissary Receivable Ledger—detail balance by officer.

Purchase Journal—record of commodity purchases by account classification.

Inmate Trust Fund

This fund represents all monies belonging to the individual inmates incarcerated in the institution. These funds are deposited in banks throughout the State of Illinois and earn interest at the rate of approximately 3%. This interest is deposited in the Inmates' Benefit Fund.

Inmate Commissary Fund

Commissaries are provided where inmates may purchase items such as candy, cigars, cigarettes, tobacco, canned foods, pastry, fruit, etc., at a price slightly above cost. Profits that accrue from commissary sales are deposited in the Inmate Benefit Fund.

CLASSIFICATION OF PRISONERS

Classification is an orderly and sensible way of doing things.

To classify means to put things into groups according to some idea or plan. A good farmer grades his grain and judges his cattle. Merchandise is displayed in departments of stores for the convenience of the shoppers. Soldiers are grouped in formation for inspection and drill. People, like animals, and things, may be classified in various ways according to interest and purpose of those who deal with them. Our bodies, for example, vary in size, shapes, texture and features. Men differ in intelligence, schooling, ability and experience, and in many other respects. People tend to group themselves in play and at work, and in social activities, according to the traits and interests they may have in common. It is natural to seek the company of those who are like ourselves, and to avoid those who are different. Civilization advances as folks learn to live together agreeably in spite of their differences. Organizations, such as lodges, churches, and clubs, make it easier for people to find their places usefully in society. Living becomes increasingly difficult for those who have no organized interests. Some are handicapped in a manner and degree that they are not able to care for themselves properly. They may become subjects for charity or asylum. Others are so misfit that they do not adjust socially. They may behave antisocially and find themselves in prison. The classification of felons is dealt with in another section of this book.

* * * * * * *

LEADERSHIP

One of the things which distinguishes a prison guard who is likely to succeed in his job and to win promotion from the one who merely discharges the minimum essentials of his post is that intangible quality we call leadership. Now leadership is not easy to define or to describe; like so many character traits which we call by a single name, it is actually the combination of a number of unitary characteristics. In attempting to identify and evaluate those individual traits which go to make up the quality of leadership in a prison guard, one possible method of procedure is to select typical examples of men who possess that qualification and of others in whom it is notably lacking. Then comparison of these individuals may help us to arrive at a notion of some of the unit elements involved.

This is the method which has been followed in this attempt to single out the basic components of leadership. Five officers were selected, three of whom possess the quality of leadership in a high degree and two of whom are entirely without it, and these individuals were then carefully compared.

A thumb-nail sketch of one of these individuals would read something as follows:

Officer A is a leader. He is possessed of a dignified, one might almost say commanding, appearance and impresses one as a slow, methodical well-balanced thinker. He *never* gives way to excitement or emotional expression—it would, for instance, be almost inconceivable that he would curse an inmate. He makes every effort to be fair, and is not ashamed to admit the fact if he makes an error of judgment. His fairness and justice include not only the fact that all inmates "look alike to him," that he has no court favorites, but the further fact that his judgment is salted with a certain quality of maturity that arises from experience. He does not accept every statement made to him as gospel, but maintains a certain open-mindedness and suspension of judgment. His manner is kindly, in general, but he has no difficulty in maintaining reserve and a certain degree of aloofness which enable him to indicate, for instance, that an interview is at an end without giving offense.

Careful reading will show that this single paragraph contains mention of a number of different character traits—traits all of which are included in the general term leadership.

More detailed analysis of the character and actions of five typical officers — three, as has been said, who are leaders, and two who are definitely not leaders — was carried through. Abstracting and generalizing from these five cases, it was possible to enumerate no less than fifteen unit characters which are included in the concept of leadership. A very brief discussion of these fifteen characters follows:

Intelligence

A leader must be at least as intelligent as the average of his followers; a stupid man inspires contempt rather than respect. Now intelligence is a very broad term and covers a very large field. There are two specific types of intelligence which are necessary to the prison guard: general common sense, and the specialized knowledge of his own particular duties. The first type of intelligence is necessary to all guards; the second type depends upon the specific duties to which he is assigned. It is obvious that the keeper assigned to the radio detail, the school, or the barber shop requires detailed specific knowledge not required of the keeper in charge of a labor detail.

Good Judgment

Good judgment consists of the ability to see and to weigh not only the immediate, but also the mediate, results of a given course of action. So very often what seems to be the best way to handle a particular, temporary situation turns out to have implications and results which are anything but wise. Judgment is in part a function of intelligence, for it depends upon being able to see and to weigh a number of alternatives. These alternatives are sometimes numerous and complicated, yet decisions must sometimes be made rapidly. Good judgment, then, involves the ability to "think on one's feet." In part, however, judgment is a function of experience: the more somewhat similar situations one has previously dealt with, the readier he is to make a prompt and sound judgment in a given situation.

Fairness

This is one of the most important requisites of true leadership, and in the case of the prison guard, it is demanded in very large measure indeed. The guard, with his tremendous power over the inmates in his charge, cannot permit himself the personal likes and dislikes of ordinary civilian life. It is almost inevitable that there will be some men in his charge whom he will like and others whom, almost instinctively he will dislike. If he wishes to have even a chance of success in the performance of his duties, he must learn to rise above these likes and dislikes—to lean backwards in seeing to it that he does not unduly favor the first group nor persecute the second. There are two specific reasons for this in addition to the obvious general one. First, inmates resent above all the officer who has certain favorites or certain men whom he "rides." Nothing will destroy the respect of inmates quicker than partiality on the part of the officer. Second, it is lamentable, but true that, in general, these inmates who curry favor and seek to ingratiate themselves with officers are doing so with ulterior motives. Few, if any, inmates really have the welfare of an officer at heart; their helpfulness is nearly always a cloak for their attempts at self-advancement.

Emotional Stability

A leader cannot blow hot in one breath and cold in the next. He cannot make quick and unexpected shifts of emotional bearing. He cannot permit his personal moods to color his attitude. An officer's behavior and general attitude from day to day build up a definite reaction pattern in his charges. The men under him have a right to expect that he will be the same today as he was yesterday. Nothing could be more unfair and more disruptive of good discipline than to regard one day as a punishable offense what had up to that time been considered passable conduct. A good officer cannot afford to be "high" one day and "down in the dumps" the next.

Dignity

The leader must maintain a certain level of aloofness—he cannot permit himself to lose his dignity and the dignity of his position. For without it he is completely disarmed. True dignity, however, does not consist of insistence upon outward show and ceremonial observance; it is a deep-lying inherent character trait —the ability to evoke respect in others.

Kindliness

Kindliness is a general personality trait—a well-defined general attitude toward one's fellow-man. Its outward manifestation is kindness, and the trait depends upon a genuine liking for and sympathy with one's fellow-men, whether convicts or civilians.

The man who does not have liking for other human beings or for any specific group of human beings should not hold the position of guard. The genuine leader can maintain his dignity without austerity; he can be dignified and kindly, friendly, genial, too.

The Common Touch

Kipling, in his poem, "If," lists as one of the requisites of a true man the ability "to walk with kings nor lose the common touch." That is especially important in any position, such as that of guard, in which the man is required in his daily work to mingle constantly with his temporary social inferiors. It takes a bit of doing to feel equally at home with bank presidents and with bums, but the man who has the ability to do so will get much farther with both groups than the man who lacks it.

Empathy

Empathy is a rather unusual word, but it seems to be about the best word there is to describe a quality which is of prime importance to the prison guard. It is, in simple words, the ability to project oneself into the other fellow's boots, to see things and feel things as he does, without necessarily agreeing with him. It is the ability to put yourself in the other man's place, and to understand his viewpoint. It is the knack of seeing how the other man will be affected by a given situation and therefore how he will react to it. In one sense it is basic to general humaneness.

Ability To Take Orders

To be a good leader one must first learn to be a good follower. The officer who shows resentment at the orders of his superiors or complains of them to his charges can hardly expect better luck with his own orders. The issue arises not only with regard to new specific orders handed down from above, the reason for which, perhaps, the officer is unable to understand, but also in the matter of discipling inmates. The officer has complied with his full duty when he has reported fairly and in an objective manner an infraction of the rules which comes to his attention. He is not the disciplinary officer, and, if in the judgment of the senior captain, the offense should be dismissed with a reprimand, the keeper should not resent this. Above all, he must not adopt the attitude of lying in wait for the inmate who has "beaten his rap" in an attempt to catch him in another infraction and so "get even." Vindictiveness has no place in a decent officer's makeup.

Self Control

The officer who cannot control himself can scarcely expect to be very successful in controlling others. Discipline presupposes self-discipline, and the officer who lets inmates see him unable to control himself loses their respect. It is never necessary to curse, to shout, to lose one's temper. Prisoners are required to exercise a very large degree of self-control to curb the large majority of their impulses; it is incumbent upon the guard to set them an example in this virtue.

Courage

Another quality which a leader must possess is courage. Even animals seem to be able to sense the presence of fear in a man, and it is well known that in lion-taming, for instance, success depends in a large measure upon the degree to which the trainer is able to erase any outward vestige of fear. Just so, among human beings, the crowd will never follow a coward or a weakling. In the position of the prison guard, pure physical courage is perhaps of less importance than that much rarer quality—moral courage. One must, for instance, have the courage to admit it when he has made a mistake. This kind of courage is as important as it is rare.

Open-Mindedness

The faculty of open-mindedness is an extremely important part of leadership. It consists, in part, of the ability to give everyone a fair hearing, to accept information no matter what the source, but not to be carried away by it—to reserve judgment. Shakespeare said it long ago in the famous speech of Polonius to Laertes in Hamlet: "Give every man your ear, but few your tongue." The efficient officer cannot allow himself to be swayed by prejudice or pre-conceived notions of any kind; he must be prepared not to be surprised at any facts, no matter how much they conflict with his fondest beliefs. He must be not only willing, but actually insistent, upon hearing both sides of a question before reaching a decision. This trait is important to the guard both in his dealings with his fellow guards and his dealings with inmates, for things are not always what they seem to be, and the profoundest confidence may sometimes be abused, just as the deepest mistrust may be unwarranted.

Reserve

Both with his fellow officers and with inmates, the man who is a leader will maintain a certain reserve. He should be prepared to answer frankly and fully all legitimate questions addressed to him from whatever source, but he should refrain from volunteering irrelevant facts, opinions, etc. A man's private affairs are truly private, and the leader knows the value of keeping them so. The chatterbox is seldom highly regarded by his superiors, his equals, or those under him.

Determination

The leader should be slow in arriving at decisions; he should use all possible care to see that his decisions are correct; but, once having reached a decision he must stick by his guns. The leader who does not have the courage of his convictions, the stick-to-it-iveness and the plain guts to stand his ground does not long remain a leader. One who would hold the respect of others cannot permit himself to be swayed from his purpose; vacillation is instantly recognized as a sign of weakness. But determination can be quiet as well as noisy; it can be calm as well as belligerent. And a man has a right to be determined only insofar as he can be sure to a moral certainty that he is right.

Loyalty

Of all the virtues in the catalog, perhaps the most attractive and beautiful is loyalty. Most of us, I think, can forgive the other fellow for many shortcomings if only he is loyal—loyal to his superiors, loyal to his ideals, loyal to himself. Once more, in the same speech of Polonius, Shakespeare has phrased the importance of loyalty to oneself in words that are as beautiful today as they were when they were written, over three hundred years ago. "And this above all," he said, "to thine own self be true; and it must follow, as the night the day, thou canst not then be false to any man." Now there are all kinds of loyalty—loyalty to country, loyalty to superiors, etc., and all of them are necessary and desirable in man. But there is one kind of loyalty, which applies to every human being who has other human beings in his charge, which is, perhaps, less obvious and less thought of. It is loyalty to those for whom one is responsible.

If I may be pardoned for doing so, I should like to quote a little anecdote from my personal experience because it illustrates the point so clearly. During the World War I, I was stationed at a training camp. A contagious disease had broken out in camp, and we had all been under quarantine for some time. One Saturday I went to the Captain in command of my company and asked whether we were to be permitted leave to go to town. He replied that no leave could be given because of the quarantine. I then told him that the men of B company were to be given leave. Immediately he replied, "Well if they are going to leave, by gosh, so are you men." And with that he went to his superior officer and presented his case, and obtained leave for us. He was loyal to the men under him. So must every officer be who desires to do his full duty. It is fully as much the duty of an officer to protect and safeguard the legitimate rights of those under him as it is to repress actions not in accordance with the rules. If one's charges owe him respect and obedience, one owes them loyalty in return.

As was explained in the introductory paragraphs, these fifteen unit characters, all of which are component parts of the quality of leadership, were derived inductively by comparing and contrasting the characters of five prison guards. Five is a very small number, and it is almost certain that other characters, in addition to the fifteen enumerated, are conained in the concept of leadership. But certainly these fifteen are among the most important.

Even the fifteen qualities listed here constitute a formidable array; if you are possessed of a proper spirit of humility, you will have asked yourself before this: "Am I supposed to possess all those qualities?" Of course not, or at least of course you cannot be expected to possess them all in their highest degree. Certainly, I know no man who has them all in abundant measure—if such a one exists, he is a paragon indeed.

No; the traits I have listed compose, when taken together, an ideal—a goal at which to aim. It might be a very good idea for you to sit down right now and attempt to score your own character, to see how many of these fifteen traits you can truthfully claim to possess. Note the ones in which you are weak; mark them down for your special attention and try to develop those sides of your character. As you become better acquainted with your fellow students and with those men already employed at this institution, score them too. Try to see in just what point one excels, in what point he is deficient. For no man is perfect. You will find, though, that your fellows and your superiors exhibit marked differences in the degree to which they possess the several qualities. Try to understand why. Select those men who seem to you particularly worthy of emulation and try to analyze just why it is that they are able to command your respect. Then try to pattern yourself upon them. If you wish to be a leader, you must be willing to pay the price in hard work, perseverence, self-discipline. But before you can direct your moral energies intelligently, you must know just what it is you are after. The analysis here attempted of the complex quality of leadership will, it is hoped, make easier the intelligent direction of your energies.

Chapter 9

SENSITIVE ASPECTS OF PRISON LIFE

Sub-Chapter (A): Employees

ENTRANCE GATE

The entrance gate, or gatehouse, is the main entrance to the institution. Through it passes virtually all pedestrian traffic in and out of the institution—employees, visitors, and inmates when they are admitted or released.

Entrance gate. Stateville Branch.

Since the officer in charge of the front entrance is constantly before the public, it is important that he have a pleasant, even disposition and follow the rules and regulations carefully without becoming disagreeably officious in the performance of his duties. However, he must be thorough and efficient and must concentrate on his task. All who pass through must be searched thoroughly for weapons, munitions, narcotics, and any contraband. It is to be remembered that guns can be made in the form and shape of fountain pens, and narcotics can be disguised as gum or candy. All such items can easily be concealed on the body or in the clothing. Anyone who attempts to smuggle them into the institution is to be held and a superior notified. Items such as pocket knives, pens, pencils, medicines, candy, gum, etc., must be surrendered at the gatehouse, where the officer will deposit them in receptacles provided for the purpose. They will be returnd to the visitor as he leaves the institution.

Another prerequisite of the officer assigned to the front entrance is a good memory. All employees assigned to duty within the institution pass in and out of the front entrance, and he must positively identify each one. It would be very easy for him to pass someone about whom he was slightly uncertain; but if this happened to be the wrong person, an escape would be the probable result. Therefore, any time there is the slightest doubt about an employee's (or anyone's) identity, the officer in charge of the gatehouse must examine the I.D. Pass, or other identification, comparing the picture thereon with the bearer's appearance. If doubt as to the person's identity is not resolved, he should be held and a supervising official telephoned for further instructions.

An important function of the front entrance officer is the reception of people who come to visit inmates. Some are unreasonable, some are apprehensive, and many on their first visit are uncomfortable and ill at ease. It is important that he meet these different kinds of people in the proper way. It is not too uncommon for boisterous, intoxicated persons to appear at the gatehouse seeking to visit some inmate. Under no circumstances may a visitor who is intoxicated be permitted to enter the institution. Aggressive, offensive individuals must be dealt with courteously but firmly and accorded no more privileges than would be given to any other person. Those who are ill at ease should be given a word of assurance and treated with consideration. It is just as easy to be courteous and considerate as it is to be gruff and ill-natured, and the front entrance is no place for an officer who is temperamental or who speaks in a harsh and unfriendly voice. First impressions are lasting, and the front gate officer is the first and last representative of the prison with whom visitors come in contact.

Among the more sensitive and important assignments in the institution is that of the lady searcher stationed in the gatehouse during visiting hours. Since female visitors can easily conceal contraband about their persons, they must be searched quite thoroughly. Yet the search must be conducted in an impersonal manner and with as much diplomacy as possible.

In addition to those persons who come to the institution to visit inmates, there are also a considerable number of official visitors. They may be members of the Department of Public Safety, F. B. I. or police investigators, ministers, social workers, contractors, or businessmen. Visitors from other states and foreign countries are not uncommon. When such a visitor approaches the officer at the gatehouse and states his name and business the officer must immediately contact the proper official and arrange an escort or approve the visitor to the office or department where his business will be transacted.

Police officers or other persons entitled to carry weapons *must* leave them at the gatehouse, where they will be deposited in the vault and returned to the officer when he leaves the prison. Weapons must never be carried into the prison except by authorized employees under the direct supervision of a Lieutenant or higher ranking officer. Guns and ammunition shall be carried separately; so that if an officer should be surprised and overpowered, his assailant will not acquire a loaded weapon.

Ordinarily any inmate permitted to pass through the front entrance is a minimum security risk assigned to some special work detail. On the inmate's first trip through the gate he must be approved by the Assistant Warden. A picture of inmates assigned to details outside the entrance gate is kept in the gate-house. This card bears the inmate's name, number, picture, custody status and work assignment. The inmate is not permitted to carry any letters, written documents or anything not expressly authorized either into or out of the prison. Every inmate must be carefully searched when he passes through the gatehouse in either direction.

Prisoners being released from the institution also pass through the front entrance. Prior to that release, the Assistant Warden or other proper official will have sent to the front entrance a notice that a certain prisoner (or prisoners) is to be released. Discharged or Paroled prisoners must be accompanied to the gatehouse by the officer detailed to escort inmates through the release procedure. The escorting officer must approach the door alone and in advance of the prisoners being released, so that the officer at the gatehouse can first admit him and close the door behind him. By utilizing this strategy, the officer at the gate will know that his fellow employee is not being used as a hostage by inmates attempting to force an exit.

With the exception of the Warden's and Assistant Warden's cars, the mail and garbage trucks, no vehicle is permitted to pass through the entrance gate without the permission of the Warden or his assistant. All vehicles must be searched thoroughly, inside and out, when entering or leaving the fenced enclosure around the institution. Commercial vehicles must be thoroughly checked by the employee in charge of the gatehouse and he is to examine the invoice or bill of lading to ascertain the contents of the load before passing the vehicle to the sally port. *If any Narcotics, pharmaceutical supplies, gas equipment, arms or ammunition are included in the shipment, they must be received at the front entrance and not passed to the sally port nor permitted to enter the prison yard.* If the load contains no contraband or dangerous articles, the officer in charge of the front gate must notify the towers and the supervising officer at the sally port that the vehicle has been approved for that destination. He must include in his notice accurate description of the vehicle. In all cases only the driver of the truck or automobile will be permitted to proceed beyond the entrance gate. Passengers or helpers must wait at the gatehouse until the vehicle returns.

Another important duty of the officer assigned to the front entrance is to prevent contacts between civilians and inmates. If an attempt to contact an inmate is made by anyone, the gatehouse officer must notify his superior immediately, so that an investigation can be made. Any suspicious movement of automobiles or pedestrians in or near the assignment must also be reported and investigated. This is one assignment on which loitering either by employees or visitors, would rate as a dangerous distraction to the employees on duty. It is, therefore, not permitted.

COOPERATION

One of the principal objectives in the management of an institution is to make every employee aware of the need for unity in attaining the goals of the administration. Each department or assignment in the institution has certain problems and responsibilities. Some of these problems are confined to a particular assignment; others are related to practically every assignment in the institution.

For example, an officer assigned to the stores or kitchens where foodstuffs or commodities are accessible to inmates is faced with the problem of pilfering of these items every minute that he is on duty.

On the other hand, an officer assigned to the Master Mechanic's Shop is not so much concerned with inmates' pilfering food; he has another problem equally as great which he must cope with continuously, and that is the manufacturing of contraband articles on the various machines of that assignment. To argue which poses the greater problem would be like arguing which comes first the chicken or the egg. It must be recognized that they are equally important, for if a great amount of foodstuff is pilfered or if dangerous contraband is manufactured, the prison administrator is in trouble regardless.

The foregoing is mentioned because at one time or another every prison employee is apt to develop the feeling that he has the most important assignment in the institution. Since each may feel his assignment is the most important, it follows that each in turn believes that he has the most of the problems.

In the long haul it will pay dividends to recognize the other person's responsibilities and respect them. On the contrary, the attitude of "Hooray for me and the heck with everyone else" only tends to make everyone's job more difficult. If guards have good reason to believe that inmates are pilfering or otherwise taking advantage of a fellow employee, they should not hesitate to call his attention to it. Certainly he should appreciate their interest and assistance. If one employee admonishes another as to something amiss on the latter's assignment, the guard being advised should not take the attitude that his job is being infringed upon, or that the employee cautioning him has no right to issue the warning.

When discussing any assignment, employees should use non-technical language and not try to impress fellow employees or supervisors with six syllable words or professional terms, such as medical terms that may have been learned in the hospital, for example. Or what is worse, perhaps, is the employee who talks in the vernacular used by an element of the inmates, for example the "hole," "screw," etc. Employees should remember the importance of not making uncomplimentary remarks about other employees or superiors, in the presence of inmates.

An extra amount of coöperation between departments is often necessary in accomplishing special or seasonal jobs. As an example, the assistance of other assignments may be required at the Canning Plant at the peak of the harvest season in order to prevent waste or spoilage of food. The fact that this situation interferes with activities on the affected assignments is understood and has already been taken into consideration by the Warden and his staff. Often the inmates welcome a day or two on a different assignment, such as shelling peas or breaking beans for the cannery, since it may be a diversion or change of pace. On the contrary, however, there is always another element of inmates who resent the change and will give voice to their feelings, especially if they feel that their officer or other superiors resent it. Under no circumstances should an employee ever express in the presence of inmates complaints about assisting with other work, as this will only encourage that element of inmate objectors to manifest their feelings more strenuously. It is very discouraging to have an inmate say, "even the Officer said the job was a waste of time." Better had that officer said to the inmate, "You want to eat this winter, don't you? Let's get the beans in the cans."

The manner in which employees express themselves is very important. When talking to inmates, they should not use curse words at any time; for whether or not the curses were directed at an inmate, some will take offense and report that they were spoken directly to them. In supervising inmate activities, plain, ordinary language should be used. The officer must be fair in his treatment of the inmates, and always make sure that his directions and orders are understood.

Sometimes it is necessary to transfer inmates from one assignment to another, and for various reasons the Assignment Captain cannot explain why. It is recognized that in many cases an officer may have spent many days and weeks breaking in an inmate on a job and it may work a hardship on an assignment to transfer him. However it should not be assumed that superior officers are "taking picks" on an employee when they remove a good worker from his assignment, or that they are showing another department preference. By the same token, employees should never ask for a certain inmate just because the inmate is rated as a good worker. Neither should they tell an inmate that efforts will be made to get him transferred to their assignment. If an employee is asked by an inmate for a transfer to his particular assignment, the employee should instruct the inmate to request a transfer through the assignment captains.

If employees are working on an assignment where a relief officer takes over or where an officer on a different shift comes on duty, they must not shove the keys into the hands of the relieving officer and rush for the front gate. Instead, a minute or two should be spent explaining any unusual activity or incident that has occurred during the completed tour of duty. The relieving officer is entitled to know. And all employees should expect the same consideration in return. If there is special work going on, the approved method of completing the work should be described. Better yet, if the work is complicated or involved, instructions should be put into writing. One habit worth forming is that of carrying a notebook in which to jot down reminders of the day's incidents and of matters that deserve further attention. This is better than relying on memory for important details.

If guards are on an assignment where no relief officer appears at the end of the shift and there is unfinished work which should be attended to, they must call it to the attention of the shift lieutenant, who will relay the information to the supervisor of the next shift. When employees on a new shift take over and have to cope with a broken steam line or a disturbed inmate or whatever problem has arisen, they should be given all available information and any instructions or orders that have been issued concerning the situation. This type of cooperation between employees is mandatory.

INSTITUTION COUNTS

An accurate accounting of inmates is an indispensable element of security in a penal institution. Without an accurate system of accounting for the whereabouts of the inmates, there would be no means of determining whether or not the security program was functioning properly and effectively. The only gauge of the security program is the "count check." If the total number of inmates on all the various assignments equals the number charged to the institution through the Record Office, the count does check and the security system passes the test of another day. If the count fails to check, then obviously someone has either miscounted or the security system has broken down.

Because of the importance of an accurate count, there can be no tolerance of error on the part of employees making the count. Either an inmate is where he is supposed to be or his whereabouts are unknown and he represents a threat to security. In either event it is the custodial officer's duty to know, not to hazard a guess or turn in an approximate count.

To insure accuracy, there are certain fundamentals which must be observed during the making of counts:

1. The officer should concentrate only on the count as he makes his rounds or checks his men past him in a double line. He should not speak to passing acquaintances or permit himself to be distracted in any way.

2. When counting more than one unit (line, Cellhouse gallery or section of a shop), the officer must list the count for each unit on a temporary count sheet. Then total the whole when the count is finished. He should not attempt to carry the separate counts in his head.

3. Officers must be certain they are counting an inmate and not a reasonable facsimile of one, meaning a dummy. During day time counts the inmates are required to stand before the door of their cells while a count is in progress. Enforcement of this rule is a *must* as it minimizes the possibility of an officer being fooled by a dummy. However, night counts made while the inmates are resting or sleeping present a different situation. Then, the officer must be sure that he sees some part of the inmate's anatomy (body); that he is not being deceived by a bundle of clothing covered with a blanket.

4. Officers on assignments where there is considerable inmate traffic via tickets and passes are to check closely the inmate movement chart to make certain every entrance and departure is properly recorded and that no false entries are recorded on it. Only by close supervision of the entries made on the inmate movement chart can officers be certain that their line count is correct when leaving the assignment.

Official counts of the entire population should be made five times during each twenty-four hours. At Stateville, the institution-wide counts begin with the 5:40 A.M. count, taken by the 11:00 P.M. to 7:00 A.M. shift; the 7:00 A.M. count is taken by the 7:00 A.M. to 3:00 P.M. shift; the evening count is taken by the 3:00 P.M. to 11:00 P.M. shift, but the time of counting varies with the number of daylight hours in the various seasons; the fourth count is taken by the 3:00 P.M. to 11:00 P.M. shift at 8:30 each evening; and to complete the official count cycle, a fifth count is made at 11:35 P.M. by the 11:00 P.M. to 7:00 A.M. shift.

In addition to these regular counts, the Warden may order an emergency count by sounding the siren while inmates are at their assignments, etc. The purpose behind this is to see how quickly all inmates can be returned to the cell houses, then counted and the total figure reported to the Captain's Office.

At the time of each count a Lieutenant is stationed in the Captain's Office or the Guard Hall to receive, compile and record the count. There are two methods of relaying necessary information to the Lieutenant conducting the count. Officers in the cell houses, hospital, and Detention Hospital, may phone in their counts. Officers in the immediate vicinity of the Captain's Office deliver their count slips personally. Officers who relay their counts by telephone must follow up by sending in signed count slips, or count books. When the Guard Hall officer phones in his count he must also report the exact total of inmates in the institution at that particular moment, this information being obtained from the official count center, the Record Office.

After all assignments have turned in their respective counts, the Lieutenant conducting the count must confirm the submitted figures. If the count should fail to check, the Lieutenant must notify the Chief Guard, who in turn will order a recount. Counts will be repeated either until they check or until further instructions from the Chief Guard or the Warden. If the count is correct, the day's routine will begin or continue in the usual manner. However in the event of bad weather conditions, such as fog, a severe storm, or limited visibility, the daily routine will be suspended until such conditions improve..

In a general sense the operation of the institution count resembles the system of accounting used by a bank in keeping track of deposits and withdrawals. When a new inmate is received at the Diagnostic Depot, he is immediately added to the total institutional count. When an inmate is released from the prison by parole, discharge, writ or transfer, he is immediately removed from the institution count. The Record Office must keep an accurate daily count of the total number of inmates in the institution. A count of the number of inmates on each and every assignment is kept at the Senior Captain's Office. It is these records against which the assignment counts are checked.

The various cell houses might be likened to a teller's window in a bank. An officer may withdraw a specified number of inmates to perform necessary work on an assignment. This number of inmates is debited to him on the count slips made out at the cell house door. At the termination of his shift the officer must return either the same number of men he took from the cell house, or whatever number he has, and make a proper accounting of those absent from his line.

When an Officer leaves the cell house with an inmate or a group of inmates in his charge, he will be given a count slip on which is listed the name of the assignment and the total number of inmates assigned. In the "out" column of the count slip will also be listed the number of men working, tool men, sick call, hospital, details, Isolation, Detention, lay-ins and tickets. Numbers listed after the first two items on the count slip—"Tool Men" and "Working"—represent the actual number of men taken out of the cell house by the officer. The figures behind the other items represent the number of men from the assignment who are at the locations designated on the count slip, such as, hospital, isolation, etc. The total of the numbers so listed must equal the number of men assigned. In other words, the figure listed at the bottom of the count slip after the words "total count" must be the same as the figure listed at the top of the slip after the word "Assigned."

Any changes in the count that occur while the officer has inmates out on an assignment must be recorded on the count slip. If, for instance, an inmate is timed out from his assignment on a ticket, the inmate's number, destination and time of departure must be listed on the back of the count slip. If the inmate does not return to his assignment before the officer takes his line back to the cell house, the officer must list the inmate in the "In" column of the count slip after the word *ticket* and reduce the number after the word *Working*. By the same token any additions to the count, such as men returning from sick call, isolation, etc., must be noted in the "In" column of the count slip. Suppose, for instance, three men were on sick call when the line left the cell house and two of them were later brought back to their work assignment. The officer would increase the number of men "working" by two and decrease the number of men on sick call by two. This would keep his count correct and provide the desired information as to the whereabouts of the inmates.

There are other general precautions which must be observed by officers when they are making counts. One is that an actual physical count of every inmate must be made. The officer must never assume that an inmate is where he should be, nor take any-one's word that he is. Another is that all counts are to be made by custodial personnel, never by an inmate. And any information relating to counts must be conveyed directly from an officer to an officer, not from an officer to an inmate clerk. Finally officers must guard against any tendency to let counting become routine. The fact that an officer has counted 46 men on a certain assignment for a number of days in a row is no indication that there will be 46 men on that assignment the next time he counts it; but he may let carelessness arrive at that count, if he expects to, unless he is keenly observant. No matter how familiar an officer is with his assignment and the men on it, he should make each count as care-fully as though it were his first. An accurate count of the inmates is so vital to institutional security that there can be no allowance made for laxity or error.

REPORTS OF INFRACTIONS

It cannot be too heavily stressed that discipline is an absolute requirement for the successful operation of a penal institution. But discipline should be constructive rather than punitive in nature and the person charged with enforcing it should be certain that he fully understands the meaning of the term.

The modern definition of discipline is not "punishment," but "training which corrects, molds, strengthens or perfects." In other words, the purpose of discipline is to secure the inmate's coöperation.

You want the inmate to do something, you tell him to do it, and he responds. That is discipline. Of course, this is a simplified illustration.

In addition to obeying reasonable orders, the inmate must refrain from pursuing a course of action based on his own initiative. It is the responsibility of every employee to see that the rules of the institution are observed. Usually this can be done by careful supervision, counsel, and an occasional reprimand or warnings when necessary. Since most inmates are interested simply in "doing their own time" with as little friction as possible, harsh measures are seldom necessary. Many infractions of the rules can be prevented by a timely warning or a word of caution. The officer who feels compelled to write frequent disciplinary reports may be relying on something other than good judgment and proper supervision in the management of his assignment.

Sometimes, however, it becomes necessary to report an inmate for serious violations of the rules or for repeated minor infractions. When the necessity arises, the officer should be entirely certain of his facts and be ready to support them. In writing a lengthy report, it is helpful to make notes at the time of the incident or immediately afterward, especially where several inmates are involved. These notes not only help in the writing of the report but will serve as reminders at a later date in the event of an investigation.

When submitting a report, the officer must keep in mind that the persons who will receive the report know absolutely nothing about the incident and for that reason are dependent on his version of the affair. The reports must, therefore, be complete and accurate. They should contain only those facts known to the officer, not hear-say or suspicion.

In writing a disciplinary report, an officer should make no attempt to interpret, analyze or construe the facts. Instead, he is to make a clear and simple report of what he actually heard and observed. He must include the Date, Time, and Place of the incident and the Names and Numbers of the inmates involved.

When a report concerns more than one inmate, an extra copy must be made for each inmate mentioned. The reason for this is that a copy of the report must be filed in the record jacket of each inmate named in the report. If the violation is of a serious nature, such as involving the use of weapons, sex perversion, assaulting an officer, or anything of a comparably serious nature, copies of the report must also be sent to the warden and the assistant wardens, as well as the senior captains.

When a report is written on an inmate who has been taken to the Detention Hospital for observation, copies must be sent to each of the following:

Criminologist
Warden (2 Copies)
Assistant Wardens
Senior Captain (Isolation)
Prison Physician
Detention Hospital Keeper

The language of a report must always be in good taste insofar as the reporting officer is concerned. However, when some remark or statement made by the participants in an affair has a bearing on the case, that remark should be quoted word for word, no matter how vulgar or obscene it may be. In cases of sexual perversion there are proper clinical terms to use in describing the acts performed. If necessary, a superior officer should be consulted on the wording of the report; but it must not contain vulgar language.

When reporting inmates for fighting, officers should include all details of the fight—who the agitator was, who struck the first blow, what the fight was about, what (if any) weapons were used, and by whom. If there were weapons involved, they should be secured and preserved for evidence without altering their condition in any degree. Fortunately, violations as serious as these are not predominant. The most common violations of the rules are talking or smoking in line, leaving food on the table, having a dirty cell, oversleeping, etc. Violations of this nature should be handled calmly and through the regular channels. And their disposition shall be entirely the responsibility of the Disciplinarian.

After a report has been submitted, the inmate or inmates concerned will be summoned to the Captain's Court. There the disciplinary report will be read to the inmate and he will be given an opportunity to affirm or deny the charges, or plead mitigating circumstances. Having heard both sides of the story, the Disciplinary Captain will dispose of the case according to policies promulgated either by law, by the Department of Public Safety, or by the Warden and his administrative staff. Depending on the nature of his violation, the inmate may be reprimanded and ex-

Captains Burris and King holding court. Stateville Branch.

cused, deprived of privileges, or be isolated or segregated. In instances where the inmate violates any criminal law or statute, he will be arraigned before the Circuit Court of Will County and tried for the offense, just as any other suspected criminal would be. If found guilty, he will be given an additional sentence.

But, disciplinary reports are not the only kind of reports that an officer may write. Inmates also perform meritorious services, such as volunteering for medical research, fire fighting, aiding an employee whose life is threatened, reporting hazardous conditions, finding and turning in a dangerous weapon, or in some way making an unusual sacrifice or contribution to the welfare of the institution or the employees and inmates thereof. When this occasion arises, employees must report the event, giving all the facts and details just as in any other type of report. A copy of the report will be filed in the inmate's record jacket, which is available to the Parole and Pardon Board. Although no one connected with the prison is permitted to make recommendations to the Board of Pardons and Paroles, the Board can examine the record which the inmate makes for himself, whether it be good or bad.

INFORMATION ABOUT INMATES

Everyone in the chain of command, from the Warden to the newest custodial officer, should consider and pass on to the employees directly concerned any information acquired, relative to the security, health, emotional and mental status of the inmates.

Security involves many things—trying to escape, inciting riots, sex relationships, starting fires ... and other more common violations of the rules such as pilfering, conniving and agitating. Inmates caught instigating the most serious of these violations will be placed in lower conduct grades and denied some of the privileges enjoyed by other inmates. To make it easy for custodial personnel to identify and watch these inmates, colored shingles will be placed over their cell doors. A *red* Shingle means that the inmate has been involved in an escape plot. A *blue* Shingle covers a range of other serious offenses. Every officer is to acquaint himself with the full implications of the colored shingle and to observe closely its possessors. Cell house keepers are given detailed information on these inmates and should make it available to their relief and to the assignment officer having supervision of any inmate who is in grades.

Some inmates may try to get together on an assignment in order to steal tobacco, candy and other personal property belonging to their fellow inmates; or they may attempt to steal and peddle state commodities. If there are on any assignment inmates who are suspected to be engaged in such activities, the guard should notify the other officers working on or near the assignment so that they, too, may keep watch over the suspects. The senior captain should also be notified *in writing*. He will then advise as to what procedure to follow.

If a guard is working on a plan to apprehend certain inmates suspected of stealing or conniving, this information should not only be given to the Senior Captain but it should also be passed on to the officer who relieves the guard on his day off; and it may be well to advise late shift employees. It does no good to keep inmates under surveillance six days a week and allow them to go unwatched on the seventh. Sex acts, escapes, riots, etc., can take place any time. And it must be remembered that the inmates watch the movements of the guards just as closely as the guards watch theirs.

Therefore alertness is required at all times, and any information compiled must be distributed to all officials concerned. Anything potentially serious, should be reported to the supervising officer, who will advise on the proper procedure in dealing with the situation.

Whenever a guard is going to be absent from an assignment because of vacations or other reasons, he should get in touch with his superior, who may advise him to pass on information to the officer scheduled to substitute for him. There is always something that he will need to know, for all assignments have an inmate or inmates who bear special watching. The passing on of such information is not only for the benefit and protection of the officer who goes on the post, but it also is a safeguard to the continuing security of the institution.

If there are on an assignment inmates who are always bickering and arguing, the Senior Captain should be notified, so that the inmates may be separated. Transferring one or both of them to other assignments will not only prevent trouble between inmates, but it may also prevent more serious trouble, such as inmates taking sides in a quarrel, getting the assignment in an uproar, or perhaps starting a full-scale riot. A guard must immediately notify his superior officers of any incident occurring on an assignment, no matter how trivial it may seem.

In the event that an inmate on the assignment becomes ill, it is important that there be no delay in notifying a superior officer or the doctor so that the inmate may be quickly examined. Even if the guard believes the inmate is "gold-bricking,' he should notify the supervising officers and the doctor; for if he proceeds on the assumption that the inmate is "gold-bricking," the guard might in some instance fail to secure medical attention for an inmate who was critically ill and thereby assume the responsibility for his death. Nothing like that should be allowed to happen when medical attention is available and can often prevent such a tragedy.

Guards will also come in contact with inmates who have grave personal problems. For instance, there may have been a death in the inmate's immediate family, or a member of his family may be seriously ill, or his wife may be divorcing him. Under circumstances such as these, a guard's wisest course may be to advise the inmate to seek spiritual aid from his chaplain. Frequently the chaplains, who are experienced in dealing with bereaved persons, are able to turn the inmate's thoughts upward and prevent him from becoming a disciplinary problem.

An ordinarily well behaved inmate may become ill natured or behave in an unusual manner which might indicate that he is under an emotional strain. In such cases the Senior Captain should always be notified, so that he may talk to the inmate or refer him to the Mental Health Department for examination if that course appears necessary. The guard's report of such an incident must be submitted in writing to the Warden, the Assistant Wardens, the Senior Captains and the Mental Health Department.

The problems cited herein are but a few of the many which daily confront the officials of this institution. In order to meet and deal effectively with all of them it is necessary that every employee report in writing pertinent information concerning the fractious, ill, or despondent inmates on his assignment. Every officer should always keep on his person a notebook wherein he can put down reminders to consult fellow employees and supervising officers on matters of importance to inmates, to the proper operation of his assignment, or to the administrative officers. A passing thought is no substitute for concrete action.

USE OF FIREARMS

The Illinois State Penitentiary was one of the first penal institutions to initiate a program of instruction in the safe handling and use of firearms. Back in 1937, a firing range was created in the Rock Quarry at the Joliet Branch. All new officers, whether assigned to Stateville or Joliet, were taken there for training and practice with the weapons they might be called upon to use. As late as 1941, only seven other state penal systems and the Federal Bureau of Prisons had any type of program for instructing officers in the techniques of marksmanship.

In 1944, the use of the firing range at the Rock Quarry was discontinued in favor of practice firing from the wall towers. This decision was in part made because of the factor of illusion well known to experienced riflemen—that aiming down at a target from a point considerably above it produces a misleading sight image which generally causes the marksman to shoot over his target. Since a tower officer would have to compensate for this visual distortion, it was decided that practice firing from the wall towers would benefit officers more than practice over a level range.

Each tower is equipped with two 30-30 Winchester lever action rifles, and a 38 caliber revolver. Every male employee is required to become proficient in the use of these weapons.

During the course of training, new officers receive instructions on the safe handling, care and use of firearms, together with demonstrations and coaching by the Lieutenant in charge. The following is an outline of the points covered in the weapons course:

1. The safe handling of firearms:

(a) A weapon must never be cocked until the actual time of firing.

(b) Do not place finger on trigger until ready to fire.

(c) Never point a gun in any direction where accidental discharge will cause injury to persons or damage to property.

(d) Weapons must always be treated as though they were loaded. They are.

(e) Keep the magazine of the weapon fully loaded, but *do not* keep a live round in the firing chamber.

(f) Cartridges must be removed from the magazine by hand. Do not "jack" them through the action, as jamming or accidental firing might result.

2. The care of firearms:

(a) Be sure there is no dirt or other obstructions in the bore of the weapon.

(b) Weapon must be kept clean and properly lubricated.

(c) Ammunition must be kept free of oil and grease, or any foreign material.

3. Instructions in aiming and sighting:

(a) How to hold a weapon.

(b) How to align sights.

(c) How to regulate breathing.

(d) How to squeeze the trigger.

4. Instructions in rules at the range:

(a) Only the person firing and the Lieutenant in charge of instruction will be permitted on the catwalk of the tower.

(b) When not shooting, officers must remain inside the tower and not interfere in any way with the man on the firing line.

(e) The commands of the Lieutenant in charge of firearms instruction relative to beginning, ceasing fire and to safe positioning of the gun must be obeyed implicitly.

Whenever the Lieutenant in charge feels that an officer has satisfactorily completed preliminary training, he will direct the officer to fire for qualification, or record.

In firing for record, official targets are used. One target of ten shots slow fire and one target of ten shots rapid fire are used in scoring accuracy with each weapon. Rifles are fired at a range of 75 to 100 yards and revolvers at 30 to 45 yards.

The final results of record firing are tabulated by the Lieutenant in charge of firearms instruction. Both rifle and revolver percentages are compiled and averaged to determine the officer's final standing. The official score is then compiled and made a part of the officer's record.

Throughout the period of his employment at the institution, each officer must maintain or improve his marksmanship by periodic practice. He must fire a qualifying round of targets at least twice a month if assigned to towers or detail. In order that practice may be had under condition that might simulate an attempted escape, qualifying rounds are frequently ordered during the course of a rain or snow storm, on foggy days, or at night.

Conditions such as these are a real test of the shooter's ability.

But training in the use of firearms is just one phase of the program. There are two others equally as important—keeping possession of weapons and knowing when to use them.

Learning to control weapons so they cannot fall into the hands of an inmate is the second phase of the weapons course. It is emphasized to new employees that weapons must never be carried in proximity to inmates. With the exception of guns kept in the towers or those actually in use, all weapons are kept secure in the Armory, from which they will be issued in case of need.

To arm the Yard and Dining Room towers, which are manned only in the daytime, weapons and ammunition are carried through an underground tunnel, never across the yard. When officers assigned to these towers finish their shift, they return the weapons to the Armory by the same route.

Weapons used in the few wall towers which are not manned at night are taken to the nearest wall tower manned on a twenty-four hour basis.

Tower officers are especially cautioned not to lean or lay their guns in such a way that they could possibly fall out of the tower and into the yard. But if such an accident should occur, they are instructed to cover the weapon with their reserve gun while they notify a superior officer, and to keep it covered until the superior can retrieve it. As a further precaution against such an accident, tower officers must never unload all guns at the same time, for cleaning or any other purpose. Neither may an officer, except those assigned to the Armory, disassemble a weapon for any reason whatsoever. If a weapon is not functioning properly, the towerman must call the Armory and not undertake to repair the weapon himself.

However to insure their remaining in proper working order, all guns kept in the wall towers are used from time to time in conducting target practice. And it is the tower officer's duty to clean his weapons *one at a time* soon after they have been fired. Weapons used elsewhere are cleaned in the Armory.

The third and final phase of the weapons course deals with the matter of judgment in using firearms. For one thing, officers are cautioned to take the danger of ricochets into consideration. A bullet fired at a hard surface such as concrete, or even the firmly packed surface of the recreation fields, might glance off and injure an innocent person—even a fellow officer. The same unhappy result could be achieved by getting excited and firing wildly into a crowd, or by firing at a mutinous inmate when there are other persons in the line of fire. A high powered rifle bullet could easily pass through three or four persons.

The question of when to use firearms poses a fine point. By hesitating too long in a critical situation, an officer might fail his duty; by getting excited and firing wildly or too soon, he might take life unnecessarily.

There are two situations in which the issues would seem fairly clear. If an Officer or an inmate is being assaulted with a deadly weapon, the attack must be stopped in time; if an inmate actually attempts to scale the wall or to force an exit, he must be stopped.

In all situations the armed officer should be positive that shooting is the only method by which a threat to the security of the institution or to the safety of its employees and inhabitants can be resolved.

The training an officer receives can teach him how to handle a gun safely, how to keep it in working order, how to shoot it accurately, and how to maintain possession of it. The question of when to use it is not quite so simple. For that reason tower officers are selected both for their ability as marksmen and their apparent good judgment — a quality that can only be estimated until proven by trial.

USE OF GAS

In suppressing disturbances, the use of irritant gases is more humane than the use of firearms. These gases cause no serious or permanent damage to those on whom they are used. Unless there has been prolonged exposure to intense concentrations, the physical discomfort caused by tear gas lasts only a short time, varying from a few minutes to a few hours. Yet, tear gas provides an effective means of subduing a man or a group of men. The psychological effect of tear gas is also important, for the same man who will endure pain without complaint may panic when his vision becomes impaired.

There are two types of gas stored in the Armory for use in the event of a serious disturbance—tear gas and sickening gas. The latter is sometimes known as "K.O." gas, and is used only when ordered by the Warden or Assistant Wardens. In addition to being kept in the Armory for emergency use, tear gas is also kept in the yard and dining room towers.

Tear gas affects the tear producing glands in the eyes, causing the eyes to water. It also produces a burning sensation that makes it almost impossible to open the eyes after a few moments exposure. Its effect on the skin is to cause a burning, smarting sensation that is intensified in warm weather or whenever the pores of the skin are open.

Sickening gas has a more severe effect on the person exposed to it. It causes a burning sensation to the nose and throat, choking and vomiting. Prolonged exposure will result in a sickening headache. However, since the effects of sickening gas are not as immediate as tear gas, the two are sometimes combined in gas grenades to achieve fast and positive results. Gas should be used only in the event of a serious disturbance by an inmate or a group of inmates, and for the purpose of compelling them to leave a particular room, dormitory, dining room or section of the institution. It may also be used in cutting off access to a particular section of the institution. For instance, should a major disturbance arise in the dining room, the objective would be to get the inmates to return to the cell houses where they could be locked in the cells as quickly as possible to prevent the disturbance from spreading. To accomplish this it might be necessary to use tear gas or sickening gas. However, the latter type must not be used unless ordered by the Warden or one of his assistants. In event of a major disturbance the only place that inmates will be permitted to go is to their cell houses, and the towermen are to use every means at their disposal to prevent inmates from going into any of the shops or assignments other than cell houses.

Gas may also be used to subdue inmates who get out of control in the yard or to disperse a mass attack on any of the gates or towers. But when gas is used in the open, the user must take care not to become the victim. He must remember that gas is carried by the prevailing breeze and could envelop the person using it. Then, too, there is the danger of a gas grenade being thrown back at the user.

To lessen the danger of having an officer overcome by gas, there is a large stock of Army style gas masks kept in the Armory, to be issued with other gas equipment. Gas masks are standard equipment in the towers where gas weapons are kept, and the officers are instructed as to the proper fitting and adjustment of masks.

Another measure to insure against the "boomeranging" of gas weapons is to use gas grenades with quick fuses and explosive containers.

The safe procedure to follow in using gas grenades is to hold the grenade in the throwing hand with the release lever pressed firmly into the palm of the hand. Then, with the free hand the cotter pin can be pulled from the fuse by running the finger through the ring attached to the pin and pulling straight away from the grenade. As long as the release lever is held firmly to the side of the grenade, the grenade will not explode. If desired, the cotter pin can be reinserted, making the grenade safe once more. However, as a rule the cotter pin should not be pulled unless there is an intention to throw the grenade.

The contents of gas grenades can be identified by the color of the containers: Tear gas grenades are red, and sickening gas or tear gas combined with sickening gas is green or olive drab in color.

*Federal—Blast Dispersion—*Color: Red and Silver. Explodes with one disintegrating blast that completely destroys the container, releasing all of the gas at the point of explosion. This type eliminates an object or container that could be thrown back.

Federal—Triple Chaser—Color: Solid Red. Equipped with two second fuse. This grenade breaks into three parts and from each part tear gas is released through vents with such force that the piece works on the order of jet propulsion, flying about the area and emitting gas in a white cloud form. The Triple Chaser not only breaks into three parts but also performs the triple function of spreading gas over a large area, of eliminating the danger of throwbacks, and of creating additional harassment in that the direction of the pieces cannot be determined. CAUTION : *The pieces of the Triple Chaser may take fire and burn and since they may travel several hundred feet before catching fire, they present a definite fire hazard.*

Lake Erie—Model 34 (New Style)—Blast Type: Equipped with 1¾ seconds fuse delay, this grenade discharges with only one blast, forcing the gas out through the vent holes in the sides, and it is considered safe from starting fires. However, it may serve as an object that can be thrown at someone after it has been discharged. All Lake Erie gas is invisible.

Lake Erie—Jumper Repeater: Equipped with two seconds fuse delay, this grenade discharges with three successive blasts. As each blast occurs, the grenade jumps ten or twelve feet to a different and unexpected point. The first blast of gas occurs two seconds after the grenade leaves the hand and the two succeeding blasts at one second intervals. If this gas gets on any article of clothing worn by the victim, it gradually vaporizes and continues to gas the victim and his associates. By discharging in three separate blasts, this grenade also serves a triple purpose, spreading gas over a large area, making it impossible to throw back (without the thrower being severely gassed), and last but not least, tending to have a great psychological effect. This grenade is not a fire hazard.

In addition to grenade type dispensers, there are several other means by which gas can be discharged. In police work the most common method is to use gas cartridges fired from a weapon designed specifically for the purpose. Three separate types of gas guns are kept ready for use in the institution if the need should arise. They are as follows:

Gas Club: The gas club is very effective at short range. It shoots a shell the same size as a 12 gauge shotgun, the difference being that it is loaded with gas. The gas spreads over a limited area because the capacity of the shell is not great.

25 MM: The 25 mm shell is shot from a gas pistol made especially for the purpose. It works on the same order as the gas club. Although the 25 mm gas cartridge can be used only at short range, it has more capacity than the shell used in the gas club.

37 MM: There are a variety of shells for this gas gun. One, designed for use at a range of 20 to 30 feet, releases the gas when fired. It is very effective. Another short range projectile has a two to four second fuse and explodes on impact. Then there is a long range shell which has a maximum range of approximately 360 yards. It, too, explodes upon impact. Since this shell is the type used for shooting through doors and barricades, it is very dangerous and must never be shot directly at a man or group of men.

Tear gas may also be obtained in large capacity cylinders equipped with a valve that can be turned on and off at will. Where inmates are barricaded in a cell, a room or a building, *cylinder gas* would prove very effective in dislodging or subduing them. In a situation of that kind the gas should be turned on for about one minute; then officers should wait five minutes before going in. By that time the inmates will have had more than they want and will be ready to surrender.

When Federal gas is used, however, there is a possibility of inmates using garden or fire hoses to wash it out of the air. Having a powder base, the Federal gases can be rendered ineffective by a fine spray of water. This problem can be met in one of two ways: by turning off the water for that particular building or by using Lake Erie gas which, having a liquid base, is not affected by water.

In choosing the type of gas to use, some consideration must be given to whether or not it will be necessary to use the building soon afterwards. The liquid based gas is more difficult to clean up because it continues to give off fumes until it has completely evaporated. And the acid quality of the liquid may cause considerable irritation to the skin. The process of evaporation can be speeded up by washing the area with hot water and giving it a prolonged airing.

To rid a building of the powder based gas, it is best to blow out the fumes with a fan before they have a chance to settle. But if that cannot be done, then the best procedure is to wash everything down with hot water and washing soda or a five percent solution of trisodium phosphate. There should be a suction fan to pull the fumes out of the building as the gas crystals are dissolved by the hot water.

Another, and perhaps more practicable method of clearing gas from a building, is to heat the building as much as possible and use fans to pull out the gas fumes.

If an officer should be accidentally exposed to tear gas he should not become alarmed. It positively has no permanent or serious effect on anyone. In fact, one can even become immune to low concentrations of tear gas if he breathes it for long periods.

In weak solution tear gas smells like apple blossoms, but will make the eyes burn and tears flow. In high concentrations tear gas causes both the eyes and nasal passages to burn and tears to flow so heavily that it is nearly impossible to open the eyes, or to see when they are opened.

The best way to recover from the effects of tear gas is to stand facing a breeze with the eyes open. The eyes should never be rubbed or dabbed with a handkerchief as that merely increases the irritation. After the worst effects of the gas have been dissipated, the eyes may be washed out with pure water or soothing eye drops. Skin areas which sting or burn should be washed with soap and water. No other treatment should be necessary.

PREVENTION OF RIOTS

In recent years there have been an unprecedented number of riots and disturbances in the prisons of the United States. Occurrences such as these are the concern of every prison administrator and his staff even though they may have taken place in a distant state. Failure to prevent riots and disturbances, or to control them with efficiency and dispatch, is a reflection on all penal institutions, for the public's knowledge of prisons is not extensive and its opinions of them are formed from reading or listening to the stories that are considered news—usually accounts of violent and dramatic events. As those of us who are actively engaged in prison work know, such events are far from representative of the normal prison scene. Yet, when mass violence does occur in prison, it is destructive of life, of property, and of the public's confidence in the penal program of the nation and of individual states.

In order to protect life and property, the administration of every prison has an obligation (a) to follow a program designed to eliminate the causes of riots and (b) to develop a plan to control riots with as little loss of life and property as possible, if they occur despite well-intentioned efforts to prevent them.

The first step in preventing riots is to keep informed of what the inmate body is thinking and how it is feeling. There are a number of ways in which the administration is enabled to keep its fingers on the pulse of the inmate body: the reports of officers and staff members are one means; the tabulation and analysis of disciplinary reports are another, because the composite behavior of inmates is a good barometer of their morale and censorship of inmate mail is invaluable in this respect.

However, since knowledge without deeds is useless, the administration must do more than keep informed. Within the dictates of sound policy it must also act on its knowledge. Legitimate grievances must be corrected, just as baseless agitation must be prevented.

In an institution where there is fair treatment, adequate amounts of wholesome food, and an opportunity to participate in a constructive program of work or training, the majority of inmates want no part of a riot.

Most disturbances are engineered by an element of the prison population which is interested, not in correcting any grievances that may exist, but in turning a riot to personal advantage, such as using it to cover an escape attempt or the settlement of grudges, etc. These agitators and troublemakers are seldom found in the forefront of a disturbance. Their forte is manufacturing the "bricks" which are tossed by unwitting "chumps" who, often as not, are unaware of the real motivation behind their acts. If the riot fails, as it invariably does, the instigators are content to sit back and let the "hot heads" reap the consequences.

But the concern of a prison administration is to prevent trouble. That can be best achieved by learning the identity of agitators and keeping them under close surveillance, perhaps placing them on assignments where they have limited contact with other inmates, or even segregating them completely if the circumstances warrant that measure.

The program of fair treatment and close supervision has successfully averted major disturbances in the Stateville-Joliet prison units for many years. This is cause for gratification, but not for complacency. All must endeavor to make the program a continued success, but be prepared to meet any emergency that may arise.

The institution's *Emergency Plan* is printed in booklet form and a copy of it is on every assignment. Employees must study the emergency plan and be certain that they understand the procedures to be put into effect in the event of a storm, a fire, or a riot. The existence of an emergency will be made known either by the wailing of a siren, by successive short blasts of the steam whistle, or by word of mouth.

A key feature of the institution's plan for suppressing riots is the mobilization of emergency squads at each branch of the institution. These squads, consisting of twelve men each, are thoroughly trained in the use of all weapons and constitute a mobile task force which can form and equip itself within a matter of minutes. Well trained and heavily armed, the emergency squads can quickly reach the scene of a disturbance and restore order before a full scale riot or insurrection can get under way.

The concept of an insurrection is not unlike that of a fire. If it can be attacked promptly and with sufficient personnel and equipment to contain it in the area of initial combustion, it will be relatively easy to suppress and little damage will result. But, if through dilatory or inadequate measures, it is allowed to gain momentum and spread to surrounding areas, then a greater effort will be needed to gain control and the cost in destruction will be multiplied.

For this reason the emergency squads have purposely been designed as fast moving units which make up in training and equipment what they lack in size. In many respects they are similar to wartime commando units.

Although each member of an emergency squad is trained in the use of firearms and gas equipment, there are on each squad men chosen for their knowledge of the entire lock and key system, for their ability to operate cutting torches, for their experience with fire fighting equipment, and so forth. The result is a versatile squad capable of dealing with any type of emergency, whether it be suppressing a disturbance, fighting a fire, or conducting rescues after a disaster.

Since the existing squads are well trained and under the command of either a Captain or a Lieutenant, it would seem pointless to attempt to detail their instructions, which in fact must remain flexible enough to accommodate the circumstances that may exist in any unusual situation. But the knowledge that these emergency squads can be mobilized, equipped, and sent to the scene of an emergency or disturbance within a few minutes should be reassuring to every employee, as well as to the public.

In the belief that it will serve as a deterrent to possible adverse behavior, information similar to this is given new inmates during the Orientation Program. They are cautioned against becoming the tools of agitators and warned not to become involved in any disorder. To avoid becoming implicated in a disturbance not of their making, the inmates are instructed to proceed immediately to their cells, or to some cell, and shut the door. That would leave only the active participants in a disturbance to be dealt with by the emergency squads.

A thought worth remembering is that if every employee supervises his assignment according to the rules and regulations, and reports any unusual actions such as moodiness, evasiveness, formation of small cliques, defiance or slowness in carrying out orders, or refusal to work, and if an employee studies and knows his men, as well as observes and reports everything of an unusual or suspicious nature to supervising officials, it is unlikely that the emergency squads will ever have to be called into action.

PREVENTION OF FIRES

Every year many persons who believe themselves to be safety conscious suffer serious injuries or even worse, because of the mild interest exercised in the performance of their daily activities, thus making their tasks haphazard ones. All prison employees should be urged to *wake up, supervise,* and *instruct.*

They must command respect of subordinates by showing a superior knowledge of modus operandi, or "know how."

They should have all mechanical appliances securely fastened, all stock piling constructively safe, allowing a minimum 20-inch clearance from the ceiling to permit the fire department to work efficiently.

Every employee must be familiar with the location of fire extinguishers and hose cabinets; they should check their position daily until they can go to them automatically without having to stop and think about their location.

Operating instructions are clearly printed on each and every fire extinguisher. Assignment officers are advised to read these instructions and to ask questions about the phase of fire extinguisher that they may fail to comprehend. In general, they are instructed to direct the stream of the discharge at the *base* of the flame, or at the *heart* of the fire, and that they must make the most of the extinguisher's capacity by using it properly. They are also cautioned as follows:

"Do not let fire hazards escape your attention. Stay alert to any situation which might cause a dangerous and costly fire. It is easy to grow unconcerned about rusty stove pipes, unemptied waste baskets, that bundle of old cleaning rags thrown in the corner; but these represent potential fires."

"Eliminate them from your assignment. Before going off duty at the end of a shift, inspect your assignment carefully to see that electrical appliances are disconnected and that there are no smoldering cigarette ends left lying around. Your vigilance will help prevent fires and you will be repaid in peace of mind."

Failure to report fire hazards makes the prison staff morally responsible for exposing the welfare and well being of men to possible dangers and quite probably for enormous property losses.

The prison staff should talk about emergencies, the time when coolness and patience are most needed. The composure of officials will have a quieting, reassuring effect on all employees and inmates. If a fire breaks out on an assignment, the officer in charge must immediately make the *fire call* and specify the exact location. All *fire calls* must be made to the *switchboard operator* who in turn should *call everyone concerned,* including the *Fire Department.*

In the event of fire the responsibility of guards towards their charges is clear cut. They must be removed to safe areas at once. The inmates are to be marched out of the building in an orderly manner, with as little commotion as possible. As soon as the line is out of the building, the officer is to make a count. The reasons for making an immediate and accurate count are twofold: It will assure the guard that all inmates and employees are safely out of the danger zone; it will help to prevent escapes or sabotage. If necessary, another officer should be called on to march the inmate line into the cell house. The guard must remain at his assignment until he is relieved by a superior officer or until the fire chief arrives to take over.

After the fire call has been made and the safety and security of the inmates accounted for, the guard should try to put the fire out, if it is at all possible. He must exercise care in the opening of windows or doors, unless they have to be used as avenues of escape, because these openings tend to create drafts which often fan the flames to greater proportions.

When the fire has been brought under control, a detailed report is to be sent to the Warden as soon afterwards as possible. It should state the exact location, the time, what was damaged, who discovered the fire (if an inmate, give his name and number), and any other pertinent information relative to the fire.

If employees understand the nature of a fire, they may better know how to combat it. The components of fire are *fuel, air,* and *heat.* If any of these elements are removed, the fire is quenched. It is, of course, rarely feasible to remove the fuel. For example, if a flame is feeding on a building, it would not ordinarily be wise to destroy the building in order to put out the fire. Therefore, extinguishing agents have been developed to eliminate either the oxygen or the heat. Carbon dioxide, dry chemical, and carbon tet act to choke off the oxygen. Result: The fire vanishes. Foam or water extinguishers put out the fire by removing the heat. But the only way to keep fuel from a fire is by keeping a clean assignment. If guards do not let inflammable materials accumulate, they cannot burn.

On some assignments it is, of course, necessary to keep inflammable materials, such as oil, grease, paint, etc. But if these materials must be kept on assignments, they positively must be stored in safe containers in a safe place, and every precaution exercised in handling them. Whenever employees are in doubt as to the inflammability of a substance, they are urged to seek information about it. If necessary, they should call the fire chief or a superior officer. These officials will advise whether the substance is dangerous and if so, how to handle and store it.

In conclusion, it should be pointed out that fires are listed in three categories: A, B and C.

Class "A" fires: wood, cloth, rubbish, etc.

Extinguishing agent: water, soda-acid and foam.

Class "B" fires: oil, gasoline, grease, paint, etc.

Extinguishing agent: dry chemical, carbon dioxide, carbon tet and foam.

Class "C" fires: Electrical equipment.

Extinguishing agents: dry chemical, carbon tet and carbon dioxide.

The watchword of every prison employee should be:

"REMEMBER . . . Don't assume that you can cope with the situation yourself and put out the fire, CALL THE FIRE DEPARTMENT."

TRANSPORTING INMATES

The handling of inmates while on transfer between institutions and while being taken to and from courts encompasses three categories:

First — Equipment:

When the Lieutenant gets a call or is notified that there is a transfer to be made, the first thing he must do is find out how many inmates are being transferred. Then he must call the Armory Officer and tell him how many chains will be required and the kind wanted. Also, how many cuffs will be needed, adding about three extra pairs as there are usually other inmates put on the transfer list at the last minute. Now that the cuffs and chains have been ordered, the Lieutenant in charge of the transfer can arrange for officers. If he is going to use the Mail Truck, he can get by with one officer; if he is going to use the Bus, he will need two officers. The officers should be reminded never to let an inmate fumble with the handcuffs as they can be opened very easily, not only with a key but also with a small piece of metal or plastic.

Second — Transportation and Records:

The Warden's Office should be requested to make arrangements for the Mail Truck or Bus and the Squad Car for the time set for the transfers. The officer in charge of transporting the inmates should make certain the vehicles are ready and waiting before taking the inmates to be transferred to the Guard Hall. After all arrangements have been made for chains, cuffs, and transportation, the officer in charge is to check the records and transfer orders to see that all are properly signed and to see that all watches, typewriters, and other personal possessions are ready to go with the inmates. There will be four (4) copies of the transfers from Stateville to the Joliet Branch or Diagnostic Depot, and four (4) copies for transfer from Joliet to Stateville, but only three (3) copies of transfers from the Diagnostic Depot to Stateville. The original goes to the Record Office; the second copy goes to the Senior Captain's Office; the third copy to the Guard Hall Officer; and the fourth copy goes with the transfer.

Third — Last, but Not Least, is the Safety of the Transfers:

The insuring of safety in transferring inmates should be undertaken systematically. When putting cuffs on an inmate, the officer should make sure they are put on right side up and are properly adjusted. The key hole on the cuffs should be toward the front or nearest the person putting on the cuffs. It must be ascertained that the inmate does not have a deformed, crippled or very small hand which might allow him to "slip" the cuff off. If he has a bad hand or wrist, he should be put on the other side of the chain so he cannot get loose from the chain or his cuffs. It must always be remembered that any man who has feet can and may run, and any man who has hands can and might put up a good scrap some place along the line. Guards should always regard each and every man they transfer as the most dangerous of all. And in that way they will avoid becoming careless.

When making a transfer with a Bus, as from Stateville to Menard, there should always be two officers in the Bus—one up in front on the right side; the other in the middle of the back seat. In these positions they can observe what is going on in the Bus. None of the officers in the Bus are armed . . . and never should be while in the Bus.

The officer or Lieutenant in the Squad Car behind the Bus should be armed and should have a bag containing equipment consisting of two (2) thirty-eight caliber pistols with ammunition for them; one gas club with extra shells. The Lieutenant in charge will have a 30-30 rifle in his hands at all times, and extra ammunition for same in the bag.

When putting on handcuffs, officers must make sure they are properly adjusted but not too tight, so as to avoid the need for changing them or loosening them on the way. When each cuff has been properly adjusted, the officer should be sure to "set the cuff" with the key so it cannot be tightened or loosened while in transit. A cuff set too tight, which may have to be loosened en route, can cause as much trouble as one that is too loose.

Officers must make sure that the inmates to be transferred have been carefully searched, that the cuffs are on and properly "set," that all the records and the personal property of the inmates are on the Bus and all accounted for, that the Bus is gassed and has plenty of oil, and that both of the State Police cars are ready. Officers must also see that the inmates are properly dressed and in winter, that blankets are on the Bus.

If the Bus has to stop for any length of time, other than for a "Stop Light" or "Stop Street," both sides of the Bus should be under close observation while it is stopped. Officers must always be alert to see that the inmates are getting along well, that they are seated and that there is no commotion in the Bus.

When leaving the Diagnostic Depot with a transfer, guards are ordered to call the Record Office and report they are leaving and the time. If going to Menard, they must on arrival call the Warden or Assistant Warden at Stateville and advise him of the time of arrival and anything of importance that happened on the way. If a breakdown should occur en route, the escort body must get word back to the institution, to the nearest state police station or to the sheriff of the county in which the breakdown occurs. The object, of course, would be to arrange supplemental transportation or to get additional help in guarding the prisoners until repairs can be effected.

When taking a prisoner into court, guards are urged always to take inventory of the court room for the exits, stairways, halls . . . any place where a man might try to get away. They must keep within reach of the man at all times, unless he is on the witness stand. A prisoner must *never* be permitted to go into a toilet or wash room alone. The guard must either stand in the doorway or accompany the prisoner into the wash room.

If a prisoner must be turned over to the sheriff or to the police, the guard must always get a receipt for the prisoner from the sheriff or the police chief as the case may be. When custody of the inmate is regained, the guard must search him thoroughly even though the jailor may give assurance that the prisoner is "clean." It is better to risk offending the jailor than to take a chance. Some visitor may have slipped the prisoner some type of contraband, even a gun. So, when it is known that a prisoner has received visits in the jail or in the bull pen, he must be searched with special care and thoroughness.

The guard should always make sure that he has the proper papers or records before leaving the Record Office with a man on transfer or writ, whichever the case may be.

If a judge continues the case to a later date, the guard should have the court clerk put the ruling of the court on the back of the writ showing the date and time the inmate is to appear in court. In all cases it should be requested that the action of the court be recorded on the back of the writ so that the Record Office may be notified promptly. If the inmate is remanded to the Warden that order should be recorded on the back of the writ.

When it is necessary to stop and feed the men in transit, the guards must always explore the possibility of arranging for an extra squad car or extra officers to secure the inmates while they are being fed.

Another point which must be borne in mind while transporting prisoners, is that when the vehicle being used for that purpose is parked, there is a possibility that someone may conceal weapons in the prisoner's seat or compartment.

When an inmate is being walked from one location to another, the lead chain should, if possible, be between the prisoner's legs. And whether in the institution or outside, the guard should always walk behind the inmate, never in front. The inmate should always precede the guard into an automobile, and no inmate should be permitted to sit directly behind or next to the driver of the car or bus, unless the vehicle is loaded so that other seating space is not available. The officer driving or sitting in the front seat must keep an eye on the prisoners at all times. He is to use the rear view mirror and to be especially watchful of men who fumble with their handcuffs. While wearing a gun, officers must be very careful not to sit, stand or walk next to an inmate. They must remember that a gun can be grabbed very quickly. Before an inmate enters a car or bus, officers are to conduct a preliminary search of the vehicle to make certain that no one has overlooked or concealed a weapon where the inmate might lay hands on it.

FUNCTIONS OF THE ARMORY

At each branch of the institution the Armory is the focal point of internal security. Within the Armory are kept the tools of institutional security—the keys, guns and gas. Since these devices protect the institution and are in turn secured at all times from inmates, it follows, then, that the Armory is by all odds the most vital and sensitive assignment within the institution.

Because officers assigned to the Armory have greater than ordinary responsibilities, they must be especially alert and cautious during every moment of their shift. They must follow implicitly the rules and regulations governing the operation of their assignment.

The Armories at Stateville-Joliet prisons are protected by two doors and the keys to both are kept inside the Armory. No one

Armory interior. This shows a small portion of arms, shells and weapons. Stateville Branch.

except personnel authorized by the Warden, the Assistant Wardens or the Chief Guard may gain admission. When an authorized person wishes to enter the Armory, the officer in charge hands him the key to the outside door. The incoming officer then enters the first door, locks it behind him and returns the key to the Armory Officer. Only then may the Armory Officer open the door admitting the approved officer to the Armory proper. In the event that a visitor to the institution should be authorized to enter the Armory, he is to be admitted only after the Warden or Assistant Warden accompanying him has entered and all doors have been locked behind him. Then the Warden or Assistant Warden escorting the visitor will notify the Armory Officer that the visitor has been officially authorized to enter the Armory. This procedure removes the possibility of an employee or administrative officer being used as a hostage to gain access to the Armory.

As a further precaution, the officer assigned to the Armory must always be certain that no inmates are near the Armory Door and that the Guard Hall gates are closed while anyone is entering or leaving the Armory.

Among the various duties of the Armory Officer, probably the most frequent one is that of issuing out and checking in keys to the officers in charge of all other assignments. Kept in theArmory are two identical keyboards, each containing a full set of keys for every assignment. Upon receipt of the assignment officer's identification tag, the Armory Officer issues him a set of keys and hangs the "dog tag" or receipt in their place. When a shift ends, this procedure is reversed. The Armory Officer puts the keys back on the proper hook and returns the identification tag or receipt to the officer who had the keys. Since the purpose of the duplicate keyboard is to insure that a set of keys will always be available for emergency use, the Armory Officer must promptly duplicate all keys which become worn or broken so he can be positive that the reserve set will work in the event of emergency.

When the service window to the Armory is not being used to issue or receive keys and other equipment, it must be kept securely locked. If the Armory Officer answers the phone or leaves the window for any purpose, the service window must be secured.

Other duties of the Armory Officer are manufacturing new keys, repairing arms and locks, and reloading ammunition. He must also keep a perpetual inventory of all the stock and equipment on hand and prepare quarterly requisitions for needed supplies.

A degree of mechanical ability is an asset to the Armory Officer. He must be able to operate the key making machine installed in the Armory; to make simple repairs on locks; to disassemble and inspect weapons, cleaning and oiling them when necessary; to check gas cannisters for leaks or deterioration of potency in storage; and to reload ammunition for the various firearms used for training purposes. The latter is a somewhat complicated process, involving the resizing of cartridge cases, the inserting of new primers, the accurate measuring of powder, and the crimping of new bullets. Dies, tools and powder scales provided for reloading must be used accurately.

Aside from the keys to the institutional assignments, the devices most frequently used are handcuffs and chains employed in transporting inmates to and from the institution. These must be kept in proper working order, ready for almost daily use. Since open handcuffs are easily damaged, officers should make sure they securely fasten them before placing them into the carrying bag. And it should be remembered that this type of equipment, properly used, can obviate the need for more drastic methods of restraint.

However, the Armory Officer must keep all of the equipment in proper condition so that it will be ready for any emergency that arises. The institution has trained "Emergency Squads," skilled in the use of all firearms and gas equipment. In the event that it is ever necessary to bring these "Emergency Squads" into action to quell a riot or prevent an escape, the officer in charge of the Armory will be instructed by the Warden or ranking official present as to the type of equipment to issue.

But, obviously, this equipment would be of little value unless it were functioning properly. To insure readiness for instant service, the Armory Officer must inspect all weapons returned from the firing range or the towers and make any minor repairs or adjustments that are necessary.

All weapons are kept loaded, ready for instant use. They must be handled safely. If any weapon requires extensive repairs, the Armory Officer must so report to the Lieutenant in charge, who will arrange for the weapon to be serviced by the manufacturer.

An adequate supply of ammunition for all weapons must be kept on hand in the Armory, and the various tear gas dispensers must be recharged at specified intervals. Fresh batteries must be kept in stock for all portable lighting equipment, including flashlights. These precautions will enable the Armory to supply the means of coping with any emergency.

It is especially important for the Armory Officer to brief relieving officers on any unusual circumstances or matters requiring prompt attention. Because the Armory is the repository for the equipment used to maintain institutional security, there should be and must be the fullest coöperation between officers assigned to the Armory. They have a common obligation to keep this equipment ready for use whenever it is needed and to keep it safe when it is not.

Employees assigned to the Armory must register in and out, showing the time and date of reporting to and leaving the assignment. While on duty they will frequently receive various items not related to the operation of the Armory, but deposited for temporary safe-keeping. Typical of such items would be contraband found during the night shifts, shipments of drugs and narcotics received at the institution after the pharmacist has left for the day, or money deposited by Lieutenants for the Red Cross and other charitable fund collections, etc. Officers assigned to the Armory must not open, examine or molest anything of this nature, but are to keep it safe and intact until claimed by the person or department to whom it properly belongs.

There is, however, one type of material which must never be accepted or taken into the Armory—INFLAMMABLES. All volatile substances are to be stored outside the walls, never in the Armory. And whenever any inflammable material is being brought into the institution through the Guard Hall, the service window to the Armory must be secured and every precaution taken to prevent "firing" the Armory, either accidentally or by design. A properly supervised Armory should be virtually impregnable. It could be immobilized by fire.

MAINTENANCE OF LOCKS AND KEYS

The security of the institution depends to very great extent upon the proper use of locks and keys. It is therefore essential that every lock and key be of a type best suited to meet the security requirements of the location at which they are used and that they be maintained in good working order.

In an institution of this size, where thousands of locks and keys are in constant usage, it is imperative to have an efficient system for the accounting and distribution of keys. The system used by the institution calls for two identical keyboards, each containing a complete set of keys for every assignment. These keyboards are, of course, kept in respective Armories of each branch of the institution.

When an officer draws the keys for his assignment, he is required to deposit his identification tag with the armory officer who hangs the "dog tag" or receipt on the vacated key ring hook. In this way it can be determined at a glance what keys are out and who has them. In the event that the officer who drew the keys from the Armory finds it necessary to give his keys to a relief officer, he must request the relief officer's "dog tag" or receipt. Then if he leaves the institution without retrieving the keys to his assignment, he can exchange the relief officer's "dog tag" or receipt for his own and the keys will then be properly charged out.

The Armory maintains a Key Book in which there is an accurate listing of the locks and keys on each assignment. In it the ring numbers, key numbers and the location and description of locks are given. An alphabetical and numerical index to all key rings and keys is plainly posted in the Armory to facilitate the handling and control of keys.

On the assignments themselves every lock is clearly identified with the Ring and Number of the key which operates that lock.

These numbers are, in nearly all cases, painted on the door imme-diately adjacent to the lock, though in a few instances the locks are identified only by the numbers stamped on them with a metal die. All keys are stamped in this fashion. For instance, there will be painted on the door of an assignment the legend "R-31 K-25." This means that the key which will open this lock is kept on Ring Number 31 and that the key itself is numbered 25. The key ring numbers, together with the name of the assignment to which the ring belongs, are stamped on a metal disc attached to the key ring. To simplify the problem of finding a particular key among others of similar appearance, keys must be placed on the key ring in numerical order, with the key ring tag serving as the divider between the lowest and highest numbered keys.

Because of the great number of locks and keys used through-out the institution care must be taken not to let obsolete keys accumulate. If a lock becomes broken, is condemned, or removed from an assignment, the armory officer must be notified, so that he can remove the keys for that lock from the ring belonging to the assignment. If this system were not followed, the key system would become confused and overburdened with a lot of useless and unaccountable keys.

On some assignments there are locks on doors and windows which are intended for emergency use only. These locks must be tried occasionally and if they fail to operate properly, that fact must be reported to the Lieutenant in charge of the Lock and Key System. Locks that are seldom used or locks that are ex-posed to the elements require periodic maintenance. They must be flushed with a solvent and lubricated with fresh graphite, but only an authorized person, such as the Lieutenant in Charge or an officer appointed by him is to do this. Many of the locks on important but seldom used openings, such as man hole covers, emergency exits, and electrical vault entrances, are equipped with flat type covers which give them a degree of protection but this should not eliminate the need for testing and maintenance. For, if they fail to open when needed, loss of human life or extensive property damage might be the result.

It may be of interest to know that the cost of maintaining the lock and key system at the Stateville-Joliet prisons, averages about $3,500 per year. In order to decrease the wear and tear on locks and keys officers should handle them carefully. When a padlock is dropped on the concrete floor, it will invariably strike near the hole into which the hasp fits, knocking it out of round and making the lock difficult or impossible to close. After a padlock has been opened it must be snapped back on the hook. Keys must also be handled with the utmost care, as they are made of light metal and will easily bend or break. A key must never be thrown to another person or skidded across the floor. Instead it should be carried to the other person, or he should come and get it. Keys to the various gates and to the cell house doors are in constant use and it is necessary that they operate smoothly at all times. Occasionally an officer will thoughtlessly slip into the habit of pushing the door open and pulling it closed with the key. This should never be done, for if the key should break off in the lock, there is a possibility that the part remaining inside the lock could not be removed and the entire lock would then have to be replaced. Keys are not intended for handles; door pulls are installed for that purpose. When, through normal wear, keys start to catch in the locks and operate with difficulty, they should be replaced. Continuous forcing of the keys in the locks will also cause them to break.

Although some inmates are issued keys to their tool boxes, work benches or desks, keys bearing any strategic importance must never be allowed in the hands of an inmate. It would be very easy for him to palm a piece of soap and make an impression of the key. And from the impression it would not be very difficult to make a duplicate key in any of the mechanical shops. If certain keys were duplicated, they would present a real threat to the security of the institution. If any were duplicated they would certainly result in the costly replacement of a number of locks. For these reasons officers must never carry their keys in such a way that they could be easily stolen nor place them where they could fall into the hands of an inmate. Keys must not be carried so as to permit visual inspection by the inmates, since a skilled mechanic might duplicate one by observation and memory, just as he can select a 3/16" drill bit by sight. Employees must also remember that a key can be made by smoking a piece of light metal or cardboard and fitting it into the locks. The pattern of the tumblers will show on the sooty surface of the material inserted into the lock, and a key can be made from the impression thus obtained. This makes it important not only to keep the keys away from the inmates, but also to keep the inmates away from the locks.

Every key in the institution must be properly accounted for at all times. The officer in charge of an assignment should know his exact key count, the lock number and location so that he can make an instant check of the keys to his assignment. However, he is required to keep on the assignment a "Key and Lock Location Card." These cards are checked periodically by the Lieutenant in Charge of Keys and Locks, when inspecting same on assignments. Any changes of locks and keys are to be made only with the approval of the Lieutenant or locksmith in charge of the Lock and Key System and the Armory Officers must be notified in writing of any such changes.

On the first Friday of every month each officer in charge of an assignment must fill out an official "Key Location Chart" form, noting any additions, replacements, or needed repairs, and forward it to the officer in charge of the Armory.

If a lock fails to function properly, this must be reported to the Lieutenant in Charge immediately. A lock is only as good as the supervision given it. Officers should always "try" a lock or door after locking it. This is a practical test which should reveal whether or not the lock is properly engaged.

WHAT IS CONTRABAND?

Speaking generally, contraband is "whatever comes into or goes out of the penitentiary without official sanction of the prison administration."

In practice this definition is extended to include items that are manufactured or altered without express permission of the administration, or any item found in a location other than the one to which it has been officially assigned.

Contraband. Display of different types of harmful items confiscated over
a period of years. Joliet Branch.

Many items are never permitted within the institution at any
time or for any reason. Articles of this nature, which include
guns, knives, money, and narcotics, fit into the first definition.
And, of course any uncensored communications or the smuggling
of any state property would fall into the same category.

Contraband manufactured within the prison takes an infinite
variety of forms. In Stateville-Joliet prisons' contraband Display
Boxes are dozens of potentially dangerous contraband items collected through the years. They range from black-jacks to soap
pistols. There are many kinds of contraband occasionally manufactured within the prison that are not included in the display.
For instance, alcoholic beverages are brewed from time to time,
but none are preserved for exhibit.

The ingredients of alcoholic brews might be cited as examples
of legitimate materials ingeniously converted to illegal use or

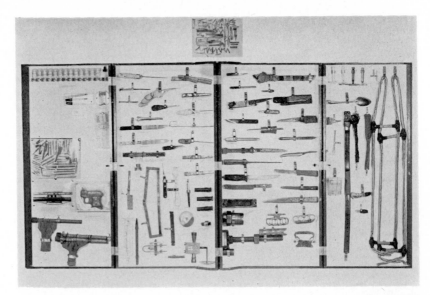

Contraband. 1959 display of different types of harmful items. Stateville Branch.

transported to an unauthorized location. Sugar, yeast, fruits, potatoes, etc., are staple items of food. Used or stored as intended, they are not contraband. But when they are stolen from the store rooms or kitchens and converted into liquor, they become contraband.

More pertinent examples would be common tools and equipment altered in such way that they become dangerous weapons. Nearly anything made of metal can be sharpened and transformed into a crude but effective knife. This is one of the reasons why tools and materials are so carefully guarded and so frequently counted. In the tool kit of an electrician a screwdriver is a constructive and necessary piece of equipment; in the hands of an inmate it can become a deadly weapon, fully as dangerous as a knife.

An ordinary machine bolt or an innocent looking length of pipe may be the component parts of a bar spreader. When searching a cell or an assignment, officers should collect all suspected items of contraband as they go through a location because, quite often, the best means of concealing an escape device, such as a bar spreader or a ladder, is to disassemble it and hide the parts in scattered locations.

Much of the contraband discovered within the institution is of the type mentioned thus far—legitimate items converted to illegitimate uses. However, that is not always the case. In the past, contraband has been successfully introduced from outside sources. And many unsuccessful attempts to do so have been made. Sometimes the offenders have been members of an inmate's family, but more frequently they have been criminal associates or confederates. For these reasons visitors to the institution are carefully screened, searched and supervised. All inmate correspondence is censored to prevent either the introduction of contraband or the development of escape plots.

The mail and visits of narcotics addicts require especially close scrutiny because of the various forms in which narcotics can be obtained and the ease with which they can be concealed. Available as liquids, tablets, powders and, in the case of marihuana, as cigarettes, narcotics are difficult to detect.

There is yet another type of contraband that deserves mention: regulation items, not harmful in themselves, which have been altered or misappropriated in violation of institutional rules. These would include tailored clothing, such as form-fitting shirts, spiked or pegged trousers, bleached clothing, and, of course, any item of apparel or any personal property stolen from another inmate. Commissary items in possession of an inmate who has not purchased them or has acquired them in excess of the amounts permitted are also regarded as contraband.

Medicines are something that can also become contraband, even though they may have been prescribed and issued by the prison physician. This can come about if an inmate palms medications and hoards them in excess of the dosage prescribed. This practice is so dangerous that officers dispensing medications must be very careful not to permit it. For many remedies contain ingredients that can prove fatal if taken in large quantities. There is not only danger that a despondent inmate may commit suicide, but there is always a possibility of an innocent person being drugged or poisoned.

Obviously, it is not possible to list here everything that might conceivably be an article of contraband. Instead there has been an attempt to direct attention to the basic fundamentals of identifying contraband items. As has been shown, an item that is both permissible and necessary in one location may be dangerous and undesirable in another.

In order to identify contraband, officers must consider several questions:

Was the inmate permitted to purchase this item in the commissary? Has it been altered in any fashion? Is it being used for the purpose intended?

This kind of thinking, plus reference to the Rule Book, should enable officers to recognize contraband when they encounter it.

But if any doubt exists, a superior officer should be consulted.

SHAKEDOWNS

The importance of vigilance in searching for contraband on the person, in cells and on the assignments of inmates, cannot be overemphasized. Laxity in the searching (shakedown) of an inmate's person, cell, and assignment can and will jeopardize the security of the institution. No one is to take anything for granted when it comes to searching an inmate. Some officer may figure that because an inmate is in a responsible job or is a runner and has been placed on the job with the sanction of officials of the institution that it is not necessary to search him thoroughly. If guards take that attitude, they are making a big mistake . . . and one that may be their last.

As an example of what can occur because of carelessness in the searching of inmates, a riot and escape in the Colorado State Penitentiary at Canon City stand out.

In that riot, which took place on October 3, 1929, seven officers were killed. The direct cause of their death was *failure to search inmates properly.*

Later investigation disclosed that prior to the Canon City riot, inmates were going from one assignment to another and passing out weapons.

Another good example is what took place right here at Stateville in 1942. The guns used in the escape of Roger Touhy, Basil Banghart and their accomplices were carried into the institution by Percy Campbell, a trustee assigned to work on a front lawn, outside the prison walls. Campbell took the two pistols from beneath a bush where they had been concealed by a brother of one of the escapees, folded a flag, concealed the guns inside and carried this lethal package all the way to the clothing room inside of the prison without arousing suspicion.

Being a "jive and good time boy" who diverted officers with his breezy line, Campbell succeeded in establishing himself as a harmless sort of individual, not so much above suspicion as beneath it. But if the officers on the gates had followed instructions and searched all inmates, as they should have done, Campbell could not have brought the guns into the institution and there probably would have been no escape. Since it did occur, the blame must rest directly on the employees who allowed the weapons to be brought into the institution through negligence in not searching an inmate.

The purpose of searching inmates is to prevent smuggling of contraband such as weapons, saws, drugs, money, etc., into the prison; to detect the manufacture of contraband, within the prison; to discourage petty thievery; and to enforce institutional security rules.

It must be remembered that many men confined in any prison are expert mechanics or machinists. It is not inconceivable that they could make a gun, not in a day or two, of course, and not all at once, but over a period of a year or two. To a man serving a life sentence, a year or two spent in making a weapon to aid his escape would not be time wasted. Officers must never permit an inmate to make anything in the prison shops except the item on order, for any prison employee could well be the victim of a contraband weapon.

The basic techniques of searching, or "shaking down," are taught all new employees while they are attending the Stateville-Joliet Prison Personnel School. However, proficience is attained through alertness and experience. In searching an individual, care must be exercised, not only to avoid overlooking concealed articles, but also to insure that the one doing the searching is not in a vulnerable position. The officer should always stand behind the person being searched and insist that those who are waiting to be searched stand apart a sufficient distance to prevent contraband from being passed.

It must be remembered that contraband may be concealed anywhere on the person, in the clothing being worn, or on or within the body of the person. Generally, contraband is concealed between the legs, in shoes (heels and soles), in hems of trousers, around the waist, within mittens or handkerchiefs, in the hat, or under the arms. Objects being held in the hand of an inmate as well as the hand itself should always be checked.

When searching a large group of inmates, such as a work detail, the men should be ordered to line up and present themselves one at a time, with their arms extended and their backs towards the searcher. As each man is searched, he must be required to place himself at a distance from those not yet searched. Have the first man start a new line far enough from the other so that contraband cannot be passed between the men who have been searched and those who have not. After the guard has completed the "shakedown" of the line, he should look over the area where the men were standing for any contraband that might have been dropped or thrown away so it would not be found on the inmate.

If packages, bundles, boxes, barrels, etc., are being searched, the guard should remember that the container as well as the contents must be examined. Contraband may be concealed within liquids, bulk materials, or semi-solids. Milk, paint, flour, or any similar material may be used as a place of concealment for contraband.

When checking vehicles, an officer must search the entire vehicle very closely. A person may conceal himself or dangerous contraband within a very small space. The underside of the vehicle, the trunk, the motor compartment, and any place that offers a possibility of concealment must be examined. A systematic approach should be made so that nothing is missed. The officer should begin at one end and work toward the other, and not allow himself to be distracted or steered away.

In searching living quarters (cells or dormitories), guards should check the walls for cracks where contraband could be concealed; check lighting fixtures; ventilating shafts; inspect the washbowl and toilet thoroughly; examine shelves and articles upon them; search all clothing hanging or stacked in the cell; run their hands over the top covering of the bed with enough pressure to detect anything hidden under the blankets or sheets or mattresses; check the bedsteads, pillows and extra blankets; be certain to examine the books, magazines, newspapers, etc., as these are favorite hiding places for contraband notes and messages. Guards should be sure there are no false bottoms on large tobacco cans, ashtrays, drawers, or medicine cabinets and they should examine window bars, window frames, and the overhead ventilators.

In searching work assignments, the same procedures are followed. Some places to check are, lockers, work clothing, tool chests, around pipes, holes in tile and plaster walls, within machinery where possible, desks, the underside of chairs and stools, in short, any place that could possibly conceal contraband.

All contraband items discovered during the "shakedown" must be confiscated and turned over to the superior officer or to the disciplinarian. A report covering the contraband should tell the story completely and concisely. Generally a report to the Disciplinary Officer is sufficient, but in the event something out of the ordinary is found, such as a bar spreader, gun, knife, etc., the Warden, the Assistant Wardens and the Senior Captains must be notified immediately.

When there is any doubt concerning an item, guards are to consult their rule book, or if one is not immediately available, consult a superior officer. They must be sure that any article confiscated is contraband; but at the same time, not neglect to examine an article just because it is permitted. Such innocent appearing things as mechanical pens or pencils can be converted into dangerous weapons by removing the functional parts and replacing them with small blades or stilettoes.

Although routine "shakedowns" within the institution are absolutely necessary to safety and security, officers should not fall into the habit of searching cells, dormitories, or work assignments at regular intervals. That would permit the inmates to observe their pattern of searching and move contraband from one place to another and back again.

While frequent, though irregular, searches of the inmates' cells are necessary in maintaining security, officers should remember that personal property authorized to be in the possession of the inmates has a special value to him and should be respected. Ordinarily, "shakedowns" can be conducted without completely tearing up the cell. There is little reason why any article in an inmate's cell cannot be returned to its original position after it has been examined, or placed on the desk or bed. An inmate's personal items are never to be thrown on the floor. To do that will only cause friction and resentment.

Inmates usually come to realize that only the possessors of contraband, the connivers, the escape artists and planners, and the troublemakers have any reason to fear "shakedowns."

EMPLOYEE AND INMATE RELATIONS

If the two prime objectives of this institution, security and rehabilitation of the inmates, are to be realized, all employees must first gain an understanding of the problems faced by the inmate. And it must always be possible for the inmate to seek the help and advice of prison authorities in dealing with his problems.

Since an inmate's conditions of existence are abnormal by any standard, he sometimes has problems that may appear to be very trivial, but which may in all seriousness seem like a near catastrophe to him. Thus when listening to an inmate's troubles, employees must bear in mind that to a person who has but little, any loss is a great loss and that slight variation in the closely ordered routine of an inmate's life may be very disturbing to him. Patient listening to the inmate's problems and prompt referral of them to the proper authorities, will do much to promote harmony and a better understanding between the employee and the inmate.

The inmate should always be encouraged to take advantage of

the religious, educational, vocational and recreational facilities provided him. It is through benefits derived from these programs that he may eventually be able to solve his own problems, or at least learn to live with them. By utilizing these programs for self benefit, the inmate can make time serve him.

Sometimes employees worry about the fact that they are not "liked" by the inmates, and possibly at times do things in an effort to be "liked" by them. A worthier goal is to attempt to gain the inmates' respect. If employees can do this, they have accomplished a great deal and achieve something more durable than a temporary rapport between individuals.

Respect can be gained by conducting oneself in such a manner as to warrant it. This involves many things—being courteous, reasonable, fair and consistent. The officer who lets his temperament be governed by his feeling of the moment will be markedly unsuccessful, for no one can predict his moods and he will be judged by his worst ones. The essence of consistency is to conduct oneself always as a gentleman, even under the most trying conditions. Neither the inmates nor officials have anything to do with an employee's private affairs and they should neither benefit nor be penalized because of them.

In their association with the inmates employees can and must be firm and positive without being rude. Discourtesy never gained anyone's respect. To curse and use strong language is to indicate that one is not capable of expressing himself without it. Shouting and cursing never gained anyone's respect nor contributed to good order.

The fact that certain elements among inmates will stoop to the lowest levels of deceit in order to embarrass guards or their superiors is never justification for responding in kind. Even though an inmate makes false charges against prison authorities, the latter must counter with truth, not deceit. If employees have in all things conducted themselves according to the rules and regulations, the truth will suffice.

Repeating gossip or making insulting remarks about either an inmate or another employee is something that must never be done. Familiarity with the inmates must be guarded against.

Under no circumstances should any prison employee convey a private message, either written or oral, from one inmate to another or from an inmate to someone outside the institution.

An insight into the way human beings think and act is helpful to the custodial officer. If guards will study the inmates on their assignments and try to see their problems from their point of view, without letting sympathy interfere with good judgment, they will eliminate many problems before they grow to major proportions.

In the Employees' Library are a number of good books on penology and criminology which should prove helpful to all employees in this, as well as in other areas of their work. It is recommended that they avail themselves of these books.

Whether in custodial service or elsewhere, the mark of a good supervisor is that he knows his work well and has the ability to instruct others in clear and simple language. He must also possess the patience to repeat instructions and, when needed, the skill to demonstrate the task.

If he also possesses a sense of fairness and the wisdom to counsel his subordinates in times of stress, then he is indeed a valuable employee.

Like nearly everyone else, an inmate occasionally finds himself confronted by a situation he is unable to manage alone. It may be a family problem, an income tax return, a veteran's service benefit, or a matter relating to his case. Whatever his problems, some department of the prison can assist him. Every inmate must be shown due consideration by the proper officials on any request that merits attention.

Fair and impartial treatment of all inmates is a must.

Certainly it is better to return the inmate to his home community satisfied that he has been given fair and impartial treatment, than to release him embittered and resentful over the manner in which he has been handled while in the institution.

ACCIDENT REPORTS

The Stateville-Joliet prison has a population of approximately 5,000 inmates and 600 employees. Among a group of more than

5,000 persons engaged in various occupations, accidents are bound to occur from time to time. Whenever an accident resulting in personal injury does happen, the full circumstances must be reported on the form supplied for that purpose.

The accident form adopted by this institution consists essentially of statistical data: statements of the how, when and where of the accident, names and statements of witnesses, suggestions for prevention of similar accidents by victims and the officer reporting the accident, classification of cause and responsibility for the accident, and required signatures of responsible personnel. The reports for both employees and inmates are similar. It is important to get as exact information on the above items as possible. In case of employee accidents, an inaccurate or no report may jeopardize any claim for compensation or sick leave credit.

Statistical Data, includes exact name, number, date, work and cell house assignment, and what subject was doing at the time of the mishap: for example, performing assigned work or playing in the recreation yard.

There is a tendency to use only last names on reports. This is not sufficient. First, middle and last names, including register numbers of inmates, must be listed. The precise date and time are required. This information should be noted at once as memory is fallible. The location of the accident should be described precisely and accurately.

A brief opinion of how and why the accident occurred should be stated.

Suggestions for prevention of the particular accident are important, as the victim, the witnesses, if any, and the assignment supervisor are in the best position to realize what could be done or changed to prevent a recurrence.

It is important to note as soon as possible the names and numbers of witnesses. Statements of witnesses should be obtained, preferably by having each witness give his statement alone so that voluntary and involuntary influences may be avoided.

The back of the form lists a classification of responsibility and cause of accidents. These are used for reference and the proper number and letter of the form code should be listed and checked. However, if desired, the statements of responsibility and cause may be written out.

Although doctors and nurses are on call around the clock, it should be borne in mind that certain types of injuries require immediate application of first aid measures. For instance, if a wound induces profuse bleeding, indicating a severed artery, a pressure bandage or tourniquet, should be applied immediately.

Another type of injury requiring prompt action is that which involves getting alkalies or other chemicals into the eyes. In that event the eyes must be irrigated with tap water at once. Any delay in washing out the eyes may result in serious damage.

In general patients who suffer cuts and bruises may be sent to the hospital for treatment. If their injuries are relatively minor, they can be sent to the hospital alone; if their injuries are severe, they should be transported on an ambulance cart. However, should a bone injury be suspected or should there exist any doubt as to the wisdom of moving the patient, the doctor should be called.

If a person has succumbed from injuries or has died under any circumstances, the body must not be moved except by permission of the coroner or his assistant.

ACCIDENT CAUSE CLASSIFICATION

RESPONSIBILITY FOR ACCIDENT:

A. INJURED PERSON	C. OFFICER IN CHARGE
B. FELLOW WORKER	D. INSTITUTION

ACCIDENT CAUSES

__ 1. OPERATING MACHINERY OR OTHER EQUIPMENT OR WORKING WITHOUT AUTHORITY.
__ 2. OPERATING OR WORKING AT UNSAFE SPEED.
__ 3. MAKING SAFETY DEVICES INOPERATIVE.
__ 4. USING IMPROPER TOOLS OR APPLIANCES.
__ 5. PILING OF MATERIALS.
__ 6. MATERIAL HANDLING.
__ 7. ASSUMING HAZARDOUS POSITION OR POSTURE.
__ 8. WORKING ON MOVING OR DANGEROUS EQUIPMENT.
__ 9. DISTRACTION, TEASING, ABUSING, AND STARTLING.
__10. FAILURE TO USE OR IMPROPER USE OF SAFE ATTIRE OR PERSONAL PROTECTIVE EQUIPMENT.
__11. FAILURE TO GIVE OR RECEIVE PROPER SIGNALS.
__12. WORKING WITHOUT INSTRUCTION.
__13. FAILURE TO COORDINATE AND COOPERATE.
__14. NO FOLLOW-UP OF INSTRUCTIONS.
__15. ERROR IN JUDGEMENT.

___16. VIOLATIONS OF SPECIFIC INSTRUCTIONS.
___17. FAILURE TO RECOGNIZE AN UNSAFE CONDITION OR PRACTICE.
___18. LACK OF INSPECTION AND MAINTENANCE.
___19. FAILURE TO COMPLY WITH PREVIOUSLY SUBMITTED RECOMMENDATIONS.
___20. FAILURE TO ESTABLISH SAFE WORKING CONDITIONS.
___21. FAILURE TO ENFORCE ESTABLISHED SAFETY RULES.
___22. IMPROPERLY GUARDED EQUIPMENT.
___23. FAULTY DESIGN AND INSTALLATION OF EQUIPMENT OR BUILDINGS.
___24. FAILURE OF MACHINERY, EQUIPMENT, STRUCTURES, MATERIALS.
___25. HAZARDOUS ARRANGEMENT, POOR HOUSEKEEPING, ETC.
___26. IMPROPER ILLUMINATION.
___27. HAZARDOUS DUSTS, GASES, FUMES, AND MISTS.
___28. PHYSICAL DEFECTS OF INJURED.
___29. ACTS OF GOD.

ACCIDENT REPORT

EMPLOYEE..
INMATE...REG. NO. ....
DEPARTMENT...............................TIME OF   . A.M DATE OF
                                                        INJURY .... P.M. INJURY ....
PART OF BODY INJURED...
JOB POSITION (WHEN INJURED)..
WHAT WORK WAS INJURED MAN DOING?..............................
....
....

EXACT LOCATION OF ACCIDENT...
HOW DID THE ACCIDENT OCCUR?...
....
....

WHY DID THE ACCIDENT OCCUR?..
....
....
....

WHAT DO YOU SUGGEST TO PREVENT RECURRENCE?...................
....
....
....

SUBJECTS RECOMMENDATION TO PREVENT RECURRENCE ....
....
....
....

LAST NAMES OF WITNESSES: BOTH EMPLOYEES AND INMATES
....
....
....

OFFICER IN CHARGE .... OFFICER.............................
WHAT ACTION DO YOU RECOMMEND?.......................................
....
....

RESPONSIBILITY................Department Superintendent ....
                            Copies Must Be Sent to: Warden, Hospital,
CAUSE ....Assistant Warden, Industrial Office (If
                            Occurring in an Industry)   FILE COPY

MERITORIOUS SERVICE

In 1872 legislation was first enacted in Illinois which provided for the reduction of prisoners' sentences because of good conduct. When an inmate of a penitentiary or reformatory earns time off from his sentence for good conduct, it is referred to as "Good Time Earned."

The Director of the Department of Public Safety in Illinois has the authority to prescribe terms for the earning of good time. These rules and regulations can be changed at any time. However, changes are not retroactive. The rules in effect at the time the prisoner begins his sentence govern the amount of good time which he may earn. Inmates received prior to February 1, 1952, may earn good time as indicated in the following table:

1st year	1 month
2 "	2 "
3 "	3 "
4 "	4 "
5 "	5 "
6 "	6 "

and six months for each
year thereafter.

On February 1, 1952, the Director of the Department of Public Safety changed the method of computing good time with reference to the maximum time that must be served on a sentence so that total good time credit cannot exceed *one-third* of the sentence.

If a prisoner commits more than four violations of the institutional rules, the Director of the Department of Public Safety may, upon recommendation by the Warden, deprive the prisoner of all or any part of the good time that the prisoner may have earned, or may earn in the future.

The Merit Staff meets at the Joliet Branch and Stateville once each month for the purpose of reviewing cases of inmates who have been reported for serious violations of the institutional rules. The Merit Staff recommends to the Warden whatever action may entail the loss of good time. If the Warden approves the recommendation of the Merit Staff, he then submits it to the Director for his concurrence.

A "progressive Merit System," distinct from the "good time" allowance, has also been adopted by the Department of Public Safety for the purpose of encouraging and rewarding good conduct and industry. The "progressive Merit System" affects only those inmates who have appeared before the Parole Board and have been denied parole but given a "set" date for another parole hearing. Time earned under the "Progressive Merit System" enables these inmates to reappear before the Parole Board at a date earlier than the one set.

Under this system five grades designated as A, B, C, D and E have been established. When received in the institution, all inmates are automatically placed in C grade, where time is neither earned nor lost. If the new inmate's behavior is satisfactory, he is promoted to B grade after three months. In grade B an inmate earns five days a month off his "set." If his behavior remains satisfactory, he will, after three months in B grade, be promoted to grade A. In that classification he earns ten days a month off the "set" date for his parole hearing.

For cause, an inmate may be demoted to D grade, in which status he loses five days a month, or to E grade, where he loses ten. When this occurs, the inmate loses all previously earned good time and must remain in the grade to which he was demoted three months for each grade dropped. Thus an inmate demoted from grade A to grade E would have to spend twelve months in the latter grade.

With the approval of the Parole and Pardon Board, the Warden can advance credits to inmates not exceeding sixty days in dimunition of time after their case has been reviewed by the Board. At each branch of the institution there are several assignments on which inmates can earn sixty days. A few of them are the Farm Detail, Administration Building, and Hospital. Within the Merit System there is also provision for giving an inmate ninety days credit towards his set. But this amount of Merit Time is given only as a reward for unusually meritorious service.

Occasionally the Warden has recommended thirty or sixty days credit for an inmate on assignments which do not ordinarily give the inmate extra credit. These special recommendations have been earned by finding and surrendering a dangerous weapon, for helping to put out fires, or for going to the aid of an employee or another inmate when their lives were endangered.

Many, many inmates have been given letters of commendation for their contributions to the Federal Government's Malaria Project and to other government sponsored medical experiments, some secret. In several instances the sentences of men participating in medical experiments have been commuted by the Governor. It is not unusual for state's attorneys to quash pending warrants because of an inmate's participation in the Malaria Research Project, which was started during World War II and is still being carried on, despite some successful discoveries.

This administration is always gratified when a deserving inmate is rewarded for outstanding conduct. It would much rather commend inmates for good behavior than to condemn them for bad. Every employee is well within the rules of this institution in submitting written reports on inmates who perform any service above and beyond that normally expected of them. Such reports must be sent to the Warden so that he may act upon them in keeping with the merits of the situation. In all instances a copy of the report will be included in the inmate's record jacket.

Awards and letters of commendation for meritorious service are not limited to inmates. Any act of heroism or exceptional service performed by an employee of the institution is also gratefully acknowledged, made a part of the employee's record, and in some instances rewarded by payment of a small sum of money.

Any employee who detects an escape plot, halts or averts a serious disturbance, discovers a fire, or anything of similar import will be nominated for a $25 reward, in addition to receiving commendation.

Proficiency in marksmanship, exceptionally good supervision of an assignment, and related accomplishments are also acclaimed.

Since promotions are made from within the ranks of the employees, these awards and commendations might well have an additional value to the employee, for in any consideration of his record they would weigh favorably.

OVER-ALL PROBLEMS OF SECURITY

When the subject of institutional security arises, one immediately thinks of escapes, guns, keys, tools, and contraband articles of every description. Coming quickly to mind, too, is the caliber of personnel, the extent of their training in institution operational techniques and, perhaps most important, their loyalty and interest. Obviously the most perfect operational regulations and procedures will only be as good as the personnel who are charged with the responsibility of carrying them out.

In the past the problems of security in prisons were fewer than in the present day, because prisoners were simply locked up and virtually ignored until their sentences expired or until they died. This was accomplished with the aid of dungeons, where inmates were chained to the walls. When it was necessary to remove them from the dungeons, a large iron ball was attached to the chain that was permanently riveted around their bodies. Some countries banished their prisoners to distant islands, such as Devil's Island. A smaller number of guards was required to accomplish a high level of security under these conditions.

However, to achieve the second goal, rehabilitation, modern institutions are obliged to have work programs, academic and vocational training, recreation, and to take care of the necessities of life of the inmates in custody. As a result of such programs, which involve movements of inmates from one part of the institution to another with tools and materials, the problems of over-all security and custody have been made more complex.

A careful analysis of the numerous breaches of institution security that have occurred in institutions indicates just as positively, however, that the over-all program for treatment and handling of inmates in the institution is as important in the success of any institution's operation as the physical restraints used to detain inmates.

It would be useless to say that inmates will be happy in prison; nevertheless, that somewhat intangible and difficult term to define—"Morale"—plays an important part in the total security.

The records show that the big majority of inmates who are receiving decent food and humane treatment and who are busily engaged in useful programs, carefully organized and purposeful leisure time activities, and programs of self improvement seldom resort to disturbances or escape attempts.

This is not to say that these things alone will assure a high degree of security without the customary specific physical restraints, but the more successful administrators have come to realize that force and restraint alone are not sufficient to prevent troublesome incidents. There must be a considerable measure of coöperation from the inmates toward a well organized program.

It should be realized as the suggestions and reminders that are included on the control of weapons, contraband, and other threats to security are read, that this matter of inmate morale is equally important to prison security.

An insight into the way human beings think and act is a very useful tool to the custodial officer. If prison officials will study their inmates carefully and try to see their problems from their point of view, without letting sympathy affect their judgment as custodial officers, they will eliminate many problems of institutional security. Most inmates can be a great hazard to the security of the institution, or almost no hazard, depending on how they are handled.

In order to maintain a high level of security and still be successful in achieving rehabilitation constant alertness and good supervision are necessary. Supervision means not only "to direct," but also "to inspect." And that is among the prison officers' most important functions—to inspect, observe and examine:

Inmates—their persons, clothing, cells and possessions.

Buildings—bars, floors, walls, tunnels, basements, lockers, furnishings, machinery and equipment.

Grounds—recreation fields, lawns, shrubbery, roadsides, manholes, sewers, etc.

Vehicles—the merchandise or commodities carried, the engine compartment, undersides, trunk, passenger compartment, hub caps, and every possible place of concealment.

What to Watch For: Escape hazards, fire hazards, accident hazards, and health hazards.

Where anything unusual is observed and there is any doubt as to its import or as to the correct method of dealing with the situation, the superior officer must be contacted immediately. Nothing of a suspicious nature should be passed over as being too insignificant or too inconclusive to bother a superior with. Plots to tunnel out of institutions have been foiled because someone observed and became suspicious of a small pile of fresh earth.

Conditions and Equipment Necessary to a High Standard of Security: Discipline of officers and inmates. Walls, gun towers, firearms, gas dispensers, lights (fixed and portable), handcuffs, leg irons, restraining belts, straight jackets, keys and locks. And last but by no means least, *organization*.

It may be said that the best organizational structure for an institution is that one which best serves to carry out all of the objectives of the program. At the Stateville-Joliet Branch those objectives are the following:

A. To achieve the maximum results with available facilities and personnel.

B. To encourage the development and improvement of personnel through in-service training.

C. To attain high standards of professional competence, sincerity, industriousness, good order, morale, and an absence of tensions.

D. To be prepared at all times to meet and cope with emergency situations.

E. To coördinate the work and activities of the various institutional departments.

F. To maintain a constructive system of communications with both employees and inmates.

G. To develop sound and friendly relationships with the surrounding community and the public at large.

In this, as in every organization, there is an appreciation of the differences that exist among individual employees. Every effort is made to assign each employee to the type of work he is most capable of performing. It is frequently necessary to assign an officer to several different posts in order to ascertain his qualifications. Some men handle inmates better than others, some are more suited as towermen, relief men, or gate men. A few have specialized skills, either mechanical or clerical, and some have the qualifications required of supervisory personnel. In a big, or relatively large prison organization, there is room for all to advance to the limit of their abilities, and opportunity, too, for all advancements should be made from among the ranks of the employees.

Each employee should be encouraged to familiarize himself with the rules, regulations, and operational procedures of the institution with a view towards both his personal welfare and the orderly, secure and efficient functioning of his assignment. However, employees must remember that policy making is the prerogative of the Administration, which is responsible for the success or failure of the institution program. They should never attempt to make their own rules. There can be no hesitancy in enforcing firmly but fairly the rules that have been developed for the disciplining and reformation of inmates.

Then, there is another phase of security—winning recognition of and voluntary obedience to institution regulations. In large measure this can be achieved by positive and constructive discipline that substitutes useful activity for idleness and meaningless, or trouble producing, chatter. This type of discipline results in good inmate morale, reduces the number of disciplinary problems, and brings about a better adjustment of inmates to the problems generated by their restricted environment.

Employees are also expected to discipline themselves, not only while they are in the institution but when they are away from it as well. It is to be remembered that the public forms its collective opinions of a tax supported institution by its contacts with the persons who represent it. For this reason employees must pay their bills and conduct themselves as gentlemen and good citizens. They should never frequent disreputable establishments. Employees who do so may find themselves in serious difficulty, for there are persons who would try to turn an officer's indiscretions into an advantage for some inmate.

Many jail breaks owe their success to the fact that some officer permitted himself to become entrapped by a gambling debt or a designing female.

To avoid becoming involved in anything illegal or disgraceful, employees should choose associates carefully and not establish any kind of relationship with former inmates or the relatives of inmates currently serving time.

ESCAPE RISKS

It is a fundamental of prison administration that each new inmate should be evaluated with respect to his status as a security risk before he is assigned to a job within the institution. The study of prisoners' records should be a continuous process. When a new prisoner is received at the institution, a review of his case is made within a very few days of his admittance. The statement of facts, the F.B.I. sheet and the report of the Classification Board are studied with a view to establishing the inmate's pattern of life outside and, if previously convicted, inside the institution. By this means the administration is better enabled to determine what can be expected of the inmate. A number of factors are considered in evaluating the inmate's security status — his record of escapes, AWOL'S, length of sentence, and type of offense, and the absence or existence of close family ties. To a great extent these govern the inmate's future assignments.

If the record indicates that an inmate is a serious escape risk, he should never be assigned to any job in the institution where he would have less than maximum supervision.

For example, such an inmate would not be assigned to the Yard Detail where he would have access to dangerous tools and perhaps would be able to hide out or take advantage of the cover offered by a sudden storm in attempting an escape. He would in all probability be assigned to cell house help or a closely supervised shop, where his movements would be restricted and he would be under the constant supervision and surveillance of an experienced officer.

Information about inmates who have escaped or attempted to escape from this or any other institution is passed along to the Captains, Lieutenants, cell house keepers, and officers in charge of the division to which the inmate has been assigned. The identification board, or "shingle," over the inmate's cell door is painted *red;* and it serves as a constant reminder to supervising officers.

Although a known escape risk is never made a runner or given any opportunity to travel from one point to another unaccompanied by an officer, he is sent on call tickets when requested by the supervisor of another division. Since call tickets are timed at both departure and arrival, there is little chance for the inmate to do anything that would endanger the security of the institution, if the tickets are closely supervised.

In assigning inmates to work details outside the walls, to the Honor Farm, or to the Administration Building, consideration is given to the inmates institutional record, sentence, time remaining until he sees the Parole Board or is eligible for discharge, visits from his friends and relatives, and mail.

Never, at any time, is a man put on the farm detail or outside the walls who has a sex offense record, or has committed arson, extortion, kidnapping, aggragated assault and similar acts of violence. Neither are men who have escaped or attempted to escape from a jail or institution, who have deserted from the Armed Forces, or who have warrants lodged against them, ever considered for assignment outside the walls.

Drug addicts or inmates convicted of selling drugs are not assigned to outside details, unless they have been granted parole or have fewer than 90 days left to serve. Even then they are kept under the direct and constant surveillance of an officer at all times.

Despite the care that is exercised in assigning men outside the walls, there is no guarantee that one will not try to escape, nor does such an assignment make the inmate a "trusty." Supervision of inmates is as essential on the outside details and the Honor Farm as it is within the walls. For without supervision they could and perhaps would escape or commit acts in violation of our laws or the rules of the institution.

There are, of course, certain legal penalties that make it unwise for an inmate to escape or to aid anyone else in escaping.
For leaving the institution either by stealth or force, an inmate
can be tried and sentenced to a term of not less than one year
nor more than ten years. However, if he helps another inmate
to escape, he will upon conviction be given that inmate's sentence
however great it may be, except that he cannot be sentenced to
death.

State laws with respect to aiding a prisoner to escape apply not
only to inmates but to all persons, including employees of the
institution.

There are in addition state laws pertaining exclusively to the
personnel of institutions. They are cited here from Chapter 38,
Illinois Revised Statutes, Criminal Code:

227 Officer of the Penitentiary Allowing) p. 91.

If the warden or any officer, guard, agent, servant of, or person employing convicts in or about the penitentiary, shall contrive, procure, aid, connive at, conceal or assist the escape of any convict from the penitentiary,
or conceal or assist any convict after he has escaped, he shall be imprisoned in the penitentiary not less than one nor more than ten years.

228 Aiding Escape) p. 92.

Whoever conveys into the penitentiary, or into any jail or other place of
confinement, any disguise, instrument, tool weapon or other thing adapted
or useful to aid a prisoner in making his escape, with intent to facilitate
the escape of any prisoner there lawfully committed or detained, or by any
means whatever aids, abets, or assists such prisoner to escape or attempt
to escape from any jail, prison, or any lawful detention whether such
escape is attempted or effected or not, or conceals or assists any convict
after he has escaped, shall upon conviction thereof be given the same penalty as the prisoner who he aided or abetted, except that in case the prisoner is sentenced to death, the penalty for such aid shall be imprisoned for
life in the penitentiary. (As amended by act approved July 6, 1927. L.
1927, p. 398).

**228-A Aiding Escape or Attempt to Escape From Correctional or
Charitable Institution. Penalty) p. 92a.**

Any person who knowingly shall aid the escape or attempted escape of
a person committed to any state correctional or charitable institution, or
who shall knowingly conceal or assist any inmate after he has escaped
therefrom, or any person who knowingly conveys or attempts to convey
into any such institution any disguise, instrument, tool, weapon or other
thing adapted or useful to aid an inmate to escape, whether the escape is
attempted or effected or not, shall be guilty of a misdemeanor, and, upon
conviction, shall be imprisoned not exceeding one year, or fined not ex-

ceeding one thousand dollars $(1000), or both in the discretion of the court, Added by act approved July 9, 1943. L. 1943, vol. 1, p. 584.
455-A Employees Communicating With Prisoners. Penalty) p. 210a.

Any employee assigned to duty at a penal institution or division thereof of the State of Illinois who communicates with any prisoner or person confined within any such institution or division or who conveys any letter, writing, package, literature, reading material or any other article to or from any prisoner or person confined therein in violation of the announced and effective laws, rules and regulations of the Department of Public Safety pertaining to such penal institutions or divisions thereof, shall be fined not exceeding $500.00 or imprisoned in the county jail not more than one year, or both. Added by act approved August 6, 1951, L. 1951, p. 2086.

INMATES IN QUARTERS

The actual methods and techniques of supervising prisoners in quarters necessarily vary with the structural design of the cell houses. At the Stateville-Joliet Branch of the Illinois State Penitentiary System there are three large rectangular cell houses of conventional design with the cell blocks built in the center of the structure and separated from the exterior walls by a corridor. Then there are four panopticons, or circular cell houses. Unlike the rectangular cell houses these have cell tiers around the perimeter of the building and each cell has a window opening to the outside. The glass enclosed fronts of the cells face a central rotunda in which the control tower is located. Needless to say, these two different types of cell house structures present different problems of management and supervision.

In the roundhouses, for example, it is necessary for an officer to enter every cell every day in order to check the window bars for possible tampering. But since there are no window openings in the cells of the rectangular cell houses, the barred fronts of the cells, which face out upon a corridor separating them from the windows and walls of the building, can be checked without entering the cells. This is known as "rapping" the bars.

From one point of view the rectangular cell houses seem more secure: The cell bars can be examined without unlocking or entering the cells; the inmates cannot easily observe the approach of an officer as he makes his rounds. But that situation has its reverse side, too, since an officer cannot observe the inmates, except as he passes in front of their cells.

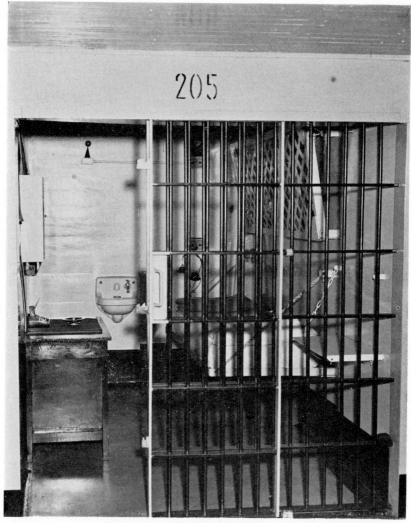

Rectangular type of new cell in 'B' House, Stateville Branch.

The round cell houses may seem less secure because of the windows opening to the outside and because of the necessity of unlocking cells in order to examine the bars. But on the other hand, the fact that an officer must enter the cells daily lends itself to an inspection of the cells. And though inmates may observe their officers constantly, the reverse is also true. With one officer

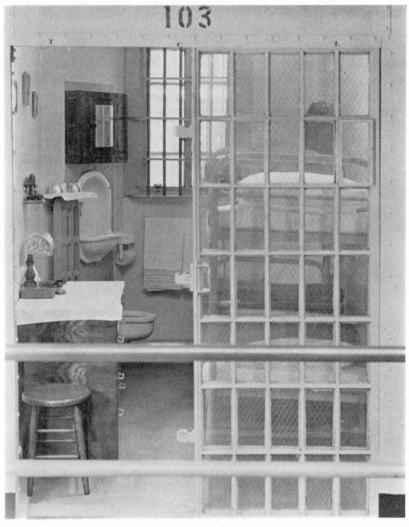

Interior view of cell in circular cell house, 1959. Stateville Branch.

posted in the central tower of the round house and another patrolling the galleries, any disturbance or irregularity can be quickly discovered.

Since cells are designed for the purpose of controlling inmates, one of the first things an employe should learn is the proper method of operating the cell locking systems. All of the cell houses at this institution have two separate locking devices—a mechanical system for locking and unlocking half a tier at once, and two individual key locks on each cell.

After the 7:00 A.M. count check, the multiple cell locking system is ordinarily employed. But, at night or in times of disturbance or poor visibility due to inclement weather, each cell door must be locked with the key locks as well as with the multiple locking mechanism. No cell may be unlocked at night except in an emergency, such as an illness or a serious disturbance, and then only at the direction of a superior officer.

The supervision of inmates in quarters entails many things: Overseeing the work of inmates assigned to the cell house; taking counts; enforcing rules; issuing supplies; distributing mail; promoting good housekeeping and personal hygiene; preventing the pilfering of cells; and supervising the inmates' general welfare.

Fundamentally, supervision should be constructive and positive, not a demoralizing "cat and mouse" situation in which officers and inmates are continually trying to outmaneuver each other.

The cell house supervisor's goal, as well as that of all employees, should be to prevent difficulties or violations of the rules through constructive approaches. The attitude of institutional employees toward the prisoners has much to do with the success or failure of the rehabilitation program. It is frequently possible to encourage the inmates to form constructive attitudes towards themselves, their associates and the institutional authorities; but this cannot be accomplished by using rough, vulgar language or by abusing authority in order to penalize inmates. By wise counsel and firm leadership more can be accomplished in the interests of discipline than by the frequent filing of disciplinary reports.

Specifically, there are certain rules which must be enforced through constant supervision. The general conduct of inmates should be orderly. Excessive noise, such as loud singing or whistling, or shouting back and forth between cells is forbidden. Inmates who are known troublemakers, escape risks, or sex perverts must be given extra close supervision. *Officers must remain alert to discover any such tendencies among the inmate population and report them to the proper official when they are observed.* Any suspicious or unusual circumstances should be reported so that corrective measures may be taken.

The "Inmates' Rule Book" and the bulletins issued by the Warden acquaint inmates with what is expected of them in the way of good housekeeping, but officers should routinely review them with any inmate who seems to have difficulty in following instructions. It should be impressed on the inmate that his cell is his home and that it will contribute to his health and sense of well being if he keeps it clean and orderly.

It is the duty of the cell house keeper to issue necessary cleaning supplies and equipment. He must also keep an inventory of such supplies and make requisition requests for needed supplies at a given time monthly.

In an institution of this kind, where large groups of men are confined in close proximity to one another, personal cleanliness becomes extremely important. Every precaution must be taken against the spread of infectious diseases. Taking baths and getting shaves and haircuts at specified times is mandatory for the inmates. Cell house officers should make sure that every inmate accompanies his line to the bath house and barber shop unless he has a valid reason for not doing so. In that case the inmate who misses a shave or haircut shall be sent on the miss-out line which exists to remedy such situations.

Letters, newspapers, magazines, books or packages which may be permitted to inmates are sent to the officer in charge of the cell house. The magazines and newspapers are distributed to the proper cells by inmates designated by the officer. Whenever an inmate fails to receive his paper or magazine at the proper time and registers a complaint, it is the duty of the cell house keeper to see that the difficulty is corrected. This may involve inquiries of the mail and censor's office to determine whether the magazine or newspaper was received. If the inmate runner delivered the paper to the wrong cell, it is up to the officer to check with the various cells and make sure the paper gets to its rightful owner.

Letter mail is distributed by the cell house officer in charge of the second shift and he is responsible for seeing that it is put into the proper cell.

Except in emergency situations, the officer in charge of the cell house must schedule maintenance and repairs so that they do not

Overall view of 'B' House, 1959. Stateville Branch.

conflict with or disrupt the routine of the institution. Necessary work on locks, plumbing and electrical equipment must be done after the lines have left the cell house and completed before they return if it is at all possible.

The cell house keeper is responsible for his work detail and must supervise the housekeeping duties essential to the proper maintenance of the cell houses. In addition to his work detail, he is also responsible for inmates remaining in their cells for various purposes, such as "lay-ins" ordered by the physician, men awaiting sick call, etc. He must keep an eye on these groups and see that they have the necessary care and supervision to prevent any kind of irregularities.

To accomplish his duties efficiently and remain on the time schedule that has been worked out for the best operation of the institution, the cell house officer must be mentally alert and intimately acquainted with the details of the routine outlined by the administration.

ESCORTING INMATES

One might, after looking at the 32 foot wall and gun towers surrounding the institution, be inclined to wonder why any precautions might be necessary in escorting inmates from one point to another within the institutional compound. Yet, there are many sound reasons why extreme caution is both prudent and essential.

In the first place, when an officer is required to escort a single inmate or a small group of inmates, it is generally because of some unusual circumstance. An inmate may be temporarily deranged, which in prison jargon is known as being "bugged up;" he may be a dangerous individual confined in the segregation unit; he may have had a fight with another inmate; or he may be an apparently well behaved inmate who becomes ill in his cell or on the assignment and must be taken to the hospital. Any or all of these situations contain a certain element of danger to the escorting officer and to the security of the institution.

The irresponsible or violent inmate could create a disturbance that might provoke other inmates or even some of the personnel into committing an act that could precipitate a riot. The quiet type of inmate may have feigned illness so that he could get out of his cell at a time when conditions were favorable for an escape attempt. In either case damage to the security and safety of the institution and its personnel could be the result.

Unnecessary risks must be avoided in transferring violent inmates from one area to another. If it becomes necessary to take an inmate out of segregation for any purpose, he must be handcuffed and chained; and the lead chain passed back between the inmate's legs so that he can be instantly subdued if he should attempt to create a disturbance. The correct position for the officer escorting an inmate is about an arm's length behind and slightly to one side. This puts the officer out of range of a sudden blow, but he is in a position to act quickly if the need should arise.

When an inmate becomes mentally or emotionally unbalanced, he must be restrained from harming himself or others. If the situation permits, nurses should be summoned to assist officers in transferring a disturbed inmate to the Detention Hospital for observation and treatment. In handling a disturbed inmate, or one who is deliberately mean for that matter, the best method is to request sufficient help to overwhelm him by force of numbers. This makes physical force or bodily assault unnecessary on the part of the officers and violence impossible on the part of the inmate.

Although the escorting of inmates under special circumstances requires a high degree of alertness and caution on the part of the officers, a more important aspect of an officer's escort duties involves supervision of lines of inmates moving to their daily routine—to work, to the dining room to the Chapel, etc.

While lines are filing out of their cells, officers must be stationed on the flag and the galleries in a position to observe every movement. If the lines are going to the dining room, officers must be strategically deployed in the tunnel connecting the cell house and the dining room. Other officers must be stationed in the dining room to maintain proper supervision of the lines, to see that they are seated in order and that each place is set with the proper silverware. At the conclusion of the meal, a bell is rung just before the lines are signaled to move out. At the sound of the bell each officer must resume his station in the dining room tunnels and in the cell houses. Those officers assigned to supervise the dining room sections must usher the lines away from the tables, observing any waste of food and keeping a close watch for contraband left lying in the dining room. The officer in charge of the dining room exit point must check the silverware as it is deposited in the trays at the rear of each section.

If a line of inmates is going anywhere other than the dining room, it must be counted through the door of the cell house by both the officer in charge of the line and the cell house doorman. Their counts must agree before the line can be marched to its destination.

Officers escorting lines from one place to another must walk on the left side of the line and maintain a position so that approximately three-fourths of the line is ahead of them. In this position an officer can readily observe the majority of his line and by turning his head occasionally can observe the remainder. The officer must keep his lines quiet and orderly. They must march in paired up fashion. Talking or smoking in lines is prohibited.

When the lines are going to the Chapel for Church Services, to view motion pictures, or to the prison ballpark for a baseball game, the seating of the inmates will be directed by a superior officer. As the lines approach their destination, the officer should go to the front of his line to receive or give instructions and to direct the inmates into the proper section of the Chapel or bleachers. He must make sure that all seats are filled in rotation. As the lines leave the Chapel after viewing a movie, the officer in charge of each section must inspect the floor and seats to see that no debris, such as candy wrappers and popcorn bags, is left.

Officers must conduct themselves in a gentlemanly and respectful manner whenever they escort inmates to the Chapel for Church Services. Loud and profane language will not be tolerated in Church, at any time or place.

Every inmate is granted a daily recreation period in the yard, unless that privilege has been temporarily suspended for disciplinary purposes. The same rules and procedures pertaining to counts and orderly marching of lines apply to the yard lines. While the inmates are on the recreation field, it is the duty of the officer to patrol the yard and keep a watchful eye for any disturbances or disputes that could lead to a fight. Shoving, pushing, tripping or any unnecessarily rough contact between men in the yard is forbidden. When the recreation period ends, the men should be lined up as nearly as possible in cell formation, so that there will be a semblance of order when they re-enter the cell house.

Undoubtedly many officers are perplexed by the problem of maintaining discipline in a line of fifty or sixty inmates. In any group of that size there are always a few non-conformists who persist in violating the rules. It is not easy to deal with such inmates. They do not all respond alike to the same measures. Sometimes halting the line and verbally reprimanding the offenders may be effective, for many of these petty violators are "show-offs" who like to think they are doing something that their more sensible associates are afraid to do or are not clever enough to get by with. The loss of face may hurt them more than a disciplinary report. Again, it may be advisable to talk to the inmate privately and try to enlist his coöperation. With some inmates persuasion works better than threats. But, of course, if all attempts to gain coöperation and obedience to the rules fail, then the problem should be passed on to superior authority.

BUREAU OF IDENTIFICATION

Historical Outline of Fingerprinting: More than eleven hundred years ago the Chinese monarchs used thumb prints on documents as sign symbols. This was the first recorded use of fingerprints.

In 1823, fingerprint impressions were discussed by Purkinje, a German Professor of Physiology and Pathology in Breslau, Germany. His ideas were not accepted.

In 1858, Sir William Herschel, an administrator in charge of the Courts of the Hoogly District of Bengal, India, dug further into the subject. Though his ideas were not accepted, they were later the foundation upon which Sir Walter E. R. Henry was able

View showing modern Bureau of Identification with inmate being fingerprinted and photographed. Stateville Branch.

to establish a fingerprint system of sound merit. In 1893, English
authorities appointed a committee headed by Sir Francis Galton
to look into the proposed "Henry System." Their recommendations were followed, and since then the fingerprint system has
been used with wonderful results.

Henry used many ideas of Herschel and Galton, but he improved them and made them practical. His system was adopted
by the Government, and today that system—known as the
"Henry System"—is used through the United States and England, and other English speaking countries. There are other systems, of course, but any fingerprint analyst who understands the
"Henry System" will find it easy to comprehend all the others.

The Bertillon System is not a fingerprint system—as most people are inclined to believe. It is a system which confines itself
to physical characteristics and measurements, such as height
weight, color of hair and eyes, complexion, the size and shape of

the nose, chin, forehead, etc. For years it was used here in conjunction with the "Henry System." However, in 1919 it was dropped in its entirety and the "Henry System" adopted, because the latter system is simpler in operation and gives unfailing results. In fact, the "Henry System" is recognized by the courts and law enforcement agencies as the only infallible system of identification in existence today.

All prisoners are received at the Diagnostic Depot, except in those rare cases where a prisoner in need of immediate medical attention is received at Stateville. Upon entering the Diagnostic Depot, the prisoner immediately becomes an inmate . . . entrusted to the custody of the Warden of the Illinois State Penitentiary at Joliet. The duties of the Warden and his assistants are to hold the inmate in security, to guard him, to defend him from danger . . . while exercising extreme precaution and vigilance as to their own protection and defense.

Thus the Bureau of Identification enters the picture. Within less than one hour after the inmate has been admitted to the Diagnostic Depot—during which time . . . as was explained in an earlier discussion . . . the inmate is assigned a number, searched, his hair cut, fed, bathed, etc.—he is ready for processing through the B. of I. That process consists of the following:

(A) What are termed "Mug Photos" (photos from the waist up) are taken of each inmate . . . both front and side view, while he is wearing the same shirt he wore upon entrance.

(B) Six sets of fingerprint cards are made on each inmate:
1. One for the Institutional MASTER FILE.
2. One for the Institutional Sub-Master File.
3. One for the Federal Bureau of Investigation, Washington, D. C.
4. One for the Illinis State Bureau of Identification.
5. One for the Chicago Detective Bureau.
6. One for the Criminologist's Record File.

(C) Each inmate is stripped and all physical characteristics, such as height, weight, color of hair, eyes and beard, facial complexion, the shape of his nose and chin, the condition of his teeth, all marks, scars, moles, tattoos, etc., are recorded.

(D) Subsequently, he is questioned as to age, date of birth, marital status, nearest of kin, military service, education, prior encounters with law—all of which information is recorded on a Descriptive Data Sheet, the original copy being retained in the Stateville B. of I. files, and a duplicate in the Diagnostic Depot B. of I. file.

Thereafter, the inmate's Master Fingerprint Card is classified according to the "Henry System" which has been explained—and a diligent search made of the B. of I. Master Card File to determine whether the inmate has ever been previously incarcerated in the Illinois State Penitentiary at Joliet. It is not unusual to find that an inmate, who claims never to have been arrested before, has actually served two, three, or more previous sentences in this same institution. Evidently he is living on a prayer that no one will recognize him . . . and perhaps they might not, if the Bertillon System were still being used instead of the infallible "Henry System."

True, institution files cover only those inmates who have at some time or another been received at the Illinois State Penitentiary, Joliet. But said files consist of more than 200,000 fingerprint cards, that is, 100,000 Master Cards and an equal number of sub-master cards . . . each serving as a cross-index to the other; together with approximately 90,000 descriptive data sheets and an equal number of book entries, together with an approximate 400,000 card Alias File . . . each of which also serves as a cross-index.

The Federal Bureau of Identification, the Illinois State Bureau of Identification, and the Chicago Detective Bureau—upon receipt of the Fingerprint Cards forwarded to them—furnish this institution with a complete criminal history of the subject as contained in the files of those respective Bureaus. Such procedures serve a dual purpose. They keep all agencies of the government and state informed as to the whereabouts of its subjects, and they furnish the institution with a complete picture of the entire criminal record of each inmate received. If it were otherwise, a person could actually hide behind prison walls; or, by merely leaving the state in which he might be wanted, be secure in his further pursuit of crime.

The Responsibilities of the Bureau of Identification Office: The Master Card Files and Photos are kept at Stateville, under lock and key. No inmate is ever permitted to enter the Master Card File Room, or the Photo Vault Room, except under the immediate supervision of the Fingerprint Technician or his assistant.

The Master Card File is used constantly. Not only is there occasion to use it when a new inmate is received, or when one is released on writ, paroled, or discharged, it is used for many other reasons.

For example, assume that Joe Doe surreptitiously purchases five or six dollars worth of commissary, usually edible goods, so that he can please his stomach while destroying the evidence, on another inmate's account. When the victimized inmate discovers that his account balance is five dollars less than it should be, he complains to the Officer in Charge of the Commissary. After the matter is investigated at the Commissary and reported to the Warden's Office, it is directed to the attention of the B. of I. The reason: All inmates are required to place their thumb print on their commissary slip in the presence of the Officer in Charge. The Officer might not know who each inmate is . . . but that infallible thumb print knows, and it cannot be fooled. Thus inmate John Doe has been fouled up by his thumb print.

Security Precautions Taken When Releasing Inmates on Discharge, Parole or Writ: Often one reads in the newspapers something to the effect that the wrong man was released. In fact, within the past years there have been three such cases, wherein inmates were released in error from the Cook County Jail. Such an error cannot happen here, for no inmate ever leaves this institution on parole, by order of writ, on expiration of sentence, or even upon death, without first having his fingerprints and photo taken—and a minute comparison made between those and the ones appearing on his Master Fingerprint Card . . . the same Master Card that was made of him the day he entered the Diagnostic Depot.

Procedure Used in Regard to Institutional Personnel: All applicants for positions at the Institution are processed through the

B. of I. Office, that is, four sets of fingerprint cards are taken:

1. One F.B.I. Card is forwarded to Washington, D. C., for checking.

2. One State of Illinois Card is forwarded to Springfield Office for checking.

3. One I.S.P. Card is forwarded to the Chicago Detective Bureau for checking.

4. One I.S.P. Card is retained in our applicant files.

A thumb print is taken for the purpose of the Identification Pass, which is issued to all employees. Three photos are made of each applicant: one side-view; one front-view; and one reduced front-view for the I.D. Pass. Each applicant is required to fill out in his own handwriting an Application Form, upon which is recorded all visible characteristics, such as color of hair and eyes, age, weight, build, complexion, etc.

Such information is, of course, copied and recorded on each fingerprint card before mailing. Whether the applicant is accepted or not, his complete file is made a part of the permanent records of the B. of I. Office.

This might appear to be a rather unusual procedure, insofar as applicants or employees are concerned. However, there have been cases where such records have proven to be very beneficial:

Not too long ago it was discovered that one of the civilians employed as a construction worker at the Joliet Branch had previously served time at this institution as an inmate. Was his purpose in entering under the guise of a construction worker motivated by evil intent? Did he return here to assist a friend? Was he planning to drop a gun or two at some point available to his friend, Joe Inmate?

The answers can only be surmised. However, if it were the latter, and that friend did get his hands on a weapon . . . the big question is: Who would be the target for that weapon? Another supposition, of course, but is not life more worth while than to chance throwing it away . . . needlessly . . . when a tiny bit of precaution would have erased, or at least squelched, that possibility in the first place?

If it were otherwise, any inmate leaving here could return again under the guise of a construction worker, or a guard, and play havoc within prison walls. It is dangerous enough as it is . . . without inviting such troubles.

The Functions of the B. of I. Office: The B. of I. Office—which, incidentally, is also the photographic department of the institution—has all the latest photographic equipment, for color, dye transfer, and black and white work. Seldom a day passes that the photographic department is not required to turn out hundreds of pictures of some nature. For example:

1. Fourteen photos are required on each inmate received, whether he is a parole violator, a transfer, a writ return, or a fish.

2. Six to fourteen photos are required on each inmate discharged on expiration of sentence, parole or writ.

3. Dozens of detail photos are required each day; six year photos are practically always in the making. The detail photos are necessary to identify men approved for work outside the walls. Six year photos are the re-photographing of an inmate after he has served that length of time. Thus any physiological changes are recorded.

4. Eight photos are required on each applicant for employment.

5. Photostatic copies of Applicant's and Inmate's Service Discharge Records are always in the making.

6. Photostatic copies of Parole Warrants, etc., to be used for Extradition Proceedings.

7. Pre-medical and post-operational photos of inmates who undergo facial operations and various members of the hospital staff, including the Malaria Staff.

8. Photographic work for the Elementary, High, Vocational and Barber School Programs.

9. Photographic work for the Sociologist's Office, Record Office, Industrial Office, etc.

10. Mounted Photos and Fingerprint Card Photos for the various Federal and Police Agencies and Courts throughout the United States.

11. Photographs of evidence resulting from contemplated escapes, attacks made on officers, destruction of cells and state property by inmates.

12. Photographic work for various other Illinois State Penal Institutions, such as Dwight (Reformatory for Women), Sheridan (Boys' Industrial Training School), etc.

13. The Photographic Department must always be kept ready to handle the photostatic copying of hundreds of fingerprint cards, photos, and other data required in the event an inmate escapes.

SUPERVISING MEALS

A wholesome, nutritionally balanced diet, fully adequate to maintain life and health, is a basic human right which should not be denied to prisoners.

Food is important to people everywhere, and equally so to inmates of penal institutions. At best their life is regimented and monotonous and they are permitted few personal choices in their daily routine. Since they cannot choose their food in accordance with their individual tastes, the menus should be varied enough to provide a little selectivity and the food should be wholesome in appearance and taste.

Good quality foodstuffs are ordered by the institution and upon receipt they are inspected closely to see that they conform with specifications. But a successful food service program requires much more than the procurement of good food. Constant supervision and inspection are necessary to keep the food in good condition while it is being processed through the kitchens and serving lines. Improper handling can rob foods not only of their nutritional value, but of their flavor and palatability as well. It must be remembered that the purpose of cooking is to enhance these qualities, not to destroy them.

While mass feeding of several thousand inmates is a difficult task, the problems attendant to it are not insurmountable. The institution cook who boils or steams food endlessly until all vitamins and other nutritive values have been lost is failing to fulfill his responsibility in maintaining high standards of health among the prisoners and is wasting food and the money it represents. For instance, even though potatoes play a large role in a low cost menu, the cook is not always required to serve them boiled. They can be baked, oven browned, made into potato salad, and prepared in numerous other ways.

During the last few years a great deal of new equipment has been added to the kitchens and bakeries. Increased oven and grill capacity make it possible to prepare foods in a variety of ways. But to secure maximum results from the available equipment, planning and supervision are necessary.

The institution menus are prepared by the Dietary Consultant. It is the duty of the steward assigned in each kitchen to see that the proper amounts of each item on the menu are prepared in the manner directed and to check or sample the food at each step of its preparation. If anything goes wrong, changes can be made before meal time. As a further precaution against the serving of bad food, every meal must be tasted by some official prior to its being served. This practice serves to minimize the possibility of a disturbance arising because of bad food. It also helps to keep the kitchen staff—employees and inmates—on their toes, so to speak.

Since food service represents one of the most important problems in a penal institution, secondary only to security and contributing directly to it, there must be the fullest coöperation between all employees in matters relating to the feeding of inmates. *Strict Supervision* of each phase of the program, from garden to dining table, *must be maintained.*

Sanitation is vital in the preparation and service of food. All personnel and inmates assigned to food handling jobs must have prior approval of the prison physician. It then becomes the duty of the supervisory personnel to enforce sanitary rules for the handling of foodstuffs.

Both employees and inmates must abstain from smoking while they are handling food. This is not to imply that they are forbidden to smoke at all, but they must not have a cigarette, pipe or cigar dangling from their lips while preparing or serving food. Ashes, butts and burnt matches must be deposited in the proper receptacles and not carelessly tossed about.

Cleanliness must be stressed at all times and at every phase and operation of the food service program. Personal cleanliness —hands, fingernails, hair and clothing—is indeed important, but hardly more so than the proper cleansing of cooking and serving utensils. There is little gained by enforcing sanitation throughout the handling and cooking of food if at the last moment it is

served on a plate contaminated with flecks of garbage from preceding meals. Sanitation must be continuous and complete, or it
is not sanitation at all.

These employees who are assigned to some phase of the food
service program are actively conscious of the need for sanitary
practices in the handling of food. Every employee should become so, for eventually nearly everyone is called upon to supervise a dining room post during the serving of meals.

When an officer is sent to the dining room to help feed, he
reports to the dining room officer who issues him a form on which
is listed the post number, the menu and the ration that is to be
served at that particular meal. The officer should then proceed
immediately to his post and ascertain the following:

1. Are the inmate waiters wearing clean white uniforms and are their
hands and fingernails clean?
2. Are those required to touch the food wearing clean white canvas
gloves?
3. Is the steam table clean and sanitary?
4. Are the utensils used in serving the food clean and of the proper
size?
5. Are the plates, bowls, and silverware *clean?*

If any of these items fail to check out affirmatively, the officer
must see that they are corrected before the serving of the meal
commences. Since a new employee might not be expected to
know the nomenclature and sizes of serving utensils, each new
officer is schooled in their identification during the period he
spends in the Officers' Training School.

While the lines are being fed, the officer supervising a post
must see that each inmate receives the portion of food due him,
but not more than one ration at the steam table. Inmates serving
meat are to be watched closely so that they do not pass out extra
portions to their friends or save the best and biggest pieces for
them. Sometimes it will happen that an unwisely cut piece of
meat will be nearly all fat or all bone, or there may be something
else wrong with a plate of food. If an inmate calls an employee's
attention to something obviously wrong, the employee should

order it rectified. If in doubt, he should call a superior officer.

There are lieutenants moving about in the inner and outer circles of the dining room during the serving of each meal. If an officer feels that anything requires their attention, he should let them know immediately.

For instance, one of the areas might be running short of an item on the menu. If so, the officer in charge of that section should notify a lieutenant or the dining room officer in order that the supply may be replenished. It may sometimes be necessary to prepare additional quantities of the short item or a last minute substitution. Prompt notice of an imminent shortage will allow a few minutes in which to begin making up a shortage and thus prevent halting the lines and causing unnecessary delay.

Since food is not inexpensive, waste must be held to an absolute minimum. The total amount of raw food used daily in preparing meals for 5,200 inmates averages about 20,000 pounds. And the cost per meal in 1960-61 was .2406 cents or a total of $1,570,162. It would take but little waste to increase that figure substantially, because food discarded or wasted costs just as much as food eaten.

Visitors to the institution are usually impressed by the size of the inmate dining rooms and almost invariably ask how many persons they seat. At the Joliet Branch the dining room consists of six sections, each of which will seat 186 inmates, or a total of 1,116. At the Stateville Branch there are eight sections in the dining room and each section seats 241, or a total of 1,928.

When that many inmates are brought together, institution security becomes a prime concern. Officers who are not given posts to supervise must place themselves in strategic places in and around the dining room. They are to avoid congregating and talking with one another. Every officer should be in a position to quell a disturbance of any kind before it has a chance to spread and involve more than two or three inmates.

The importance of moving swiftly to stop trouble in its incipient stage cannot be too strongly emphasized. At the same time officers must be very careful not to give an appearance of exercising undue force in subduing an inmate or inmates. A calm, dispassionate attitude is the best approach to nearly any situation. Inmates are awakened at 6:15 A.M. for breakfast, which is served from 6:30 A.M to 7:00 A.M. Dinner, the second meal, is consumed between 11:30 A.M. and 12:10 P.M. Service of the final meal, supper, starts at 5:15 P.M. and continues until 6:00 P.M.

After the supper period, inmates are lodged in their cells. Lights out time is 9:00 P.M., when all are expected to go to bed.

Following is a typical menu of all meals for inmates during a one week period:

BREAKFAST	DINNER	SUPPER
Sunday		
Apple Butter	Roast Beef	Sliced Bologna
Sugar Corn Pops	W/Natural Gravy	Cream of Tomato Soup
Milk	Mashed Potatoes	Soda Crackers
Butterine	Creamed Corn	Cottage Cheese
Bread and Coffee	Mustard - Relish	Mustard - Cookies
	Bread and Coffee	Bread and Coffee
Monday		
Stewed Apples	Sliced Pimento Cheese	Potted Braised Beef
Dry Cereal	Potted Red Beans	W/Natural Gravy
Milk and Sugar	W/Meat & Tomato Sauce	Boiled Potatoes
Sweet Rolls	Mustard	Fresh Vegetables
Bread and Coffee	Apple Sauce	Piccalilli
	Bread and Tea	Baking Powder Biscuits
		Apple Butter & Butterine
		Bread and Coffee
Tuesday		
Apple Butter	Sliced Luncheon Meat	Baked Beef Casserole
Creamed Rice W/Raisins	Potted Macaroni	W/Tomato Sauce
Milk and Sugar	W/Meat & Tomato Sauce	Buttered Green Beans
Bread and Coffee	Boiled Cabbage	Mustard Sauce
	Spice Cookies	Apple Butter
	Bread and Tea	Bread and Coffee
Wednesday		
Stewed Prunes	Sliced Swiss Cheese	Braised Pork Steak
Dry Cereal	Fresh Beef Hash	W/Country Gravy
Milk and Sugar	(Southern Style)	Buttered Potatoes
Coffee Cake	Creamed Corn	Creamed Carrots
Bread and Coffee	Mustard Sauce	Mustard - Apple Butter
	Apple Sauce	Bread and Coffee
	Bread and Tea	
Thursday		
Stewed Raisins	Creamed Hamburger	Steamed Franks
Rolled Oats	W/Diced Carrots	Baked Navy Beans
Milk and Sugar	Boiled Potatoes	W/Diced Smoked Jowls
Butterine	Peanut Butter & Jelly	Mustard Sauce
Bread and Coffee	Piccalilli	Fresh Vegetables
	Bread and Tea	Ice Cream and Cookies
		Bread and Coffee

Friday

Stewed Mixed Fruit	Sliced American Cheese	Deep Fried Perch
Dry Cereal	Macaroni - Potted	W/Au Gatin Potatoes
Milk and Sugar	W/Cream Sauce	Creamed Corn
Raisin Bread	Fresh Vegetables	Piccalilli
Butterine	Graham Crackers	White Cake W/Icing
Bread and Coffee	Bread and Tea	Bread and Coffee

Saturday

Apple Butter	Sliced Luncheon Meat	Meat Balls and Spaghetti
Dry Cereal	Chili Con Carne	W/Italian Cheese Sauce
Milk and Sugar	Mustard Sauce	Mustard and Relish
2 Boiled Eggs	Soda Crackers	Fresh Vegetable
Bread and Coffee	Stewed Mixed Fruit	Chocolate Pudding
	Bread and Tea	Bread and Coffee

FRESH FARM VEGETABLES ARE SERVED DAILY IN SEASON

THE CHAPLAIN IN A CORRECTIONAL INSTITUTION

The role of the chaplain in correctional institutions has gone through various phases during the past century. In the middle of the nineteenth century, the chaplain was librarian, physical education director, mail censor, cell inspector, welfare worker, teacher. Our own law in Illinois, framed in the 1870s, indicated that the chaplain should make a weekly inspection of each cell in order to check on the reading of each inmate, should teach English and History at the discretion of the warden, should be in charge of the library and conduct religious services.

The reason for the law was obvious. Back in those days, there was almost exclusive emphasis on custody and so the greatest part of all other functions recognized as standard procedure in prisons today was relegated to the chaplain.

Two factors, specialization and a changing concept of the purpose of penitentiaries, have removed the chaplain from the library, the mail room, the playing field and the class room, and have left him free to fulfill in a more capable manner his own proper functions. These functions are outlined in the *Manual of Standards for State Institutions,* issued by the American Correctional Association. They are:

1. Conduct of a sacramental ministry.

2. Conduct of a counseling ministry.

3. Ministry to inmates' families and concerned persons.

4. Service to staff and operational personnel.

5. Interpretative ministry to the community.
6. Educational ministry for future chaplains.

Quite obviously, the conduct of the sacramental ministry is the basic function of any priest or minister. With reference to the Catholic Chaplain, this includes the Sacrifice of the Mass on Sundays and Holy Days of Obligation, frequent opportunity for Confession and Communion, periodic opportunity for the sacraments of Baptism and Confirmation, administering the sacrament of Extreme Unction to the sick; burying the dead; offering other religious services which are considered helpful for the moral advancement of the men, e.g., Holy Hour, First Saturday devotion.

There is a corollary to the above paragraph. All the items listed (with the exception of burying the dead!) demand a certain amount of knowledge on the part of the recipient. It is an obvious truth that a man should not be baptized until he knows the great privileges and the great responsibilities which come with Baptism. A man cannot go to Confession unless he knows what he is doing. The same is true of all the other points mentioned. But very many of the men who enter a correctional institution have had little or no basic religious training. The deficiency must be remedied and so it becomes the duty of the chaplain, in order to carry out his basic functions, to give adequate instructions to the men desiring to avail themselves of his sacramental ministry.

In his service to the inmate, the chaplain's duty goes beyond the sacramental ministry. It involves much personal counseling. There are various recognized factors in a large prison which make this part of a chaplain's ministry very important. These factors are: separation from loved ones, complete routinism, impersonality of authority, utter lack of privacy, abnormality of exclusively male companionship. A man must seek relief occasionally from the tensions caused by these factors. Many turn to the chaplain who, in the course of a single day, finds himself used as a safety valve, a source of information, a referral service, a confidant, a trusted guide. It can be an enlightening and a humbling experience. Out of it come many lessons. No matter how trivial a problem may seem to the chaplain, to the man who brings it to him, the problem is big. He should receive the courtesy of having the problem treated as he sees it and not as the chaplain regards it.

The chaplain comes in contact quite frequently with the families of the men confined in an institution. It some cases this contact begins quite early in the man's career. The families of many inmates suffer from the same misconceptions in regard to prison treatment as will be found among other members of the population. A communication from the chaplain helps to change such misconceptions.

Then there are many occasions in the course of the inmate's prison life where the chaplain will find it necessary to write to the man's family. Such occasions may occur when tragedy strikes the man or the family. It may be necessary at times to make known to the family if he is seriously ill. At the same time, letters from the family announcing some serious incident will generally be brought to the attention of the chaplain so that he may discuss the message with the man. In cases where there is obvious neglect on the part of parents or relatives, the chaplain may find it necessary to remind them of their duty to give as much support and encouragement as possible to the man during his imprisonment.

Any services which a chaplain extends to the men in an institution he is willing to give also to any member of the staff or operational personnel.

In addition, he is willing to explain the operation and the ideals of the institution he serves to interested outside groups. This he does because he is convinced that a more active interest on the part of outside groups is needed if the ideals of the institution are ever to be realized.

RELATIONS OF OFFICERS AND CHAPLAINS

There are problems in connection with caring for the needs of incarcerated men, which custodial officers and chaplains have in common. Each may have his various theories about what is wrong with the world and why crime continues to flourish, and what could or should be done to diminish it, but after all the theorizing is over, the facts still remain.

Since officers and chaplains are in this responsibility together, they must work together. They must not only understand their respective jobs, but in order to function for the best interests of all concerned, each must know something about the problems of the other.

There is always the possibility that a custodial officer may never look beyond the horizon of his own responsibility, and thus have little or no appreciation of what the chaplains are trying to do. There is also the possibility that a chaplain may lose his perspective and become unreasonable in what he expects of custodial officers.

Much of the effectiveness of officers and chaplains depends upon the attitude they have towards their respective jobs. Regardless of what people do for a living, it helps tremendously if they can enjoy what they are doing, and the only effective way of doing that is to visualize their jobs as in some way rendering a service to humanity. Perhaps it may seem to some that chaplains should find it easier to think of their work in that way, but a chaplain is human and unless he keeps his perspective where it ought to be, he is apt to look upon at least part of his task as a round of duties to be fulfilled. He may be tempted to discouragement when men for whom he had built such high hopes of what they would do when paroled or discharged, utterly fail and disappoint him. Instead, he keeps his mind on those who do make good, and goes on doing what he can to inspire men to start life over.

A chaplain with proper perspective realizes that custodial officers view a side of inmate life he never sees. He knows that guards may see the insincere inmate after he has been to church or Bible class, or just returned from an interview in which he gave his best song-and-dance to the chaplain. He realizes that guards may see the way the inmate acts, hear the way he talks, observe the various means he uses in getting out of work or acquiring something he is not supposed to have. In other words, officers are apt to see incarcerated men at their worst, whereas chaplains are apt to see them at their best. Unless chaplains keep reminding themselves of things as they actually are, they are liable to grow starry-eyed and too idealistic to be of any practical help to those who really mean business about becoming rehabilitated.

If a chaplain runs the risk of becoming too optimistic about the number of potential saints he has among his penal parishioners, then, on the other hand, the custodial officer must guard against becoming caught in the undertow of cynicism. He must not allow himself to think of a chaplain as engaged in a hopeless task, just because there are inmates who are insincere or others who seem to start out on a religious journey with very promising prospects but who end up in a spiritual shipwreck. A Chaplain is unhappy when he encounters an officer who nurtures the opinion that it is useless to offer religion to these men. He feels badly about it not only because he knows that such an attitude jeopardizes the officer's own spiritual future, but also because such an attitude will tend to make the officer less coöperative with what the chaplain is trying to do for the men. When religion really "takes," it works in prison as well as elsewhere.

It would be profitable for officers and chaplains to have periodic joint-sessions in which they could informally discuss their mutual problems.

Sub-Chaper (B): Inmates

PROCESSING NEW INMATES

All adult male prisoners convicted in the courts of northern Illinois are received at the Diagnostic Depot where they are held for study and classification with the objectives of determining the program of treatment and training best suited to their needs and of deciding to which institution they should be transferred. Thirty days or more may be required for the members of the professional staff to make a thorough diagnostic study of new inmates. This is the average length of time an inmate remains at the Diagnostic Depot.

In order to handle the turnover of inmates, which averages

Entrance to Diagnostic Depot. Joliet Branch.

about 200 per month, it is essential to process the inmates without unnecessary delay, so that they may enter an active work or training program in the institution to which they are assigned by the classification board.

The majority of prisoners received at the Diagnostic Depot come from Cook County, usually arriving in sizeable groups. For that reason the security measures used in admitting them into the institution compound varies somewhat from those employed in the reception of prisoners from less populous counties. The Cook County Sheriff's van unloads in the Sally Port, where the manacled prisoners are locked between gates until the Sheriff's van, with the deputies' weapons deposited in it, has been driven to the front entrance out of the reach of inmates. Then the Cook County prisoners are marched into the building through the recreation yard.

Deputies from smaller counties deliver their prisoners to the Guard Hall and deposit their weapons in the Armory before uncuffing their prisoners. In both instances the Captain in Charge of the Diagnostic Depot appears immediately to inspect the credentials of the deputies and to accept the Mittimus and Travel Vouchers. If everything is in order, he signs the Travel Voucher and returns it to the deputy, or Sheriff. From that point on all prisoners are processed in an identical manner.

The first thing required of a new inmate is that he surrender his personal property. The Captain counts the inmate's money before him and lists it, together with his other possessions, on the temporary property sheet.

Next on the agenda is a trip to the Barber Shop, where the inmate receives a hair trim in preparation for being photographed.

He is then taken to the Bureau of Identification to be photographed and fingerprinted. That process completed, the inmate is taken to the shower room where he must strip, submit to a naked search, take a shower, have the pubic hair clipped from his body and blue ointment applied to the denuded area.

After the foregoing procedure, he is issued a clean set of khaki fatigues, clean underwear, and a pair of shoes. Then he is assigned to a cell and advised to study the *Inmates' Rule Book*. At this time such of his personal property as is permitted in the institution is returned to him. The inmate is informed that on the second or third day he will be interviewed in regards to compiling a correspondence and visiting list. He is told he will be permitted to list six persons with whom he may wish to correspond or receive visits during his incarceration.

Emphasis is placed on the fact that he should concentrate on the immediate members of his family as they are more apt to stand by him while he is in prison than are mere friends and acquaintances. This fact has been borne out time and time again.

During an inmate's stay at the Diagnostic Depot the Captain is often confronted by inmate requests for interviews. These concern many problems of the new inmate. Answers to the type of questions most frequently asked are usually supplied in the orientation program. Some of the requests are of a nature which are referred to the chaplain of the inmate's faith. All others are handled within the policies of the rules and regulations governing the request. All requests are honored.

On the second day the inmate is summoned to the Captain's Office, where he is shown the personal property not returned to him and informed that he has an option of mailing the articles home or of having them confiscated as contraband. In either event the disposition of the property is noted on his personal property sheet. An inmate's cash and other valuables, including his social security card, are forwarded to the Chief Clerk at Stateville. All Military papers are sent to the Veteran's Service Officer.

By agreement all clothing worn into the Diagnostic Depot becomes the property of the state, since all inmates leaving the institution either on parole or discharge are given a complete issue of new clothing furnished by the state. The used clothing is sent to the State Penal Farm at Vandalia.

After the personal property issue has been settled by the Captain, the inmate then goes to the Bureau of Identification for a thorough processing. The fingerprint technician examines the inmate's body and notes all scars, deformities and other personal identification factors such as height, weight, color of hair, color of eyes, etc. The inmate is also interrogated as to his past criminal record and his statements recorded on the B. of I. record.

Once again the Captain interviews the inmate and asks him a series of questions designed to elicit his complete life history. The inmate's responses are recorded on a work sheet which is later compared against the B. of I. records and the Mental Health Department's records. If these records check with one another, the information contained in them is transcribed onto the official record forms.

During the remainder of the inmate's stay at the Diagnostic Depot he undergoes medical examinations, blood tests, vaccinations, dental and eye examinations. He is interviewed by the Mental Health Staff, who analyze his emotional condition, test his mental powers, and finally determine his classification.

If an inmate is classified as being improvable, he will be sent to Pontiac; criminally insane or borderline mental defective, to Menard; an occasional offender with short sentence, to the Joliet Branch; and inmates with long term sentences, recidivists and trouble makers, to the Stateville Branch.

When the Mental Health Department notifies the Captain of the Diagnostic Depot that an inmate has been classified, he then rechecks all the records for accuracy, making certain that the Medical Records, Mental Health Reports, and the Statement of Facts are intact and that an Isolation Card has been prepared. The inmate's Isolation Card will state whether or not he is eligible to handle food, whether he is a drug addict, or whether there are any pending warrants on him. All warrants are marked in RED.

After the Captain has satisfied himself that the records are complete, he forwards to the Warden a triplicate transfer form, showing the name of the inmate, the register number assigned to him and the branch of the Illinois State Prison System to which the inmate is being transferred. The Warden then schedules the inmate for transfer to the institution where he will commence serving his time.

Thus far little has been said of the responsibilities of officers assigned to the Diagnostic Depot. They do not take an active part in conducting the diagnostic study of the inmates. The professional staff does that. But this in no way minimizes the importance of officers' general duties, nor does it indicate that officers cannot be helpful in the orientation of new inmates.

At the Diagnostic Depot security measures must be undertaken as seriously as they are at Joliet or Stateville. Officers should be experts at conducting searches of an inmate's person and apparel in order to make certain that no dangerous contraband is smuggled into the institution. It should also be remembered that new prisoners are frequently despondent and may have suicidal tendencies. On the other hand, there are escape risks and some of them may make a rash and desperate attempt to escape. Because of these possibilities, officers must closely observe the actions and attitudes of all new inmates. If for any reason an officer suspects the attitude of a prisoner or detects signs of emotional disorder, he should immediately report the matter to the Captain in Charge, who in turn submits this information to the Warden and the Staff Psychiatrist.

The absolute necessity for carrying out effective sanitary measures is another matter to which officers at the Diagnostic Depot must give special attention. Not infrequently inmates with communicable diseases or body vermin are brought into the Diagnostic Depot, hence use of the blue ointment. It is true that the doctors will soon discover these cases and either isolate them or begin treating them. But, meanwhile, the germ will have spread. Therefore, it is imperative the officers at the Diagnostic Depot should see that everything, clothing, bedding, kitchen and dining room utensils, and the inmates' quarters, are scrubbed well and frequently.

Although there is an established orientation program, which is conducted by an assistant warden, the officers at the Diagnostic Depot should have sufficient general knowledge of the prison's organization to enable them to answer a new inmate's questions as to prison regulations, the academic and vocational training available to him, the possibility of attending church services of his choice, etc. If the man newly committed to prison does not receive advice from his supervising officers, he will seek it from other inmates, usually those who have had previous experience in the institution and may have established uncoöperative attitudes. Well informed officers can do much to prevent this from happening.

ASSIGNING INMATES TO PRISON JOBS

In assigning inmates to jobs, one must first determine the capability and mentality of the inmate as a guide to placing him properly on an institutional assignment. For this purpose a copy of the psychometric report compiled on the inmate at the Diagnostic Depot is kept in the files of the Senior Captains at Isolation. The intelligence quotients of inmates fall into one of the following categories:

1. Very Superior.
2. Superior.
3. High Average.
4. Average.
5. Low Average.
6. Dull.
7. Borderline Mental Defective.
8. Mental Defective.

Inmates with low average intelligence may be assigned to the simpler tasks. Those with high average intelligence may be assigned to the more complex tasks. However, in placing the inmate, consideration is also given to:

1. *Interest*—The inmate, despite a low I.Q., may show a high mechanical interest. He, therefore, would be assigned accordingly.

2. *Behavior*—He may be a disciplinary problem or may be erratic and have a tendency to fly off the handle. Consequently, he would not be placed on essential assignments where he could be a disturbing influence.

3. *Stability*—He may request frequent changes because of inability to get along with others, or may "burn out" on an assignment after a short period.

4. *Judgment*—A person with high intellect may be a liability because he lacks perception and good judgment.

5. *Supervision*—He may require more than the usual amount of supervision because of gambling, escape risk, homosexual tendencies, etc.

After the Assignment Captain has made a preliminary evaluation of these factors, he must also consider the inmate's needs, interest and legitimate wishes insofar as practicable. When making assignments, the training of inmates for productive work is kept in mind. There are many assignments where constructive on-the-job training can be given inmates as an aid to rehabilitation.

If an inmate has less than an eighth grade education, and if the factors in his case warrant it, he is usually assigned to the grade school. In some cases the inmate may not be capable of absorbing secondary or advanced education; but if he has a sound intellect, the academic facilities provide him an opportunity to develop it. When an inmate has reached the limit of his academic potential, he is then assigned either to vocational training, maintenance or service jobs, or to one of many industrial jobs.

In order to employ as many inmates as possible in constructive and satisfying work it is necessary to examine every aptitude to determine the extent to which inmates may be usefully employed. Even jobs that require little skill or training can have rehabilitative value, for there is satisfaction to be gained from doing a real day's work. However, the work must be of a type that is demonstrably useful or necessary. The inmate cannot gain any satisfaction from "boondoggling" jobs that provide work but accomplish nothing.

Some assignments, however, are made primarily in the interest of institutional security. If an inmate is considered an escape risk, he will of course be assigned where he can be closely supervised. In quite a number of cases other factors are taken into consideration in assigning jobs. Inmates are not assigned in a haphazard manner to jobs for which they may not be fitted or to which they aspire for questionable reasons.

Although the duties of the Assignment Captain are in some respects similar to those of a personnel manager for a large industrial concern, there are many factors which the Assignment Captain must consider in addition to finding a man capable of performing a specific job. In prison, where rehabilitation is the goal, the Assignment Captain must not only ask himself "How well can this man do the job?" but also "What can the job do for this man?"

Stone Quarry at Joliet Branch

INMATE WHO RESENTS JOB ASSIGNMENT

In an institution the size of the Joliet-Stateville Branch, one must remember that there are numerous jobs to be filled by inmates in order to keep the institution operating in the prescribed manner.

As in any other type of endeavor, some jobs are more desirable than others and this is where resentment on the part of some inmates enters the scene.

To begin with there are many utility jobs throughout the institution which must be performed daily. Typical assignments that handle these chores are: the coal divisions, the inmate's dining room, and the Yard Detail. As a general rule inmates newly received from the Diagnostic Depot are assigned to these tasks and remain on them for a short period of time before they are reassigned to other jobs. It may happen that a new inmate receives a disciplinary report for some infraction of the rules and then feels that he is being discriminated against because he is kept on a service assignment for a period of time. His feeling would not be justified by the facts, for all new inmates are required to start at the bottom and work toward better assignments. The same holds true in any type of an organization.

In every group of new inmates there are likely to be a few malcontents who feel that it is beneath their dignity to perform menial tasks. These inmates not only perform their tasks in a slipshod manner, doing as little as possible, but they also attempt to agitate their fellow inmates and to belittle those who would do a good job if left to their own devices. Fortunately, the unstable, malcontented, and trouble making inmates are a distinct minority. The average inmate just wants to do his time as peacefully as possible and get out of prison as quickly as he can.

However, wanting to get along in prison and wanting to get out of prison do not necessarily imply an active interest in the task at hand. One of the common denominators of the majority of prison inmates is a poor employment record. Few of them have ever been able to decide what they want to do in life. Consequently, few of them like to work at all. And their records bear evidence that they will do almost anything, except work at a job that they do not like.

How to interest these inmates in their work is one of the institution's biggest problems. It has been shown that many varying considerations enter into the assigning of an inmate to a prison job. Where to assign the new inmate is the biggest and most important decision the Senior Captains have confronting them. Another problem of major proportions is in keeping an inmate satisfied with his environment after he has been established on an assignment.

Some guidance in meeting these problems is available to the Senior Captains, for during the course of the Classification Program information is compiled which gives the Assignment Captain an insight into the inmate's problems, preferences and possibilities. Typical classification reports give a brief resumé of the inmate's personal history—his age, education, mentality, skills and work record. This kind of information helps the Assignment Captains to place the inmate on the type of job for which he is qualified. Also available to the Assignment Captains are the results of the aptitude and preference tests given to the inmate. These not only tell what kind of work the inmate is capable of performing but they also indicate his likes and dislikes, thus disclosing probable areas of interest.

Because many inmates have never shown an inclination to apply themselves to any task, it devolves upon the assignment officer to try to interest the inmate in the job to which he has been assigned. Even on the less attractive jobs in the institution there are some redeeming features. The formation of good work habits can be cited. It may also be pointed out that performing a needed service for one's fellow men is a worthy undertaking. On the other hand most assignments provide an opportunity for the inmate to learn a valuable trade. Officers should remind the inmate that gaining competence in some trade may enable him to stay out of prison.

There are two other areas of inmate discontent that pose problems which must be dealt with. One concerns those inmates who have been granted parole or are soon to be discharged. The institutional policy is to assign these men either to the Farm Detail or to the Outside Coal Detail. Oftentimes these men fail to comprehend the reasons for this policy and will moan and groan, "I don't want to go to work out there. Why can't I stay where I am?"

Well, there are some sound reasons for putting them on outside details. For one, they constitute a reservoir of low security risks for work outside the walls. For another, it makes jobs available for other inmates who have good work records. A third reason is that outside work hardens them physically and puts them in condition to do an honest day's work after they are released. Finally, it may be pointed out to them that they have kept warm and eaten well through the efforts of inmates who have preceded them on the Outside Coal and Farm details, and that it is now their turn to do the same for others.

One of the stricter forms of discipline employed against inmates is the practice of transferring an inmate from some assignment that he may have striven for years to obtain. When an inmate has shown considerable competence and worked hard and well for a number of years to earn one of the better assignments in the institution, it becomes a severe disappointment to be sent to the bottom of the ladder for some violation of the rules. More often than not he will fail to show much interest in his new assignment. The sensible way to encourage such an inmate is to explain to him that through hard work and good behavior he can redeem himself in the opinion of the Officials and perhaps regain privileges lost because of his own misdemeanors.

As a rule most inmates will respond well to any personal interest shown in them. There are countless examples of inmates "finding" themselves in prison and later going out and creating a highly satisfying life for themselves. It is more than reasonable to suppose that the human equation helped them to solve their problems. There is little satisfaction to be had from doing a job well if there is no one around to acknowledge that it has been well done and to encourage them to do it even better next time.

Assignment officers should guard against falling into the habit of constant fault finding. It is easy to criticize an inmate's short comings. It should also be possible to give him credit for something now and then. One way to be sure of finding something praiseworthy in an inmate's performance is to assign him a project that you are sure that he can handle, give him directions that he can understand, and then turn the job over to him. In that way you can give the inmate a feeling of responsibility that should cause him to take pride in his work and to do a job that deserves an honest compliment.

It is essential on jobs that require different levels of skill or training to promote a feeling of progress by assigning the inmate to more difficult phases of the work as he develops skill. In this way his interest can be maintained, for the work will always present a challenge to his ability.

Thus far we have attempted in various ways to define the attitudes that officers may encounter among the troublesome inmates on their assignment and suggest ways of altering those attitudes to conform with accepted standards. There is one thing every officer may be certain of, that in supervising inmates he is still dealing with people. True, an inmate's bad habits may be firmly set and his attitudes completely anti-social, but underneath his veneer of toughness are the same hopes and wishes that exist in everyone, although the inmate himself might be the last to admit it.

At all times it must be remembered that this is a prison and that officials will encounter troublesome and even dangerous inmates in most assignments. Inmates of this type cannot all be assigned to one division, therefore, they are assigned to various divisions where they are apt to cause the least trouble. If officers have troublesome inmates in their division, they should not request their removal because they may be a problem to them. Rather they should keep the Captains and other Supervising Officers informed of any unusual situation regarding troublesome inmates. These officials should work with officers and give all the assistance that is needed in handling difficult or recalcitrant inmates.

A fundamental of human behavior is that whatever we do in response to others is based upon our anticipation of how they will react towards us. That is why the administration should constantly stress that officers must be fair and consistent in their dealings with inmates. Employees can imagine how difficult it would be to work for a man if they could not recognize things that annoyed him and if, in fact, they could not even tell when he was annoyed. In such a situation either they would soon be out of a job or they would be a nervous wreck. It is certainly not reasonable to expect maladjusted inmates to endure a situation that even well adjusted persons could not tolerate. If, therefore, a correctional officer would be effective, he must keep an even temper, show no favoritism, be absolutely fair with the inmates, and employ his best judgment in advance of every action that he takes.

This course will win him, if not the admiration, at least the respect of the inmates. And from that vantage point he is in a good position to win their coöperation and to influence their interests.

RECREATION ACTIVITIES

Recreation plays an important part in the over-all program of rehabilitation. It not only teaches a man the lessons of sportsmanship and coöperation, but it also relaxes his mind and conditions it to accept new ideas and to form new attitudes.

Like work, recreation gives an inmate an outlet for tense emotions that might otherwise build up until they are released as a destructive force. Unlike work, participation in sports, either as a player or a spectator, tends to stimulate the inmate's interest and cause him to follow his favorite games on the radio and in the newspapers. Thus he gains an additional benefit from the recreational program because cell time spent in listening to, reading about, or talking over a hotly contested game is the time that will not be spent in worrying about his troubles.

Apart from its mental health aspects, recreation, also contributes to the physical well-being of inmates. The man who gets out doors, takes regular exercise, and breathes deeply of the pure air is going to remain healthier than the one who stays inside.

These are some of the reasons why officers should encourage inmates under their supervision to participate in the recreation program, which offers something for men of all ages and conditions of health.

At the Stateville Branch there are five recreational yards, one for each of the cellhouses. In addition there is a baseball field which would be the envy of many a major league ball club. The Joliet Branch also has a recreational yard for each cellhouse and a separate baseball diamond.

Each recreational yard has one or more softball diamonds, an area abutting the wall set off for handball courts, a basketball court, several horseshoe courts, badminton courts, a set of parallel bars for gymnastics, and weight lifting bars. There is also played here a variation on horseshoe pitching, called "washers" in which an iron washer about $2\frac{1}{2}$ inches in diameter is tossed at a cup embedded in the ground. The playing of touch-football is also permitted during the football season.

Softball is perhaps the most popular sport in the institution. There are sixteen teams composed of men on the various assignments throughout the institution, and patterned after the major leagues. One league is called the American and the other the National. At the close of the season a "world series" is played and then the "series" is followed up by an "all star" game.

Each team chooses its own captain and manager, but all league games are played under the supervision of an officer, who sometimes finds himself acting as a referee because, as sports fans know, close games produce heated discussions. The softball schedule is formulated by the Athletic Director. He also arranges the schedule of weekly baseball games.

Every Saturday during the baseball season (hard-ball league) either a semi-pro or a service team is invited from the outside to play against the institution nine. These games have a large and vociferous group of fans who invariably root for the outside team and inform it of the weakness of the inmate players. Despite these handicaps the inmate team has had fair success against good service teams from the Great Lakes Naval Training Station, Glenview Naval Air Base, Chanute Air Force Base, and Fort Sheridan, to name a few.

Spectator interest in these baseball games is so great it has been found by the officials that suspension of an inmate's privilege to attend them is an effective punishment for minor infractions of the rules.

In winter when mud and snow and cold make the outdoor recreation unpleasant, motion pictures replace the weekly baseball games. On Saturdays the Chapel doubles as a theatre where inmates can view the show on the new cinemascope screen.

Whenever inmates are in their cells, they may listen to their choice of three different radio stations tuned in on the centrally-controlled and monitored institutional radio system. These inmates assigned to late details or night jobs generally are permitted to have a radio or television set on their assignment. Television sets have been installed in the hospitals.

The institutional policy is to encourage interest in sports of all kinds by seeing to it that all major sporting events are carried over the institutional radio system. Certainly they are preferable to crime stories, for instance, which are never permitted on the institutional radio system.

Other forms of recreation which the inmates may enjoy are art and music. With permission they may purchase art supplies through the Inmates' Commissary. The possession of art supplies is, however, governed strictly by permit. Some of the men are really excellent artists and have created pictures which have won favorable comment both from visitors to the institution and from critics at local art exhibitions. Inmates may also own a musical instrument and play it in their cells at specified periods. Many of the inmates owning musical instruments are members of the Stateville Band, which plays at all the ball games and in addition upon many other special occasions.

Chess, checkers, dominoes and playing cards are lighter forms of diversion permitted. However, these are for recreation only and may not be employed in gambling.

It has been found that the various recreational privileges, which are highly valued by the inmates, give the institution a powerful lever against disobedience and misbehavior. Not infrequently an inmate reported for some infraction of the rules asks the Disciplinary Captain to put him in isolation rather than to take away any of his recreational privileges.

Officers who supervise recreational yards see to it that certain inmates do not monopolize the fields in various events, and are on the alert for undue roughness, especially during football season. They make sure that all damaged equipment is reported to the proper authority, so that it may be repaired or replaced as the case may be. All wilful damage of athletic equipment must be reported immediately to the Senior Captains.

It should be obvious that the institution has a moral obligation to release back into society, when his time is up, a man who is in as good or better mental condition than he was upon arrival. That obligation cannot be fulfilled by locking a man in a cell with nothing to do but worry and hate. There must be some outlet for pent-up emotions and excess energy. Recreation of some kind is essential to good mental health. The institution is also morally obliged to protect the health of the inmate as well as it can, not only for humane reasons, but so that upon release he may be physically able to earn an honest living. Therefore, daily periods of outdoor recreation must be given and encouraged.

INMATE SCHOOLS

To establish an effective school system it is first necessary to determine the intelligence rating of its prospective students. Obviously a student cannot learn beyond his inherited intellectual capacity. Some of the inmates received are mentally deficient and cannot be expected to meet the usual academic standards. It is the duty, however, of the administration and officers to encourage all men to participate in the school program to the limit of their ability.

What will education do for the inmates? One of the lesser

advantages is that it gives the men something to do. This is especially important in prison where most of the inmates spend many
hours daily in their cells. If some of this time is spent in study,
the opportunity for mischief and more serious trouble is markedly
reduced. In this institution where hobbies are almost non-existent,
it should be recognized that the encouragement of academic
learning and regular study habits contributes greatly to the
morale and security of the prison.

The biggest value of education, of course, is that it increases
the inmates' power to get and hold better jobs when they are
released, and thus may become a lesser burden on society. Even
for inmates with low mental ability, education has an advantage.
Such inmates come in contact with better educated men, and since
men are imitators by nature, they begin to imitate the better men.

Grade School and Book Bindery. Stateville Branch.

They adopt a more reasonable attitude and begin to attach some
purpose to their lives. When an inmate comes into the school

system he is given every opportunity to advance as far as he can. However, if he is unable to maintain the required academic pace he is dropped from the school and transferred to another assignment.

In order to provide for all levels of intelligence or previous training, the Stateville schools give all levels of instruction. There is an elementary school which starts at first grade and ends at the eighth grade. When a man finishes this school he is awarded a diploma from the recognized school system of Will County, Illinois. This diploma does not show that the man has even been in prison.

The Stateville High School offers a general high school curriculum, the completion of which entitles an inmate to a General Educational Development certificate awarded by the Lockport, Illinois, Township High School. These certificates are awarded

A modern High School that meets the exacting requirements necessary outside the prison walls. Stateville Branch.

only after the successful completion of a battery of tests given over a two day period by the Veterans' Testing agent for this area. The certificates may be used for entrance to any university.

High School. Professor Givens supervising instruction of class in the use of the slide rule. Stateville Branch.

Also, available is a visual type of higher education, at the college level, over television. Regular tests are given which may qualify TV students for college degrees.

Libraries

Libraries have made great strides during the past half-century. Working hand-in-hand with publishing houses, printing companies, book binderies, artists, engravers, and authors, libraries have done much to realize their ambition of a "book for every reader and a reader for every book."

Realizing the therapeutic value of reading, prison administrators should try consistently to improve the facilities and service in their libraries and should abandon the old prison idea that it was sufficient to put a Bible into each cell and hope for the best. However, the Bible in each cell is important.

Joliet-Stateville does have one central library, but we also have many branch libraries and books are always available. It is felt that only a central library in a prison would result in decreased circulation and inferior service. Instead of just one central library, the library catalogue is divided in various collections. There are fifteen of these:

(1) Four general collections—one each at the Diagnostic Depot, the Honor Farm, the Joliet Branch and the Stateville Branch.

(2) Two collections of books on philosophy and religion—one at the Joliet Branch and one at Stateville. These are in charge of the full-time chaplains.

(3) One useful arts' collection in the vocational school at Stateville.

(4) One school library housed in the high school at Stateville.

(5) Seven fiction collections. One in each cell house at the Joliet and Stateville Branches. All collections are rotated.

Inmate librarians are in charge of all collections. These men have received some training in the use of the Dewey Decimal classification system and the book of Cutter numbers. There is no comprehensive cataloging system. Author and title cards are kept of the collections.

Many men in the prison who are assigned to pay jobs, to the vocational school, or to jobs relating to their trades are not disposed to attend school on a full time basis. The school program extends to them through the medium of correspondence courses. These men prepare their lessons in their spare time and send them to the school for grading. They are called to the school at regular intervals for tests and for tutoring if they require aid. Inmates at the Joliet Branch also participate in this program. In fact, there are usually several students in correspondence study from the State Industrial School at Sheridan, Illinois. There are usually six or seven hundred correspondence courses in force at all times.

Some of the men who are high school graduates take correspondence courses from outside universities. These courses carry credit toward college degrees and are offered in a wide range of subjects. Tuition charges for these courses are paid by the inmate and lessons are mailed through the school office. Relatively few men can take these courses because of the cost, but all men who qualify and who can afford it are encouraged to take advantage of this method of earning college credit.

All of the teaching at Stateville is done by inmate teachers supervised by qualified civilian teachers and herein lies one of the most serious problems. It is difficult to find inmates who have the educational background, interest, disposition, patience and personality which are necessary requisites for effective teaching. It is a problem to attract and hold inmate teachers because they are the type of men most often sought by other assignments because of their natural abilities, previous training and generally high calibre. Teaching also becomes burdensome since all correspondence lessons as well as classroom lessons must be graded on holidays, Sundays, evening and during any other spare time. No compensation is given to teachers, and jobs which offer pay or other advantages constantly attract them away from the school.

There are always men in the institution who have not taken part in the academic training program. Many of these men will be found on all assignments throughout the prison. Some of these men do not belong in the school program but many of them should be encouraged to participate. It is quite possible that officers can encourage a man who is thought to be lazy and shiftless to find some meaning in his life and to become a useful citizen.

VOCATIONAL SCHOOL

The vocational school training program is a very important element in the operation of the institution and in the rehabilitation of inmates. It provides useful employment for inmates who, if it were not for the vocational school, would have to be placed on other assignments. Since the close of World War II, the vocational school has had a tremendous growth. Today there are twenty-four (24) different trades and vocations being taught

Vocational School. Warden Ragen speaking with inmate of the Vocational
School. Stateville Branch.

and additional building space had to be erected to house all the
facilities. With all these trades being taught a reservoir of me-
chanically skilled inmates who can be placed in various jobs in
and around the institution is created. Vocational training not
only teaches inmates to work, but also equips them with a trade

which will enable them to take their place in society thoroughly qualified to earn an honest living.

A good number of inmates arrive at this institution with a chip on their shoulders. They believe that the world owes them a living. They have seldom worked at anything worthwhile when they were on the outside. Inmates of this calibre almost have to be challenged to accept the opportunity to learn a trade. But, all inmates enter the vocational school on a voluntary basis. Reports of the Classification Board are studied and evaluated on all applicants. Inmates are given personal interviews in which it is attempted to learn the feelings and attitudes of the individual, what he expects to derive from vocational guidance, his aims in learning a trade, what his past work record has been, and his educational background.

Many inmates request interviews stating that they wish to take up radio, television or electrical work. Often these inmates do not have the educational requirements to enter these fields, and are then referred to the superintendent of education. When an interview has been successfully concluded with an inmate and it is felt that he will fit into the program, a letter is sent to the Senior Captain requesting that he be assigned to the Vocational School. If the inmate has had a satisfactory institution record, the Senior Captain will approve the request and assign the inmate to the vocational school.

Among the 24 trades offered, there are nine (9) basic trades. They are radio and television, Typewriter Repair, Printing, Auto Mechanics, Electrical Refrigeration, Welding, Sign Painting, Body and Fender Repair, and Wood Working.

In the printing class all institutional printing is done. It would be impossible to itemize all the various forms that come off the presses. The typewriter repair class maintains and repairs all state owned typewriters as well as typewriters owned by inmates. It also repairs adding machines, calculating machines, recorders and various other business machines.

Radio and television classes handle the repair of many of the employees' sets, in addition to all institutional owned sets, plus

Vocational School. Carpenter Shop where boat building for the Conservation Department takes place. Stateville Branch.

the institutional communication system.

The sign class makes and maintains all signs for use by the institution. It also makes signs and displays for the Department of Conservation, many of them being used at State and County fairs.

The auto mechanics class handles all repairs of institutional trucks, busses and squad cars, and some State Police cars.

There are three Vocational Guard Instructors assigned to the vocational school. Their jobs consist of more than just serving as instructors. Security and discipline are the first requisites, as after all this is a maximum security institution. The guard instructors must maintain continuous surveillance.

By observation they can detect any indication of inmate unrest and any threat to the institutional security. Discipline must be maintained at all times. Guard instructors must have the ability to develop and supervise inmate instructors, of whom there is one for each of the trades being taught. Some of the inmates selected as instructors have had previous experience in the trade which they are helping to teach; others have learned their trade in the Vocational School.

In addition to the above, Vocational Guard Instructors supervise and oversee all work that is being done. They must be especially alert to see that there is no waste of material or mishandling of tools and equipment. They instruct inmates in the proper use of all tools and equipment and also teach safety precaution measures.

It is to be noted that the vocational school carries almost 4,000 tools on its inventory in addition to materials from which almost anything could be made. Therefore, it can readily be seen why strict discipline must be maintained at all times and why, as previously mentioned, inmates must be approved by the Senior Captain before they can be assigned to the vocational school.

Every tool that leaves the tool crib must be checked out by one of the Vocational Guard Instructors or by the Superintendent of Vocational Training, and the tools are checked back into the tool crib in the same manner as they were issued. At no time and under no circumstances are inmates permitted to check in or out any tools. In view of the many tools in use and the materials available, it is necessary that constant shakedowns be conducted of the various departments within the vocational school as a security measure.

There are no cash appropriations made by the State of Illinois to conduct operation of classrooms in the vocational school. The vocational school is maintained by profits derived from the Inmate's Commissary, although from time to time the State has purchased some of the larger pieces of equipment now in use.

It is believed that if the vocational school has been instrumental in teaching a man good work habits, it has accomplished something worthwhile. Many inmates who have taken courses in the vocational school have later written the Warden thanking him for the help the vocational school has given them in obtaining jobs after release and in restoring them to their places in society. Former inmates who make a success of their lives after release are seldom heard from. Only the failures make head-lines. Fortunately a great many do become good citizens and take their place in society and do not return to a life of crime.

BARBER SCHOOL

The Joliet-Stateville Branches of the Illinois State Penal Sys-tem have a charter granted by the State of Illinois which permits operation of a Barber School within the institutions. At both branches of the institution, the Barber Schools are supervised by a Registered Barber.

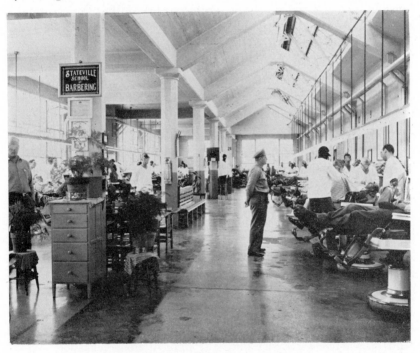

Stateville Barber School and Shop.

In addition to operating the Barber Schools in a manner con-sistent with safety and security, the Barber Instructor is required to teach the practice and theory of barbering — practice, by demonstrating correct methods of shaving and haircutting;

theory, by teaching anatomy, physiology, bacteriology, recognition and care of skin diseases, and the sterilization and care of equipment.

Before an inmate may be enrolled as a student barber, he must meet these requirements: Pass a thorough medical examination by the prison physician; have the equivalent of two years high school education; and finally he must have a satisfactory prison record so that he can gain the approval of the Assignment Captain.

After an inmate has been transferred to the Barber School, an application to register him as a student barber is made to the Department of Registration and Education. This application must be accompanied by two photographs of the applicant, his high school accreditation, his health certificate, and the sum of five dollars to cover fees. If the application is accepted, a student barber license is issued by the Illinois Department of Registration and Education. From that date on the student is officially credited for his hours of barber training. The student training period occupying nine months, or 1,872 hours, of which 234 hours are devoted to theory and 1,638 hours to practice. Weekly tests of the student barber's progress are given, graded and recorded.

After the inmate has completed his student barber training, he may take an apprentice barber examination, conducted at the institution by the Illinois Barber Board. If the inmate passes the test, he may upon application and payment of another five dollar fee, be licensed as an apprentice barber. When the apprentice barber satisfactorily completes the required twenty-seven months' training under the supervision of one or more registered barbers he becomes eligible to take an examination admitting him to full status as a registered barber. Since all barber licenses must be renewed annually, the inmate barber does not receive his registered barber's license until the date of his release.

In conjunction with the Barber School and in addition to the main shop, there are eleven other barber shops throughout the institution. Altogether they employ about 85 inmate barbers, most of whom have received their training in the institutional barber school. All of these shops are under the direct supervision of a registered barber, whose duties include the ordering of all barber supplies and equipment.

In the main Barber Shop at Stateville an average of 1,000 shaves and 200 haircuts are given daily. On a weekly basis this amounts to somewhat more than 5,000 shaves and 1,000 haircuts. To accomplish this amount of work, the Barber Shop must maintain a very strict schedule and this can be done only through the coöperation of officers in bringing their lines into the shop on time. A fifteen or twenty minute delay by any one line can upset the schedule for an entire day.

With the large number of inmates who are constantly coming and going through the waiting room of the barber shop, a problem of maintaining security and discipline is posed. Ordinarily there are three or four different assignments in the waiting room at one time. Therefore, it is the duty of each officer to watch everyone and see that there is no contact between inmates on the various assignments. Neither is talking permitted in either place.

Officers assigned to the Barber Shop must be especially careful in the handling of razors and shears. Counts of them must be made and checked several times daily. Each inmate barber is issued a tool kit containing two razors and one pair of shears. With the exception of tools assigned to relief barbers, each kit is numbered the same as the chair to which the barber is assigned. A record is kept of each kit and the inmate barbers are instructed never to lay their tools down so that someone else might pick them up. Neither may they trade tools without permission.

If permission is granted, the records are changed to correspond. Thus, at any time, the officer can look at the records and ascertain the number on the tools assigned to an inmate barber.

For reasons of sanitation a clean steam towel and face towel are provided for each inmate shaved. There are some inmates who might want to take these small towels to use as washcloths. In the event that one is found in the possession of an unauthorized inmate, a disciplinary report must be written.

Barber Shop units are operated in the Administration Building, the Hospital, the Officers Kitchen, the General Kitchen, Isolation, Detention, Cellhouse "C" (Farm Detail) and at the Honor Farm, thus making it possible to provide barber services to all segments of the institutional population without undue loss of time, inconvenience or risk. Hospital patients are barbered in portable chairs carried into the wards.

In the Detention Hospital and in Isolation and Segregation no straight razors or shears are used. For security reasons inmates confined there are shaved with locked safety razors or electric razors and their hair is cut only with electric clippers.

Although the Barber Shops provide a necessary service for both the officers and inmates of this institution, it should be remembered that training student barbers is an equally important function of the Barber School. In it, as in every department of the institution, the inmates should be encouraged to learn their trade and to prepare themselves for eventual release. Barbering is a vocation admirably suited to the needs of former inmates. A Master Barber rarely encounters any difficulty in obtaining a job wherever he may go. There is a good reason for this. Under Illinois law three years of apprenticeship are required to earn a registered barber's license, and no barber may tutor more than one apprentice at a time. This creates an obstacle for most men desirous of learning the barber trade in civilian life. Therefore, barbers have little competition either in finding jobs or in operating their own establishments. Few businesses can be started with less capital than is required to open a small barber shop. Yet that small capital outlay can set up a location where the barber can practice his trade, earn good wages for his own labor and possibly reap a profit from the labor of employees.

Officer's barber shops are located in both branches of the Institution and at the Diagnostic Depot. These shops are maintained solely for employees of the institution. Barber cards may be purchased at the Chief Clerk's Office for one dollar. In addition to obtaining barber services, employees may also use their barber cards to have their automobiles washed. Barber cards last the average employee two to three weeks.

Employees patronizing the Officer's Barber Shop must carry their barber cards when entering the shop and have sufficient number of punches left on their card for the services they want. Under no circumstances are employees to ask inmate barbers to work on them unless they have their barber cards. No extra, or free service, will be given.

MAIL AND THE CENSOR'S OFFICE

To men deprived of normal family and social contacts, as they are in prison, the privilege of corresponding with family and friends is one means of making their existence more endurable.

It is often a determining factor in their adjustment to prison life and their tractability under strict discipline. Correspondence with approved persons is not only permitted but encouraged by the administration.

When an inmate is received at the diagnostic depot, he is advised of the rules pertaining to inmate correspondence and is requested to fill out a form known as the "Inmate's Mailing List." On it the inmate is required to list the names and addresses of all members of his immediate family. He may also list friends with whom he wishes to correspond. But he is urged to give preference to relatives. It is well known to prison officials that a prisoner's family is more apt to stand by him during his incarceration than are mere friends.

Since the number of persons listed on the "Inmate's Mailing List" frequently exceeds the maximum number with whom he is allowed to correspond, the inmate must choose from his list the six persons he would like most to correspond with. The interviewer then places a "C & V" after the names of these persons, thus identifying them as the ones chosen for correspondence and visits. However, mother and father, brother and sister-in-law, sister and brother-in-law, aunt and uncle, may be counted as one on the correspondence list, if they are living at the same address. And if the inmate's parents are divorced, he is permitted to increase his correspondence list by one, making a total of seven.

The inmate is advised that during his first ten days at the diagnostic depot, he may write to his closest relatives, such as his father, mother or wife, because it takes about ten days to receive a reply to the correspondence and visiting questionnaires sent out to the persons listed by the inmate.

There are, of course, certain qualifications and limitations affecting an inmate's discretion in selecting his list of correspondents. For instance, if an inmate is separated from his legal wife, but has been living with another woman in common-law, and there is a child or children born of this union, the mother of the children may be listed even though common-law marriages are not legal in Illinois.

However, if an inmate wishes to write to the wife of an acquaintance, he may not do so unless her husband signifies his approval by counter signing the form sent to her. Generally an inmate will not be permitted to write to a person who has been convicted of crime. However, by special permission of the warden, the inmate may be granted permission to write a close relative such as father or brother even though that person has been involved with the law. Friends of short acquaintance may not be listed if there is any question as to whether they are law-abiding citizens.

Within this framework of rules inmates may request and receive permission to write to four relatives and two friends, or they may write six relatives and two friends, or they may write six relatives if they prefer, provided, of course, that these persons indicate their desire to correspond with the inmate by filling out and returning the form sent to them.

When correspondence and visiting questionnaires are returned, they are received by the Record Office at Stateville. Then they are sent to the Joliet Branch Information Desk and Mail Office; the Stateville Branch Information Desk and Mail Office, and finally back to the Record Office at Stateville where they are filed in the inmate's jacket.

After an inmate's mailing list has been established, he may write to any person on it in whatever rotation or proportion he chooses. However, he is permitted but one letter each week.

An inmate in E or D grade may write only to members of his immediate family.

An inmate is privileged to obtain "special" letters for use in urgent or important matters concerning his welfare. In order to obtain a "special" letter the inmate must request it from one of the wardens, captains or lieutenants. The Institutional Parole Officer and the Record Clerk are also authorized to approve "special" letters for use in matters pertaining to parole, such as obtaining a place of residence, contacting a prospective employer, or matters pertaining to judges, courts, attorneys, etc.

This brings us to a consideration of the purposes of censorship. They are multiple and require an exercise of good judgment on the part of censors. Since an inmate's letters are almost certain to reflect his feelings, attitudes and opinions, the censor is in a position to gather reliable information which, if brought to the attention of the proper authorities, can bulwark both the safety and security of the institution. At the same time, the censor must not interpret his instructions in such a way that the effect is to deprive the inmates of the privilege of correspondence. Although censors are expected to enforce the institutional rules governing inmate correspondence, they are also expected to understand the importance attached to it.

An inmate's letters serve many purposes that are desirable from the institutional point of view. Among them are easing the inmate's adjustment to prison life, helping him to maintain approved and desirable contacts, and contributing to his family's peace of mind. Intelligent censorship of these letters will reveal information that will help to assure the safety of the inmate, to protect employees from violence, and to strengthen the security of the institution.

Whenever any letter by an inmate indicates that he is unduly disturbed, contemplating suicide, or planning an escape, the censor should notify the mail officer immediately, who in turn will call it to the attention of the warden or proper authority. Conversely, should an incoming letter bear a message pertaining to serious illness or death in the inmate's family, or contain papers relative to a divorce suit or to matters of child custody, it must be forwarded to the Senior Capain at the branch of the institution to which the inmate is assigned. It is especially important that such a letter never be delivered directly to any inmate assigned outside the walls. To do so would be to invite an escape attempt by an emotionally disturbed inmate.

Because of the volume of mail passing through the mail office, it has become impossible for the civilians employed there to censor all of it. For that reason certain officers working the night shifts on assignments marked by little activity are required to censor mail, though not at the expense of proper supervision of their assignment. Since any employee might conceivably be called upon to censor mail, it is necessary for all to acquaint themselves with the rules of the mail office as set forth in the employees' rule book.

An employee assigned to censorship duties should first inspect the letter to see that it is proper in form. After this has been ascertained, the censor should then read the contents of the letter to determine whether it contains anything of an alarming or offensive nature.

In general, an inmate's letter must not contain obscene, libelous or threatening statements. It may not be written in code. If it is addressed to anyone within the United States, it may not be in a foreign language.

It is to be remembered that some inmates may try to include secret messages to members of their family or friends by mail. This may be done by writing a short letter or writing between lines by using what is known as invisible ink, which in most cases may be achieved by using orange juice, lemon juice or urine. This can be detected by running a hot iron over the surface of the paper. The mail office is required to use this hot iron process on a number of letters each week.

Whenever a censor has cause to suspect the contents of an inmate's letter, he should note his opinion on a separate piece of paper, giving the page and line numbers of the material to which he objects. Then the note should be clipped to the letter. Under no circumstances are rejected letters to be mixed with the approved ones. The rejected letters must be put into a separate compartment in the censor's box and returned to the mail room.

It should hardly be necessary to remind employees that all correspondence is confidential and may not be discussed with anyone other than the warden, the assistant wardens, the senior captains, or the mail officer. To provide fuel for gossip is not one of the functions of the censorship.

One of the more important contributions which the mail office makes to the security of the institution is the maintaining of a "Watch List" of inmates whose records indicate that they should be closely observed. On this list are known troublemakers, escape risks, drug addicts, etc. All letters written by or to these men are censored by the mail officer himself.

This is, however, another indication of the importance of censorship. Employees should remember that the Mail or Censor's Office is a main artery of the institution. Through it flow the attitudes and feelings of the inmate population. And a conscientious and alert censorship of inmate mail will enable the administration to sense the fluctuating moods of the inmates, individually or collectively, and to anticipate and prevent trouble before it occurs.

INMATE CLOTHING

When a new inmate is received at this institution, he is taken to the clothing room, measured and issued a complete outfit of clothing that fits him. All of the inmate's clothes are stenciled with his register number. This stencil should be renewed when necessary; for if it fades to the point of illegibility, the item of clothing will become lost.

In the event that an inmate is assigned to an outside work detail, he is issued additional work clothing: two pairs of work pants, two work shirts, a storm coat, one pair of gloves, one pair of overshoes, and two sets of winter underwear.

When an inmate's clothing needs repair, it should be sent to the clothing room immediately. Remember the old adage that

"A stitch in time saves nine." Clothing more than 4,000 inmates is an expensive proposition and repairs should not be neglected. It is the duty of an officer to see that the inmates wear their own clothes in a prescribed manner: buttons buttoned, shirt cuffs turned down, etc. It follows that he should also be responsible for seeing that the inmate's clothing is kept in proper repair, being neither torn, ragged, nor extremely ill-fitting. Neatness, as well as cleanliness, contributes to good morale and reflects credit upon the institutional standards.

Inmates are issued three shirts and three pairs of pants. Each of these items of clothing is consecutively numbered, one (1), two (2), and three (3), in addition to the register numbers. Whenever new clothing or replacement clothing is issued, it is recorded on the inmate's clothing record card.

When an item of clothing becomes unserviceable, the clothing room officer will condemn it. The condemnation of clothing is handled twice a week. Tickets are sent to inmates who have had clothing condemned in order that they may receive replacement of same. The inmate is measured for size and he signs a receipt for the replacement. Ordinarily, pants and shirts may be expected to last a year unless the inmate is assigned to work which is unusually destructive to clothing.

If an inmate deliberately destroys his clothing he should be reported. If possible, the report should state how the destruction was accomplished.

It should be interesting to note that it costs the State of Illinois $44.70 to clothe each new inmate. Since inmates are received at the rate of about 200 per month, the clothing bill amounts to more than $8,940 a month, or $107,280 a year. Whenever an inmate leaves the institution, it costs the state $58.95 to dress him out. The annual clothing bill for inmates at the Joliet-Stateville Branch is $250,000.

In the repair of shoes at the Stateville Branch, four tons of leather are used annually to repair 6,654 pairs of shoes. Also, on an annual average basis, are repaired 14,220 pairs of pants and about the same number of shirts. In addition, inmates assigned to the clothing room make 2,300 belts from scrap leather, 1,500 pairs of mittens, 700 cloth helmets, and 400 pairs of ear muffs.

Clothing room records are kept pertaining to cleaning supplies such as mop handles, mop heads, brooms, scrub brushes, etc. These records disclose the quantity of such items normally used by the various assignments. Therefore, when ordering these items, more than are actually needed should not be requested. In one year the institution spent a total of $5,376 just for mop heads and brooms alone.

INMATE VISITING

The administration acknowledges that the morale of inmates is aided materially by visits from their loved ones. For that reason a visiting room has been provided where relatives or friends may see and confer with the inmate under close supervision.

When an inmate first arrives at the Diagnostic Depot, he is requested to fill out a form on which he lists the names and addresses of six persons from whom he would like to receive visits or mail. The institutional policy is to encourage the inmate to list his parents, wife, and relatives, as it is believed that these persons are more likely to remain interested in the welfare of the inmate.

Each of the persons listed is sent a Correspondence and Visiting Questionnaire. One side of the questionnaire contains a brief résumé of the rules and regulations governing visits and correspondence. The other side contains questions pertaining to the name, address, relationship or length of acquaintance, marital status, occupation, and criminal record, if any. Whenever possible, verifications of the statements made on these questionnaires is sought through local authorities.

During the time the inmate is being processed at the Diagnostic Depot he is not permitted to receive visits. After that, if his behavior remains good, he may receive visits every fourteen days (visits from lawyers, social workers or ministers do not count as regular visits). The visiting hours are from 8:00 A.M. to 3:00 P.M. However, only two persons whose names appear on the inmate's approved visiting list are admitted at one time, with the exception of Saturday, when only one person is permitted to visit. No visits are permitted on Sundays or holidays unless they have been approved by the warden.

Visitors are required to register at the gatehouse, listing their names, addresses, and the name and number of the inmate they wish to see. After registering, the visitor must proceed directly to the search room where he or she is searched by an employee of corresponding sex. There is a repository provided for personal effects of the type regarded as contraband in the institution.

After being cleared through the gatehouse, visitors proceed to the Information Desk and register with the officer in charge. If the visitor is on the inmate's approved list, the officer at the Information Desk telephones the number of the inmate to be visited to the officer in charge of the visiting room, who in turn sends a ticket by runner to the assignment where the inmate works, or to the inmate's cellhouse as the case may be.

When the inmate's ticket arrives at his assignment, the officer times him out and sends him to the hospital gate. There the inmate tenders his visit ticket to the officer in charge, who notifies the visiting room that the inmate is awaiting his visit. The officer in the visiting room then telephones the inmate's number to the officer at the Information Desk, who in turn informs the visitor that arrangements have been completed and directs the visitor to the visiting room.

Employees in the visiting room should remember that they are dealing with the general public and should be courteous at all times. If there is any unnecessary delay in getting an inmate to the visiting room, the officer in charge of the visiting room should investigate the delay in order to expedite the visit. Many visitors come a long distance or have busy schedules and they should not be kept waiting longer than necessary.

After the visitor and inmate have entered the visiting room, which is divided into two sections, one for the visitors, and the other for inmates, they are permitted to greet each other with a handshake or a kiss. At the conclusion of the greeting the inmate must display opened hands and mouth to show that nothing has been passed to him.

Visitors and inmates must keep their hands and belongings at least a foot from the dividing glass in the center of the table. Children accompanying visitors must remain in their seats during the visit, and adult visitors are also expected to conduct themselves in an orderly manner.

Pictures or other permitted items which the visitor wishes to give the inmate must be sent to the mail or record office. There they will be censored and forwarded to the inmate. But if the visitor has some pictures or papers which he wants the inmate to see but not keep, the visitor may hand them to the officer in charge who will inspect them and pass them to the inmate. After the inmate has looked at the pictures or papers, he will hand them back to the officer, who will return them to the visitor.

Under no circumstances may anything be passed over the visiting table by an inmate or visitor.

The time allowed for the usual visit is one hour, but persons coming from a distance of 150 miles or more may be permitted to remain two hours. If a visitor makes a reasonable request for an additional five or ten minutes, the request should be granted if the visiting room is not overcrowded.

When the time allotted for the visit has expired, the inmate's ticket will be timed and placed before him and he must get up and leave the table immediately. However, the officer must detain him at the desk for a few moments until the visitor has left the hall. This is for the purpose of preventing contact between visitor and inmate as they leave the visiting room.

On occasions when an inmate assigned to the Administration Building receives a visit, he should not be permitted to leave the visiting room until the officer at the Information Desk notifies the visiting room officer that the inmate's visitor has left the building.

Records indicate that only 30 per cent of the inmates receive visits after 2 years of incarceration.

For security reasons and to avoid confusion, neither visitors nor inmates may be permitted to enter or leave the visiting room during a change of shifts.

Immediately before and after visiting hours a thorough inspection of the visiting room is to be made. The officer in charge must look underneath the tables and chairs on both sides of the room to make sure that no contraband has been concealed there. Until this inspection has been completed, inmates assigned to the visiting room must not be permitted on the visitor's side of the room. Neither may they be permitted to contact visitors in any way. No loitering by employees, visitors or inmates should be tolerated in the visiting room.

The security of the institution must remain uppermost in the minds of employees assigned to the visiting room. They must remain constantly alert to see that no contraband items are passed over the visiting room tables.

Incidents of visitors having attempted to pass contraband articles such as drugs, saws, money, etc., to an inmate are not unknown. Every precaution should be taken to prevent such an occurrence, and at least one chair at either end of the visiting room must be occupied by an employee at all times. Visitors under the influence of liquor will not be admitted to the visiting room, nor will visitors be permitted to bring edibles, liquids or drugs into the visiting room.

Ex-convicts are not permitted to visit at any time and should an ex-convict be recognized, the visit is to be terminated immediately. Employees are to report any violations of visiting rules directly to the warden. If the violation is of a serious nature, the warden should be notified immediately.

PRE-RELEASE PLANNING

The Pre-Release classes and associated programs have been designed to bridge the gap between closely ordered life within prison walls and freedom of normal living, or the relative freedom under parole. The purpose, operation and effect of these programs are outlined as follows:

1. The Pre-Release Planning School is conducted for the purpose of acquainting the prospective Parolee or Dischargee with

the changed conditions in the outside world and of helping him to re-establish himself in society and to conduct himself as a good citizen.

2. It is difficult to pin-point any specific step in the screening of new prisoners at the Diagnostic Depot that has a direct bearing on the pre-release program. Every step in classifying and assigning the inmate has as its ultimate objective the successful planning of rehabilitation for the prisoner. It follows, therefore, that pre-release planning actually begins on the first day of the prisoner's incarceration.

3. Since the sum of a man's experience in prison will surely affect his outlook on life, the fact of his eventual release either by parole or expiration of sentence should be kept always in mind. The process of preparing an inmate for re-entry into society is a continuing one, extending throughout his imprisonment and even beyond, when he is released on parole.

4. It is obvious that an inmate being released on parole must have the financial security of regular employment and the stabilizing influence of family, friends or a benevolent social organization in order to successfully fulfill the requirements and conditions of parole. It is imperative that the parolee obtain a good home and suitable employment before he is released. Without these he might find himself in financial difficulty and would soon return to crime.

5. A person on parole is closely supervised by his parole agent, whose duty is to help the parolee by guiding and advising him in the problems that arise, so that he can live as an upright citizen and not get into the difficulties which originally caused his imprisonment. The following rules have been established to govern parolees and any violation of these rules will cause the parolee to be returned to prison:

Do not carry weapons of any kind.

Do not frequent disreputable establishments nor criminal "hangouts."

Do not associate with anyone who has a police record.

Do not write to any inmate of any penal or correctional institution.

Do not become intoxicated.

Do not use drugs or narcotics.

Do not get married without first obtaining permission from your agent or the Superintendent of Paroles.

Do not be away from your home or place of abode after 10.00 P.M.

Do not drive or ride in a car for pleasure without first obtaining permission from your agent or Superintendent.

Do not leave the county in which you are paroled without permission.

You are required to notify your agent in advance before changing your address or place of abode.

Before changing employment you are required to notify your agent in advance and obtain the necessary permission to do so.

These rules are constantly before the parolee, as they are printed on the back of every report form which the parolee must fill out and submit to his agent at the end of each month.

Parole and Discharge School Class. Inmates being counseled in preparation for release. Stateville Branch.

6. The objectives of the Discharge School are not different than those of the Pre-Parole School. Both attempt to advise the inmate on matters of social conduct and the necessity of obtaining gainful employment. Representatives of the John Howard Association, the State Employment Service, and other interested organizations, such as Alcoholics Anonymous, instruct the pre-release classes on these matters. Motion pictures entitled "How to Get a Job" and "How to Hold a Job" are shown to each class. Unlike parolees, men going out on discharge at the expiration of their sentences are not required to obtain a job prior to release. However, the various organizations which participate in the Pre-Release program are quite as eager to assist them in straightening out their lives as they are to be of aid to parolees.

7. The real test of rehabilitation takes place in the state of freedom. During the fiscal year July 1, 1960,-June 30, 1961, a total of 734 men were granted paroles from the Stateville-Joliet Branch. This was an average of 62 paroles for each monthly parole docket and constitutes 44% of the 1664 men who were granted parole hearings on the dates specified by law. Of the 734 men granted parole, only 644 were able to meet the conditions imposed and to effect their release. Since in Illinois paroles extend for periods of 3, 4 or 5 years, there were on parole at the end of the year a total of 1,073 men. During the year 265 warrants were issued on violators. The rate of parole violation was thus 24%. Unfortunately, there is no coordinated system with which to determine how many of the 701 inmates released last year on expiration of sentence returned to crime and were reimprisoned in some other state or federal institution.

Every employee can help to combat recidivism by encouraging inmates to work towards their own reformation by furthering their educations, learning trades, joining Alcoholics Anonymous (if drink was a factor in their crimes), and attending church services regularly. These are the salient features of a rehabilitation program designed to help men leaving prison to lead better lives than they led before.

BORDERLINE MENTAL CASES

On the subject of borderline mental cases, there are two pertinent questions and answers. First, who classifies an inmate as a borderline mental case? Second, who is concerned with the handling of inmates so classified?

Let's consider the first question. It is essential to understand that the professional staff of the Criminologist determines whether or not an inmate is a borderline mental case and, therefore, custodial personnel as laymen, do not interfere with the Criminologist and the classification. The staff of the Criminologist provides reports covering the individual psychiatric and sociological interviews with inmates.

The Senior Captain's office studies the cases of inmates who are classified as borderline mental cases and who have been recommended for placement in the general population at Joliet and Stateville.

The primary problem is to place the inmate under adequate supervision and to help him adjust within the institution scene so that he will conform to rules.

Secondly, his adjustment is considered. Sometimes it is necessary to feel one's way in dealing with the placement of these cases and learn from experience how to adjust the assignments of the inmates according to their conditions and needs, in relation to their classification.

Initially, some thought is given to trade training or schooling. The borderline mental case may be encouraged to start school and accomplish as much as possible and later be placed in a vocational assignment.

In the vocational school the instructor may uncover in the inmate some interest in a trade which the inmate will be able to sustain himself when released. Furthermore, the vocational training may enable the inmate to utilize natural aptitudes he may have along mechanical lines.

The school and vocational instructors allow a reasonable period of time to elapse in which to observe the inmate and test his adjustability.

If the inmate fails to profit from a school or vocational training program, he may be given an opportunity in some assignment in which he expresses an interest, such as gardening on the lawns and terraces; or a manual job, such as carpenter work; or he may be placed on an assignment not requiring initiative or complex skills such as cellhouse help. Once the inmate is found to be apparently getting along satisfactorily on his assignment, he is permitted to remain in that status.

Finally, it is worth emphasizing that any inmate in this category may at any time exhibit unusual or bizarre behavior. Again, the custodial personnel should not undertake to determine if he is malingering. A professionally trained person, such as a psychiatrist, is best qualified to evaluate his mental condition.

The Detention Hospital was set up for the purpose of taking care of inmates who become mentally disturbed. Therefore, if an inmate develops peculiar patterns of behavior, he should be admitted to the Detention Hospital and a report submitted covering his behavior. A copy of the report should be forwarded to the State Criminologist, Warden, Assistant Wardens, the Psychiatrist, Detention Hospital Keeper, Prison Physician, and the Senior Captain.

HONOR FARM

The Honor Farm, which borders the walls of Stateville on three sides, embraces an area of 2,200 acres, or nearly four square miles. The land has been surveyed and mapped into 80 acre fields, which are the units of measure employed in drawing up planting schedules and crop rotations. About 200 acres are occupied by buildings, yards and roads. The remainder is pasture and crop land.

On the 1,700 tillable acres, 350 of which are planted to garden crops, a five year rotation is followed: two years of corn, one year of oats, and two years of hay. This rotation, together with the use of lime from the quarry, phosphate, the spreading of stable manures, and the growing of leguminous hay, has greatly improved the soil. Back in the 30's the Farm lands produced only 30 to 35 bushels of corn per acre. In recent years the corn yield averages 80 bushels per acre. Improving soil productivity has, of course, increased the capacity of the farm to support livestock.

On the farm is kept a herd of 400 brood sows that farrow approximately 2,400 pigs every six months. In one year more than 400,000 pounds of dressed pork are delivered to the General Store at Stateville for use in the institution.

There are more than 300 head of dairy type cattle on the farm in an average year. Of this total in one year 110 are on the milking line, 10 are dry, 50 were under two years of age, 50 were less than one year old, and 135 were classified as dairy beef and slaughtered for institutional usage. The total dressed weight of dairy animals slaughtered in a typical year and delivered to the butcher shop is nearly 55,000 pounds.

Milk production is at its highest peak in the history of the farm and there have been in the milking herd five of the highest producing cows in any state owned herd. Good stock and good management have brought milk production up to the rate of 15,000 gallons per month. During the fiscal year ending June 30, 1961, the farm dairy delivered 180,000 gallons of raw milk to the milk room at the General Store. After being pasteurized, this milk was consumed by employees and inmates either as fresh milk, ice cream, or milk used in cooking.

The dairy unit's record of production was achieved without "contented" cows, for there are few, if any, bulls kept on the farm. All breeding is done by means of artificial insemination. It is believed that in this way the milking herd can be upgraded by using only the finest production tested bloodlines. What the cows think of this, is a matter for conjecture.

Breeding herds of beef cattle are not maintained on the farm, but every spring young cows of the beef breeds are bought and put in pasture. The number of feeders averages about 500 per year, depending upon the pasture and roughage available for them. After the beef cattle have been fattened, they are slaughtered as needed for use in the institution. The total weight of dressed beef slaughtered on the farm and delivered to the butcher shop in a recent year was 439,051 pounds.

The greatest volume of food production per acre is, however, achieved on those acres planted to garden vegetables. On 350 acres are grown a full year's supply of many staple items for the diets of 5,000 officers and men. The garden crops are planted with two objectives in mind: one, to produce fresh vegetables for the dining rooms over as long a period as possible; the other, to supply the canning plant with a steady flow of produce rather than to swamp it with a larger harvest than it could process without spoilage and waste.

Since the basic objective is to produce as much as possible of the institutional food supply, there is the closest kind of coöperation between the farm, the canning plant, the General Store, and the Dietician. One year this program paid off in the amount of $420,734.28, the market value placed upon the foods produced on the farm.

Of course, this result was not obtained without a great deal of labor. There are 320 inmates assigned to the Honor Farm. In addition to performing chores, they operate and maintain the farm machinery required to plow, plant, cultivate, and harvest hundreds of acres. Two garden tractors and six large field tractors furnish the motive power for the various implements. Altogether the farm has machinery and equipment valued at $100,000 which is not an excessive investment in machinery considering the acreage involved.

The Honor Farm is one of the few farms in the country on which may still be found several teams of horses and mules. Although these animals are used more for pulling wagons than for field work, there are a total of 38 head, or 19 teams of work stock on the farm. Twelve riding horses are used for patrolling the institutional grounds. Caring for these fifty head of horses and mules is a big chore and one with which few of the younger men are familiar.

In scientific livestock raising, as practised on the farm, the health of the animals is not left to chance. They are inspected regularly by State Veterinarians and are given shots and vaccinations to protect them from disease. They must be dipped and drenched to rid them of parasites. Some of them must be castrated and dehorned. Stalls and pens must be kept in a sanitary condition.

Inmates assigned to work on the Honor Farm are carefully screened and selected. They are not transferred from inside the walls directly to the Honor Farm. Rather, they are first assigned to the Farm Detail where they work on the farm, the front lawn or in the gardens during the day but are returned within the walls each night. Whether an inmate is eventually transferred to the Honor Farm on a full time basis depends on his initiative and conduct.

When an inmate is chosen for assignment to the Farm Detail, the Senior Captains at Isolation prepare a record of the inmate's past assignments and send it to the lieutenant in charge at the farm so that he may know something of the inmate's skills and capabilities.

The farm, like the institution proper, is a self contained community. It not only employs men in the fields and in the barns, but it also has need of cooks, bakers, barbers, painters, mechanics, etc. Frequently the possessors of these needed skills have learned their trades while they were incarcerated within the walls at Joliet or Stateville.

Although an inmate may be a well-trained and well-behaved workman, that fact in no way lessens the necessity for supervising his activities. Officers assigned to the Honor Farm must be just as security conscious as those working within the walls. Every officer must keep a perpetual count of inmates on his detail. And should an officer receive information or have any cause to suspect that an inmate plans to escape the farm, he must make an immediate report of the details to his superior officer.

Mounted patrol officers keep under constant surveillance the inmates working in the area of their assignment. Patrol officers must watch for passing vehicles and note anything of a suspicious nature. They are to be especially watchful for any items of contraband that may have been thrown along the roadside. Although mounted officers are expected to be polite and courteous to the public, they must bar trespassers from the institutional property.

An assignment on the prison farm offers a challenge to the good judgment of an officer. He is in a position to contribute much to the welfare of the institution. If anything is important in the management of an institution, it is the provision of an adequate and healthful diet for the inmates. By careful and informed supervision of field work, the feeding and care of livestock, and the harvesting of crops, an officer can do much to augment the production of food for use within the institution.

Officers assigned to supervise field work must make sure that all tilling, fertilizing, planting and cultivating are done properly. At harvest time they must see that the crops are gathered cleanly and handled in such a way as to avoid damage and loss.

Officers who are charged with livestock production must see that the animals have plenty of fresh water available at all times, that they are fed as directed by the Farm Superintendent, and that they are correctly handled. It should be remembered that clean surroundings are as important to the health of livestock as they are to the health of humans. In the slaughter house, the dairy barn and the milk house the watchword is not just clean, but SANITARY. The stalls, utensils, cans,—everything must be thoroughly scrubbed and sterilized after each use.

In an average year, there are approximately 200,000 gallons of fruit and vegetables preserved. In addition to canned goods, more than 100 barrels of pickles and sauerkraut are put up. The production of the Cannery is, of course, governed to some degree by natural forces affecting the yield of farm and garden crops. If cold weather and heavy rains delay plantings, or if crops are attacked by plant diseases, then the reduced yields tend to lower canning plant production, though this is somewhat offset by purchase of produce when necessary.

The following is an itemized list of products and the amounts canned during 1957:

Assorted Jellies	8,619	gals.
Turnip Tops	240	gals.
Greens and Spinach	9,457	gals.
Early June Peas	5,765	gals.
Green Beans	35,178	gals.
Beets	2,760	gals.
Cabbage	1,995	gals.
Creamed Corn	14,986	gals.
Tomatoe Puree	20,020	gals.
Tomatoe Paste	5,278	gals.
Tomatoe Catsup	6,152	gals.
Sauerkraut	8,123	gals.
Pumpkin	3,953	gals.
Carrots	19,905	gals.
Apple Butter	10,030	gals.
Apple Sauce	7,998	gals.
Pork and Beans	1,960	gals.
Total Cans Processed	162,418	gals.
Dill Pickles	34	bbls.

Not all of this food was consumed at the Joliet-Stateville Branches. A considerable amount of it was transferred to other state institutions on requisition.

CANNING OPERATIONS

In recent years, the canning plant of the Illinois State Penitentiary, located at the Stateville Branch, has undergone a program of modernization and expansion which has made it one of the finest canning plants of its size in the state. At least that

Shelling beans for the Cannery. Stateville Branch.

is the expressed opinion of some commercial packing company representatives who have inspected the plant at Stateville.

During the past four years nearly $40,000 have been spent for new machinery and equipment. As a result, the plant's capacity to pack fruits and vegetables for institutional use has been greatly increased. An improvement in the quality of its products has also been achieved.

It is doubtful that casual observers appreciate the complexities involved in the operation of the canning plant. Unlike commercial canning plants, which are often set up for processing a single crop grown in the area to which it is best adapted, the plant at Stateville cans almost every kind of fruit and vegetable grown locally, as well as some that are shipped in from southern Illinois and Michigan.

To can such a variety of products requires both planning and versatility. As a matter of fact, the successful operation of the canning plant depends greatly upon the long-range planning of the farm superintendent and the head gardener, who schedule plantings with the canning plant in mind.

By staggering planting dates of the various crops, they can usually avoid over-burdening the canning plant at harvest time with too much of any one crop or with too many varieties of crops. In this way spoilage and loss are held to a minimum. Since many crops such as peas, for instance, are highly perishable and must be processed immediately after they are harvested, it would not do to have them ripening in greater quantities than the canning plant could handle. And the only way to prevent that is by close coöperation between the canning plant and the farm. However, there are times when weather conditions interfere with planting dates or delay the ripening of a crop. When that occurs, every effort must be made to salvage the crops even though all of them ripen at close intervals.

At harvest peaks inmates are taken from other assignments to prepare the huge volume of product for the cannery. Sometimes as many as seven or eight hundred inmates are employed at the canning plant in addition to the men regularly assigned there.

Last year approximately 70,000 man hours were expended in preparing and canning foods for institutional use.

The largest output of canned products in a single day was 10,000 cans. On that day work commenced at 7:00 A.M. and ended at midnight. This makes it obvious that inmates assigned to the canning plant must be screened for security and approved to work on late details during the busy season at the canning plant.

Inmates assigned to the canning plant must also pass a physical examination just as any other inmate who handles food. Cleanliness and sanitation are of utmost importance on this assignment. Personal cleanliness is stressed day in and day out. The inmates' finger nails are inspected; their clothing must be clean; they must not smoke while working over the food; in short, high standards of sanitation must be maintained.

Since food processed in non-sterile utensils or sealed in non-sterile cans will quickly spoil, it follows that continuous sterilization of canning machinery, piping, vats, and the containers is absolutely necessary, not only to preserve the food but to protect lives as well. There is a type of bacteria, BACILLUS BOTULINUS, which develops only in canned foods and is difficult to detect because of its lack of odor. It proves fatal to 40% of the persons who consume food that contains it. This alone should be sufficient reason for observance of extreme caution and precise sanitation in cannery operations.

Another fundamental that must be considered in the operation of the canning plant is that of preserving institutional security.

During the canning season many tons of fruit and sugar are brought into the canning plant and there are undoubtedly some ex-bootleggers around who would not be above brewing a gallon or two of moonshine, if they are not closely observed. The canning plant must be searched daily to prevent such an occurrence.

Earlier there was mention of the seven or eight hundred men who are sometimes drawn from other assignments such as the schools and shops to work at the cannery. For preparing certain fruits and vegetables which must be peeled, cored, or sliced, these men are issued paring knives. The officer in charge of a line must

Beet harvest. Stateville Branch.

take the name and number of every inmate to whom he issues a knife. During the working day the officer must patrol his line constantly and carefully, being always on the alert for arguments or incidents that could lead to serious trouble. Before the officer returns his line to the cellhouse, he must collect ALL of the knives he has issued, checking them off against the name and number of the inmate as they are turned in. Then the officer's total knife count must be checked against the number he drew from the lieutenant in charge. After the knife count has checked, the officer must shake down his line to make certain that no inmate has on his person any other kind of contraband. These precautions also apply to inmates regularly assigned to the canning plant.

Speaking generally, prisons are not considered as money making concerns, but the farm and the canning plant, working together, contribute to a substantial saving of the taxpayers' money.

Without the quantity of fresh and canned foods produced by

these units, an increased state appropriation for the feeding of prisoners would be necessary. And it is safe to assume that the inmates would not receive as large a quantity of good wholesome food as is now being served in the institution.

The canning plant searches continuously for new and better ways of preserving food. However, in order to turn out an attractive product, it must have the coöperation of officers assigned to supervise the inmates who prepare the raw foods for canning. Officers must instruct the inmates on how to stem, pare, or core the fruits and vegetables. They must instruct the inmates to trim or discard any portion of the fruit that is discolored, bruised, wormy or rotted. Finally, the officers must supervise the work closely to see that their instructions are carried out.

The appearance of food is almost as important as its taste, and every officer should remember that the results of his supervision will be served him in the Officers' Dining Room.

INDUSTRIES

The use of inmate labor in the manufacture of various commodities in prison industries serves several purposes. It employs the inmate in productive work and it teaches him a vocation or trade with which he can earn a living after release. Also, it teaches him the habit of working.

Not only is Prison Industry of vital significance in the economics of correctional administration, it is also an invaluable aid in reducing the problems of discipline and security and helps to step up the program of rehabilitation.

It is a known fact that sustained idleness among inmates is disastrous to an institution of this kind. Productive labor not only benefits the inmate but also the taxpayer. In general, society has opposed the extensive use of inmate labor in prison industry for various reasons. There have been many ways in which inmate labor has been used and exploited prior to the systems, functions, and purposes of industrial employment now in force.

Most prisons in this country adopted the "Contract Labor System" by 1835. Under this system the State retained the inmate but sold his labor for a stipulated sum daily for each inmate used. This system was particularly vicious since the inmate worker was at the mercy of the contractor's supervisors. Under this system the contractor furnished the machinery and raw materials and supervised the inmates.

This was later replaced by the "Piece Price System" which was merely a variation of the "Contract Labor System." The contractor furnished the raw materials and machinery and received the finished product, paying the prison administration a stipulated amount of money for each finished unit accepted. Under this "Piece Price System" the prison administration hired its own supervisors. In this manner the exploitation of inmate labor was minimized somewhat.

Another variation was the "Lease System" which allowed the contractor to assume control of the inmates including their maintenance and discipline. All of these systems were particularly opposed by citizens and free labor alike, not only for humanitarian reasons but also competitive reasons.

The severe panic of 1873 and the ensuing years stimulated the activities of free labor and the contract labor system was finally abolished from Illinois Prisons in 1904.

The fact that there was an abundance of rock that could be quarried in the vicinity of Joliet was one of the deciding factors in moving the prison from Alton to Joliet in 1858. The Rock Quarry was the first industrial project at the Joliet Penitentiary. Other industries were added and by 1867 there were a cooperage, a wagon shop, a machine and blacksmith shop, and facilities for cigar making.

In 1872 the sale of articles made in the prison industries brought a return greater than the expenditure for operating the prison. Therefore, no tax money was required to maintain the prison in that year. In fact, a profit of $36,000 was shown.

The next few years brought about the realignment of the industrial set-up and by 1884 the principal industries were the Harness Shop, Boot and Shoe Shop, Cooperage, Stone Quarry and the Knitting Mills. Throughout most of this period, Illinois was a growing, thriving area and prison made commodities were much in demand. But in 1886, the economy of this area suffered reverses. This caused great public resentment against the sale of prison made products, accompanied by threats of a boycott.

Ten years later prison industries were again prospering and in 1895-1896 the industrial shops at Joliet were enlarged at a cost of $700,000. This prosperity continued until the start of World War I, at which time there was such a shortage of labor in the Joliet area that wages outside of the prison were far in excess of those paid the custodial officers. This caused an exodus of custodial officers who sought jobs in private industries. This migration created a shortage in custodial and supervisory personnel making it necessary to curtail the operation of prison industries. The industry hurt most was the Rock Quarry which was unable to supply enough crushed stone for the improvement of State and Township roads.

After the end of the war, prison industries enjoyed another brief period of activity and prosperity until the depression era of the 1930's.

At that time many people were out of work and sustaining themselves on the bread-lines or were on public relief rolls or government building projects. This situation again brought bitter opposition to the sale of prison made products. The people protested that every day's work performed by an inmate represented a day of unemployment for them.

The most serious blow to prison contract labor was the passage of three Federal Statutes, the Hawes-Cooper Act in 1929, the Ashurst-Summers Act in 1935, and the Congressional Act of October, 1940. The first divested prison products of their interstate character on their arrival at the destination point. The second prohibited transportation companies from accepting prison made products for transportation into any state in violation of the laws of that state and provided for the labeling of all packages containing prison made products in interstate commerce. The third excluded almost all products made in state prisons from interstate commerce. Under its provisions parties shipping such goods across state lines were subject to a fine of $1,000 and one year's imprisonment.

Legislation in Illinois was patterned generally after the Federal Statutes. The "State Use Acts" enacted in Illinois went into effect three years before the effective date of the Hawes-Cooper Act. This "State Use Act," passed in 1931, limited the sale of prison made products to only public institutions and tax supported bodies of the State of Illinois.

In 1934, this Act was amended to make it unlawful to sell or exchange any goods, wares, or merchandise manufactured or mined by convicts of other states. The "State Use Act" did, however, specifically authorize the Department of Public Safety to employ inmates in the manufacture of such items as are used within the Department or by all other tax supported bodies. The "Act" also stipulated that any article manufactured by the prison

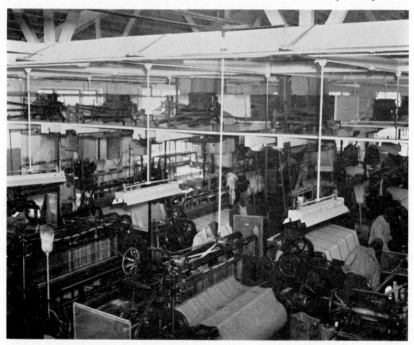

Overall view of the Textile Plant. Joliet Branch.

industries could not be purchased from any source other than the Penitentiary Industrial Department.

At the present time, Joliet-Stateville Prison Industries manufacture numerous items. Not only do they manufacture staple items, but many specials, particularly in the Furniture and Sheet Metal Departments. There are at present eleven different industrial departments within the prisons.

A total of 42 trades are taught in our prison schools and shops.

The Menard Branch contains a knitting factory and tobacco factory, while at the Pontiac Branch there is a sign shop where all State Highway Signs are made, and a foundry.

At the Joliet-Stateville Branch there are approximately 1,200 inmates employed and carried on the Industrial Payroll. While their salary is nominal they do have an opportunity to learn skills which will be advantageous to them upon their release to civilian life.

The prison's industrial department is eager to employ as many inmates as possible for more than one reason. Besides learning a skill or trade, the inmate also becomes accustomed to the habit of working on production lines and there is also a personal satisfaction achieved in knowing that he is able to produce useful commodities.

At the Joliet-Stateville Branch we have a Bookbindery, Box Factory, Furniture Factory, Soap Factory, Garment Factory, Textile Mill, Shoe Factory, Glove Department, Mattress Factory, Upholstery Department and Sheet Metal Department. We manufacture cotton mattresses which are used by all mental hospitals in the State of Illinois. In our Box Factory we manufacture many different sizes of chipboard and corrugated boxes which are used by all the Industrial Departments of our institution.

Our Bookbindery Department repaired approximately 50,000 damaged books for the public schools throughout the State of Illinois in the months between April and October last year. In processing these books, prison inmates were able to effect major savings for the public schools of the State. Not only was there a monetary saving effected, but they obtained far superior materials which gave the books longer life because the materials used are superior to those used by outside binders. Besides text books our Bookbindery Department binds numerous periodicals and refurbishes library books for public libraries throughout the State. Our binding facilities cover books of all types, including law books. During the Fall and Winter months when the text books are being used by the schools, our Bookbindery Department is busy making boxes. Many chipboard and corrugated boxes used in our various Industrial Departments are made in this department. We employ an average of 60 inmates during the fall and winter months, and in the summer months when text books are being bound, there are as many as 100 inmates employed.

In the garment factory clothing of every description is manufactured. Approximately 300 inmates are employed in this department at all times and the commodities are used by all state institutions. Many different kinds of materials are used and a full range of sizes are manufactured.

There are approximately 200 different items manufactured in the Garment Department.

The Furniture Factory manufactures not only a complete line of office equipment but also many items of household furniture. The Cabinet Department in the Furniture Factory lays out and manufactures many special items of cabinets and counters. These are drawn up from sketches and specifications submitted to us by other tax supported organizations. The inmates, of which there are approximately 300 in this factory, have the opportunity to learn not only to operate each individual machine used in making up standard milled parts, but also the specialized art of cabinet making.

In the Upholstery Department which is also a highly skilled trade, the inmates learn the complete art of repairing and upholstering furniture of all types.

The Mattress Factory manufactures highest grade cotton mattresses. State Hospitals in Illinois have standardized on the cotton mattresses manufactured here.

In the Soap Factory, employing approximately 100 inmates at all times, are made the highest grade soap products. These products cover a complete line from laundry soap to the best sanitizer.

At the Joliet Branch are located the Textile Mills where any of the 300 inmates employed can learn all phases of weaving, from winding cotton yarn on tubes through dyeing and looming. They also learn all phases of wool processing, from the raw wool through the carding, dyeing, spinning and looming process. In other words, this Textile Mill is complete from raw materials in both cotton and wool to the finished cloth product. In this department are manufactured both huck and terry towels, wash cloths, blue denim, hickory shirting, ticking, wool suiting and overcoating, and woolen blankets.

In the shoe factory every stage of shoe manufacturing is taught to approximately 100 inmates. This consists of knowing what quality raw material is necessary through each operation, from cutting the hides to the boxing of the finished shoes. We manufacture a complete line of men's work and dress oxfords and shoes, women's, girls' and children's shoes for all ages and sizes and foot needs.

In the glove department are manufactured full leather and leather palm canvas back gloves which are purchased by all other State Institutions.

In the Sheet Metal Shop many different items are made, from drinking cups to large canopies of stainless steel. The 80 inmates employed in this shop learn all phases of the sheet metal trade which include welding with Argon gas, a highly specialized trade in itself, and the welding of aluminum and stainless steel. In this shop men are taught to lay out special work from specifications submitted by tax bodies.

Products from all of these departments are sold to the 25 separate Department of Welfare Institutions, to the four Youth Commission Institutions and to all institutions under the Department of Public Safety. They are also available to all State Parks, State Game Farms, Public Health Institutions, Public Schools, Libraries, Counties, Townships, Villages and Cities in the State of Illinois.

Gross sales for the last fiscal year amounted to $1,867,685.16. The cost of raw materials purchased amounted to $1,091,030.46.

Wages paid inmates totaled $116,764.11 and manufacturing expenses amounted to $317,442.68. The manufacturing expenses include among other things the salaries of the superintendents, foremen and guards, the costs of repair and maintenance, depreciation, freight, tools and selling expenses. The net profit of our Industrial Department during a recent fiscal year was $222,372.05.

Although a profit is desirable in the operation of any business, it is not the only reason for operating prison industries. The fundamental function of an Industrial Department is to give the inmate worthwhile or productive employment, something with a meaning, to teach him skills and sound work habits so that he can be better prepared to accept the responsibilities he will face when he again enters society. And there is a great possibility that he will again be an integral part of society, for approximately 95 per cent of all inmates in this institution eventually return to free society.

The Industrial Department is one part of the total effort to combat recidivism. It also attempts to lighten the taxpayers burden by teaching an inmate ways and means of self-support; and during the inmate's incarceration, supplying public institutions with far superior products than could be purchased from other sources at comparable figures.

Our shop superintendents and foremen along with their production supervisors, also have the same problem as the guards assigned to these units, in that security is a prime requirement.

In addition to other duties there is a constant check and careful accounting of all tools and equipment used. Complete tool checks are made at least four times daily by the superintendent and foremen of each department, and while they are being used in production, they are supervised not only by these men, but by the custodial officers assigned to the departments. All employees supervise the actual work done by the inmates. The superintendent and foremen teach the inmate. Inmates of long experience and proven ability are sometimes used as lead men or instructors, augmenting the instructions given to unskilled inmates in the various phases of complicated manufacturing processes. Not only is security and production a problem of superintendents, foremen, and custodial officers but safety precautions must also be stressed.

It is necessary that all officers assigned to the supervision of industrial production should have a full understanding of the problems and responsibilities of other departments and they should understand the general technique of handling inmates and instructing them in job methods. The help and support of each individual employee is needed in the Industrial Departments, especially the help of the lieutenants to give over-all custodial supervision.

An in-service training program is designed to acquaint every officer not only with the specific problems and requirements of an individual assignment, but also with inter-related public problems involving other departments of the institution.

RELIGION

The importance of religion is recognized at Joliet-Stateville and I frequently state that an officer who does not recognize this importance has no place in a correctional institution. Complete coöperation with the religious program is demanded at Joliet.

The basic work of a prison chaplain is identical with the work of every minister, priest, or rabbi on the outside. Just as the minister of religion is an essential part of right living on the outside of a prison, so the prison chaplain is essential for the proper conduct of any prison. Leave religion out of the prison and you might just as well throw away the key on the men confined. No amount of education, vocational training, or physical work will be effective without the practical acknowledgment that this must be correlated with character building and religious motivation. In my opinion, the chaplain, if used in other capacities within a prison, lessens his value as a chaplain.

There are two full-time chaplains at the prison, one Protestant and one Catholic. Six part-time clergymen are authorized and do conduct the services of their particular denominations each week and are welcome to come in at any time to counsel the members of their flocks, and they do spend much time at the institution.

Outside priests, ministers, and rabbis are at all times given preferential treatment in the institution and are permitted and encouraged to visit their parishioners. Just as important as the conducting of religious services in a penal institution, is the counseling of individual inmates by the various chaplains.

The institution recognizes that if a man is faithful to his God, he cannot be anything but faithful to his fellow man. Each chaplain has a library and there also is a general library.

Reading is by far the most popular pastime at Joliet-Stateville. The circulation figures of the general and fiction collections show an average of five books per man per month. More than one thousand titles are always in circulation from the chaplains' libraries. The schools have many volumes in the hands of their students.

Recently it was decided to add pocket editions to the cell house collections. Through an arrangement with a local news agency, seven copies (one for each cell house) of some forty titles are purchased each month. These books are not classified. They are "put on the route" and pass from cell to cell. Circulation figures are, of course, impossible, but it is safe to say that these books are read and re-read, many, many, times.

Men at Joliet-Stateville read much. Their reading is a hopeful sign for the future.

ALCOHOLICS ANONYMOUS

In order to understand the reason for the organization and meetings of Alcoholics Anonymous in an institution where drinking is not permitted, it is necessary to understand something of the problem of alcoholism, and what can be done to effect a recovery from it.

Several clinics have been founded to try to find the basic causes of drinking. These studies have brought to light several factors which have been helpful to alcoholics, and to people living with them or trying to help them recover. Alcoholism is now recognized as an illness which is brought on by an allergy to alcohol. Men and women who compulsively persist in its use as a beverage become sick from a unique illness known to medical science as

Alcoholic Anonymous. View showing inmates attending a group meeting
which is supervised by a civilian employee. Stateville Branch.

alcoholism. It is unique in that it adversely affects the drinker
physically, mentally and spiritually. Because it is an illness, will-
power alone is not always effective in recovering from it. Nobody
would tell a diabetic to use his will-power to overcome his illness,
but it is understood that a diabetic must have the will to recover
and must be willing to do whatever is necessary to recover. The
same is true of the alcoholic.

One factor which is often overlooked in the treatment of alcoholics is the fact that little can be done until he is absolutely
convinced that he is powerless to resist alcohol and is willing to do
anything to stop drinking because of what alcohol is doing to him.

Alcoholism is also recognized as a progressive illness. Once a
drinker becomes an alcoholic he rarely confines drinking to small
quantities of alcohol without setting up a compulsion which
makes him powerless to stop at one or two drinks.

Alcoholics Anonymous is a fellowship which originated in 1935, and whose membership is composed of ex-problem drinkers, banded together in order to help each other recover and to maintain their sobriety. The members try to live by the "12 steps to recovery." Each in his own way tries to live up to the principles involved in the steps.

In the early 1940's A. A. was introduced to the inmate alcoholics in the San Quentin Penitentiary in California. The success of the program aroused the interest of the wardens of other states, and groups have been started in 290 prisons throughout the United States. Canada and other foreign nations have also instituted groups in their penal institutions.

It is estimated that 45% of the inmates serving time in prisons on a national basis, became violators because of addiction to alcohol, and that 15% are there because alcohol was involved in committing the crime for which they were sentenced.

Further, it is estimated that 90% of alcoholic inmates who are paroled or discharged but who have made no effort to correct their problem will be returned to prison. If they return to drink, they will return to prison. Abstinence from alcohol (whether voluntary or compulsory) over a long period of times does not enable the alcoholic to drink normally. If he resumes drinking, he generally is powerless to stop at one or two drinks.

Alcoholics Anonymous was organized at Joliet-Stateville to help alcoholic inmates solve their drinking problem. The philosophy involved in A. A. is not new, but the approach used causes members to admit their problem and to see their shortcomings. Resentment is a common characteristic of the alcoholic. Until he learns to overcome it he cannot live in peace with himself or the people around him. A. A. members learn the futility of resentment and are urged to adjust to life, whether they are living inside or out. Many men who have a record of being chronic rule breakers learn to accept the institutional rules and try to live within them. They not only strive to stop breaking rules, but in many instances they become an example of model behavior which leads other men to change their attitude towards the rules.

The philosophy of A. A. is not only effective with men who will some day be released; it works as well for inmates who have little or no chance of ever being released on parole or by expiration of sentence.

We have no way to keep track of the inmate members of A. A. who leave on parole or discharge. The assumption is they have not returned to drinking or they would have returned to this or some other penal institution.

Very few inmates who have returned claim to have been active in A. A. after their release. Many admit they felt they did not need to follow up in A. A. and, therefore, returned to drinking. However, we do know that 49% of the members who have been paroled have completed their parole and have had no further trouble, while 64% of the members discharged after expiration of sentence have managed to stay out of trouble.

A. A. as a fellowship does not let failure of a member interfere with trying to help others. A. A. members who visit the "inside" groups do not come down with the idea of being of help as much they they are concerned with saving their own sobriety. We have records of A. A. members who come into the institution to give the inmates the benefits of their experience.

There is no way, nor is any attempt made, to determine who is sincere in the groups. There is no way to tell when the meetings will start to make sense to an insincere member and cause him to become serious in his efforts to live by the 12 steps. If a member comes to meetings and continually asks to be excused, he is dropped from the roll. If a call ticket is issued for a member and he does not appear at the meeting room, it is assumed that he is needed on his assignment and his membership is continued until it can be determined that he is missing meetings because he does not wish to attend, or he asks to be dropped from the roll. For this reason members should be allowed to go to the meeting room and be excused if it is at all convenient and possible.

Nobody is forced to attend meetings, but membership should not be cancelled if a member cannot attend due to his work assignment. However, it should be remembered that being permitted to attend meetings may well be the deciding factor in whether the alcoholic inmate stays out of prison or returned after his release.

HOMOSEXUALITY IN PRISON

In most studies of homosexuality in prisons there have been attempts made to estimate the percentage of prisoners who engage in homosexual activities.

Little agreement concerning the prevalence of abnormal sexual practices, either in prison or in free society, has been evident. The estimates have ranged from a very high percentage to a very low one. It is not our purpose here to join that controversy, but simply to acknowledge that the problem does exist and that it is difficult to eliminate or repress.

One aspect of the problem of sexual deviation which presents an obstacle to its control is the difficulty of identifying certain types of homosexuals. The known deviates can be closely supervised or even segregated from the main population of the institution, but the "X" quantity, or unknown perverts, are not as easy to restrain from practicing their peculiarities.

Although perversion takes many forms, homosexuals may, for the purpose of classification, be designated as belonging to one of the following three groups:

1. The frank homosexual.
2. The feeble-minded, mentally ill, or insane.
3. The occasional or situational.

The frank homosexual is easily identified by his feminine mannerisms, speech, clothes, habits, etc. This type is, aside from his sexual proclivities, usually not a behavior problem. He tends to form groups and is undisturbed by the ridicule and revulsion created in others. At times he seems to invite ridicule by flaunting his inversion before the group. Because of his frank homosexuality, he is easily identified and can be carefully guarded, segregated and kept from becoming an object of contention among the aggressive types of homosexuals.

Undoubtedly, the type of pervert representing the gravest

threat to the security of the institution is the active homosexual, or the prison wolf. He is crafty, sly, and will go to any extreme to gain his prey, not infrequently committing murder when he becomes jealous. This jealousy is easily aroused if any attentions, favors or gifts are given to his "punk." Care must be taken at cell count, especially if there is a new guard, that these misfits are in their proper cells, for they are not above switching cells to get in with a "kid" and will stop at nothing to gain sexual gratification.

During the Orientation Program at the Diagnostic Depot new inmates are warned of the prison "wolf" and acquainted with his usual tactics. The younger inmates in particular are cautioned to be skeptical of any form or method of approach.

Generally, the aggressive pervert attempts to achieve his ends by one of four means: (a) He may try to purchase sex relations with commissary items, or he may give them to his prospect as "gifts" so that he can later claim that his selected victim is indebted to him; (b) he tries various conversational approaches to establish a rapport and try to ingratiate himself into the confidence of the younger inmate, from which vantage he will soon be "advising" his victim on how to do "easy time"; (c) he may play on his victim's fear of other wolves and then offer "protection" from them; or (d) he may simply try to frighten his victim into submission by direct threats of violence.

The psychcotic or feeble-minded individuals comprising the second group may also be either active or passive homosexuals. The passive feeble-minded type may submit to indignities because he either fails to realize the nature and probable consequences of his acts or lacks sufficient intelligence to repulse improper advances. The behavior of an insane person may be caused by his delusions and is, therefore, not predictable. This kind of prisoner must be carefully isolated from the rest of the prison population for his own protection and the safety of the other prisoners. Dependent on the nature of his aberrations, he may assault others, or he may be preyed upon.

The third group consists of individuals who may under stress of confinement, threats of violence, or some other motivation participate in an occasional act of perversion. It sometimes happens that an individual who recognized within himself a latent homosexual tendency will be extremely fearful of such contacts and go into an absolute panic if he is propositioned. And in the grip of panic he may kill or injure his would be seducer. The situational or occasional homosexual may also become emotionally disturbed by feelings of guilt after an act of perversion.

Those individuals who frankly accept their homosexuality show no guilt reaction. They are the ones most in need of psychotherapy, for they have deluded themselves into the belief that there is nothing immoral, abnormal, and repulsive in their sexual habits. If at all possible, they should be given intensive treatment by a psychiatrist.

Although homosexuality may or may not be more prevalent in prison than it is in society, it may be said that the prison environment, isolating men from female companionships and stripping them of their individual dignity and self-respect, tends to bring out latent homosexual impulses. This is particularly so with respect to the younger inmates for a two-fold reason:

In the first place they are deprived of normal relations at the period of life when their sex drive is at its peak; in the second place, they are the natural target of the aggressive type who would use them as a substitute for women.

And this use is not always by consent. Prior to the "cleaning up" of penitentiary morals in Joliet-Stateville, it was not uncommon for a gang of tough perverts to strongarm an unfortunate youth and rape him. Nor was it uncommon for them to force him into prostitution. This sort of thing has been and must continue to be prevented by strict and constant supervision of all areas of an assignment.

Officers in charge of assignments that have shower baths, storerooms, closets, etc., on the premises must keep these areas under constant surveillance to prevent their becoming the scenes of brutal and immoral assaults. Always watch stock rooms to prevent items being placed in such a manner as to form hiding places. The time to prevent such acts is before they occur. It has been learned through experience that the example of punishment has little deterrent effect on confirmed homosexuals. The only known solution to the problem of controlling them is either to keep them segregated or keep them under constant supervision. This is the primary reason why they are not given certain assignments, but are kept where they are under the direct supervision of an officer at all times.

Related to the administration's efforts to repress homosexuality in the institution is its constant battle to eliminate pornographic materials from the prison. Books ordered for the institutional libraries are thoroughly scrutinized for obscene passages before they are placed in circulation. The librarian has what is known as a "hot list" of book titles and authors whose works are barred from the institution. Despite the care with which books are censored, objectionable ones sometimes do get into circulation. Such books are invariably found in the cells at some later time. Certain inmates cannot resist underlining risque passages, and officers will notice these as they thumb through a book searching for contraband. Books underlined in this manner must be sent to the Captain's Court together with a proper report of the circumstances. It will then be determined whether or not the book is to be placed back in circulation or withdrawn from the library.

The institution has a permitted list of magazines to which inmates can subscribe. But today even the most popular family-type magazines contain pictures of semi-nude women. Some inmates take a perverse delight in altering these pictures in various ways, usually superimposing drawings of enlarged mammary glands or sexual organs. Magazines defiled in this manner should also be located during cell searches.

Periodically, love letters enroute from one inmate to another are intercepted. The contents of some of these letters are almost unbelievable. The average person, having no experience with perverted passions, would find it difficult to comprehend the depth of a genuine romance between homosexuals. Nor could he understand the depths of degradation to which the professional ones can sink.

In some instances drawings of persons in the various postures of perversion are discovered. Frequently these are passed along from one pervert to another, though sometimes the distribution of lewd pictures may become a commercial enterprise. Inmates have been caught reproducing lewd pictures on copying machines located on various assignments or with the photographic equipment in the B. of I. The pictures thus produced find a ready sale among the inmate population. In order to prevent this sort of thing, officers must keep such equipment securely locked up when it is not being used under close supervision.

Although the inmates who wish may obtain permission to purchase art supplies to make drawings and paintings, any inmate found to be abusing this privilege by drawing or painting pornographic pictures will have his drawing permit revoked and disciplinary action will be taken.

As was stated at the beginning, sex perversion within the confines of a prison is a real problem, a grave one. It is not less so in civilian society, as witness the numerous criminal laws enacted against it. For the very reason that most acts of perversion are not only morally reprehensible but also criminally liable, officers of the institution must be very careful not to indulge in loose speculation or to make reckless accusation against any inmate. Whenever they have grounds for suspicion, they should report them to their superior officer and let him direct a thorough investigation of the case. Officers must not jump at conclusions. On the other hand if they catch any inmates in an act of perversion, they must secure their names and numbers and make an immediate report in detail to the supervising officer. Then they are to make a written report of the incident to the Senior Captain. Again, guess work must never be indulged in. Report exactly what was seen, and what, if anything, was said. In such a report the correct terminology should be used to describe the act committed. Slang and vulgar terms may not be used in a report of this kind except when reporting verbatim anything that the inmates involved may have said. If officers do not

Isolation Cells, Stateville Branch, Joliet, Ilinois.

know the proper terms to employ in such a report, the supervising officer should acquaint them with the appropriate wording.

Officers are cautioned that in all matters, especially in this one, they must keep an open mind, neither believing nor disbelieving that an inmate is a homosexual. The inmate creates his own record. The duty of a correctional officer is to supervise his assignment closely enough to discourage and prevent violations of the law and rules.

Sub-Chapter (C): Sanitation, Hospitals, Veterans' Aid, Inmates as Guinea Pigs

SANITARY INSPECTIONS

In any area where people are gathered closely together the practice of rigid sanitary measures becomes a necessity in order to preserve health and life.

In general, sanitation encompasses three areas: cleanliness of the physical plant and equipment, preventing of the spread of contagious diseases, and personal hygiene.

Inspection of the physical plant and equipment includes the water supply, kitchens, dairy and food processing areas. These inspections are conducted by the prison physician. Employees in charge of these assignments are required to inspect these assignments daily to insure that a rigid sanitation program is being enforced.

Clean, odorless, and neutral tasting water is essential for the general well being, morale, and good health. It must be free from contamination, especially by water from sewerage containing human or animal wastes. This is rather well controlled by the Chief Engineer's Department which periodically sends out samples of water to be tested by the proper laboratories. The initial installation and construction of the deep wells and plumbing in the proper and approved manner keeps the water almost automatically clean and pure. When the bacterial count goes up chlorine is added.

Modern inmate Shower Room. Stateville Branch.

An adequate number of convenient toilet facilities contribute to cleanliness and good morale. Means for washing hands after using the toilets should be provided on food handling assignments in order to prevent or limit dissemination of diseases, particularly those of the group causing diarrheas.

Personal and area cleanliness should be insisted upon. Food handlers must wash their hands thoroughly after using the toilet facilities. Food handlers with skin infections, boils, and diarrhea should immediately be sent to the hospital to determine their fitness to return to the handling or preparing of food. This is a responsibility of all officers and employees coming in contact with inmates on food-handling assignments.

Garbage should be stored in closed containers with close fitting covers in order to minimize odors which attract flies, insects and rodents. Because of the natural history of the fly, garbage should be collected daily to prevent the completion of the fly's larval-

Old time bath tubs. Joliet Branch.

feeding period of five days. In addition to carrying disease germs, the flies and other insects are a nuisance. They make sleep and recreation difficult. The control of flies and other insects by proper garbage collection and disposal, general cleanliness, and the use of sprays and chemicals in a proper manner is essential for control of disease and general comfort in the institutional population.

Inspections of the kitchens, dairy and food-processing facilities are made to check general cleanliness of the areas, proper screening, garbage disposal, and individual hygiene among the personnel. Infectious conditions such as carbuncles or furuncles are especially looked for. Clean fingernails and hands are important. Deficiencies in the sanitation as it may affect the general health and well being are reported directly to the warden who may take such action as he deems necessary.

Food handlers and barbers are inspected for infections and other conditions of health which might disqualify them either temporarily or permanently. It is an institutional policy to disqualify inmates with a past history of syphilis although after proper treatment they might be qualified as this disease is not considered infectious then.

Inmates who have recently recovered from certain contagious illnesses, such as tuberculosis or hepatitis, are automatically disqualified for food handling and are segregated by recommending cell alone or sick bay assignments until there is no danger of recurrence.

Sick inmates are immediately treated or hospitalized as the case requires. Immunization against small pox and typhoid is given at the Diagnostic Depot. Special immunizations against tetanus, influenza, and possibly poliomyelitis can be and are given after the inmates have been assigned here. Generally inmates on the farm and the farm detail are immunized against tetanus because of the frequent contamination of wounds by soil and animal waste.

Blood donors are qualified by referring to the records of medical history and physical examinations compiled here and at other institutions. (All employees and inmates are typed as to their "blood type" and it is noted on all their medical records.

Individuals with a history of syphilis and hepatitis are automatically disqualified by this hospital and by visiting blood banks. However, the visiting blood banks determine the qualifications of the donors they select. We qualify donors for our own hospital only.

Each inmate upon arriving is examined and questioned as to his past medical history. All of this information is recorded on the proper forms and is a permanent record which accompanies the inmate if he is transferred to other institutions. The record is kept up to date by data taken while he is a hospital patient, or whenever he is treated for injuries or is examined, or medication is prescribed on sick call visits.

It is important to see that each inmate keeps himself clean by regular bathing. The clothes should be washed or cleaned at proper intervals to insure cleanliness and personal comfort.

Bedding such as the mattresses, sheets, and blankets should be aired and cleaned at regular intervals, weather permitting. Bedding and blankets should be examined regularly and condemned or replaced when necessary. This is a housekeeping procedure usually taken care of and supervised by the cellhouse keepers.

Officers and employees in contact with inmates in the cellhouses and various work assignments can increase efficiency of public health measures by referring obviously ill, injured, or disabled inmates to the hospital.

Hospitals

The medical services and prison hospitals at Joliet-Stateville are operated as one would expect in an average community hospital outside prison walls. The medical staff consists of four civilian physician-surgeons, two at each institution (one a resident on call twenty-four hours a day and the other on a part-time basis); a dentist at each institution, an oculist, and an eye, ear, nose and throat specialist whose services are shared by both institutions.

All incoming inmates must go through a medical, psychiatric, psychological and sociological processing at the Diagnostic Depot before being transferred to one of the state prisons. A prison physician interviews and examines each new inmate, recording medical history and significant findings and defects so that the prison physician of the institutions to which the inmate is transferred may take corrective measures. Inmates requiring mental treatment are sent to the psychiatric division at the Menard institution. Active cases of tuberculosis are transferred to the modern tuberculosis hospital at the Pontiac Branch of the Illinois State Penitentiary for treatment, with fine results. All inmates have chest x-rays and routine blood Kahn tests and immunizations are started, and if possible, completed during their stay at the Diagnostic Depot; otherwise, immunization is completed by the medical department of the institution to which the inmate is transferred. Treatment for venereal disease is given immediately, if indicated. Immunizations against small pox, typhoid fever, tetanus and poliomyelitis are now given routinely.

The prison physician at the institution to which the inmate has been transferred examines each medical jacket accompanying a new inmate and follows through on immunizations, etc., as indicated. Inmates requiring dental work are referred to the prison dentist. Those in need of dental work are taken care of, and if dentures are needed, they are supplied by our own dental laboratory. Men needing spectacles or hearing aids are referred to the eye, ear, nose and throat department where their defects are given attention and corrected if possible.

Annual chest x-rays are taken on all inmates; inmates having a history of arrested pulmonary tuberculosis, syphilis, or infectious hepatitis are routinely barred from food handling assignments.

Formal sick call is held at prescribed times, three days a week; sick inmates are hospitalized as indicated. However, anyone becoming ill may be brought to the hospital any time of the day or night.

Practically all of the unusual medical and surgical cases are sent to Stateville from the other branch prisons. Most of the medical treatment and surgery is handled by our own institutional physicians and surgeons. However, when necessary, top specialists in the Joliet and Chicago areas are called in unusual chest, ophthalmologic, orthopedic, neurological, and urological cases. We have established rapport with the medical departments of the University of Illinois and the University of Chicago. On many occasions, outstanding doctors from these universities are called to examine and perform surgery on inmates. Fairly recently, the Chief of Surgery of Billings Hospital, Chicago, Illinois, performed the repair of a femoral aneurysm (a dilation or communication between major blood vessels). This particular surgical repair included an artery graft. One of Joliet's leading chest surgeons has performed pneumonectomies and lobectomies here, along with the pre-operative work-ups that in some cases included bronchoscopies and biopsies. A Joliet neuro-surgeon has performed delicate brain operations, which were necessary to aspirate a brain tumor in order to save a man's vision.

Considerable plastic surgery has been done by one of Chicago's top plastic surgeons. Included among his cases were the removal of unsightly facial scars, and plastic repair of facial defects that undoubtedly caused the persons involved great psychological damage in the past. Statistics prove that plastic repair of this type has tremendous rehabilitative value.

From a rehabilitation standpoint, the repair of hernias, varicosities, and other functional and organic defects that effect a man's employability are, of course, of prime importance. It is the aim of the medical department to return men to the free community in the best possible physical condition.

One of the real problems that confronts the prison physician is the physical rehabilitation of inmates suffering from crippling effects of gunshot wounds. Particularly difficult are the cases of wounds to the spine. We receive one or two paraplegics each year. They usually require long-term hospitalization with special emphasis on physical therapy. We have, however, had the satisfaction of seeing some of the admission paraplegics walk out of the institution unaided, and reasonably capable of holding their own in a competitive world.

Outside of the physicians, pharmacist, and required guard personnel, all other hospital assignments are filled by inmates. Nurses, laboratory technicians, x-ray technicians, dental nurse, dental technicians, and medical record librarians are recruited from the inmate population. They are trained through an "on-the-job" training program. Most of the inmates are intensely interested and dedicated to their hospital work. Many of them become very proficient and compare favorably in ability with personnel in similar occupations in outside hospitals.

HOW INMATES SERVED AS VOLUNTARY GUINEA PIGS TO HELP SAVE GI LIVES IN WORLD WAR II

Army Research Projects have been carried on at Stateville by a staff of medical experts under the supervision of Dr. Alf S. Alving, Professor of Medicine, University of Chicago, since September of 1944.

The research originally conducted concentrated on discovery

of a cure for malaria as well as an antidote to prevent malaria among military personnel.

Needless to say ,the research efforts of Dr. Alving's staff were successful in finding the answers they sought, with the help of inmates who served as volunteer guinea pigs for the experiments.

Inmates volunteered to expose themselves to the so-called bite of malaria insects. Many suffered intense pain during the experiments but all survived.

None submitted with the promise of any reward or thought of favor; however, two governors, first, Governor Dwight H. Green, and later, Governor Adlai E. Stevenson, awarded all of the inmate participants in the experiments with benefits in the form of commuted sentences, some more, some less, depending on the nature of the crime and length of sentence.

As Dr. Alving points out, the anti-malaria experiments were launched in September, 1944.

While the malarial tests have been completed, other experiments continue. Since some of these are still classified as secret by Army authorities, I am not at liberty to discuss them.

I merely point this out to show that Stateville and Joliet prison inmates still are contributing to the nation's security.

So far as the author is concerned, the following is a testimonial to the inherent patriotism of our inmates, despite their criminal records.

They offered themselves to undergo experiments which could have proved fatal or, at least, damaging to their bodies. The fact that none suffered permanent injury does not detract from the fact that they offered to sacrifice themselves in the national interest.

Dr. Alving describes in the following how the inmates of Joliet-Stateville prisons aided in the military effort during World War 11, the Korean War and other research projects:

"Clinical investigations at Stateville Penitentiary involving volunteers as experimental subjects, and later employing volunteers as technicians, nurses, secretaries, and other personnel in research, was initiated in late September, 1944. At this time malaria was the primary military medical problem in the Southwest Pacific Theater of Military Operations. It was the cause of more deaths and disability in the overall war than were Japanese bullets. In military operations, whoever best controls a plague or disease, has that disease or plague working on his side as an aggressive military weapon. This is a form of bacterial warfare in reverse, so to speak, which all armies and all military leaders have utilized since very early times. Malaria has been one of the most important diseases, not only economically, socially, and medically, but also in military operations since before the birth of Christ. Rome was saved on several occasions because the invaders who had no immunity to malaria from previous exposure to the disease would be decimated, while the defenders of the Roman cities simply waited within their walls until the attacking armies were destroyed by the disease.

"The first assignment that the Army gave to us, at Stateville, was the evaluation of an experimental antimalarial drug, known to be better than quinine, but thought to be more toxic. This drug was known by the name SN-7618 and is now called chloroquine. It has been proved far superior to any other drug in the suppression of malaria because it can be taken once a week. It was used exclusively in the Korean war to protect the troops that were fighting. Our first job was to test the toxicity to make it practical for use by he Army. This research was supported by the Office of Scientific Research and Development, a special organization created by Congress for Research in World War II. This Office also organized the development of the Atomic Bomb. Research was supported by the United States Army by the assignment of Army Medical Officers to participate in the work.

"The second research program grew out of the first. It concerned the development or discovery of a curative antimalarial drug. Fifty-four have been studied at Stateville. Primaquine, the thirty-fifth drug studied, cures most strains of relapsing malaria occurring in the world in non-toxic doses. It was used in Korea, being administered once a day to each soldier returning to the United States by MSTS transports.

"A third project concerned the use of soaking soldiers' clothes in insecticides or mite repellent compounds in order to combat a serious disease in Korean troops called Hemorrhagic Fever. Hemorrhagic Fever was the cause of many deaths and still is a disease that cannot be cured. The prevention of the Hemorrhagic Fever has been made possible by soaking soldiers' clothes in mite repellent chemicals. The correct dose that could be used to impregnate soldiers' clothes was solved in three or four months by a medical research program conducted by Army Officers at the Joliet prison.

"Finally, we are testing the toxicity of primaquine which, in twice the dose necessary to cure Korean veterans of vivax malaria, will cause an acute destruction of blood in about 10% of American Negroes, 20% or more of Sardinians and Southern Italians. 30% of Sephardic Jews, and many other racial and ethnic groups. Twice the dose necessary to cure Korean vivax malaria would be necessary to cure the malaria existing in Guadalcanal, if military operations were to resume in the Southwest Pacific. We have found that by giving a large dose of primaquine once a week, instead of small doses once a day, the toxicity can be avoided while the effectiveness of primaquine as an antimalarial agent is unimpaired. This discovery promises to be of great practical value.

"We have conducted many other investigations, which have occurred to us, as sidelines. Some of these have become of major importance, both from a practical and theoretical point of view. As an outgrowth of the finding that certain races or peoples are sensitive to primaquine we investigated the sensitivity of these individuals to many other drugs. It has been found that some unexplained blood transfusion reactions and other bad reactions to drugs that are commonly used in the United States can be explained on the same basis as the destruction of blood that occurs with administration of daily large doses of primaquine. This has been of great importance to the Army. It is also of interest to biochemical investigators in cancer research and it has been found to have practical value and application in blood banks and in the storage of blood. This basic research which was begun incidental to the practical research in malaria, has answered other problems that no one dreamed were related to our investigations. It has created a great interest also among the geneticists to know that the sensitivity to drugs is transmitted by heredity through the female who only gets a mild disorder, to the male offspring who gets a severe reaction to certain drugs. Anthropologists in Peru are using this genetic trait in a study of the possible origin of the Polynesians by westward travel over the Pacific, as did the raft, Kontiki.

"It was also found by us that antimalarial drugs were of value in arthritis. Although the drug which we first used, primaquine, has been displaced as an arthritic drug by other antimalarial compounds that are less toxic, it was the investigations at Stateville, undertaken simply because of curiosity, that led to very practical important discoveries. Much of the development of the investigations that we started at Stateville have been pursued elsewhere; but, the developments would never have been possible if the original investigations had not been made at Stateville.

"Other investigators at the University of Chicago have also carried on research as an outgrowth of our clinical studies. Dr. Dragstedt and his group studied the cutting of the vagus nerve for ulcers of the stomach, and Dr. Eisele studied a form of diarrhea which ,though not serious, was debilitating and of interest in Public Health.

"In all of these investigations, the inmates have participated enthusiastically of their free will, and we have received the finest coöperation from you and your entire staff. No volunteer has been permanently injured by the clinical investigations that have been performed."

As former warden of the Illinois State Penitentiary at Joliet, I should like to say that the above mentioned are not the only medical research projects in which inmates of the institution have participated and coöperated. Other universities, the State Department of Public Health and various scientists have carried on a number of other medical projects in which the inmates have participated.

PHARMACEUTICAL MANAGEMENT

The pharmacist in charge of drugs and hospital supplies is also a member of the State Pharmacy Committee, which supervises the purchase of all pharmaceutical supplies, equipment, and x-ray materials for all state institutions.

As a member of that committee, he is directly concerned with maintaining the quality of drug supplies used by state institutions. Those which fail to meet the highest standards are rejected. The pharmacist must also concern himself with economy in the purchasing and dispensation of drugs.

Over the past several years the pharmacist has been able to effect savings on purchase of drug supplies which have made possible the purchase of needed equipment for the prison hospitals. As a result the hospitals at Joliet-Stateville have acquired modern facilities equal to or excelling those of any hospital in the state. Saving ways are profitable and serve a distinct purpose.

As a full time employee, he also compounds drug prescriptions for the 4,500 men at Joliet-Stateville and supervises the program of drug control within the prison.

Three times weekly, a sick call is held for the benefit of the inmates. If upon examination of an inmate the prison physician determines that any medication is required, he writes the ailing inmate a prescription which may ordinarily be filled at the hospital drug room. Staffed by inmate nurses who have been well trained in their duties, this drug room is stocked with medicines considered safe and routine.

However, within the hospital drug room is a locked compartment to which only the officer in charge has a key. In this compartment, which may be opened only in the presence of the officer, are kept medicines of a classified "hot" nature, such as barbituates, ethers ,vasopressors, surgical medicines, or any kind of medicine that could prove dangerous in the hands of a person not properly qualified to handle them.

If a medication is prescribed which is not stocked in the hospital drug room, the prescription is forwarded to the pharmacy for filling. The pharmacist himself fills these prescriptions and places them in a locked box for delivery to the respective cell-houses by an officer. Upon receipt of the medicine, the officer in charge of the cellhouse signs for it and then locks it in his desk to be dispensed according to directions.

Neither medicines in multiple form nor medicines considered dangerous are ever given to an inmate personally. Medicines of this kind must always be dispensed by an officer who will exercise proper vigilance to see that the inmate takes his medication and does not palm or hoard it.

Several years ago medicines in the form of pills or tablets were given directly to the inmates and little attention was paid to whether or not they took the medicine. Consequently some inmates stored up quantities of medicine which, if taken at one time, could have been extremely dangerous.

Now, medications of the "hot" category are bought in liquid form and dispensed by the spoonful. This policy makes it difficult for the inmates to hoard medicine. But, needless to say, any unusual or suspicious looking medicines found in the institution should be taken to the pharmacy for testing and analysis. The date on which prescriptions were issued is marked on every container and unused prescriptions more than two weeks old should be returned to the pharmacy.

Preparations such as narcotics are kept in the pharmacy and are dispensed only by the pharmacist. All narcotics are kept in a strong box especially provided for the purpose. A perpetual inventory of narcotics must be kept in a ledger in the pharmacy which is to remain in the strong box. Entries in the narcotics ledger show the date of withdrawals and additions. Narcotics may never be administered to an inmate unless they have been prescribed by a physician, and given in the presence of an officer.

Whenever a narcotic is to be administered, the employee in charge is to dissolve it and syphon the liquified drug into a syringe. Nurses must be observed closely to make certain they do not switch syringes and thus retain the narcotic for any purpose other than the one for which it was prescribed.

Items such as eyedroppers, which could be used by a narcotics addict, are issued to inmates when prescribed by a physician. A record is kept of them and they must be returned to the pharmacy after a period of time has elapsed—two weeks in most cases. All syringes used in the hospital are numbered and records of them are kept in the pharmacy. Routine checks are made to see that the total number is always correct.

Hypodermic needles are controlled in the same manner. It is, therefore, almost impossible for a syringe or hypodermic needle to fall into the hands of an inmate.

As a result of this meticulous handling of medications and hospital items, there have been no untoward incidents in recent years. There should be none, if every officer exercises proper caution and vigilance in the handling and dispensing of toxic medicines.

Sometimes the purpose of this rigid program of drug control is misunderstood and resented by employees and inmates alike. But, in truth, it works no hardship on a person who is genuinely ill.

It may even safeguard his health by causing him to report to the physician in time to check progressive diseases. A prison pharmacy has to be attuned to the nature of its environment. If toxic drugs were available to unauthorized persons, they could prove detrimental to the security of the institution. The methods used to control drugs have been designed to guard against such an eventuality. Their purpose is not to deprive any person of needed medications.

VETERANS' SERVICE OFFICER

Inmate Veteran Count	World War I	World War II	Korean War	Peace- time	Span.- Amer.	Al- lied	Total
As of 1 Dec. 1946	195	309		92	2	8	606
As of 1 Jan. 1958	49	1302	364	219	1	5	1938

Following World War II, the veteran count at Joliet-Stateville soared.

Many of these veterans had served honestly and faithfully in the nation's armed forces and were eligible to file for various federal and state benefits due them on the basis of their military service, but the claim filing situation here was considerably mixed up due to insufficient or improper evidence being submitted and because letters were addressed to the wrong governmental agency.

The Department of Public Safety was requested to appoint a full-time Veterans' Service Officer and, on July 1, 1946, a Veterans' Service Officer was installed at Stateville. The function of this office is as follows:

Veteran Laws: To find, study, interpret, and distribute pertinent information relating to the laws governing veteran benefits.

Filing Procedures: To obtain appropriate forms with which to file veteran claims. To know which governmental agency has jurisdiction of these claims at the various stages of processing. To locate claims filed before incarceration and to change the veteran's address to Stateville.

Evidence: To assist the veteran to obtain and submit various needed evidence in his claim:

Periods of service.
Type of discharge certificate.
Evidence from military hospitals.
Evidence from civilian doctors and hospitals.
Evidence from lay people.
Evidence by affidavit from the veteran himself.

Institutional Regulations: The responsibility of censoring correspondence to and from governmental agencies was given to the Veterans' Service Officer. This duty includes assisting to execute various forms and affidavits, affixing appropriate notarizations and witnessings, granting Special Letters or writing in a veteran's behalf over the Warden's signature. On direct order from the warden, the veterans of Joliet-Stateville are given the fullest possible assistance to prosecute any claim for any benefit due them as a result of their military service.

In ten and one-half years there has never been a complaint that, because of his incarceration, a veteran had been denied a claim to which he otherwise had been eligible. The contrary holds true, for veterans incarcerated in Joliet-Stateville were obtaining New York World War II Bonuses at a time when veterans living in the town of Joliet were being denied this benefit because they had given up New York residency at the time of filing their claims.

Hospitalization and Domiciliary Care: To obtain information, forms, and entrance requirement. To assist with applications, and to obtain necessary documentary evidence.

Selective Service Act: To assist in change of address. To furnish the Selective Service System with commitment information for the purpose of reclassification. To determine whether or not all subject inmates being released on parole or discharge are registered under this act and, if not, to register the inmate before release. To visit Local Board 212, Joliet, Illinois, each week for the purpose of coördinating records. To assist the Federal Bureau of Investigation in investigating violations of the Act. And to assist inmates to follow Federal Bureau of Investigation suggestions where it is necessary to correct records under this Act.

Veterans Administration: To maintain liaison with the Chicago Regional Office, the St. Paul District Office, and various hospital and Domiciliary Facilities of the Veterans' Administration. To expedite requests for information either from the Veterans' Administration or from Joliet-Stateville. To assist the Veterans' Administration doctors when they visit Joliet-Stateville to examine inmate-veterans for compensation purposes. To act as technical advisor to policy making level personnel at the Veterans' Administration Chicago Regional Office relative to the veterans' needs of the inmates in other prisons and jails.

Pay and Bonds Claims: To assist in filing claims with various armed forces or other governmental agencies. To collect and submit the factual evidence needed in the claims.

Government Insurance: To have a working knowledge of three types of government insurance: World War I, World War II, and Korean. To obtain specific information as requested by a veteran. To assist in:

Change in Beneficiary
Cash surrender
Change of address

Conversion

Correction of the record

Dividends

Loans

Change of Option

Premium—credit, deduction, payment, and waiver.

Power of attorney

Reinstatement

Renewal

Family Aid: To assist in obtaining temporary relief under the Illinois Borgardus Act. To obtain aid for Dependent Children. To expedite claims with the various relief agencies. To assist in providing eligibility and veterans' preference in public housing. To assist in all claims based upon veteran dependency.

INSECT AND RODENT CONTROL

Whenever there is a densely populated area, or where large groups of people are closely confined, sanitation, the control of insects and rodents, is highly important in promoting and preserving good health.

In order to show the contrast between an institution where sanitation and rodent control are in force, and where such a program is absent, here is a brief picture of Joliet Penitentiary as it was in 1930, and as Joliet-Stateville is now that a program of control has been effected. At that time—in 1930—almost every cell at the Joliet Branch was infested with bedbugs. Cockroaches were prevalent in most buildings and tunnels. Also, most buildings were infested with rats and mice. The only program for insect and rodent control was that practiced by the inmates, who, in their cells, would use burning paper in attempts to destroy the bedbugs around the steel frames of their beds.

Inmates at that time were permitted to have pets in their cells and as some of the inmates failed to properly care for their pets, this aggravated a bad situation.

In 1931, a program for the combating of bedbugs and roaches was inaugurated and consisted of an inmate going about with a blow torch and burning insects. Kerosene was also used in this program. Needless to say, this program was not very effective. It failed to prevent the breeding of insects and rodents. Of course, it must be realized that there was not available the effective insecticides that have since been developed.

In 1935 a program was inaugurated to rid all parts of the Joliet-Stateville Penitentiary of insects and rodents and within a short time a noticeable improvement could be observed. By adhering rigidly to this carefully planned program, and using all available aids, the Joliet-Stateville Penitentiary was gradually brought to the high state of sanitation that is now maintained. Following are the methods used in the institution program of insect and rodent control.

An officer is permanently assigned to direct the extermination program. Three inmates are assigned to aid him, two of whom are assigned to the day shift, spraying those assignments that can be sprayed with insecticides during the working day. The third inmate is assigned to the night shift and, under the supervision of a Lieutenant, sprays those assignments that cannot be sprayed during the day time.

Three types of spray insecticides are used, DDT; a liquid insecticide with DDT added, that is manufactured here; and a liquid insecticide having an oil base and an additive of 2% Chlordane. Each of these insecticides has a specific purpose. The liquid insecticide with DDT added will kill all insects, but is not used where food is being stored or processed. Therefore this insecticide is used in tunnels, manholes, basements, etc.

The mill type spray for use in the dining room, kitchens, canning plant, store rooms, etc., is manufactured in the institution. The liquid insecticide with 2% Chlordane added (which is also manufactured here) has an oil base and is used as a "space spray." It will stick to walls and other surfaces.

Included in the program is the spraying of all tunnels, basements, and out-of-the-way places. Every assignment is covered by the spraying schedule and a record is kept of the date each assignment is sprayed, and the type and amount of material used.

At the present time approximately 2,000 gallons of insectitude and 40 pounds of insect powder are used each year at the Stateville Branch. As it is poisonous to humans, the insect powder is not manufactured here.

The Joliet-Stateville Fire Chief has the responsibility for rodent control, and makes periodic inspections of buildings and areas throughout the institution. Decon, a highly toxic substance, is used to kill rodents.

Naturally, care must be exercised in the use of these various insecticides and powders, not only from a standpoint of health, but also from the standpoint of institutional security.

All of the insecticides manufactured here are non-poisonous, although they are toxic, and they do not carry a poison label. Being toxic means that a person could be sickened by the spray, but would not be in danger of death. Should anyone, inmate or employee, become ill from one of these insecticides (through inhaling too much, or for any other reason), the person should immediately be taken to the prison physician, who is aware of the ingredients of the insecticides used here, and can give prompt treatment.

Cockroach powder, being poisonous, is used only where inmates cannot have access to it, either before or after application. Rules governing the handling of poisons and narcotics, as outlined in the Officers Rule Book, are strictly adhered to in handling this powder.

All non-poisonous insecticides are kept locked in the exterminator locker when not in use, and can only be taken out and used under the direct supervision of an officer. *No Insecticides or Insect Powders are to be left on any Assignment!*

There are many aspects of sanitation, insect and rodent control, such as the treatment of incoming inmates at the Diagnostic Depot, and rules governing housekeeping within the institution. In order to completely cover the subject many more pages would be necessary, and therefore just the highlights have been presented here.

Sanitation is everyone's business, and can only be maintained through the complete coöperation of every employee. All parts of this institution must be kept scrupulously clean. If an employee finds evidence of insects or rodents present anywhere within the institution, he should report this to a superior officer. If, after a reasonable length of time, action has not been taken, a report of the condition should be sent to the Warden.

TOOL CONTROL

Officers new to custodial work are generally prone to take tools for granted. There is nothing unusual in their attitude because tools are so much a part of this mechanical age. Yet, in a penal institution ordinary tools acquire a special significance. If there is anything that can be compared to keys and guns as a threat to the security of the institution, it is tools.

Even the most common sort of tool, a wrench or screwdriver, may be used in an escape attempt. Bars can be twisted off with a small wrench. Locks can be removed with a screwdriver. Either item may be used as a weapon. It is, therefore, necessary that all personnel learn to regard tools not just as a normal complement of every assignment, but as a potential weapon against the safety and security of the institution and individual employees and inmates.

Desirable as it would be from the standpoint of security, tools cannot be dispensed with. They are used throughout the institution. It could not long operate without them. The solution to the problem, then, is careful control and supervision of all tools. This supervision and control of tools must be of concern to all personnel no matter what rank or classification.

The first step in the control of tools is to make a complete inventory. This is the responsibility of the officer in charge of each assignment, for he is charged with all tools and equipment on his assignment. The over-all inventory of tools is supervised by the Assistant Warden and the Chief Engineer. In addition to the annual tool inventory, which must be made once each year and submitted to the above mentioned officials, verification of the tool count must be made twice monthly, by the assignment officer. Standard forms are provided by the institution for both the bi-weekly "Tool Reports" and the "Assignment Tool List," or annual tool inventory. An officer taking over an assignment should make a tool inventory at once.

Sometimes officers are confused by the fact that a tool may appear on both the Fixed Assets Inventory and the Tool Inventory. If it is kept in mind that the one concerns finance and the other security, the confusion will resolve itself. In the instance of power machinery, such as band saws, and meat slicers, the machine itself is carried on the Fixed Assets Inventory, the cutting blades on the Tool Inventory. This is purely a security measure.

Making an Inventory

In making a tool inventory, officers should list tools according to their location in the tool crib. This eliminates the necessity of skipping around from one tool box or shadow board to another. If, for example, all the items in tool box number 4 are listed in order on the same page of the "Assignment Tool List," it is easy to check those tools by turning to the proper page and checking off each tool one by one.

Classifying and Supervising Dangerous Tools

Although every tool allocated to an assignment must be controlled and accounted for, some tools are obviously more dangerous than others. This would include such tools as welding torches, hack-saws, pipe cutters, bolt cutters, jacks or bar spreaders. Tools of this type must be given maximum supervision. Such tools as are not kept in the Armory must be kept in a secure locker or cabinet which is within the officer's sight and supervision at all times. This precaution must be observed not only with workable tools, but with broken ones as well. When a saw blade breaks, officers must be sure to collect all the pieces, since a two or three inch section of hack-saw blade will readily cut a bar.

Identity of Tools

All tools must have the assignment code marked or stamped on them. For instance, tools assigned to the Master Mechanics' Shop must be marked with the letters MM; those assigned to the Power House with PH; and so forth. This not only keeps the tools where they belong, but also averts any dodging of responsibility for them in the event of any difficulty.

Use of a Check System

When tools are issued to anyone, a list of them must be kept by the person in charge of the tool crib. The list must accurately describe each tool, giving the kind, type and size, to ease the matter of identification. This list must also include the name and rank of the person drawing the tools, the date and time they were issued, and where they are to be used. A copy of this tool list must be kept on file until the tools are returned and checked.

Get a Signed Receipt for Tools

When issuing tools to anyone, the employee in charge of the tool crib must secure a signed receipt from the person drawing the tools. If an inmate draws tools to work on a detail, the employee must list on the back of the inmate's work ticket the tools he drew. These tools must be checked in and out of the M & M Shop and all assignments by the officer in charge who must also initial the tool list, usually on the back of the work ticket. When the inmate arrives at the assignment where the work is to be done, the officer in charge of the assignment must check the tools in and out, also signing the work ticket. If an inmate goes to an assignment to perform some job and his tools *do not* check with the list the M & M officer has signed him out with, the assignment officer must get on the telephone and find out why the list does not check. *Under no circumstances should the officer sign for the tools or let the inmate commence work until the tools and the ticket check with each other,* or until the discrepancy has been cleared up by the M & M Shop Officer. Even then, the assignment officer must not sign for any tools other than those brought into his assignment.

Use Shadow Boards to Facilitate Tool Checks

If tool crib permits, tools should be kept on shadow boards, a board or section of wall on which the outline of the tool is painted in the position that it rests and in a contrasting color to the background. With such an arrangement it is possible to see at a glance what is missing from its usual place. The shadow board is no substitute for carefulness in checking tools, but it does provide a quick method of detecting and identifying missing tools.

Custody of Ladders

For obvious reasons ladders are very carefully supervised in an institution of this type. With the exception of step ladders under five feet in height, all ladders must be securely chained to a post or column so that they cannot be moved or carried from the spot until they have been securely locked by a Lieutenant. Ladders more than ten feet long are kept, not within the walls, but in the Sally Port. When a ladder is to be taken from the Sally Port to some location within the walls, the officer at the Sally Port calls all towers and the Chief Guard, stating that a ladder of certain length is going to a certain destination, carried by a certain number of inmates, escorted by a certain Lieutenant. He also describes the route they are to take to reach their destination. When finished with the ladder, the Lieutenant calls the towers and advises them that the ladder is being carried back to the Sally Port by so many inmates, escorted by Lieutenant Brown or Jones or whatever his name is, and describes the route they are to take. When the ladder is back in the Sally Port, the Sally Port officer notifies the towers and the Chief Guard that the ladder is secure.

(D): *Business Management and Other*
Physical Controls

INVENTORY CONTROL PROCEDURES

Employees should bear in mind that all State Property of a permanent or semi-permanent character is identified and governed according to the Legislation of the State Property Control Act. This is designed to regulate the supervision, accountability and control of state owned properties, both real and personal. It provides certain penalties.

This property consists of all equipment and household items in some 600 major object classifications. Employees are cautioned to observe that every major object on their assignment carries an inventory number, with the exception of surgical and dental instruments, which are controlled only by count and description. Inventory numbers are charged to an assignment, not only in the records of the institution, but also in the records of the Property Control Division in Springfield.

The Property Control Division maintains a set of four cards used in the control of all state owned property. The A and B cards, which are administrative cards, remain in the offices of the Property Control Division. The C and D cards are sent to the institution. The D card forms our permanent inventory record. The C card is used as a traveling card on which notification of inter-departmental transfers of equipment, or requests for condemnation proceedings of equipment, is conveyed to the central offices of the Property Control Division in Springfield, the State Capitol. Although the institution has its own forms for handling transfers between assignments, every such transfer must be forwarded on a 3-C card to the property control division, where four new cards, A, B, C, and D, must be made out in order to complete the transaction. Since so much detail is involved in making transfers, none should be requested unless they are reasonably essential to the operation of the assignment.

Every inventory card contains the following information: the card number, tag number, description of propery, location code, year purchased, purchase price, object code, voucher number and transaction code. Every time a change is effected in our inventory, this information is recorded on a 3-C card. For example, if an item is transferred from one assignment to another within the institution. If the inventory officer believes that an item should be condemned, he conveys that information to the Property Control Division through the medium of a 3-C card, showing it as "transferable property." The Property Control Division then sends a field representative into the prison to inspect the property and he decides whether to condemn the property or to make some other disposition of it.

In the event the institution wants to transfer a piece of equipment to another state agency the property is offered as surplus equipment. The Property Control Division then publishes a list of surplus equipment from which the agency wanting any particular piece of equipment may requisition it through the Property Control Division.

Periodically and at least once each year the Auditor of Public Accounts shall make a physical check of the records and property under the control and supervision of the warden. This check must be sufficient to satisfy the Auditor of Public Accounts as to the accuracy thereof.

INSTITUTIONAL LIBRARY

Long before most other aids to rehabilitation were admitted within prison walls the necessity of providing books for prisoners was recognized.

But only in comparatively recent years has the difference between *books* and a *library* been understood.

A good library must consist of a collection of books and periodicals sufficiently diversified to meet within reason the needs and interests of a prison population.

With that objective in view the library at Joliet-Stateville has accumulated a total of more than 17,000 books, which are almost evenly divided between fiction and non-fiction.

To distribute these books among the inmates, the library system operates, through the main library at Stateville, a division library at the Joliet Branch and a branch library in each of the cellhouses, in the Farm Dormitory and in the Diagnostic Depot.

In addition, mobile library carts are operated in the hospitals. Even the unfortunate patients in the contagious wards are given a choice of reading materials which are destroyed after they have been read.

The circulation of library books is based on the fluctuation of the inmate population. For the year ending December 31, 1957, the circulation of the Stateville Branch was 125,533 books, while the monthly circulation was 10,461. The annual circulation of the Joliet Branch was 43,632 books, while the monthly circulation was 3,619. The combined total for the year makes an over-all circulation of 169,165 books, or 14,980 per month.

A substantial appropriation makes it possible for the library to purchase new books each quarter. This, together with books that are donated, keeps the library system up to date and satisfies the heavy demands made on it by an avid reading population of some 4,400 inmates.

The Main Library is staffed by six inmates who are under the direct supervision of an Officer-Librarian. The staff classifies all books under the Standard Dewey-Decimal Classification and the Cutter-Author System. They sort and fill requests, check returns for repairs, and repair damaged and worn books. The Library Bookbindery repairs and rebinds an average of 300 books each month.

Such magazines as the *National Geographic, Popular Mechanics, Popular Science,* and other current popular magazines are bound into volumes, either quarterly, monthly, or weekly, for circulation in the branch libraries. Bound volumes of the *National Geographic* magazines dating as far back as 1920 are still in demand.

Each cellhouse has two inmate librarians, who work under the supervision of the cellhouse keeper. Their duties are to distribute and pick up non-fiction books which are issued from the Main Library once a week (technical books are issued on a study basis) and to issue fiction books from the cellhouse library.

The choice and selection of the books purchased is made by the librarian, who is given the best available material from which to compile the quarterly requisitions. Book reviews which appear in the Saturday Review of Literature and in the *New York Times* and *Chicago Tribune,* current book lists, and all of the latest book publishers' catalogues are received periodically by the library.

It is surprising to note the taste pattern in individual reading material, and the popularity which it has taken as follows: biography, current events, travel and semi-technical books in the non-fiction category. In fiction, the preference is shown in this sequence: western, mystery, historical and adventure novels.

The Diagnostic Depot, where all new inmates are received and held during their classification and before transfer to one of the state prisons, has a branch library which is serviced from the Joliet Branch. It is in the Diagnostic Depot, where men start a different kind of life, that they acquire a taste for reading to combat their boredom and to occupy their idle evening hours. Therefore, the branch library at the Diagnostic Depot is well patronized.

It would be impossible to estimate the true value of the library in terms of mental therapy, education, and rehabilitation. But, to resort to a well-accepted platitude, even in prison, books are to the mind what food is to the body, and our adherence to this maxim is another step in the rehabilitation procedure.

A fiction book is classified by white letters on a black background, while a non-fiction book has black letters on a white background. Also, a fiction book always starts with a letter, while a non-fiction book starts with three numbers. Example: (G 845 M) fiction—(940.458) non-fiction.

Cellhouse keepers and officers assigned to the cellhouses, or any other assignment on which inmates are permitted to keep books, must inspect the books when conducting shakedowns. Regardless of whether a book has been issued from the Inmates' Library, the Grade or High School Libraries, or the Chapel libraries, the officer should determine whether the book is overdue, and whether it has been mutilated in any way. Some inmates have a nasty habit of underlining words, sentences and whole paragraphs. Whenever an officer picks up a book that has been defaced in that or any other manner, he should write an appropriate report on the inmate involved.

Some books may be "hot," that is, they may not be properly stamped or permitted. Any book found that is not permitted over the signature of the Superintendent of Education or one of the

Chaplains or that is not plainly identified as belonging to the library, the schools or the chapel, is an illegally possessed book. The officer finding such a book must confiscate it and send it to the Senior Captain together with a report of the circumstances under which it was found.

FUNCTIONS OF THE BUSINESS MANAGER'S OFFICE

A long established principle of democratic government is that public monies can be expended only by authorization of the legislature. The budget, or appropriation bill, is approved by the General Assembly as it deems necessary for the operation of all state agencies.

Funds appropriated for the operation of this unit of the Department of Public Safety during the 70th Biennium were in the following amounts:

Personal Services	$ 4,340,000.00
Contractual Services	241,000.00
Postage	14,500.00
Commodities	3,568,000.00
Paroled and Discharged Prisoners' travel expenses and allowances....	72,000.00
Equipment	125,000.00
Stationery, Printing, Office Supplies	40,000.00

The appropriation having been made for these seven funds, they cannot legally be transferred from one fund to another, no matter how desirable or necessary that action might seem. To cite an example. If there were in the Equipment Fund $10,000 and in the Commodities Fund no balance, it still would not be possible to make purchases of commodities and pay for them out of money appropriated for Equipment. All expenditures from monies appropriated for specific budget requests are checked by the General Office of the Department of Public Safety, by the Department of Finance, by the Auditor of Public Accounts, by the State Treasurer, and the Auditor General.

It is, therefore, the concern of the business manager's department to formulate a program between the administration and the various department heads with respect to anticipated expenditures, so that the prison may operate throughout the budget period without having to restrict or curtail any program.

Expenditures of an institution or unit of the Department of Public Safety are governed by, and limited to, the amount of money allowed in the budget. These budgets are initiated by the individual institutions and it is essential that the budget request include all necessary funds to implement any continuing or proposed program. Considerable thought must be given to ascertain that all necessary items are included.

On more than one occasion the appropriation committee of the State Legislature has seen fit to curtail suggestions that were submitted by the warden concerning allocations in the various funds. This and various other factors are the reasons why emphasis is made on economical purchasing and use of equipment, supplies and materials. Employees of the institution should be in a position to make sure that they can justify the purchase of all items.

One of the functions of the business manager's office is the checking and receiving of requisitions. All requirements for the operation and maintenance of the institution are placed on quarterly, semi-annual, and annual requisitions, in addition to special or emergency requisitions.

Each department within the institution (department heads) is required to make requisitions according to specifications. Each word, items and cost must be checked to see that the requisition is correctly prepared. After requisitions have been received in the business manager's office, they must be checked against the remaining stores in order to eliminate unnecessary stock piling of antiquated materials or supplies. And, on the other hand, it is necessary to make certain that the amounts ordered are sufficient to insure the proper functioning of each departmen. Employees can coöperate by studying the actual requirements of their assignments and filling out their requisitions accordingly.

With further reference to emergency requisitions, only authorized persons are permitted to purchase items locally, in case of emergencies, and then only with approval of the warden or business manager. All such purchases must be accompanied by an invoice or paid receipt which is to be promptly delivered to the business manager's office.

Once the requirements of a department have been estimated, requested, and approved, they should be used as economically as possible. The fund for Commodities, second in amount only to Personal Services, is one area of expenditures which might by substantially reduced.

As an example, the electric bill for one year is approximately $67,000. A saving of 5% would amount to $3,350, which in effect means that if electrical equipment operates needlessly three minutes out of an hour, there has been an actual loss of $3,350. Employees should understand why it is so important to conserve electricity.

Most employees are of the opinion that water is free because the institution has its own wells. This is far from the truth. It costs about $40,000 to drill and equip a well. It takes electricity to operate the motors in the well houses, which means that any water saved is actually a saving in the electric bill. There are additional expenses involved in the purchase of repair parts and chlorine gas.

In this connection it may be well to remember that water and coal are used to produce steam. When steam leaks are permitted to exist or when radiators are turned on unnecessarily, both coal and water are being wasted. The coal bill for one year amounts to approximately $198,000. A 5% saving would amount to $9,900. Obviously it is very important not to use more water and steam than necessary.

Cars, trucks and buses cost money. It is important that employees who drive these vehicles or supervise the inmate drivers see to it that they are lubricated on schedule. It is also important that vehicles be repaired when needed and not driven until they are beyond repair. The same holds true for all mechanical equipment in the institution. The cost for vehicles and mechanical supplies for one year amount to about $32,500.

It would take over $125 million dollars to replace this institution. This indicates the importance of maintaining the institution's fixed assets. Their loss by negligence or fire would be very costly to the taxpayers of the state.

Many employees may wonder why they cannot get a piece of equipment as soon as it arrives in the receiving room. In the first place all equipment must bear an inventory tag. Before this tag can be affixed it is necessary that the invoice covering the article be vouchered and sent to Springfield for payment. After the invoice reaches the Property Control Division of the Department of Finance, the institution is furnished with an inventory card showing the description, cost, and location of the particular piece of equipment. That is why it is so important that the Inventory Office be notified before any piece of equipment is sent out for repairs or moved to a different assignment. If any equipment is beyond repair or not needed on an assignment, the supervising officer must notify the Inventory Office before making any disposition of the equipment.

It is also important that the officer in charge of an assignment become familiar with all the equipment items on his assignment.

The department of finance employs field inspectors who drop into the institution from time to time for the purpose of making spot checks of various departments. It would be embarrassing both to the prison staff and to the institution to have a faulty inventory. In many instances spot checks have revealed that items have been transferred or destroyed without receiving the proper authorization. Those who handle state property must bear in mind that they are governed by the laws of the state and that those who carelessly or knowingly violate a law can be prosecuted.

No individual or group can violate laws of the state. Neither can they change the operation of the institution. We live and are governed by laws.

While a salary raise for employees was made recently by the legislature and the governor, and other raises will be coming periodically, the fact remains that state employees are not overpaid.

It seems reasonable that efficient use and handling of the various items covered by the summaries of the Chief Engineer and the Business Manager would make it possible to reduce the appropriations for those items and, perhaps, result in securing an increased appropriation for personal services, the bill for which amounted last year to $1,903,252.42. In other words, the more economically and efficiently the employees operate this institution, the better chance they stand of getting an increase in salary.

It is the consensus that the In-Service Training Program enables every employee to become better acquainted with the other man's problems and builds improved coöperation between all departments of the prison on a realistic basis.

There is an old saying that "nothing succeeds like success" and, as everyone knows, when there is a unified effort, success is the natural result.

MAINTENANCE AND CONSERVATION OF PHYSICAL RESOURCES

An institution the size of the Joliet-Stateville prison is tremendously expensive to maintain. At present, maintenance operations total about $120,000 a year. As the buildings and equipment deteriorate with age, these costs will increase greatly unless every employee does his part toward proper maintenance with proper supervision.

Whenever officers have difficulty with any of the equipment on their assignment, they should not attempt to diagnose the trouble themselves. That is a function of the maintenance department. It has men trained in the diagnosis and repair of all institutional equipment. Neither officers nor the inmates on any assignment should attempt to make repairs, without prior approval of the Maintenance Department.

In case of emergencies the chief engineer or one of the foremen at the Machine and Maintenance Shop should be contacted. They in turn will take care of the situation. In all such instances it is necessary that a phone call be followed by a written report giving all the details of the incident. If it is not an emergency, a work order is sufficient.

Under no circumstances should officers dispose of, or permit any inmate to discard, materials or parts of machinery. Nothing may be junked or replaced until after it has been inspected by a foreman. When there are parts or materials to be disposed of, officers must call the M.&M. Shop and secure prior approval from one of the foremen.

For all normal maintenance of equipment, materials are available from stock and may be requisitioned from the mechanical store by one of the foremen. However, if a request is made to manufacture or redesign some piece of equipment or structure, the material may have to be ordered especially for the job. This kind of request must be evaluated to determine the practicability of the project. It may be approved, modified, or rejected for the time being.

Preventive maintenance is established by planning and regular inspection. Work is planned on a long-term program and correlated to the life expectancy of the machinery. The approximate length of time a machine will run before it needs overhauling is known, and critical parts of the machine, are usually replaced in advance of a major breakdown.

However, this maintenance schedule may be upset by improper servicing or reckless handling of machinery. This is particularly true with respect to automotive equipment. Employees who operate state owned vehicles should use and treat them as if they were their own, complying with all the rules and regulations of the institution governing these vehicles. Furthermore, employees are to report any mishandling of trucks by inmate drivers. There is to be no joyriding, speeding, cowboy antics, or any form of reckless and abusive driving.

In this institution there are buildings and equipment, as pointed out, that would cost $125 million dollars to replace. Practically every kind of facility that would be found in a small city may be found here, and many different kinds of skills are required to keep the institution functioning properly. The most effective way to prevent breakdowns is to schedule a sound program of preventive maintenance. Officer may contribute to that program by making constant and careful inspections of their assignments. If any of the machinery seems to be operating improperly or if the building itself needs repairs, that situation should be made known to the mechanical foremen whose duty it is to see that the necessary repairs are effected.

All of the utilities, water, steam, electricity, etc., are most important in the operation of this institution and every employee must help to conserve them. Our water supply, perhaps the most important utility, is derived from deep wells. There are five wells which supply water for Stateville and three for the Joliet Branch. These wells are approximately 1,600 feet deep and are equipped with turbine pumps. At Stateville we use about a million gallons of water a day. The five pumps here are capable of pumping 1½ millions gallons a day. There is a reservoir with a storage capacity of a million and a half gallons. At certain times of the year, as in the summer months of July and August, as much as 1,300,000 gallons of water are used each day. A large amount of water has to be used on the flowers and lawns. Also, in warm weather months water in large quantities is used by the farm through irrigation systems. These pumps must be maintained and kept operating at all times.

If trouble develops with one pump, it becomes necessary that all departments of the institution conserve on the use of water and everyone is notified so that he will be aware of the problem.

One experience like that occurred in August 1956, when water consumption was at its highest. During a bad electrical storm, lightning struck several transformers at the Farm Colony and put the farm power plant out of action. All departments were notified at once and practically every one started conserving water at once. Although this farm pump had been pumping approximately 380,000 gallons of water a day, the loss of this amount of water was hardly noticed because of the effective conservation of water practiced by the majority of the employees. This points up clearly that water can be conserved during an emergency.

The natural water table in this area has been dropping about ten feet per year. As the water table drops the pumps have to be set deeper. When pumps are set deeper, horse power of the electric motors that drive these pumps has to be increased commensurately, and as the horse power goes up so does the electrical and maintenance cost.

Fifteen years ago the pumps were set around 300 feet and were driven by 50 or 60 horse power motors. Today the pumps are set at 500 feet and are driven by 125 and 150 horse power motors, thus increasing the cost of pumping water. Therefore, whenever officers discover on their assignment any leaks, such as showers or faucets, they must notify the Maintenance Department who will stop the loss of valuable water.

All of the steam used for heating and processing is generated in the powerhouse at Stateville and Joliet. At Joliet there are three boilers and at Stateville six. The boilers at Stateville have a rating of 350 horse power each or a total of 2,100 horse power. These boilers may be operated with a 50 or 60 per cent overload. About 800,000 pounds of steam are generated each day and this requires approximately 80 tons of coal per day. The boilers at Stateville were installed in 1923. They are old and their efficiency is poor. Considering the age of these boilers the men at the powerhouse are doing a very good job. But there seems to be a lot of wasted steam after it leaves the powerhouse. Officers and other personnel can help in many ways to conserve heat. One way would be to refrain from opening windows over heated radiators. Another is to shut the heat off if it is too warm for comfort and then open the windows. Still another is by reporting to maintenance any steam leaks that are noticed. Many rooms and buildings are vacated at night and sometimes over the weekend. Proper supervision of the heat in these buildings and rooms at such times would save many valuable pounds of steam, water and coal.

All electric power used at Stateville and Joliet Branches is purchased from public utilities. Two 33,000 volt lines feed both institutions. Through transformers this voltage is dropped to 2,400 volts at Stateville and 6,900 at the Joliet Branch, and is again reduced by transformers to 40, 220 and 1140 volts to be used at the assignments where a given voltage is required. About 15,000 kilowatts per day are used at Stateville. As everyone knows electricity is dangerous and as high voltages are used throughout the institution, officers are forbidden to make any repairs, or to allow an inmate to repair anything unless he has been assigned to do so by one of the civilian foremen.

MAINTENANCE OF STRUCTURES AND BUILDINGS

For reasons of appearance, utility and economy all buildings and structures should be periodically inspected for minor as well as major defects. Since the greater portion of the value of this institution is represented by the many large and expensive buildings, it clearly follows that a comprehensive program of building maintenance is essential.

Buildings have a mortal enemy which is not always recognized as such. To many persons, water leaks are merely a source of annoyance. They are much more than that: Water causes paint to peel, wood to rot, steel to rust and concrete to crumble. Unrepaired leaks in the exterior of a building will destroy it, not spectacularly, but just as surely as a fire or a tornado uproots everything in its path. Officers should be ever alert to detect and report them.

Leaks in a roof are generally easy to discover, though sometimes a bucket is placed under the drip and no report made. But water entering side walls of a building and seeping into the concrete structure may not be easily detected, at least until after it has caused deterioration of the masonry bond. If officers notice any place where the paint is peeling or plaster is loose from the walls, they may assume that the difficulty is being caused by water penetrating the walls. They should report it.

The building defects which should command attention are broken window panes or windows and doors that close improperly. If water enters through these openings it may cause window and door frames to rust or rot. Besides, if they are not properly sealed during cold weather, they can cause a substantial increase in the fuel bill.

It is also important to detect leaks in the plumbing or in the vast network of steam lines. Such leaks not only endanger the interior of a building, but they can also be responsible for increased operating expenses. The latter consideration is especially applicable to the hot water return lines. When steam cools sufficiently to condense it is piped back to the steam boilers as hot water. Much less fuel is required to convert this heated water back into steam than would be the case if cold water were added to the boilers.

On the prison grounds are structures other than buildings, which also require preventive maintenance. Among them, of course, are the walls, the reservoir, the water tower, the exhaust ducts and dust bins over the furniture factory. If these structures are of masonry, any cracks which develop in them must be cemented and sealed. If they are of metal, they must be kept painted to protect them from rust. Wire fences and gates must be similarly protected.

Occasionally employees may be placed in charge of a detail assigned to maintenance and repair. In that eventuality an M & M foreman will give instructions concerning the proper procedures. Officers must make certain that they clearly understand his directions. Whenever officers are assigned to supervise work requiring the use of scaffolding, they must insist that it be solidly put together and safe to work on. Scaffolding, whether it be built up from the ground with timbers or suspended on ropes or cables, offers a potential threat to security. Carelessly guarded, scaffolding could be used to scale the wall.

Although tools are essential in performing necessary work, many of them are dangerous and should be handled with caution. Improperly used tools may cause injury to the person using them or to anyone in the immediate vicinity. If officers observe anyone using a tool unsafely or for some purpose other than the one for which it was designed, they should command him to stop and then instruct him in the safe and proper handling of that tool. Tools must be counted often and any shortage reported immediately, for tools must never be allowed in the possession of an inmate except when he is using them under the supervision of an officer.

Undoubtedly many officers may wonder why they have been instructed on procedures which, on the surface, would appear to be the concern of the Maintenance and Machine Shop employees. One reason, of course, is that the program of In-Service Training has been instituted to familiarize all employees with the operation of every department within the prison. Another is that officers are the persons who will have the best opportunity to inspect assignments and to discover the need of maintenance and repairs. Although an inspection team could tour the buildings for that purpose, this is a sizeable institution and it would be difficult for them to know each assignment as intimately as the person who works there daily. Therefore, it is most important that the officer on an assignment supplement the efforts of the maintenance department to keep the institution in a state of good repair. By doing so he can contribute to the preservation of the physical assets and to the efficient and economical operation of the institution.

A nut tightened, a nail driven, or an ounce of lubrication applied when needed will prolong the service life of many costly buildings and machines.

HIGH VOLTAGE INSTALLATIONS

The institution purchases its electricity from the Public Service Company of Northern Illinois. The electricity is fed into the transformer yards at both Joliet and Stateville at the rate of 33,000 volts. In the transformer yards, located outside the walls at the west side of both institutions, the voltage is stepped down so that 2,400 volts feed into Stateville and 3,600 volts into the Joliet Branch. Carried underground to the sub-stations, the electricity then passes through numerous switches which distribute it to the various transformer vaults. From these vaults it is fed into the buildings and assignments at different voltages. Usually an assignment will have two or more lines carrying 120, 240, or 480 volts.

At Stateville the electrical vaults are placed underground, while at Joliet they are set flush with the surface of the ground. In both instances they are protected by heavy iron covers. No one should ever be allowed access to the transformer vaults unless he is accompanied by one of the electricians or the Master Mechanic. Since these vaults enclose HIGH VOLTAGE, an employee not trained in servicing high voltage lines might touch the wrong things. Then new employees would be assessed by the Good Will Club. One may also imagine the Warden's embarrassment if the coroner were to ask him what John Doe was doing in that transformer vault in place of one of the electricians employed here.

Whenever there is work to be done on 480 to 6,900 volts, it is necessary that two electricians work together for the safety of each other. With HIGH VOLTAGE, a man only makes one mistake, his last one. Electricity is always ready to maim or kill if given the opportunity, and this applies not only to HIGH VOLTAGE but to LOWER VOLTAGE as well.

The transformer vaults are kept locked for security as well as safety. If an inmate with knowledge of electricity were to get into certain of the vaults, he might be able to endanger the security of the institution; certainly he could cause a great deal of damage. REMEMBER THAT ALL OF THE ELECTRICAL VAULTS ARE DANGEROUS, AND IN MORE WAYS THAN ONE.

On one occasion a 240 volt line shorted in a transformer vault. It blew the cast-iron cover off the vault and shot flames and molten copper ten to fifteen feet into the air. The electrical cable, about an inch and a half in diameter, burned up, and about eight feet of its length just disappeared into thin air. It is not difficult to visualize what would have happened to a man had he been in the vault at that instant.

The sub-station is very HOT. It must be remembered that 2,400 volts feed into the sub-station and that men working there are never more than a few feet from disaster. The area around the switches in the sub-station must be kept clear of debris and refuse. Not only are such materials a fire hazard, but they constitute a grave violation of good safety practice. Should anyone trip over such material and fall into the switches, he would pay dearly for his carelessness or that of someone else. Besides, in case of fire on any assignment the personnel working in the sub-station must be able to pull the switches immediately and cut off the voltage feeding into that assignment. What has been said here applies to all fuse boxes throughout the institution. The area around them must be kept clear so that in emergencies the switches can be shut off quickly.

If at any time a pole or wire breaks, it is to be left alone. Employees must KEEP EVERYONE AWAY FROM IT and call an electrician at once. He will handle it from there on. Remember, keep everyone away and let the electricians handle the repairs. Another thing to keep in mind is that when men are working on electric lines, one may endanger others' lives by distracting them with needless talk and foolish questions. An electrician's work is dangerous and requires his full concentration to avoid a possible fatal mistake.

There are a number of precautions which employees should observe in operating or supervising the operation of electrical equipment in their assignments:

1. Burned out fuses must not be replaced with fuses having greater amperage capacity than that marked on the burned out ones. Electric wiring of any given size has a definite amperage capacity and is protected from overloading by fuses of a size specified by the National Electrical Code. Putting in a larger fuse will cause the insulation on the wires to break down and let the exposed wires come into contact either with each other or some part of the structure, thus causing a fire or a dangerous electrical short.

2. Keep water away from all fuse boxes, switches, plugs, and electric motors. Water is a good conductor of electricity and so is the human body. Keep water away from anything that might give out an electrical shock.

3. When leaving an assignment turn off all lights except those used as night lights. Do not permit a machine to be left running while the operator is absent, even if he has only gone for a drink of water. Someone else might be seriously injured by such carelessness, for it is difficult to see the teeth of a whirling

saw or the spokes of a rapidly rotating flywheel.

4. Since telephones are vital to communications and, therefore, to the security of the institution, they should be handled with care. The telephone is a delicate instrument and should not be dropped or tossed around, for rough treatment will soon put it out of commission. However, the telephone repairman often finds that transmission difficulties are the fault of the person using the telephone. Failure to speak directly into the transmitter, or mouth piece, will result in faulty transmission of your voice. In the transmitter is a diaphragm which vibrates when sound waves hit it. This vibration of the diaphragm sends sound over the wire; so talk directly into the mouthpiece of the telephone, not over or under it.

From time to time one of the Electrical Foremen may request of the Chief Guard an officer to take charge of an inmate electrician. When an officer is assigned to such a detail, he should not try to direct the actual work if he has had no training or experience as an electrician. In a situation like that the officer's job would consist of guarding the inmate electrician and seeing to it that he confined himself to the job specified on the work ticket. The officer should, for safety's sake, keep other persons away from the immediate area where electrical work is being done.

GENERAL AND MECHANICAL STORES

The responsibilities of an institutional storekeeper are many. At Stateville the storekeeper is in charge of and must supervise the General and Mechanical Stores at Stateville, the stores of the Joliet Branch and the Farm. He controls all departments within the General Store, all stock and equipment, all keys and all records. Because of the nature of his duties, he is a bonded employee.

Among the principal obligations of the storekeeper are checking inventories, preparing quarterly requisitions, and verifying invoices. In order to know how much stock is on hand and how much was used in preceding quarters, he must keep a system of perpetual stock inventory. These inventory records are invaluable in preparing quarterly requisitions to meet institutional needs for commodities and office supplies, as its needs have to be placed several months in advance.

Before he sends a quarterly requisition to the General Office at Springfield, the storekeeper must be certain that he has ordered sufficient stock to supply institutional needs throughout the period covered by the requisition. When the supplies thus ordered arrive at the institution, he checks the invoices and sees that no merchandise is issued out or placed in stock or posted to the records until it has been checked against quantities, qualities and specifications listed on the purchase order. The only exception to this procedure is in the handling of pharmaceutical supplies and items ordered for emergencies. All drugs and pharmaceutical supplies are received by the prison pharmacist at the Front Gate where they are inspected prior to entry into the prison.

Every shipment must be checked by the storekeeper for overage or any shortage. Over-shipments are discouraged because the quantity of merchandise listed on the purchase order controls the amount which may be accepted. Invoices for shipments which exceed the amounts listed on the purchase order contract by more than 10% cannot be approved. Undershipments must not be confused with "partial" shipments that may have been requested for the convenience of the institution.

Invoices against purchase orders must agree in every detail with the purchase order. The name of the shipper, the address of the shipper, the purchase order number, the quantity, quality and price must coincide.

If any merchandise shipped to the institution is of inferior quality or fails to meet specifications, a letter of complaint is written to the vendor and a copy of the letter sent to the Purchasing Office at Springfield. Should the vendor fail to pick up and replace the inferior merchandise within a reasonable time, a "Status of Complaint" is issued and sent to the Purchasing Department at Springfield and a copy sent to the vendor (A "status of complaint" is in effect a request to the Springfield Office to take further action).

In the event that the vendor, or supplier, then refuses to adjust the complaint, he will in all probability be barred from further consideration in the business operation of the institution.

There are in addition to the office, six other assignments at the General Store—the Loading Platform, the Receiving Room, the Butcher Shop, the Milk Room, the Basement, and the Stockroom.

Most of the merchandise coming into the institution is received at the Platform and forwarded through the Receiving Room, where it is checked for contraband and against the purchase order. Meat, potatoes and other foodstuffs are checked at the outside platform to determine whether they have been stamped with the U.S.D.A. stamp of approval for shipment into the State of Illinois. If they have not been so stamped, they are rejected.

The Butcher Shop handles all meats for Stateville, the Joliet Branch, the Diagnostic Depot, and the Farm. Some of the meat is slaughtered at the Farm and sent into the Butcher Shop for processing and storage. Other meats such as luncheon meat and fish are purchased from packing companies. The Butcher Shop also renders lard and tallow from the carcasses slaughtered at the Farm, thus utilizing as much of the carcass as possible. Approximately 1,500,000 pounds of meat are processed annually. The value of meat consumed in the institution in one year is slightly more than $500,000, but the greater portion of it is produced on the Farm.

Each day the milk sent from the Farm into the milk room must be pasteurized, and some is separated to obtain the cream used in the institution. All of the Ice Cream used at Stateville, the Joliet Branch, the Diagnostic Depot and the Farm is also made in the Milk Room. The annual consumption of milk within the institution is approximately 175,000 gallons, valued at $70,-000. Nearly 23,000 gallons of ice cream, valued at $15,000, are manufactured annually.

Sanitary measures must be rigidly enforced in the Milk Room and throughout the Store. Although it is certainly necessary to handle all foods in a sanitary manner, few are more perishable or more easily contaminated than milk. Therefore it requires efficient processing in clean utensils and surroundings, and it must be kept refrigerated.

The Store's basement is used for storage of bulk items such as sugar, flour, vegetables, and cleaning compounds. During the canning season vegetables harvested on the Farm are stored in the basement until they can be processed by the Canning Plant.

The General Store at the Joliet Branch stores and distributes all meats and groceries alloted to the Joliet Branch and the Diagnostic Depot. These commodities are requisitioned from the Joliet Branch Store as needed and the requisitions are forwarded to the Stateville General Store for extension of unit prices and total costs. The Joliet Store also forwards a monthly report of items issued, received and on hand at the time. This report must agree with the ledgers at the Stateville Store.

Merchandise for the Mechanical Store comes through the Receiving Room of the General Store and Stateville and is held there until an invoice has been received and cleared for payment by the Store Office, which keeps a register by accounts of all Mechanical Store Purchases. At the end of each month the Mechanical Store's records must check with the figures in the register.

All commodities requisitioned from the General or Mechanical Stores must be listed on a "Request for Requisition" form. The items requested should be identified by stock number if known or, if not, by an adequate description. Since there are 9,500 items stocked in the Mechanical Store, it is not possible to fill orders unless the stock wanted is adequately described. Requests must be written legibly or typed and they must be signed by the head of the department ordering. Requests for items stocked in the Mechanical Store must be signed by a foreman or the Chief Engineer. Nothing is ever issued without a properly signed request. All requisitions are finally approved by the Warden.

The General Store Loading Platform is a sensitive assignment, from the standpoint of security. Nearly everything coming into or going out of the institution passes over the platform and it has been the scene of more than one escape attempt. The officer assigned there must be especially alert. No vehicle may be loaded or unloaded at the Platform without supervision by an officer. All barrels must be probed with a rod, all boxes and sacks must be checked to make sure that no inmate has concealed himself within them. The unloading of trucks that do not belong to the institution must be supervised not only by an officer but also by a Lieutenant. In addition the Loading Platform is under constant surveillance by tower guards at the Sally Port.

Packages received at the General Store are immediately searched for contraband, and if the shipment contains "hot" items such as razors, knives, files, and saws, they are locked in the General Store vault at once. The vault may be opened only by the storekeeper or his assistant.

Officers must watch everything that is being loaded or unloaded in order to prevent theft of any merchandise. In addition, they must conduct frequent shakedowns of their assignment to see that nothing is being concealed, that no liquor is being brewed, and that the supply of coffee is not being depleted by informal or "midnight" requisitions.

Each year the General Store handles and stocks commodities in approximately the following amounts:

Groceries	$ 666,000
Meats	513,000
Household and Stationery	192,000
Annual Total	$ 1,371,000

These are sizeable sums and they represent a great quantity of food and supplies. Unless these stocks are properly stored and carefully managed, they could be subject to considerable spoilage and loss. The duty of an officer assigned to the General Store is to prevent such an occurrence and at the same time to maintain security on a sensitive assignment.

LAUNDRIES

It should be emphasized that a laundry is a very necessary part of any large institution, not only for reasons of cleanliness and economy but also to provide work for inmates.

The institution laundries provide vocational opportunity for inmates interested in learning various phases of the laundry business. An inmate who learns his trade in the institutional laundries should be employable anywhere. The methods used are approved by the American Institute of Laundering. The machinery and equipment are up to date and similar to that used in commercial laundries.

In order for the laundries to operate efficiently and economically all equipment now in use has been selected for the utmost durability, thus giving the maximum service with the minimum number of operations.

In order to handle and keep pace with the huge volume of laundry being processed at the Joliet-Stateville Branches, approximately 40,000 pounds per week, close coöperation between assignments and the laundries is an absolute necessity. This can only be accomplished by adhering to the "laundry schedule" and avoiding all unnecessary delays. Officers in charge of assignments such as cellhouses, hospitals and officers' quarters, must be sure that all items to be washed are ready to be picked up and carefully counted and that their laundry slips are made out properly.

The laundries at the Joliet Branch and the Stateville Branch differ somewhat in that the Joliet Branch has a smaller inmate and officer population and does not have a "shower room" in conjunction with the laundry. The shower room is housed separately.

At the Stateville Branch the laundry and shower room are located in the same building. With inmates coming into the shower room throughout the day a great amount of traffic in and out of the building is created. Therefore, the officer in charge of the laundry cannot be expected to take charge of inmates who pass through the assignment for showers. Officers in charge of "bath lines" must assume full responsibility for their lines. Also time is an essential factor in the shower room. Officers are ordered to move their lines in and out without undue loss of time. Also, they are to see that each inmate is given his full allotted time under the shower. Some inmates may try to avoid taking a shower, and under no circumstances will this be permitted unless they have *written permission from the prison physician.*

On the other hand, some inmates may try to "hog" the showers, thus preventing another inmate from his allotted time. This applies especially to lines of 50 or more inmates.

Inmates on coal or work divisions entering the shower room are given clean work socks daily, but only if they turn in a dirty pair. Officers in charge of these lines should see to it that this order is carried out.

At the Joliet Branch, in addition to the regular institutional laundry, contractual work is done for the Sunny Hill Sanatorium and the Joliet Nursing Home. During 1957, some 51,000 pounds of laundry were processed for the Sanatorium at a cost of $2,450 and 12,000 pounds processed for the Nursing Home at a cost of $550.

Security measures enter into handling outside laundry. Each and every piece of laundry must be properly searched to insure that no contraband is smuggled into the institution or that nothing is smuggled out. Officers assigned to searching in an out going laundry must be especially alert and take nothing for granted. A few of the items found while searching incoming laundry that are regarded as "hot" contraband have been pocket knives, a match box filled with new razor blades, address and telephone numbers, money, and "eight pagers," or pornographic booklets.

Recently the laundry at the Stateville Branch installed a new mangle and six dryers of 125 pound capacity. Both the Joliet and Stateville Branch laundries would compare favorably with laundries outside and, in many instances, would excel them. All soaps and detergents used in these laundries are manufactured in the Stateville Soap Factory. It is the responsibility of the Officer in Charge of the laundry to make sure that these cleansing agents are mixed and used in the proper quantities. Carelessness in this respect could have several results: if too little were used, the clothing might not be well laundered; if too much were used, there would be a waste of cleaning compounds; and if far too much of them were used, the clothing might be damaged. It is, therefore, most important to use the recommended proportions of cleansing agents in the wash water.

Institutional personnel are admonished to observe laundry instructions and schedules. When sending in their laundry, they are warned to remember there is a security measure involved and instructions governing laundry must be carried out to the letter. A laundry list must be submitted. Each and every item must be listed and fully described. When listing a shirt, an employee is not to just list "shirt." If it is a uniform shirt, he is to list at as such. If it is a white or blue dress shirt, he is to say so, and the amounts must be listed, whether it be one, two, three, or more articles. When sending in "T" shirts, the employee is to list them as "T" shirts or as undershirts; in other words he is to give the correct description. When laundry is received and checked for washing but fails to correspond with the owner's list, the laundry will be returned, *unwashed*. All laundry must be properly marked so that it will not be lost. The same procedure is to be followed when sending in uniforms for dry cleaning.

CENTRAL FILING SYSTEM

The Record Office of the four branches of the Joliet-Stateville Prison is located at Stateville, and in this office the records of each inmate are kept.

When an inmate is received at the Diagnostic Depot, his commitment papers are forwarded to the Record Office. From these papers the Record Office file, which we refer to as "JACKET," is partially prepared. Also a similar jacket is prepared which consists of a set of the commitment papers and is sent to the Parole and Pardon Board at Springfield for their files.

This is just the beginning of an inmate's record jacket. When the examination history sheets are received from the Captain at the Diagnostic Depot, a mounted photo and reports from the Bureau of Identification, the Criminologist, the Prison Physician and the FBI record from Washington, the inmate's jacket is well on its way.

However, as time goes on and the inmate remains here, a great deal of additional information is recorded and filed in the inmate's jacket. This would include inquiries and answers from interested persons on the outside, reports of violations of the institutional rules, warrants by other authorities, promotion or demotion in grade, previous criminal record, Parole Board date or discharge date, plus many other bits of information.

At the present time there are nine civilian employees and seven inmates assigned to the Record Office. I refrain from detailing duties of the personnel in the Record Office because a considerable amount of the work consists of preparing reports, filing, correspondence, compiling statistics on inmates, and recording the daily count.

Reports of any act or movement concerning an inmate should be written and filed in the Record Office. And, officers must submit as many copies of written reports as there are inmates mentioned in the report. In an institution as large as this, no one can remember from day to day the many happenings or movements of individuals. Therefore, complete records are essential. And today this institution has a functional record system which is accurate, efficient and dependable.

One of the most important duties of the employees in the Record Office is the computing of an inmate's time so his Parole Board date or discharge date may be recorded on the face of his jacket. At a later date the proper officials and officers are notified either when an inmate is scheduled to appear before the Parole Board, or when his expiration of sentence date is coming up.

Whenever inmates are scheduled for transfers to Pontiac or Menard, a list of transfers is prepared in the Record Office. Copies of the list are distributed to approximately twenty-two separate departments so that they may adjust their records accordingly and forward to the Record Office any vital records which should accompany the inmate.

When the Warden receives a writ or order that an inmate is to be produced in one of the various courts, the order is sent to the Record Office and the proper officials are notified as to the court location, the date and time the inmate is to be produced.

The Senior Captains notify the Record Office of change of assignments of inmates. These transfers are recorded on the back of the jackets and in a permanent master ledger.

In case of serious illness or death of an inmate, the Record Office notifies the nearest relative by telegram. Also in the event of death (unless it is a coroner's case) a medical certificate of death is filled out, signed by the Record Clerk, and forwarded to the funeral director. The information consists of the age, marital status, place and date of birth of the deceased. The cause of death is recorded on the certificate by the prison physician.

During 1956 there were over four thousand petitions from or for inmates received in the Record Office for mailing to various attorneys, courts and judges. The services of a notary public are available in the Record Office to any inmate who desires legal papers notarized.

Due to the fact that there are inmates assigned to the Record Office, reports which the Warden considers confidential are filed in a lock vault. All the employees have access to this file, but never an inmate.

Each month a statistical report is prepared in the Record Office which lists the number of men received from court; transfers from other institutions; violators returned; men released on writ, parole or discharge; the population classified by crime; number of inmates from each county, age and when received; the state or foreign country each inmate was born in; religion; deaths; escapes and escapees returned; military status; marital status and previous convictions of a felony. This report is furnished to the State Statistician at Springfield as well as to the Director of the Department of Public Safety, Superintendent of Prisons, Parole and Pardon Board and the Chicago Crime Commission.

The Parole Board meets at Joliet-Stateville Divisions ten times each year for the purpose of considering those inmates' cases who are eligible for release on parole. The parole docket is prepared in the Record Office, where approximately forty copies are made and distributed to various persons interested in the docket.

Each evening, before closing time, all jackets are returned to the fire-proof vault and accounted for. If an inmate's jacket is lost, it would be almost impossible to replace because of the fact that his original commitment papers are kept in the jacket which is the only authority the Warden has to hold a prisoner. When an inmate is released certain offices forward their records to the Record Office where they are placed in the inmate's jacket. Then they are taken to the Administration Building vault or the vault in the basement of the new officers' quarters, for filing.

Another important duty of the employees in the Record Office is to be able to identify any present or former inmate, whether he served here under an alias or correct name. In fact, records are maintained on every inmate who has been confined at the Joliet institution since 1858, the year in which the Joliet Prison was opened for the confinement of prisoners.

Since the first prisoner was received at the Joliet Prison, register numbers have been issued to inmates as follows:

SERIAL NUMBER From one (1) to	DATE STARTED
A - 10,000	1 - A - 5-25-1858
B - 10,000	1 - B - 6-22-1876
C - 10,000	1 - C - 12-14-1899
D - 10,000	1 - D - 11-28-1906
E - 10,000	1 - E - 7-10-1925
F - 2,000	1 - F - 8- 2-1934
52,000	
10,001	11-1 1935
20,000	3- 5-1943
30,000	7-10-1950
41,606	2-20-1958
41,606	High Number as of February 20, 1958
10,001	High Number as of November 1, 1935
31,605	Total Number Received Since November 1, 1935
52,000	Total Number Received Prior to November 1, 1935
83,605	Total Number Received Since 1858

During the early history of the prison system the Record Clerk was literally the keeper of all prison records—administrative or otherwise, including the Warden's records, official orders, Commissioners' journal of proceedings and the prisoner's commitment papers. The duties of the Record Clerk have, with the growth of the prison system, been modified.

In the Record Office is one of the old time rule books which was adopted by the now defunct Board of Commissioners of the Illinois State Penitentiary at Joliet and printed in 1899. It is one of the oldest rule books now in the Record Office. However, there are older records dating from 1840 up to the present time which pertain to the Commissioners' reports regarding the management, discipline, etc., of the Illinois State Penitentiaries. It is noted in this old rule book that former authorities were very strict with the employees. In fact, if an officer failed to give thirty days' notice of his intention to resign, all pay due would be forfeited. Pay schedules averaged approximately $70 per month at that time. The officers worked twelve hours per day, seven days per week, with the exception that they could alternate and be dismissed one-half day per week so that they might attend church on Sunday.

An inmate's jacket includes among other vital documents the Commitment papers, the indictment, penitentiary mittimus statement of facts signed by the trial judge and state's attorney and other forms from the Record Office. The court papers are very carefully examined to make sure they are complete, and that the sentence and crime correspond throughout the set of papers.

When an inmate leaves the Institution on writ or court order, the transporting officer is given the writ, a certified copy of the penitentiary mittimus, a photograph of the inmate and a sheriff's receipt to be signed by a jailer or sheriff in the event the inmate is remanded to the custody of the sheriff. The same person will also acknowledge receipt of the certified copy of the mittimus.

In transporting a prisoner some distance, if it is necessary that he be kept in jail over night, a copy of the inmate's mittimus should be left with the sheriff, if requested. However, in all cases a receipt is obtained for the prisoner. As long as the inmate is in custody, the transporting officer should always let the jailer know where he can be contacted.

Chapter 10

RULES FOR PRISON EMPLOYEES

The Illinois Department of Public Safety endeavors to select for employment persons who are citizens of Illinois with good reputations in their communities. All applicants are fingerprinted, thoroughly investigated, and required to pass a physical examination before appointments are approved. All employees are required to be re-examined annually.

Discipline is of prime importance in a prison and must be maintained without fear or favor, both among the inmates and regularly assigned employees. Every employee, regardless of his assignment, is responsible for the security and discipline of the institution.

The most unpredictable things happen in and around prisons when they are least expected. In most cases, it is because some employee working an assignment becomes careless in the performance of his or her duties. No employee or official should be lulled into a sense of false security by thinking: "IT CAN NEVER HAPPEN HERE!" Only constant vigilance on the part of every employee of the institution will guarantee the welfare of other employees, the safeguarding of the inmates, and an efficiently operated prison.

A committee, consisting of the warden, assistant warden, and chief guard of each institution, makes suggestions, recommendations, and constructive criticisms to employees regarding the handling of their assignments. Employees will be expected to follow these suggestions, or disciplinary action will result.

Any person employed in the penal institutions must live up to the rules of the institution. Trading, trafficking, aiding or abetting an inmate is prohibited by law and anyone violating this law

437

will be prosecuted by the Department of Public Safety.

Only through rigid, but fair, enforcement of these rules can the desired degree of discipline be attained. It is the duty of each employee to enforce the rules governing inmates and to obey each of the rules laid down for employees. Success in controlling inmates depends to a great extent on the employee's own deportment. A close observation of the manner in which successful employees perform their duties will greatly benefit the inexperienced officer. Lieutenants should encourage new officers whenever they can in order to help them get started on the right foot. It is also a good policy to give all employees a word of encouragement.

It is important, of course, that an employee or inmate who violates rules be reported. Information and/or rumors of an unusual nature should be reported to a superior. However, it must be remembered that the best employee is not always the one who writes the greatest number of reports. Few reports are necessary under proper supervision and guidance. Employees must be honest in all their activities. TRUTHFULNESS IN MAKING REPORTS AND ANSWERING QUESTIONS IS MANDATORY.

The following general rules, together with the special rules and bulletins published from time to time by the warden, shall govern the employees of this institution. Strict adherence to these rules is required at all times and any violation shall be cause for disciplinary action against the offender. Employees are to accept disciplinary action and not be thin-skinned about it. When such action is taken it is for a specific reason and no one is to hold grudges as a result of being disciplined. All employees must consult the bulletin board daily for any general or special orders issued during the day. Each new order will be read at roll call, then posted in a ledger containing copies of all orders issued. This ledger is kept in the vicinity of the guard hall. No one is authorized to place, change, or annul an order on the bulletin board without the signature of the warden.

1. Any person employed by the Department of Public Safety, whose assignment is in the institution, will not be permitted to associate with friends or relatives of any inmate presently con-

fined in the institution, nor with parolees, dischargees, or any of their friends or relatives.

Persons holding positions in the Illinois state penal system must conduct themselves in such a manner as not to bring discredit upon themselves or the authority under which they hold such position. Therefore, it will be regarded as cause for disciplinary action or dismissal if any employee (a) frequents or loiters about places of ill repute, (b) gambles or loiters around gambling houses, or (c) disregards his personal obligations so as to acquire an unsavory reputation. Intemperance will not be tolerated in an employee and it is strictly prohibited to keep or use intoxicating liquors in or about the institution.

2. A military atmosphere must prevail at all times and employees must show due respect to superior officers. While on duty, each employee will salute his superior officers in a military manner. Such salutes shall be properly returned by the superior. Courtesy is demanded at all times and fellow employees should be treated with mutual respect and kindness. The discussion of controversial subjects shall be avoided at all times. The conduct of an employee of the institution should be that of a gentleman at all times and under all conditions, whether or not the situation is specifically covered by these rules.

3. Smoking while on duty is prohibited, except in properly designated areas. No employee will attempt to carry on a conversation or meet a fellow-worker or visitor with a cigarette, cigar or pipe in his mouth; nor will he fail to remove his cap when introduced to ladies, or upon entering the office of a superior.

4. All employees, shall, while within the prison, refrain from whistling, scuffling, immoderate laughter, boisterous conversation, exciting discussions, and all other acts which might tend to disturb the harmony and good order of the institution.

5. All innocent amusements on the part of employees will be encouraged to a reasonable extent; however, gambling in any form is strictly prohibited.

6. Every employee must report for duty at the specified hour,

unless properly excused by the warden or his authorized representative; each shall be available for duty and consider himself subject to call 24 hours each day. In case of an emergency, all employees — regardless of classification — shall cheerfully perform any duty assigned to them by a superior officer. Regular assignments to duty will be made by the captain of the guards and requests for transfer to another assignment will be ignored, unless accompanied by valid reasons. Superior officers will be the sole judge of each man's ability, and due recognition will be given those with special qualifications. Wherever possible, all promotions and advancements will be made from the ranks.

7. Each employee will be issued an identification card and metal identification tag, and such identification must be carried at all times. Regulation uniforms, required by the Department of Public Safety, will be issued as soon as possible, and ONLY such regulation uniforms shall be worn by employees while on duty. Uniforms will not be worn away from the institution, except when on duty. Neatness and cleanliness in dress and personal habits are required at all times. Employees not in proper uniform, or dressed in a slovenly manner, shall be reported by their superior officers.

8. Upon being given an assignment, it shall be the duty of each employee to familiarize himself with the special rules governing that assignment or post. He will ascertain immediately the location, care and use of any equipment, firearms, ammunition, keys, tools, light switches or other items pertinent to his post. He shall make special preparations necessary to fulfill the requirements of the assignment.

a. Employees who wear side arms shall not remove them while on duty. Rifles always are to be within reach.

b. Horsemen are to be informed by the officer in charge of the farm and outside detail whenever inmates are assigned in their areas.

9. Supplies for all assignments will be procured by requisitions. It will be the duty of the employee in charge to make certain that an ample supply of all items is on hand and that requi-

sitions are properly submitted at the direction of the business manager or chief clerk of the institution. But care should be taken to avoid an over-abundance of supplies at any time—especially items of a perishable nature, or those which would become stale or deteriorate in value. Every assignment, other than stock centers, will order supplies monthly by requisition. Such requisitions shall be submitted to the general store-keeper not later than the last day of each month. At no time shall an over-supply of any items be on hand or on order.

10. A perpetual inventory of all tools must be kept on each assignment. Tool reports shall be submitted every two weeks to the assistant warden. Assignments shall be so divided that one half of them will make their reports the first and third week and the other half the second and fourth week, at the time specified by the warden. However, a list of new and/or condemned tools is to be submitted each week, even though it may not be the scheduled week for the routine tool report.

a. In addition to an actual physical check each morning, noon and night, the employee in charge of each assignment must be able to account for every tool at any time throughout the working day. This rule will apply to every assignment and under no circumstances will any employee deviate from this procedure.

b. When a tool is taken from one assignment to another, in order that a special job may be done, a receipt must be given to the officer by the master mechanic or foreman, and the officer on the assignment where the tool is to be used must always give the master mechanic or foreman receipt for same. When the tool is returned to the original assignment, the same procedure must be used.

c. Purchases made for a specific assignment by the master mechanic must be brought to the mechanical store stockroom and issued only when a signed requisition is submitted from that assignment.

d. Lists of tools issued from the mechanical store stockroom to a specific assignment are to be sent daily to the assistant warden's office.

11. Every piece of furniture or item of equipment is designated for a particular assignment and becomes a part of that assignment's inventory. It is so registered in the general office. Articles may not be transferred from one assignment to another without the permission of the business manager or chief clerk.

12. Except in an emergency, all property worn out or broken is to be taken to the condemning office on a day set by the warden. New property will not be issued for replacement until the old property has been condemned and turned in. Copies of all condemning orders must be sent weekly to the assistant warden's office.

13. Knives, saws, welding torches, jacks, bar-spreaders, wrenches or any tool or instrument which could be used as an escape weapon, must be under the constant supervision of an employee when in use; all such items shall be locked in the place provided, when not in use.

14. At no time shall sedatives, narcotics or poisons be permitted to fall into the hands of inmates; nor shall such items be permitted on assignments where food is being handled or stored, nor allowed in the institution proper unless authorized by pharmacist, prison physician or warden, and all gatemen are to make certain such authorization has been given. All poisons will be kept in vaults provided for that purpose; all drugs and medicines will be administered under the direct supervision of an employee. Each officer on all shifts must familiarize himself with instructions concerning drugs to be administered as prescribed by prison physicians.

A monthly inventory is to be sent to the pharmacist before the 5th of each month by the department officers, listing names of all poisonous chemicals, liquids or compounds on hand, and their locations.

Employees living in the institution are to report to the chief guard when their physician has prescribed medication for their own use which contains drugs, sedatives, narcotics, poisons, etc. Such medicines must be locked securely so they do not fall in the hands of an inmate, when they are not on the person of the employee.

15. All inflammables shall be kept outside the walls, securely locked in the proper storage places. All such items shall be requisitioned for use inside the walls only when and where needed and must be under the direct supervision of an employee at all times. Inmates will be permitted to transfer such items ONLY when accompanied by an employee.

16. All ladders more than twelve (12) feet in length are to be kept outside the walls. When necessary for ladders to be used within the walls, they shall be under the direct supervision of a lieutenant or other superior officer. Such items shall be returned immediately to the proper storage places after use. All towermen are to be notified before ladders are brought into the yard.

17. All employees must familiarize themselves with the use of call tickets, pass tickets, and other printed forms in general use; know the general system used for searches and shakedowns; the proper method of looking for contraband; the meaning of the power house whistles, emergency whistles, sirens, etc. It is especially important that each employee know the location of various assignments, buildings, towers, etc.

18. Too much cannot be said about the searching for contraband on the person of inmates, in the shops and the various assignments, bed-posts, mattresses and cells in general. No inmate is going to leave contraband where it can be seen. It will be carried on his person, usually between his legs, in his shoes, in the hem of his trousers, or around his waist. In making searches, it is important that all these places be covered. It must be remembered also that we have inmates who are highly skilled mechanics and capable of making any sort of escape weapon, including a gun. This can be accomplished by working just a little each day, perhaps only ten minutes at a time. Bars can be sawed with emery dust and twine string, and, of course, with better equipment.

19. When searching a cell go through all books, magazines, beds, bedclothing, commode, ventilators, and any place where it would be possible to conceal anything, but DO NOT DESTROY ANYTHING in making the search. It is to be remembered that per-

mitted articles are the inmates' private property and may be of great value to them. Searches should be systematic.

20. When searching a person, ask him to take everything out of his pockets. Always search from the back, going over the arms, down the front and back as far as the shoes, to make certain there is no article concealed on his body in such places as the armpits, between the legs, at the small of the back, or around the belt.

21. There are specific items of clothing and personal property which inmates are permitted to have. Anything found on an inmate's person or in his cell which is not considered a permitted item will be considered as contraband and should be confiscated immediately. These contraband items include weapons and tools of any description; outside clothing; or any state property not issued or unnumbered. If money is found in the possession of inmates or on assignments, it is to be confiscated and placed in the Inmates' Amusement Fund. Reports covering any confiscation shall be made to the disciplinarian, who will take the proper action. Inmates reported for having contraband of a serious nature may be reduced in grade and/or lose statutory time, as recommended by the Merit Staff.

22. Call tickets for inmates to report to the hospital, visiting room, disciplinarians, office, etc., will be delivered directly to the employee in charge of the inmates assignment. When the inmate leaves his assignment, the time of his departure will be noted on the ticket. Upon arriving at his destination, the calling official will note the time of arrival and, when he leaves, the time of departure. Upon the inmate's return to his assignment, the employee will again note the time of arrival. Any delay in the inmate's movement between the two places shall be reported to the disciplinarian. All such call or pass tickets will be sent to the chief guard's office at the close of each day, where the proper inspection will be made.

23. No employee shall receive any personal service while on duty. Such personal service will include barber work (hair cuts, shaves, etc.), shoe shines, tailor work or that of like nature.

These services are a privilege, and under no circumstances will this privilege be abused. Inmates shall not be paid or compensated in any way for service rendered.

24. Under no circumstance will any employee leave his place of assignment, until he has been properly relieved. The relieving officer is to count the inmates and equipment before accepting an assignment.

25. In case of a general alarm, day or night, every employee living in the institution who is not on duty must report immediately to the guard hall for orders. Employees living away from the institution are subject to call. Those on duty shall remain at their posts until properly relieved. The siren or whistle will be sounded any time there is an emergency, such as an escape, fire or fire drill. When such signal is sounded, it shall be the duty of every employee in charge of inmates, regardless of the location of his assignment, to return all inmates to their respective cellhouses. Permission to hold inmates on an assignment during an emergency can be granted by the chief guard or his authorized representative. It is to be remembered, in counts of this sort, that tools and the security of the institution shall be taken into consideration and the proper checks made.

26. Employees in charge of assignments must be able to identify personally each inmate assigned to his division. He will carefully scrutinize and, if possible, ascertain the background, personality traits and pertinent data concerning the newly assigned inmate. Personal knowledge of inmates is very important. Employees in charge of inmates must be prepared, when called upon, to write a complete history covering all phases of the inmate's work record, his attitude, his personality, his adaptability, and his ability to coöperate and work with other people.

27. It must be constantly kept in mind that the safekeeping of the inmates is paramount to all other considerations, and that escapes shall be prevented at all hazards. Obedience to the rules and regulations of the prison on the part of the inmates will be enforced, even at the sacrifice of life. Discipline is the first and highest consideration in a prison and the official who maintains

such discipline with the least difficulty will receive the highest commendation from the warden. It is to be remembered that no one can escape nor can a serious incident occur, if each employee does his or her duty. Therefore, if an inmate does escape, it can be charged to the negligence of someone.

28. In case of a serious or major disturbance, such as an escape, a riot, murder, suicide (or an attempt at such), it shall be the duty of any employee to notify immediately his superior officer. Employees shall proceed to prevent any unusual happening and, in case of a serious storm, flood, fire, etc., good judgment is to be used always. To prevent loss of life or property, employees in charge of inmates should move them to their respective cell houses, whenever possible.

29. Employees must be vigilant at all times in guarding against surprise or an attempt to escape on the part of an inmate. Under no circumstance shall any box, barrel, package, container of any kind, truck, wagon be passed out of the enclosure, unless approved in person by the employee who supervised the packing. Barrels of garbage and other material of any description will be thoroughly probed by a rod provided for that purpose, to make certain that no inmate or contraband is concealed therein.

30. Under no circumstance shall any person, inmate, or visitor be passed into any enclosure without first being thoroughly searched by the employee in charge of the gate. Nor will any outside vehicle be passed into the institution, unless properly approved by the warden and then only after it has been thoroughly searched.

31. The warden is the only official of the institution who has the authority to pass anyone in or out of the institution proper. The warden may, however, delegate such authority to the assistant warden or the senior captains, when the occasion warrants. All passes out of the institution shall be approved in person by the official having such authority. Under no circumstances shall anyone be passed out of the institution by telephone approval or a written pass. When inmates or visitors, accompanied by an employee, are to be passed out of the institution, the official in

charge of the gate must assure himself that the accompanying employee is not being forced to release an inmate who may be attempting to escape. Such gateman must, if the group entered the institution prior to his reporting for duty, require the group to halt at least thirty (30)) feet before reaching the gate. The accompanying employee will advance to the gateman and identify the group. The gateman, after receiving proper identification, will then pass the group. No gateman shall pass through his gate anyone wearing the uniform of an employee, unless such person is positively known to be an employee and not an inmate.

a. Inmates being released from the institution on discharge, parole, or on writ must be approved by the warden or his assistant through No. 1 gate after release authority in the record office has been signed by the approving official. The official must then notify the officer in charge of the Entrance Gate the names and numbers of the men being released, as well as identifying himself to the officer.

32. In the event that any employee suspects a fellow-worker, regardless of his rank, of dealing in or transporting contraband articles, or becomes suspicious of the actions of such fellow-worker, it shall be his duty to report such information and cause a search to be made of the suspected employee. Any employee of the institution may be searched at any time for security reasons. A complete report of such information or search shall be made to the warden.

33. While on duty, generally all employees will be on their feet. No employee shall be asleep, dozing, or reclining in a lazy position, while on duty; neither shall he be engaged in reading or writing other than necessary reports. Constant vigilance is required at all times, and nothing should be permitted to divert the attention of any employee. Radios and television will be permitted on assignments only by permission of the warden.

34. It shall be the duty of any employee to note the license number and/or letters of any airplane, car, or truck which may pass his assignment, if suspicious, and report it to his superior.

35. Upon interception or receipt of any information pertinent

to the discipline or safety of the institution, the employee receiving such information shall not attempt to make an independent investigation, but shall make a complete report to his superior officer. However, in emergencies where a delay may bring serious consequences, any employee is authorized to proceed immediately to quell any disturbance or forestall any attempted disturbance. At the earliest opportunity a full report of the incident will be made, in writing, to his superior officer.

36. Cleanliness and neatness are expected and demanded in every department of the institution at all times. Each employee shall make certain that such conditions prevail throughout his assignment; he shall arrange for the proper disposal of all useless scrap, shavings, chips, or other combustible waste or materials at the end of each working day. Needless waste, however, shall be avoided and any salvageable materials must be returned to the proper department. It should be uppermost in the mind of every employee that conservation of supplies is a necessity. This institution is supported by the taxpayers, who are entitled to the full return on all monies expended. It is the duty of every employee to aid the administration in obtaining the maximum of efficiency at the least expense.

37. Employees always shall guard against the hazard of fire. Before leaving his department or shop at the noon hour or close of day, the employee in charge shall make a personal inspection of his assignment to make certain that all inflammable refuse has been removed from the building. All assignments are provided with fire extinguishers and equipment necessary to combat small blazes. It will be the duty of all employees to make daily inspections of the fire-fighting equipment on their particular assignments and to fully understand the use of such equipment.

38. All electric lights and switches, water faucets, etc., shall be turned off when not in use. Electricity, power and water are expensive, and it is the duty of each employee to guard against waste. Leaks, breaks, etc., must be reported to the master mechanic at once.

39. Each employee will return to his assignment at the earliest

possible moment, after having been relieved for meals or for an emergency. Employees on duty are permitted one-half hour for a meal. Under no circumstances will any employee be permitted to leave the institution, nor shall he loaf or congregate with fellow-employees or inmates during working hours.

40. Employees assigned to the dining room or the kitchen are to familiarize themselves with all rules governing those assignments, including the preparation and serving of foods.

41. Employees assigned to duty in the cellhouses and recreation yards will stay at their posts, constantly on the alert. Employees shall walk the cellhouse galleries and the recreation yards continually, and must not congregate nor converse with inmates other than in the line of duty.

42. Pictures may be taken of the institution outside the front gate only, provided no inmates are in view.

43. Under no circumstance shall loitering by employees or outsiders be permitted in or around any assignment at any time.

44. No employee shall have any pecuniary interest—directly or indirectly—in any business wherein the prison is a party. Neither shall any employee receive, directly or indirectly, any fee, commission, or gift from any person or corporation tendering, or furnishing supplies to, or doing business with the institution. Nor shall any employee accept any fees or any form of payment from anyone having business with or at the prison or with any of the inmates therein.

45. At no time will the institution or the Department of Public Safety be held responsible for any personal property loss.

46. Employees who expect to receive mail at the institution should make every effort to advise friends and relatives of the correct mail address. Employees shall not bring into the institution, nor permit to be sent to them in care of the institution, anything which might be used as a weapon, such as a gun, razor, saw, knife, etc. Whenever an employee is absent from the institution on vacation or sick leave, he shall notify the mail office accordingly and instruct that office to either hold his mail or forward it.

All hospital mail should be sent to the pharmacist for disposition. This does not include mail addressed personally to a hospital employee.

47. All employees shall list their addresses, telephone and automobile license numbers with the warden or assistant. In the event a change in any of the foregoing occurs, prompt notification is required.

48. Parking facilities are furnished for automobiles. In some cases garages are furnished. The keys to all cars shall be removed and the doors to cars and garages shall be kept locked at all times.

49. Employees living within the walls of the prison, and who remain out later than twelve (12:00) o'clock midnight, must register and record the time of arrival at the front gate before admission will be granted. Under no circumstance will an employee under the influence of alcoholic liquor be admitted to the institution.

50. To obtain a leave of absence for thirty (30) days or longer, application must be made in writing to the warden. Leaves of absence will be granted only in cases of illness, injury, or military duty. The institution has a right to demand, and does demand, the same continuity of service as a private corporation. The warden should be notified promptly by telephone or telegraph when an employee is detained or unable to report for duty. In case of illness, it is a good policy for an employee to obtain a statement from his attending physician, stating the nature of the illness. Employees unable to report for duty because of illness must notify the institution or disciplinary action will folllow. Continual absence from duty may cause suspension or dismissal; absence from duty without proper authorization, is cause for immediate discharge.

51. Each employee must take one day's rest in seven, unless the warden or his authorized representative finds it necessary to request such employee to remain on duty because of unusual conditions. Accumulation of days off will not be permitted, unless circumstances require continuous duty. Substituting one employee

for another defeats the purpose of the one day's rest provision and will not be permitted, unless institutional conditions require such a modification.

52. No employee will be considered eligible for compensation when he becomes injured or sick while on duty in the institution, unless a complete examination has been made by the prison physician and a proper report made to the warden covering all details of the accident, injury, or illness.

53. Any female employee going beyond the guard hall must be accompanied by a male employee.

54. No employee or inmate is permitted to enter any vault, file or desk which contains records of any description, unless so authorized and in the performance of his or her duties.

55. Cooperation between employees is important. It is often necessary to seek information from a fellow-worker; such information should be given without hesitation. Lack of cooperation on the part of any employee should be promptly reported and will be cause for disciplinary action. All information given to superior officers will be kept confidential.

56. It shall be the duty of all employees and inmates not working or occupied to stand when a supervising officer or visitor enters an assignment.

57. Under no circumstance will any institution business or information concerning inmates or occurrences which take place within the institution be discussed in public. Reports to the press and to other public agencies will be made by the warden. However, there is nothing about the general operation of prisons at Joliet which the public should not know and, when inquiries are made, it is important that the proper information is given. If you are unable to answer such inquiries, you should consult someone for the correct information.

58. Inmates who are assigned to positions of trust, both inside and outside the wall, are known as "trusties." When it is necessary for any one of them to remain out of their cells or dormitory quarters after the evening count, proper written approval must be given. A copy of this approval should be filed (a) in the in-

mate's jacket in the senior captain's office and (b) in the captain's office where the supervising officers on the second and third shifts will have access to it.

59. Officers and employees are prohibited from discussing within the limits of the institution the manner in which any employee performs his duty, and from making remarks which might tend to reflect upon the character or management of such employee. It is further prohibited to discuss, in the presence of inmates, matters relating to the discipline or management of this or similar institutions. Violations of this and other rules should be reported immediately to a superior officer and will be cause for disciplinary action. Constructive suggestions, however, always will be appreciated.

60. Inmates assigned to the handling of food must be approved by the hospital and have a health certificate from the prison physician, before being placed in such an assignment.

61. Under no circumstance will an inmate be granted special privileges or shown partiality. The granting of favors to inmates eventually will lead to the dismissal of the employee. A prisoner receiving such favors usually reports the employee for so doing.

62. Employees in charge of inmates marching in line will see that all lines are kept in a military, orderly fashion, with no straggling. Generally speaking, inmates are not to converse while the lines are marching, in the chapel, or during the movies. However, good judgment is to be used at all times.

63. Employees taking the count must see that each inmate is standing with both hands on the cell door. Do not count a dummy! All doors must be in the proper place, securely closed and locked. It should be remembered that the chief administrative principle in the operation of a prison is an accurate count at all times— day and night.

64. Cellhouses are known as "banks," and every man removed from a cellhouse is charged to the employee removing him. Employee is directly responsible for all inmates on his assignment and must know their whereabouts at all times. Counts should be made at frequent intervals and, should a prisoner be missing

from his assignment, an immediate report must be made to the superior officer. Upon returning inmates to the cellhouse, the cellhouse keeper is to give credit to the employee returning them and maintain a perpetual record as to the whereabouts of every inmate.

65. Employees in charge of inmates must be constantly alert to guard against acts of perversion. Distasteful as the subject may be, the fact remains that there are known perverts among the inmates who will not stop at anything in accomplishing their purposes. Any acts of perversion must be reported in writing immediately to the disciplinarian.

66. In the event there is trouble on any assignment, the employee in charge should immediately notify his superior officer. If circumstances prevent calling for help, either over the radio or telephone, the employee should, if at all possible, knock the telephone receiver off the hook, thus getting the attention of the operator, who, in turn, must notify the proper officials. It is important that you make certain your telephone is properly placed in the cradle and/or the hook so there will be no difficulty in reaching you when necessary. If an emergency arises and the line to the assignment you wish to converse with is busy, advise the operator it is an emergency call and it will be his or her duty to cut in on the line.

67. Inmate runners are assigned to each assignment by the disciplinarian to run errands and deliver materials and supplies to other assignments. These inmates are provided with a paddle on which is stenciled or painted the inmate's assignment and his number. All officers are permitted to stop an inmate runner who may enter his assignment, to ascertain the reason for his being there. Whenever an inmate is in an assignment other than his own, a lieutenant should be called, to make proper investigation and disposition of the matter.

68. Inmates are confined to this institution for various periods of time and under various sentences, and it is not unusual for an inmate to ask an employee for information regarding his case. All such inquiries should be referred to the record clerk or the

warden for proper disposition. It is the duty of all employees to care for and confine the prisoner in accordance with the terms of his sentence, as imposed by the courts. It will avail nothing to commiserate with him or to discuss his sentence. All inmates must be shown due consideration by the proper officials on any request that merits attention.

69. A full report of all unusual incidents is to be made, in writing, to the warden. Such reports must cover all phases of the incident, including all injuries sustained by employees or inmates, fires, escapes, etc.

70. All reports should be kept in the files provided for that purpose and all necessary notations made therein. Verbal reports should be avoided whenever possible, but it is of vital importance that all events taking place during an employee's tour of duty should be properly and promptly reported to his superiors. Where there are records to be kept, it is necessary that all notations be properly noted and accounted for.

71. It shall be the duty of every employee to report an inmate whom he sees violating a rule, even though such inmate may be in another division. It is to be remembered that violations of the rules will cause trouble in a penal institution, and every employee should help his fellow-workers maintain strict and fair discipline at all times. Do not consider an assisting fellow-worker officious; he is only trying to help you.

72. When reporting inmates for violations of the rules, the report should be made on the regulation form. In making a report, TRUTHFULNESS IS MANDATORY. First, be sure that the inmate you are reporting is the one who violated; second, give facts in detail so that the disciplinarian may fully understand the circumstances; third, sign your full name to the report. However, if an inmate's violation is serious, it will be your duty to send for a lieutenant immediately.

73. No employee shall ask for the removal of an apparently unmanageable inmate. The proper action is to report such inmate to the disciplinarian, giving an accurate account of the inmate's action. No employee shall ask for a special inmate to be as-

signed to his department, shop or division. When in need of additional inmates, the employee in charge of the assignment should notify the assigning officer. Whenever possible, it is suggested that the assignment of inmates be discussed thoroughly with the assigning officer, outlining the need for specially trained inmates. The placement officer will be the judge of an inmate's ability to perform certain duties; he will assign inmates with special qualifications to divisions where their abilities can be utilized best. However, it is to be remembered that, if we are to be successful, we must train inmates, whenever possible, not only for our own use but also with a view toward their rehabilitation.

74. Under no circumstance shall any employee trade or traffic or become familiar with inmates; nor shall he convey any message—written or verbal—from one inmate to another or to any person outside the institution. In their relationship with inmates, employees must take nothing and give nothing.

75. Employees must speak to inmates in a firm, mild tone, using no offensive, profane, vulgar or rough language. At the same time, the employee shall be positive in a dignified manner, which almost invariably commands instant obedience. After giving an order, the employee should not argue with the inmate, but should quietly and mildly explain his order and be certain that it is understood. If the inmate does not then obey, he should be reported to the disciplinarian. CORPORAL PUNISHMENT IS PROHIBITED AT ANY TIME. No employee shall strike an inmate except under extraordinary circumstances, such as stopping an attempted escape, the assaulting of another inmate or an assault upon an employee, and then, only if he is unable to subdue the inmate without resorting to the use of force.

76. Employees and inmates shall not be permitted to use profane or loud language under any circumstances.

77. Inmates shall not be permitted to handle keys of importance, such as those to doors, gates, warehouses, tool rooms, etc. In some instances, when inmates are given the responsibility and charged with the maintenance of a locker or desk which is to be kept locked, the keys will be checked to such inmate every morn-

ing and returned to the employee in charge at the end of the day, or whenever such inmate leaves the assignment.

78. No employee shall be permitted to send or take, either on foot or by private or institution conveyance, any inmate from the grounds of the prison except with the proper authority.

79. If any known inmate is observed away from the prison, it shall be the duty of every employee, whether on or off duty, to return such inmate to the prison. If, for any reason, it is impossible for the individual employee, alone, to return such prisoner, he shall call for help either from bystanders or by telephone. A complete report of the incident shall be made at the earliest possible time.

80. Inmates are issued a regulation prison uniform and they shall wear same at all times when outside their cells. Under no circumstance will civilian or outside clothing be permitted, except those items sold by permission in the inmates' commissary.

81. When forming opinions with respect to the industry of a prisoner, employees must bear in mind that one prisoner may be able to do more work in a given period of time than another. If, however, an inmate shows evidence of a desire to do all the work of which he is capable and does it correctly, though slowly, he should be credited accordingly. In other words, an amount of work which may be sufficient for one man might be insufficient for another. Each inmate is required to do an ordinary day's work, and it shall be the duty of each employee to see that no one shirks his work and that all are treated alike in every respect. An order which cannot be executed by the inmate should never be given; however, when an order has been given, it is the duty of each employee to see that such order is carried out to the best of the inmate's ability.

82. Inmates shall not be permitted to speak in a disrespectful manner about, or to, any employee. All inmates must address each employee by his proper title at all times. Employees must never permit inmates to become familiar or to discuss the administration of the institution.

83. Inmates will not be permitted to accept or place any calls

over an outside telephone. On specific assignments, it will be permissible for inmates to use the institution telephones in the performance of their duties.

84. If an inmate desires to converse with the warden or assistant warden in a shop, he may do so provided such officials are not accompanied by visitors. An inmate is always permitted to communicate with the warden in writing. Such messages shall be written and dropped in the mail box provided for that purpose in each cellhouse.

85. If, at any time, an inmate reports himself ill or unable to turn out for work, the employee in charge of such inmate shall immediately report this information to his superior officer and give the inmate permission to attend sick call. If necessary, the inmate may be sent to the hospital on a ticket approved by a lieutenant or other superior officer. If an inmate is injured, it is the duty of the employee in charge to get him to the hospital as soon as possible, keeping in mind institutional safety at all times.

86. Inmates will be permitted to prepare their own petitions for writs in regard to their own cases, after which the papers are to be forwarded to the record office. However, under no circumstances, will inmates be permitted to prepare or advise other inmates in the preparation of writs. Inmates requesting such advise are to be referred to the senior captain, assistant warden or warden. The State of Illinois has no desire to confine any man illegally and he is entitled to his day in court. Inmates are not to have more than six (6) law books in their possession. If they feel it necessary to have another law book in their library, they may request it and, upon delivery of same, one of the other books will be picked up and forwarded to the destination given by the inmate. Inmates with surplus law books may donate them to the institutional library. It will be permissible for inmates to request law books in the library, the same as they request other library books.

87. It is not possible to include in this Rule Book every situation which arises on any particular assignment, nor provide the precise answer to every conceivable circumstance. To be too exact

would only destroy the initiative of employees and would tend to lose flexibility of operations. When established regulations, policies, or procedures do not provide the answer to a particular situation, the employee in doubt should consult his superior as to what course of action should be taken.

88. All rules and regulations governing the prison are promulgated by the warden, on the authority of the Department of Public Safety and are not to be modified or rescinded, in whole or part; nor will such rules be interpreted contrary to their letter and spirit.

Employees are urged to ask questions of their superior officers, if the purpose or meaning of any rule or regulation is ambiguous. Only a thorough understanding of the rules, and the necessity for each, can bring the obedience required to maintain discipline in a penal institution.

It is impossible to over-emphasize the importance of prompt, complete compliance with these rules and regulations; it is likewise impossible to place too much stress on the importance of reporting every incident to your superior. It is imperative that we have a complete, concise picture of every event which takes place in the day-to-day life of the prison, so that the warden may properly administer the affairs of the institution.

Only through the wholehearted cooperation of every employee can the desired results be obtained; the cooperation can best be given by the cheerful performance of any assigned duty and complete obedience to these rules and regulations.

We always welcome suggestions. Do not hesitate to offer them.

PROCEDURE FOLLOWED UPON RECEIPT OF NEW INMATE

1. When a new inmate is received at the Diagnostic Depot, his full name is to be checked against the mittimus accompanying him to be sure they correspond.

2. The inmate is requested to turn in any money or valuables he may have in his possession. The money is counted and listed along with all valuables.

3. Personal property is placed in a bag bearing his name. The

inmate must be searched thoroughly to be certain he has turned in everything.

4. Cash and personal property are to be forwarded to the chief clerk's office and deposited for safe-keeping. Any property which has no value is to be considered contraband. The inmate is requested to sign a release granting authorization for the officer in charge to dispose of the contraband items. All of the inmate's personal possessions which are permissible are to be returned to him.

5. The date of delivery of the prisoner and the register number assigned to him are stamped on the mittimus; also, the signature of the sheriff and/or deputy who delivered the prisoner is affixed to the mittimus at this time.

6. The travel voucher is returned to the sheriff and/or deputy who made the delivery after necessary information has been entered, the voucher signed and the seal placed thereon.

7. The Examination of Prisoner sheet is filled in with the inmate's committed name, term of court in which he was sentenced, date he was received at the depot, crime for which he was committed, the sentence as directed by the court, his race and other pertinent information.

8. The cash and valuables are entered on the reverse side of this sheet. The inmate is asked to read information entered and instructed that this sheet is also an authorization for the institution officials to censor all incoming and outgoing mail. This sheet is to be signed by the inmate and countersigned by the officer in charge.

9. The inmate is then to be shaved and his hair trimmed, after which the Bureau of Identification will photograph, fingerprint, make its regular examination, and complete Bureau of Identification papers pertinent to each new inmate.

10. Following this, the inmate is returned to the bathroom where all hair on his body is to be removed and instructions given to him to take a shower before the examination by the doctor who is to report any vermin, contagious disease, etc. He is then dressed in prison garb.

11. During the next few days the new inmate receives a thorough examination by the prison physician and prison dentist. The physical examination includes a series of typhoid shots, Kahn and undulant fever tests and vaccination.

12. As soon as possible after his admittance, a complete history is to be compiled by the captain at the Diagnostic Depot indicating the past life of the inmate, including religion, marital status, life history prior to his conviction, and a list of relatives or friends whom he expects to correspond with, or receive visits from.

13. The inmate is then examined by the classification board and after their work is completed the captain's office is notified by the mental health department and a transfer is made out and forwarded to the warden for his approval. Upon receipt of approval from the warden, the inmate is outfitted with regulation state issue clothing and is transferred to the branch designated.

14. During the stay of all inmates in the Diagnostic Depot, it shall be the duty of the captain in charge to issue each inmate a rule book provided by the institution. At intervals the captain in charge should go over the rule book explaining the rules in detail. The inmates should be encouraged to ask questions. An assistant warden will hold an indoctrination program for all new inmates during their stay in the Diagnostic Depot and go over each rule and regulation and answer each and all questions, and attempt to familiarize them with the operation and program of the institution and the importance of furthering their educations, both academic and vocational, while serving the sentences the courts have imposed.

15. The chaplains interview each inmate during his stay in the Diagnostic Depot.

CLASSIFICATION PROGRAM

1. For many years the state of Illinois has enjoyed a position of leadership in the application of scientific methods to the study of delinquents and offenders incarcerated in correctional and penal institutions. On July 1, 1933, the classification program

was organized according to law and set in operation under the general direction of the state criminologist and his staff. The Diagnostic Depots or receiving stations were designated, one at Joliet and one at Menard. Since the majority of persons who are admitted to the penitentiary come from the northern portion of the state, the Diagnostic Depot at Joliet became the main receiving station and center of professional activity.

2. Following admittance, the inmates receive individualized studies and examinations by trained sociologists, psychologists and psychiatrists who compose the classification board. When these studies are finished, usually after an observation period varying from three to six weeks, each inmate is then classified according to his personality makeup, his capacity for improvement, and his disposition to respond to correctional treatment. Inasmuch as the criminologist and his staff do not have administrative authority, recommendations are outlined in each case as to the branch of the penitentiary system which is best adapted to the inmate's adjustment and training. Broad suggestions are offered, too, as to such assignments, as cell partners, work, school, vocational training, health requirements, and follow-up counselling. These are advisory only and are submitted for the approval of administrative officials in the Department of Public Safety.

3. The purpose of this professional program is manifold. It is important to acquire new and increasing knowledge about criminology so that the cause of crime and the treatment of the offender may be understood more correctly. It is essential to understand sympathetically the personality of the offender so that he may be aided intelligently to better himself. It is desirable always to inspire in the inmate and to encourage an increasing desire to learn new and better ways of living. Another purpose, perhaps the most significant one, is to further the aims and facilities of education so that all who have to do with the supervision of inmates may become qualified to deal helpfully and efficiently with the many problems that arise among the prisoners, constantly having in mind their essential betterment and future adjustment in society.

ENTRANCE GATE

1. The entrance gate, or gatehouse, as the name implies, is the main entrance of the institution. Through this assignment must pass the relatives and friends of the inmates, all visitors, employees, and inmates who have been assigned to duties outside the institution proper.

A view from the top of the Administration Building showing driveway leading to Highway 66. Stateville Branch.

2. It must be remembered that relatives or friends of some inmates assigned to or outside the gatehouse may attempt to further the escape plans of some inmates within the walls, by delivering contraband intended for this use to inmates in the entrance gate area. Therefore, it is imperative that employees assigned to the entrance gate do a thorough job of searching everyone.

3. No person under the influence of liquor shall be passed through the gatehouse.

4. Visitors will be required to register, listing their names, addresses, the parties they wish to see, and, their relationship, if visiting an inmate. Upon departure, they are to sign their names again, and it will be the duty of the employee to see that the signatures correspond. After registering, visitors are to proceed directly to the search room, where they are to be asked to place their personal property on the table provided for that purpose. At no time will an employee go into the purses or pockets of visitors, unless there is reason to believe they are concealing contraband, or if the visitors do not respond to the request to display their personal effects.

5. Pigeonholes are provided for depositing the personal property taken from each visitor. Such property should consist only of such articles as drugs, files, or anything which might be considered contraband. An identification tag with a number corresponding with the number on the pigeonhole shall be issued to the visitor. Upon leaving the institution, visitors must return the tag before their personal effects are relinquished.

6. Each visitor shall be given the usual search of the entire body and passed through the electric eye before being released to the administration building.

7. One of the most important assignments in the institution is that of the lady searcher, who is regularly stationed in the gatehouse during visiting hours. Female visitors can readily conceal contraband around their breasts and under their dresses. It should never be taken for granted that, because they are women, they will not attempt to carry contraband articles in the institution. Female visitors, after entering the gatehouse, will be requested to register and then proceed directly to the search room.

8. A visitor shall not be permitted to enter the washroom before being thoroughly searched. When a visitor is given a body search, the employee should first request the visitor to turn his back. This rule is for the protection of the employee and is to prevent any possibility of an assault.

9. Close watch is to be kept to prevent anyone from smuggling medicines, drugs, or narcotics of any type into the institution.

Fountain pens, pencils, or other items of this type should be examined carefully to ascertain if they contain gas or drugs.

10. Any box, bag, or package brought into the institution through this assignment must be properly searched, except those that are approved by an employee who is accompanying them. Liquids and medicines are prohibited, unless approved by the Warden or his authorized assistant. THIS RULE APPLIES TO EMPLOYEES ALSO.

11. Guns, razors, knives, or any other weapons will not be permitted to pass this post, but shall be confiscated immediately and reported to the supervising officer. The confiscated articles are to be held in a locker until the officer to whom the incident is reported arrives on the scene.

12. A law enforcement officer, or anyone authorized to bear arms, must leave such weapons with the employee in charge of this assignment before being permitted to enter the institution. The weapons will be locked in the vault until his or her departure, at which time they are to be restored to the owner.

13. No weapon is to be carried to the outside gate or into the administration building, without permission from the warden or his authorized assistant. When employees return from a manhunt or from court, it is the duty of the gateman to see that they do not carry any weapons inside alone: one employee should carry the guns, another the ammunition, and they should always be accompanied by a lieutenant.

14. No one wearing a mask or sun glasses is to be permitted to enter or leave the gatehouse without first removing them, or until the employee in charge is definitely satisfied as to his identification. Employees are not to permit anyone to leave the institution, even though he may be in uniform, whom the employees do not know or recognize. Any visitor who entered prior to the employee's tour of duty will not be permitted to leave until he has been properly identified by another responsible employee of the institution.

15. Positive identification is required of all persons wishing to be released through the door leading from the yard into this

assignment, as there is always the possibility that some inmate may have dressed in civilian clothes and attempt to pass out as a visitor.

16. All inmates released on parole or discharge pass through this gate. The employee in charge of these men will appear at the door by himself, and the men to be released will not be permitted to enter until the door has been closed behind the employee. This is done to prevent any attempt to force a release.

17. Since it is never permissible for anyone with a prison record to visit the institution, all dischargees will be carefully scrutinized, so that each one may be readily recognized in the event he attempts to reënter as a visitor.

18. An employee who has been released from service, either by discharge or resignation, shall not be permitted to reënter the institution without permission of the warden. In the event such permission is granted, the ex-employee will be searched thoroughly before being passed into the institution.

19. Under no circumstance is an employee to accept anything from, or give anything to, the relatives or friends who are visiting an inmate. The employee is to enforce the rule which forbids inmates conversing with or contacting the persons who pass this post. If inmates on other assignments violate rules, the employee will treat them as if they were on his assignment. ALL inmates who pass this post must be searched and passed through the electric eye.

20. It is the duty of the employee in charge to receive approval for all persons being passed through, if they are not known to him, even though they may be accompanied by the warden, assistant wardren, or another employee. ANY employee accompanying a person not known by the employee in charge of the post is to separate himself from that individual, as there is always the possibility that an inmate may be trying to escape and is using an employee as a hostage.

21. Outside tradesmen, professional men, or anyone carrying tools or instruments, are not permitted to enter the institution unless they are accompanied by an employee. The employee

is to make a list, in triplicate, of all the tools or instruments. The original copy is to be retained by the accompanying employee, one copy left at the gatehouse and one copy left at Gate No. 1. When the party leaves the institution, the list is to be rechecked at both assignments, to make sure that all tools or instruments are accounted for. The lists then will be sent to the assistant warden's office. In the event the accompanying employee is relieved before the tradesmen or professional men leaves, he is to give the list to the relieving employee, so that proper check can be made and the tools or instruments accounted for.

22. The employee assigned to this post is to issue passes and complete all records used at the information and registration desk for all special visits and hospital visits conducted after hours, and between the hours of 8:00 A.M. and 4:00 P.M. on Sundays and holidays. The passes shall be signed by the employee in charge of the visits and will be returned to this assignment. The information and registration desk is to be informed for their records.

23. All visitors, other than relatives or friends of inmates on regular visits, are to be approved by the warden or his authorized assistant before being permitted to enter the institution. Anyone wishing to see the business manager, chief clerk, superintendent of industries, or master mechanic, is to wait at the gatehouse until the employee has made sure that the person asked for is in the institution. The employee is to ask the official to meet the visitor at the entrance to the administration building and accompany him to his office.

24. There will be no random public visiting to the institution. If an outsider inquires about visiting, he will be informed that visits can be made only with permission obtained in writing by the warden in advance.

25. Visitors to be shown through the institution will be given tickets which they are to sign at the gatehouse, and which the employee in charge is to initial. They will then be searched, passed through the electric eye, and permitted to proceed into the institution. The visitors will be accompanied by an officer or

an official of the institution. On leaving the institution, the visitors are to sign their tickets again, between Gate No. 1 and 2, and have them initialed by the official or officer accompanying them. Only after properly identifying each visitor will the employee at Gate No. 1 permit the visitor to pass his post. When the visitors have returned to the gatehouse, all of the signatures and the initials will be checked, and they must correspond. These tickets are to be forwarded to the warden's office.

26. If, at any time, there are more than five people in the group, the right hand of each visitor will be stamped with the approval stamp provided for this purpose. The employee is to make sure that the stamp is genuine, before releasing the visitors after their visits.

27. Church groups accompanying chaplains must be accorded the same treatment as any other visitors and will be searched thoroughly and passed through the electric eye.

28. When transferring inmates out of the institution to another assignment, it will be the duty of the employee in charge to see that such inmates are properly accompanied by officers of the institution and to make certain that a force-out is not being attempted. Inmates being transferred into the institution must be accompanied by the employee with the authority to make that transfer. Armed employees are to remain outside of the enclosure when the truck or bus enters the yard proper. After the inmates have entered the administration building and have had sufficient time to pass through Gate No. 1, the arms are to be deposited in a vault provided for that purpose.

29. Visitors or inmates are not permitted to enter or leave the main building during the transfer of inmates.

30. With the exception of the warden's and assistant warden's cars, the mail truck, and the garbage truck (which trucks are permitted to enter the institution once a day), no vehicle is to enter the enclosure, except by permission of the warden. All vehicles will be searched thoroughly, inside and outside, when entering or leaving the enclosure. When a car is being driven out of the entrance gate, the employee in charge is not to open the gate

until he is certain that a force-out is not being attempted and has made certain the occupants of the car are legitimate. Any stranger in the car must be identified before being passed out.

31. Inmate chauffeurs will not be permitted to drive cars outside the enclosure without specific authority from the warden or his authorized assistant.

32. Employees driving a car out of the enclosure must get out of the car and step to the rear before the gate is opened, and under no circumstance will the keys to the driveway or exit of the institution be in the hands of anyone other than the employee on duty at the gate. No one other than the employee on duty is to operate the buzzer and electric locks.

33. Before any trucks can be passed by this post, they must be thoroughly checked by the employee in charge to ascertain that the trucks are not loaded with men who might attempt to "crash" the sally port. Pass the driver only. Trucks returning from the sally port must also be checked to prevent any inmate from the farm detail or the farm from trying to escape. After passing any vehicle to the sally port, the employee is to notify the supervising officer at the sally port of its coming. Notify towers by phone or radio of any passenger cars or trucks driving around the wall.

34. Lights are provided as an aid in identifying people at night, and they must be used.

35. If, for any reason, a car parks in the driveway and arouses suspicion, the employee is to take the license number of the car, the make and model, and attempt to identify the occupants. If an attempt to contact an inmate is made by anyone, the employee will notify the supervising officer at once, that an investigation can be started immediately. Should anyone inside or outside the building arouse your suspicion, it will be his duty, and that of the employee who has the authority, to search him.

36. The employee in charge of the gate also has the authority to designate other employees to check trucks, buses, and taxi cabs, or any suspicious movement of automobiles or pedestrians near

the assignment.

37. Pictures may be taken of the institution outside the front gate only, provided no inmates are in view.

38. No reading material, writing, television, radio, shaving, in fact anything which may serve to take the employees' attention from his duty, will be permitted.

39. The employee is not to call, or permit anyone else to call, for any employee on duty except in an emergency.

40. Under no circumstance will any loitering, either by employees or visitors, be permitted around this assignment at any time.

41. The side door, which will permit anyone to enter or leave the institution, will be opened only at the direction of the superior officer in charge of the gatehouse.

42. Every assistance will be given visitors who are uncertain of the assignment of the inmate they wish to visit.

WARDENHOUSE AND ADMINISTRATION BUILDING

The administration building is one of the most important assignments in the institution. All persons who have business within

View showing the front of the Administration Building. Stateville Branch.

the institution must enter this building. They should report at once to the employee in charge of the information and registration desk in the lobby, who will direct them to their destination. In the event any visitor should ask an employee for information, the visitor should be courteously referred to the proper official. Inmates must not engage in conversation with visitors at any time; employees should limit conversation with visitors to business matters.

The supervisor of the administration building will assign rooms to those employees residing in the officers' quarters, according to their shifts. They are required to conform to all regulations governing the care of such quarters and are expected to be congenial with other employees sharing the same room. All employees are expected to conduct themselves in a gentlemanly manner at all times and under all conditions.

Under no circumstances are employees permitted to bring visitors into their quarter without permission of the warden or his authorized assistant. Neither shall anything be brought into the quarters that inmates could use as a weapon. Each employee's room is his, and he is responsible for all state property therein.

Alcoholic liquors and individually owned razors are banned from institutional grounds and any found will be confiscated and the owner reported to the warden. GAMBLING IN ANY FORM WILL NOT BE PERMITTED AT ANY TIME.

Each employee is provided with the necessary uniform, as directed by the Department of Public Safety and a locker is provided for the safe-keeping of all uniforms that are not in use. Regulation uniforms, caps, and civilian clothing never are to be left where there is a possibility that they may fall into hands of an inmate, who might use such apparel in an attempt to escape. Carelessness on the part of employees in the care and maintenance of state property will not be tolerated and shall be reported to the warden immediately.

Employees never are to leave money or other valuables in their lockers. A vault is provided for this purpose, and neither the institution nor the Department of Public Safety will be responsible for any loss of personal property. On the contrary, employees who permit their personal property to fall into the hands of an inmate will be subject to disciplinary action.

When an employee is suspected of removing state property or the personal belongings of any other employee, it shall be the duty of the employee in charge of the building to search, or cause to be searched, the baggage and/or the person of such suspected employee. A superior officer should be notified immediately of any suspected theft or removal.

Female employees are not to enter any part of the building that is not under the general supervision of an officer.

The waiting room is to be occupied only by visitors who are waiting to be called for visits. No inmate shall be permitted to enter the waiting room while visitors are present.

The employee in charge of the administration building and wardenhouse shall act as supervisor of that part of the building outside of Gate No. 1, including the living quarters of the employees. He shall be in charge of all inmates assigned outside of Gate No. 1, the offices, etc. Civilian employees in the administration building are to coöperate in the security and safety program of the institution. Employees in charge of offices where inmates are assigned should know their whereabouts at all times and never permit inmates and outsiders to converse. They are custodial employees under the supervision of the officer in charge of the administration building, so far as safety and security are concerned.

In addition to abiding by the general rules applicable to all employees, the administration building officers will conform to the following rules and regulations specifically designated for this assignment.

1. Upon assignment as officer in charge of the administration building, the employee will immediately familiarize himself with the location of all locks, keys, and light switches on his assignment. Keys and locks shall be properly numbered and maintained. All lights shall be turned off when not in use.

2. Any violation of the rules on the part of a visitor, em-

ployee, or inmate shall be promptly reported to the proper official.

3. Frequent daily inspections shall be made throughout the building, including the employees' living quarters and the offices. Accumulation of newspapers, magazines, etc., in the room or hallways is prohibited.

4. A complete check must be kept of all linens, towels, bed-clothing, furnishings, etc. Such items will be issued in accordance with instructions, and all employees are to be accorded equal consideration.

5. An inspection of the fence enclosing the administration building shall be made in each shift by the officer in charge of the building. It shall be examined carefully for breaks and the lawn in the vicinity of the fence shall be searched for contraband articles.

6. The officer in charge is the custodian of all property in the building. He shall make certain that needed repairs are made promptly, making a report to the master mechanic whenever necessary.

7. If, at any time, it becomes necessary to do repair work on the roof of the administration building or to open the door leading to any tower, all tower men in the vicinity of the building shall be notified. Such repairs shall be made only under the direct supervision of an employee. Under no circumstances will any employee be permitted to let himself into any tower in or on the administration building. Another employee must always lock and unlock the door for entrance and exit.

8. All outside workmen shall be under the constant supervision of an employee.

9. Whenever it becomes necessary for the officer in charge of the building to leave the institution at any time in the performance of his duties, he shall immediately notify the gatehouse and the employee on duty in the gatehouse tower. All keys will be left at the institution with the officer in charge of Gate No. 1.

10. The officer in charge of the administration building shall be responsible for all tools, knives, utensils, etc. Under no cir-cumstance will inmates be permitted to carry tools or keys, ex-

cept when necessary in the proper performance of their work. All tools and lockers shall be checked periodically, and keys used by inmates shall be turned in to the employee on duty at Gate No. 1 before such inmates leave their assignments.

11. The officer in charge of the building shall have supervision over commodities and materials coming from the general store and will check all such items against requisitions. He shall make any necessary purchases of supplies, which may be required daily. When such purchases are made at downtown stores, it shall be the duty of such employee to make certain that only first class merchandise is received and that the prices charged are in line with those prevailing.

12. Supplies for the building will be ordered on monthly and quarterly requisitions, or as directed. Such requisitions shall be properly prepared and submitted to the chief clerk or the business manager.

13. The employee in charge of this assignment shall be responsible for all institution cars assigned to the garage inside the fenced enclosure and shall assign such cars to officials as the need arises. Under no circumstance will any employee be permitted to drive a car from the institution property, unless he has a driver's license.

14. A sufficient number of inmates are assigned to the garage to maintain properly all cars on the premises, and it shall be the duty of the employee in charge of the building to make certain that all cars are in good order and have proper maintenance and care. When inmate chauffeurs have cars outside the enclosure, the officer in charge will check to make certain of their whereabouts at all times. No inmate shall be permitted to drive any motor vehicle off state property.

15. There are a number of inmates working within this assignment, and while they are carefully selected, it is possible that any one of them may try to use a civilian as a hostage in an attempt to escape. Therefore, all must be carefully supervised.

16. It shall be the officer's duty to receive and count the inmates each morning when they report for the day's work; other

counts shall be made at noon and at the end of his tour of duty. Checks throughout the day must be kept of all inmates on the assignment. Upon being relieved from duty he shall count and check each assigned inmate, accompanied by his relieving employee. In the evening, when the official count is made, the employee on duty shall again check all inmates to make certain they are on the proper assignment.

17. Special details for maintenance or construction purposes shall be permitted to work outside Gate No. 1 only when absolutely necessary and, then, only under the direct supervision of a properly designated employee. Such details shall be returned immediately inside the enclosure upon completion of the work.

18. Under no circumstance shall anyone be given meals in the quarters of the warden or assistant warden, unless authorized by them. Inmates assigned to these quarters shall not be permitted to take advantage of their position by passing food to other inmates, nor shall they be permitted to remove any article from the apartments without direct permission.

19. Inmates assigned to the administration building are to remain on their assignments and shall not be permitted on floors other than the one to which assigned, except in the performance of their work. Any inmate who has a detail authorizing him to remain on assignment after evening check count, shall be returned to the inside, if found not employed at his work.

20. No inmate will be permitted to accept or place calls on an outside telephone.

INFORMATION AND REGISTRATION DESK

1. The information and registration desk is provided so that an accurate record may be kept of all persons who visit inmates confined in the institution. It is located in the main lobby of the administration building. A regularly assigned employee is to be in charge of the desk at all times during visiting hours.

2. Visiting records are important. Frequently, they are checked by the courts, law enforcement agencies, government authorities, etc. When an inmate has been released on discharge or parole,

his visiting record should be forwarded to the record office, to be filed in his jacket.

3. Employees are required to be courteous to visitors at all times, but shall refrain from discussing matters pertaining to the institution, religion, politics, or any controversial subject. Proper requests for information will be handled promptly and courteously, in conformance with institution rules. However, in the event the information requested is not available, or the employee on duty feels that such information should not be given, the visitor will be referred to the warden or his authorized assistant.

4. After having been properly registered, all visitors must retire to the waiting room provided for them. No loitering will be permitted in the vicinity of the desk or reception hall. Immediately after the registration has been completed, the visiting room will be notified and the employee on duty there will be given the number of the inmate receiving the visit.

5. Every precaution should be taken to prevent visitors from contacting inmates within the range of the assignment. Any such attempt should be reported immediately to the warden or his assistant.

6. Loud talking, boisterous conduct, or any disturbance by employees and inmates near the assignment will not be permitted.

7. If, for any reason, an inmate is denied a visit, the reason for the denial will be noted on the records for future reference.

8. Inmates in good standing may receive visits from relatives every two weeks. Under no circumstance will any person other than relatives be permitted to visit any inmate, unless such person has been approved and the visit authorized by the warden. Visits by the clergymen, attorneys, welfare workers, or by the person who expects to employ the inmate on parole, are not to be considered as regular visits.

9. In the event there is doubt as to the truthfulness of a visitor's claim of relationship to the inmate, the records containing a list of all the inmate's relatives shall be consulted. If the visitor is not listed among the relatives, he shall be denied admittance, and the matter referred to the warden or his authorized

assistant.

10. Not more than two persons shall be permitted to visit an inmate at any one time, except in unusual instances, when a divided visit may be authorized by the warden or his assistant.

11. Under no circumstance will any person under the influence of intoxicants be permitted to visit.

12. Any suspicious persons or ex-convicts seeking to visit an inmate will be reported immediately to the warden or his assistant.

13. When inmates assigned to the administration building receive visits, they shall not be permitted to return to their assignment until the visitors have left the building. The employee in charge of the registration desk will notify the visiting room when such visitors have left, and only then will the inmate be permitted to leave the visiting room and return to his assignment.

14. Inmates assigned to the administration building will not be allowed to congregate in the reception hall, nor will such inmates be permitted to converse with visitors at any time.

15. It will be the duty of the employee in charge of the registration desk to scrutinize every inmate who is released from the institution by discharge or parole, so that he may be able to identify him at a later date if he attempts to visit anyone confined.

16. When a group of visitors enters the institution on an escorted tour, a careful scrutiny shall be made of each visitor in order to eliminate any possibility that relatives or friends of inmates may gain admission to the grounds. Any employees who recognizes a friend or relative of an inmate among such visitors shall immediately report the incident to the warden or his authorized assistant.

17. Frequent inspections shall be made of the visitors' waiting room and all offices in the immediate vicinity of the assignment. Immediately before the start of the visiting day, a thorough inspection shall be made of the waiting room to see that inmates have not deposited notes, letters, or contraband for visitors. At the close of business each day, the waiting room will again be carefully inspected for contraband that may have been left by

visitors for inmates assigned to the building.

18. No inmate assigned to the administration building will be permitted to enter any other room or assignment at any time, unless authorized to do so. Under no circumstance will any inmate be permitted to enter the visitors' waiting room, unless he is accompanied by an employee and, then, only in case of necessity or in the proper performance of his assigned duties.

19. The officers' commissary, which is for the convenience of employees and visitors, shall be under the direct supervision of the employee in charge of the registation desk at any time the regularly assigned employee is called away from the assignment for any reason. The employee in charge of the registration desk shall approve all purchases which are to be forwarded to inmates.

20. Visitors or inmates will not be permitted to enter or leave the administration building at a time when inmates are being transferred. The reception hall is to be kept clear of traffic while the transfer is passing through.

21. Violation of any of the institution rules by visitors, employees, or inmates shall be immediately reported to the warden or the properly designated superior officer.

OFFICERS' COMMISSARY

1. The officers' commissary is operated for the convenience of the employees and visitors.

2. Employees are permitted to have a charge account not to exceed twenty (20.00) dollars, which must be paid in full each month. When payments are made, a receipt must be issued to employees. If any employee fails to pay his account in full at the end of the month, his credit is to be stopped.

3. Persons who visit inmates may purchase from the officers' commissary for delivery to inmates. These purchases are not to exceed the amount designated by the warden in a written order. Every package delivered to an inmate must be inspected personally by an officer. Each item in the package is to be checked against the sales slips. The officer then supervises the delivery of the packages to the gate leading into the institution yard,

where they will be turned over to another officer for delivery to the inmates.

4. A well balanced stock must be maintained by the employee in charge of the commissary. When merchandise is needed, he shall submit an order to the chief clerk for transmittal. It is a duty of the officer in charge to receive the shipments of merchandise at a place designated by the warden and to inspect all the deliveries. Inferior merchandise shall not be accepted.

5. Only the employee in charge and the inmates assigned to the commissary are permitted to handle money or stock.

6. The accounts must be posted, the credit ledger balanced and the cash checked daily to see that it balances.

7. The receipts of the day are to be turned over to the chief clerk at the end of each day with the exception of ten ($10.00) dollars, which is to be kept in the cash register as petty cash. After hours, it will be the duty of the commissary clerk to put the money in a cash box and place it in the armory. The armory officer will give a receipt for the money. The following morning the commissary clerk will surrender the receipt to obtain the cash box.

8. An inventory based on cost price is to be taken as directed.

9. Any employee assigned to the commissary will be accountable for the money and merchandise while on duty.

10. When necessary to be absent from his assignment, the commissary officer is to inform the officer in charge of the information and registration desk who, in turn, will supervise the commissary.

11. The commissary must be kept immaculately clean and the merchandise displayed in neat order.

MAIL OFFICE

1. The mail office is an important assignment, and the officer in charge is responsible for all matter transmitted between inmates and their friends or relatives, including letters, books, newspapers, periodicals, or other items sent through the mails.

2. The officer's responsibility does not end with routine in-

spection or censorship of such items for objectionable material, but must include the exercise of judgment in all matters affecting the welfare and safety of the institution which come to his attention through the mail. For example, letters to inmates assigned outside the walls which contain such disturbing news as the death of a relative, etc., must be turned over to the assistant warden or the senior captain, who in turn will summon the inmate and deliver the letter or message to him in person. Since it is also possible for the mail officer to get the "feel" of the institution from inmates' correspondence, he must notify a superior immediately if at any time he senses anything that indicates trouble.

3. All mail addressed to the institution and to the warden must be forwarded to him immediately after sorting. Employees' mail is deposited in boxes provided for that purpose in the guard hall. Packages addressed to them should be sent to the reception office in the administration building, to be picked up personally. Mail for employees on vacation or on sick leave, if not to be forwarded, should be held in a safe place until called for when they return.

4. Packages addressed to inmates are to be returned to the sender, except in cases of authorized purchases of books, etc.

5. Inmates are permitted to write one letter each week to persons on their mailing lists. Special letters, in cases of emergency or when it is clear that personal business might suffer for lack of a letter, are granted on the approval of the assistant warden and other supervising officers. Letters to persons not on an inmate's mailing list are permitted only after investigation, or when the mail officer is satisfied such letters will not be detrimental to the best interests of the institution. Inmates sometimes secure from newspapers or other sources the names and addresses of persons unknown to them and to whom they write letters, which may result in complaints or embarrassment to officials.

6. It is the institution's policy to encourage inmates' contacts with relatives and others who will assist in their rehabilitation, but at the same time it is contrary to policy to permit any inmate to maintain contact with ex-convicts or undesirable persons, espe-

cially those who may have been associated with them in the offenses which brought them to prison and who may have a bad influence upon them when released.

7. Inmates may receive as many letters as are addressed to them, providing the letters contain nothing objectionable. A record is to be kept of the names and addresses of all persons who write to each inmate, together with the date such letters are received.

8. The mail officer will keep a record of all outgoing mail, on forms provided. Letters addressed to more than one person on the same letterhead are not to be approved.

9. Inmate letters containing criticism of the administration, the institution, or its employees are to be given to the warden or assistant warden. Letters which are objectionable should be returned to the inmate for re-writing or, in some cases where a letter may be considered valuable for the records, it may be placed on file.

10. There are problem inmates in every institution who would take advantage of every opportunity to cause trouble for the institution, and they may have connections on the outside who would assist them in any way possible. The names and numbers of these inmates should be placed on a "watch list." Incoming and outgoing mail for anyone on this list should be censored by the mail officer personally.

11. Tests with a hot iron should be made of all letters which the mail officer has reason to suspect may contain invisible writing done with citrus juices, urine, or other such fluids.

12. Written material, other than legal documents, which an imate wishes to send out via his visitors is to be given to the mail office three days beforehand for inspection and censorship. All legal documents for inmates are to be forwarded to the record office.

13. Care should be taken so that clerks under the supervision of the mail officer are instructed to prevent inmates from securing extra letters by using another inmate's name and number on a letterhead and addressing it to a correspondent on his own list.

14. Letters which request money for dental work, medical supplies, or the like, are to be investigated to see that the request is genuine and not an attempt to obtain money, often from relatives who can ill afford it, for the payment of gambling debts or other such unauthorized purposes.

15. Cash is never to be accepted when sent by mail, but is to be given to the chief clerk for return to the sender. Money orders, checks, drafts, etc., are to be listed according to the cell house of the inmate receiving same and delivered to the chief clerk's office. That officer will see that they are endorsed by the chief clerk for deposit in the inmate's account.

16. A record of all printed matter addressed to inmates must be kept, not only in the mail office but also in the cellhouse, to insure delivery of periodicals and newspaper to the proper person.

17. Only newspapers and magazines which appear on the permitted list on file in the mail office are to be accepted for delivery to inmates, and all such material must be sent direct from the publishers.

18. Inmate complaints about mail are to be investigated.

19. An annual report shall be made of all incoming and outgoing mail on June 30th of each year.

BUSINESS MANAGER

1. The duties of the business manager may be broadly defined as the supervision of the business activities of the institution under the regulations set out in the statutes of the State of Illinois and the policies formulated by the Director of the Department of Public Safety, his administrative assistants, and the warden of the institution. The functions of the business manager's office may be compared to those of the office of the comptroller of any large corporation. As chief fiscal officer of the institution, the business manager is directly responsible to the warden for the efficient and proper management of the business of the institution.

2. The business manager must establish and maintain in his office such proper methods and practices as will insure the orderly, efficient, handling of the business transactions of the insti-

tution. He must delegate responsibilities to and properly supervise the work of the personnel assigned to his office.

3. He must prepare, after consultation with the warden, the recommended operating budget for the institution for each biennial period for submission to the director. Once a definite budget has been established by the general office, after legislative appropriations, it is the duty of the business manager to establish and maintain such budget controls as may be required for the efficient financial management of the institution.

4. It is the duty of the business manager to establish and maintain in his office such accounting records and practices as will make possible the proper recording of the daily business transactions of the institution. Such records and systems must be established by the State Auditor of Public Accounts, the general office of the Department of Public Safety, and in keeping with standard, accepted, accounting records and systems. One of the prime responsibilities of the business manager is the approval of payment of all invoices rendered the institution by suppliers of materials and equipment delivered to the institution. Such approval may not be given until and unless the business manager determines that the materials or equipment covered by the invoices have actually been received by the institution; are covered by a bona fide order issued by the proper purchasing authority; that the invoice is rendered in accordance with the terms set out in the order, and that materials received are of the quality ordered.

5. The business manager must also supervise the requisitioning of all materials required for the operation and maintenance of the institution. The quarterly requisitions for all institutional departments are forwarded to his office for inspection, determination of the proper purchasing classifications by accounts, and recapitulation and approval of encumbrances by accounts, prior to the submission of such requisitions to the warden for final approval and transmittal to the general office of the Department of Public Safety. All special requisitions covering emergency requirements of the institution must be processed in the same

manner. As chief fiscal officer of the institution, the business manager must, through his budget controls and inspection of requisitions, prevent the building up of abnormal inventories of supplies and equipment. Equally important, he must insure an adequate supply of materials required for the orderly, efficient operation of the institution.

6. It is the duty of the business manager to compile the monthly payroll for the personnel of the institution and to maintain such records as may be required for this purpose.

7. It is his duty to supervise the maintenance of the general ledgers and subsidiary ledgers, invoice journal, sale journal, and the accounts receivable records pertaining to the operation of the prison industries and to offer such information and assistance to the superintendent of industries as may be required to further the efficient operation of such industries. He must be familiar with the statutes governing the operation of the industries and with the types of products and services offered by them to the tax supported bodies of the state.

8. The business manager must coöperate closely with administrative officers of the various departmental units of the institution. He should be familiar with the functions of the various departments, their general requirements insofar as materials and equipment are concerned, and offer such assistance as may be required to obtain materials and equipment, within the limits prescribed by his budget controls, for the efficient operation of the various departments.

9. The business manager is the supervising officer of the perpetual inventory covering all institution property. He must make certain that all items disposed of are condemned and proper record kept of same. The inventory records should be kept in order at all times.

10. As one of the chief administrative assistants of the warden, the business manager must provide such information and statements as required on the fiscal affairs of the institution to permit proper program planning and efficient management of the institution's affairs by the warden.

CHIEF CLERK

1. The chief clerk has charge of all funds, including the inmates' trust, benefit, and commissary funds, the officers' benefit, commissary, barber, badge and tag funds. He also has charge of the industrial working capital, miscellaneous collections, etc. He has custody of all inmate personal property not permitted to be in the inmates' possession.

2. The chief clerk is to purchase all supplies for the inmates' commissary, the officers' commissary, and the officers' barber shop by taking bids. If possible, the lowest bidder is to receive the order, however, quality is always an important factor as inferior merchandise should not be purchased or accepted. Prices for the sale of these supplies are to be established by the chief clerk. All transactions shall be approved by the warden.

3. He supervises the accounting records of the inmates' and officers' commissaries and exercises direction of both commissaries with the assistance of civilian commissary clerks.

4. All fiscal reports for the general office in Springfield are directed and supervised by the chief clerk. He must keep employees' payroll records and distribute salary checks, supervise all deposits and withdrawals from the inmates' trust accounts, purchase permitted items for inmates when requested, and handle all transactions dealing with outside sources in connection with inmates' personal property.

5. The chief clerk purchases all athletic equipment, band supplies, school supplies, radio equipment, motion pictures, and other items necessary for either the benefit or education of inmates, the money for such purchases being obtained solely from the profits of the inmates' commissary. He disburses all funds from the inmates' and officers' commissaries and inmates' benefit fund only when supported by proper documents. He must record and remit all industrial collections and miscellaneous revenue, handle all banking and bank transactions, receive all monies, execute all orders and wishes of the warden, and general orders from Springfield dealing with the operations of the chief clerk's office.

6. The chief clerk has charge of purchasing defense bonds for employees and inmates, and also for the collection of group insurance from employees.

7. All monies forwarded by check and money order to inmates must be properly endorsed and deposited by the chief clerk as directed by the warden.

ASSISTANT WARDEN

On occasions when it is necessary for the warden to absent himself from the institution, the assistant warden is to assume responsibility. He should have a thorough knowledge of every phase of prison life. He must be able to make decisions quickly and justly, both in routine matters and in time of an emergency, and must file a report on any unusual occurrence.

1. The assistant warden is to make daily periodic trips into the yard and around the institution to see that the various shifts are being properly operated and that instructions of the supervising officers are being obeyed. During his tours of inspection he is to counsel and instruct employees as to the operation of their particular assignments, giving credit or criticism where it is due. This routine check of the institution should include the employees' living quarters to make certain there is no gambling and that state property is not being misused.

2. The assistant warden and one senior captain are authorized by the warden to pass out men who are being released on parole, on writ, or on discharge, and pass outsiders into the institution proper for visits or business when the warden is not available.

3. It is the duty of the assistant warden to have each department head submit tool inventories at regular intervals and to submit at a specified time a tool check slip signed by the department head, notifying him that the count of all tools check. He also makes sure that a complete check is made throughout the entire institution at frequent intervals by a lieutenant. Requisitions for tools require the signature of the assistant warden and the master mechanic.

4. Where typewriters, watches, musical instruments, and school

supplies are permitted, the assistant warden is to receive them, see that they are properly stamped and numbered, and have permits issued to the inmates for same. Supplies for the chaplains also must clear through the assistant warden.

5. The assistant warden is to coöperate with the record clerk and see that petitions are prepared and presented to the County Court at least fifteen days prior to the release of inmates who are sentenced for sex crimes to determine whether they are insane, feebleminded, or criminal sexual psychopaths. He must see that the inmates are taken to court on the day set for a hearing and he may attend the hearing as a representative of the Director of the Department of Public Safety.

6. It is also the duty of the assistant warden, as a member of the merit staff, to see that meetings are held as near the first of each month as possible in order that the staff may act upon violations of the inmates during the previous month. The merit staff consists of two senior captains, the assistant warden, and a clerk or any other designated employee.

7. The assistant warden is to identify and pass in or out of the institution everyone not otherwise authorized to pass through the gates.

8. A complete set of files covering the personnel, including photographs and identification cards, is to be maintained in the assistant warden's office.

9. The assistant warden together with the warden and two senior captains approve the inmates to be assigned outside the walls. He is to check all records of inmates, personally interview inmates, and approve, or disapprove, all inmates for outside details on write-ups submitted by captains and the record clerk. On those approved by the warden, the assistant warden is to see that a regulation form is filled out to be filed in the inmate's jacket, giving the crime, sentence, and description of the inmate, as well as his mailing and visiting record. In the event of an escape this information is available for broadcast purposes.

10. The assistant warden is to maintain a record showing the name, address ,and telephone number of every employee; and in

the event any employee owns a car, the description and current license number of the car.

11. Permit cards are issued by the assistant warden to all officers living in the institution, and reports are to be made to the business manager when an officer moves in or out of the institution.

RECORD OFFICE

1. The institution record office is a repository for all information obtained about each inmate who enters the prison; his complete biography may be written from the entries filed and cross-filed here during the period between his entrance and eventual discharge. Filing this information in such a manner that it is possible to answer instantly the unending stream of inquiries about prisoners, past or present, and to insure that each incoming prisoner is promoted from grade to grade, given his day before the parole board, or discharged when due, is the responsibility of the record clerk.

2. This responsibility and clerical routine begins with the arrival of a new prisoner at the diagnostic depot. Notice of the arrivals is sent to the record office and their numbers are included in the total institution count. The office not only must keep an accurate daily count of men assigned but also of those who are on parole, absent on writ or court order, or absent for other reasons. This count is furnished daily to the Department of Public Safety in Springfield.

3. Assigned numbers and commitment papers of new inmates are brought to the record office. Information from the mittimi— the sentencing court's formal and legal description of the offense and the term to be served—is immediately circularized to more than forty other interested departments. Copies of the state's attorney's statements are also made for the psychiatrist and the Division of Correction files. Data taken from these commitment papers and from the examination sheet prepared at the receiving depot is then recorded on the face of a jacket which in time will contain all papers and information pertinent to the inmate.

This data is also entered in a number of registers:

(a) a day book, listing all persons taken in or out of the prison;

(b) An alphabetical register;

(c) a master register which lists in numerical order everyone received at the prison since its establishment;

(d) an alphabetical directory which also lists assignments. Aliases and variations in the spelling of a name are entered in a separate alias register.

4. In addition, cards are made for each new man for each of five separate card indexes. Two of these indexes are date systems which show the prisoner's status in relation to eligibility for parole consideration or discharge by expiration of sentence. These dates must be computed carefully by the record clerk, who must take into account two types of "good time" allowance fixed by law—one for determinate and one for indeterminate sentences. Two more card files give the prisoner's grade status and history of punishment reports. The fifth card index is a statistical file of all men in the institution's active roll, whether inside the walls or out.

5. The minutiae of paper detail connected with a prisoner's release is also the record clerk's responsibility. In the case of those under indeterminate sentence, this begins six months before the prisoner is eligible for a parole hearing, at which time the office sends each prospective parole applicant a form on which he is to list past employers and references. The completed forms are returned to the record office and forwarded to the Parole Board at Springfield. Two months before a given meeting of the division some twenty-five copies of a list of those to be heard are sent to the departments and department heads who will furnish medical, sociological, and other reports for the Parole Board's information. Lists also are furnished to the Bankers' Association, the Chicago Crime Commission, the Chicago police superintendent and bureau of identification, and the local parole office notifies the state's attorney, complaining witness, and sentencing judge in the county from which the prisoner was sentenced. Copies of the list furnished to the Springfield office of

the division are marked for corrections or additions and returned to the institution. From this corrected list the advance docket is prepared by the record clerk and copies forwarded to the necessary assignments of the institution.

6. Because of the time between creation of the first list and actual board hearings, cases are added or dropped constantly until the docket is officially closed ten days preceding the board hearing. Then copies of the final docket are sent out.

7. Results of the board's actions are usually supplied to the record office about a week before the next board meeting. These actions are entered on jackets, registers, and card files, and original notices are given to the institution's senior captain for distribution to the inmates concerned. A list of men ordered paroled is sent to the clothing room, the prison bureau of identification and others, while a summary of all actions taken by the agency is supplied to the warden.

8. The required number of copies of a list of men to be discharged by expiration of sentence are made and sent to the departments affected two or more months prior to their release. Some of those to be discharged may be sex cases. In such cases the law requires they must be given court examinations prior to release. Separate notices are made of these cases and petitions for their hearings are prepared in the record office and filed in the county court. After the court sets a date for the examinations, the record office notifies relatives of the men concerned, as well as the institution psychiatrist, physicians, and others whose reports are presented in court.

9. The record office is similarly concerned with the several other methods by which a prisoner may be released. These are: Discharge by court order; transfer to another branch of the penitentiary, or death. In each case, various institutional departments are notified so they may close out their files and forward them to the record office, where they are placed in the jackets and (except in the cases of men transferred to another branch) moved to an inactive file. In the case of men transferred, the office makes out the usual formal release orders, sees that the

proper records accompany the prisoners to their destination, arranges for the vehicle used, together with an adequate police escort, and notifies the prisoners' relatives of the move.

10. The hospital keeps the office posted on the condition of patients who may be seriously ill and relatives of such patients are informed by telegram. If death occurs, the office follows through to final disposition of the body, whether claimed or buried in the prison cemetery.

11. The foregoing outlines record office activities connected with the receipt and release of prisoners. In between receipt and release are the day-to-day activitis of the office which are linked to the prisoner's life and movement within the institution. Almost everything that happens to him, short of the meals he eats and the form of recreation he takes in the yard, is the subject of office concern in one way or another.

12. Changes of assignment, disciplinary reports, and requests from the prisoner himself for copies of his commitment papers are routine daily matters which require the full-time services of several clerks. His criminal history, as furnished by the Federal Bureau of Investigation, is posted in detail in the master register and on his jacket.

13. Inquiries are received from relatives by telephone and by mail as to the prisoner's health, his eligibility for parole or discharge. Inquiries also come from county, state, and federal officials who often can supply only a misspelled name or a variation of it which must be traced through the alias registers until identified. Also there are interviews with the prisoner at his request, often for notarization of legal papers, since the record clerk also is a notary public.

14. There are regular weekly and monthly reports covering the receipt and release of prisoners which must be submitted to the office of the director of the Department of Public Safety, copies of which are also furnished to Chicago police officials.

15. There is a monthly statistical report furnished to the department's statistician, classifying every prisoner by location, color, religion, crime, sentence, age, when received, occupation,

education, prison terms served, etc.

16. The record clerk is to meet with the warden each morning, bringing to his attention all correspondence and other current matters which require his personal attention.

17. There are warrants, issued in the record office at the request of the Division of Superintendent of Parolees, for detention or return of parole violators, and the attendant entries and reports related thereto. Notices also must be sent to police officials and other authorities who have warrants on files for men about to be paroled or discharged.

18. Finally, there are the quasi-legal duties of the record clerk in connection with prisoners' petitions for writs of habeas corpus, certiorari, coram nobis ,etc.—duties that require of him more than a nodding acquaintance with the laws of the land. The record clerk must inspect these petitions before notarizing them. Most of them he is obliged to read entirely. The inmate involved must be seen at the time of notarization. The record clerk then forwards the petitions to the proper courts, together with supplementary motions, notices, and other correspondence related to them. In addition numerous copies of FBI reports must be made and furnished to the attorney general's office so that it may adequately represent the state in these cases. In those cases where court hearings have been granted the petitioners, the record clerk must note the date and time of the court appearance, notify the captain's office and clothing room, and prepare release orders and other receipts which must be signed when the prisoners are turned over to court authorities.

19. Working in the record office is a merit staff secretary who acts as liaison officer between the former and the captain's office, noting grade promotions or other actions taken by the staff. The secretary also assists in the careful screening program used in connection with prisoners to be assigned to work outside the wall, wherein the record office prepares history sheets containing jacket information for the supervising officer in charge of the outside detail. The staff secretary also searches the file for data on the individual's past behavior to indicate the kind of risk he might

be outside the prison wall, passing this along with the captain's letter of recommendation to the warden and assistant warden, both of whom must approve the assignment before any prisoner is given a job as trusty.

20. In view of the valuable and confidential matter filed in the record office, all jackets and master registers are stored in a fireproof vault which is locked except when the custodian is present. No jacket is permitted outside the office except to the warden or authorized assistants and then only after the vault file clerk has charged it out. This clerk also keeps a record of jackets removed from the file by those in the record office, so that their whereabouts are known at all times.

21. Where there is a veterans' office established, it is to work in close coöperation with the record clerk and all files of the veterans' office are the property of the record office. After an inmate has been released, the files in the veterans' office on the inmate are to be forwarded to the record office for filing in the inmate's jacket.

PAROLE OFFICE

1. The parole officer is an employee of the Division of Supervision of Parolees and acts as a liaison agent between the Division of Correction, the various other institutional departments, and the inmates.

2. He is in complete charge of the business activities conducted by his office. No other employee has the authority at any time to direct or to issue instructions concerning such business matters. The employee charged with the custody of the inmates assigned to work in the parole office has the duty to supervise them, insofar as discipline and institutional safety are concerned.

3. The parole officer handles all petitions for executive clemency, rehearing, etc., except those filed in an inmate's behalf by an attorney, relative, or friend on the outside.

4. Any inmate may request an interview with the parole officer concerning his own case, insofar as it pertains to parole, execu-

tive clemency, rehearing, etc. The inmate's request should state the exact question he wants answered or the exact nature of the business about which he desires to see the parole officer. All inmate requests will be honored, but inmates should be instructed not to send a large number of requests to the parole officer.

5. An inmate's petition for executive clemency should be typed, if possible, and contain: (1) A brief summary of his life, that is, date of birth, where born, parents' name and address if alive, if not state when they died, what schools he attended and how much schooling he has, places at which he has worked after leaving school up until the time of his arrest, etc. In other words he should give a general account of his life from the date of his birth until the time of his arrest. (2) The inmate's version of the crime, (The state's version is on file.) It is desired to know just what the inmate has to say about it. He should give details of his arrest, identification, trial, and conviction and just how the crime was committed. (3) Reasons why executive clemency should be granted. Seven copies of the petition should be sent to the parole office at least sixty days before the date of the meeting of the Parole and Pardon Board at which they are to be considered.

6. Only one copy of a petition for rehearing is necessary. The rules of the Parole and Pardon Board require that an inmate must serve an additional year from the date of denial of a petition for rehearing before he may again make application for rehearing. If one year has not elapsed since the date the inmate was last denied a rehearing, he should not submit another petition.

7. Each employee should familiarize himself with the foregoing, so that he will be in a position to properly advise any inmate who asks his advise.

INTER-INSTITUTIONAL TELEPHONE OPERATORS

1. The switchboard is one of the central nerve areas of the institution and an alert operator is in a position to stop trouble if it starts. Courteous and fast service is important. If at any time an emergency should arise in the yard it will be the duty of the institutional telephone operator to give THREE SHARP RINGS ON THE TELEPHONE to each of the following assignments:

Towers
Front Gate
Armory
Gate 1
Sally Port

2. It will not be necessary for anyone to answer his phone in this event. However, it will indicate to everyone there is an emergency, that they should be on their toes and be ALERT, until such time as advised that the situation is under control.

3. Whenever an officer calls in and asks for a certain number or party, stating it is an emergency call, and that line happens to be busy, it will be your duty to break the connection on the desired line immediately, and connect the officer making the emergency call with the number or party he has requested without delay.

4. At any time there is disturbance or trouble within the institution, the information is to be given to the telephone operator immediately, and it will be his (or her) duty to notify the warden's office without delay.

5. At any time an escape or attempted escape is reported, it will be the duty of the civilian telephone operator to notify all towermen. Should there be an inmate relief operator, it will then be the duty of the officer in charge of the guard hall to notify the towermen.

6. At any time serious trouble occurs, such as an escape, riot, insurrection, etc., each employee who may have any information relative to same must call the warden immediately, giving the information to anyone who may be there, making certain, of course, that it is not an inmate. In the event there is no one in the warden's office, all available information should be given to the telephone operator on the institution switchboard, so he (or she) may spread the alarm and notify the assistant warden and captains, etc.

7. In the event of an emergency, where an employee may be in need of assistance and is near a telephone, he (or she) should take or knock the receiver off the hook or cradle and it will be the duty of the operator to get the information to a captain, lieu-

tenant, the warden, or assistant warden, who will investigate and ascertain the trouble.

8. Whenever officers are sent out on a manhunt, the telephone operator shall notify the employee in charge of each assignment in the administration building, as well as the entrance gate and the entrance gate tower. The employees in charge must keep inmates on their assignments until such time as notified by the operator that all the officers have been dispatched.

9. In the event of a fire it is the duty of the officer in the guard hall to order the telephone operator to notify the fire chief first, then call the power house so they may regulate the water supply accordingly. The sub-station must be notified so that if high tension wires are in the area of the fire, and endangering the men fighting the fire, the power shall be shut off immediately. If necessary, the fire departments from the nearest communities are to be called by the supervising officer in charge. Then notify the master mechanic, mechanical foreman, and the warden or assistant warden as soon as possible.

10. Civilian telephone operators are to be relieved for short periods of time, but under no circumstances are they to be away from their assignment too long, or too often.

11. The switchboard operator is to report to the proper authorities any employee who fails to adhere to the rules of the institution concerning emergency telephone use.

12. Employees assigned to the guard towers are to call the operator every 30 minutes. A record is to be kept by the operator and those missing calls reported to a supervising officer.

13. Unless permission has been granted, inmates are not to use the institutional telephones. Under no circumstances will inmates be permitted to use outside telephones.

14. Institution, as well as outside telephones, are to be used for business only.

15. Employees on duty are not to be summoned to the telephone unless the call is an emergency. Public phones in the institution are to be used by employees for their personal calls, but only after they are off duty.

GATE NO. 1

1. The employee assigned to duty at Gate No. 1 holds one of the most responsible posts in the entire institution. This gate controls the entrance to and exit from the institution proper, and strict observance of all rules and regulations is imperative, if the safety and efficient operation of the prison is to be maintained.

2. Constant vigilance must be maintained at all times, for even the slightest error in judgment or mistake in identity could bring dire consequences. Permitting an unauthorized person to enter or leave the institution could bring great discredit to the governor, the director, the warden, and everyone connected with the Department of Public Safety, with resultant trouble and disgrace to the responsible employee and his family. Therefore, the face of every person who attempts to pass through Gate No. 1 will be carefully scrutinized to insure that only those authorized are permitted to enter or leave.

3. No person shall be permitted to pass through this gate until he is approved by the warden or his authorized assistant. In the case of visitors going to or coming from the visiting room, a ticket authorizing the visit and properly signed by the employee in charge of the information and registration desk will be considered sufficient authorization to permit such visitors to pass through the gate. However, should the individual seeking to enter be recognized as a former inmate or a person not authorized to enter the institution, entrance should be denied and the matter referred to the warden.

4. Gate No. 1 will not be opened when large numbers of inmates are passing through the guard hall, and under no circumstance will Gate No. 1 and 2 be opened at the same time.

5. During the night hours when one employee is serving as turnkey for both Gate No. 1 and Gate No. 2, the key to Gate No. 1 must be left in the armory, except when actually in use. During such hours the gate will be under surveillance of the armory officer. Guard hall and gate men are to use the alarm system provided for that purpose in an emergency.

6. No inmate or prison official, who is not personally known

to the employee on duty, will be passed through Gate No. 1. When there is any question as to the individual's identity, entrance or exit shall be denied until proper identification has been established by the warden or his authorized assistant. This applies to any person, whether in uniform or civilian clothes, for it is not beyond the realm of possibility that an inmate or inmates may obtain uniforms or civilian clothes and masquerade as employees and officials in the hope that they will be permitted to pass through the gate.

7. Visitors to be shown through the institution must be approved by the warden or his authorized assistant and must be accompanied by an employee in regulation uniform before they will be permitted to pass through the gate. The employee accompanying such visitors must identify each of them upon leaving, before they will be permitted to pass through the guard hall. After identification tickets have been signed and signatures compared, a count will be made of all visitors entering the institution and a check count made upon their exit.

8. When an employee is accompanying any outside visitor, it will be his duty to remain with that person until visit has been completed.

9. No employee while on duty will be permitted to pass in or out of this gate, unless he is properly authorized to do so. Men who are assigned to relief duty on the towers, etc., are not to be passed through this gate until fifteen (15) minutes before the regular relief time.

10. Individuals who have entered the institution while the previous shift was on duty, or while a relief employee was in charge of the gate, will not be permitted to leave the institution until proper identification has been established, even though such individuals may be in uniform.

11. Every package, box, basket, etc., carried through Gate No. 1, either by an employee or inmate, must be inspected carefully. Such packages will be opened by the receiving officer before being admitted to the guard hall. However, if there is any reason to suspect that proper inspection has not been made, the

employee on duty at Gate No. 1 may make any search or inspection he deems necessary. Laundry from the administration building must be inspected and approved by the employee in charge of the building before being passed through the gate. All packages being taken out must be accompanied by a gate pass signed by the officer in charge of its origin, showing destination, etc.

12. The time of arrival and departure of those employees who sign the time sheet at Gate No. 1 will be checked by the employee assigned to duty at this gate.

13. When an employee has been released from duty, either by discharge or resignation, he will not be permitted to pass through Gate No. 1.

14. Inmates who have been assigned to work outside this gate must first be approved and passed through it by the warden or his authorized assistant. After the original approval has been given, the employee in charge of the administration building must always receive this group of inmates and identify them, to make certain no unauthorized inmate is passed through. Lines waiting to pass through must be kept in an orderly manner and absolute silence maintained.

15. Inmates are not to be passed to the administration building until the employee in charge of that assignment is present to take charge of them. In his absence they may be turned over to the official in charge of the information and registration desk.

16. Any inmate runner assigned to the administration building must sign the register at Gate No. 1 showing his name, number, destination, and time of departure, before he will be permitted to go beyond Gate No. 2. Upon his return, the time will be noted in the space provided.

17. Any inmate passing through this gate may be searched at any time, if there is reason to believe he has unauthorized articles in his possession.

18. If it becomes necessary for an inmate assigned to the administration building to go to the hospital because of illness, he will be passed through Gate No. 1. Emergencies are always to be given proper consideration; however, great care will be exer-

cised, as it is possible the inmate may be malingering in an attempt to contact some person beyond this post.

19. Inmates who carry keys to desks and lockers on their assignment must deposit keys before entering the guard hall. Each key and all necessary tools will be checked in and out by the employee on duty at Gate No. 1.

20. No one will be permitted to pass through this gate if he is wearing colored glasses or anything that might obstruct a full view of his facial features.

21. Under no circumstances will loitering by employees, inmates, or outsiders be permitted around this gate at any time.

GATE NO. 2

AND GUARD HALL

1. Gates No. 1 and No. 2 never are to be open at the same time. All inmates passing through Gate No. 2 must be thoroughly searched for contraband.

2. The employee in charge of Gate No. 2 is also in charge of the guard hall. He must maintain a constant watch on the armory. When necessary to open the armory door, he must take every precaution to prevent the possibility of an inmate seizing a gun or other weapon from the armory or one that is being transported to or from the Armory through the Guard Hall. Employees admitted to the armory are to be passed through door No. 1 of the armory and this door locked behind them before the armory door is opened. In no event shall any inmate come in contact with the officer in the armory by giving or receiving anything through the window.

3. In the event of an escape it will be the duty of the officer at Gate No. 2 to notify the farm, the farm detail, and the officer in the armory. The latter officer will in turn notify all towers through the speaker system.

4. If fire is reported it shall be the duty of the guard hall officer to see that the telephone operator first notifies the fire chief and then the supervising officer in charge of the shift, and the warden.

5. Should trouble develop in the lighting system he must make

View of Guard Hall leading to Gate 2. Stateville Branch.

certain that the master mechanic and the electrician are notified immediately.

6. If the inter-institutional switchboard breaks down, he must, at once, advise the warden, the assistant warden, the chief guard, and the armory officer. The armory officer in turn shall notify all towers through the speaker system.

7. Strict attention must be paid by the officer at Gate No. 2 to every visitor who enters or leaves the visiting room, and he must be positive of every person's identity before passing him through the gate in either direction.

8. Other than those going to the inmates' visiting room, no visitor is to be passed in or out unless he is accompanied by the warden, the assistant warden, or by some other authorized employee.

9. When an inmate is transferred to work outside of Gate No. 2, he can be admitted to his assignment for the first time only

upon the approval of the warden, assistant warden, or senior captain. All inmates returning to the farm from the institution must be accompanied by an employee from the farm. No inmate is to be passed outside of Gate No. 2 without proper approval.

10. After business hours, the officer assigned to the guard hall will receive all telephone calls and telegrams addressed to the institution. Proper report, in writing, should be made of all important calls received and distribution made to the warden, the assistant warden, or to such employees as may be concerned. It is important that an effort be made to notify an employee when a telephone or telegraph message is received regarding his or her family. Triplicate copies of messages received for inmates shall be made, one copy going to the supervising officer in charge of the shift for delivery to the inmate, one copy to the warden's office and one copy to the record office.

11. It is the guard hall officer's responsibility also to check and report to the proper destination the calls received regarding the housemen assigned to the dwellings and other assignments on the institution reservation.

12. The guard hall officer shall make certain that all inmates being transferred or who are going out on writs are handcuffed before being passed through Gate No. 2.

13. He also will make certain that all inmates leaving their assignment by permission, or on an errand and unaccompanied by an officer, sign the sheet for absentees, giving number, name, time, and destination. When these inmates return, the guard hall officer will make certain they sign the sheet, giving the time of their return and check on any overdue absence. When making the count, he must not accept the word of anyone regarding the whereabouts of an inmate. He must see every inmate counted.

14. He will not permit loitering in the guard hall by either employees or inmates.

15. He must not permit passage of packages and bundles through Gate No. 2, unless a thorough inspection has been made. Inmates outside Gate No. 1 are prohibited from carrying anything back through the guard hall, except a watch, a handker-

chief, or material required for their work in connection with the institution.

16. All inmates coming from the farm to go on writ, on discharge, or on parole, or any inmate assigned to temporary work, shall be placed on the institution count; and it is the guard hall officer's responsibility to see that the record office is notified of all such movements.

17. He must keep an accurate count record in the guard hall of all inmates who are admitted and who are released from the institution proper. He also must keep a count of all visitors (other than those going to the visiting room) who pass through the gate.

18. It shall be his duty to see that the bars on the windows in each office adjoining the guard hall are inspected daily. He also must see that these offices as well as the guard hall itself are kept immaculately clean and in good order.

19. He must not permit female employees to go beyond Gate No. 2 unless they are accompanied by a male employee.

20. The armory officer, after finishing his meal, is to spend thirty minutes outside the armory before returning to his post. During this time he will relieve the Gate No. 2 officer for his meal. The latter, when finished, will relieve the officer at Gate No. 1 before returning to his own assignment.

ARMORY

1. This assignment is the most vulnerable position in the institution. The entire institution would be lost if an inmate or any accomplices should gain possession of the armory. The key to the armory is NEVER to be left in the door. Generally speaking, the officer in charge of this assignment should keep watch on the guard hall, as well as the gates leading from same. Watch should also be kept on persons entering or leaving through the gates adjoining the guard hall, so that no one rushes the officer there. This is especially important for officers assigned on the second and third shifts.

2. Only one gate in the guard hall is to be opened at a time.

During the hours when only a single officer is serving as turnkey for both gates, the key to Gate No. 1 is to remain in the armory when not in use.

3. The officer in charge of the armory must quell disturbances and prevent escapes, using firearms if necessary, but remember that care should be taken, as bullets may ricochet.

4. The armory officer is in charge of all firearms and equipment. The day officer is to repair all equipment, such as guns, lights, keys, and manufacture and re-load shells for practice. If, for any reason, an article cannot be repaired in the armory, a report must be made to the business manager, who will make arrangements for repairs. It is very important that all equipment be kept in first-class condition at all times. A duplicate key for each assignment and each lock in the institution is to be made and kept properly tagged and numbered for emergency use.

5. Only one door leading to the armory should ever be open at one time. This has reference to the door leading into the armory, the cage adjoining the armory, the tunnel and guard hall. The armory door leading to the guard hall should never be opened when an inmate is sufficiently close to rush it and possibly gain entrance. The outer gate to the armory is to be locked behind anyone before the inner door is opened for his entrance.

6. Other than regularly assigned employees, no one is to enter the armory, except on orders of the warden or his authorized assistant. In case of an emergency, only a recognized employee will be admitted to assist the armory officer. Any visitor wishing to be admitted to the armory must be approved by the warden or his assistant, and the approving person must first enter the armory and the door locked behind him. After he has given verbal approval, the officer is to admit the visitor.

7. Inmates are not permitted to communicate directly with the employee on duty in the armory at any time. Any official business should be taken up with the employee at Gate No. 2. Inmates are not permitted to receive anything through the window of the armory.

8. The employee in charge shall wear a pistol at all times

during his tour of duty.

9. The day shift armory officer is to accompany the lieutenant in charge of target practice to each of the towers once every month for the purpose of checking the various munitions used therein.

10. The warden or his assistant may authorize the entrance of an employee to the tunnel with a detail of inmates. Red lights are provided for the safety of personnel in the tunnel, and whenever any person or detail is in the tunnel the lights must be turned on. The employee at the power house must be notified whenever anyone enters the tunnel from the armory, and the employe at the power house shall notify the armory officer when anyone enters the tunnel from that end. If, by any chance, inmates are employed in the tunnel, never enter an assignment you may be relieving unless there is a locked gate between the inmates and yourself. When an employee draws the keys for the tunnel and enters through the power house, the keys are to be returned to the armory while the change of shifts for employees assigned to towers within the yard is being made. The keys are not to be taken inside the wall until the tunnel has been cleared. The dining room tower officers and all yards tower officers are to be notified when inmates are working in the tunnel. Officers at these posts must not leave their respective towers until the inmates are out of the tunnel.

11. The communication system should be checked every two hours during each tour of duty. Any irregularities are to be reported immediately.

12. All armory windows are to be kept in their places at all times. The service window is to be latched, except when in use. All equipment contained in the armory is to be kept out of reach of anyone.

13. A register is provided for employees assigned to the armory, in which each one is required to sign in and out, showing the date and time of reporting. Reliefs assigned to the armory shall register also.

14. A perpetual inventory of all articles in the armory must

be kept, and a check made immediately after reporting for duty. A sufficient number of flashlights must be on hand at all times with at least five (5) dozen reserve batteries. Each time an article is issued a receipt or identification tag must be obtained, and the officer in charge must be positive that an employee is receiving it. Officers on the second and third shifts who issue or exchange articles from the armory are to leave a list giving the necessary information for the day officer.

15. All necessary supplies are to be ordered on quarterly requisitions. Do not attempt to keep records in your head; a book is provided for that purpose, and all necessary notations should be made.

16. The armory officer is to spend 30 minutes outside the armory after returning from meals, during which time the officer at Gate No. 2 shall be relieved, and the regular guard hall officer shall relieve the officer at Gate No. 1 for meals.

17. Generally speaking, all officers assigned to the armory are to see that the floor and furnishings are kept clean, but it will be the duty of the officer on the last shift to mop the floor daily and wash windows when necessary.

18. It will be the duty of the day officer to dispose of any accumulation of junk or contraband upon the assistant warden's approval.

19. INFLAMMABLES ARE NEVER TO BE TAKEN INTO THE ARMORY.

VISITING ROOM

1. Institution officials recognize the fact that the morale of inmates is aided materially by visits from their loved ones. To encourage regular visits, a visiting room has been provided where relatives and friends may meet and talk with the men confined. As a general rule, only relatives are permitted to visit inmates; however, with the permission of the warden, friends also may visit.

2. No ex-convict will be permitted to visit at any time. Should an employee in charge of the visiting room recognize a visitor

Inmates visiting room. Visits are under the direct supervision of two employees. Stateville Branch.

as a former inmate, the visit will be terminated immediately and a report of the incident made to the warden.

3. No person who is under the influence of intoxicants will be permitted to enter the visiting room.

4. Visiting hours are from 8:00 A.M until 4:00 P.M,, Mondays through Saturdays. No visits will be permitted on Sundays or holidays, unless approved by the warden, and then only in unusual cases.

5. The time permitted for each visit will be one (1) hour on weekdays and thirty (30) minutes on Saturdays. Persons coming from a distance of 150 miles or more, and those who do not visit regularly will be permitted to remain one and one-half (1½) hours on weekdays and one (1) hour on Saturdays, unless conditions make it impossible to permit extended visits.

6. The visiting room is to be under constant supervision of an

employee, whose duty it is to make certain that all visits are conducted in a proper manner. Every courtesy is to be extended all visitors and they in turn, will be expected to conduct themselves in an orderly manner and observe all rules and regulations of the institution pertaining to them.

View showing visiting room before 1935. Joliet Branch.

7. At least one of the chairs at either end of the visiting room must be occupied by an employee at all times, to insure proper supervision of all visits.

8. Visitors and inmates are to enter the visiting room through the proper doors.

9. On entering only, visitors and inmates may kiss and shake hands in front of the visiting room desk, occupied by the employee in charge. Following such greeting, the inmate will be required to show his opened hands and mouth to the employee in charge who is to make certain nothing has been passed from the visitor to the inmate.

10. Visitors will sit on one side of the table and inmates on the other side; no personal contact will be permitted across the table. Inmates will be required to keep their hands at least one foot away from the dividing glass during the visit, and visitors will keep their hands and belongings the same distance from the glass. Children accompanying visitors must remain in their seats during the visit.

11. Inmates and visitors shall be passed out of the room without being given an opportunity to contact each other. Their exit should be so regulated as to prevent any attempt to pass notes or contraband to each other.

12. Visitors will not be permitted to bring edibles, drugs, etc., into the visiting room. It should be remembered that there have been cases where friends or relatives attempted to pass contraband articles such as drugs, saws, etc., to an inmate while in the visiting room. Every precaution must be taken by the employee in charge to prevent such violation.

13. In the event a violation should be observed ,the visit is to be terminated immediately, the visitor escorted to a supervising officer of the institution, and a complete report of the incident made to the warden. If the violation is serious, such as attempting to pass any article to an inmate, the visitor will be escorted to the warden's office and a full report made of the incident.

14. Inmates assigned to the administration building should not be permitted to leave the visiting room until the employee assigned to the information desk advises that their visitors have left the building.

15. Inmates who are assigned to the visiting room will not be permitted to contact visitors.

16. Pictures and/or papers which the visitors wish to leave for the inmates, or which the inmates wish to send out with visitors, must be sent to the mail office or the record office where they will be censored and forwarded.

17. Legal documents which have been prepared by an inmate to be taken out by a visitor are to be sent to the record office at least three days prior to the visit. Such papers are not to be taken

to the visiting room. Sometimes attorneys bring legal documents to be handled the day of the visit. In this case it is necessary for the officer in charge to consult the warden, assistant warden, or record clerk, who will grant approval.

18. In order to avoid confusion in the guard hall during the change in shifts of employees or when any large group is passing through the guard hall, visitors will not be permitted to enter or leave the visiting room until approval has been given by the employee in charge of the guard hall.

19. A thorough examination and inspection of all furniture is to be made immediately before and after visiting hours have terminated to see that no contraband has been left. No inmate will be permitted to go on the visitors' side of the room until such inspection has been completed.

20. NO LOITERING BY EMPLOYEES OR VISITORS WILL BE PERMITTED AROUND THIS ASSIGNMENT AT ANY TIME.

HOSPITAL AND OFFICERS' KITCHEN

1. Inmates assigned to the handling of food must be approved by the prison physician. A health certificate signed by the physician must accompany the inmate when he is transferred to any assignment where food is handled.

2. White uniforms must be worn by inmates handling the food; they must wash their hands after using the toilet. Inspection of their hands and fingernails is to be made frequently.

3. The employee is charge is to supervise the preparation and serving of all food, and must see that the dining room and kitchen are kept immaculately clean and in good order at all times.

4. All meals must be prepared in accordance with the menus compiled by the institution steward.

5. Food will not be served except during scheduled meal times.

6. No special diets will be prepared for anyone except by order of one of the prison physicians. Inmates, other than those assigned, are not to receive food from the kitchen without proper authority.

7. Hospital patients will be served their meals under the

supervision of an officer and as the physician prescribes. All inmates employed in the hospital must go to the inmate dining room with the line, regardless of whether they care to eat or not, except those who have authorization to eat in the officers' kitchen.

8. A record of all garbage weights—edible and inedible—is to be kept, and there is to be no food wasted at any time.

9. All cleansing agents, such as lye, sani-flush, etc., must be stored in a locker provided for that purpose and will be used only at the direction of the employee in charge. When it is necessary to use such agents, the officer is to see that they are properly distributed and not placed in foodstuffs.

10. A close check is to be kept of all tools and silver issued, and all must be accounted for.

11. Inmates delivering provisions and supplies to this assignment will be permitted in the officers' kitchen, and in every instance the vehicle carrying the supplies and every package and container on it must be closely inspected and thoroughly searched before it will be permitted to enter or leave.

12. No inmates, except those delivering provisions and supplies and otherwise authorized to be in the hospital and officers' kitchen, will be permitted to enter.

13. Extreme care must be exercised when taking the count of inmates on this assignment.

GENERAL HOSPITAL

1. The hospital, generally, shall be under the supervision of institution physicians and surgeons. Their orders prescribing treatment and medication shall be followed to the letter by all employees and inmates. The maintenance of discipline and enforcement of the rules of the institution, however, shall be the function of employees assigned to duty within the hospital. This rule shall be their first consideration at all times.

2. In many instances specialists or other outside physicians are called in to treat certain cases or to consult with staff physicians concerning treatment or surgery. Orders and recommendations of such consultants, upon approval by staff physicians, shall be

followed. Every courtesy must be extended to consulting physicians by all employees; however, institution rules shall be enforced at all times.

3. The hospital is small and all available space is needed to care for those inmates actually in need of hospitalization. It should be remembered there are inmates who will make an effort to gain admission to the hospital in an attempt to further their

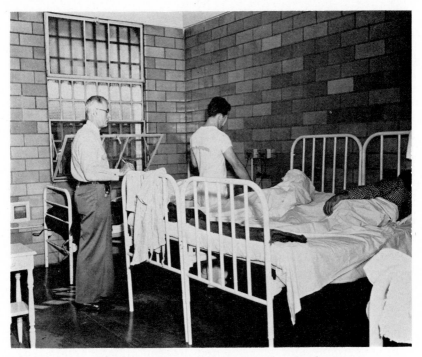

Modern hospital ward. Stateville Branch.

own personal aims, such as to obtain better food, to loaf, or to make an effort to escape. If an inmate known to be an escape risk or suspected of being a dangerous character should be admitted to the hospital, it shall be the duty of the employee to notify the warden or assistant warden immediately so that proper precautions may be taken and necessary supervision maintained.

4. Institution doctors and employees assigned to duty in the hospital unit will be expected to coöperate fully with each other

at all times. The doctors will make certain that employees are fully informed on all pertinent facts concerning each case in order that the employees can properly supervise the work of the nurses.

5. The sick line will be held in the room designated for that purpose by one of the institution physicians at the time specified by the warden. All examinations are to be held in the emergency

View of old hospital at Joliet Branch before remodeling.

dressing room unless prohibited by conditions. Contacts between inmate nurses and inmates in the sick line must be closely supervised.

6. Patients may be admitted to the hospital only after being properly checked in by the employees in charge or at the direction of the attending physician. In an emergency, any superior officer of the institution may direct that a patient be admitted temporarily, pending an examination. In such cases, the diet of the patient will be liquid only until ordered otherwise by the physician.

7. It is the duty of the state to take care of any employee injured in the line of duty. However, it is not the duty of the state to take care of an employee who may become ill or injured while off duty.

8. Upon admission to the hospital of any employee or inmate because of injury or sickness, the employee in charge of the hospital shall make certain that first-aid is administered without delay. He shall make a complete report in writing to the warden and assistant warden, giving all details of the incident, including the statement of the injured person.

9. Whenever an inmate is admitted to the hospital the employee in charge shall notify immediately, in writing, the cellhouse keeper and/or the inmate's assignment, giving the date and time of admission. Similarly, upon the release of any inmate from the hospital, the employee in charge shall notify the cellhouse and/or the assignment of the inmate.

10. The diet of the patient will be indicated on the check-in slip, one copy of which will be sent to the nurses' chart room, another to the hospital kitchen. Special diets will be given only when prescribed by the attending physician. Commissary foodstuffs, unless prescribed, are banned for hospital patients.

11. For no reason whatsoever, personal judgment or disciplinary action notwithstanding, shall any employee or inmate nurse alter the medications or diet prescribed by the attending physician as indicated on the hospital chart. Medications and diets prescribed by the physician are based on his skill, knowledge, and experience; hence, it is mandatory that his orders be executed precisely.

12. Whenever it is necessary for any doctor to be consulted over the outside telephone regarding a patient, the doctor will prescribe to the employee who will, in turn, transmit the doctor's instructions to the inmate nurse. The employee will always be governed by the doctor's recommendations.

13. Blood transfusions will be made only on the direct instruction of the attending physician. Blood will not be taken from any inmate without the approval of an institution physician and it

must be voluntary on the part of the donor.

14. No hospital patient shall be transferred to the detention ward except at the direction of the attending physician; but in the event an inmate or patient becomes violent, he may be transferred to the detention ward by a superior officer, pending an examination by a staff physician.

15. Hospital patients who have been transferred directly from another institution and are to be dismissed as patients will remain in the hospital until a proper transfer from the senior captain is received.

16. An isolation ward has been established for the treatment of those patients suffering from contagious or infectious disease. No one shall be permitted to enter such ward except under the direction of a staff physician. The doors and windows of such ward may be sealed when necessary to prevent the spread of disease. Supervision, however, must be maintained at all times.

17. A complete record of each case, employee or inmate, shall be kept in the hospital office file. This record shall contain detailed information regarding the patient's illness or injury and shall indicate medication prescribed, treatments and surgery. All clerical work of the hospital will be performed in the hospital office by the properly assigned personnel. A complete report of all hospital activities will be submitted daily to the warden or his assistant.

18. After every major surgical operation a report of same will be made to the record clerk who will, in turn, notify the next of kin regarding the operation. If any patient is seriously ill, a telegram is to be sent to the next of kin, using the form provided. A report of any surgery or serious illness will also be made to the assistant warden, senior captain and chaplain of the inmate's particiular faith.

19. When surgery is performed and results in scars of any description, or where plastic surgery alters an inmate's features in any way or leaves a scar of any description, the bureau of identification shall be furnished with a complete report of the case so that proper notations may be made on the records.

20. Every consideration will be given inmates in need of medical attention, but this should not be taken advantage of by inmates.

21. Inmates assigned to the 24-hour or outside detail should, whenever possible, be examined on a particular day specified by the warden.

22. Certain patients who are ambulatory, but of necessity hospitalized, may be given yard privileges at the direction of the attending physician and senior captain.

23. Hospital patients shall be under the constant supervision of an employee.

24. Inmate nurses must never be permitted to prescribe medication or perform any sort of operation, regardless of how minor it may be.

25. The employee in charge of the hospital shall generally supervise traffic throughout his assignment. Such traffic will be kept at a minimum, and assigned inmates will be permitted to enter rooms or wards only in performance of their duties.

26. No one, inmate or employee, will be permitted to enter the hospital without proper authority.

27. The employee in charge of the hospital unit must immediately familiarize himself with all keys used on his assignment, the locations of locks and light switches, and all other items pertinent to the assignment.

28. He shall maintain an accurate count of all tools, instruments, etc., used throughout the assignment.

29. At frequent intervals throughout the day inspections will be made of each bed, ward, corridor, bathroom, department and office.

30. Every part of the hospital must be immaculately clean at all times, beds properly made, etc.

31. Inmates assigned to one floor of the hospital will not be permitted to loiter or congregate on any other floor, nor will inmates not assigned to the hospital unit be permitted to enter the assignment except on sick call.

32. All laundry for the hospital (incoming and outgoing) will be inspected by the employee in charge.

33. The employee in charge shall make daily inspections of all outside walls, windows, and doors to make certain that no attempt is being made to escape. At no time shall any article of furniture such as a chest of drawers, a bed, a cabinet, etc., be placed in any position which obscures sight of the outside prison wall.

34. During the absence of the prison physician the employee in charge shall see that his orders are carried out so far as is possible; however, do not prescribe, or permit an inmate nurse to prescribe without consulting the prison physician. Make certain the rules covering the prison physician, drug and compounding room, and narcotics are carried out to the letter.

HOSPITAL REGULATIONS AFFECTING EMPLOYEES

1. Employees not on duty in the hospital shall not request medication or supplies from the inmates. All such requests will be made to the prison physician or the pharmacist (if the prison physician is not in the institution).

2. Employees must not enter the dispensary for the purpose of receiving non-emergency treatment, such as diathermy, foot clinic care, etc., without first contacting the employee in charge of the hospital unit. The man in charge of an assignment shall be advised of any activity within his department, regardless of its importance.

3. Employees under the care of physicians outside the institution shall not make requests for x-rays, prescriptions, or laboratory orders with the institution medical department.

4. Indicated treatment and examination will be instituted promptly by the prison physicians where illness or accidental injury occurs in the line of duty. A report in detail shall be sent to the warden.

5. All records concerning the medical history of employees and inmates must be kept in the hospital record office, except current charts of hospital patients. No employee other than the

resident prison physicians shall have access to these medical records, except in extreme emergency and then only through the employee in charge; nor shall any information concerning same be divulged except in the line of duty.

DENTAL OFFICE

1. Unless there is an emergency, inmates in need of dental work shall make their request to the dentist in the daily sick line.

2. After examination, if the inmate is in need of fillings or extractions, his number will be placed on the calendar and taken in turn until his work is completed.

3. If the inmate needs bridge work, inlays, crowns, full or partial dentures, his name will be placed on a list and called for this work when his name is reached. An inmate may be placed ahead on the list for the following reasons:

    a. If he is about to be discharged or paroled from the institution.

    b. By order of the prison physicians to safeguard his health.

    c. When it is an imate's desire to pay for work which requires material not furnished by the institution. The dentist is to have the inmate sign a money transfer for only the actual cost of the work done on the outside.

4. Where it is impossible to complete work of an unusual nature in our dental office and laboratory, the dentist is to consult the warden for authority to have the work done in an outside dental laboratory.

5. Tickets are issued to indicate the time the inmate is to appear at the dental office. Employees should have inmates report as close to scheduled time as possible.

6. A day specified by the warden will be set aside to take care of inmates on the farm and outside detail except, of course, in the event of an emergency.

7. Diet cards are issued to inmates when it is impossible for them to digest their food properly. These cards may cover a period of 7 to 30 days. They may be renewed if necessary.

8. All gold removed from an inmate's mouth is to be placed

in his personal property jacket.

9. There will be absolutely no dental services for employees at any time.

10. Haphazard work will not be tolerated.

11. Supplies must never be wasted.

12. The dentist is the supervisor and instructor of the dental laboratory and it is under his direct supervision. He is to request the number of inmates needed as aides and supervise their training as dental technicians.

PRISON PHYSICIANS

The institution is staffed with qualified resident physicians, as well as part time physicians. In addition to this group, we call upon specialists in the various fields of medicine from time to time when, in the opinion of the prison physicians, they are needed.

The general duties of the prison physicians are as follows:

1. *Sick Line:*

   a. Conduct sick line and prescribe necessary medical treatment. An inmate must never be permitted to diagnose a case or prescribe treatment for anyone. Sick line procedure consists of physical examinations of inmates, prescribing medications as indicated; referral of cases to the dentist; eye, ear, nose and throat doctor; foot clinic; dressing room; diathermy; x-ray and pathological laboratory; and mental health department, as the symptoms indicate.

   b. Extreme care should be taken when prescribing medication. Not more than two or three items should be deemed necessary at one time since sick line is held daily.

   c. Medication containing a sedative should be delivered to the cellhouse keeper with instructions regarding the administering of it. Such medicine must never be given directly to inmates.

   d. All prescriptions should bear the inmate's name and number on the container in which it is placed.

   e. Sick line for inmates on the farm and farm detail will be held at a time specified by the warden.

f. Follow up cases requiring continued treatment or physiological relief of pathology.

g. Hospitalize inmates for observation and treatment if results of the examination so indicate.

h. Daily visits to inmates confined in isolation and segregation, and order their removal if their physical condition becomes impaired or if they are in need of medical care.

2. *Surgery:*

a. Perform surgery and assist all institution or visiting surgeons during operations.

b. Serve as anesthetist when required.

3. *Hospital:*

a. Medical service for hospitalized inmates.

b. Train inmates as nurses.

c. Advise the warden of the progress of seriously ill patients.

d. Quarantine any resident employee or inmate who has a contagious or infectious disease.

e. Daily visits to all patients in the general hospital and detention ward.

f. Issue required certificates in the event of a natural death by known causes.

g. Make certain that absolute sanitary conditions exist in and around the hospital, the kitchens, store, etc.

h. Report to the senior captain any inmate who violates a rule of the hospital or institution.

4. *Public Health:*

a. Inspect all assignments where food is handled, including kitchens, dining rooms, storerooms, dairy, etc. Make reports to the warden on anything that is unusual or not up to health standards.

b. Follow-up venereal disease control programs.

c. Screen inmates who are being considered for assignments where food is handled.

d. Immunization treatment for inmates according to public health regulations.

e. Physical examination of employee-applicants. Immunization treatment, and annual booster inoculations.

f. Coöperate with State Health Department and report anything of an unusual nature.

5. *Administrative:*

a. Written reports to the warden on cases where a special physical examination has been requested.

b. Make examinations and submit reports, when requested by the parole authorities.

6. *General:*

a. Administer treatment and prescribe medication for any employee injured on institution property, and perform surgery if necessary.

b. Make up, verify, and authorize all sedative and narcotic medications as directed by law. Never permit an inmate to handle narcotics at any time.

c. Generally supervise the hospital, and recommend necessary supplies, medications, and equipment.

d. Subject to 24-hour call.

7. *Diagnostic Depot:*

a. Complete physical examination, including blood and urine, of all newly admitted inmates.

b. Screen all incoming inmates for health class which governs work assignments as follows:

Class A—Excellent	(Free from physical handicaps.)	
" B—Good	(Able to do moderate work.)	
" C—Fair	(Able to do light work only.)	
" D—Poor	(Not able to work at all.)	

c. Screen all newly admitted inmates with a view to recommending treatment or surgery which will be helpful to them in serving their time and assisting in eventual rehabilitation.

d. Transfer inmates in need of treatment to the hospital.

DRUG AND COMPOUNDING ROOM

1. The pharmacist is in charge of the drug and compounding room, and of all drugs, medical, dental, and x-ray supplies received at the institution, as well as the dispensing of same.

2. He personally must attend to all compounding, and supervise milk tests and bacteria counts. The laboratory will be under his supervision.

3. He will prepare quarterly requisitions for supplies. Upon the receipt of any items a check must be made against the proper quarterly requisition or O.F.D., and the receiving ticket listing these items is to be made in triplicate, two copies of which are to be sent to the general storekeeper, and one copy retained for the pharmacist's file.

4. A perpetual inventory must be kept in balance with the stock and a record kept of all drugs received and dispensed.

5. All drugs and poisons are to be kept locked in the drug and compounding room. Insecticides stored in the vault at the greenhouse must be checked at intervals.

6. Drugs will be dispensed as needed upon the presentation of a requisition properly signed by a physician; they are to be issued only under the close supervision of an employee.

7. Inmates, except those assigned, are not permitted in the drug or compounding room. They must be kept under close supervision by the employee in charge. Each inmate must be searched thoroughly each time he leaves the room.

8. At regular intervals, phenobarbital tablets and sodium dilantin capsules prescribed by the physician for patients are to be put in suitable containers properly labeled with the date, the inmate's name and number, and the physician's instructions for the dispensing of same. These containers are to be sent to the employee in charge of the cellhouse who will sign for them in the book presented to him by the employee making delivery. The officer making the delivery is to witness the signature of each cellhouse officer in accordance with the instructions on the label. provided. The medicine shall be dispensed to the inmate by the cellhouse officer in accordance with the instruction on the label.

9. The mesh door of the compounding room shall be kept locked at all times. When the pharmacist leaves this room, he shall lock the main door, always checking to be sure he has locked it.

10. Tools which are kept in the compounding and dispensing rooms are to be checked, and a report sent to the assistant warden and the master mechanic at specified times.

NARCOTICS

1. The narcotic reserve stock is to be kept in a strong box especially provided for same. Any withdrawal from the stock must be by requisition which is to be signed by the prescribing physician. A continuous inventory must be kept in a ledger which is to remain in the box. Entries should show the dates on which withdrawals are made or stock added.

2. When narcotics are ordered, instructions should be given to the supplier to address them to the warden. When they are received at the institution they are to be delivered to the warden or his authorized assistant, who will notify the pharmacist. They are never to be delivered to the general store.

3. Never permit an inmate to have possession of any narcotics.

4. Narcotics are not to be administered to an inmate unless prescribed by a physician.

5. When a narcotic is to be administered to a patient, the employee in charge is to dissolve the tablet in a spoon, syphon it into a syringe, and then carry the syringe to the patient to whom the nurse is to administer the shot. The nurse must be watched very closely to make certain two syringes are not used or a switch made or the patient in need of the shot is given water or some other fluid instead of the narcotic.

6. The amount of narcotics which the officer in charge of the hospital is permitted to have on hand at all times is limited to the following quantities:

10 tablets ¼ gr.H. T. Morphine
"　　"　　¼ gr. H. T. Codeine
"　　"　　½ gr. T. T. Codeine
"　　"　　⅙ gr. and ⅛ gr. H. T. Morphine
　　　　　(or equivalent)

POISONS

1. It must be remembered there are inmates in the institution

who would not hesitate to put poison in food or water, thus possibly causing the death of a large number of persons. Drugs containing poison, prescribed by the physician, are to be administered only under close supervision of the physician or an employee. Remember that it is possible for an inmate to hold a tablet under his tongue and remove it when supervision ceases. Thus over a period of time a sufficiently large quantity could be accumulated by an inmate to poison people or use it in some way to further his own interests.

2. A monthly inventory is to be sent to the pharmacist before the 5th of each month by department officers, listing names of all poisonous chemicals, liquids or compounds on hand, and their location.

DEATH

1. In the event of a death of an employee or inmate, whether it be in the hospital or elsewhere in the institution, the prison physician shall be notifiied so that he may examine the body and sign the death certificate, if he can properly do so. The supervising officer on duty should be nofified immediately of a death and after proper examination and fingerprints have been taken, the body shall be removed from the place of death to a room provided for that purpose until the undertaker receives the body and signs receipt for same. It is to be remembered, however, that in case of sudden or unusual death a coroner's inquest will be held and the body is not to be removed until permission is given by the coroner.

2. The next of kin is to be notified by wire regarding the death of an inmate, advising the name of the undertaker to whom the body is released.

3. If death occurs as a result of an accident or violence, a complete report should be made to the warden. Anyone who may have been a witness to the death or who has any knowledge of it, should be interviewed and statements taken. If inmates are involved, they are to be separated during the interrogation so there will be no possible chance of fixing a story.

DETENTION HOSPITAL

1. Detention hospital was set up for the purpose of taking care of inmates who become mentally disturbed during their stay in prison. Tact, firmness and good judgment are essential on this assignment, and close supervision must be maintained over the inmate-patients constantly.

2. At the time an inmate-patient is admitted to detention hospital a report covering his actions and apparent condition should be made by the officer most familiar with the situation. A copy of this report should be forwarded to the psychiatrists, senior captain, warden, and assistant warden.

3. Unless permission is granted by the warden or his authorized assistant, patients will not be permitted to leave the ward and they are never to be permitted out of their cells after the evening count without such permission. Inmate nurses will be locked in their cells at 7:00 P.M. when not on duty. Also, inmates not assigned to detention hospital will not be permitted to enter the ward; however, when it is necessary for inmates to enter or leave this assignment they are to be searched thoroughly.

4. Inmates regularly assigned to detention hospital are to have their regular recreation period, and a plan worked out so there is an inmate nurse on duty at all times.

5. All precautions must be taken to prevent attempted suicide by inmates or attempts to harm themselves or others.

6. If an inmate becomes physically ill, the prison physician is to be notified at once and his instructions followed. All instructions regarding treatment and medication will be made in writing by the physician or psychiatrist to the employee in charge of the hospital. This includes drugs and narcotics. A surplus quantity of these items is never to be kept in the ward at any time. The administration of medication and treatment will be carried out under the close supervision of the employee in charge of the assignment.

7. A report should be submitted to the senior captain, psychiatrist, record office, and warden's office whenever an inmate is received or released from detention hospital.

8. All keys must be under the supervision of the employee in charge at all times; inmates NEVER are to be given keys.

9. Instruments, tools, ropes, in fact anything which might be used in an escape or possible suicide attempt, will be kept out of the hands of inmate patients. Any article which might be used as a weapon must be kept under lock and key, and the employee in charge is to keep an accurate count of all tools and instruments at all times.

10. Excess food is not to be kept in detention hospital but is to be returned to the kitchen from which it came, after completion of the meal.

11. Complete records must be kept on all patients covering all treatments and doctors' orders.

12. Medication prescribed by the psychiatrist will be sent to the prison physician for his information and approval.

13. When patients are released from detention hospital all medication is to be returned to the pharmacist. This also shall be done if medications are changed.

OFFICERS' BARBER SHOP

The officers' barber shop has been established as a privilege. The fee charged for services is set by the warden to cover the necessary expenditures for equipment, supplies, etc. Employees are not to take advantage of inmates assigned to the barber shop, and the following rules and regulations must be obeyed or the privilege will be revoked:

1. Under no circumstances will any service be given unless the employee is in possession of a barber card, which must be punched for the correct amount after the work has been completed.

2. Extra service is not to be expected or given.

3. Employees are to take their turn as vacancies occur in the chairs.

4. Under no circumstances will work be done for any employee while on duty.

5. Only tonics and other barber supplies furnished by the institution are to be taken to the barber shop.

BUREAU OF IDENTIFICATION

1. It is the duty of the employee in charge of the institutions' bureau of identification to photograph all newly admitted inmates at the diagnostic depot before their hair is cut. For sanitary reasons, after the picture is taken, the inmate's hair is entirely removed; then he is stripped and bathed, at which time physical scars and deformities are to be noted. All surgical and bullet scars, trunk line scars of dope addicts, amputations, etc., are to be noted on the records.

2. The inmate is then fingerprinted and copies of the prints sent to the Federal Bureau of Investigation in Washington, the Bureau of Identification in Springfield, and the Chicago Police Department. Two cards remain in the prison files; one, stamped "MASTER," is classified and placed in the active permanent file of the institution's bureau.

3. This card is referred to from time to time and always must be carefully compared when an inmate is going out on a writ or being released by parole or discharge—to make certain the inmate being released is the same one as described on the Master card—and to certify all outgoing inmates to the record office. Inmates are then photographed in their civilian clothes and the picture becomes known as the "dress-out" picture.

4. Fingerprint cards and film negatives must be kept in the vault until ready to be processed. The negatives are developed and printed in the bureau of identification office as soon as possible. When fingerprint cards are typed, they must be mailed to the bureaus referred to above in Paragraph 2 from where transcript sheets are returned showing the entire criminal history of the subject. Fingerprint cards retained by the bureaus are kept in the active file forever. When the transcript sheets are received they must be checked carefully to ascertain if inmates are wanted by other authorities. The constant check of reports from the various fingerprint departments may uncover escapees or parole violators.

5. The employee in charge of the bureau of identification must make periodic checks to ascertain if the original picture of

the inmate is still a good likeness. New pictures often are neces-sary when an inmate has been incarcerated over a period of years.

6. The hospital shall notify the employee in charge of the bureau of identification when surgery is to be performed, espe-cially when fingers are to be amputated, which would change rec-ords of the police and law enforcement agencies to be checked.

7. It is most important that new pictures be taken after plastic surgery alters the facial features of inmates.

8. All employees are to be photographed and fingerprinted and their prints mailed to the various bureaus to be checked for criminal records, etc.

9. The employee in charge of the bureau is responsible for the safekeeping of all fingerprint cards, which never are to be in the possession of an inmate. This department is a safeguard for the entire institution, insofar as identification is concerned. The Master fingerprint cards and original photographs are never to be removed from the files.

10. It is important that bureau of identification employees study and becomes familiar with all new phases of fingerprint work and photography, including color film and latent print work. We find the extreme identification in all its phases is akin to black magic. The secrets involved can only be unfolded in their true light in the hands of experienced operators.

11. Photographing institutional buildings and activities is also a duty.

12. All deceased prisoners are fingerprinted before their bodies are removed from the institution.

GATE NO. 3 ADMINISTRATION BUILDING TO YARD

1. Only inmates with proper authority will be permitted to pass through this gate.

2. Each inmate must have in his possession either a call ticket which has been properly signed by the employee in charge of the department sending for him and stamped with the signa-ture of the senior captain, or a work ticket properly made out and signed. This does not apply to an inmate, or inmates, being

escorted by an officer to the hospital for treatment, or to some other destination.

3. Reports should be made on inmates who do not have an authorized call ticket or work ticket, the inmates detained, and a superior officer called to handle the situation.

4. When call tickets are sent out by the psychiatrist, the sociologist, the parole officer, or the parole board, not more than ten inmates should be waiting at any one time, and those waiting must be from the same cellhouse.

5. Do not keep any of the above referred to officials waiting to see inmates summoned by them. It should be so arranged that the tickets are delivered in such a manner as to insure there will be a group on hand at all times until each inmate sent for has been interviewed.

6. Inmates who are waiting for visits, to see employees or members of the professional staff of the institution, are not permitted to smoke.

7. The employee in charge of this gate is to make certain the inmates go only to the place designated on the ticket.

8. Loitering or congregating around this gate will not be permitted.

9. Inmates must be searched thoroughly upon entering or leaving this gate, and those waiting to be searched and passed through must maintain absolute silence. They must also stand at attention when visitors, the warden, the assistant warden, captains, or lieutenant pass.

10. Before morning check count and after evening check count, any inmate passing through this gate must be in the custody of an officer and an accurate count must be kept by the employee in charge of this assignment.

11. All packages, bundles, or boxes being taken through this gate must be inspected carefully and searched, unless they are accompanied by an officer who will give the necessary approval for the package, etc.

12. All officers must be in regulation uniform before they

are to be permitted to go through this gate into the yard.

13. Employees who work in civilian clothes must be known by the employee on this assignment before they are to be permitted through the gate, since it is possible for an inmate to secure civilian clothes and attempt an escape.

14. If an officer appears at this gate with anyone who is not known to the employee in charge, the officer should be at least twenty steps ahead of the visitor, or visitors, and he should be admitted first in order to make certain the people accompanying him are legitimate.

15. A count of all visitors who enter the yard through this gate must be kept. Under no circumstances will a visitor be permitted to pass in or out of this gate unless accompanied by an employee of the institution. A count of all visitors who have entered the yard must be made when they return, and the count must check.

16. Every male person not employed in the institution should be searched thoroughly before he is permitted to pass in or out of this gate. It is essential that this be done, for a visitor might attempt to bring contraband in or to take something out for an inmate.

17. The employee in charge of this gate must not leave it unlocked at any time.

18. All inmates in line passing through this gate must be counted by the employee in charge of the gate, as well as by the officer in charge of the line. Before the line is permitted to proceed to its destination, the count will be compared and any inaccuracy corrected.

19. The employee in charge of the gate will assist the officer in charge of a line of inmates passing through to search thoroughly each inmate in the line.

CHAPEL

1. The chapel is a house of worship, where different religious services are conducted each week. Every encouragement should be given to inmates to attend the service of their choice.

Chapel. Protestant Service, Rev. Sorensen. Stateville Branch.

2. It always must be remembered that some inmates may attend services for purposes other than worship, purposes that may cause trouble. With this in mind, great care should be taken to prevent improper contacts by inmates, especially those who are either escape or sex problems.

3. Inmates who desire to attend a religious service will be issued a church card for the denomination they specify. No inmate will be permitted to have cards, simultaneously, for more than one denomination.

4. It will be the duty of all employees to see that no inmate uses a card issued to another. Church cards are not transferable. If an inmate no longer wants his church card, he must surrender it to his officer, who will return it to the chapel with a proper notation.

5. Church lines will assemble on the flag of each cellhouse and each inmate will hold his church card where it will be plainly

visible. The officer in charge of the cellhouse will then pass along
the line, inspecting it to see that each inmate in the line has his

Chapel, Catholic Service, Father Brinkman. Stateville Branch.

church card. Then, and only then, will the cellhouse officer give
the signal for the line to leave. If an inmate appears in the line
without a church card and claims that he has lost it, he should be
permitted to attend the services if, in the judgment of the employee, the inmate is sincere. However, no inmate should be
permitted to use this excuse indefinitely; he can obtain another
card by making the proper request to his chaplain.

6. When the line of inmates reaches the chapel, each one
will surrender his card when passing through the doorway.
Later, each card will be returned to each inmate.

7. Employees assigned to escort lines to the chapel for
services are responsible for the inmates in the line. These inmates
must be returned to their respective assignments immediately

View showing old Chapel. Joliet Branch.

after the services. To attain this end, all chaplains should arrange to have regular interview days so that it will not be necessary to detain inmates after the services are over, unless there should be an emergency.

8. Employees who escort lines to the chapel may remain in the rear if they do not desire to participate in the services. They must, however, place themselves in a position where they can supervise the inmates in their custody, so that no inmate will be unobserved and thereby able to make contacts or to act in any other improper manner.

9. All inmates are to remove their caps immediately upon entering the chapel. However, inmates attending Jewish services are required to keep their caps on while in the chapel.

10. There will be no smoking either by employees or inmates during religious services.

11. Inmates called to the chapel on a ticket for interviews

will not be permitted to smoke.

12. Inmates assigned to work in the chapel will be given specific instructions regarding their smoking.

13. No inmates are permitted in the chapel except those who are regularly assigned and those on call tickets. THIS RULE MUST BE ENFORCED AT ALL TIMES.

14. Inmates assigned to work in the chapel should be searched upon entering and leaving. If at all possible, inmates called to the chapel on tickets are to be searched thoroughly upon entering and leaving. In any event, spot searches are to be made daily.

15. Inmates called to the chapel on tickets are to be seated in the space allotted for each cellhouse. Inmates from one cellhouse are not to mingle with those from another cellhouse.

16. Inmates will not be permitted on the stage when visitors are present, except those needed to operate the lights, curtains, etc.

17. Under no circumstance will inmates be permitted to associate with or contact visitors who attend religious services, evening motion picture shows, or visitors being conducted on tours.

18. The chaplains of the various denominations are to use good judgment and never at any time call a large number of inmates to the chapel on tickets, especially if it should be a day when specific religious services are scheduled. For instance, if the Catholic Chaplain has a specified day for hearing confessions, other chaplains should hold their tickets to a minimum. This same procedure should be followed when special services are being held by one of the other chaplains. The chaplains are to personally sign their own call tickets. All tickets must be originated by them, and care should be taken to see that inmates' friends or accomplices are not called for the purpose of contacting each other.

19. Every chaplain will be assigned a sufficient number of inmates to do the work required and these inmates will work on that particular assignment only. However, if the employee in charge deems it necessary, inmates may be borrowed for other

work if it will not cause any difficulty for the chaplain to whom they are formally assigned.

20. In general, the offices of the chaplains are reserved for their use. While the employees assigned to the chapel are to be the supervisors of the inmates, they are not to make a habit of placing themselves in a position where they may interfere with the chaplains in the giving of instructions or religious advice to inmates. The employee in charge of the chapel may, at any time he deems it necessary for institutional safety, enter any office in the chapel. However, he must use good judgment at all times.

21. In addition to being a house of worship, the chapel is also a recreational center, with motion pictures provided periodically for the inmates.

22. The lines of inmates coming from the cellhouses to the chapel to attend motion pictures are to be seated as directed by the lieutenant in charge, and each officer is to be seated on the aisle with his own line.

23. It will be the officer's duty to supervise his line and prevent loud talking, profanity, "horse-play," or any exchange of commissary merchandise, contraband, etc., between the inmates.

24. It must be remembered by all employees that the chapel is darkened during a motion picture show, that certain inmates are sex problems and might attempt to take advantage of the situation to commit acts of degeneracy, crime vs. nature, etc. Therefore, every employee during the showing of a motion picture must be alert at all times, must not become absorbed in the picture, and must constantly keep the inmates in his section under observation. The foregoing rule is very important. The employee must remember they are not at the motion picture show for their own entertainment; they are to supervise the inmates in their custody.

25. Ordinary applause by the inmates is always welcome and should be encouraged. However, there will be no loud whispering, stamping of feet, etc.

26. There will be no smoking either by employees or inmates during a motion picture show.

27. If an inmate leaves the chapel during a motion picture in order to go to the toilet, his name, number and cellhouse must be taken by the employee in charge of the chapel and sent to the senior captain's office, and the inmate returned to his cellhouse immediately.

28. Under no circumstance will anyone, other than those persons assigned, be permitted on the stage or in the motion picture projection booth. Only the inmates who have been approved by the officer in charge of inmate assignments as accompanists for religious services and motion picture shows are permitted to use the organ.

29. If an inmate's work requires him to have tools in his possession, they are to be itemized on a work order and a check is to be made to see that they are returned.

30. The employee in charge of the chapel will make periodic daily inspection tours but will not do so at the same time each day. He must inspect each room carefully, especially the toilets. All rooms, toilets, etc., must be kept clean at all times.

31. The doors of the fan room, electric vault, tunnel, projection booth, chaplains' offices, and all outside doors are to be locked, except when actually in use. The employee in charge of the chapel will check the doors before he leaves.

32. There are many groups of men and women participating regularly in the religious services, as well as visitors passing through the chapel frequently. Under no circumstances should profane language by the inmates be permitted.

33. The officer in charge should see that none of the radios in the various departments of the chapel are allowed to disturb a religious service. Nor should there be any boisterous conduct or loud talking in the lobby of the chapel while such services are in session.

34. Inmates assigned to the chapel are not permitted off their immediate assignments, except in the performance of their duties.

CHAPLAINS

1. Chaplains are assigned to the institution to minister to

the spiritual needs of the men. It is the thought of the administration that rehabilitation is primarily a spiritual problem. It must be the desire and effort of the chaplains to make themselves as completely available for service as possible. They are to hold interviews, at which time counsel is offered concerning the inmates' spiritual problems. Often many special problems may be uncovered by the interviews thus held.

2. Church cards will be issued by the chaplains entitling men to attend their services. These cards are a means for the chaplain to check the attendance, and to call and encourage those who do not come.

3. Inmates are not permitted to have more than one church card, as there is reason to suspect that a man holding a number of such cards is doing so for purposes other than to attend services.

4. If a man wishes to attend a church service of his faith and has no church card, the cellhouse keeper shall pass him through and send his name and number to the respective chaplain. Sometime in transfer or through carelessness a church card may be lost. This is not to be considered sufficient reason to bar a man from church attendance.

5. Cards are unnecessary on Christmas, Easter, Mother's Day, or any special occasion which may be requested by the Chaplain.

6. All records of the chaplains shall be considered confidential. The position of the chaplain as inmate counsellor of the men should not be jeopardized by arousing suspicion in the inmates that their records are subject to scrutiny.

7. Full time chaplains shall visit the various parts of the institution periodically including isolation and segregation. Special emphasis shall be placed on the hospitals.

8. Chaplains shall refer problems which they cannot handle personally to the various officers or agencies, inside and outside the institution, equipped to handle them. Frequently problems are presented which involve features that can be handled only by the warden, the captain, the doctor, the veteran adminis-

trator, or by social agencies, etc. A full referral report by the chaplain will save time and trouble for all involved.

9. When necessary or expedient, the chaplain shall contact the relatives of an inmate, but a practice should not be made of this. It is necessary, especially in the case of new inmates, to explain the prison set-up to their relatives and stress the morale problems which are present in a penitentiary. Often such matters are more favorably received by outsiders when they are explained by a chaplain. Sometimes it is of great value to the chaplain in attempting to help an inmate if he has information regarding the man direct from his relatives.

10. Correspondence between chaplains and relatives of inmates should be cleared through the warden's office. Most often chaplains will be confronted with problems presented by inmates or relatives which should be brought to the attention of the warden for disposition.

11. Chaplains are welcome to attend meetings of the classification and pre-parole progress boards of the institution. It is felt that the specialized position of the chaplain in the institution makes him particularly suited for service in the initial consideration of an inmate's program and evaluation of his success in following that program while in the institution.

CAPTAINS IN CHARGE OF INMATE ASSIGNMENTS

Offices of captains in charge of assignments and discipline are located in the Isolation and Segregation building. They are overall supervisors of all activities in the building.

1. The security of the institution being of major importance, the assignment of inmates to various departments must be made with that security in mind. It must be remembered that some inmates are more dangerous than others and security should be first and foremost watchword at all times.

2. The captain in charge of inmate assignments will instruct all incoming inmates as to the rules governing them. They will be given a good general outline of what is expected of them and of the deportment they will be required to maintain. Each

one is furnished with an inmate rule book at the diagnostic depot.

3. Each incoming inmate will be interviewed by the captain in charge of inmate assignments to determine where he is best fitted to work, and he will be assigned accordingly.

4. The captain in charge of inmate assignments must consult medical, psychiatric, and classification reports as to inmate placement and will be guided by them if possible.

5. Whenever possible, inmates should be given the opportunity to choose their assignments so they may learn a trade that will be beneficial to them upon release. We are responsible for rehabilitating men who have been committed here and it is our duty to help them in this respect, providing their choice does not interfere with the security of the institution and the welfare of other inmates. Always be guided where possible by aptitude test classification report made by professional staff at the diagnostic depot.

6. Care must be exercised in the placement of inmates. It sometimes happens that an inmate has testified against his associates in the crime who may be "out to get him." In such cases, the inmate is to be assigned to a department where his associates will never come in contact with him.

7. In assigning inmates to jobs, consideration should be given to merit and seniority. Inmates should be obliged to work their way to better assignments. Good conduct, general attitude, etc., are factors that should be taken into consideration.

8. Every assignment is to have a full complement of inmates at all times. When vacancies exist or occur they are to be filled immediately.

9. Inmates with little or no education must be assigned to the grade school.

10. All inmates with venereal diseases are to be assigned to a single division known as the "shot line," and this assignment is to be in one cellhouse where the inmates may be given work to do and, at the same time, be given treatment by the prison physocian. They are to eat at a designated place in the dining room and use only the utensils provided for their division. Under no

circumstance will these utensils be used to serve food to other inmates. Their clothing and bedclothes shall be laundered separately, as directed by the warden. No transfers are to be made from this division without a "cured" or "non-infectious" report signed by the prison physician.

11. Each inmate who requests a transfer to another assignment must be interviewed. If, in the judgment of the captain in charge of inmate assignments, the transfer should be made, he will so order it.

12. An accurate list of all inmates and warrants filed against them is to be kept in the office of the captain in charge of inmate assignments, and a notation of the existing warrant is to be placed on each picture card. Before any assignment is made, this list is to be consulted and inmates whose names appear on this list are not to be assigned to positions that require them to be out of their cells after evening count, unless permission of the warden has been secured.

13. All inmates must be celled according to their work assignment, in consecutive cells in the cellhouse, unless an exemption has been granted by the warden or his authorized assistant.

14. The captains in charge of inmate assignments will interview those inmates who may be adjudged worthy of placement in trusted positions inside and outside the wall. If, after questioning, an inmate is found to be worthy of such an assignment, all available information concerning him, such as the crime for which he is committed, his sentence, age, mail, visits, etc., is to be incorporated into a report. This report is to be forwarded to the record office, where it will be checked with the information found in his jacket. The record clerk will make pertinent notations on the report, showing warrants or detainers, prior escapes, whether the inmate's military record, if any, shows irregularities, etc. The report will then be submitted to the assistant warden, who will then interview the inmate, check his record, and indicate either his approval or disapproval of the proposed assignment. The report will then be submitted to the warden for final approval or disapproval.

15. Inmates who are or have been drug addicts; who have warrants or detainers on file; who have been convicted at any time of arson, kidnaping, extortion, or a sex crime of any kind; who have escaped or have AWOL records, are not to be given consideration for any position outside the wall.

16. All special and/or night details are to be handled in the manner set forth in the two preceding paragraphs.

17. The captain in charge of assignments will provide the captain of guards, fire chief, and all night supervising officers with the names and numbers of inmates who have been approved to move inside or outside the wall on emergency work assignments, such as a fire or disaster.

18. All inmates detailed to work before or after regular hours are to have an order signed by their respective department heads and by the captain in charge of inmate assignments. Such orders are to be effective for one month only and may be renewed, if necessary.

19. The night lieutenant must be provided with a list of inmates available for night details.

20. Close supervision must be kept over files and records to make sure they are accurate and that the assignment of each inmate is known at all times. These files and records are confidential. No employee other than the one in charge of inmate assignments is authorized to refer to them.

21. The office of the captains in charge of inmate assignments is to be locked at the end of each day.

22. The captains in charge of assignments and discipline should pass out the farm detail each morning as well as any other inmate working outside the wall who goes out through the sally port. The identity of each inmate is to be carefully examined to make certain that every inmate passing through the gate actually has been assigned to the farm detail or outside the wall.

23. The captains in charge of inmate assignments are to transfer to the detention hospital at once any inmate who appears to be mentally unbalanced and a complete report is to be sub-

mitted to the psychiatrist, with copies to the warden and the assistant warden.

24. This employee also is to notify the cellhouse keepers of inmates who are known as escape risks or degenerates, and, if for any reason an inmate must be watched carefully, he is to submit a detailed report to the cellhouse keeper. The cellhouse keeper will relay such information to the relief officer and the officer in charge of the inmate's assignment, so that all persons concerned will have full knowledge of his character, potentialities, etc.

25. If, at any time, an inmate receives a death message or bad news of any kind, as a denial of pardon or parole, the captain in charge of inmate assignments is to inform the inmate accordingly and provide him with a special letter permit, if necessary. Inmates assigned outside the wall, or in trusted positions, are to be removed from their assignments if they receive news of this kind. It is to be remembered that any man may become mentally upset and attempt to escape. Such inmates assigned outside the wall are not to be returned there until approved by the warden.

DISCIPLINARIAN

1. Since all activities of an institution revolve around its standard of discipline, it is imperative that good conduct be maintained at all times. This can be accomplished with a minimum of punishment, consistent of course with established policies. Good counsel, sometimes, can accomplish more with an unruly inmate than isolation punishment.

2. The disciplinarian shall furnish the officer in charge of isolation with any pertinent information that may be helpful in supervising an inmate during his stay in isolation, such as potential suicide, escape risk, homosexual, etc.

3. Before an inmate is placed in isolation, his physical and mental health must be checked and the medical record consulted. Under no circumstance will any inmate be placed in isolation should his condition indicate that he might be unable to undergo the confinement.

4. Heart cases, asthmatics, diabetics, and epileptics are not to be placed in isolation at any time. When it becomes necessary to discipline inmates with such afflictions, other methods will be used, such as confinement in detention hospital, loss of privileges, etc.

5. Any inmate who gives cause for questioning his mental health is to be transferred to the detention hospital immediately. A complete report is to be submitted to the psychiatrist, the warden, and the assistant warden.

6. No inmate is to be confined in isolation for a period longer than fifteen (15) consecutive days.

7. Rule violation reports that are not specific and detailed or that show either an inaccurate number or name are to be returned to the officers submitting them for rewriting. Reports must be properly dated and signed by the officer witnessing or discovering the violation. Where contraband is involved the evidence, when possible, must accompany the report.

8. An investigation should be made in every case to determine if the inmate is guilty of the offense for which he has been reported.

9. An inmate whose case is being investigated is not to be placed in isolation until after the investigation has been completed. The inmate is to be held in segregation and given full rations until all phases of his case have been investigated. Participants or witnesses should not be permitted to contact each other, to avoid any opportunity for them to agree on any prearranged story.

10. When an inmate appears in captain's court, the report of the complaining officer is to be read to the inmate, and he must be given an opportunity to state his side of the case. All statements made by the inmate should be seriously considered.

11. In a case where the violation is of a serious nature, such as an attempt to escape, attacking an officer, perversion, etc., and the maximum isolation punishment has been awarded, the disciplinarian will write a report to the warden and to the secretary of the Merit Staff in order that the case may be con-

sidered at the next monthly staff meeting. If the recommendation of the staff results in a demotion in grade or loss of statutory time, the disciplinarian will call the inmate involved to his office and notify him. He will also notify the inmate to whom a promotion in grade or to whom a restoration of statutory time is granted.

12. No inmate is to be punished by isolation confinement on the mere word of another inmate. In the event two or more inmates are reported for the same offense, and one is blamed by the others, their respective statements should be weighed carefully before any action is taken.

13. In the event several inmates are reported for the same offense and contraband is involved, the ownership of which is in doubt, all are to be treated equally; however, if ownership can be determined, the owner is to be the only one punished.

14. Inmates who are potential suicides or who are belligerent are to be placed in a stripped cell.

15. Corporal punishment shall not be imposed at any time.

16. Each inmate released from isolation shall be shaved, given a bath, clean clothes, etc., and is to be returned to his regular assignment, unless otherwise dealt with as the warden may direct.

17. If anything unusual, such as a fire, riot, fighting, escape, attempted escape, assaulting an officer, suicide, etc., takes place, it will be the duty of the disciplinarian to interrogate all who participated or who may have knowledge of it. He should obtain a signed statement from each one, if possible. The statement should be properly witnessed and should contain details as to the signer's activities or connection with the incident. The statement with the disciplinarian's report of the incident is to be forwarded to the warden as soon as possible.

18. The disciplinarian will make daily reports to the warden, the assistant warden, and the record office, showing the name and number of each inmate in isolation, the charge against him, the name of the officer or officers who submitted the report, and the extent of punishment imposed.

19. A monthly report will be submitted to the warden and to the assistant warden. This report will list all disciplinary reports acted on during the current month, will set out the various punishments, total cases reprimanded and excused, total number of days served in isolation, number of inmates in isolation for the month, percentage in relation to the institution population, percentage in relation to reports received, etc.

20. An annual report will be submitted to the warden, summarizing all disciplinary actions during the twelve preceding months.

21. Close supervision is to be given all files and records to see that they are kept accurately and that all disciplinary actions are entered therein.

22. The files and records of the disciplinarian are confidential. They are not be be examined by other employees, since they contain a copy of all pertinent information regarding each inmate.

23. The office of the disciplinarian must be locked at the end of each day.

ISOLATION

1. Maximum efficiency in the operation of any penitentiary can be reached only when strict discipline is maintained among inmates (and employees) of the institution. The required degree of discipline can be attained only by enforcement of every rule of the institution, by promptly reporting each violation to the proper official, and by the equally prompt and efficient disposition of such reports by the disciplinarians.

2. The majority of the inmates will make a serious effort to abide by the regulations, but there will be repeated instances where institution rules are broken, some thoughtlessly, others through design. Regardless of the circumstances, it is the duty of every employee to report in detail to the proper official each observed infraction of the rules. The proper disciplinary official will determine the seriousness of the offense and what steps should be taken to prevent a recurrence of the violation.

3. In cases where a breach of discipline is minor, denial

Corridor in Isolation Block. Stateville Branch.

of certain privileges will be sufficient to impress on the inmate the necessity for strict observance of the rules. In cases involving major or repeated violations, it becomes necessary to isolate the offender from other members of the inmate body, in addition to denying him certain privileges. To handle these latter cases, isolation has been established and has become an integral part of the institution's behavior pattern.

4. If it were possible to enforce discipline by other methods, officials would abandon the use of isolation. But, because a small percentage of the inmates refuse to obey instructions, continually break rules, or refuse to accept suggestions, isolation punishment, as it is now administered, becomes necessary.

5. Inmates will be ordered to isolation for various lengths of time when, in the discretion of the disciplinarian or senior captains, such punishment is warranted. Under no circumstances

will any man be held in isolation more than fifteen (15) consecutive days.

6. When an inmate is ordered into isolation, the disciplinarian or the senior captain, through the isolation officer, shall notify the employee in charge of the inmate's assignment, cellhouse keeper, and other pertinent officials.

1959 view showing isolation cell. Stateville Branch.

View showing old isolation cells at Joliet Branch before 1935. (Note men hand cuffed to bars.)

7. Inmates who have been ordered to punishment cells will be stripped and searched thoroughly. While the search is being made, all doors must be locked and not reopened until the search has been completed and the inmate locked in the assigned cell.

8. Regulation isolation clothing, approved by the warden, will be issued to each man upon his commitment to isolation.

Interior view of isolation cell, 1959. Stateville Branch.

He will receive three blankets and, during cold weather, additional blankets will be issued.

9. The employee in charge of the isolation building will be responsible for all inmates in the punishment cells, as well as those assigned to work in the building. Only those inmates who have tickets properly marked for this department will be admitted to the isolation building. Under no circumstance will any inmate assigned to the building be allowed to contact or converse with inmates confined in the punishment cells.

10. Each isolation cell will be inspected at frequent intervals (at no time shall more than 30 minutes elapse between inspections). It shall be the duty of the employee in charge to maintain constant vigilance to prevent any violation of rules. Smoking, passing of notes, talking, and unnecessary noise is strictly prohibited at all times.

11. Inmates confined in isolation cells will be served a noon meal, which will be the same as that served in the inmate dining room. Each inmate will be given as much food as he can eat at the time the meal is served, but no foodstuffs are to be kept in the cells (or in the isolation building) at any time. Pans and utensils provided for feeding inmates are to be returned to the dining room immediately after the meal has been served.

12. All punishment cells must be kept clean and sanitary at all times.

13. The prison physician will visit inmates in isolation cells once during every twenty-four (24) hour period. Following his visit to any inmate, the physician will write a complete report showing the treatment given, together with recommendation for further treatment. If at any time the employee in charge feels that an inmate needs the attention of the physician, he will notify his superior officer or call the physician.

14. It is not uncommon for an inmate, after being placed in isolation, to feign insanity or attempt to destroy the furnishings of the cell. When an inmate becomes unruly or is creating a disturbance, the superior officer in charge shall be notified immediately. In most cases it will be found that the inmate

is only attempting to gain his release from isolation. However, in the event an inmate becomes physically or mentally ill during his stay in isolation, the physician is to be notified. Removal of an inmate to either the general or detention hospitals is to be made only upon recommendation of the prison physician and/or at the direction of a superior official.

15.   Attempted suicide on the part of inmates is not unusual in any assignment in the prison; therefore, all inmates are to be observed closely and frequent checks are to be made to prevent any such attempt by an inmate. When a suicide risk is confined, close supervision must be maintained at all times and solid doors must be left open.

16.   At no time will any inmate who is a degenerate or who has the reputation of being a degenerate be confined in isolation cells with other inmates. Specified cells are provided for inmates being treated for infectious or contagious diseases (commonly known as the "Shot Line").

17.   Where possible, inmates employed outside the walls on assignments such as the farm detail or in the administration building are to be confined in an isolation cell assigned for that purpose.

18.   No man who is old, feeble, epileptic or physically unfit is to be placed in isolation. If for any reason such a person should be committed, the matter shall be called to the attention of the prison physician and the senior captain immediately.

19.   Many contraband articles of all descriptions are turned in to the employee in charge of the isolation building. It shall be his duty to mark such articles, identify each with an accompanying report, and securely lock all contraband in the room provided for that purpose.

20.   Only one inmate is to be admitted to the senior captain's office at any time, unless otherwise directed. No inmate will be permitted within hearing distance of the senior captain's office while another inmate's report is being heard or discussed.

21.   There are occasions when inmates are brought to isolation in such a mood that any agitation may cause them to at-

tempt to assault an employee. When an inmate's temper has been aroused, he must be handled with care, and never in such a manner as to provoke an assault. Employees are prohibited from striking any inmate except in self-defense. All questions on the punishment of an inmate will be decided by the senior captains or their superior. An unruly inmate, however, may be locked in an isolation cell pending investigation and decision of the senior captain.

22. In the event of fog or other unusual weather conditions, no cell door in isolation is to be unlocked; the usual morning clean-up will be postponed until the unusual condition ceases to exist, or until otherwise ordered by the senior captain.

23. When there is only one employee on duty in the building, no door in isolation is to be unlocked except at the direction of a superior officer and then only when the employee in charge is accompanied by another employee, the outside door is locked, and the key is in the possession of an employee on the outside of the building.

24. No employee except those assigned to isolation will be permitted to go to an isolation cell or to talk with any inmate confined therein unless granted permission to do so by the senior captains. (Such permission will be granted only when the senior captains believe the request is warranted.)

25. Under no circumstance will any employee assigned to the isolation building be permitted to inspect or obtain records of any inmate. Only those records pertaining to the assignment will be consulted by the employee on duty.

26. The employee in charge of the building is responsible for all tools, knives, razors, etc., used by personnel assigned to isolation. Any tools issued to inmates will be checked carefully to make certain all are returned.

27. Before an inmate is released from isolation and returned to his assignment he must be given a shave by the barber assigned to the building, under the supervision of the employee in charge.

28. In the event ladders, rope, wire, or escape devices of

any kind are delivered to isolation for evidence or safekeeping, they will be dismantled under the direction of the employee in charge (after the purpose has been served) and turned over to the master mechanic.

29. All clothing or other material coming into this building shall be properly searched for contraband. Any clothing in need of repair or to be laundered will be sent to the laundry after being searched properly.

30. Every bar in the building must be checked and inspected daily by employee on duty during the day shift.

31. Isolation cells must be ventilated properly at all times and an even temperature must be maintained. At specific times, temperature readings should be taken and recorded for future reference.

Special Notes for Employees on Duty at Night:

Under no circumstances shall any cell door in isolation be unlocked unless so directed by a superior officer in charge and then only when such superior is present. The outside door of the building should be locked with the key to the outside door in the possession of an employee stationed outside the building.

Any inmate taken out of isolation during the night must be released to the custody of the lieutenant in charge. At least one other employee in addition to the lieutenant must accompany the inmate.

SEGREGATION

1. Inmates in segregation are never to be removed from their cell nor is the cell door to be opened, except with the approval of the superior officer in charge. The key to the outside door of the building is never to be in the building when a cell of the segregation unit is open. Under no circumstance should more than one inmate be released from his cell at one time.

2. All inmates confined in segregation are to be given a bath and shave each week, and a haircut every four weeks.

3. These inmates should have a recreation period daily; however, only one inmate will be released for recreation at one time.

The men are to be searched before they go to the yard and also upon their return to their cells. During the time an inmate is in the recreation yard his cell is to be searched for contraband of any kind. Inmates who do not take the recreation privilege are to be removed from their cells periodically and their cells searched.

4. If a disturbance should occur in the recreation yard, or in the building proper, no one officer should attempt to break it up. It is to be remembered that the disturbance may be a fake, the inmates may try to get control of the officer and hold him as a hostage. Officers are to remember that the inmates confined in segregation are desperate; however, officers are not to assault or strike an inmate, except in self-defense.

5. Suicide attempts are always a possibility; care should be taken to prevent them.

6. Cell furnishings will consist of bed, bedclothes, and radio earphones, unless otherwise directed.

7. During their stay in segregation, inmates will be permitted to have the following personal property: six law books, papers, toilet articles, and one cup. Inmates in grade will be given commissary privileges, unless they are denied by the disciplinarian. Each inmate must keep his own cell clean and orderly at all times.

8. Porters assigned to the segregation building and inmates on work assignments therein are to be searched before they enter the building proper and before they leave. No inmate is ever to be permitted to enter the corridor in front of the cell block, except when supervised by the officer in charge.

9. Officers on the second and third shifts can best supervise these inmates by using the peep-holes in the utility tunnel and they must make their rounds regularly, never entering the corridor in front of the cells except by permission of a captain or lieutenant.

10. At mealtime, the food is to be served on plates or in bowls and passed under the door to the inmates under the supervision of the officer in charge. They are to be given full rations of food, but there is to be no waste. The cell door is never to be

opened at meal times. All pans, dishes, spoons, etc., will be returned to the general dining room after each meal for washing and sterilization.

11. All inmates confined in this unit will be permitted one visit every thirty (30) days, but visits are not permitted on Saturday, Sunday, or holidays. The inmate must be accompanied to and from the visiting room by a lieutenant.

12. All mail received by the inmates, as well as the letters they write, are to be read by the officer in charge of the 7:00 A.M. to 3:00 P.M. shift, and copies are to be made of all incoming and outgoing mail.

13. A vault where records are deposited for safekeeping is located in the basement of the segregation building. Under no circumstance will records be removed or turned over to anyone, except an employee of the particular office requesting the record. A book is provided for charging records to the person removing same. The inmate assigned here is to be searched before entering and again when leaving this room. It will be the officer's duty to supervise this inmate and his activities, to see that he keeps this room in perfect order at all times and that records are filed chronologically. The room is to be kept locked and no one shall be permitted to enter it without permission from the senior captain.

14. The execution chamber and the utility room in the basement are never to be opened, except upon authorization of a supervising officer.

DEATH CHAMBER

1. When an inmate is under death sentence, the employee assigned to supervise him must exert every effort to prevent suicide or an attempt at same, and extreme care should be taken to make sure the inmate does not receive any article that could be used as a suicide weapon.

2. All visits to the condemned person must be approved by a superior officer, but the chaplain of the inmate's faith will be permitted to visit him at any time without permission, between the hours of 8:00 A.M and 3:00 P.M. Inmates are never to be

permitted to visit or contact a condemned man.

3. The officers' conversations with the condemned man are to be short and are not to refer to his case in any way.

4. A report is to be made by each officer on duty as to what may have transpired during his particular shift.

5. Every article for the condemned man must be inspected thoroughly before it is permitted into, or out of, his cell.

6. The inmate is to be given all he cares to eat at each meal.

7. Daily papers and library books will be permitted after they have been closely inspected.

8. A radio will be installed outside his cell.

9. Weather permitting, the inmate is to be given a daily exercise period in the segregation yard, but he must be accompanied by an officer at all times.

10. Unless permission is given by a superior officer, the cell

The Electric Chair. Stateville Branch.

door is never to be opened, except when the inmate is being taken to the segregation yard for exercise, to an authorized visit, or to prevent an attempted suicide.

11. The chamber and utility room are never to be opened, except upon authorization of a superior officer.

CHIEF GUARD, CAPTAIN and LIEUTENANTS

1. The chief guard has supervision over all custodial officers and has full authority to assign them to various posts throughout the institution; to see that all posts are adequately covered; to designate each employee's day off, and to arrange the vacation schedule. He will be required to maintain the payroll record, to check the attendance of all employees each day, and to submit a report of all absentees.

2. The chief guard is to see that all towers are properly equipped with guns, shells, and gas. In choosing officers for assignment to duty on wall towers, only those who meet the required standard of efficiency in handling of weapons are to be selected. Each man chosen must have a clearly defined understanding of what his duty will be in an emergency; he also must have a determination to perform that duty. No employee is to be assigned to a tower position who is not properly trained in the use of firearms. A lieutenant is to be assigned to train all new employees in target practice, and men assigned to towers are to practice twice a month. Before change of shifts and before a relief officer is sent to a tower, the captain or lieutenant in charge is to call all towers and advise as to the identity of the relief officer, etc. Where guns are used inside the wall in towers, the chief guard is to see that the officers filling these positions are properly covered while guns and munitions are moved through the yard or tunnel system. The captain and lieutenants in charge of shifts are to make periodic checks, to see that the towermen are constantly on the alert and that they make proper calls to the switchboard operator every thirty (30) minutes.

3. During fog, poor visibility, or in the event of a "blackout," the chief guard is to assign officers to patrol the area between the inside wall towers.

4. During any unnatural condition, no inmate is to be released from his cell until authorized by a superior officer. All doors are to be closely guarded, and inmates who are authorized to be on their assignments, such as in the bakery, kitchen, dining and vegetable rooms, must remain at their immediate working places. During poor visibility resulting from any cause, meals are to be served in the cellhouses.

5. The chief guard and lieutenants are the police officers of the institution. Throughout the day and night they are to make inspections of all shops, cellhouses, and assignments, to see that employees and inmates are doing their work as directed.

6. The chief guard is to insist that all captains, lieutenants, and guards are absolutely fair and impartial in their supervision of inmates; their personal feelings are not to influence their actions concerning inmates.

7. The chief guard is to instruct all custodial officers that it will be their duty to stop and investigate prisoners who are away from their assignments, checking their tickets to ascertain if they are properly authorized; if there is any doubt about the inmate's authority to be absent from his assignment, an investigation should be made. No inmate is to be permitted to leave his assignment without proper authority.

8. There is to be a continuous count kept of all inmates at all times. Generally, there will be institution counts of all inmates at 7:00 A.M., noon, 5 P.M., 8:30 P.M., 12 midnight, and 6:00 A.M. Weather conditions and seasons, of course, will vary these times.

9. Employees are never to be permitted to congregate in groups, whether in the shops, cellhouses, or yards.

10. The chief guard is to insist that all of the shops, assignments, tunnels, and cellhouses are maintained at a high standard of cleanliness and must pass inspection at all times.

11. All employees must be equipped with a proper uniform, identification card, and tag. An inspection should be made at least once each month to see that all employees are attired in proper uniform and have their cards and tags.

12. The chief guard is to make sure that the lieutenants and, if necessary, the officers, have a working knowledge of the fire equipment in the institution, so that in the event of an emergency fire they could be of assistance.

13. Each institution is provided with a siren or whistle, which is to be used when an emergency occurs, such as an escape or a fire, etc. When the siren or whistle is blown, all inmates are to be returned immediately to their cellhouses. Fire drills are to be held periodically, and a record kept of the time required for their completion.

14. In the event of accident to inmate or employee, the chief guard, captain, or a lieutenant is to see that the injured person is immediately brought to the hospital for proper attention and treatment, and that a full report of the incident is made to the warden.

15. Lumber, pipe, rope, wire, or any equipment which might conceivably be used in an escape attempt, is to be kept in the mechanical stockroom or in the proper place designated for the storage thereof.

16. Ladders more than twelve (12) feet in length will not be permitted inside the enclosure, except when under the supervision and surveillance of a captain or lieutenant.

17. At least one captain or lieutenant or more, if possible, is to be stationed in a position where he will be able to see all movements of lines going to or from the dining room at meal times. They are to see that the guards are stationed properly throughout the dining room and that an officer is assigned to supervise each serving table, with instructions to see that all inmates are given proper portions of food—no more and no less. A lieutenant is to taste the food at each meal before it is served to make sure that it has been properly prepared and is palatable. Any food that is not satisfactory is to be replaced.

18. A captain or lieutenant must be present in the chapel during all church services and during the showing of motion pictures.

19. At least once a week the greenhouse, all basements,

and all buildings situated near the wall are to be inspected thoroughly for tunneling or other attempts at an escape.

20. All tools and accessories in all assignments are to be checked and accounted for each day, and any shortages are to be reported immediately. A weekly tool report from all assignments is to be made to the assistant warden and the master mechanic.

21. There is to be a periodic inspection of the numbers on inmate clothing. When an inmate is in need of clothing replacement, a report of his need is to be sent to the condemning officer.

22. Inmates in need of medical attention shall be passed to the hospital with the approval of a lieutenant or captain.

23. A lieutenant shall be assigned to general supervision of the hospital. He is to make daily inspections, to see that the employees are carrying out the instructions of the doctors and that proper security and cleanliness are maintained.

24. Each morning the chief guard is to send an officer around the inside of the wall to see if any contraband has been thrown over the wall during the night, and he is to be instructed to gather up any such items, turn them in, and submit a report.

25. A lieutenant shall be assigned as general supervisor of the administration building. He is to see that it is kept in good order and that discipline, cleanliness, and proper supervision are maintained.

26. All cellhouses are to be maintained and operated in a uniform manner. A lieutenant is to be assigned to each cellhouse as a general supervisor, and it will be his duty to make proper inspections as to security and cleanliness. He will listen to complaints or needs of inmates and handle them, when possible. Cells are to be searched daily. Officers assigned to duty in the cellhouses are to maintain a constant patrol of the galleries. Each inmate is to remain in his cell unless he has permission to be elsewhere. No cell transfers are to be permitted unless authorized by the lieutenant in charge or the senior captain. However, cell changes should be made within the division, if cellmates are having trouble. Cellhouses may be classified as "banks," and inmates

released from any cellhouse to an officer are to be charged to the officer. It will be his responsibility to return all inmates he has taken out and to account for the whereabouts of any who may have been called from his division on tickets.

27. The bars in all cellhouses or any other place where inmates may be confined, such as the hospital, are to be inspected daily by assigned officers. Periodically, a lieutenant shall be assigned to check the bars, to verify that the officer has performed his inspections properly.

28. The lieutenant in charge of night shifts shall not hesitate to call a nurse in case an inmate becomes ill in a cellhouse and, if necessary, remove him to the hospital. Whenever an inmate becomes mentally disturbed at night, he is to be transferred to the detention hospital and a report made to the psychiatrist and warden.

29. If an inmate becomes seriously ill, the chaplain of his faith should be notified.

30. In case of death, the prison physician should be notified at once, and a telegram sent to the nearest relative of the deceased inmate. In the event of the death of an inmate from other than natural causes, the lieutenant in charge is to call the coroner. The body shall not be removed until permission is given by the coroner. Should a death occur from natural causes, the lieutenant is to call the undertaker. However, before a body is removed from the institution, the fingerprints of the deceased must be taken and a full report submitted to the warden. All personal property of the deceased inmate should be sent to the chief clerk's office and a proper report made covering same.

31. After the evening count, the cellhouses, hospital, isolation and segregation buildings are to be locked and the keys removed. These buildings will not be opened during the night, unless a lieutenant is present. It will be his duty to see that one employee remains outside with the keys, the first door to be locked after the building has been entered.

32. A list of inmates eligible for night duty in case of an emergency must be posted in the captain's office.

33. Employees living in the institution will not be permitted to enter if intoxicated. All employees are to conduct themselves as gentlemen, whether on or off the institution grounds.

34. It will be the duty of the captain and lieutenant in charge of shifts to demand a report in writing from an officer who has been absent from duty. If, for any reason, officers do not report, and the chief guard or lieutenant deems it necessary, investigation should be made.

35. There is to be no loitering by anyone in the captain's office or on any assignment.

36. It will be the duty of all supervising officers to submit a report in writing of any rule violation on the part of any employee.

37. All visitors being conducted through the institution must be under the supervision of a lieutenant. He is to see that the visitors sign in at the front gate, have their hands stamped, and receive tickets properly initialed by the employee witnessing the signatures. Each visitor is to keep his ticket in his possession until he returns to the front gate. When the tour has been completed, each ticket is to be signed in the guard hall by the visitor in the presence of an officer, who is to compare the signatures and show his approval by initialing same. He will then notify the gateman of such approval and identify the visitors before they are passed out.

38. The chief guard, captain, and lieutenants are to devote their time to the inspection and supervision of the institution, and are to instruct, encourage, and supervise all employees in the performance of their duties, giving credit where it is due and making reports of any violations.

39. Except in cases of emergency, no employee will be called to the outside telephone or permitted the use of same; nor will he be permitted to receive visits while on duty.

40. Under no circumstance will inter-assignment visiting be permitted employees while on duty. Nor will employees off duty be permitted to loiter on or near any assignment.

INMATE DINING ROOM

1. Before any inmate is assigned to the inmate dining room, he must be approved by the prison physician and a health certificate signed by the prison physician must accompany the inmate when he is transferred to this assignment.

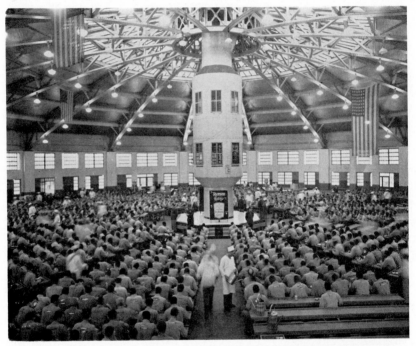

1959 view of Dining Room during meal time. Stateville Branch.

2. The inmate dining room is not to be used as a short cut to other assignments, and inmates not assigned to the inmate dining room will not be permitted here unless on an authorized mission.

3. Loitering or congregating will not be tolerated at any time. This also applies to the inmates assigned to the inmate dining room.

4. It is the desire of the institution management to have the food prepared and served properly so that the inmates may receive the maximum benefit from it. The food is not to be sent

Dining Room during the 1920's. Joliet Branch.

to the dining room before mealtime, as it will become cool and unpalatable. This also applies to preparation and serving of coffee.

5. Employees detailed to the dining room at mealtime should report to the employee in charge upon their arrival.

6. It is imperative that an employee supervise the distribution of food at all times, as frequently the inmates serving food will take advantage of an employee's temporary absence to "take care" of their friends by not giving other inmates the portions due them. Every inmate is to receive the portion of food due him, and it is the duty of the employee in charge at each serving table to see that this rule is enforced. Seconds are to be served when possible, with the exception of meat. Only one portion of meat is to be served each inmate. No favoritism is to be shown at any time.

7. The employee in charge at each serving table will see

that the line is kept moving in an orderly manner; that each inmate is served no more than one ration of each item at the serving table (the inmate may request the waiter to give him less than one ration or he may pass up any item he does not want) ; and the employee is to see that no arguments develop between the inmate being served and the inmate waiter.

8. Each inmate shall carry his own cup to the dining room. Each inmate must use his own cup.

9. Smoking will not be permitted in the dining room during mealtime or when food is being served. Inmates, after being seated, may converse in a low or moderate tone during meal time but loud or boisterous language is never permitted.

10. Inmates at the diet table must produce a diet card before being served. This diet card must be signed by the prison physician and countersigned by the senior captain. The employee in charge of the diet table will inspect each card to see that it is in proper order before the inmate is served. He must also make certain that no inmate uses a card issued to another. Diet cards have an expiration date shown on them. Do not serve any inmate at the diet table after the expiration date on his card. Inmates who have been issued diet cards are to eat at the diet table only.

11. Inmates receiving treatment for contagious diseases are to be served in dishes set aside for their use. This applies to silverware. The dishes and silverware used by these inmates must never be mixed with the utensils used elsewhere in the dining room. These inmates are to be served and seated at tables set aside for their exclusive use.

12. Every utensil or tool which might be used as a weapon is to be securely locked in a compartment under the immediate supervision of an employee. Knives, forks, spoons, and tools of every description are to be checked each morning, noon, and night, and every item must be accounted for. Any shortage is to be reported at once to a superior officer.

13. It is imperative that this assignment be kept scrupulously clean at all times, and it is the duty of the officer in charge of the dining room to make frequent inspection tours to see that

this rule is complied with.

14. Each inmate waiter must wash his hands carefully immediately before he handles food or utensils and also immediately after he uses the toilet. He must keep his fingernails clean at all times. The officer in charge of the dining room will make frequent inspections of the inmate waiters' hands.

15. Inmates assigned to the dining room are to wear gloves at all times when serving food or handling utensils. These gloves are to be kept thoroughly clean and inspected frequently. If an inmate waiter is temporarily without gloves, he is not to be permitted to serve food or handle utensils.

16. During mealtime, the employee in charge of each group of inmates will watch them carefully to see there is no unnecessary talking. Playing at the table and arguments will not be tolerated. Each employee in the dining room at mealtime must be vigilant for when a large number of inmates are present, anything could happen.

17. An inmate may call an employee's attention to his food and there is something obviously wrong with it, the employee must order it rectified. If the employee is in doubt, he should call a superior officer.

18. The employee in charge of the dining room must see that a sufficient number of inmates has been approved for the serving of early and late details. If short for the early and late details, make request of the senior captain to obtain approval for additional help.

INMATE KITCHEN AND BAKERY

1. Hungry men may become vicious men. Therefore, it is the responsibility of employees assigned to the kitchen and bakery to see that inmates receive food which has been properly prepared and served.

2. A record of all ingredients used in the preparation of meals is maintained by the steward. Menus are outlined at least one week in advance and posted on the kitchen bulletin board. No change is to be made in the menus without good reason.

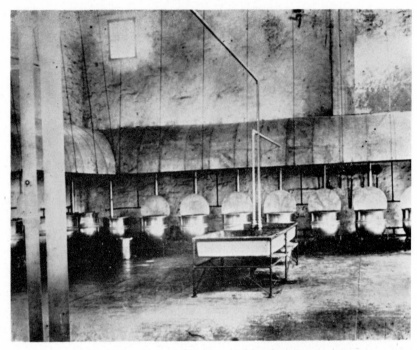

1944 view of kitchen. Joliet Branch.

3. Foodstuffs used are of good quality and it is the duty of the officers in charge to supervise closely the preparation of same, according to the direction of the steward. All food and baked goods should be tasted before serving to insure proper preparation and to make certain that no foreign matter has been added.

4. Food supplies and utensils are to be requisitioned when needed. It is important that only necessary supplies be requested or removed from the general store. Officers in charge will see that requisitions are drawn so that additional items cannot be added, and that all items requisitioned are received.

5. It is important that sufficient food be prepared so that no shortages occur at mealtime. If because of spoilage or other unforeseen circumstances a shortage does occur, there should be enough food in the kitchen to carry through the meal.

6. No waste is permitted at any time. A record of the

weights and types of garbage — edible and inedible — is to be kept, and that which is suitable for feeding livestock on the farm is to be kept separate from other types.

7. The cold storage room is to be kept in perfect order and locked at all times. Only inmates assigned to work in this room are permitted in it.

8. Inmates assigned to handling food must be approved by the prison physician, and officers in charge of the assignments will see that no inmate is accepted in the assignments without a health certificate signed by the physician.

1959 view of modern kitchen. Stateville Branch

9. With the exception of those inmates assigned to the kitchen and bakery, no others are to be permitted in the assignments.

10. Loitering and unnecessary noise are not permitted, nor is visiting in other assignments.

11. At no time shall officers or inmates receive special meals

except upon order of a prison physician. There is to be absolutely no favoritism.

12. Knives, tools, and anything that might conceivably be used as a weapon are to be kept locked in a safe compartment and issued only under supervision. A daily check must be kept of all such items and any tool shortage is to be reported at once to the supervising officer.

13. When lines are passing into the dining room or when knives are being used, the kitchen and bakery doors are to be locked.

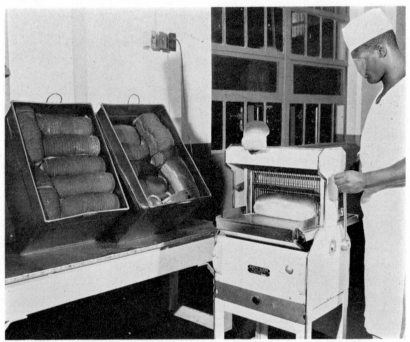

View showing new slicing machine in Bakery. Stateville Branch.

14. All cleaning agents, such as lye, sani-flush, insecticides, etc., must be locked in a locker and used only under supervision. The officer will see that no opportunity arises for any such items to be placed in foodstuffs.

15. All inmates leaving or entering the assignments must be searched thoroughly. The tool and work orders of those

doing temporary work on the assignment must be examined and checked carefully.

16. Inmate lockers on the assignment must be examined periodically to insure they are kept in order and that no contraband is stored in them.

View showing old slicing method in Bakery, 1920. Joliet Branch.

17. It is imperative that the bakery and kitchen assignments be kept scrupulously clean at all times. Inmates must wash their hands before handling food, particularly after using the toilet. Their fingernails are to be inspected regularly. There is to be no smoking while handling food.

VEGETABLE ROOM

1. Inmates assigned to the handling of food must be approved by the prison physician and a health certificate signed by the physician must accompany each inmate to this assignment.

2. The employee in charge of this assignment is to super-

vise it closely at all times, and he is to make certain especially that foodstuffs are prepared in accordance with instructions received from the institution steward. A great waste of vegetables and fruits can occur through improper paring.

3. Knives and other equipment used in the preparation of vegetables for the kitchen are to be checked out to the inmates and a record kept of same. Proper search will be made of any inmate leaving the assignment. Any tools or equipment that may have been checked out to an inmate must be returned to the employee in charge before the inmate leaves. Should a shortage occur, no one is to leave the assignment and the supervising officer is to be notified immediately.

4. When not in authorized use, all knives, tools, or utensils of any type that might be used as a weapon must be kept in a locked vault provided for that purpose, and the keys are never to be permitted to fall into the hands of an inmate.

5. All cleaning agents, such as lye, sani-flush, insecticides, etc., must be stored in a locker provided for that purpose. Only an officer will have access to the locker. When it is necessary to use the above mentioned agents, the employee in charge is to see they are properly distributed and that there is no chance at any time for any of it to be placed in foodstuffs.

6. No loitering will be permitted and inmates from other assignments are not to visit with or contact inmates in this assignment.

7. This assignment is to be kept scrupulously clean and in neat order at all times. Inmates must wash their hands after using the toilet, and their hands and fingernails are to be inspected frequently by the employee in charge to make certain they are always clean.

8. No smoking is to be permitted on this assignment while handling food.

BAND

A good band and orchestra are great assets to the institution and those who desire to study music may do so providing they pass the required aptitude test.

1. It shall be the duty of the bandmaster to instruct and encourage inmate students who are interested in learning music.

2. The bandmaster will be responsible for all musical instruments and equipment purchased by the institution and must see that all instruments are carefully checked and kept in first class condition at all times. In the event an instrument becomes damaged, it is to be so reported, and the bandmaster is to make arrangements for its repair.

3. The bandmaster will also see that all instruments owned by inmates are recorded as follows: Four (4) copies of the instrument permit are to be made and signed by the bandmaster, the inmate owner, and the assistant warden. One copy of permit is to be filed in the assistant warden's office, one in the chief clerk's office, one in the band room, and the remaining copy is to be retained by the inmate owner. Should an inmate wish to send his instrument out of the institution, the instrument and permit covering same must be taken to the assistant warden's office for disposition.

4. Under no circumstances is any inmate permitted to trade or give his instrument to another inmate. If he is leaving the institution by discharge or parole and does not want his instrument, it is to become the property of the state and will be so identified and used as other state-owned instruments.

5. Strings for all string instruments shall be ordered through the bandmaster and the chief clerk's office. New strings are to be distributed by the bandmaster who will pick up old strings and destroy them. Old strings are not to fall into the hands of inmates.

CELLHOUSES

Security or safekeeping of prisoners is the most important factor in the administration of a penal institution. The proper degree of security can be attained only through careful enforcement of institutional rules and maintenance of proper discipline among inmates and employees.

Constant vigilance is demanded of every cellhouse keeper and other employees assigned to duty within each cellhouse. Every employee should be aware of the possibility that an inmate in any of the cellhouses might effect an escape through long hours of work, conniving, and with the help of a confederate who may be assigned as a clerk or runner in the cellhouse. For example,

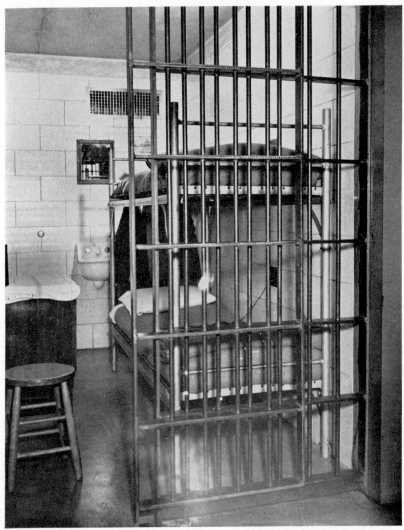

A view of an "old prison" cell after remodeling in 1959. Juliet Branch.

a bar may be completely cut through with a handful of emery dust and a piece of twine string. Such a feat could not be accomplished in one night, to be sure, but an inmate serving a long sentence has plenty of time. This is just one of the methods that can be used by a desperate criminal in an attempt to escape. There are others too numerous to mention. Cellhouse keepers

Interior view of old prison cell before remodeling. Joliet Branch.

should anticipate the germination of an escape plot and make every effort to stop such preparations before the plot reaches a menacing stage.

It should be pointed out that being constantly on the alert, proper searching of inmates and cells, frequent inspection of bars, and the instant removal of an unauthorized article, will break up an escape plot and perhaps save the life of an employee or inmate of the institution. Therefore, it is essential that the cellhouse keeper and every employee assigned thereto conscientiously execute all duties assigned to him and enforce the rules and regulations to the letter.

In addition to the general rules and regulations governing employees of the institution, the following rules pertaining to cellhouse assignments shall be enforced by employees assigned:

1. The employee in charge of the cellhouse, hereinafter referred to as the cellhouse keeper, shall have general supervision over all employees assigned to duty within the cellhouse, all inmates assigned to his cellhouse, and all employees or inmates going into or out of the cellhouse.

2. An accurate record of the whereabouts of every inmate assigned to the cellhouse shall be maintained at all times. If an inmate leaves the cellhouse on a ticket or for any other purpose, the time of his departure and return shall be noted on the inmate movement chart provided for that purpose. At no time shall any inmate be permitted to leave the cellhouse without proper permission.

3. Employees assigned to duty within the cellhouse must maintain constant vigilance throughout their tours of duty. They will, when not otherwise detailed, walk the galleries at all times; they will not be permitted to congregate on the galleries, stairs, or main floor of the cellhouse; they will not fraternize with inmates, nor talk to any inmate except in the line of duty. It is strictly prohibited to traffic or barter with any inmate. No employee shall be permitted to carry messages, written or oral, from one inmate to another.

4. Church lines will assemble on the flag of each cellhouse;

inmates will hold their church cards where they will be plainly visible for inspection. Then, and only then, will the cellhouse keeper give the signal for the line to leave. If an inmate appears in the line without a church card and claims that he has lost it, he should be permitted to attend the services if, in the judgment of the employee, the inmate is sincere. However, any individual inmate should not be permitted to use this excuse indefinitely; he can obtain another church card by making the proper request of the chaplain.

5. Each employee in charge of a line leaving the cellhouse must count the men and account to the cellhouse keeper for every man on his assignment. Upon returning the line to the cellhouse, the employee in charge must count the inmates as they enter, account for any absentees, and provide the cellhouse keeper with the correct count. After his count has been checked, such employee will accompany the inmates to the proper gallery, make

Circular Cell House at Stateville.

certain that each enters the proper cell, and lock and test cell doors. He shall then patrol the galleries, unless properly relieved by the cellhouse keeper.

6. At no time will the count of the cellhouse clerk be accepted without verification by the cellhouse keeper or employee in charge of inmates.

7. When making a check of inmates, undivided attention must be given to the task. All inmates shall be required to stand at their respective cell doors while the count is being made. Men, not shingles, must be counted. Employees on duty at night must make certain that men — not dummies resembling men — are counted. Night rounds should be made at intervals so that the employee does not become mechanical. Be positive that every inmate is in his proper assignment or cell.

8. During the night one employee should be posted near the telephone while others patrol the galleries. In circular cellhouses, one employee must be posted in the tower (tower doors will be kept locked and the key left in the tower, except when the employee on duty there is being relieved). At no time should the telephone be unattended. It should be remembered that an emergency can arise when it will be necessary to call for help. If, at any time, an emergency should arise when it is impossible to make the proper telephone call, knock the telephone receiver from its hook. This will alert the operator who, in turn, will notify the proper officials.

9. No cell is to be unlocked at night except in an emergency, such as illness, etc., and then only at the direction of a superior officer. More than one employee must be present when the door is unlocked and every precaution is to be taken.

10. After the evening count checks, only one outside door to the cellhouse shall be unlocked at any time and the employee with the key shall remain outside. The cellhouse door shall not be opened from the outside until approval is given by the cellhouse keeper or his assistant.

11. Before unlocking a cellhouse door to relieve any employee for meals or change of shift, every precaution shall be

taken to make certain that an employee is being released and not an inmate who may have tied up the employee and is wearing his uniform.

12. Employees assigned to cellhouse doors shall keep a continuous count and check on all inmate movements passing this assignment. All inmates not accompanied by an employee shall be searched before entering or leaving the cellhouse. Under no circumstance will any package or bundle be permitted to pass through the cellhouse door without being inspected properly.

13. It shall be the duty of the cellhouse keeper to post employees at strategic points commanding a full view of the galleries while lines are entering or leaving the cells.

14. Daily inspection shall be made of screens and cell bars. The bars should not only be tested with the aid of a looking glass and rod provided for that purpose, but should also be carefully scrutinized to make certain no attempt is being made by an inmate to cut the bars. From time to time, minute examinations will be made of the cell doors, walls, ceilings, and switches, to make certain they are in good and secure condition. At irregular intervals mattresses and other cell furnishings should be thoroughly searched for contraband articles.

15. At least fifteen cells shall be searched thoroughly each day, but under no circumstance should cell searching become routine; skip cell searching is the proper method.

16. If and when an inmate is transferred out of his cell for any reason, as to isolation or the hospital, his cell is to be thoroughly searched. If his personal belongings are to be removed from the cell, a list is to be made of same and held until his return.

17. At no time will any article of furniture such as chest of drawers, bed, cabinet, etc., be placed against an outside will in any cell. It is important that a daily inspection be made of all outside walls to prevent any attempt to tunnel through the wall.

18. Inmates shall never be permitted to enter the basement of any cellhouse or any utility tunnel, except when accompanied by a regularly assigned employee. Under no circumstance shall

any work be done in basements, unless authorized by the proper official.

19. Inmates shall move to and from their respective cells in cell formation, and each prisoner must be in full regulation uniform at all times when leaving his cell.

20. Each inmate must go to each meal with his respective line. No inmate will be permitted to lie in without permission from the prison physician or the warden.

21. Talking by any inmate while on the galleries will not be permitted. Any unnecessary noise, booing, or yelling will not be tolerated at any time, and any inmate causing such disturbance shall be immediately reported to the disciplinarian.

22. All inmates who have regular assignments must report to them daily, unless given permission by one of the prison physicians or a superior officer to lie in. All cells should be checked after lines leave the cellhouse to make certain that no inmate has remained in his cell without proper permission. It should be remembered that escape plots may begin with inmates lying in without permission.

23. Care must be exercised in the assignment of cell partners and the cellhouse keeper must take all factors into consideration when making a cell assignment. Every inmate is to be assigned to a cell in the group allotted for his particular work detail; no exceptions will be made except by special permission of the warden or his authorized assistant.

24. Cell transfers shall be permitted only with the approval of a superior officer.

25. An inmate will not be permitted to enter any cell other than his own, except in the performance of his work and, then, only when under the supervision of an employee.

26. A report should be forwarded to the clothing room listing the names and numbers of inmates in need of new items of clothing. A separate list should be submitted whenever clothes are in need of repair.

27. A report is to be made to the supervising officer of any inmate caught in the act of sexual misconduct. After the inmate

has been properly dealt with, he shall be assigned to a 1-man cell. At any time suspicion arises concerning the actions of a sex pervert, a report of same is to be made to the warden.

28. Each inmate will have a shingle showing his name and number, which must be hung outside his cell at all times when the inmate is carried on the cellhouse count. In the event an inmate is removed to the hospital or isolation, his shingle shall be removed from the cell and kept in the custody of the cellhouse keeper, until such inmate is returned to the cellhouse.

29. A record shall be kept of all known escapees, dangerous, or unusual prisoners and all information concerning them shall be transmitted immediately to the employee in charge of such inmates' assignments. All employees assigned to duty in the cellhouse, especially those on night duty, shall familiarize themselves with the names, numbers, and appearances of such prisoners. The cells of these inmates shall be closely supervised and searched at frequent intervals to make certain that no contraband is concealed to be used in an escape attempt.

30. Under no circumstances will papers or debris of any sort be permitted to accumulate in any cell. Such debris furnishes a breeding place for vermin and it shall be the duty of the cellhouse keeper to make certain each cell is kept clean. Windows, walls, and floors must be washed regularly; cells and beds must be kept in a neat, uniform order and ready for inspection at all times.

31. The galleries and flag of each cellhouse are to be swept and mopped so that they are spic and span at all times.

32. Each inmate is provided with sufficient blankets, as well as 2 sheets and pillowcases. Mattresses and pillows will be replaced when necessary. Nothing except permitted articles shall be in any cell. (See inmate rule book for permitted items.)

33. Commissary supplies exceeding the amount specified shall not be accumulated by any inmate. It should be remembered that commissary items may be used to pay gambling debts and gambling in any form is strictly prohibited.

34. All books and magazines, except school books, pur-

chased by inmates will be permitted in their possession for a period of ten days, unless additional time is granted at the direction of the warden. After that period all such items shall become the property of the state and sent to the institution library for proper disposition.

35. Letters, newspapers, and magazines which have been sent to the cellhouse from the mail office are to be delivered only to the inmate to whom they are addressed, after there is sufficient indication that such mail has been properly censored. Cellhouse keepers shall not permit other employees and/or inmates to inspect incoming or outgoing mail.

36. Inmates are to be provided with regulation institution stationery on Saturday afternoon. If such stationery is accidentally spoiled, it shall be picked up by the cellhouse keeper before additional paper is issued. All outgoing mail will be picked up in each cellhouse on Sunday evening and forwarded to the mail office on Monday morning.

37. The employee in charge of the hospital shall be notified when an inmate becomes ill. If any inmate is admitted to the hospital or isolation, the cellhouse keeper shall be immediately notified; such inmate will be removed temporarily from the cellhouse count, the shingle removed from his cell and kept in the custody of the cellhouse keeper. When such inmate is released from the hospital or isolation, the cellhouse keeper will be so notified. It will be the duty of the cellhouse keeper to check daily with the hospital and isolation concerning patients from his cellhouse.

38. If at any time an inmate who is confined to the hospital requests his earphones or any personal property in his cell, such articles may be forwarded by the cellhouse keeper.

39. Inmate's name and number must be on all bottles or boxes of medicine issued to him. Medicines containing poison or sedatives shall be dispensed to the inmate by the cellhouse keeper as prescribed by the physician. Second and third shift employees are to administer drugs, etc., only as directed.

40. The cellhouse keeper shall dispense all medication for

epileptic patients. This medicine is delivered to him in suitable containers properly labeled with the date, the inmate's name and number, and the physician's instructions. The cellhouse keeper shall sign for these containers in the book presented to him by the employee delivering them. The officer delivering the medicine is to witness the signature of each cellhouse keeper and is to countersign the book.

41. It is permissible for flowers or other plant life to be kept on the cellhouse flag; however, under no circumstance shall the walls or any part of the cellhouse be decorated.

42. Employees assigned to the cellhouses should make certain that inmates do not pilfer from other inmates' cells. When searches are made, care should be taken that inmate's property is not destroyed. Any permitted articles are the personal property of the inmate and should be protected by all employees.

43. Under no circumstance will an inmate be permitted to carry tools, etc., to his cell. An accurate accounting of every tool required for cellhouse maintenance shall be made daily and any shortage immediately reported. Tools will be kept in a locked cabinet and issued to maintenance men under the direction of the cellhouse keeper.

44. It is the duty of the cellhouse keeper and all employees assigned to thoroughly familiarize themselves with all locks and they are to be kept in perfect working condition. Any defect must be reported and repairs or replacements are to be made at once.

45. Employees patrolling the galleries shall have an unobstructed view of every cell. Curtains or anything that would conceal a portion of the cell from full view will not be permitted.

46. Any unusual occurrence or happening within the cellhouse shall be immediately reported to the cellhouse keeper. He, in turn, shall make a report of such occurrence to the proper officials.

CELLHOUSE DOORMAN

1. In order to insure that an accurate record is kept of the movement of inmates to and from the cellhouses, one employee shall be regularly assigned to duty as doorman at each cellhouse.

Such doorman will work at all times under the direct supervision of the cellhouse keeper and, during his tour of duty, will be responsible for the count of all inmates leaving or entering the cellhouse and for the security of the cellhouse door.

2. He must at all times be able to account for the whereabouts of every inmate of the cellhouse. He will constantly check the work of the inmate door clerks and verify entries on the inmate movement chart.

3. Outside doors will be kept locked at all times and only those authorized will be permitted to enter or leave the cellhouse.

4. At any time it becomes necessary to feed the inmates in the cellhouse because of weather conditions, trouble of any kind, or other unusual situations, it will be the duty of the doorman to lock both inner and outer cellhouse doors and remain between them until such emergency ceases to exist or until he is otherwise directed by order of the warden.

5. In case of rioting or any other serious trouble outside the cellhouse, the majority of the inmates will, in all probability, attempt to go to their cells to keep out of trouble. In that event, it will be the duty of the doorman to permit such inmates to enter the cellhouse. The cellhouse keeper will make certain that these inmates go to their proper cells and that they are securely confined therein.

6. When a line enters or leaves the cellhouse under the supervision of an employee, it will be the duty of the employee and the doorman to count every inmate in line. All counts must check when a line leaves the cellhouse and every inmate must be accounted for when a line returns.

7. The doorman will carefully supervise all lines entering or leaving the cellhouse, checking the personal appearance of each inmate to make certain that all are properly and neatly dressed and not in possession of contraband.

8. Unless otherwise instructed by the cellhouse keeper, the doorman will station himself in a position where he can observe all lines passing to and from the dining room. He will make certain that proper order is maintained and that all lines proceed

in a quiet manner.

9. Every inmate entering or leaving the cellhouse, except those in lines accompanied by an assigned employee, must be searched for contraband. All wagons, carts, bundles, and packages will be carefully examined to make certain that no contraband articles are contained therein.

10. All clerks and runners entering or leaving the cellhouse will be timed in and out, carefully searched upon their departure, and again upon their return. The doorman will make certain that the trip is strictly business and fully authorized.

11. In the event any inmate should be absent from the cellhouse on a ticket for an unusual length of time, the doorman will notify the cellhouse keeper, advising him of the inmate's destination and time of departure. It will be the duty of the cellhouse keeper to notify the proper officials.

12. All traffic in the cellhouse tunnel and, whenever possible, traffic on sections in the immediate vicinity of the cellhouse, will be under the constant surveillance of the doorman. He will not permit loitering by employees, outsiders, or inmates in or near the assignment; any attempt by inmates to contact other inmates shall be reported promptly to the proper officials.

13. Any inmate authorized to do necessary work in the cellhouse must be in possession of a work slip, listing the tools he is permitted to carry, unless such inmate is accompanied by an employee. All such tools must be checked in and out by the doorman and any unauthorized tools will be held and the incident reported to the proper officials. Under no circumstance will any tool be left in the cellhouse without the approval of the cellhouse keeper and, even then, it is to be securely locked up.

DORMITORY

1. Employees assigned to duty in the dormitory shall be under the general supervision of the dormitory keeper and shall be expected to coöperate with him at all times. They shall not congregate in one place, nor shall they visit with inmates. No employee is permitted to give to or receive from an inmate

anything whatsoever.

2. Inmates are not permitted to be out of their rooms without proper detail or permission. Regulation dress is required for all inmates outside their rooms.

3. Inmates shall not be permitted to leave the dormitory without a properly executed ticket, except those in a division and under the supervision of an employee.

4. Every inmate must go to each meal with his respective line. Under no circumstance will anyone be permitted to lie in without permission from the prison physician or the warden. Any illness is to be reported immediately to the hospital.

5. If, at any time, an inmate is confined to the hospital, it will be permissible to forward his earphones and other personal property to the hospital, if requested.

6. Employees working out of the dormitory must count their men before leaving, while at work, and again upon returning to the dormitory. Inmates are to hold their respective places in line until properly checked.

7. Inmates shall be in line in room formation and will be assigned to rooms according to their work assignment.

8. Unless accompanied by an employee or in a regular work line, all inmates will be searched upon entering or leaving the dormitory.

9. The entire dormitory shall be kept clean and neat at all times. Beds are to made up in a uniform manner and every room shall be ready for inspection at any time.

10. Nothing shall be permitted in any room which will obstruct a full view of same. Pieces of furniture, such as the bed, chest of drawers, etc., must not be placed against an outside wall or window.

11. Inspection of bars, windows, and rooms shall be made daily. Outside walls are to be checked daily to make certain an effort is not being made to tunnel through them.

12. Unnecessary noise, booing, loud talking, etc., will not

be permitted.

13. Every inmate must be out of the shower room by 8:00 P.M.

14. Under no circumstance shall any unassigned employee or inmate be permitted to loiter in or around the dormitory.

LAUNDRY

1. There is a proper way to launder various types of clothing and the formulae that are set up must be followed so that the best results are obtained, such as using the required amount of soap, bleach, etc., including proper rinsing. Unless the officer in charge properly supervises this assignment, inmates will take advantage of the situation by not following the required procedure, which could result in waste of materials and destruction of clothing.

2. Employees' clothing which is to be laundered must be picked up and delivered while the day officer is on duty. Laundry for employees will be done on a specified day; each package must be accompanied by a laundry slip bearing the employee's badge number and name, and the contents accurately enumerated. The finished clothes are to be checked against this laundry slip; if a shortage occurs it should be reported immediately.

3. Each cellhouse has a designated day at the laundry, and inmates' clothing is to be sent on that particular day. Each item must bear the register number of the inmate to whom it has been issued, and the number must be clear and legible. This applies also to any commissary clothing sold to an inmate. All items are to be returned the following day, except sheets which are to be returned as soon as possible after laundering. Inmate clothing is not to be starched or ironed unless proper authorization is given.

4. Denim overalls will be laundered every two weeks and are to be picked up in the cellhouses. Work clothes are to bear the identification, "Work' 'or "W-K", and are to be picked up in the shops. A slip showing the count and description of these articles of clothing must be signed by the officer in charge when the pick-up is made, and the slip is to accompany the clothes to the laundry and be checked.

5. Inmates' sheets and pillow slips will be laundered once a week, on a specified day, and that schedule is to be adhered to unless an emergency should arise.

6. Good judgment is to be used in the care and supervision of all laundry machinery, and it is never to be neglected or improperly operated. Daily inspections for fire hazards, grease, and lint are to be made.

7. No employee in charge of this assignment may leave until all wet or damp clothing has been properly spread out so that it will not be a fire hazard and there will be no opportunity for combustion.

8. Cleanliness on this assignment must be maintained at a high level at all times.

BATH HOUSE

1. Unless excused by the doctor, all inmates are to bathe at a specified time. A complete change of clothing is to be issued each man.

2. A sufficient length of time will be allotted under the shower so that each inmate will be able to soap and rinse himself properly before the water is turned off.

3. Each inmate will be provided with a towel and will not be permitted to use any article of clothing as a towel or floor mat.

4. In the bath house are containers which hold a drug solution to eliminate athletes' foot and fungus; as the inmates step out of the shower, they are to rinse their feet in this solution.

5. The officer in charge of the bath house is to see that the facilities are in proper working order at all times; that the shower room is thoroughly cleaned after each line is finished and that there is no soap or debris in the drains.

6. There is to be no loud talking, scuffling, or any other unnecessary noise in the bath house at any time.

SCHOOL

1. Many inmates find their way into crime and finally into prison because of lack of education. Our school program has

been provided for the rehabilitation of inmates lacking education. It is the duty of all employees to encourage inmates to educate themselves properly before release from the institution, so they will have a way of earning an honest livelihood and not go back into crime.

2. It is important that an inmate take advantage of the opportunities offered him. The desire of the department is to see that everyone gets at least an 8th grade education before being released from the institution.

3. If for any reason he does not coöperate in the educational program offered, and sufficient time has elapsed for him to benefit from the opportunities, such inmate is to be reported to the assigning officer and recommendation made by the Superintendent of Education that he be removed because of the impossibility of furthering his education. The discipline of the schoolroom should be firm but fair. Patience is important because men without schooling are slow in learning.

4. Inmates should be encouraged to take courses in the high school and college subjects offered. Through the educational facilities of the Superintendent of Schools and the G.E.D. test system, we are able to present diplomas to inmates who have met the requirements. Such diplomas contain no reference to where they were earned. The same applies to TV courses of college level.

5. It is important that security be maintained. All inmates entering and leaving the school are to be searched.

6. Supplies are to be issued to inmates at a specified time in school periods. When supplies are exhausted, replacement will be made. Each inmate will be responsible for the books and supplies issued to him. Anyone who defaces any of the state property will be reported to the disciplinarian. Permission may be granted inmates to take books and supplies to their cells for study.

7. The use of tobacco in any form will not be tolerated except during periods specified by the Superintendent of Education. Inmates will not be permitted to leave the classroom unless permission has been granted.

VOCATIONAL SCHOOL

1. Vocational training is a very important phase in helping to rehabilitate an inmate.

2. Primarily, it teaches him to work and to have an interest in something other than crime. Any hidden talents or aptitudes the inmate may possess are directed toward a useful and productive life upon his release from the institution. This gives him a sense of responsibility and a feeling that he can and will become useful, not only to himself but also to society. Keeping an inmate busy while serving time in any prison is very important, as idleness causes unrest which, in turn, leads to trouble.

3. The institution also benefits by the vocational school. Men trained in our schools are, upon graduation, given assignments in various forms of maintenance and industrial work throughout the prison. This procedure gives them an opportunity to practice and apply the knowledge they acquired while learning their trade. The motto "Learn by Doing" is to be closely followed whenever the opportunity presents itself.

4. Part of the cost of maintaining and operating the vocational school is financed through receipts of the inmates' commissary which also provides revenue for the general Inmates' Benefit Fund.

5. A percentage of the tools and equipment used in the vocational training program is paid for out of the Benefit Fund and used solely for the inmates' benefit. Up-to-date equipment is furnished whenever deemed advisable as it enables our school to keep abreast of new trade methods and techniques as they arise.

6. A competitive spirit is encouraged throughout the student body as just and fair comparison with the work of others teaches the inmate the truth of the axiom that "a job worth doing is worth doing well."

7. The vocational school personnel is comprised of a superintendent, custodial officers, school supervisors, and inmate instructors on the teaching staff.

8. Qualified inmates are selected to teach in the school.

They are men who have had experience in a particular trade on the outside or are graduates of the school.

9. The training followed here adheres strictly to the curriculum used in trade schools on the outside. The various methods employed are so devised that ALL students may acquire the maximum amount of knowledge and skill in the particular subject in which they are enrolled.

10. The school was created for the benefit of those inmates who desire to learn a trade. They are expected to apply themselves. An inmate who does not show an interest or lacks aptitude for such training is removed and his place given to another inmate who has the ability and interest to make good. Any student who makes the effort and is willing to learn will be given coöperation and encouragement.

11. All tools and equipment must be kept in good order and repair. A constant check is to be made on tools and any shortage must be reported to the supervisor or a lieutenant. Inmates will not be permitted to leave the assignment until the shortage has been investigated and cleared. All tools must be signed for when taken out for use.

12. Classes will be dismissed sufficiently early so the assignment may be cleaned before leaving school.

13. Inmates who study in their cells will be permitted to carry books out of the school in the evening only, and they can only be returned in the morning. Nothing may be carried out of this assignment during the noon hour.

INDUSTRIES AND SHOPS

1. The duties of the superintendent of industries may be broadly defined as the carrying out of the administrative policies pertaining to the prison industries as have been established by the statutes governing their operations, and the programs formulated by the director of the Department of Public Safety, his administrative assistants, and by the warden of the institution.

2. He is required to delegate duties to, and supervise the work of, the personnel assigned to his office. It is his duty to

A few samples of furniture manufactured at the furniture factory. Warden Ragen speaking with Mr. Hartfield, Superintendent. Stateville Branch, 1959.

establish and maintain in the office of the superintendent of industries such business procedures and office records as will insure the proper recording of the business activities of the industries.

3. He must coöperate closely with the individual departmental superintendents and, in turn, require their coöperation to insure the efficient, orderly management of the industries. He must be familiar with the plant and equipment facilities of each unit and with the manufacturing operations carried on in each department. He must maintain close contact with each department to determine that established operating policies of the prison industries are being carried out.

4. It is his duty, after consultation with the warden and the business manager of the institution, to prepare the recommended operating budget for the industries for each biennial

period. Once a definite operating budget has been established by
the director of the Department of Public Safety, after legislative approval, it is the duty of the superintendent of industries
to establish such necessary budget controls as will insure the
proper allocation of funds to the departments required for their
efficient operation.

View showing Reed Factory in 1920's. Joliet Branch.

5. It is the duty of the superintendent of industries to inspect and approve all requisitions for materials and equipment
required for the operations of the various departments. The installation of proper inventory control records and the supervision
of their maintenance are an important function in this respect,
inasmuch as the industries annually utilize materials and equipment in their manufacturing operations.

6. The superintendent of industries must approve all invoices rendered by suppliers for materials and equipment required
in the industries. He must establish and maintain such office pro-

cedures as will provide a check on the receipt of materials and a register of all orders placed for materials and equipment. He must maintain a record of all official orders placed for products of the industries and shipments of any materials not covered by a bona fide order.

7. He must require the establishment and maintenance of such cost records in the individual departments as will insure the proper recording of all necessary cost data and the correlation of such information in his office to insure the proper pricing of all industrial products. He must issue price lists at regular intervals and exercise general supervision over the pricing policies to insure the profitable operation of the industries.

8. It is the duty of the superintendent of industries to inspect and approve the monthly payrolls covering inmate industrial bonuses for all departments and to compile such payrolls in his office each month for vouchering.

9. The superintendent of industries must make every effort to promote a good supplier-customer relationship with the many institutions utilizing the products of the industries. This entails frequent consultations with the departmental supervisors on the quality and design of products and their packaging and shipment. He must contact the administrative officers of the state and local tax-supported bodies frequently on orders placed with the industries and offer such suggestions and recommendations to them on the utilization of industrial products as may be helpful.

10. The superintendent of industries must cooperate closely with the other administrative officers of the institution since operations of the industries constitute only one of the important phases of the over-all institutional program, and, as one of the chief administrative aides of the warden, the primary function of his office must be the efficient, orderly management of the industries so that they may contribute their full share of the success of that program.

11. The duties of departmental superintendents and foremen of the various departments of the prison industries may be broadly defined as those of a supervisory nature normally con-

nected with the operation of any large manufacturing plant. Such duties include the supervision of employees and inmates assigned to the department, the procurement of necessary equipment and materials, the efficient planning of departmental operations, the scheduling of production, the establishment of specifications for the design, construction, and finishing of items manufactured, the maintenance of proper standards of workmanship, inspection of finished items, and the shipment of completed items against orders for delivery approved by the Department of Public Safety.

12. It is the duty of every departmental superintendent to carry out the general industrial program and policy established for his department by the warden of the institution and the superintendent of industries. He must cooperate fully with the custodial officers in carrying out the security regulations of the institution as they may affect his department. Discipline and institutional safety will be the foremost consideration at all times.

13. The various industrial departments manufacture hundreds of items involving cutting, milling, assembly, and finishing operations. The departmental superintendent must be familiar with each of these operations and offer such technical assistance and information to the shop personnel of his department as may be required. He must thoroughly familiarize himself with the general regulations governing all employees of the institution and with those special regulations which pertain to the operation of the prison industries in order that he may properly supervise his department in a manner that will promote the general industrial program.

14. If he is to efficiently discharge his duties, the superintendent must realize that his department, as a unit of the prison industries, serves a two-fold purpose: that of providing worthwhile work activities for assigned inmates and that of furnishing materials and equipment to state institutions at the lowest possible cost. He must be actively interested in the operation of his department and determine that it will contribute its full share to the over-all program of the industries and the institution.

15. The superintendent of each department may delegate

responsibility to the various foremen assigned as his administrative assistants. He will, however, carefully supervise the shop activities of such foremen and work in close harmony with them to insure that efficient and practical shop operations are being utilized.

16. He will approve the work assignments of all inmates in the department and exercise such general supervision over their work habits and technical abilities as will promote the orderly and efficient flow of work through the department.

17. He must plan shop operations in a manner that will insure prompt handling of all orders, schedule production in his department, determine what items are to be manufactured, when they are to be made, and make certain that proper authorization exists fo rtheir manufacture.

18. The superintendent will submit requisitions for required materials and equipment at fixed intervals or when emergency requirements arise, and must inspect all such requisitions originating in his department to determine that the materials are actually required. After approval by the departmental superintendent, all requisitions will be forwarded to the office of the superintendent of industries for further handling. .

19. He must guard against the unnecessary accumulation of materials and maintain such records in his department as will insure a proper check on quantities in stock, normal operating requirements, and current costs. It is his duty to maintain adequate inventories of materials to insure efficient and orderly manufacturing operations and, as far as possible, should be familiar with the proper quality of the basic materials used, to insure the proper quality of the finished product.

20. He shall personally inspect each shipment of merchandise delivered to his department against purchase orders or O.F.D.'s issued to various suppliers, in order to determine that such merchandise meets the specifications as to quality and kind of material as specified in the order. The receipt of any inferior merchandise shall be reported immediately to the warden and the superintendent of industries.

21. Each superintendent must check the quality of workmanship in his department and must not permit the shipment of any completed item that fails to meet the accepted standards of materials and workmanship. He must be familiar with the specifications of the items manufactured in his department and recommend to the superintendent of industries any changes in construction or design which he may deem warranted.

22. In addition to his responsibility for the actual production activities of his department, the superintendent must be familiar with the maintenance of office and stock records required for the efficient management of his department. He must make certain that the necessary daily and monthly reports are properly compiled and submitted to the superintendent of industries.

23. Of paramount importance is his duty to maintain such necessary cost records as will reflect accurately the manufacturing costs of each item produced in his department. Cost records are essential for the proper pricing of products; it is the duty of the superintendent to establish the correct selling price for all items manufactured in his department. Such prices, together with detailed cost information, will be submitted to the superintendent of industries for approval.

24. The superintendent must supervise the maintenance of the industrial bonus records for his department and, at the end of each month's business, will submit detailed time sheets showing the shop hours credited to each inmate assigned to his department in that particular month. When bonuses are paid, he must supervise the maintenance of the proper industrial records.

25. Maintenance of discipline, security of inmates, and institutional safety shall be the responsibility of all departmental superintendents, foremen and employees of the institution assigned to duty in any department. However, it will be the duty of each superintendent to make certain that all institution regulations are closely followed by employees assigned to his department.

26. A room is provided in each assignment for the storage of tools and any article that might be used by an inmate in an

attempted escape. Such tools may be checked out to an inmate when necessary to perform his work properly, however, an accurate record must be kept of all tools issued. It will be the duty of each departmental superintendent and foreman to make certain that all tools are checked and returned to the tool room daily. Under no circumstances will anyone, except men assigned to that duty, be permitted to enter any tool room.

27. Boxes, barrels, crates, or anything in which an inmate could conceal himself should, whenever possible, be made ready for shipment and locked in the shipping room overnight. This will permit several counts of inmates to insure that none has concealed himself in an attempt to escape.

28. Any rope, wire, twine, or ladders will be carefully checked in and out by an employee. At no time will such articles be left in charge of an inmate.

29. Inflammable articles must be under the constant supervision of an employee assigned to the department. At no time will any inmate be permitted to transport or deliver such inflammable articles, except under the direct supervision of an employee.

30. In case special work details are required to complete work by a certain time, and when such details have been approved, it will be the duty of the department foreman or any other authorized employee to remain with the detail until the work has been completed.

31. Inmates on tickets are to be searched thoroughly upon entering or leaving the assignment. Work lines will be searched thoroughly before being permitted to leave the assignment.

32. When it is necessary for inmates engaged in repair work to have tools in their possession, such tools will be listed on the work order and must be carefully checked when brought into or out of any assignment.

MASTER MECHANIC

1. The master mechanic is responsible for all maintenance work within the institution. He is subject to twenty-four hour call, and when away from the institution (except on vacation), must give the guard hall officer his telephone number. As the

master mechanic, he is in charge of all foreman of the various mechanical trades.

2. He is to plan the work for all foremen, instruct them as to their duties, and see that they have the tools and materials needed for the jobs assigned to them.

3. The mechanical stockroom, warehouses, and records are to be checked to see that a sufficient amount of stock for repairs and spart parts are on hand at all times. No material shall be drawn from the stockroom or warehouses without a requisition properly authorized by the master mechanic and assistant warden.

4. The master mechanic and the foremen in charge of the shops are to keep in mind that it is the aim of the institution to rehabilitate men. Every effort should be made to see that inmates are encouraged to learn the various trades. It is important that a sufficient number of inmates (who can qualify for various vocations) be assigned to the shops, so that when an inmate is released or transferred another inmate is qualified to replace him.

5. He has complete supervision of all automotive equipment and is to see that it is properly cared for and inspected in accordance with state requirements, in addition to keeping a record of the cost of operation.

6. He is to see that all utilities, such as gas, electricity, steam and water are adequate, safe, tested daily, and in good working order. A record is to be kept showing daily consumption, cost, etc.

7. All coal received must be checked to ascertain if it is the quality as ordered, the correct size, and if the supply is sufficient.

8. At a time set by the business office, quarterly and annual requisitions are to be made to cover necessary equipment and supplies needed in the maintenance of the institution.

9. Fire equipment must be kept in good working condition at all times. Any recommendations made by the State Fire Marshal must be followed, insofar as possible.

10. The master mechanic is to make certain that all communication lines and equipment are in good working order at

all times.

11. A constant check is to be kept to make certain that the water supply is sufficient and that the equipment is in proper working order. All water must be properly chlorinated and fit for drinking purposes.

12. The master mechanic is in charge of the maintenance of all powerhouse boilers, pumps, water softeners, etc. No boiler is to be added or taken off the line by the fireman or employee in charge of any shift, unless authorized by the master mechanic, except in emergencies. A record is to be kept indicating the efficiency of all boilers.

13. It is his duty to see that the ice machine is in good working condition and instruct the employee in charge of the machine regarding its complete operation. A record must be kept of ice manufactured, as well as the cost of same.

14. The locking system used in the institution is an important function, and he is to see that all necessary repairs are made immediately.

15. All work in the master mechanic's shop is to be completed as soon as possible, after proper authorization has been given.

16. All buildings of the institution are to be properly maintained and he must see that necessary repairs are made on all buildings, including painting.

17. All new construction projects must be inspected to see that the work is being done according to specifications.

18. A monthly report must be submitted to the Springfield Office showing the operation of boilers, ice plant, gasoline and oil consumption, water chlorination, water, power and light, pumping records and coal. The master mechanic shall make a report to the warden of all construction work, stating location, date started, date finished, and cost.

19. The master mechanic's department will take care of all maintenance work in and around the institution. Superintendents, firemen, foremen, and maintenance employees in this department are under the supervision of the master mechanic, and will

perform the duties assigned them in accordance with his directions. Safety measures will be observed at all times. Foremen supervising a work assignment are to see that the job is completed, whenever possible, without asking for a late detail. These details are to be asked for only in an emergency.

20. No work is to be performed without a work order, signed by the proper authorities. It is positively prohibited to manufacture knives or tools of any kind without the proper authorization. Equipment such as emery wheels, lathes, etc., which might be used to make contraband articles is to be under the supervision of an employee at all times.

21. If steam, water, or electricity is to be turned off for repair work, notify the senior captain's office, as well as the departments which might be affected.

22. No major changes in equipment or buildings will be made without the authorization of the warden and the master mechanic. This specifically has to do with the cutting of any bars, holes in buildings, holes in walls, or any other work of this type.

23. Inmates must remain on their particular assignments within the shop and will not be permitted to leave them, unless authorized to do so. When it is necessary for an inmate to leave any shop to make repairs, all tools and materials shall be listed on the work order. A timed work order is to be carried by the inmate when he is moving from one assignment to another.

24. The employee in charge of the master mechanic's shop is to time the inmate out and check the time he arrives at the point designated on the work order; thereafter, at intervals, he is to check with the employee where the work is being done as to the inmate's presence.

25. Foremen are to supervise the inmates making repairs. After the work has been completed, foremen are to make final inspections and give their approval so there will be no opportunity for any imperfect work.

26. Tools are essential in performing necessary work, but it is to be remembered that those same tools are a great source of danger. Therefore, tools are to be accounted for every minute

of the day and are not to be left out of the tool room when not in use, nor used other than in the manner for which they are prescribed. An inspection of all tools and equipment will be made at regular intervals; any shortage is to be reported immediately. Worn-out or broken tools are to be condemned and deposited in a place designated for that purpose. Tools are not to be in the hands of an inmate at any time, unless he is supervised. All tools are to be marked as indicated.

27. A copy of the tool report will be sent to the assistant warden each week and will be signed by the employee designated to make tool counts and checks. Any additional tools or condemned tools, will be included in this list. All tools must be stamped with the identification mark assigned for each department (See form to be used).

28. All rope, twine, wire, ladders, or anything which might be used to accomplish an escape must be carefully checked in and out. Under no circumstances will equipment of this type be permitted to leave the shop in the custody of an inmate. Inmates bearing such equipment must be accompanied by an employee.

29. The mechanical foremen are under the direct supervision of the master mechanic; however, each foreman is directly responsible for his individual department and the inmates assigned to that department. Foremen, like the master mechanic, are on twenty-four hour call. They are to notify the guard hall when off duty and away from home (except during vacation), so that, if an emergency arises, they may be located.

30. Foremen are to supervise all work done by the inmates assigned to their departments. There are places in the institution where inmates are not permitted; therefore, the foremen will be required to do the work necessary in such areas.

31. Foremen are to keep an accurate check of all the work scheduled, work completed, and work being completed. A full report will be made out monthly and submitted to the warden and the master mechanic.

32. Inmates experienced in the trades should be selected with extreme care to do the work; however, you are always to

have student helpers and attempt in all ways to rehabilitate inmates before their final release on parole or discharge. It is the duty of the foremen to give them every opportunity to learn and master a trade.

33. Discipline must be maintained at all times by the foremen in charge, reports made of any irregularities, and cooperate in all ways with custodial employees.

34. All tools, equipment, etc., must be returned to the shops when not in use or at the close of the work day. This includes worn out or replaced parts. When a project is finished, left over supplies are to be returned to the proper storage places.

35. Safety for everyone is of utmost importance on all work projects.

36. With the exception of one foreman who is to remain in the master mechanic's shop, all others are to have their meals at the same time the inmates do.

MECHANICAL STORE

1. The mechanical store is a branch of the general store and is used for the storing of needed supplies requisitioned by the master mechanic and foreman in charge of maintenance, etc. All stock deposited in the mechanical store must be kept on the books in the general store, and the books of both stores are to be kept in balance. The mechanical store is in possession of many tools and various pieces of equipment which could be used by inmates for assault, escape, and destruction of property. Saws, wrenches, files, paints, oils, and inflammables of all descriptions could be put to nefarious use by inmates, and a careful and positive check and search must be made at the time supplies are received from the general store. Paints, lacquers, and liquids are to be opened and stirred to see that no contraband is deposited therein. This applies to any box or container.

2. Saws which could be used in cutting steel must be sent directly to the armory by the receiving officer, and the employee in the armory must sign the receiving ticket. Anyone in need of a saw is to get it at the armory, sign a receipt for same, and return it to the armory the same day.

3. Duplicate requisitions for new tools to be drawn from the mechanical store stock must be signed by the master mechanic and the assistant warden, and submitted to the mechanical storekeeper.

4. The storekeeper is to note on one copy of the requisition what merchandise has been issued, initial same, and return to the sender. In this way the employee making the request for supplies will know what part of his requisition has been filled. Before being issued by the mechanical store, tools must be stamped with the identification mark assigned to each particular department.

5. Merchandise is not to be delivered nor given to anyone without a proper requisition. A space should be left blank between each item on all requisitions so that the stock number of such item may be listed; after the last item shown on the requisition, a line should be drawn diagonally toward the bottom of the sheet so nothing more can be added.

6. All tools must be condemned when they are of no further service and deposited with the condemning officer. When a replacement is asked for, it is to be properly noted on the condemning order, signed by the officer with the authority to condemn property, and a copy is to be sent to the assistant warden's office as well as to the mechanial storekeeper, and checked against tools that have been condemned before replacements are issued.

7. When unpacking freight packed in straw, paper, excelsior, or any other inflammable material, such material should be removed to the yard incinerator as soon as possible after unpacking. Inflammable articles must be under the constant supervision of an employee. Inmates are never to be permitted to supervise or handle an article that is inflammable unless they are accompanied by an officer.

8. A gate pass signed by the mechanical storekeeper must be made for all material going outside the wall.

9. All receiving tickets that accompany stock from the general receiving room to the mechanical store must be signed

by the officer checking same and, if correct, the tickets and receiving reports are to be returned to the general store.

10. Light bulbs must be signed for by the master mechanic.

11. All articles must be piled or stacked in order, and an accurate account kept of each item. Rope, twine, wire, ladders, etc., are to be carefully checked at all times and should at no time be left in charge of an inmate.

12. Only one door at the entrance is to be open at any time. No unassigned inmate will be permitted to enter the mechanical store except when accompanied by an employee, whose duty it will be to supervise that inmate during his stay in the store. Before an inmate leaves this assignment he is to be searched thoroughly. If an inmate's work requires him to have tools in his possession, they are to be listed on a work order and a check is to be made to see they are returned.

CONDEMNING OFFICER

1. The employee in charge of the inventory also acts as the condemning and survey officer for the institution. Each institution must have a perpetual inventory of all state property. Each piece of equipment is to be given a number indicating the department to which it is assigned. It is the duty of the condemning officer to make certain this identification number is removed at the time the article is condemned.

2. Any article of clothing or equipment deemed unfit for further use is to be inspected before being condemned. Any usable portions should be salvaged before the items are destroyed or junked. Condemning reports are to be made and signed by the condemning officer and by the employee in charge of the department wherein the articles or equipment are located. This report is to be forwarded to the chief clerk or business manager for proper handling. The condemning officer is to work in close cooperation with the business manager's office and store at all times.

3. The condemning of property is of major importance to the institution. A great saving of the taxpayers' money is possible if every article is inspected properly so that nothing of

value is condemned.

4. No replacements are to be made until condemned items for disposal have been turned in to the condemning officer who, in turn, is to deposit the condemned equipment in a place provided for that purpose.

CLOTHING ROOM AND SHOE SHOP

1. All clothing issued to an inmate must pass through this department. The handling of these articles is done in a specified manner and it is a MUST for the employee in charge to see that the inmates in his care do not deviate from the prescribed rules.

2. Each inmate is required to have only those clothes designated by the institutional rules and is never to be given more nor less than his allotment. It is the duty of the employee assigned to this department to see that all of the men are properly fitted and clothed.

Tailor Shop. Inmate being measured for his release clothing, Stateville Branch.

3. Inmates being released on parole, discharge, or writ, are to be furnished with clothes and shoes that fit them and, when possible, they may choose the color, etc. If they are dressed-out before the day of their release, the employee in charge of the clothing room will accompany them to the transit cells. The dress-out clothing then will be removed and placed in a secure locker until the inmates' release.

4. An inmate is never permitted to wear or carry a civilian suit outside the clothing room unless accompanied by an employee.

5. The stenciling of clothing and the stamping of shoes must be done under the supervision of an employee. Stencils are never to be given to an inmate. Numbers on clothing and shoes are not to be altered in any way. Any number which becomes faded or blurred is to be re-stamped so it is plainly visible at all times.

6. Clothing and shoes are to be repaired when needed

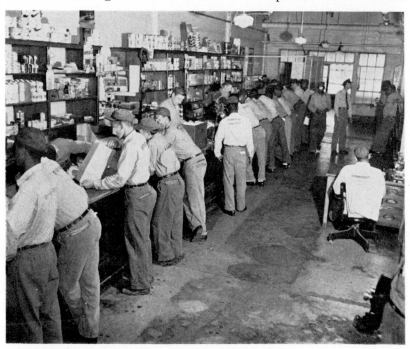

1936 view showing old inmate Commissary. Stateville Branch.

and such repairs are not to be delayed until the apparel is beyond repair stage. Good workmanship is a must in all repair work.

7. An accurate check of all clothing and supplies must be made daily and any shortage reported immediately.

8. Tools are to be accounted for every morning, noon, and evening, and shortages reported at once.

INMATE COMMISSARY

1. The inmate commissary has been set up as a privilege for inmates in good standing to purchase such items as are permitted under the rules of the Department of Public Safety. These

1959 view showing modern inmate Commissary. Stateville Branch.

items are sold at near cost, the margin of profit being turned into a fund which supports the prison's athletic and educational program.

2. All inmates, except those not in grade, have the privilege of making purchases at the commissary, providing they

have sufficient funds in their account, over and above that amount specified by the institution for those men assigned to industries. The employee in charge is to consult his ledgers to make certain of this before releasing any merchandise. Out-of-grade prisoners may purchase only dental necessities, shoes, and similar items on the exempt list.

3. To avoid forgeries and prevent inmates from making purchases on any account except their own, each must sign a voucher and place on this his thumb print. The print must be legible so that it may be classified by the prison bureau of identification should that become necessary. When it is impossible for an inmate to go to the commissary personally, he must sign a voucher and place his thumb print on it in the presence of an employee who will attest to this by initialing the voucher.

4. The employee in charge of the commissary is to be constantly alert for forgeries, and must notify the supervising officer when one is attempted. The suspected voucher will be taken to the bureau of identification.

5. Inmate purchases from the commissary must not exceed a specified amount each week, except when the purchase includes shoes and other items on the exempt list on file in the commissary. All items of clothing, including shoes, must be taken to the clothing room and stamped with the purchaser's register number before delivery is made. Worn-out clothing and shoes must be turned in to the commissary officer before replacements may be ordered.

6. No merchandise may be added to the commissary list without the approval of the warden. When new items are added, the cellhouse keepers must be notified so that inmates may have prior notice before their commissary day.

7. No merchandise is to be exchanged and no credit extended to any inmate.

8. A perpetual inventory shall be kept of all stock.

9. The commissary is to be kept scrupulously clean and in perfect order at all times. Unnecessary noise is not to be tolerated and inmates who create disturbances are to be reported

for disciplinary action. There is to be no smoking in the commissary during trading periods, except by inmates regularly assigned there. If inmates from other assingnments violate any of the rules they are to be treated as though part of the division under the commissary employee's supervision.

10. All inmates leaving the assignment must be thoroughly searched, except those lines accompanied by an officer.

11. Commissary clerks who handle food must be approved for the assignment by the prison physician and a health certificate must accompany an inmate when transferred to work there.

12. If an inmate's work requires the use of tools, these are to be listed on his work order and a check made to see they are returned.

INMATE BARBER SHOP AND WAITING ROOM

The barber shop, in addition to being a service department, is a school and student inmates are to be given every encouragement to learn the trade and better fit themselves for society after their release.

1. The instructor and employee in charge of the shop are the custodians of all razors, tools, and instruments used in the operation of the barber shop. All such items will be checked and charged to the inmate receiving them, and will be returned to the instructor or employee before the inmate leaves the shop. During working hours the instructor and the employee will periodically check the articles mentioned above and ascertain that they are not being mishandled. A safety locker is provided for the shop tools, etc., and under no circumstances will this locker be left unlocked or ungarded. Inmates who have been given razors, tools, and instruments with which to work will turn them in when requested. No inmate is to handle such tools unless he has been assigned to the barber shop.

2. All barber chairs will be kept in perfect alignment at all times and the shelves, brushes, towels, cups, etc., are to be kept neat, clean, and in a uniform position. All tools are to be properly sterilized. Special tools and towels will be used on the inmates who may have a contagious infection.

3. The employee is responsible for all inmates assigned to the barber shop, and at no time will an inmate leave this assignment without proper authority. If an inmate is permitted to leave on a ticket, he will turn in his allotment of tools and be searched before he leaves the shop.

4. When not occupied, barbers are to stand beside their chairs when visitors enter the shop.

5. The employee in charge of inmate divisions leaving the shower room for the barber shop will place at the front of the line those who wish to trade at the commissary. After having been barbered, those inmates who trade will not be permitted to return to the waiting room.

6. Employees in charge of a line are to supervise the seating of the inmates in an orderly manner. There will be no smoking, loud talking, or visiting among the inmates. This applies to both the waiting room and the barber shop. Employees are to maintain discipline in their particular divisions and are not to congregate.

7. Inmates in the waiting room are to remain seated when any visitors enter the building.

8. When necessary, inmates will be given permission to use the toilet at the rear of the waiting room by the employee in charge. There will be no loitering or congregating permitted.

9. As a chair becomes vacant in the barber shop an inmate will be called in and assigned that chair. At no time will an inmate be permitted to choose his own barber, nor a barber permitted to select any special inmate.

10. As each division is finished with their barbering, they are to return to their assignments, leaving the waiting room in an orderly manner, one row at a time.

11. Under no circumstances will any loitering be permitted, and inmates from one assignment will not be permitted to intermingle with the inmates of another assignment.

12. All razors, tools, and instruments are to be deposited in locker provided at end of the work period.

GENERAL STORE

1. The storekeeper is charged with the responsibility of receiving all merchandise and equipment. It will be his duty to inspect all items received and make certain the quality and quantity are as ordered.

2. The storekeeper and his assistants are responsible for the temperatures of the refrigerators, ice plants, and pasteurizing plant. It is important that the mechanism of these units is always in proper working order.

3. Before any item can be removed from the store it is necessary that a signed requisition be submitted. The storekeeper is responsible for the filling of requisitions and for the delivery of merchandise to the proper destination. A signed gate pass is to accompany all orders to be delivered outside the walls.

4. When milk is delivered to the general store, it should be sent immediately to the milk room and poured from one can to another to see that no contraband is contained therein. Cans are to be returned to the dairy at the close of the day's business but not before. All crates and containers are to be returned to the supplier as soon as possible. This includes divisions of the institution which supply the store, such as the farm.

5. Vegetables delivered from the farm are to be processed as soon as possible after being received. When it is necessary to keep vegetables overnight, they should be placed where they will be best preserved until the next day.

6. A workable program shall be laid out by the storekeeper, under the supervision of the chief guard, to see that all divisions of the store are properly supervised by an employee. The procedure which has been set up in the general office for the handling of merchandise shall be followed precisely.

7. Cleanliness and neatness are very important on this assignment. All inmates assigned to handle foodstuffs must first be approved by the prison physician, and a health certificate signed by the physician must accompany the inmate when he is assigned to the store. Inmates working in the store must keep themselves neat and clean, and frequent inspections should be

made to make certain this is done. Inmates not assigned to the store will not be permitted to enter unless they are accompanied by an employee.

8. Because of the many activities of the store, it is essential to make certain that dangerous tools, knives, etc., are carefully checked and a correct tool count maintained constantly.

CANNING PLANT

1. The canning plant is set up for the purpose of processing as much foodstuffs for institution use as possible.

2. Inmates assigned to the handling of food must be approved by the prison physician and a health certificate signed by the physician must accompany each inmate when he is transferred to this assignment. Inmates who work in the canning plant are to keep themselves clean; are to wash their hands after using the toilet, and their fingernails and hands are to be inspected reguarly by the employee in charge.

3. Fruits and vegetables should be processed as soon as possible after they arrive from the farm or market, according to the canning manual. The officers and superintendent are to see there is no waste.

4. A daily count of all production is to be kept so the employee in charge can give a total account any time a report is requested. Each can must be properly marked as to its contents. After a product is finished and cooled it is to be turned over to the storekeeper.

5. All crates and containers are to be returned to the farm as soon as possible, and it will be the duty of the employee in charge to supervise the loading and transporting of same through the gate, keeping alert for any contraband or hideouts. He also is to see that boxes and crates are not stacked so they form a possible place of concealment for inmates.

6. An accurate check of all tools and equipment must be kept at all times. Since there are a number of knives in this assignment, the employee in charge shall count them out to the officer who has men working in the preparation room; he in

turn will check them out to the inmates and, when gathered up, they are to be checked back to the officer in charge. The tool and equipment count is very important and a perpetual inventory is to be kept of all knives and equipment. If an inmate's work requires him to have tools in his possession, they are to be listed on a work order and a check is to be made to see that they are returned before the inmate leaves the assignment.

7. In the event a tool or knife is missing, a report is to be made immediately to the captain. Careful search is to be made and no inmate is to leave the shop until he is released by the captain or officer in charge of the search, or until the missing item is found.

8. Officers working in the shop are to take work orders from the employee in charge of the plant.

9. All garbage is to be placed in containers provided for that purpose and disposed of as soon as possible.

10. No one is to smoke while working over food.

11. It is very important that the shop and equipment are kept clean at all times.

12. When the officer in charge of this assignment is not busy, he is to assist in the general store.

SALLY PORT (OUTSIDE GATE)

1. Generally speaking, the rules governing the supervising officer of the sally port cover the gates proper; however, it is important that the employee assigned to the gates realizes that his assignment is one of the most important in the institution. Through this assignment contraband may be passed, therefore, every person and vehicle passed through the sally port must be searched thoroughly. It is not impossible for institution or outside trucks to have contraband concealed in or about them, and the driver not aware of it. Close scrutiny of all vehicles is very important. Employees are especially warned to inspect boxes, barrels, garbage, or anything in which an inmate could be concealed as a means of escape. The harness, tails, and manes of horses must be searched.

2. The gates are always to be under the control of the officer located in the tower above the sally port, and both gates are never to be opened at the same time.

3. Materials, equipment, and supplies are not to be passed in or out of this gate unless proper requisition or a gate pass accompanies same. Gate passes are to be forwarded to the warden's office each evening after work.

4. In the event of fire, the supervising officer is authorized to pass the fire chief, fire equipment, and inmates assigned to this detail through the sally port and into the institution proper. Fire department units from surrounding communities which may come to assist are to be permitted to pass through the sally port provided they are accompanied by an officer and after proper search has been made. All persons permitted to enter the institution at the time of a fire are to be identified by a supervising officer before they are passed out.

5. An accurate count should be kept at all times of inmates who pass out of the gate in the morning; those who return within the walls during the day, and the final return of all inmates in the evening. When the final count of the day is made and all inmates returned inside the supervising officer in charge is to be notified immediately.

6. The supervising officer in charge is to be notified when a railroad switch is to be made, and when it is completed.

7. The officer in charge of the sally port is to familiarize himself with all the rules governing the outside detail.

POWER HOUSE

1. The power house must be operated as efficiently as possible and at a minimum cost. An accurate record must be kept of all coal and water consumed. The employee in charge is to see that proper steam pressure is maintained at all times; that proper firing is being done; that fires are pulled clean, leaving no clinkers on the side or back wall of the fire box and, in order to save fuel, tubes, and brick work inside the fire box, fires should be pulled as quickly as possible. The flues must be blown properly three times daily. The boilers must never be

left untended; a fireman must be present at all times.

2. The employee in charge must see that no one is permitted in the pump room or over the boilers except those inmates assigned there. The water tender and maintenance men are the only persons to be permitted on the water mound. The water tender is the only person permitted on the catwalk in front of and between the boilers.

3. Coal must be burned properly and without waste. Ashes are to be removed properly. All boilers and other apparatus, the windows, walls, and floors must be kept clean and in perfect order at all times. The door to the power house is to be kept locked and only assigned inmates permitted to enter at any time.

4. The maintenance man must keep all equipment in proper working order and report any breakdowns immediately.

5. When necessary to turn off the steam, water, or electricity, the employee in charge is to notify the captain as well as the various departments which will be affected. This should be done at least one hour in advance, if at all possible.

6. The employee in charge must report to the telephone operator every 30 minutes.

7. In case of fire it shall be the duty of the employee in charge of the power house to determine the exact location of the fire; to shut off water in all mains except the one which leads to the fire area; to shut off the water softeners in the power house and notify the ice plants at cold storage, the general kitchen, and the farm dormitory to shut off their ice machines.

8. The door to the sub-station must never be opened except when necessary. No inmates are to be admitted except those assigned or accompanied by an officer.

9. The officer in charge of the power house is to make periodic inspections of all departments to see that everything is in proper working order.

10. The red lights in the tunnel must be turned on when anyone enters from the power house and the armory must be notified. In turn, when anyone enters the tunnel from the armory, the power house is to be notified.

11. Rope, twine, wire and ladders are to be checked in and out very carefully, and at on time will they be left in charge of an inmate.

YARD DIVISION AND SUPERVISION OF GARDENS

1. The employee in charge of this assignment has general supervision over all inmates assigned to the yard detail. It is his responsibility to see that the necessary work is accomplished. Safety is the first consideration and men with escape or bad records are to be assigned only where they can be under close supervision. A correct list giving the names, numbers, and assignments of all inmates in this division is to be kept at all times.

2. No inmate is to be assigned as a truck driver, gateman, bucketman for the towers, runner or any other job calling for a detail, until permission has been given by the senior captain and the necessary details signed. Under no circumstances will any inmate, other than those assigned, be permitted to ride in a truck.

3. Every truck and wagon must be inspected before it is loaded. The yard division officer must place himself in a strategic spot while the vehicle is being loaded so that he may make certain no inmates or contraband are concealed therein. When this inspection has been made, approval should be given to the employee in charge of the sally port. The employee in charge of the vehicle is to ride on the outside of the truck and never in the cab with an inmate. As towers are passed, the towermen are to be signaled so they are assured the vehicle is in full command of an employee. The employee in charge is to remain with the truck or wagon until it has gone through the gate.

4. The employee in charge of this assignment is to make certain the power house is supplied daily with the necessary coal and that railroad tracks are in good condition at all times.

5. All assignments within the yard division are to be kept clean and in an orderly fashion. The tunnels and walks must be kept clean and free of any debris. If they become glazed in

winter they are to be kept sanded until the ice can be removed. Flowers, shrubs and grass are to be tended properly, as directed by the gardener. Garbage and trash must be removed from the hospital, shops, and other assignments and disposed of in the proper manner.

6. The employee in charge of the coal division will take all men not needed for any work to the bath house every afternoon for a bath and return them to the cellhouse before the change of shifts.

7. When leaving the various assignments, all inmates are to be searched thoroughly. In the event an inmate's work requires him to have tools in his possession, they should be listed on a work order which is to be carried by the inmate. All tools and equipment must be kept serviceable and all must be accounted for before this assignment is left in the evening. When the tools are returned they must be checked and counted.

TOWERS

The guard towers, strategically placed on the walls surrounding the prison and located at critical points within the walls, form the backbone of the institution's security system. If armed men were not assigned to the towers, there would be innumerable attempts to escape, to start riots, to assault officials, to start fires, etc., some of which would succeed or result in the serious injury or even death of employees and the wanton destruction of state property. Only the constant vigilance of employees assigned to duty in the towers can prevent such disturbances.

Employees assigned to tower duty must be outstanding in their alertness, judgment, marksmanship, and ability to act promptly and efficiently in an emergency. The assignment is one of the most important in the institution and absolute compliance with all rules of the institution and the special regulations governing the post is mandatory.

It should never be forgotten that many prisoners have friends or relatives on the outside who may attempt to provide guns, saws, explosives, or even narcotics by throwing them over

Tower No. 9. Thirty-two feet high, nine feet in ground. Stateville Brancn.

the wall or try to smuggle such articles through the gates by a trusty or runner. There is also the possibility that an inmate inside the walls may try to obtain explosives and attempt to bomb or burn out the towerman in an effort to gain possession of his firearms and thus effect an escape.

Should an escape be attempted, it will be the duty of any employee of the institution to do everything possible to prevent its success. Firearms should be used when, in the opinion of the employee, the escape cannot otherwise be prevented. Firearms, however, should be used with discretion. A trained marksman can so place his shots that the desired effect can be obtained without endangering the lives of innocent persons. It should be kept in mind at all times that a bullet may ricochet and cause untold damage.

The ingenuity of the desperate prisoner attempting to

escape is almost unbelievable. His plan may be foolhardy, but he will stop at nothing to gain his objective — even if it means killing prison officials. Only the alertness of the employee on duty in the tower and the promptness with which he acts can prevent attempts to escape. The personal safety of the towerman, himself, as well as that of his fellow-employee handling inmates inside the walls, depends entirely upon the efficient functioning of employees manning the towers.

In addition to the general rules and regulations governing all employees of the institution, the following shall pertain in particular to those assigned to duty in the towers:

1. At no time and under no circumstances shall any person be admitted to any tower unless such person is known to be an employee of this institution. Regardless of whether the individual seeking admittance is in the regulation uniform, he shall not be admitted unless personally known to and recognized by the towerman then on duty, and after receiving the approval of the lieutenant or captain in charge. When a change in shifts is to be made, the towerman on duty shall be notified by his superior officer of the identity of the relieving employee. He shall make certain that only the designated employee is admitted to the tower. The tower door shall be kept locked at all times and the key kept in the possession of the towerman. When the proper relief appears, and has been identified and recognized, the key shall be lowered to him by a rope provided for that purpose.

2. It shall be the duty of the towerman to maintain a constant watch in all directions, always being on the alert and observing everything that takes place near his tower. In the event there is activity on both sides of the wall, he shall maintain supervision to the best of his ability over such activity. Any unusual incident shall be promptly reported to the proper officials.

3. In the event that an attempt to escape is made, all towermen in the vicinity shall immediately take any action necessary to stop the inmate or inmates.

4. It is not beyond the realm of possibility that an attempt may be made to deliver contraband articles to an inmate through the use of an airplane or helicopter. If, at any time, either should land or attempt to land within the walls of the institution, all towermen are instructed to use firearms to disable the machine so it will be unable to rise. In the event an airplane or other flying machine should drop an article within the walls, firearms should be used to prevent any inmate from reaching the object. The incident should be reported immediately to the warden or superior officer on duty.

5. The license numbers of automobiles passing close to any tower, and the identifying letters and numbers of any aircraft flying at a low altitude in the vicinity of the institution shall be recorded and a report made without undue delay to the proper officials.

6. Should any attempt be made to place a ladder against the inside wall, or to throw a rope, wire, etc., over the wall, the towerman must stop such a maneuver at all costs. When necessary to make repairs on the wall, wall-lights, etc., ladders may be placed against the OUTSIDE OF THE WALL at the direct order of the warden or his authorized assistant. Any work detail using ladders or ropes in the immediate vicinity of the outside wall shall be under the direct supervision of a superior officer of the institution.

7. When it becomes necessary for arms and/or ammunition to be transferred from one tower to another, all towermen in the vicinity shall be notified and the officer making such transfer shall be fully protected by neighboring towermen.

8. In the event a tower inside the walls is to be occupied by an armed employee, he shall be accompanied to his post by a superior officer of the institution. When it becomes necessary to transfer arms within the walls, the transferring party shall be supervised by a superior officer. Arms and ammunition shall never be carried by one person; firearms shall be transported by one employee and the ammunition by another. In all cases where munitions are transferred, the group shall be fully

covered by an armed employee at a safe distance to make certain that no inmate attempts to gain their possession.

9. Each tower will be equipped with six flares, two rifles, one revolver, three gas grenades, adequate ammunition, and a pistol-grip light. Weapons must be kept within reach at all times. The towerman is directly responsible for the cleanliness and working condition of all equipment; he must make certain that all arms are cleaned, well oiled, and in good working order when he goes on duty; he will check all equipment personally and account for each item before signing the equipment slip for the towerman being relieved. Weapons or supplies issued from the armory must be in first class condition before being accepted by towermen. Necessary repairs to all ordnance equipment will be made by the armory man. The towerman, while on duty, must never attempt to make repairs, replace burned-out light bulbs, or perform any other task that may interfere with the proper performance of his duties. Should repair or replacement of any item of equipment become necessary during the towerman's tour of duty, the superior officer in charge shall be notified immediately.

10. The towerman must exercise discretion in the use of emergency equipment. Flashlights, battery-lights, and flares should be used only when absolutely necessary (in the event a storm or any other disturbance causes a failure in the lighting system). Care should be taken to preserve batteries for use in such emergencies.

11. In any emergency the towerman should throw his flares in such position that the top of the wall is in view at all times. He should, generally speaking, use his pistol-grip light to supervise the area to the right of his tower; however, it should be remembered that the lights from neighboring towers may not reach his tower and each towerman should make every effort to maintain complete supervision of the surrounding area.

12. During a fog or other unusual weather condition, employees are detailed to patrol the inside of the wall, while cars are provided to supervise the outside area, and, it shall

be the duty of the towerman to be especially watchful during such emergencies to prevent any escape or attempt to escape.

13. The large lights on the towers are to be turned on during the day only in the event of unusual weather conditions, or at the direction of the warden or his authorized assistant.

14. During the hours of darkness, towermen will challenge anyone approaching the tower from either side of the wall by flashing their lights on the approaching person or party. If the person is a supervising officer or other employee, the challenge will be answered by a return flash. If, for any reason, the challenge is not properly answered or the towerman is in any doubt as to the identity of the approaching person or party, he shall keep his light concentrated on the person and immediately notify his superior officer.

15. In the event that cars or other vehicles pass his tower the towerman shall turn his light on the occupants (regardless of the fact that the driver may be blinded), permitting no car to pass on institution property unless the occupants are known to have legitimate business in the vicinity. Should any car or vehicle pass the tower before the towerman has identified the occupants, he shall immediately notify his superior officer and other towers in the vicinity of the passing vehicle.

16. Where towers operate outside existing gates the towerman on duty shall open only one gate at a time, and then only when given the proper signal by the employee in charge of the gate. It shall be the duty of any towerman to order a search of any vehicle passing the immediate vicinity of his tower when he has reason to suspect that undetected contraband has been concealed in such vehicle.

17. Towermen on duty at a point where coal is passed through the wall shall be especially watchful during the time such openings are in use to make certain that no contraband articles are passed.

18. If the tower is in the immediate vicinity of any shop, building, or other assignment where there is activity or where inmates are employed, the towerman must supervise all activity

to the best of his ability. He shall be especially watchful to guard against contacts being made among the inmates, or the passage of any article in or out of the assignment. He shall immediately notify his superior officer (and if possible, the employee in charge of the inmates) of any unusual activity and report any incident that he deems important.

19. AT NO TIME SHALL ANY INMATE OR GROUP OF IN-MATES LOITER OR CONGREGATE NEAR THE WALL OR UNDER ANY TOWER.

20. The towerman shall be on the alert constantly for any distress signal given by a fellow-employee who may be supervising inmates in the vicinity of the tower. It should always be uppermost in the mind of every towerman that he is the first line of protection for his fellow-employee inside the walls. It is impossible to over-emphasize the importance of breaking up an attempt riot or escape before it can gain headway. Only constant alertness and prompt action by the towerman can assure a safe institution.

21. Parties of visitors passing in the vicinity of inmates should be carefully watched, not only to prevent contact by inmates but also for the protection of such visitors. It should be remembered that it is not impossible for an inmate to hold a visitor, especially a woman or child, as hostage, nor is it beyond the realm of possibility that an inmate may attempt to indecently expose himself while visitors are touring the institution.

22. Officials of the institution and superior officers passing any tower must be saluted by the towerman on duty.

23. Some towers are provided with catwalks but, generally speaking, they are not to be used. The tower itself furnishes protection, and it should be remembered that a group of inmates bent on escape can disable the towerman if he is on the catwalk by throwing rocks or bricks at him.

24. The towerman should be especially careful in handling guns while outside the tower. Guns should not be set on window ledges or placed where they may be knocked or dropped off.

In the event a gun should fall inside the wall, the towerman should immediately report such fact to his superior officer and use his relief gun to cover the fallen weapon until help can arrive.

25. Towermen will be notified whenever it is necessary for an inmate to be on the roof of any building. However, in the event that a towerman has not been notified and he observes one or more inmates on any building, he shall immediately report their presence to his superior officer.

26. Whenever it becomes necessary to take an inmate repair man into any tower, the towerman and all arms and munitions will be removed to the nearest neighboring tower while the necessary repairs are being made.

27. Employees assigned to tower duty must furnish their own meals from outside the institution and must carry their own drinking water. Water containers can be refilled only by an employee of the institution. Never shall any towerman accept any food or drink whatsoever from an inmate during his tour of duty. (This rule is primarily for the protection of the employee, because of the possibility of meals being poisoned or liquids drugged by an inmate who plans to attempt to gain possession of firearms or to escape.)

28. Where towers are occupied only a portion of the day, the employee last on duty in such tower shall make certain that all windows are closed and the tower is properly locked before he leaves.

29. Employees assigned to the dining room tower should keep in mind the fact that the dining room is one of the most vulnerable spots in the institution. Such employees must be especially watchful during the time inmates are in the room and make an immediate report of an unusual action or incident to their superior officer. Should a riot or any major disturbance take place, the employee on duty in the central tower shall use tear gas, placing the charge at the point nearest the seat of the trouble. Firearms should be used only when absolutely necessary and, then, with the greatest of care. It must be remembered that the building is constructed of hard material

and bullets may ricochet. However, protection of life and property is essential and any riot or disturbance must be quelled at all costs.

30. In towers where coal stoves provide heat, it is the duty of the towerman to keep a sufficient supply of coal in the tower at all times. The stoves must be kept clean and in good repair at all times, and ashes are to be removed during each shift. It is imperative that the entire assignment be kept scrupulously clean at all times.

31. In some instances towers are provided with runners; it will be the duty of the towerman to prohibit such runners from trading, contacting, or dealing in contraband with anyone.

32. Towermen will report every thirty (30) minutes, either by reporting to the telephone operator, or by using the radio (or both).

33. Sleeping, cooking, reading, listening to the radio, writing (other than essential reports), shaving, or in fact doing anything that might distract the attention of the towerman from his duty, is strictly prohibited. Any such neglect of duty will be cause for severe disciplinary action.

34. If, for any reason, it is necessary for the towerman to be relieved from duty because of sickness, etc., he shall immediately call his superior officer, and request such relief. At no time shall any towerman leave his post without first having been properly relieved.

INSTITUTION TOURS

1. Visitors escorted through the institution should know they have been granted a privilege, and they will be expected to abide by all rules at all times.

2. First, and most important, relatives or close friends of inmates will not be permitted to tour the institution under any circumstances. Employees who are assigned to take visitors through must know who they are and be able to vouch that they are not connected with any inmate.

3. Tours should be conducted in approximately one-half

hour. Under no circumstance will any visitor or visitors be taken, without permission, to places in the institution which are not designated in the tour route laid out by the warden. Groups are to enter through the gatehouse, where all will be properly searched, registered, and (when groups contain more than five persons) one hand of each visitor stamped. Registration is to be supervised by the employee at the gatehouse, and a ticket issued to each visitor when the group is over five. The employees conducting the tour are to make sure the visitors sign their names and addresses. The tickets are to be carried during the tour, and on the return trip through the guard hall, they are to be signed again by the visitors under the supervision of the officer in charge of the guard hall to make certain the signatures are identical. Upon leaving, the tickets are to be picked up at the gatehouse and checked again to see that the signatures are identical.

4. Visitors must remain in pairs during the entire tour. Loud talking, boisterousness, or any unnecessary noise will not be permitted. The employees conducting the tour must see that the visitors conduct themselves as ladies and gentlemen; any who cause difficulty are to be returned to the gatehouse immediately. There is to be absolutely no contact made between visitors and inmates.

5. Employees are to answer all reasonable questions asked by visitors; however, if they do not know the correct answers, they are to advise the visitor accordingly, as it is important that only correct information be given.

6. Employees are to place themselves in a position where they have complete supervision of the group, as we have men confined here for various types of crimes and some would not hesitate to commit an immoral or immodest act while visitors are passing, causing embarrassment to all. It must also be remembered that we have civilian clothes inside the yard and in the administration building, and it would not be impossible for an inmate to obtain clothes and attempt to fall into the group and be passed out as a visitor. The tour guide must know the number of persons in the group!

TRANSPORTING INMATES

1. In moving prisoners between the institutions, whether on writs or to return escapees, etc., the prisoners are to be securely handcuffed; leg irons, as well as lead chain, should be used for additional security. Remember, in handling or moving a prisoner, it is not impossible for someone to slip him a weapon. This especially applies where there is a crowd, as in a depot, courthouse, or on a train. When handling court cases, you are to contact the sheriff, police department, or United States marshal as soon as you arrive at the court and be guided by their orders as to movement.

2. If an inmate is remanded to jail by the judge to await further action in his case, the guard must receive a copy of the court order, if possible. Always secure a receipt from the sheriff, police department, or marshall when a prisoner is turned over to them.

3. To move a prisoner across a state line, it is essential that the governor of Illinois and the governor of the state from which the prisoner is being extradited grant authority to travel between the states, unless the prisoner waives extradition. If extradition is waived, insist on having the prisoner sign an extradition waiver. This applies in all cases except federal writs, where a man is being removed from the institution to the federal courts. When transporting prisoners, never remove the hand-cuffs until the prisoner is delivered to the place of confinement or to the court issuing the writ for his appearance.

4. If it becomes necessary to travel overnight, the escorting officer must never go to sleep or turn the prisoner over to any-one. If necessary, it is permissible to spend the night where the prisoner can be confined in a secure jail, but always search a prisoner before moving him after he has been in jail or out of sight. Do not permit a prisoner to enter a toilet or lavatory unless the guard accompanies him, and NEVER close or lock the door.

5. If a guard is careless, it is not impossible for a prisoner in transit to seize his gun. At no time should the guard remove

the gun or place himself in a position where an inmate may attack him.

6. When transporting men in an automobile, it is to be remembered that an attempt could be made to grab the wheel and wreck the car, or assault the driver so that the car may be wrecked.

7. Inmates on writs are not to be permitted visits without permission of the court or police department in whose jurisdiction you may be located.

BUS DRIVER

1. The institution bus is furnished for the convenience of employees in getting to and from work, and any passenger violating the rules covering the operation of the bus will be barred from riding in it.

2. Under no circumstances will boisterousness, loud talking, or profanity be permitted, and passengers must remain seated at all times. The bus will not be permitted to leave the designated route, and special stops will not be permitted. Deliveries are not to be made for anyone and special runs are not to be made at any time, except with the permission of the warden.

3. It will be the duty of the bus driver to make sure that he has sufficient oil and gas and that the bus is in proper condition to make the run before leaving the institution. When the bus is turned over to a relieving employee, he should be fully advised as to the condition of the bus.

4. Complete stops must be made at all railroad crossings, all traffic rules must be obeyed, and a speed in excess of 35 miles per hour is not permitted.

5. Before starting the bus, make sure the door is closed. It is not to be opened to discharge passengers until a complete stop is made. The utmost precaution must be exercised at all times for the protection of the passengers.

6. In case of accident, a report shall be made to the warden and either the city or state police, giving them the full details

of the accident, together with the license number and name of the person operating the vehicle involved in the accident.

7. Never leave the bus during a run, except in case of an emergency.

8. The bus driver is to make certain that the necessary equipment is in the bus at all times, including a flashlight and at least four flares, which are to be properly placed on the highway in the event of an accident, breakdown, etc.

9. It is the duty of every employee riding the bus to do his part in keeping the interior of the bus clean.

10. Inmate bus hostlers, on 24-hour detail, will pick up the bus at the front gate to repair any faulty condition. It will be necessary for the employee in charge of the bus to make certain the repairs have been made properly.

FARM SUPERINTENDENT

1. The farm superintendent and all other employees are responsible for the proper care of all livestock, and for the maintenance of the buildings, farm machinery and equipment. Extreme care should be taken by the superintendent to safeguard against fires and keep fire hazards at a minimum.

2. Crops are never to be neglected nor permitted to mature beyond their full value. The land is to be properly fertilized, irrigated, well planted and cultivated to insure good crops.

3. The care of the livestock is very important and every effort should be put forth to raise healthy stock so that peak production is attained. The farm superintendent is to call the veterinarian whenever he deems it necessary. If this is done, disease and sickness among the livestock will be kept to a minimum. Daily reports must be made to the warden on all activities and unusual occurrences.

4. Complete records for every phase of the farm are to be maintained, and reports made to the business office and general store indicating the crops harvested, dairy produce yielded, and hogs and cattle raised and slaughtered.

5. A store is to be maintained at the farm for all ordinary

needs. The superintendent is to requisition all farm needs at designated times. Ample stocks of supplies, feed, repair parts, etc., should be kept on hand. Requistions for any item in the store must be approved by the farm superintendent or lieutenant.

6. The superintendent is to inspect and account for all equipment and supplies purchased, and under no circumstances will inferior quality be accepted.

7. It is necessary for the superintendent to keep himself well posted on new and better ways to operate the farm, such as planting and harvesting crops, feeding of livestock, as well as keeping a constant vigil against insects and rodents. The superintendent should consult with representatives of the state Department of Agriculture and government and county farm advisors to enable him to keep the institution farm operating in as up-to-date fashion as possible.

8. The farm superintendent, like any other employee, is responsible for the safety of all inmates assigned to the farm. The security of the farm should be his first thought at all times and under no circumstances should any chances be taken which might afford an inmate an opportunity to escape.

9. The superintendent is to visit all assignments and buildings on the farm, including the inmates' quarters, at least twice a day to make certain everything is in order and every employee is doing the work assigned to him.

10. It is the duty of the superintendent to lay out the work for the gardener, swine herdsman, dairyman, garageman, implement repairman, etc. He is to keep the farm lieutenant informed as to the number of men needed in all the assignments so that proper details can be arranged. However, the lieutenant is to make all assignments of inmates to the various details as requested by the superintendent.

11. During the canning season the farm superintendent, storekeeper, steward, and superintendent of the canning plant are to consult daily to make sure the needs of the kitchens are met and that the cannery is kept supplied.

12. Cleanliness and good housekeeping are most important

at all times and no excuse will be accepted for assignments to be otherwise.

13. Violations of the rules on the part of employees or inmates on the farm are to be reported.

14. When not under the direct supervision of an employee all poisons must be locked securely so they will not be accessible to inmates.

15. Marijuana is a perennial plant and must never be permitted to grow on prison property; neither shall it be permissible for inmates to have it in their possession.

FARM LIEUTENANT

1. The lieutenant assigned to the farm is to work and coöperate with the farm superintendent. Security is extremely important on the farm and the superintendent and lieutenant are to take every precaution to insure that inmates are under supervision, thereby eliminating chances for escape.

2. As chief custodial officer of the farm the lieutenant is responsible that the officers under his superivision execute their duties properly.

3. A sufficient number of inmates will be assigned by the lieutenant to operate the various assignments under the supervision of officers. The officers are to keep a continuous count of their men and report immediately to the lieutenant or superintendent if anything unusual should occur. The inmates must be counted when they get on and off the trucks and equipment and the officer in charge of them is to place himself in such a position whereby he can see each inmate.

4. A daily inspection should be made of all doors, bars, entrances, and exists of the dormitory to see that an inmate has not attempted to escape.

5. When an inmate or officer violates a rule of the institution he is to be reported.

6. All meals are to be served at a specified time and special meals are not to be prepared except upon the recommendation of the prison physician.

7. When not under the direct supervision of an employee all poisons must be locked securely so they will not be accessible to inmates.

8. During the inmate visiting hours at the farm, demonstrations of affection will not be permitted with any woman visitors other than the permissible form of greeting.

SUPERVISING OFFICER OF OUTSIDE DETAIL

1. The supervising officer of the outside detail is in full charge and it is his duty to enforce the rules and regulations governing this assignment. These rules cover both employees and inmates.

2. When an officer is first assigned to duty at the sally port, he will be accompanied to his assignment by the chief guard, who will identify him and approve his passage through the sally port. Thereafter, he will be permitted to pass through only in the performance of his duties. Pictures of all employees and inmates approved for this assignment will be on file at the sally port office.

3. Employees will not be permitted to pass through this gate on their way to and from work.

4. Employees in charge of receiving supplies and equipment at the sally port also have complete supervision of inmates assigned.

5. Inmates who have been approved for outside detail assignments or for special work details outside of the enclosure will be accompanied by the senior captain via the guard hall on their first trip to their assignment; thereafter, they may pass in and out of the sally port after being thoroughly searched. The senior captain is to be present each morning when the inmates on the outside detail pass through the gate.

6. Inmates who have been approved for special work outside of the walls, such as maintenance or construction work, will be permitted to enter or leave the institution proper through the sally port after their first trip via the guard hall, only when they are accompanied by an approved employee and have an

authorized work order approved by the senior captain. Employees supervising such inmates are responsible for their custody while outside the wall.

7. When an inmate has been taken off the outside detail for any reason, he is not to be permitted to pass through the sally port, unless officially assigned.

8. An inmate assigned to a 24-hour detail may leave his assignment only by permission from the supervising officer or the officer in the nearest tower. The officer giving the permission is to keep a check on the inmate and always be sure of his whereabouts.

9. After the supervising officer of the outside detail goes off duty, the 24-hour inmates may remain in the area surrounding the nearest tower, where they will be in full view of the towerman at all times. They are to be locked up 45 minutes before dark, and the towerman is to make the count and telephone it to the guard hall or captain's office at the time specified.

10. Inmates assigned to an outside detail will not be permitted to return within the enclosure during working hours except when called into the institution on a ticket or in case of an emergency. They will not be permitted to return outside of the walls unless the senior captain is present to approve their passage.

11. A room has been provided where inmates working outside of the wall are to change clothes. It will be the duty of the officer in charge to see that inmates remove their issued clothes, pass nude before an officer into another room where they are to dress in their work clothes. When the inmates are brought inside the wall, the reverse procedure is to be followed.

12. Inmates on the outside detail are not permitted to associate with or visit inmates assigned to the farm.

13. If information is received that an inmate is planning an escape, he is to be taken inside the wall at once and a report in writing is to be made to the supervising officer, giving all the details. Never wait for an attempted escape to occur.

14. Everyone, visitors or inmates, in the company of the

warden, the assistant warden, or a captain with pass-out privilege, is to remain at least one hundred feet from the gate inside of the wall while the official or employee enters the gate. After approval for the passage of the visitors or inmates has been given, the officer in charge of the gate will then reopen it and signal them to enter. Each visitor or inmate must be thoroughly searched.

15. All buildings and assignments in the immediate vicinity of the sally port are under the jurisdiction of the supervising officer in charge of the outside detail. All supplies, provisions, commodities and farm products that pass through the sally port must be listed on a signed requisition or pass, and all must be carefully inspected by an officer before approval is given for the load to be passed.

16. A check of all shipments received should be made against the bill of lading to make sure the merchandise quantities as well as quality are correct.

17. Institution trucks and wagons which pass through the sally port from the outside are to move to the fenced enclosure after being properly searched; at that point an inmate driver from the inside of the wall will take charge of the vehicle and make the necessary deliveries. Under no circumstances will inmates assigned to handling such vehicles within the wall be permitted to enter the sally port proper. All vehicles are to be under the constant supervision of an officer who will give the approval.

18. All vehicles that pass through this cage from inside the walls must be searched, and all barrels and boxes must be punched with a sharp pointed steel rod to make certain there is no contraband or an inmate concealed in therein. It is to be remembered that contraband can be concealed in the harness, or under the mane or tail of the horse. All trucks and cars must have locked gas tank caps. When the officer in charge of the gate is certain the vehicle has been thoroughly searched, he may pass it within the cage, never permitting both gates to be opened at the same time.

19. Officers in charge of inmates assigned outside the walls who are loading vegetables, manure, straw, or anything which may be sent inside the wall, are to supervise every crate or load and make certain that it does not contain contraband.

20. Inmate lines, wagons, etc. inside the walls, may pass in the vicinity of this enclosure, as long as the wire gate inside the wall is properly locked.

21. It may be necessary for trains to enter the institution property to make deliveries, but they will not be permitted to enter the enclosure until after the evening count is completed nor until all inmates have been locked up. Only those trucks and railroad cars which cannot be loaded or unloaded outside of the enclosure are to be permitted to enter the institution. Before the railroad switch is started, the supervising officer of the outside detail will telephone the captain's office and notify the lieutenant in charge that the switch is ready to be made and receive his aproval. After the switch has been completed, the lieutenant in charge will be notified accordingly.

22. All railroad cars must be thoroughly searched, and it is important to make sure there are no false ends or bottoms. Each car must be unlocked, and an employee is to enter and search the interior before it is permitted to pass into or out of the institution. After the employee has completed the search, it is to be relocked until time for loading or unloading.

23. The supervising officer is in charge of the delivery and unloading of coal through the coal door in the wall and the officer in charge of the inmate detail is to be properly instructed. The key to the door is to be held by the officer in the nearest tower, and the officer in charge of the coal detail must constantly supervise all coal put through the wall.

24. It is to be remembered that inmates have friends on the outside who would attempt to conceal guns, dope — or any other material which may be used in an attempted escape — into coal cars, box cars, or packages shipped to the institution from any outside source. Also, even though the institution buys from reputable suppliers, it is not an impossibility for a supplier to

hire a person who, unknown to him, is dishonest and would attempt to conceal contraband in supplies shipped to the institution. All boxes, barrels, packages, etc., received are to be opened and carefully searched, after which they are to be turned over to the storekeeper and a receipt signed for same.

25. Bundles or packages passed through must be accompanied by a gate pass signed by the officer forwarding them; the pass and the items in the packages must correspond. All gate passes are to be sent to the warden's office at the close of each day.

26. Association between inmates and civilian truck drivers, railroad men, or anyone from the outside is forbidden. No outsider is to enter the enclosure except by approval of the warden or assistant warden.

27. In the event of fire, the supervising officer is authorized to pass the fire chief, fire equipment, and inmates assigned to this detail through the sally port and into the institution proper. Fire equipment from surrounding communities which may come to assist is to be permitted to pass through the sally port, provided it is accompanied by an officer and proper search has been made. All persons who may have entered the institution at the time of a fire are to be identified by the supervising officer before they will be permitted to return outside of the wall.

28. It is imperative that waste of all descripion be kept at a minimum. Scrap, junk, etc., must be salvaged and put to good use whenever possible. Garbage suitable for hog consumption is to be kept separate from that which has no stock feed value, and is to be sent to the farm daily.

29. The sally port is to be used daily but a designated time for closing will be set by the warden. It is to be remembered that both gates and bars must be closed when not in use.

30. Inmates are never to be permitted to operate the mechanism of the gates.

DAIRYMAN

1. Maximum production is important to the institution and

every effort must be made to attain the maximum through proper feeding of the dairy cattle. Feeding the cattle is to be in accordance with the specifications laid out by the farm superintendent. The required amount of feed is to be kept at the dairy, and while there should not be a vast amount of it on hand at any time, precaution should be taken so a shortage does not occur. Complete production records of each animal are to be kept as well as a correct count of the annimals, and both are to be submitted to the farm superintendent.

2. Cleanliness in the dairy is of major importance and is demanded. Machinery and utensils used are to be washed and sterilized, and the floors of the barn and milk room are to be thoroughly scrubbed. Manure is to be removed from the barns periodically during the day. The dairy, as well as the cows, are to be sprayed to keep down flies and insects.

3. The dairy machinery, buildings, and grounds surrounding the dairy must be properly maintained.

4. Cows are to be bred at the time recommended by the superintendent of the farm. Complete breeding records are to be kept. Heifer calves from good cows and bulls are to be raised. Each calf should be tagged and treated as recommended by the state Department of Agriculture under the supervision of the state veterinarian.

5. Sick cattle should be given good care and a veterinarian called when needed. Cows are to be curried and brushed daily. Cows' udders must be washed and tails kept clipped to insure cleanliness.

6. Milking is to occur at the same time, both in the morning and in the evening, and in some instances it will be necessary to milk cows three times a day.

7. The dairyman is to make thorough inspections of the dairy for fire and fire hazards. Smoking is not permitted in the dairy barn.

8. The dairyman is responsible for the security and custotodial care of all inmates assigned to him, and he is to keep a close check on them throughout the day.

FARM MAINTENANCE

1. It is the duty of the men assigned to the farm maintenance shop to keep in good repair all cars, trucks, tractors, buses, and farm machinery. They are to be greased, oil changed, tires and batteries checked, and winterized at the proper time. Inspection of the vehicles should be made periodically as directed by the safety lane authorities.

2. A stock of repair parts, grease, oils, etc. must be maintained to keep equipment in repair; however, there should not be an excessive quantity of any item on hand. Accurate records must be kept on the number of tires, batteries, and quantity of grease received and used. Tools must be checked daily and a weekly report submitted indicating any changes in the inventory.

3. State owned vehicles ONLY are to be inspected and repaired at the farm.

4. Close contact and full coöperation should be maintained with the master mechanic and the business manager.

5. All poisons, combustibles, explosives, and inflammables should be used with extreme care. When in use they should be closely supervised by an employee, and when not in use they are to be stored in a safe place and the key kept by an employee so inmates will not have access to them.

6. Inmates are to be supervised by the maintenance employees, and the security of the institution should always be remembered.

GARDENER

1. The duty of the gardener is to see that the land used for gardening is fertilized, irrigated, planted, and cultivated correctly. He is responsible for the planting and harvesting of all crops. Each step from planting to harvesting must be done at the right time of the season. The crops must never be neglected nor permitted to mature beyond their full value.

2. The hotbed boxes are to be supervised by the gardener to make certain they are seeded with the various kinds and types of seeds at the proper time. They are to be watered, cultivated,

and ventilated with extreme care so losses are kept at a minimum.

3. When crops have matured and are ready for consumption they are to be delivered to the store, kitchen, and canning department. When it is practical, the tops of the vegetables should be removed before they are weighed, otherwise allowance should be made for them. All vegetables must be cleaned before delivery to the above mentioned places.

4. All garden equipment, including implements, tools, knives, hotbed sashes, crates, etc., are to be kept in good repair.

5. Garden seeds are to be requisitioned at the time specified by the warden.

6. A constant vigil should be kept to exterminate insects and rodents as they are detrimental to the gardens. All plants should be sprayed in accordance with specifications set up by the state Department of Agriculture.

7. In addition, the gardener is to supervise the inmates' work, and he is responsible for the security of all assigned to him.

8. The gardener is to give full coöperation to the farm superintendent, the storekeeper, canner and steward, and set up a working arrangement for delivery of vegetables. The full value can only be had of farm produce when all concerned work together.

FARM DORMITORY

1. Inmates assigned to the farm are housed in the dormitory. The dormitory officer must keep an accurate count and always know the whereabouts of the inmates who are under his supervision. Counts shall be taken before each meal, and at 8:30 p.m., 10:30 p.m., and immediately after the officer on the third shift takes over at 11:00 p.m.

2. The dormitory officer is responsible for the preparation of all meals. They are to be cooked, seasoned, and served properly with the least amount of waste. The meals are to be served at specified times and special meals are not to be prepared for anyone except upon the recommendation of the prison physician. A record shall be kept of all meals served and

amount of food required to serve the meal.

3. The officer in charge of the dormitory is to keep the kitchen supplied with an ample stock of groceries by requisitioning them from the general store. There is not, however, to be an excessive amount of foodsuffs on hand.

4. Every effort is to be made to eliminate fire hazards, therefore, an accumulation of newspapers, magazines, etc. around the dormitory is forbidden. Debris is to be kept to a minimum and it is the duty of the officer in charge of the dormitory to see that inmates abide by this rule.

5. If an inmate violates a rule of the institution he is to be reported.

FARM DORMITORY (Night Men)

1. All inmates are to be in bed at a time specified by the warden. Congregating and gambling will not be permitted. All windows, doors, entrances, and exits are to be locked at a time specified by the warden. No inmate is to be released unless the officer in charge has received the approval of the night lieutenant or supervising officer.

2. Night details for inmates are permissible, providing they have been approved by the lieutenant and/or superintendent of the farm, and whatever supervision is stipulated in the written approval must be adhered to by the employee in charge. Inmates assigned to work nights without supervision are to call the dormitory office every 30 minutes to report their presence.

3. When an employee is assigned to the outside of the dormitory at night he is to make periodic inspections of the grounds and buildings to make certain there have been no attempts to escape. He is to check the dormitory to see that it is securely locked, keep the keys in his possession, and check all inmates working on night details.

4. Counts must be made at hours specified by the warden.

5. In case of sickness or serious injury to an inmate the lieutenant or supervising officer is to be notified immediately and the inmate removed to the hospital if necessary.

FARM INMATE VISITS

1. Inmates may be permitted visits on days specified by the warden. Each man will be permitted five visitors but their names must be registered on his visiting list. It is very important that the visitors are checked carefully to make certain ex-convicts do not attempt to visit.

2. Visitors will not be permitted to enter any building or room other than the farm office and the room provided for visiting in the dormitory. Weather permitting, visits will be held in the yard; however, regardless of where visits are held, they are to be closely supervised by officers who are to place themselves in a position where inmates and visitors will be in full view.

3. Foodstuffs, except fruit, are permissible when approved by the warden but they are to be closely inspected.

4. Careful searches should be made so that alcoholic beverages or any other contraband are not brought on institution property.

SWINE HERDSMAN

1. At a specified time the swine herdsman is to supervise the breeding of sows. The sows are to be selected from the pig litters for breeding purposes, and the boars must be changed to follow good breeding practices and to produce the best results, as prescribed by the Department of Agriculture. Sows are to be removed to the brooder house at a specified time so the pigs may be born there. Pigs shall be removed from the brooder house as soon as practical and vaccinated immediately after being weaned. Pigs are to be castrated according to the recommendation set up by the state department of agriculture and the state veterinarian. Cholera vaccination is to be injected as recommended by the above.

2. At the proper time, the pigs are to be placed in fattening lots. Care in feeding them as they grow to maturity is most important and must be supervised carefully by the swine herdsman. Hogs also must be fed a proper diet. All garbage fed

them must be free of bones, cans, glass, coffee grounds, egg shells, etc. Feed should not be wasted and strict supervision is demanded for the proper mixing of commercial feeds. Fresh water always should be available for the pigs and hogs. Pasture locations for hogs must be changed each year.

3. Cleanliness in the farrowing pens and brooder houses is demanded. At a specified time they are to be sterilized with an electric steam sterilizing machine before the sows are permitted to occupy them.

4. Daily and monthly reports are to be made according to specifications and submitted to the warden.

5. Inmates assigned to the swine herdsman are to be under his supervision and custody and he is to see that each man does the work assigned to him.

HORSE BARN

1. All horses should be given good care, kept clean, and properly fed. The employee in charge of the barn is to give the inmate hostlers the amount of feed required for their horses. Fresh water should always be available for them.

2. Horses are to be properly harnessed and hitched, each horse wearing his own properly fitted harness and collar.

3. Horses are never to be mistreated by anyone. The work assigned for the day should be accomplished but the horses are not to be overworked. Sore shoulders, necks, etc. must be washed and treated following the day's work. When necessary the veteraniarian should be called.

4. The officer in charge of the barn is responsible for the teamsters when they are in the fields as well as when they are in the barn. Teams are never to be left unsupervised.

5. The barns and surrounding grounds are to be kept neat and clean.

6. All equipment on the assignment, including the harnesses, saddles, etc. are to be kept in good repair.

MOUNTED PATROL OFFICERS

1. Employees assigned to mounted duty are to maintain

a constant patrol of the route laid out, watch over the entire region assigned to them, keep on the move, be alert to prevent escapes. Make sure no contact is made between inmates, working on outside detail assignments or farm, and civilians. Patrol officers must remain on duty until the entire outside detail has been returned inside the wall. Never leave an assignment except in an emergency, such as an escape or making necessary investigation.

2. It is not uncommon for horsemen to find contraband articles, such as guns, liquor, drugs, etc., deposited in or near their assignment. Check the assignment immediately upon going on duty and report anything unusual. In fact, anything of an unusual nature which is observed should be reported to your supervising officer.

3. All vehicles passing on the roads adjacent to institution property are to be kept under surveillance to make sure nothing is left which could be picked up later by an inmate. Note the license number of any vehicle giving cause for suspicion and, likewise, the identifying number of any plane. Check all cars parked in or near an assignment and question any occupant; if unoccupied, remove the keys and notify your supervising officer promptly.

4. No one shall trespass on institution grounds, except on designated roads. Patrolmen are to be courteous to people who may stop them; however, conversation should not be encouraged, as there is a possibility the officers' attention might be divided to effect an escape from some other portion of the assignment.

5. In the event of an escape or attempted escape, telephone the superior officer at once or enlist the aid of someone to do so. Guards will find people coöperative in such emergency. All state farm houses are equipped with telephones; however, do not hesitate to request the use of a neighbor's telephone in case of an emergency. Do not take unnecessary chances; telephone the office immediately for assistance.

6. Patrolmen should place themselves in a position where

they will have full view of their entire assignment. They must remain in the immediate vicinity of the state property boundaries. A distance of thirty (30) feet should be maintained between themselves and inmates, so that there will be no chance of a horse being seized. Never place yourself in a position where an inmate may grab your gun. Do not follow a set route, as it would enable inmates to know your specific location.

7. A shelter is provided on each assignment for the patrolman and his horse to use during bad weather. It is to be remembered that inmates will attempt to escape during fogs, heavy rains, snow storms, etc. If there is not proper supervision from the tower, guards should make periodic rounds to make sure everything is secure.

8. Inmates are not to leave the prison grounds at any time. If an inmate is off state property, officers will deliver him to a supervising officer and return to their post as soon as possible.

9. A wire cutter is provided for each rider to be used in cutting fences, etc., in the event of an escape, to enable an officer to follow the prisoner or prisoners. Do not hesitate to cut a fence if necessary; the state will assume responsibility for making repairs and replacements.

10. The horse assigned to an officer must be kept under his full command at all times. He must remain mounted while on duty, except for occasional dismounts to rest.

11. The horse must be treated well and handled with good judgment; the equipment must be in first class condition at all times. Examine the horse daily, before saddling, for back sores, etc. Never ride a lame horse. The horse should not be ridden on any hard-surfaced road. If a shoe is pulled, report it to a supervising officer immediately.

12. Always ride upright in the saddle, as hanging or swinging will cause a horse's back to gall. It is important that the saddle be properly cinched at all times.

FIRE DEPARTMENT

1. The institution is provided with a truck and pumper,

properly equipped for the handling of institution fires, and it is the duty of the fire chief to keep all equipment in first class working order at all times.

2. A sufficient number of inmates will be assigned to the fire chief to enable him to make necessary inspection of equipment and to keep it up to standard.

3. It will be the duty of the fire chief to eliminate fire hazards and to make routine inspection of all shops, buildings, and homes on the reservation.

4. The fire chief is to report in writing to the master mechanic, with a copy to the warden and assistant warden, of any unsatisfactory or defective wiring or heating equipment, improper storage of materials, oils, or other inflammable or combustible items.

5. Men assigned to the fire department are to be trained by the fire chief in the handling of all fire equipment, and fire drills are to be held at least once each week to keep the men properly acquainted with the handling of the equipment and routine to be followed.

6. During the absence of the fire chief, the chief guard is to assign a properly trained assistant chief to take care of this assignment. The assistant chief must acquaint himself with all necessary details and equipment, so that he may give proper protection to the institution and surrounding state property.

7. Inspection of all fire extinguishers, hose, fire plugs, and the water system is to be made monthly by the fire chief. The fire chief is to submit to the business office a written order of necessary parts or equipment needed to keep the department up to standard, as soon as they are needed.

8. When a serious fire occurs, outside fire departments are to be called in and every effort made to coöperate so that the utmost efficiency will be obtained in extinguishing the blaze. Outside firemen and equipment must be thoroughly searched before passage inside the wall is approved, and all care must be taken when men and equipment are passed out.

9. If the institution fire equipment is outside of the wall,

it will be the duty of the supervising officer to see that the employee in charge, the fire equipment, and the inmates assigned thereto, are permitted within the walls as soon as possible after the alarm is sounded. It must be remembered, however, that proper search should be made before they are permitted to enter or leave.

10. Monthly reports regarding all activities of the fire department and detailed reports covering any fire or smudge discovered are to be made to the warden. ANY necessary recommendations for safety or any fire hazards found are to be reported in writing to the warden.

11. Keys are available for all locked buildings and the supervising officer of each shift must permit the fire chief or his assistant, entrance to any building for inspection or extinguishing fires.

12. Proper drying and inspection of all hose and equipment after it has been used is very important; under no circumstance will hose be stored which has not been properly dried.

OUTSIDE CONSTRUCTION EMPLOYEES

1. Outside contractors often are asked to bid on the remodeling of old buildings or on the construction of new buildings. After the contract has been granted, it becomes necessary for the contractor to bring his own tools, equipment, and workmen inside the institution.

2. These workmen are to be treated courteously, but they are not to be given favors or permitted to violate any rule of the institution. They are always to be searched properly and accompanied in and out of the gates by the officer assigned to them. Their equipment will be under this officer's supervision.

3. A room will be made available in the administration building or outside the walls, where workmen, who desire, may change their clothes.

4. All employees of an outside contractor are to be fingerprinted, their photographs taken, and identification cards, properly signed by the warden issued to each one. At the end of

each day, these cards are to be deposited at the entrance of the institution and are to be picked up by the workmen when they enter the institution the next day.

5. Triplicate copies of an inventory listing all the contractor's tools and equipment must be made. The tools and equipment are to be checked against this inventory before such tools and equipment are permitted to go through the gates. One copy of the inventory is to be left at the front gate, one copy is to be carried by the officer in charge of the workmen, and the third copy is to be carried by the outside workman in charge of the tools and equipment. If the sally port is used, the same procedure is to be followed. However, all workmen must enter through the guard hall.

6. Under no circumstance will any inmate be permitted to work for a contractor or his employees.

7. Every officer of the institution will be vigilant to see that no inmate associates with or contacts the contractor or his employee.

8. It is imperative that we give coöperation to all outsiders who may be employed at the institution so that their work may be completed as soon as possible.

9. The whereabouts of each outside workman must be known at all times by the officer in charge of the workmen while they are inside the institution. All tools must be checked and accounted for at all times, and properly safeguarded at the end of the day.

10. If the employee who accompanies workmen must be relieved for any reason, he is to see that relief is properly instructed as to their identification and the whereabouts of all tools and equipment.

11. The same procedure is to be followed, if work is being done outside of the walls on institution property.

FORM GOVERNING EMPLOYEES LIVING IN INSTITUTION HOUSES

(FORM TO BE SIGNED BY EMPLOYEES LIVING IN PRISON HOMES)

Date.........................

I, ..., THE UNDERSIGNED, AN EMPLOYEE OF THE ILLINOIS STATE PENITENTIARY, JOLIET BRANCH, RESIDING IN A HOUSE BELONGING TO THE STATE OF ILLINOIS, LOCATED ON THE PRISON RESERVATION, JOLIET, ILLINOIS, UNDERSTAND THAT IT SHALL BE MY DUTY TO SEE THAT THE FOLLOWING INSTRUCTIONS AND ORDERS ARE CAREFULLY ADHERED TO, AND SHALL INSTRUCT MY FAMILY AS TO THE FOLLOWING REGULATIONS:

I understand that one inmate is to be assigned to the house but AT NO TIME WILL HE BE PERMITTED TO ENTER THE HOUSE EXCEPT IN MY PRESENCE OR IN THE PRESENCE OF ANOTHER EMPLOYEE.

I shall instruct my family that a violation of any rule is to be reported immediately.

The inmate houseman may enter the basement to fire the furnace, but the entrance to the house must be kept locked. I shall instruct my family that if it is necessary for anyone to go to the basement or another building while an inmate is present, he will request the inmate to remain outside until the person who entered the basement or building has left. In addition to taking care of the furnace, I understand the inmate is to take care of the yard.

I understand it will be my duty to maintain the house and premises where I reside, including the buildings, grounds, garden and shrubbery, in tip-top shape at all times. I shall not expect extraordinary expenditures for unnecessary equipment or repairs, but will report to the warden, in writing, when necessary repairs are needed.

If more help is needed for maintenance, I am privileged to request from the farm superintendent or farm lieutenant the need for same two hours in advance, and I shall be assigned men from the farm to work under my supervision. I understand I shall be held responsible for the men assigned to me and that it shall be my duty to pick up the men so assigned and return them to their proper assignments.

I will be responsible for having a member of my family call the guard hall each day at the time specified by the Warden to report inmates working on the premises.

I fully understand that violation of the above orders by myself or any member of my family will be cause for the denial of inmate help, or my removal from the home provided for me.

SIGNED...........................
SIGNED...........................

GENERAL RULES (SUPPLEMENT)

All state property issued to employees such as clothing, badge, dog tag, identification card, rule book, etc., must be turned in upon leaving the employ of the institution, or the employee's last pay check will be held until such items are turned in.

No state property is to be removed from the institutional reservation without approval of the warden or his authorized assistant in writing.

The foregoing rules are for employees' help and guidance. At no time shall any of them be modified or rescinded without the approval of the warden. In some instances there are rules which overlap one another so far as security, production, etc., are concerned. However, the employee in the assignment is to see that all rules are carried out and that good judgment is always used.

If you work for a man, in Heaven's name work for him.

If he pays you wages that supply your bread and butter, work for him, speak well of him, and stand by him, and stand by the institutions he represents.

If put to a pinch, an ounce of loyalty is worth a pound of cleverness; If you must villify, condemn, or eternally disparage, resign your position.

But as long as you are a part of the institution, do not condemn it. If you do, you are loosening the tendrils that hold you to the institution, and the first high wind that comes along, you will be uprooted and blown away, and probably you will never know why.

IN-SERVICE TRAINING PROGRAM — OUTLINE OF PROCEDURE

ILLINOIS STATE PENITENTIARY
JOLIET-STATEVILLE BRANCH

The following outline is covered in the instructions to student officers in order to acquaint them with their duties and how they are expected to fit into the Institutional Program. (Subjects taken from Illinois State Penitentiary, Officers' Training School Text Book, by Joseph E. Ragen, Warden.)

(1) REQUIREMENTS OF EMPLOYEES: (It is emphasized to the new that honesty, loyalty and good citizenship are requirements that are mandatory and that they are expected to set an example for the inmates by their bearing and action.)

(a) Fraternization.

(b) Trafficking with inmates; cleverness, trust, inducements, apparent innocence, seriousness.

(c) Boisterous conduct at institution.

(d) Keeping conversation with inmates on a business level.

(e) Gentlemen at all times.

(f)   No abusive language.
(g)   Supervise and instruct inmates. (Don't do the work yourself.)
(h)   Personal behavior and sense of fair play does much to gain respect of inmates.
(j)   Respect to superior officers.
(k)   Conduct away from institution.
(l)   Institution — judged by conduct of its employees.
(m)   Embarrassment to self, superiors, institution, department and State.
(n)   Repeating gossip.
(o)   Honesty and truthfulness.
(p)   Selection and promotion of employees. (From the ranks.)

(2)   SECURITY, CUSTODY AND DISCIPLINE: (It is pointed out to the new employee that this phase of the training program is their first and principle function.)
(a)   Safe handling and use of firearms and gas.
(b)   Contraband, preserving same for evidence.
(c)   Shakedowns and searches.
(d)   Use of inter-institutional communications.
(e)   Emergencies; escapes, insurrections, fire, weather conditions, etc.
(f)   Rules —Two types:
    (1)   Those governing employees.
    (2)   Those governing inmates.
        (A)   Why there must be firm but fair rules in order to maintain discipline.
        (B)   Rules apply to all alike. (No partiality.)
        (C)   Who meets out disciplinary action for inmates — (Captains Court).
        (D)   Punishments involved; R & E, privilege denials, isolation, reduction in grade or loss of good time.
(g)   Report writing — Two kinds:
    (1)   Disciplinary reports.
    (2)   Detailed reports for the records.
    THINGS STRESSED; Accuracy, honesty and thoroughness.
(h)   Methods of obtaining discipline: Inmates;
    (1)   Punishment as mentioned above for rule infractions.
    (2)   More desirable jobs and opportunity to take advantage of the educational facilities, recreation, etc., as a result of a good record.
(i)   Detecting signs of unrest and trouble.
(j)   Mail censorship.
(k)   Safety; prevent injuries and accidents.
(l)   Cleanliness, housekeeping.

REHABILITATION PROGRAM:
(a)   Consistant, firm, fair and impartial treatment.
(b)   Instill Discipline. (Often lacking in inmates.)
(c)   Adequate housing, food, clothing, medical attention.
(d)   Encourage inmates to attend religious services.

(e)   Encourage inmates to participate in educational program.
(f)   Encourage inmates to participate in recreational program.
(g)   Work Program; Trade training and habits of work.

Inter-Institutional   ILLINOIS STATE PENITENTIARY
Correspondence   Office of the Warden
                                                Joseph E. Ragen
                                                 January 9, 1957

MEMORANDUM TO: Captains, Lieutenants, Maintenance Employees,
                 Industrial Superintendents, Industrial Foremen

Our first in-service training program will be inaugurated on January 22 at 3:15 p.m., in the chapel at Stateville. Various persons in the above Classifications have been assigned topics, and every effort should be made by the speaker to cover the topic that is assigned to him.

In-service training has long been recognized by private industry and organizations that we are working in. It has proved to be educational and valuable to all that participate and take an interest in it. It makes for better working, understanding of your fellow employee's responsibility, and promotes more of an interest in everyone's well being in performing a capable and worthwhile service while on the job.

It is understood that it will inconvenience some employees by participating in these programs, but I am sure great dividends will be derived from those who do participate. Similar programs will be held for all divisions in our organization. All of us, including myself, understand it will be impossible to assemble everyone and cover all the subjects the different branches and departments of the institution would be interested in.

Those in charge of various assignments at the Joliet Branch and Diagnostic Depot, who will be working at the above stated time, are to contact the chief guard and arrangements will be made to cover your assignment. Those who do not have transportation are to contact either Assistant Warden Acord or Assistant Warden King.

You will be expected to cooperate, and your cooperation will be very much appreciated. I am sure you will find the program worthwhile to you in every respect.

All persons in the above mentioned categories will be expected to attend.

/s/ Warden.

jer ebs do
Employees' Bulletin

January 10, 1957

BULLETIN NO. 9

An in-service training program is being inaugurated January 22, and notices are going out to the Captains, Lieutenants, Maintenance Foremen, Industrial Superintendents, and Industrial Foremen, to attend the first class for these particular assignments.

This program will cover every employee in the institution, and as time goes on we will work out a system whereby employees will receive credit for the time spent in these meetings if it is not during working hours. This time off, however, will be given at vacation time, or at the convenience of the chief guards.

I am sure this in-service training program will benefit everyone, and it will be to your advantage to attend. I also feel it will compensate everyone in that you will become a better employee, and it will give you an opportunity to work with more ease, and certainly more safety to yourself and the institution.

An attendance record will be kept, and each man graded. This record will become a part of your personnel file. These courses will cover the necessity and reasons for the various rules and regulations, and you are invited to question the teachers and supervising employees for further explanation.

Your complete cooperation is expected and it will be appreciated.

Warden.

jer ebs do
Employee's Bulletin
SB JB DD FARM

ILLINOIS STATE PENITENTIARY
JOLIET-STATEVILLE BRANCH

SUBJECT: PROPOSED METHOD BY
PRESENTING AN "IN-
SERVICE TRAINING
PROGRAM.

1. Approximately fifty-five (55) subjects including introduction and Round Table discussions of Knotty Problems. This will involve approximately fifteen (15) total hours, covering a period of fifteen weeks, from January 22, through May 7, 1957. (There is a possibility due to unforeseen circumstances at this time that the time element may extend beyond the time estimated herein.
2. Classes will be held every Tuesday afternoon at 3:15, unless otherwise specified, and for one (1) hour duration.
3. Captains, Lieutenants, Superintendents and Foremen, will comprise the first class and it will be mandatory that they attend, unless they are otherwise excused by the Warden.
4. The class of Captains, Lieutenants, Superintendents and Foremen, will be based on a "guinea-pig" or trail run basis.
5. The same subjects will be covered in the class of Catains, Lieutenants, Superintendents and Foremen, as will be dealt with when the course is offered to the Custodial Officers. However, it will be understood that Captains, Lieutenants, Superintendents and Foremen may be called upon to instruct in some of these subjects in future classes.
6. After the Captains, Lieutenants, Superintendents and Foremen's course is completed and the necessary corrections have been made in our pro-

posed outline, the same course will then be offered to the Custodial Officers. And, it will be pointed out to the officers that only a limited number may be accepted for each class, and it will be on a FIRST COME, FIRST SERVED Basis.

7. Recognition will be given each employee completing the course by a Diploma and an entry in their personnel record. . . .

ILLINOIS STATE PENITENTIARY
JOLIET-STATEVILLE BRANCH

IN-SERVICE TRAINING PROGRAM FOR
CAPTAINS, LIEUTENANTS, INDUSTRIAL
PERSONNEL AND MAINTENANCE FOREMEN

INTRODUCTORY OUTLINE: **PURPOSE OF THE TRAINING PRO-GRAM.** The purpose of our projected training program may be considered in three parts.

PART 1: To point out that private industries have long since recognized the importance of a training program for supervisors and foremen, primarily in order that they may deal more effectively with the men under their supervision as well as with management. Comparing private industry with our own work, we find:

1. The Foremen's position in private industry is not too unlike that of the custodial officer who stands between the inmate and the administration. This applies especially to Captains and Lieutenants who have this relationship not only between inmates and administration, but also between custodial officer and administration.
2. Qualities of leadership, recognized by industry as being important in foremen, are equally as important in custodial officers.
3. Where supervision of inmates is concerned, there are no **unimportant** jobs **or un-important employees.** All are extremely important and leadership is one of the principal requisites of a custodial officer.
4. Captains and Lieutenants have been promoted to their positions because of their proven ability as leaders. Therefore it is important that they be able not only to recognize traits of leadership in custodial officers, but also to teach leadership to those officers under their supervision.
5. Captains, Lieutenants, Superintendents, Industrial Foremen, Maintenance Foremen — all are expected to teach leadership.
6. **Definition of leadership:** The means and methods employed by an individual to get others to perform in a desirable manner in any given situation.

PART II. To show that the custodial officer is, in the best sense of the term, a **Professional Person.** Professional by reason of:

> Interest in his Job
> Devotion to duty
> Attitude

Highlighting this term a bit more, we may say:

1. A professional person is one who has learned to do something extremely well. A paramount need in correctional work is for people who are willing to take the time and make the sacrifices necessary to learn their work well.
2. We assure that all of our Captains and Lieutenants are according to the preceding definition. The burden of making professional personnel of the custodial officers rest on their shoulders.
3. In recent years it has become an accepted fact that professionalism is needed in every phase of correctional work, from custody to treatment of inmates. There is only one school that forms professional men and that is the prison itself.
4. We cannot stress too much the dignity and importance of correctional work. Every employee is important. Every assignment is important. It is the duty of each captain, each lieutenant, each foreman to develop this sense of Professionalism.

PART III. To achieve various specific objectives, among which may be mentioned:

1. To aid each individual employee to perform his own particular job in the institution more efficiently by understanding his own job in relation to the job of others; — in other words, to understand the total program and the relation of his job to the total program.
2. To weld the entire staff into a harmonious unit striving for a common goal.
3. To reduce or entirely eliminate some of the problems and misconceptions which exist in an institution of this kind. These include:
    a. The lack of understanding on the part of custodial officers of the part they play in the Big Business of conducting a correctional institution and the tremendous responsibility of the Warden toward his charges his employees, his superiors and the State.
    b. The lack of understanding on the part of many employees of the many personality and behavior problems with which they must deal with daily.

ILLINOIS STATE PENITENTIARY
JOLIET — STATEVILLE BRANCH

In the conduct of the In-Service Training Program a proposed outline is sent to each of the various department heads requesting that they prepare an outline or talk of their own from the proposed outline. They are requested to have these outlines in the hands of the Assistant Warden approximately two weeks in advance of the date scheduled for their appearance at the in-service training school. He may add other subjects than those contained in the proposed outline. When his outline has been submitted and gone over, he may be called in to clarify some point or another or possibly make some changes.

This policy of calling on each department head has proven to be quite successful and has been received quite enthusiastically by the personnel attending these sessions. The success of a program of this kind has its advantages. (1) There is no necessity of having to call upon outside help in conducting these classes. (2) The personnel called upon to talk to each class are thoroughly trained in their own particular field, (in our own particular case, every department head has worked his way up from the ranks). (3) No one man can be expected to know everything there is to be known about each and every phase of a department within the confines of a penitentiary. (4) Each Captain, Lieutenant, Superintendent, Foreman, etc., has the opportunity of presenting the views of his particular department which he may believe would be of benefit to the institution and to those who may not be familiar with the various duties connected with that department. (5) It acquaints each employee with the problems of the other employee, and much good can be made of this later on in the Round Table discussion of Knotty Problems.

The references found in our "In-Service Training Program" as referred reading does not mean that we endorse these books or pamphlets as guides governing the policies of the Illinois State Penitentiary. These references are merely used as a topic of pro and con. Some of the materials found in the references may coincide with some of the subjects being used in our "In-Service Training Program" which fit into the objectives of a maximum security prison. Each prison has its own particular policies and methods to certain procedures and therefore, cannot endorse nor condone policies and methods of other institutions as good as they may be. It is entirely up to the prison administrator as to the policies and methods used in an in-service training program. The references noted herein have been given to our "In-Service Training Classes" as referred reading to show the contrast between various prisions throughout the United States and the differences between minimum, medium and maximum security prisons and other related matters. Some of these policies fit into our own type of institution and are good policies, and the others just don't happen to fit our required needs.

ILLINOIS STATE PENITENTIARY
JOLIET — STATEVILLE BRANCH

IN-SERVICE TRAINING PROGRAM
SUBJECT: REFERRED READING MATTERS

N O T E :

TO ALL EMPLOYEES ATTENDING THE IN-SERVICE TRAINING CLASS.

It will be noted on various subjects throughout the proposed outlines being introduced that reference will be made by *1, *2, etc. These asterisks and numbers will denote reading material, which may give you a broader viewpoint and insight on the subjects being presented.

Again it is to be mentioned that referred reading matter (as herein listed), is not necessarily endorsed as policies governing this institution.

INDEX TO REFERRED READING

* 1   Correctional Employees Training Manual No. 2, State of California.
* 2   Correctional Employees Training Manual No. 3, State of California.
* 3   Correctional Employees Training Manual No. 6, State of California.
* 4   Prisoners Transportation Manual, State of California.
* 5   In-Service Training—Custodial Personnel, Oklahoma State Penitentiary.
* 6   A Manual of Correctional Standards, The American Correctional Association.
* 7   Jail Administration, Myrl E. Alexander.
* 8   New Horizons in Criminology, Barnes and Teeters.
* 9   Proceeding of the 85th Annual Congress of Correction of the American Correctional Association, Des Moines, Iowa.
*10   The Training of Prison Guards in the State of New York, Walter M. Wallack.
*11   Prisoners' Case Records, Howard B. Gill, Department of Sociology and Anthropology, University of Wisconsin.
*12   The Way to Prison Work, Vol. II, Staff of the Bureau of Prisons.
*13   Prison Problems—Answers to some Pertinent Questions., U. S. Bureau of Prisons.
*14   Institutional Food Sanitation, University of Illinois.

For further information on referred reading matter you may contact the Assistant Warden. See Bulletin No. 164 in reference to the time limit on books from the employees library.

ILLINOIS STATE PENITENTIARY
JOLIET — STATEVILLE BRANCH

LIST OF PROPOSED SUBJECTS TO BE INTRODUCED
IN THE INSTRUCTIONS OF THE IN-SERVICE
TRAINING OF PERSONNEL

INSTRUCTIONS ARE CLASSIFIED INTO FOUR PARTS

       PART I   ADMINISTRATION
       PART II   INTER-DEPARTMENTAL RELATIONS
       PART III   SPECIAL PROGRAMS
       PART IV   SECURITY AND SUPERVISION

PART I. **ADMINISTRATION**

A.   The Illinois Prison System
B.   Work Program
C.   Maintenance of Structures and Grounds
D.   Conserving Institutional Equipment and Supplies
E.   Conserving Utilities
F.   Pharmaceutical Management
G.   Institutional Sanitation and Housekeeping
H.   The Employee's Responsibility for prevention of injuries and fires
I.   Proper care of inmate clothing by the Institution and by the inmate

PART II. **INTER-DEPARTMENTAL RELATIONS**

A. Over-all view of Inter-Departmental Relations in an Institution
B. What to look for when inspecting inmate letters and how to channel pertinent information
C. Current inmate visiting policies and methods
D. Looking for and passing pertinent information about an inmate on to other employees

PART III. **SPECIAL PROGRAMS**

A. Correct procedures for receiving inmates
B. Admission Orientation
C. The Classification Program and its objectives
D. Inmate Recreational Activities Program
E. Academic and High Schools
F. Vocational School
G. Pre-release School
H. Library for inmates — Fiction and Non-fiction
I. High voltage, etc.
J. General and Mechanical Stores
K. Canning Plant operations
L. Farm
M. Industries
N. Barber School and Shops
O. The inmate's personality and I. Q. as factors in assigning inmates to prison jobs
P. Care of inmates who are borderline mental cases
Q. Interest the inmate in his work who resents his job — assignment
R. Catholic Chaplain
S. Protestant Chaplain
T. Alcoholic Anonymous program for inmates

PART IV. **SECURITY AND SUPERVISION**

A. Sizing up all-over problems of security in the institution
B. Handling inmates while on transfer between institutions and while being returned to and from courts
C. Reorganization of lock and key system
D. Functions of the Armories
E. Counts
F. Tool Control
G. Items that are contraband and the reason why each is contraband
H. Shakedowns
I. Employee and inmate relation
J. Meritorious Service
K. Report writing
L. The Record Office as a central filing system
M. Control of Serious Escape Risks
N. Escape Plan ... Blockade System and Emergency Squads
O. Supervising inmates in Quarters

P. Escorting inmates individually and in groups
Q. The custodial officer's conduct and attitude while supervising meals—preparing of food stuff and dispensing of same
R. Transporting prisoners from or to the institution
S. Safe use of firearms
T. Use of gas
U. B. of I.
V. Round Table discussion of Knotty Problems

PART I   Consists of 9 subjects
PART II   Consists of 4 subjects
PART III   Consists of 20 subjects
PART IV   Consists of 22 subjects
TOTAL SUBJECTS..................... 55

Movies on prison industries from Maryland State Penitentiary and Correctional Institutions, shown to In-Service Training Class during month of April, 1957. (added subject.)

ILLINOIS STATE PENITENTIARY
JOLIET — STATEVILLE BRANCH

SUGGESTED LIST OF ITEMS OF INSTRUCTIONS   Part I
FOR IN-SERVICE TRAINING OF PERSONNEL   Administration
SUBJECT: THE ILLINOIS PRISON SYSTEM
SPEAKER: WARDEN

1. Historical backgrounds
2. The development of Illinois Prisons
3. Organization of the Illinois Prisons
4. Basic objectives of a prison system
5. The present program in contrast to the past

ILLINOIS STATE PENITENTIARY
JOLIET — STATEVILLE BRANCH

SUGGESTED LIST OF ITEMS OF INSTRUCTION   Part I
FOR IN-SERVICE TRAINING OF PERSONNEL   Administration
SUBJECT: WORK PROGRAM & MAINTENANCE OF STRUCTURES
          AND GROUNDS
SPEAKER: CHIEF ENGINEER, CHIEF MECHANIC OR MAINTEN-
          ANCE FOREMEN

1. Quick mention of types of construction and preventive maintenance carried on by the construction and mechanical service
2. Construction and alteration of buildings
3. Construction of minor items of equipment and furniture
4. Work order procedures
5. MAINTENANCE OF STRUCTURES AND GROUNDS: Common maintenance defects

6. Miscellaneous structures and facilities
7. Roads, fences and landscaping

ILLINOIS STATE PENITENTIARY
JOLIET — STATEVILLE BRANCH

SUGGESTED LIST OF ITEMS OF INSTRUCTIONS　　Part I
FOR IN-SERVICE TRAINING OF PERSONNEL　　Administration
SUBJECT: CONSERVING INSTITUTIONAL EQUIPMENT
　　　AND SUPPLIES
SPEAKER: CHIEF ENGINEER, CHIEF MECHANIC OR MAINTEN-
　　　ANCE FOREMEN

1. Know what equipment and supplies that should be used to do the job you undertake
2. Instruct inmates in proper use of equipment
3. Keep clean any equipment assigned to you, from mops to complicated machinery
4. Report immediately any necessary repairs of equipment before the need for repairs and replacement becomes extensive
5. Know the kind and quantity of supplies that should be used to do the job correctly
6. Ask for information rather than guess when not certain, particularly in housekeeping operations

ILLINOIS STATE PENITENTIARY
JOLIET — STATEVILLE BRANCH

SUGGESTED LIST OF ITEMS OF INSTRUCTIONS　　Part I
FOR IN-SERVICE TRAINING OF PERSONNEL　　Administration
SUBJECT: CONSERVING UTILITIES
SPEAKER: BUSINESS MANAGER or ACCOUNTANT

1. State amount of money spent annually by institution for:
    Coal, Electricity and Water
2. Point out number of dollars that would be represented by a reduction of 1% per quarter in cost of utilities
3. Conserving of utilities is a matter of good housekeeping
4. The employee's example in conserving utilities influences the inmate
5. Report leaky faucets and pipes via regular channels
6. Turn off lights, faucets and showers when not needed
7. Duty of officer to see that heat is not wasted in quarters where heat is not controlled automatically, etc.
8. Let inmates whom you supervise know that utilities conserved result in additional funds for other needs of the institution
    Note: Cost estimate of cleaning materials, amount of water used per month or quarter.

REFERRED READING
*2
*5

ILLINOIS STATE PENITENTIARY
JOLIET — STATEVILLE BRANCH

SUGGESTED LIST OF ITEMS OR INSTRUCTIONS
FOR IN-SERVICE TRAINING OF PERSONNEL

SUBJECT: PHARMACEUTICAL MANAGEMENT

SPEAKER: REGISTERED PHARMACIST

1. Duties of a prison pharmacist
2. Requisitioning of supplies for an institution
3. Control of drugs, medicines, etc., precautions used to keep inmate nurses from handling "hot drugs"
4. Dispensing of medications prescribed by prison physician
5. Control and records of eye droppers issued to inmates (narcotic addicts)
6. Control, numbering and checking of syringes and other surgical instruments
7. Why hot medications are bought in liquid form
8. Show a comparison of monies saved by control buying of supplies and surgical instruments
9. List some of the new equipment purchased during the past year
10. Mention of yearly x-rays and the use of the mobile x-ray unit

ILLINOIS STATE PENITENTIARY
JOLIET — STATEVILLE BRANCH

SUGGESTED LIST OF ITEMS OF INSTRUCTIONS   Part I
FOR IN-SERVICE TRAINING OF PERSONNEL   Administration

SUBJECT: INSTITUTIONAL SANITATION AND HOUSEKEEPING

SPEAKER: PRISON PHYSICIAN AND/OR EXTERMINATING
OFFICER

1. Sanitation particularly necessary in institution due to concentrated living conditions
2. Sanitation promotes good health habits
3. Institution sanitation achieved mainly through proper use of soap and water
4. Periodic sanitary inspections of entire institution necessary
5. Control of rodents and insects necessary
6. Care used in delousing in Receiving Unit essential at time of every admission

ILLINOIS STATE PENITENTIARY
JOLIET — STATEVILLE BRANCH

SUGGESTED LIST OF ITEMS OF INSTRUCTION   Part I
FOR IN-SERVICE TRAINING OF PERSONNEL   Administration

SUBJECT: THE EMPLOYEE'S RESPONSIBILITY FOR PREVENTION
OF INJURIES AND FIRES

SPEAKER: PRISON PHYSICIAN AND INSTITUTIONAL FIRE CHIEF

1. Be safety conscious
2. Good housekeeping is essential in preventing injuries, and fires
3. Look for and report to Safety Officer conditions in the area which you supervise, that might cause an injury or a fire hazard
4. If condition is mior, such as a heap of papers in a closet, or on assignment, or in a cell, correct it yourself
5. Set an example of safety, instruct inmates under your supervision in the safe use of tools or equipment assigned to them
6. When asking to stack or otherwise handle material, show them the safe way to do it
7. Insist that inmates follow safety instructions
8. Know the functions of each type of fire extinguisher in the institution and how to instruct others in the use of same
9. PRISON PHYSICIAN: — COVERING OF ACCIDENT REPORTS; When and how to make out accident report forms, getting all pertinent information to accident and names of witnesses, etc.

ILLINOIS STATE PENITENTIARY
JOLIET — STATEVILLE BRANCH

SUGGESTED LIST OF ITEMS OF INSTRUCTIONS   Part I
FOR IN-SERVICE TRAINING OF PERSONNEL   Administration
SUBJECT: CLOTHING, SHOES AND INVENTORY CONTROL
SPEAKER: INSTITUTIONAL CLOTHING OFFICER, INVENTORY OR BUSINESS MANAGER

1. Importance of fitting clothing and shoes well
2. Issuing of clothing appropriate to work to be done
3. A STITCH IN TIME — Repairing of clothing and shoes before it is too late
4. Commendation to inmates for care of clothing and shoes
5. Disciplinary action for deliberate destruction of clothing and shoes.
6. Explain system of keeping records of all clothing issued
7. Explain the issuing of clothing and shoes
8. The importance of keeping all inmate clothing clearly stenciled
9. Estimate the approximate cost per quarter and year on clothing and shoes
10. Explain the general functioning of inventory control, i.e., Transfers from one assignment to another, from one institution to another, etc.
REFERRED READING:
*6

ILLINOIS STATE PENITENTIARY
JOLIET — STATEVILLE BRANCH

SUGGESTED LIST OF ITEMS OF INSTRUCTIONS Part II
FOR IN-SERVICE TRAINING OF PERSONNEL   Inter-Departmental
                                          Relations
SUBJECT: OVER-ALL VIEW OF INTER-DEPARTMENTAL RELA-

TIONS IN AN INSTITUTION

SPEAKER: WARDEN OR ASSISTANT WARDENS

1. Ease of communication between departments facilitates entire program of institution
2. Use of non-technical language when talking about your department to an employee of another department assists in building good inter-departmental relations
3. Through visiting each part of the institution as often as possible the employee gains an over-all view of the physical facilities of the respective departments and thus, an understanding of the various activities of the different departments is gained
4. See what the other person's responsibilities are, and respect them
5. Finances for the administrative, culinary, custodial, farm, mechanical services and hospital all come from the same fund, and that is from the "taxpayer"
6. Transfers of inmates from a job in one department to a job in another may frequently be necessary for the benefit of the institution and also the inmate
7. An understanding of sound disciplinary practices by employees in all departments decreases contradictory approaches in supervising inmates
8. Cooperation between departments is necessary in accomplishing special or seasonal jobs
9. An extra amount of cooperation between departments may be necessary when any kind of an emergency may arise

ILLINOIS STATE PENITENTIARY
JOLIET — STATEVILLE BRANCH

SUGGESTED LIST OF ITEMS OF INSTRUCTIONS Part II

FOR IN-SERVICE TRAINING OF PERSONNEL   Inter-Departmental
                                                                          Relations

SUBJECT: WHAT TO LOOK FOR WHEN INSPECTING INMATES' LETTERS AND HOW TO CHANNEL PERTINENT INFORMATION

SPEAKER: MAIL AND CENSOR OFFICER

1. Purpose of inspecting the inmate's mail
2. Persons with whom inmates may correspond
3. Number of authorized correspondents permitted
4. The number of letters allowed. (Outgoing.)
5. Reasons for which a letter to or from an inmate may be rejected:
   (a) Containing material or wording which violates postal laws
   (b) Discussing criminal activity
   (c) Containing malicious or libelous information about individuals
   (d) Containing the names or addresses of employees of the institution
   (e) Illegible writing
   (f) Incorrect addresses (on outgoing mail)
6. Nature of special letters

7. Types of information to be channeled to the Warden, Assistant Warden or Senior Captains

ILLINOIS STATE PENITENTIARY
JOLIET — STATEVILLE BRANCH

SUGGESTED LIST OF ITEMS OF INSTRUCTIONS   Part II
FOR IN-SERVICE TRAINING OF PERSONNEL   Inter-Departmental
                                           Relations

SUBJECT: CURRENT INMATE VISITING POLICIES AND METHODS
SPEAKER: VISITING ROOM OFFICER

1. Policy and principles
2. Visiting facilities
3. Visiting regulations
4. Explain procedures to be followed in the visiting room
5. The importance of courtesy at all times
6. What to guard against
7. Describe how the mailing and visiting lists are compiled at the Diagnostic Depot

REFERRED READING:
*7

ILLINOIS STATE PENITENTIARY
JOLIET — STATEVILLE BRANCH

SUGGESTED LIST OF ITEMS OF INSTRUCTIONS   Part II
FOR IN-SERVICE TRAINING OF PERSONNEL   Inter-Departmental
                                           Relations

SUBJECT: LOOKING FOR AND PASSING PERTINENT INFORMA-
          TION ABOUT AN INMATE ON TO OTHER EMPLOYEES
SPEAKER: SENIOR CAPTAIN

1. Suspicion of conniving between inmates (pilfering)
2. To relieving officer; work plans for the following day
3. To relieving officer; in the event of days off or vacation, the passing on of pertinent information relative to such inmates as may be in question
4. Bickering between inmates; to Senior Captain
5. Signs of being physically ill; to Medical Officer
6. Signs of concern about family; to Chaplain's
7. Signs of unusual behavior or emotional disturbances; to Warden, Senior Captains, and Mental Health Department

ILLINOIS STATE PENITENTIARY
JOLIET — STATEVILLE BRANCH

SUGGESTED LIST OF ITEMS OF INSTRUCTIONS   Part III
FOR IN-SERVICE TRAINING OF PERSONNEL   Special Programs
SUBJECT: CORRECT PROCEDURES FOR RECEIVING INMATES

SPEAKER: SENIOR CAPTAIN — RECEIVING OFFICER
1. Have Sheriff leave weapons outside of institution.
2. Be courteous to Sheriff and to prisoners
3. Check commitment papers
4. Searching prisoners for weapons, etc.
5. Escorting prisoner to Receiving Unit
6. Procedure used in handling cash and other personal property
7. Fingerprinting and photographing
8. Bathing, examining prisoner's body for money, narcotics, pieces of hacksaw blades, etc.
9. Examining body for evidence of disease and filth
10. Method used in disposal prisoners clothing
11. Issuing of institutional clothing
12. The making of institutional records on newly received prisoners
    REFERRED READING:
      *5
      *6

ILLINOIS STATE PENITENTIARY
JOLIET — STATEVILLE BRANCH

SUGGESTED LIST OF ITEMS OF INSTRUCTIONS   Part III
FOR IN-SERVICE TRAINING OF PERSONNEL   Special Programs
SUBJECT: ADMISSION ORIENTATION
SPEAKER: ASSISTANT WARDEN
1. Read the introduction of the inmate rule book
2. No personal attitude toward new men
3. Rules and disciplinary action involved for infractions of same
   (a) R. & E.
   (b) Privilege denials — shows, ball games, etc.
   (c) Isolation
   (d) Demotion in grade
   (e) Revoking of good time
   (f) Segregation
4. Violations of serious nature
   (a) Escape
   (b) Assaulting an officer
   (c) Destroying State Property
   (d) Sex perversion
   (e) Refusing to work, etc.
   (f) Cursing an officer or inmate
   (g) Threatening the officials
   (h) Fighting
   (i) Contraband
5. What is offered to them by the institution and the many benefits to be gained by taking advantage of these
   (a) Education
   (b) Church

(c) Medical attention
(d) Recreational activities
(e) Visiting and correspondence
(f) Veterans Service Officer
(g) Alcoholics Anonymous
(h) Work program
6. Some of the contrasts in other prisons as well as a number of years
ago here
7. The importance of a man taking advantage of the present program
8. Various types of people they will encounter here

ILLINOIS STATE PENITENTIARY
JOLIET — STATEVILLE BRANCH

SUGGESTED LIST OF ITEMS OF INSTRUCTIONS   Part III
FOR IN-SERVICE TRAINING OF PERSONNEL   Special Programs
SUBJECT: THE CLASSIFICATION PROGRAM AND ITS OBJECTIVES
SPEAKER: MEMBERS OF THE CLASSIFICATION BOARD OR SOCI-
OLOGIST-ACTUARIES

1. Background of classification
2. The meaning of classification
3. Types of classification systems
4. Admission classification meetings
5. Reclassification
6. Contributions made by classification
7. The future of classification
   REFERRED READING:
        *6
        *9
        *8

ILLINOIS STATE PENITENTIARY
JOLIET — STATEVILLE BRANCH

SUGGESTED LIST OF ITEMS OF INSTRUCTIONS   Part III
FOR IN-SERVICE TRAINING OF PERSONNEL   Special Programs
SUBJECT: INMATES RECREATIONAL ACTIVITIES PROGRAM
SPEAKER: RECREATIONAL OFFICER

1. Reason for having a recreation time for prisoners
2. List and give description of inmate recreation activities currently
scheduled in the institution
3. The part recreation periods play in rehabilitation
4. Why it is so important to give inmates recreation out of doors, weather
permitting
5. Comparison with past and present in recreational activities
   REFERRED READING:
        *2
        *8

ILLINOIS STATE PENITENTIARY
JOLIET — STATEVILLE BRANCH

SUGGESTED LIST OF ITEMS OF INSTRUCTIONS   Part III
FOR IN-SERVICE TRAINING OF PERSONNEL   Special Programs
SUBJECT: ACADEMIC AND HIGH SCHOOLS
SPEAKER: SCHOOL SUPERINTENDENT

1. Opportunity offered to the inmates wishing to continue their education while in prison
2. The various correspondence courses available
3. What is expected of the inmate while in school
4. How education may enable the inmate to a better life upon being released
5. Assisting the inmate to improve his personality and ability
6. Approximate number of illiterates and semi-illiterates in the institution

REFERRED READING:
*2

ILLINOIS STATE PENITENTIARY
JOLIET — STATEVILLE BRANCH

SUGGESTED LIST OF ITEMS OF INSTRUCTIONS   Part III
FOR IN-SERVICE TRAINING OF PERSONNEL   Special Programs
SUBJECT: VOCATIONAL GUIDANCE COURSES
SPEAKER: VOCATIONAL GUIDANCE SUPERINTENDENT

1. Importance of a vocational training program within a prison
2. Interviews and determining what inmates are to be selected for vocational guidance courses
3. List and give brief history of the courses being taught
4. The instructors job in:
   (a) Instructional capacity
   (b) Supervisory duties
   (c) Keeping waste to a minimum
   (d) Efficient and proper use of machinery and tools
5. Give a brief discussion on the methods used and tests held to see if an inmate is adapting himself to the vocation selected, and the reassigning of the inmate if warranted
6. The necessity of maintaining strict discipline in the school
7. Mention of the display work that has been put out by the inmates in the school

REFERRED READING:
*2
*12

ILLINOIS STATE PENITENTIARY
JOLIET — STATEVILLE BRANCH

SUGGESTED LIST OF ITEMS OF INSTRUCTIONS   Part III

FOR IN-SERVICE TRAINING OF PERSONNEL   Special Programs
SUBJECT: PRE-RELEASE PLANNING
SPEAKER: INSTITUTIONAL PAROLE OFFICER
1. The purpose of the Pre-release Planning School
2. How the program originates upon the admittance of the inmate at the Diagnostic Depot
3. The reason why an inmate going on parole must have a job before being released
4. The supervision that is received while on parole
5. The objectives in the Discharge School
6. Give facts and figures on approximately how many inmates are released yearly and number of violations
   REFERRED READING:
           *6
           *7

ILLINOIS STATE PENITENTIARY
JOLIET — STATEVILLE BRANCH

SUGGESTED LIST OF ITEMS OF INSTRUCTIONS   Part III
FOR IN-SERVICE TRAINING OF PERSONNEL   Special Programs
SUBJECT: LIBRARY OF FICTION AND NON-FICTION FOR INMATES
SPEAKER: INSTITUTIONAL LIBRARIAN
1. Number of books in the library system, fiction and non-fiction
2. The approximate number of books in circulation, monthly and yearly
3. How library functions, methods used in issuing library books, cards, catalog system, etc.
4. How books are circulated in cellhouses, hospitals and farm
5. How to distinguish library books from school books. Methods used in marking books. What to look for
6. What to do when books and other periodicals are not properly marked or stamped
7. Making disciplinary reports on inmates found marking or defacing library books
8. Give the approximate cost of books now on hand
   REFERRED READING:
           *6

ILLINOIS STATE PENITENTIARY
JOLIET — STATEVILLE BRANCH

SUGGESTED LIST OF ITEMS OF INSTRUCTIONS   Part III
FOR IN-SERVICE TRAINING OF PERSONNEL   Special Programs
SUBJECT: HIGH VOLTAGE AND ELECTRICAL APPLIANCES, ETC.
SPEAKER: ELECTRICAL MAINTENANCE FOREMAN
1. High voltage — Explain the dangers connected with high voltage, care

and maintenance of same
2. Areas of danger; such as vaults, sub-station, switch boxes, etc.
3. What everyone should know in conjunction with high voltage, mainly to leave it alone if they are not assigned to handle it
4. Things not to do when around high voltage
5. Telephone — Institutional system
6. Care and maintenance of electrical appliances and motors
7. Reporting of broken electrical lines, etc. — immediately
8. To turn off lights and appliances when not in use, checking of all switches, etc., before leaving assignments

ILLINOIS STATE PENITENTIARY
JOLIET — STATEVILLE BRANCH

SUGGESTED LIST OF ITEMS OF INSTRUCTIONS   Part III
FOR IN-SERVICE TRAINING OF PERSONNEL   Special Programs
SUBJECT: GENERAL AND MECHANICAL STORES
SPEAKER: INSTITUTIONAL STOREKEEPER
1. The purpose and function of the General Store, i.e., requisitioning, receiving and issuing of merchandise, etc.
2. Butcher shop; pounds of meat prepared for institutional use, weekly, monthly and yearly (give figures for same).
3. Milk room; operation of: gallons of milk pasteurized, monthly and yearly, amounts issued; ice cream, amounts used in institution
4. Mechanical store; comment on this in regards to tie in with the General Store, and other pertinent information
5. Mention the functions of the store at the Joliet Branch
6. The proper method of requisitioning supplies from General and Mechanical Stores
7. Security in conjunction with various vehicles when loading at platform
8. Being alert in watching of supplies, conducting shakedowns, use of vault for hot stuff

ILLINOIS STATE PENITENTIARY
JOLIET — STATEVILLE BRANCH

SUGGESTED LIST OF ITEMS OF INSTRUCTIONS   Part III
FOR IN-SERVICE TRAINING OF PERSONNEL   Special Programs
SUBJECT: CANNING PLANT OPERATIONS
SPEAKER: SUPERINTENDENT OF CANNING PLANT
1. State the full operations of the canning plant
2. Give all facts and figures in regards to amount of all items canned during the past year
3. Mention the increase of last year in comparison to the years in the past
4. Tell about the new machinery and equipment that has been installed and the approximate cost of same (if any other is on order, mention that also)
5. The approximate number of man hours used in preparing last output,

and how and why men are taken from other assignments to get this work done

6. How much of the finished products are used here, and how much is shipped to other State Institutions
7. Cooperation between Head Farmer, Farm Superintendent, in regards to harvesting crops and delivery of same

ILLINOIS STATE PENITENTIARY
JOLIET — STATEVILLE BRANCH

SUGGESTED LIST OF ITEMS OF INSTRUCTIONS   Part III
FOR IN-SERVICE TRAINING OF PERSONNEL   Special Programs
SUBJECT: HONOR FARM
SPEAKER: FARM SUPERINTENDENT OR HEAD FARMER

1. Approximate number of acres on farm; acres used for planting; acres used for pasture
2. Crop planting; rotation of crops
3. Kinds of vegetables raised; number in pounds of each
4. Swine herd; number raised in course of year; pounds slaughtered in a year
5. Dairy herd; how many in herd; amount of milk produced in course of a year; institutional usage over the same period
6. Number of beef cattle slaughtered in course of a year
7. Give approximate valuation in conjunction with items 3, 4, 5 and 6, covering a one year period
8. Cooperation between the farm and the canning plant
9. Farm machinery and equipment; cost, etc., proper care of same
10. Various trades other than farming which is taught, such as cooks, painters, blacksmith's, slaughtering, etc.

ILLINOIS STATE PENITENTIARY
JOLIET — STATEVILLE BRANCH

SUGGESTED LIST OF ITEMS OF INSTRUCTIONS   Part III
FOR IN-SERVICE TRAINING OF PERSONNEL   Special Programs
SUBJECT: INSTITUTIONAL INDUSTRIES
SPEAKER: SUPERINTENDENT OF INDUSTRIES

1. Give a brief description and list all industries and over-all valuation
2. The approximate number of other institutions and agencies that purchase our products
3. The cost of the upkeep of our industries which includes, overhead, salaries, etc.
4. Total income for a year, less operating cost for same period
5. How many inmates employed in the industries, and the average compensation received
6. Give some pertinent facts concerning the history of industries; possibly, contrast to the past and present, and some of the problems encountered which may be of benefit to the school

7. Security factors used in conjunction with tools and equipment
8. How superintendents and foremen supervise and teach inmates the various trades, in regards to their respective trades

REFERRED READING:
*3
*9

ILLINOIS STATE PENITENTIARY
JOLIET — STATEVILLE BRANCH

SUGGESTED LIST OF ITEMS OF INSTRUCTIONS   Part III
FOR IN-SERVICE TRAINING OF PERSONNEL   Special Programs

SUBJECT: INSTITUTIONAL BARBER SHOPS AND THEIR FUNCTIONS THEREIN

SPEAKER: REGISTERED BARBER INSTRUCTOR

1. How all Barber Shops within the Institution operate
   (a) Main Shop
   (b) Officers' Shop
   (c) Isolation and Segregation
   (d) Hospital and Detention Hospital
   (e) Officers' Kitchen, General Kitchen
   (f) Administration Building, Farm and Farm Detail
2. The approximate number of shaves and haircuts, daily, weekly and monthly
3. The method used in bringing lines to and from the Main Shop
4. Sanitation methods used in all shops and the reasons thereof
5. The maintaining of discipline both in the Barber Shop and Waiting Room; and why
6. Explain the methods used in checking tools in the Main Shop
7. The keeping of all shop supplied with equipment and supplies
8. The necessity of keeping an accurate count on the barber towels and the reason why

ILLINOIS STATE PENITENTIARY
JOLIET — STATEVILLE BRANCH

SUGGESTED LIST OF ITEMS OF INSTRUCTIONS   Part III
FOR IN-SERVICE TRAINING OF PERSONNEL   Special Programs

SUBJECT: THE INMATE'S PERSONALITY AND I. Q., AS FACTORS IN ASSIGNING INMATES TO PRISON JOBS

SPEAKER: SENIOR CAPTAIN

1. Jobs vary in requirements
2. Inmates vary in capacities, personality and interest
3. How the inmate's I. Q. is determined during his first month in the institution
4. Types of institution jobs that can be performed by an inmate with an I. Q. of 80 and those by an inmate with an I. Q. of 100.
5. Matching inmate personality and I. Q. with job, in order to keep the

inmate satisfied and to get the job done.
6. Selling inmates on assignments which might be beneficial to themselves in learning a trade, etc.
   REFERRED READING:
   *2
   *3

ILLINOIS STATE PENITENTIARY
JOLIET — STATEVILLE BRANCH

SUGGESTED LIST OF ITEMS OF INSTRUCTIONS   Part III
FOR IN-SERVICE TRAINING OF PERSONNEL   Special Programs
SUBJECT: CARE OF INMATES WHO ARE BORDERLINE MENTAL
      CASES
SPEAKER: SENIOR CAPTAINS
1. The problem is general; over-all and specific case concerning the introvert
2. The mild psychconeurotic, and the feeble minded
3. Determining which inmates are borderline mental cases is a medical problem
4. The borderline mental case needs to be assigned to a type of work which is medically and custodially suitable for him
5. Any employee should report to the criminologist or the senior captain, any observations that seem to indicate borderline mental disorder, any bizarre behavior, epileptic or other seizures
   REFERRED READING:
   *15

ILLINOIS STATE PENITENTIARY
JOLIET — STATEVILLE BRANCH

SUGGESTED LIST OF ITEMS OF INSTRUCTIONS   Part III
FOR IN-SERVICE TRAINING OF PERSONNEL   Special Programs
SUBJECT: INTEREST THE INMATE IN HIS WORK WHO RESENTS
      HIS JOB — ASSIGNMENT
SPEAKER: SENIOR CAPTAINS OR VOCATIONAL SUPERIN-
      TENDENT
1. Point out to the inmate the advantages to him of the work to which he is assigned
2. Provide thorough on-the-job instructions
3. Develope a sense of job responsibility in the inmate
4. Show him how he can earn a recommendation for meritorious award on present assignment
5. Ask him to perform those tasks which you believe he dislikes least, that need to be done on the job, and that he can handle
   REFERRED READING:
   *13
   *6

ILLINOIS STATE PENITENTIARY
JOLIET — STATEVILLE BRANCH

SUGGESTED LIST OF ITEMS OF INSTRUCTIONS   Part III
FOR IN-SERVICE TRAINING OF PERSONNEL   Special Programs
SUBJECT: ALCOHOLICS ANONYMOUS
SPEAKER: ALCOHOLICS ANONYMOUS OFFICER (AND OUTSIDE
    A. A. MEMBERS)

1. Reason for an alcoholics anonymous program in prison
2. Alcoholism being recognized as an illness
3. When and how the A. A. program was introduced into the prison program
4. Give facts and figures on men released on parole and discharge who enter the A. A. program on the outside
   (a) How many made good
   (b) How many were returned for violations or new charges
5. Give facts and figures on men released on parole and discharge who were members who didn't follow A. A. up
   (a) How many made good
   (b) How many were returned for violations or new charges

ILLINOIS STATE PENITENTIARY
JOLIET — STATEVILLE BRANCH

SUGGESTED LIST OF ITEMS OF INSTRUCTIONS   Part III
FOR IN-SERVICE TRAINING OF PERSONNEL   Special Programs
SUBJECT: PRISON CHAPLAINS
SPEAKER: INSTITUTIONAL CHAPLAINS

In conjunction with the in-service training program for personnel, I would like to have you submit an outline or prepared talk, that can be delivered to this class.

These are a few possible suggestions that you may want to use:

1. Brief summary of a chaplain's duties
2. Counseling inmates and problem cases
3. Any given subjects or problems you feel that custodial personnel should know about
4. Chaplain and officer relationship; understanding of each other's job
5. Feel free to submit any items of your own choosing

ILLINOIS STATE PENITENTIARY
JOLIET — STATEVILLE BRANCH

SUGGESTED LIST OF ITEMS OF INSTRUCTIONS   Part IV
FOR IN-SERVICE TRAINING OF PERSONNEL   Security and
    Supervision
SUBJECT: SIZING UP ALL-OVER PROBLEMS OF SECURITY
SPEAKER: CHIEF GUARDS, CAPTAINS AND LIEUTENANTS

1. Day watch procedures

2. Evening watch procedures
3. Morning watch procedures
4. Weak points in institutional layout; gates, partitions, walls, fences, etc.
5. Purpose to analyze existing security weakness
6. The techniques of searching inmates and assignments for contraband
7. Constant awareness of security of the institution, especially beware of any unusual circumstances or conditions
8. The necessity of security checks

REFERRED READING:
*7
*5
*1

ILLINOIS STATE PENITENTIARY
JOLIET — STATEVILLE BRANCH

SUGGESTED LIST OF ITEMS OF INSTRUCTIONS	Part IV
FOR IN-SERVICE TRAINING OF PERSONNEL	Security and
	Supervision

SUBJECT: HANDLING INMATES WHILE ON TRANSFER BETWEEN INSTITUTIONS AND WHILE BEING RETURNED TO AND FROM COURTS

SPEAKER: TRANSPORTATION OFFICERS

1. Where to ride in car or bus when transporting prisoners while being armed
2. The proper searching before leaving on a trip to transport prisoners
3. Security measures taken before leaving institutions
4. Security measures taken after boarding vehicle
5. Security measures taken while in court
6. Proper procedure in turning prisoner over to proper authorities
7. Checking of records which must accompany a prisoner

REFERRED READING:
*4

ILLINOIS STATE PENITENTIARY
JOLIET — STATEVILLE BRANCH

SUGGESTED LIST OF ITEMS OF INSTRUCTIONS	Part IV
FOR IN-SERVICE TRAINING OF PERSONNEL	Security and
	Supervision

SUBJECT: REPAIR AND MAINTENANCE OF LOCK SYSTEM—AND FUNCTIONS OF ARMORY

SPEAKER: ARMORY OFFICER, LOCK AND KEYS OFFICERS, GUNNERY OFFICER

1. Estimate amount of money spent last fiscal year for locks, lock parts, keys, and for lock repairs
2. How to decrease wear and tear on locks and keys
3. Schedule for repairing of locks and replacing keys

4. Money-saving ideas concerning the repair of locks and replacing of keys
5. Ideas for improving the inventory of locks and keys
6. Brief discussion of the function of the armory
   (a) How to handle firearms in the armory
   (b) Issuing of all armory equipment
   (c) Stress importance of never permitting keys to fall into the hands of an inmate even for a few moments
   (d) Point out necessary caution of preventing inmates from gaining access to the armory at time door is opened to permit an employee to enter or leave the armory

ILLINOIS STATE PENITENTIARY
JOLIET — STATEVILLE BRANCH

SUGGESTED LIST OF ITEMS OF INSTRUCTIONS   Part IV
FOR IN-SERVICE TRAINING OF PERSONNEL   Security and
     Supervision

SUBJECT: REORGANIZATION OF LOCK AND KEY SYSTEM
SPEAKER: LIEUTENANT IN CHARGE OF LOCKS AND KEYS AND/ OR ARMORY OFFICER

1. Purpose to create new awareness of need to improve lock and key system from time to time, and to secure useful ideas on the subject
2. Ideas for improving the system of issuing keys.
3. Give example of some of the conditions to be found in the lock and key system
4. The lock and key system in regards to security
5. Dead keys
6. Extra keys
7. Keys not numbered
8. Locks not numbered
9. Having keys properly accounted for at all times
10. Dog tags and keys

ILLINOIS STATE PENITENTIARY
JOLIET — STATEVILLE BRANCH

SUGGESTED LIST OF ITEMS OF INSTRUCTIONS   Part IV
FOR IN-SERVICE TRAINING OF PERSONNEL   Security and
     Supervision

SUBJECT: COUNTS
SPEAKER: CHIEF GUARD, SHIFT LIEUTENANTS

1. No movement from one unit, line or room to another during the time of count
2. SEE your man before counting him
3. Write down your count by section when counting separate groups on the same floor or on more than one floor
4. **When in doubt RECOUNT**

5. Proper method of counting in case of an escape, and/or other emergencies
6. Method for a good counting procedure for the institution

ILLINOIS STATE PENITENTIARY
JOLIET — STATEVILLE BRANCH

SUGGESTED LIST OF ITEMS OF INSTRUCTIONS   Part IV
FOR IN-SERVICE TRAINING OF PERSONNEL   Security and
     Supervision

SUBJECT: TOOL CONTROL

SPEAKER: TOOL CONTROL OFFICER (LIEUTENANT)

1. Making of an inventory
2. Classifying of tools as to whether dangerous; hacksaws, knives, etc.
3. Identity of tools
4. Use of a check system
5. Get a receipt for tools when issued
6. Use of shadow board to check at end of day
7. Custody of ladders

REFERRED READING:
*7
*6

ILLINOIS STATE PENITENTIARY
JOLIET — STATEVILLE BRANCH

SUGGESTED LIST OF ITEMS OF INSTRUCTIONS   Part IV
FOR IN-SERVICE TRAINING OF PERSONNEL   Security and
     Supervision

SUBJECT: ITEMS THAT ARE CONTRABAND AND THE REASON
WHY EACH IS CONTRABAND

SPEAKER: LIEUTENANT IN CHARGE OF OFFICERS' TRAINING
SCHOOL

1. General definition of the term "contraband"
   Escape devices; bar spreaders, hacksaw blades, etc.
   Weapons; shives, improvised guns, simulated guns, blackjacks, etc.
2. "Home brew," nuisance items, etc.
3. Explanation of any memorandum issued in the institution which identify contraband items
4. Use of institution's "commissary list" as a means of determining what items are contraband
5. Exhibiting of a collection of contraband items found in the institution

REFERRED READING:
*6

ILLINOIS STATE PENITENTIARY
JOLIET — STATEVILLE BRANCH

SUGGESTED LIST OF ITEMS OF INSTRUCTIONS   Part IV

FOR IN-SERVICE TRAINING OF PERSONNEL   Security and
                                            Supervision

SUBJECT: SHAKEDOWNS

SPEAKER: CHIEF GUARD OR LIEUTENANT IN CHARGE OF OFFI-
CERS' TRAINING SCHOOL

1. How to shakedown an inmate
2. Desirability of having routine shakedowns at irregular intervals
3. When to shakedown inmates assigned to the storehouses, shops, schools
    and other assignments
4. How to shakedown a shop or office
5. How to shakedown a truck
6. Consideration necessary for feeling of the inmates
7. How to shakedown a large group of inmates; such as a work detail
    or transfer
8. Importance of thoroughness in shaking down and harm done by a fast
    and poor shakedown

REFERRED READING:
*6
*7

ILLINOIS STATE PENITENTIARY
JOLIET — STATEVILLE BRANCH

SUGGESTED LIST OF ITEMS OF INSTRUCTIONS   Part IV
FOR IN-SERVICE TRAINING OF PERSONNEL   Security and
                                               Supervision

SUBJECT: EMPLOYEE AND INMATE RELATIONS

SPEAKER: SENIOR CAPTAIN

1. Transmit to inmates by your day to day conduct, socially constructive
    attitudes
2. Be friendly but avoid improper familiarity
3. Friendliness without fraternization
4. Dignity without stiffness
5. Understanding without a gushing sympathy
6. Set examples; set a good example of bearing, neatness and interest
    in your job
7. Knowing your own job well, will enable you to gain the confidence
    and respect of the inmates
8. Do not carry gossip
10. Encourage the inmate to discuss his problems with you, but do not
    discuss your problems with him or in his presence
11. All qualities of good leadership are necessary in order to give con-
    structive guidance to inmates

REFERRED READING:
*8

ILLINOIS STATE PENITENTIARY
JOLIET — STATEVILLE BRANCH

SUGGESTED LIST OF ITEMS OF INSTRUCTIONS   Part IV
FOR IN-SERVICE TRAINING OF PERSONNEL   Security and
Supervision

SUBJECT: MERITORIOUS SERVICE

SPEAKER: ASSISTANT WARDEN

1. Point out to the inmate his opportunity of earning good time
2. Good time awards to inmates for exceptionally meritorious or outstanding services on the job
3. Awards for exceptionally meritorious or outstanding services of a special nature
4. Payment of compensation for exceptional meritorious or outstanding service
5. General Regulations: Procedures relative to recommendations and granting of meritorious service awards

ILLINOIS STATE PENITENTIARY
JOLIET — STATEVILLE BRANCH

SUGGESTED LIST OF ITEMS OF INSTRUCTIONS   Part IV
FOR IN-SERVICE TRAINING OF PERSONNEL   Security and
Supervision

SUBJECT: REPORT WRITING

SPEAKER: LIEUTENANT IN CHARGE OF OFFICERS' TRAINING SCHOOL

1. List and describe several reports of the type which are frequently made during the courses of a day in the institution
2. Discussion on inmate work reports; reports dealing with acts or service and injury reports
3. Characteristics of good report writing, accuracy, consciousness, which include pertinent facts, dating and signing of same
4. Give two or three hypothetical cases and ask each person receiving the instructions to write a report describing their version of the case
5. When writing a disciplinary report, be authentic and remember these facts, they are important; when derogatory remarks are made about an officer or employee, the remarks are to be quoted verbatim and the same shall apply whenever profanity is used, this shall also apply to inmates
6. When a fight occurs, try to determine if possible who was the agitator, who threw the first punch, what was said, etc
7. Be sure that you have the right NAME and NUMBER when writing any report
8. When in the Dining Room if an occasion arises whereby a report has to be written, wait until the inmate is leaving the Dining Room, then ask him to step out of line, unless you know his number or name then even this won't be necessary
9. Emphasize that telephone calls cannot be filed in record jackets, although in the event of an emergency, make your phone call and follow it up with a written report

REFERRED READING:
*1
*11

ILLINOIS STATE PENITENTIARY
JOLIET — STATEVILLE BRANCH

SUGGESTED LIST OF ITEMS OF INSTRUCTIONS Part IV
FOR IN-SERVICE TRAINING OF PERSONNEL   Security and
                 Supervision

SUBJECT: THE RECORD OFFICE AS A CENTRAL FILING SYSTEM
SPEAKER: CHIEF RECORD CLERK

1. General functions of the Record Office
2. Importance of one central filing system where records, such as the following are kept:
    (a) The over-all institutional count
    (b) Transfer records
    (c) Disciplinary and merit staff reports
    (d) Parole docket proceedings
    (e) Statistical compiling
    (f) One central file for inmate jackets
    (g) Assignment records, etc
3. Importance of Record Vault

REFERRED READING:
*11
* 7
* 5

ILLINOIS STATE PENITENTIARY
JOLIET — STATEVILLE BRANCH

SUGGESTED LIST OF ITEMS OF INSTRUCTIONS Part IV
FOR IN-SERVICE TRAINING OF PERSONNEL   Security and
                 Supervision

SUBJECT: CONTROL OF SERIOUS ESCAPE RISKS
SPEAKER: ASSISTANT WARDEN

1. Study the records of all prisoners
2. Attempt to determine the pattern of operation of each inmate who appears to be escape-minded
3. House escape-minded prisoners where physical facilities make custody reasonably secure
4. Assigned to work in parts of institution where physical facilities make custody reasonably secure
5. In quarters and at work provide as much supervision as possible, as escapes can be made from a strong cell or from a locked kitchen where there is little supervision
6. Advise all custodial personnel and employees of any escape risks on their assignment; especially lieutenants and sergeants

REFERRED READING:
*1
*5
*7

ILLINOIS STATE PENITENTIARY
JOLIET — STATEVILLE BRANCH

SUGGESTED LIST OF ITEMS OF INSTRUCTIONS   Part IV
FOR IN-SERVICE TRAINING OF PERSONNEL   Security and
                                                      Supervision

SUBJECT: ESCAPE PLAN (INCLUDING ALARM SYSTEM AND
       EMERGENCY SQUAD)

SPEAKER: ASSISTANT WARDEN

Review and discussion of the Institution's current escape plan, and
suggestions for its revision

Blockade system; complete supervision, especially outside the wall to
prevent escapes.

ILLINOIS STATE PENITENTIARY
JOLIET — STATEVILLE BRANCH

SUGGESTED LIST OF ITEMS OF INSTRUCTIONS   Part IV
FOR IN-SERVICE TRAINING OF PERSONNEL   Security and
                                                      Supervision

SUBJECT: SUPERVISING INMATES IN QUARTERS

SPEAKERS: LIEUTENANTS IN CHARGE OF CELLHOUSES

1. Know the weaknesses of the physical layout of the quarters
2. Know the posy analysis for the quarters
3. Familiarize yourself with the inmates assigned to the quarters to the
   extent of being able to recognize all or many of them when seeing
   them
4. Obtain information daily concerning attitudes, habits, and institution
   program of inmates assigned to the quarters
5. Be humane, honor reasonable requests and recognize inmate complaints when they seem just
6. Know escape risks and bugs
7. CELLHOUSE DOOR — Many ESCAPE RISKS working in cellhouse
   help

REFERRED READING:
*1
*10

ILLINOIS STATE PENITENTIARY
JOLIET — STATEVILLE BRANCH

SUGGESTED LIST OF ITEMS OF INSTRUCTIONS   Part IV
FOR IN-SERVICE TRAINING OF PERSONNEL   Security and
                                                      Supervision

SUBJECT: ESCORTING INMATES, INDIVIDUALLY AND IN
GROUPS, WITHIN THE WALL AND ON STATE
PROPERTY

SPEAKER: LIEUTENANTS

1. Escorting an inmate from one place to another inside the walls
2. Use of passes inside the walls
3. (IN GROUPS) To and from the Dining Room; to and from weekly motion picture shows; to and from recreation yards; to and from religious services
4. Checking work details in and out of the walls
5. Where an officer should walk in relation to his lines
6. Inmates in restraints (cuffs and chains) — should be ahead of escorting officer

ILLINOIS STATE PENITENTIARY
JOLIET — STATEVILLE BRANCH

SUGGESTED LIST OF ITEMS OF INSTRUCTIONS	Part IV
FOR IN-SERVICE TRAINING OF PERSONNEL	Security and
	Supervision

SUBJECT: THE CUSTODIAL OFFICER'S CONDUCT AND ATTITUDE
WHILE SUPERVISING MEALS — PREPARING FOOD
STUFF AND DISPENSING OF SAME

SPEAKER: CHIEF STEWARD

1. Close supervision of the rationing of food. (This is important.)
2. Call anything of an unusual nature immediately to the attention of a captain, lieutenant, or officer in charge
3. Officers should be alert and in an apparently relaxed manner, move about in an orderly manner without blustering actions or blustering talk
4. Officers are to avoid congregating and talking with one another whenever lines are entering or leaving the Dining Room and especially during meal time
5. Every officer should be in a position to quell a disturbance of any kind before it has an opportunity to involve more than three or four inmates, and you can't be in a position to spot trouble if you are standing around gabbing back and forth
6. Lieutenants especially should be on the alert, there are many things they can see while moving about in the inner an douter circle
7. Close co-ordination between lieutenants, kitchen and dining room officers must be maintained at all times. If you think that there is going to be a shortage of food that is being served, let it be known, don't hesitate, if it can be noted five minutes before it happens, that five minutes will allow that much more time to prepare something else
8. Do not, and it is to be emphasized, do not let your stand run out of food. Send to the kitchen in case you are running short. This is another way of letting the steward or kitchen officer know if there

is a possibility that they may be running low on any particular foodstuff

9. Cleanliness must be stressed at all times both in the kitchen and dining room. Officers assigned to these assignments cannot be laxed when it comes to this topic

10. The tool counts of these two assignments must be at all times checked with absolute care, especially the kitchen as there are many knives, etc., handled therein

11. Officers assigned to the kitchen (this applies to regular, relief and extra officers) must be constantly alert to maintaining of discipline, good housekeeping methods and be ever watchful for pilfering of food

12. Officers are to know how much of a serving each inmate is to receive over the stands before the lines enter into the dining room

13. That strict supervision is maintained at all times in the preparation of all food and that waste is held to an absolute minimum

14. Give the approximate cost of food annually

15. Why discipline must be maintained in the dining room

REFERRED READING:

* 7
* 2
* 5
* 6
*14

ILLINOIS STATE PENITENTIARY
JOLIET — STATEVILLE BRANCH

SUGGESTED LIST OF ITEMS OF INSTRUCTIONS   Part IV
FOR IN-SERVICE TRAINING OF PERSONNEL   Security and
    Supervision

SUBJECT: TRANSPORTING PRISONERS FROM OR TO THE INSTITUTION

SPEAKER: WARDEN

1. The problem of maintaining control en route without embarrassing the prisoners or the departments

2. The problem of the prisoner's comfort and protection from injury while en route

3. Use of handcuffs, restraining belt and leg irons

4. Use of sidearms

5. Purpose of transporting and special problems in connection when taking a prisoner to court

6. To transfer to another institution

7. When appearing at an inquest

8. Safety precautions to be used while in transport

REFERRED READING:

*4
*8

ILLINOIS STATE PENITENTIARY
JOLIET — STATEVILLE BRANCH

SUGGESTED LIST OF ITEMS OF INSTRUCTIONS   Part IV
FOR IN-SERVICE TRAINING OF PERSONNEL   Security and
Supervision

SUBJECT: SAFE USE OF FIREARMS

SPEAKER: GUNNERY LIEUTENANT

1. Storing of guns in the armory
2. Issuing guns from armory daily for tower use or target practice
3. Issuing guns from armory at time of an emergency
4. Use of guns at target practice
5. Use of guns in towers
6. Care of guns

    REFERRED READING:

        *5
        *6
        *7

ILLINOIS STATE PENITENTIARY
JOLIET — STATEVILLE BRANCH

SUGGESTED LIST OF ITEMS OF INSTRUCTIONS   Part IV
FOR IN-SERVICE TRAINING OF PERSONNEL   Security and
Supervision

SUBJECT: USE OF GAS

SPEAKER: GUNNERY LIEUTENANT

1. Types of gas available in the institution
2. When to use gas
3. What types of gas to use
4. Nomenclature of gas guns, etc.
5. Refer to letter from "Federal Laboratories, Inc." (copies on file in all armories and Assistant Warden Pate's Office
6. Caution in handling of gas

    REFERRED READING:

        *5
        *6

ILLINOIS STATE PENITENTIARY
JOLIET — STATEVILLE BRANCH

SUGGESTED LIST OF ITEMS OF INSTRUCTIONS   Part IV
FOR IN-SERVICE TRAINING OF PERSONNEL   Security and
Supervision

SUBJECT: BUREAU OF IDENTIFICATION

SPEAKER: FINGERPRINT TECHNICIAN

1. Brief history as to methods used in present day identification as in comparison to the past

2. When inmates are received at the Diagnostic Depot, the procedures used
3. The responsibilities of the Bureau of Identification, in respect to finger-prints, photographs and the safe keeping of same
4. Security precautionary measures taken when releasing inmates on discharge, parole or writs
5. Procedures used in regards to institutional personnel, F.B.I. reports, various investigations made, etc.
6. Give an example or two of the results which were uncovered in regards to item number five

REFERRED READING:
*7

PART III
ILLINOIS CRIME TRENDS

Chapter 11

ILLINOIS CRIME TRENDS

Major crimes are increasing in Illinois and America. This is reflected in the annual rising number of admissions to state penitentiaries, including institutions for men and women.

During a 12-year period, from 1946 to 1957, Illinois courts sentenced 16,396 men to serve time in the three state prisons — Joliet-Stateville, Pontiac and Menard. In the same 12-year period only 12,510 men left prison cells.

The total prison population, male and female, in 1956 was 9,112. It went up to 9,660 in 1957.

The Joliet-Stateville, Pontiac and Menard institutions had a population of 7,883 in 1956. It rose to 7,996 a year later.

The women's reformatory at Dwight had 252 inmates on June 30, 1955. A year later this climbed to 259 and was up to 303 on June 30, 1957.

There are sharp differences in the geographical crime pattern in the state. For example, armed robbery seems to be a violation peculiar chiefly to major metropolitan areas, as in Chicago. Almost 32 per cent of the 1,455 violators received at Joliet-Stateville units in 1957 were sentenced on armed robbery charges in comparison to only 9 per cent of the 352 inmates sentenced to Menard.

Similarly, in the same year, 7 per cent of the new Joliet-Stateville inmates were sentenced on narcotics charges as against virtually none at Menard.

The biggest category of women violators sent to Dwight in 1957 was composed of those sentenced for violation of the narcotics laws, with 36 per cent of the 138 admissions serving time for unlawful possession of narcotics, illegal sale of drugs, possession of hypodermic syringe or other violations connected with drugs.

The number of inmates sentenced to Dwight on dope charges virtually doubled between 1955 and 1957, from 25 to 51, because possession of narcotics was only a misdemeanor until April, 1957.

Prisoners from rural areas of the state fall mostly in the category of burglary and fraud, offenses against property and petty forgery induced by alcoholism for the most part.

In the Joliet-Stateville units are found a greater total of men under 30 years of age, sentenced mainly for predatory offenses.

Conversely, the older inmates in Menard compose a significantly larger group, corresponding with a greater proportion of economic offenses.

Intelligence studies and statistics show that the intelligence level of women inmates at Dwight is much lower than at institutions for men. This is explained by the nature of the offenses and crimes for which women are prosecuted, narcotic violations and crimes reflecting social inadequacy being more prevalent among feminine offenders.

In general, age and color are important factors in the crime picture. The biggest category of violators ranges in the 18 to 29 age group. In 1946 this age group composed 56 per cent of the prison new inmate population. In 1957 it rose to almost 63 per cent.

Racially, the Negro population behind bars is growing. In 1946 Negroes composed about 44 per cent of the new inmate population in comparison to 56 per cent whites. In 1957 the ratio was 46.5 per cent Negroes against 53.2 per cent white. Nearly 60 per cent of all new inmates who come from Cook County are Negroes.

In 1957 the state prison at Joliet-Stateville received its first major batch of Orientals — five Chinese and Japanese criminals, including two for robbery, and one each on larceny, burglary and narcotics charges.

The Negro new inmate population exceeded the white population in only one year— 1955. In that year the intake ratio was 51.1 per cent Negro and 48.9 per cent white.

Generally, the distribution of intelligence for men admitted to the penitentiary varies only slightly and to an insignificant degree from the intelligence quotient in the nation's population as a whole.

Intelligence ratings, however, vary among criminals, according to the type of crime committed.

Crimes associated with impulsivity, lack of reflection or critical judgment, such as murder, sex and narcotics offenses, are committed more frequently by individuals who range across the lower end of the intelligence barometer.

Robbery, burglary, and larceny involve criminals who approach a normal or average distribution of intelligence. Fraud is more frequently committed by the more intelligent and better trained individual, since this type of violation calls for greater planning and premeditation, such as passing forged or fictitious checks and engaging in a confidence game.

The Joliet-Stateville prison units, biggest in the state, clear for admission an average of from 68 to 217 inmates monthly, or a total of 1,677, at least on the basis of the year ending June 30, 1957. The smaller number came in May, the bigger number in September. Seventy-five per cent of all new inmates come from Cook County, mainly Chicago.

In the same yearly period only 1,099 left prison cells, including 632 who were discharged by expiration of sentence; 450 who were paroled; five discharged by court order, and 12 who died.

Of 1,455 new inmates in 1957 who were sent to Joliet-Stateville prison cells by courts, the crimes for which the men were committed included the following:

460, or almost 32 per cent, for armed robbery;
327, or 22 per cent, for burglary; 185, or 13 per cent,

for larceny; 140, or almost 10 per cent, for murder; 136, or better than 9 per cent, for sex crimes; 95, or almost 7 per cent, for narcotics charges; 93, or better than 6 per cent, for fraud, and 19, or more than one per cent, for arson, abortion, aiding an escapee, assault to commit a felony, concealed weapons, extortion, mayhem.

In contrast to these figures, of 352 admissions into Menard in 1957, 37 per cent were found guilty of burglary; 20 per cent of fraud; 15 per cent of larceny; 9 per cent of robbery; 9 per cent of sex violations; 6 per cent of murder, and 4 per cent of other crimes.

At Pontiac, of 588 admissions, 33 per cent were for armed robbery; 30 per cent for burglary; 17 per cent for larceny; 8 per cent for sex crimes; 5 per cent for murder; 3 per cent for narcotics charges; 3 per cent for fraud, and one per cent for other crimes.

Of 141 admissions to Dwight in 1957, 94 came from Cook County, mainly Chicago. Admissions by type of crime in Dwight in the same year are divided as follows: Narcotics, 36 per cent; murder, 19 per cent; larceny, 17 per cent; fraud, 12 per cent; burglary, 5 per cent; armed robbery, 5 per cent; sex crimes, 4 per cent, and other violations, 2 per cent, mainly driving an automobile under the influence of liquor and aiding a prisoner to escape.

What is the breakdown analysis of crimes by color and age of the 1,455 men admitted to Joliet-Stateville in 1957? Here it is by color:

Of the 460 sentenced for armed robberies, 51 per cent were Negroes; of 327 for burglary, 63 per cent were white inmates; of 185 larceny commitments, 57 per cent were white; of 136 sentenced for sex crimes, 63 per cent were white; of 90 sentenced for narcotics violations, 85 per cent were Negroes; of 93 committed for fraud, 86 per cent were white; and of the other 19 sentenced for miscellaneous crimes, 58 per cent were white.

In the age breakdown for the 1,455 men committed to

Joliet-Stateville in 1957, 31 per cent were in the 20 to 24 bracket; 23 per cent in the 25 to 29 bracket; 13 per cent in the 30 to 34 year group; 11 per cent in the 18-19 group; 8 per cent in the 35 to 39 group; 5 per cent in the 40 to 44 group; 4 per cent in the 14 to 17 age group; 3 per cent were 50 or more, and 2 per cent in the 45 to 49 group.

Of 352 admissions into Menard in 1957 the age groups were as follows:

25 per cent, between 20 to 24; 17 per cent, between 25 and 29; 14 per cent, 18 to 19; 12 per cent, between 30 and 34; 7 per cent, between 35 and 39; 7 per cent between 40 and 44; 11 per cent 50 or more; 4 per cent, between 45 and 49, and 3 per cent 11 to 17. Of the total 88 per cent were white, 12 per cent Negroes.

Among Pontiac's 588 new inmates in 1957 were 52 per cent between 18 and 20; 34 per cent, between 21 and 24; 12 per cent, between 15 and 17, and 2 per cent, between 25 and 27. Of the total 65 per cent were white and 35 per cent Negroes.

Dwight's 141 new admissions in 1957 ranged from 15 to 66 years in age. They included one at 15; one at 16; three who were 18; three at 19; two at 20, and nine at 21.

Their marital status included 44 who were married; 36 separated; 30 single; 15 divorcees; 12 widows, and four who were living in common law marriages. On the color basis, 65 per cent were Negro, 35 per cent white.

The various categories of improvability estimates, based on the diagnosis of our scientific experts, appear to remain fairly constant from year to year in each of the state's institutions.

Surveys for a 12-year period, from 1946 to 1957, show that among inmates admitted to the Joliet-Stateville units the preponderant category includes questionable and doubtfully improvable inmates, while the improvable group is next in size. Those who may be tagged unimprovable are definitely in the small minority.

For example, among the 1,455 new inmates in 1957 to Joliet-Stateville, 42.3 per cent were diagnosed as questionable improvable; 39.3 per cent as doubtfully improvable; 16.3 per cent as improvable, and only 2.1 per cent as unimprovable.

The initial and followup diagnosis do not necessarily mean that those in the doubtful, or questionable or unimprovable categories will not improve and prepare themselves for eventual release or discharge.

Since 95 per cent of our inmates eventually win freedom through parole, discharge through expiration of sentence, court order, or through commutation of sentence or pardon, most are expected to achieve a degree of reformation, although the degree may vary.

There are always inmates in prison who, while serving long, indeterminate sentences, would be good risks for parole well before their terms end or prior to qualifying for parole on a minimum basis, that is, after serving the minimum time necessary under the state's parole regulations.

On the other hand, a number of inmates achieve freedom who, at least in the firm opinion of the warden and other prison authorities, should never be released and are rated as poor parole or discharge risks. Their return to prison cells is expected and generally takes place.

Generally speaking, murderers are rated as being among the best parole risks. Holdup men fall in this category, too.

The improvable estimate ratio among admissions to Joliet-Stateville has been placed as high as 26.1 per cent among 1,130 new inmates in 1946. It fell to a low of 7.1 per cent in 1951 when 1,125 new inmates were admitted.

On the other hand, the questionably improvable category rose to a high of 58.5 per cent in 1953, among 1,469 new admissions. It fell to a low of 37.3 per cent in 1946. The doubtfully improvable rate has ranged between 38.6 per cent in 1947 to a high of 40.4 per cent in 1950 and 1955.

The improvable category has been a virtually unchanged one. The ratio has varied little, from a low of 1.8 per cent in 1953 and 1954 to 3.9 per cent in 1950.

At Pontiac, where more youthful inmates are housed, the improvable ratio is higher, with roughly one in every three inmates falling in this category of diagnosis. Thus, among 588 inmates admitted in 1957, 33.5 per cent were in the improvable class, while 66.5 per cent, the balance, were placed in the questionably improvable group.

At Menard prison the improvable group is the predominant one in recent years. Among 352 new inmates admitted here in 1957, 42.1 per cent were in the improvable category while 39.2 per cent were in the questionably improvable group; 17.3 per cent in the doubtfully improvable group, and only 1.4 per cent in the unimprovable class.

The diagnosis of 138 new women inmates at Dwight in 1957 shows a situation comparable to the one in Joliet-Stateville. Sixty-six of the new admissions were placed in the questionably improvable category; 35 were rated as doubtfully improvable; 33 as improvable; four as unimprovable or unfavorable.

It has been found that the span between the minimum and maximum terms in many cases was so short that the flexibility of the parole program was considerably limited. This was cured in February, 1952, when the statutory good time provision as applied to maximum terms was changed.

As a result, four months instead of six months now may be earned each year in good time off, after five years of incarceration.

For example, prior to 1952 an inmate serving a 20-year sentence had to serve only a maximum of 11 years and 3 months before becoming eligible for parole. Now the maximum under this sentence is 13 years and 4 months. Despite the increase in the span between minimum and maximum terms, there has been no noticeable change in the percentage of men paroled.

The majority of Joliet-Stateville inmates do not receive immediate paroles following completion of their minimum terms. However, in many cases there is a sufficient spread between minimum and maximum time spent behind bars to allow for a full 3-year period, or more, for supervision under parole status.

One of the state's problems concerns the inmate who is

scheduled to be paroled or discharged but has neither a home to go to or a place of employment waiting for him.

Outgoing inmates are given necessary clothes, including suit, shoes, hat, overcoat (if weather calls for it), and other necessities, all prison-made, plus between $25 and $50 in cash.

Since these limited resources require immediate employment, homeless and jobless dischargees find themselves in a quandary.

Such situations could create a tremendous roadblock in efforts at social and vocational rehabilitation in prison.

Prison officials, parole agents, prison chaplains and community organizations and individuals coöperate in efforts to find employment and a proper home for inmates in this dilemma, but a more constructive program is needed.

Since, as has been pointed out, about 95 per cent of offenders are eventually returned to the free community, a pre-parole program has been instituted to prepare inmates for release.

Here they are given instruction in a wide range of subject-matter, from a simple thing as how to dial a telephone to the manner and general conduct they should use in being interviewed for a job by a personnel manager. These final steps are designed to return them to society in adjusted fashion, at least as far as this is possible after years of incarceration.

The pre-parole program also highlights instruction on rules and regulations of the state Parole and Pardon Board and the danger of recommitment to the institution if they are violated.

Men who leave the prison on discharge after expiration of their full sentences depart with no strings of supervision tied to them by the Parole Board. Once they leave the prison, this category of ex-inmates is free to contact or see whomever they please and go where they wish. It is our belief that all men leaving a prison should undergo a period of parole supervision.

Chapter 12

REHABILITATION: DISCIPLINE, WORK AND EDUCATION

It has been previously noted herein that the penitentiary of today aims beyond the mere punishment of its inmates. The big majority of the men in any prison will at some time or other be returned to society, and the wise administrator will do his utmost to have the day of their release find them adequately prepared to resume their individual places in the program of civilized intercourse.

A two-fold technique is necessary to the achievement of this end. First, all possible discouragement should be given to continued criminal thinking; second, all possible aid should be offered to sincere efforts at self-betterment.

In connection with the first phase of this dual goal, it is important to realize that rehabilitation cannot be forced upon a man. If he is determined to retain an anti-social attitude, all the reformative methods known to penology will fail to effect any enduring change for the better. The facilities for mental and spiritual renovation may be available, but the constructive utilization of those facilities rests with the man himself. Further, the act of imprisonment does not insure a cessation of felonious activities. True, the latitude is drastically limited, but there still would be opportunities, if the penitentiary authorities do not carefully eliminate them, for small scale larceny and petty conspiring.

"Laissez faire," then, is not suited to penitentiary management. Rules must be adopted to govern the inmates, and the rules must be enforced. It would be worse than useless simply to inform a man that he will be subject to certain regulations, and then sit back and hope the arrangement meets with his approval. He must be imbued with a wholesome respect for the type of law and order that obtains within the walls.

Thus, while punishment is not per se the full function of a modern prison, neither is impunity the watchword.

In Joliet, the various branches of the State Penitentiary make use of a uniform system of disciplinary action, the individual officer being the point of origin of such action. If an inmate in his charge is guilty of an infraction of the rules, the officer may either reprimand him, as when the misdeed is of a very minor nature, or he may send a report of the circumstances to the Senior Captain's Court. This latter act is known in the jargon as "writing a ticket." When the Senior Captains receive the report, they will call the inmate to their office and read the accusation. If the inmate is able to prove his innocence, he will be allowed to go back to his place of assignment, and the incident will be forgotten. If, however, the charge is justified, the inmate will be subject to a penalty. Isolation confinement is the most common form of punishment, but other sanctions may be invoked. The inmate's recreational privileges may be suspended, his visits may be stopped for a time, or, if the offense is particularly serious, he may be deprived of all or a portion of his "good time," the time that the statutes permit to be deducted from a sentence for good behavior. In extreme cases, additional criminal charges may be preferred against the inmate, and he may be taken to court and re-tried.

Now, it might seem to some that the authorities are defeating their own avowed purpose in subjecting an inmate to such sanctions. It should be enough, the argument might run, to deprive a man of his liberty; additional punishment would only serve to increase the already manifest lack of sympathy with society.

This is an erroneous view, insofar as Joliet's prisons are concerned, where no inmate is punished unless he has invited punishment. The officers are instructed to use discretion in the writing of reports, that an inmate will never feel he is being discriminated against.

The fact is that strict discipline must be maintained at all times. As stated before, one of the principal causes of the original imprisonment of an inmate is an inability to govern himself, and if there is to be a successful attempt at rehabilitation, he must be taught to restrain his impulses. In a sense he must be domesticated. It will be shown later that a number of privileges are granted to the inmate body, privileges that a humane policy indicates as advisable. They are the common property of the men who behave themselves; they would cease to be privileges if they were extended to the trouble-makers. They are a reward for the obedient. Discipline is a latent force; if not disturbed, it will not sting.

But if it is latent, it is also immovable. Many inmates discover this fact, after a long and losing struggle. Their basic education has to begin in reverse, as it were. They must un-learn before they can learn. Their former habits and customs must be entirely dispensed with, and a completely new set of blueprints made for their design for living. When they have assimilated this unassailable truth, the door will open onto the second, or positive, phase of the progress of rehabilitation.

What is morality?

Philosophical treatises by the thousands have sought to define this abstraction, and no two efforts have been exactly identical. The multiple factors which make one act right and another wrong are not easily susceptible of categorization, but, more than any other single principle, civilization is based on the desire for the "greatest good to the greatest number." If personal propensities conflict with the trend of society as a whole, then personal propensities must be subordinated. This is not merely a hypothesis; it is a proven proposition, and any man with the capacity for rationalization will admit that the proof is logical.

But what if a man is unable to perceive the coördinating pattern which underlines the surface of society? He may then feel that the world is against him, that the Gods have sold him short, that he is predestined to live out his life in futility, and that there is not very much he can do about it.

Or he may take what he considers corrective action, and devote his days, and nights, to moral activity.

"There is so much good in the worst of us . . ." Rehabilitation takes as its major premise the thesis that ignorance is the root of all evil, that if a man is equally familiar with right and wrong, he will in the majority of instances choose the former. Most of the men in prison have a corrupted courage. They dared to rebel against an unsupportable environment, but they were mentally and spiritually untrained to prosecute the rebellion morally. It has for years been admitted that slums constitute the most insidious social menace known, and the greatest task of the penologist lies in counteracting the influence of the slums. Something like ninety per cent of all prison populations in this country are recruited from the marginal and sub-marginal sections of the large cities. The prison authorities must take this chronically underprivileged mass of humanity and place it on the path of morality.

Some pediatricians claim that the teachings which a child absorb during the first seven years of its life will have a more lasting effect than any knowledge subsequently gained. If the rule was invariable, the battle to place rehabilitation ahead of retribution in penal institutions could well be abandoned for the men being dealt with have had four and five times seven years of contra-constructive teaching. There will be no fresh, undefiled material upon which to inscribe the truth. Instead, there will be a heterogeneous accumulation of cerebral excrescence, which must be cleaned out before it will be possible to introduce the doctrines of decency. Human experience does not come in layers. There are no successive integuments of physical and physiological after-effects, superimposing themselves upon the body and soul and obliterating all but sporadic vestiges of the original stuff. A man matures discretely; some little thing is added here, something else taken there, and the combined sum and remainder is the man's character.

But his addition and subtraction can be controlled. Chemistry knows that carbon dioxide may be changed into carbon monoxide, a completely different compound, by simply removing one molecule of oxygen. Why, then, cannot a man's personality be radically altered by a judicious readjustment of the component parts?

The answer, of course, is that he can, through education. Show a man the superiority of pure metal over dross and he will prefer the metal, even though he had previously, in his ignorance, loaded himself down with the dross. The intelligence quotient of penitentiary inmates is very nearly identical with that of the free population, but the inmates, by their very presence in prison, admit that they have made poor use of their intelligence. Why? Because they know no better. They were under-educated.

The conclusion seems obvious. Raise the educational level of inmates, and considerable headway will be made in the direction of reducing recidivism and parole violation; in fact, toward solving the general problem of crime.

But, is it safe to extend to those of professed criminal inclinations the advantages of education? Will not the training received within the institution be turned to more dangerously felonious purpose when the inmate has been released?

Criminologists are generally agreed that such will not be the case, and they have advanced many arguments in support of their contention. The author would like to add one more. Criminals are essentially egotists. They feel that they are smart enough to "get by" without indulging in honest toil, and they consider the laborer with the lunch box a poor, misguided "sucker." But if the brain of the criminal can once be primed into using all its machinery, instead of only one or two eccentric cogwheels, there is an even chance that the true nature of the situation will be revealed to him. He will see that in reality he is the "sucker," and the working man the truly "wise guy," for the odds are so great against any continued success in crime that he who accepts them willingly is an arrant idiot.

That the work of education in prison will in many cases be slow and tedious is axiomatic. Class rosters include men of middle age who can neither read nor write. They include literate but mentally unresponsive men, men who cannot be inspired with intellectual ambition. But they also include young men, and men not so young, who will take full advantage of the opportunity for broadening their perspective and augmenting their self-sufficiency along lines acceptable to society.

There are men whose salvation is the chief concern of penology. It is in them that a social conscience will take root.

So much for the theory.

In practice, the Joliet State Penitentiary provides educational facilities, ranging all the way from first grade of elementary school to fourth year of college, and now college by TV and correspondence. The Menard, Pontiac, Joliet and Stateville Branches all maintain grade schools. Text books and equipment are supplied by the state and are the same as used in public schools throughout the country. The staff of teachers is recruited from the inmate body, those at Stateville being given a preliminary training course in a normal class. The subjects taught are arithmetic, spelling, grammar, reading, geography, and history. At the end of each school year a regulation high school entrance examination is taken by the eighth grade students. A graduation diploma is given those who succeed in this examination, and a record of the work done by all the students in all the grades is forwarded regularly to the Board of Pardons and Paroles. Promotions to higher grades are made each year, and a great many inmates receive a complete elementary school education within the prison.

There are four civilian Superintendents of Education for Joliet and Stateville. These men are eminently qualified for their positions, all having been active in the teaching profession before entering prison work. Upon them rests a many-sided duty. The superintendent in charge of the Joliet and Stateville schools, for instance, must maintain constant contact with some 450 students. He must see that they are supplied with the necessary scholastic materials; that their attention to their studies, as evidenced by the monthly report cards, is satisfactory; and that they are advanced to higher grades as soon as their work warrants. He must interview every inmate that enters either institution, to determine each man's educational needs. He must select, supervise, and integrate the efforts of inmate teachers. He must confer frequently with the warden, and settle all questions of an academic nature which may arise. In short, he is responsible for the smooth and efficient functioning of the school, with the help of three assistants and four officers.

It was found that the limited curriculum of the grade school could not satisfy the scholastic appetites of the Joliet and Stateville inmates, so the Stateville Correspondence School and Junior College were established. Between 45 and 50 men earn grade school displomas annually, while an additional average of 40 men a year are awarded four-year high school diplomas. An average of between 25 and 30 men qualify each year to study college courses by the correspondence method, most of them being enrolled with mid-western universities. More than 400 inmates have been enrolled annually since the inception of the grade schools in 1936 and start of high school classes in 1947. The following excerpts, taken from one of the school's annual reports, will demonstrate the quality of the service rendered by the school.

"Enrollment in the Junior College is voluntary and is open to all properly qualified inmates of the Stateville, Joliet, and Benard branches of the Illinois State Penitentiary, of the Honor Farm at Stateville, and the Diagnostic Depot at Joliet, and to all former inmates of these institutions, now on parole. Inasmuch as many prisoners are largely self-educated, graduation from grammar school has not been demanded as a prerequisite to enrollment; all that is required is that the applicant give some indication of his ability to carry the work for which he desires to enroll. This ability is tested by means of a standardization placement test, by personal interview, and by information taken from the student's application blanks and from the institution records. Textbooks and supplies are furnished the student without cost, but applicants with the means are encouraged to purchase their own books. The method of instruction is predominantly correspondence, but this is supplemented in some cases by oral classes and by personal interviews between teacher and student. Classes are held in geometry, French, German, Latin, and Spanish. Students at Stateville, enrolled for any subject, are called for interview when they encounter difficulties that are not easily explicable in writing.

"The student does his work in his spare time, usually evenings in the cell. In this way, enrollment in the school does not entail loss of the student's regular prison assignment. Lessons may be submitted as rapidly as is consistent with good work; each lesson is corrected, graded, and returned within twenty-four hours after its receipt. After a course has been completed, the student is called to the school and given a proctored examination. The results of these examinations have been most encouraging as evidence of the progress made.

"The curriculum covers the courses ordinarily offered in outside high schools, with the exception of courses in chemistry and physics, as well as courses presented in the first two years of college in the fields of mathematics, languages, accounting, and history. At present, nearly 100 courses are permitted. Each course consists of from twenty to thirty lessons and is intended to be the equivalent of the material covered in a semester's time by a standard high school or in a four-to-five hour course at college. The lesson sheets refer the student to assignments in accepted textbooks and include additional comment on the material covered. The comment is very much more detailed than is usual in correspondence teaching. The lesson-sheets in eight courses are adapted from those used at the University of Chicago, University of Illinois, and the University of Iowa. The remainder have been prepared by the school staff. The papers turned in by the students are all corrected by the staff. Thus, the school is entirely intra-mural in character.

"Additional incentive to organized study is afforded by the issuance of certificates of completion of the successive years of high school, and of high school diplomas. The public high schools of Chicago have agreed to accept work done in the Stateville Correspondence School as valid toward their graduation requirements, and the State High School Visitor has indicated that he will recommend acceptance of such work by any of the accredited schools of the state. Several universities recognize work done in this school without further examination."

It will be seen from the above that the Correspondence School is a valuable agent in the preparation of an inmate for his return to society. It also embodies a tremendously important outlet for the accumulated mental energy of the imprisoned men. It furnishes distraction from worry, it exercises the creative faculties, and it occupies the leisure time, of which the inmate has a plethora, in intelligently directed study.

In addition to the subjects mentioned in the report, some foreign languages are taught as well as bookkeeping and shorthand. Others are studying such divergent courses as flower gardening, typewriting, economics, journalism, short story writing, American history, Roman comedy, political science and business correspondence.

Vocational guidance and training also is given in the Illinois institutions; both by correspondence and by practical instruction, and 42 trades are taught in the factories and the shops, and the Vocational School proper.

The most effective weapon in the armory of rehabilitation is education. We know that even though most teaching is done by qualified inmate teachers, supervised by accredited civilian teachers, the students are moving forward. The County Superintendent of Schools holds eighth grade examinations and grades the papers. The Superintendent of Lockport Township High School holds examinations and grades papers. For those who pass, diplomas are issued.

But education alone often is not sufficient. From time to time, there will arise a set of circumstances which completely baffle the mind, however, highly trained it may be. On such occasions, the only source of sustenance may be not in the brain, but in the soul. Religious education will then prove its worth.

Spiritual enlightenment has been invaluable as an implement in the work of reformation. The Church takes up where the school leaves off, allocating on the moral scale the truths learned in the texts. Absolute rehabilitation, in the final instance must come from within; few men can set their spiritual house in order without a sincere faith.

Hence, Chaplains of the various denominations are important figures in penology. Their work is prodigious; the weekly services are but part of their good offices.

Consider a segment of the week as lived by the Catholic Chaplain visiting Stateville and Joliet. On interview days, in the morning, the Chaplain will be at Joliet, talking over with perhaps twenty-five or thirty men, matters of general and specific import. One will need advice concerning a domestic emergency; another will require counsel on some detail of prison life. Possibly the man himself will not have sought the interview; the Chaplain may have deemed it advisable to summon him and offer unsolicited warning or suggestion. Similar programs are carried out by the Chaplains of the Protestant, Jewish, Orthodox, Lutheran, Episcopal, Christian Science, and Colored Baptist religions.

With the morning thus spent, the Chaplain will then go to Stateville where three or four more hours will be spent in the same manner. If it seems necessary, he will agree to telephone or visit the relatives of an inmate, to relieve some difficulty or present some plan of action.

On another morning, he will attend to administrative minutiae of his two offices, assisted by his inmate secretaries. The next day there will be more interviews. Friday afternoons and Saturday mornings will be consecrated to Confession, with some three or four hundred inmates taking part in the ceremony. On Saturday evening, after the cells are locked, he will deliver addresses over the radio at both institutions.

Then comes the regular Sunday worship.

Assuredly, the Chaplain is indispensable in prison life, whether his faith be Catholic, Protestant, or Jewish, and Joliet recognizes and respects that fact. The inmates of the State Penitentiary are served by representatives of eight denominations, as well as members of the Salvation Army. A Chicago Synagogue sends a Rabbi and a social worker each week to conduct services and inquire into the personal problems of Jewish inmates.

Education. A sound mind and a soothed spirit. What forms of immorality can prevail against the combined might of these?

Chapter 13

THE NEW LOOK IN GUARDS

Until a comparatively few years ago, it was believed that a strong arm and a sadistic temperament were sufficient to qualify any man for the duties of guard in a penal institution. Consequently, thousand upon thousand of inmates were released in no fit condition to take up the struggle for existence in a highly competitive world. They were broken in body, cowed in spirit; if they had any ambition at all, it usually was to visit vengeance upon those whom they considered responsible for their suffering.

Even when society tentatively withdrew its head from the dark sand of indifference and allowed itself to see the need for a more humane prison policy, no thought was given to the influence, beneficial or otherwise, exercised by the guards. They were chosen haphazardly, and their training consisted of issuing them a uniform and leaving them to their own devices. They had to work out their own ways and means of handling the inmates, and the result was far too often incompatible with progressive penology.

Finally, however, the importance of the guards in the rehabilitory scheme became so apparent that no sincere administrator could ignore the necessity for adopting some program of selective training.

When the author first assumed the responsibility of a penitentiary warden, he was astonished at the wide variety of abilities exhibited by the individual officers. Some commanded the respect and obedience of the men in their charge with seemingly effortless ease, while others were able to obtain only an extremely low grade of discipline. Moreover, those whose charges were best behaved were the officers who submitted the least number of reports to the Disciplinarian. This may appear to be an obvious corollary; that is, the inmates who conducted themselves most obediently would naturally be the least likely to merit "a ticket." By this reasoning, the inmates, rather than the officers, would be held primarily responsible for the discipline maintained in any given group.

This misapprehension may be corrected by a specific example. Officer A was assigned to the quarry at the Joliet Branch and Officer B was stationed in the Textile Factory. The men in the quarry are for the most part the least amenable type — recidivists, incorrigibles, and potential or active agitators — yet they created very little disturbance under Officer A. On the other hand. Officer B was literally flooding the Disciplinarian's office with reports; hardly a day went by that did not see some of the inmates under his jurisdiction sentenced to isolation confinement.

This state of affairs continued until a routine shift of assignments found Officer A changing places with Officer B. Almost immediately, the inmates working in the quarry were supplying a good proportion of the population of isolation, whereas the number of reports emanating from the Textile Factory decreased almost to the vanishing point.

What, then, was the peculiar faculty which enabled Officer A to maintain such excellent order, no matter with what group of inmates he was associated? The answer lies in one word: Leadership. Officer A required only the power of his own personality to draw from his men a satisfactory type of behavior. He was a leader.

The question now arises, is this faculty inherent in some persons, or can it be transmitted through artificial media? Is it, basically, teachable? Conducted research has resulted in the conclusion that, although the ability to lead is inborn in a small minority of men, others not so gifted can be instructed and trained to a degree that will enable them to display most of the qualities of a leader.

This being so, the training of penal institution guards is an indispensable adjunct of forward-looking penal administration. To a large extent, the efficient functioning of the diverse divisions of the penitentiary depends on the officers; it is vital that they be adequately prepared for their positions.

In Joliet, the training of prospective officers follows a well-defined path. A number of men are selected by the Civil Service Commission and formed into a class, after a check by mail and state police of their complete life, and are allotted quarters at the Stateville branch. After they have been fingerprinted and photographed, and their blood tested, they are supplied with the uniform of a student officer, and a four-week course of intensified instruction begins. The course is divided into classroom and practical training. During the former, which occupies the afternoons, lectures are given on criminology, penology, sociology, and the several intangible qualities that comprise leadership. Officers from regular posts appear and talk about their duties, the warden speaks several times and the Captains and Lieutenants address the students. This classroom period is under the direction of the Lieutenant in charge of training who delivers many lectures himself.

In the mornings, the students assist the officers at their posts, where they learn at first hand how each guard contributes to the management of the institution, and how necessary it is that there be no diminution of diligence, even momentarily, at any single point in the custodial chain.

At the end of each week a two-hour written test is given the students. The grades made on these examinations, together with the reports received from the officers at whose posts the students were stationed for a day, form the basis for the rating which decides whether or not the probationers are qualified to be employed as regular guards.

Some may believe that there is little to teach a guard, that he will automatically fall into the routine of prison as soon as he is orientated. That is so, to a certain extent, but the officer who is at once thrown upon his own resources will never, unless he is the exception, develop into as competent an employee as the man who receives initial and carefully delineated assistance. In every unit of the institution, some officers maintain the balance between order and disorder, between productiveness and waste, and the man who has some experience will be of more value to the warden, and himself, than he who steps into his job with only his own wits as assets.

In the matter of productiveness and waste, it must be remembered that the principal material dealt with in prison is human lives. There would be little point in installing the most modern equipment in the tailor shop if the shop were at the same time placed under the command of a uniformed brute, for even if such an arrangement produced clothing par excellence, the loss incurred by the misery of the inmates would be irremediable. It is not desirable that officers should fraternize with the inmates, but it is desirable that each officer maintain a friendly and helpful attitude, so that the men with whom he comes in contact will feel encouraged to seek his counsel. It is said that "familiarity breeds contempt," but there are many forms of familiarity. The good prison officer will endeavor to assist in the solution of such of the inmates' problems as come to his notice, even if the problem be outside the penal sphere.

It is essential that the morale of the officer body be kept at a high level; the abnormal atmosphere of a prison renders esprit de corps a most necessary possession to all guards. It follows from this that the warden must strive to keep dissatisfaction at a distance; he must interest himself in every phase of the work of his officers, and see to it that their work is rewarded according to its desserts.

Joliet prison officers are accorded the fairest of treatment. Their working conditions are the best possible; shifts are changed every eight hours, a uniform wage scale is in effect, all advancements — as from officer to sergeant, sergeant to lieutenant, lieutenant to captain, captain to assistant warden, then to warden — are made in strict accordance with the merit system. It is to be remembered there must be a program and there must be discipline for all employees as well as inmates.

Inmates are human beings; they cannot be looked upon as so many ambulant segments of matter. They must be approached intelligently, if they are to profit from their term of servitude, and that approach can be made most easily by the officers.

The general public is gradually learning to understand the importance of the work done in penal institutions. The knowledge is being slowly disseminated that society receives returns commensurate with the attention it gives to the curing of such moral ills as result in the incarceration of some of its members.

With this changing public opinion, an increasingly high type of men are applying for prison employment. Wardens should see to it that this level is maintained.

Chapter 14

DETERMINATE VERSUS INDETERMINATE
SENTENCES AND PAROLE

To most people, a prime factor in penology is "the debt to society." It is generally held that a felon, having transgressed one or more of the rules by which the game of life must be played, has burdened himself with an obligation, and that to discharge that obligation he must surrender all his social rights for a specified number of years.

In other words, a thief must pay with a portion of his life for having stolen.

But there is an additional implication in the phrase. There is the tacit understanding that when once the malefactor has had his bill receipted by discharge from the institution to which he was sentenced, society no longer has any claim on him. He has "paid his debt," and the matter is to be forgotten.

Such an interpretation is the acme of shortsightedness. Of what value is it to imprison a man for three or five or ten years, and then take no further interest in him? For all the good that sort of policy does, the term might as well be spent at the seashore, or on a dude ranch. The only practical method of insuring society against a repetition of felonious activities by one who has been convicted and sentenced to a penitentiary, is to follow as closely as possible the movements of that man for a sufficiently protracted period after he has been permitted to leave the institution. That is not to infer that he should be hounded, or that his efforts to readjust should be impeded in any way. Indeed, in most cases it is to the benefit of the out-going inmate that he remain under benevolent supervision until he has proven himself capable of managing his own affairs in a manner that is agreeable to society.

In the State of Illinois, most crimes are punishable by inde-terminate sentences. For instance, a man convicted of operating a confidence game, or of committing any of the offenses under the heading of larceny, will be sentenced to serve not less than one year and not more than ten years. This is known as the "one-to-ten." At the end of his first year in prison, this man will appear before the Parole Board, which will determine how many of the remaining years of the sentence must be spent in confinement. If his previous life has been law-abiding, if it is shown that the crime for which he was imprisoned was the only break in an otherwise un-criminal existence, the man quite possibly will be granted an immediate parole. The board will examine thoroughly the reports of the psychiatrist and the soci-ologist, as well as the man's record within the institution, and reach their decision after all the complexities of the case have been analyzed.

It is then up to the man to provide himself with a home and satisfactory employment. These will be investigated by the Parole Supervision Department, and a report made to the Board at Springfield. If all arrangements are approved, the man will be permitted to leave the institution on parole. He will remain for three years under the supervision of a parole agent, who will see to it that the man turns in regular reports, conducts himself with decorum, works earnestly and honestly, and in every way lives up to the terms of his parole contract. If he should violate any of those terms, he immediately will be returned to prison.

Perhaps the Board will decide that a certain inmate will profit from spending more than a year in the penitentiary. He might be given a five-year "set," that is, he will serve five years, less the statutory "good time" allowance, which he can earn by good behavior while incarcerated. He then would re-appear before the Board at the end of three years and five months, at which time it would be decided whether he now was fit for parole.

But suppose the man was a chronic recidivist, with a long record of past arrests and little prospect of future improvement? Such a man should be removed from an existence with which he patently cannot cope. He should be kept behind the walls for many years, perhaps for the rest of his life.

According to law, however, the maximum amount of time he can be made to serve under a charge of larceny, confidence game, or any other of the "one-to-ten" variety, is ten years, and he can earn a reduction of three years and three months. Therefore, no matter how inconsistent with safety it may be, this man will go free in six years and nine months, if he has done nothing to lose his "good time." Surely such a procedure is unwise.

It is the opinion of the author that all sentences, regardless of the crimes committed, should be one-to-life. Under such a policy, a man would be released as soon as, but not until, expert diagnosticians had agreed that release was advisable. It must be realized that penitentiaries deal with men who have proven themselves unamenable to moderate forms of correctional instruction; possibly a short period behind the walls will produce an adequate improvement, possibly not. If not, then a longer period should be served. A man should be paroled only when he has been declared a good parole risk by competent judges.

And if he is not considered a good parole risk, he should not be released at all.

If a man has demonstrated that his tendencies are antisocial, we only invite resumption of criminal acts to renounce all control over him the minute he is free. That is not to say that every man released from prison by discharge will return to law violation, but the violation ratio will be so much greater than among those who go out on parole as to make a comparison ludicrous. The parolee should be all times under the watchful eye of his agent; the discharged inmate need account for his actions to no one but himself. The parolee must have employment; discharge demands nothing. The parolee must have a good home and the support of a reputable citizen; after discharge, a man may go where he wishes and associate with whom he pleases. Of course, there have been parole agents who either were actually dishonest or constitutionally lazy, with the result that their charges were able to violate their parole contracts with such success that only arrest on new criminal charges brought their behavior to light. But those cases in Illinois in recent years have been very, very few.

In this regard, it must be admitted that the Parole Supervision Department is understaffed in Illinois, especially where the larger cities are concerned. It is manifestly impossible for one man to know at all times what a thousand other men are doing, and not in all instances of violation is the agent to blame. What is needed is a carefully selected, thoroughly trained, and numerically sufficient force of parole agents, so that conscientious parolees may be protected from the few who do not care to respect either the spirit or the letter of the parole contract.

It should, then, be the policy to release men from penal institutions only on parole, and the Parole Board should be empowered to decide, without restriction, when the day of release may be. If all sentences were from one year to life, not only would there be eliminated the danger of an inmate's leaving prison before a reformation has been truly effected, but also the maintaining of prison discipline would be immeasurably facilitated. The author would like to see isolation confinement done away with; it is of no benefit to anyone to have an inmate locked up on a short diet up to fifteen days Discipline, however, is an important problem in prison management, and as long as no other means are available to enforce obedience to institutional rules, isolation must remain as an omnipresent threat.

But if every inmate were under a one-to-life sentence, isolation confinement could be forgotten and the punishment cells torn down, for no sane man would contravene regulations, if such a contravention could mean the difference between freedom and an additional period of confinement in prison.

Further, it might well be that a man who is considered unfit for parole today will, in the course of time, so alter his attitude that he would become a good risk.

The basic requirements for a competent parole system are absolute freedom of jurisdiction for the Parole Board and adequate supervision by trained agents. It is unfortunate that the newspapers cannot be induced to utilize their power in educating the public along such lines. It must be admitted that occasionally a parolee commits a spectacular breach of conduct, but that in itself is no reason for presenting an unfair and insincere picture of the ramifications of parole. Whenever the newspapers attack parole, they are deliberately making thousands of men who are earnestly attempting to reclaim their lives suffer for the sins of a renegade exception. That is not the Christian way.

Since crime is a sociological problem, it should be treated as such by those agencies which have as their work the correction of social evils. Contact should be made by authorized persons with the family of a convicted man as soon as possible after sentence has been passed. Often the wife and the children of the man going to prison are left without any other support than that supplied by public assistance; they will therefore be totally unable to prepare a home suitable for the convicted man to enter if he is paroled. Also the 25 dollars which has traditionally been deemed sufficient endowment in recent years for an inmate leaving a penitentiary is not enough. At least fifty dollars, or more, are needed to provide adequately for him during his initial period of freedom.

For many years, it has been admitted that the slums provide the main incubators for crime, but only sporadic efforts are made to improve conditions in those districts. The past decade has seen the spread of the marginal stratum of society. And a tremendous increase in lawlessness on the part of teen-age boys has resulted. The place to bring to these boys a realization of the sort of life for which they are laying the foundation is not a penitentiary, but the school and the home.

Chapter 15

PRISON LUXURIES

There are two major matters which must be constantly under consideration by those entrusted with the management of a penal institution. They are, the general welfare of and the privileges which are granted to the inmates.

The first of these two, is of course, the more important. Men may live without luxuries, but welfare is vital. It also is a broad term, and may include many and variegated factors. In terms of a penitentiary, however, there are five main divisions: personal hygiene, mental and physical health, food, clothing, and shelter. All are essential to the well being of the inmates, and the warden must make certain that a uniform standard of excellence is maintained for each.

A brief explanation of these individual components will show that none may be safely neglected, if the term "welfare" is to have any practical meaning.

First, personal hygiene. The old and apt saying "a sound mind in a sound body" could be altered here to read "a clean mind in a clean body," for certainly an inmate's thoughts— or, for that matter, the thoughts of any man—will fall far short in purity if he is forced to live in filth. Furthermore, dirt invites disease, and under the crowded conditions which obtain in prison, a continued lack of cleanliness would be little more than a petition for epidemics. Then there is the self-respect of the inmates. This trait is the last to die when a character is disintegrating, and everything possible should be done to pre-

713

serve it in a prisoner. No man can reclaim himself upon release if he has not kept his self-respect, and no man can keep his self-respect if he is dirty.

In Joliet institutions, personal hygiene is provided for by the barber shops, the bathrooms, and the laundries. At the barber shops, every man is given a shave at least twice a week and a haircut at least once a month. Also, a number of inmates are afforded rehabilitative assistance by instruction and training in a trade by which they will be able to live after leaving the penitentiary. It is now possible, arrangements having been completed with the proper state authorities, for an inmate to earn his student barber and his apprentice cards while serving his sentence, and the equipment with which he works is, so far as is practical, similar to that found in the better shops throughout the country.

The laundries and bathrooms are located as close together as possible, some are in the same building. This facilitates issuance of clean clothes to every inmate when the weekly bath is taken.

In the category of health, mental and physical improvement, little has been left undone to reduce sickness among the inmates. Physicians and surgeons, dentists, specialists in eye, ear, nose and throat work, psychiatrists, psychologists, and sociologists — all of these administer to the needs of the various inmate bodies. The hospital at Stateville, for instance, is a well-lighted, airy, modern three-story building, each floor of which contains twelve six-bed wards. Tubercular and contagious diseases are isolated. Tubercular patients are transferred to a modern tuberculosis hospital at Pontiac. There is a thoroughly modern operating room; and an X-ray unit, a drug dispensary, a pathological laboratory, and an extremely efficient dressing room at the Stateville hospital. The permanent staff is composed of two physicians and surgeons, a registered pharmacist, and a dentist; but specialists make weekly visits to treat the ailments calling for their particular techniques.

An adjunct of the hospital at Stateville is the Detention

Hospital, in which care is taken of the mentally sick. Trained psychiatrists and neurologists staff this department, the attendants are inmates. Thirty-two cells are here given over to the insane and the neurotic inmates, there is hydro-therapy treatment available for those needing it before transfer to the Psychopathic Division at Menard.

An opportunity is given to every inmate to join the "sick line" each morning, the line in which malingerers are sent back to the cellhouse, but in which those suffering from actual ills receive immediate attention. If any inmate is stricken while at work, at play, or in his cell, he will be taken at once to the hospital by an officer. If it should be proven that he had been merely feigning illness as a ruse to escape work, he will naturally be disciplined, but those in need of medical care will be given all the consideration necessary.

It is necessary to keep in good condition all the cellhouses and shops, for inmates will not remain alert and responsive if the buildings in which they are working and living are slowly falling apart. Ventilation and sanitation must also be maintained at a high level, both for the health and morale of the inmates.

The fourth division of the general welfare of the inmates is the food they eat. This department is in charge of a steward, who plans well-balanced meals, superintends their preparation, and oversees their being served. In addition to the inmates' kitchen and dining room, he has supervision over the butcher shop, the vegetable room, the bakery, and several storage rooms. Every precaution is taken to keep everything clean, including food, the utensils and the men who work in the many sub-departments controlled by the steward. Indeed, any inmate desiring to be employed by the steward must submit first to a doctor's examination, in order that none but entirely healthy men may have anything to do with food of the institution.

Finally, there is the matter of clothing. Inmates are dressed in regulation uniforms, consisting of blue hickory shirts, blue denim trousers, white cotton socks, shoes, and cap. In the winter, a short jacket and heavy trousers of cadet grey are issued, as well as heavy underwear. New clothes are given to inmates on arrival, and thereafter they are kept in repair until no longer usable, at which time they are condemned and replaced. Routine inspection is made of clothes weekly, after they have been laundered, and necessary repairs are made then. In addition, inmates are given the opportunity of sending torn clothes to the clothing room, where they are either patched or condemned.

There now comes under discussion the subject of privileges. Ill-advised sources periodically foster the impression that penitentiary prisoners enjoy comparative luxury, that they live better than many persons in the free world. This, to some extent, is true, for there is no starvation in a penitentiary, and there is no wondering where the next night's lodging will be obtained. But in Joliet institutions, there no longer exist conditions wherein some inmates, because of wealth, physical prowess, or "connections," appropriate for themselves unauthorized clothing, food, living quarters, and other luxuries, while the main body of men takes what the authorities provide. Necessarily, of course, there are some jobs to be performed in a prison to which every inmate cannot be assigned, and inmates so detailed are sometimes granted special favors. But in general, there is absolutely no favoritism shown. The privileges enjoyed by one inmate may be earned by all.

The most common of these privileges are: receiving mail and visits by authorized persons, making use of the inmates' commissary, and attending sports events, motion pictures and the radio. The arriving inmate actually is not required to earn these privileges, but only by continued good behavior may he expect to keep them.

When an inmate is first received in Joliet institution, he is required to sign an agreement whereby all mail addressed to him may be opened and censored before being delivered to him. Incoming mail may be in the form of letters, permitted newspapers and magazines, and post cards. No restriction is placed on the amount of mail that may be received, but correspondence with persons having criminal records is not allowed. On each

Sunday of each month, inmates are permitted to write to close friends and relatives. These letters must be respectable and decent in every respect and may contain nothing of an inflammatory nature. Close censorship is kept over all out-going and incoming mail, and accurate records are kept.

Inmates who have not lost the privilege are permitted one visit, of sixty minutes duration, every two weeks. Only relatives and close friends are permitted to make these visits, and two persons only may come at one time. Visitors from a great distance are granted an extended period.

There are, at Joliet prisons, inmate commissaries. These commissaries were established for the purpose of providing prisoners with articles not furnished by the state. The privilege of purchase is limited to inmates who have a good behavior record. The goods offered for sale include foodstuffs, a wide variety of tobacco, candy, toilet articles, and some wearing apparel. The amount that may be spent each week is limited to six dollars and is deducted from the inmate's account, no cash being permitted within the institution. The profits from the commissary are diverted into the Inmates' Benefit Funds, which are used to supply all forms of entertainment and recreation offered during the year. Shows, baseball games, the library, athletic equipment, school supplies — all these are paid for from the Benefit Fund.

The privilege of attending sporting events — such as the baseball game which brings together every Saturday morning some organization outside the prison, and the motion picture show which is presented every Saturday during the winter months, is valued most highly.

There also are softball games between teams within the institution, formed into a league and competing with each other during the summer weeks. Handball and volleyball, basketball, horseshoes, etc., are played during the recreation periods, but the movies are the most cherished privilege of all. By this visual contact with the outside world, the inmate feels more closely connected with the realities of life, and maintains a far better spirit. The radio also contributes to this end, and there is a choice of three stations.

Privileges, then, are extended to the inmates by the Warden, but he may withdraw them if he sees fit. Occasionally an inmate will be found guilty of misconduct so serious that all his privileges will be taken away from him for a protracted period, and sometimes it is necessary, for institutional discipline, to suspend some particular privilege for all inmates; but these situations seldom arise. Generally, inmates guard jealously their right to enjoy their privileges and do nothing which would place them in jeopardy.

A rather strange sight would have greeted an observer at Joliet Prison on a morning in early spring some years ago. A gondola had been shunted inside the walls and stood on the spur track behind the marble shop. It was filled with bricks and convicts. The convicts would place five or six bricks in a pile and hand the pile over the side of the car to other convicts who, in turn, would place them on iron trays. The trays would then be picked up by still other convicts and taken some fifty yards distant, where they would be piled head-high on the ground. Then the trays would be brought back, and the process repeated. There were some seventy men so employed, twenty in the gondola, twenty standing by the tracks, and thirty walking in an endless circle.

If the observer had asked one of the convicts what was going on, he would have received a reply similar to this:

"We're boondoggling. We take some bricks down to that there pile, see, an' we stack them nice an' pretty. It'll be maybe three days before we get this car unloaded, but that don't make no difference, because we ain't going nowhere. After we get all the bricks piled up down there, the Captain will probably decide he wants them at the other end of the yard, so we'll put them back on the trays an' take them where we're told. When we've done that two or three times, they may decide to build something with the bricks, so we'll take them some place else.

"It's just a jibe, see? There ain't enough work to go 'round, an' they give us this to do so we won't have to lay around in the cell all day."

However, this is not true today. Our maintenance, vocations, and industrial shops occupy most of our population.

Since he is able to command several viewpoints at once, the warden of a penitentiary can perceive that the institution which he commands is something of a chameleon. Its appearance alters with a shift in perspective. For instance, society sees it as a sort of strong box, differing from the usual type in that liabilities rather than assets are put there for safekeeping. On the other hand, the inmate looks upon it as a modified vacuum, a place where ordinary life almost comes to a full stop and where there is substituted an existence to which he must with more or less difficulty adjust himself, but which bears little relation to the natural scheme of things.

The warden, being the point of contact between the inmate and society, can appreciate each of these attitudes, even while recognizing that prejudice taints them both. His angle of observation encompasses both "the outside" and "the inside," and in addition produces images of his own.

To the warden, a penitentiary is a small city of which he is the mayor. The city has shops, schools, a church, a hospital, a fire department, a ball park, a motion picture theater, a post office. It has a court of law and a jail — the Disciplinarian's office and the isolation block — and the officers comprise its police force. The residential district is the cellhouses; the Administration Building, the City Hall. There is a farm to supply dairy products, meat, vegetables, and cereals. There is a powerhouse to distribute light and heat. There are waterworks and a sewage disposal system.

And there are industries. . . .

Land, capital, and labor are the economic fundamentals; that is a copybook maxim. Land produces rent; capital yields interest; labor is recompensed by wages. When any of this triumvirate fails to receive its due returns, the economy falters until one or both of the other two assume the additional burden.

Thus, if land and labor are unproductive — that is, if they are unrewarded by rent and wages — capital either must contribute sufficient interest to make up the difference, or reduce its own principal.

That is exactly what happens in a penitentiary. The land upon which the institution is built and the fields from which the farm produce is harvested, are a dead loss; they take in no revenue at all. Similarly, labor receives nothing, all laborers being inmates. Therefore, capital, in the form of appropriation from taxes, is forced to underwrite everything.

It could be different. The price which the taxpayers are charged for the necessary luxury of keeping their problem children in exile could be very materially reduced.

How? By allowing labor to make its proper donation to the internal economy.

The Stateville and Joliet Branches of the Illinois State Penitentiary maintain 42 vocational units. The work is all done by inmates, under the supervision of skilled officers, and the finished products are sent, as required, to the tax-supported institutions of the state. Each inmate employed in these several industries receives a small wage, not fixed but varying with the amount of goods produced during a specified period. These are the only inmates who receive any remuneration for their labor. The law demands that they be paid, else they too would get nothing.

It is obviously unfair that a man engaged in the manufacture of armchairs should be more favored than a nurse who sits up all night to save a life, or a man who shovels coal all day to keep the furnaces going, or a cellhouse helper who pushes a mop and wields a broom to prevent the living quarters from becoming filthy. The author is of the opinion that no prison inmate should be paid for his work, unless all are paid.

It is also our opinion that all should be paid.

The prime purpose of rehabilitation is to convince the inmate that he cannot live morally without assuming some fraction of the social load. He must work for his bread, not steal.

However, it is difficult to instill such a conviction in the mind of a man who has spent a number of years working for nothing. Inmates know that they will be fed and clothed regardless of their assignment; hence they take little interest in the work they are required to do. But if a wage-scale were set up for prison labor, the quality of that labor would improve immediately and tremendously.

Those who direct the destinies of the labor unions could bestow upon society a boon of incalculable value. They could do it simply by permitting prison-made goods to be sold on the open market. If such a concession were made, prisons would become largely self-sustaining, without any effect on the price of the article sold. All the penal institutions in Illinois, operating their industries at full capacity, would not reduce the work week or the wages of labor unions by one second or one cent.

They would, however, add immeasurably to the self-respect of the inmates, as well as provide them with material assistance in their struggle for regeneration. The men would know that the money with which they would go out to begin life again was earned legitimately. They would have experienced for themselves that working for a living is not a sucker's game. They would be able to look the world in the eye and tell it, not to go to hell, but to step up and be their friend. They would have learned how to transform sweat into cash on hand. They would be persuaded that not only is the laborer worthy of his hire, but also the hire of the laborer.

A large sum is appropriated each year for the operation and maintenance of prisons. If the industries of those prisons were showing annual profits in proportion to the potentialities, the appropriations would be greatly decreased, and the citizen would benefit in terms of reduced taxes.

But the public would benefit more in terms of sociological improvement, for criminals would see the futility of crime as opposed to honest industry. Suppose three men rob an office of three thousand dollars at the point of a gun. The "split" would be a thousand apiece. Suppose that after dividing the amount, two of them are apprehended and sent to the penitentiary. They serve five years each. Their earnings from the crime would then be about two hundred dollars a year, or a little less than four dollars a week. If, while imprisoned, they are put to work, made to labor diligently, and paid as much as ten dollars a week for doing so, is it not reasonable to suppose that they will decide that stealing is a waste of effort?

And there are very, very few felons who secure as much as a thousand dollars from any single crime.

No man should be released from prison with less than fifty dollars in his pocket; one hundred dollars is a more reasonable amount. There will be an unavoidable period for readjustment, and there should be available a large enough sum of money to meet his needs during that period.

Unfortunately, the city which is a penitentiary must be operated as cheaply as possible, and humans often cannot see present expenditures as future profits. The labor unions have proven to be so beneficial to the working man that one wonders how he ever got along without them. Nevertheless, they are, through their inability to see the whole picture, placing an impediment in the path of progress. They are neglecting an opportunity to put forth a much-needed hand to help those who never have been taught to help themselves honestly. They are losing sight of the woods because they persist in standing behind a dead and decaying tree.

As long as the entire population of the penitentiary-city is on the dole, as long as little work of any value is provided, as long as the work which is provided goes unrewarded, as long as prisoners are shown no advantage in toiling — as long as all these things hold true, penology will continue to struggle uphill with a halter on its hind leg.

Chapter 16

PREVENTING ESCAPES AND RIOTS

It has been previously shown that the inmates of a penitentiary must adhere to a schedule of regulations, and that a failure to adhere will bring forth disciplinary action. The same is true of the officers. There are very definite rules which they must follow, and there are very definite penalties imposed for disobediences.

The reason for this strictness is that the first objective of a prison must be maintenance of maximum security. No inmate has taken up residence on the inside willingly; they will remain in confinement only as long as no opportunity is given them to do anything else. The officers of the institution constitute the first line of defense, as it were, between society and the prisoners. To them falls the duty of keeping the convicted man behind the walls until such time as release through the proper channels is deemed prudent. The walls themselves form a considerable obstacle in the path of unauthorized freedom, but without the officers to act as preventive agencies the walls would hold few inmates very long.

Consequently, Illinois prison officers are carefully trained to respond to emergencies. They are shown the need for prompt and effective action; they must thoroughly understand that the safety of the men rests primarily with them. They are shown that they have certain specific obligations when emergencies arise.

Prison emergencies may be grouped into fires, escapes, riots or strikes, and unusual weather conditions. There are stand-

723

ardized techniques for dealing with each variety.

In the case of fire, the officer must get word immediately to a superior. This is done through the institutional communication systems, or by means of a runner. After the Lieutenant or Captain has been notified, the officer does what he can to check the progress of the conflagration until the fire department arrives. Promptly after word of the emergency has reached the officials, the siren will sound, and all inmates will be returned to the cellhouse. This will enable every officer not detailed to the cellhouse to assist in coping with the fire. It is vital that the guard at whose shop the blaze was discovered should make sure that none of his men take advantage of the situation to attempt an escape. The inmates must be returned to their cells immediately upon the sounding of the siren, to be counted and kept in safety until the danger has passed.

An escape from the prison is not necessarily a large-scale disaster, but it is the cause of a temporary rupture in the prison routine. All escapes from the Joliet and Stateville branches within the past few years have been made from the Honor Farm and other trusted assignments outside the walls. But there have been occasions on which inmates succeeded in breaking the actual custodial chain.

When an escape has been established as fact, it is the officer's duty to make a report to a superior at once, giving the identity of the escapee, the circumstances surrounding the occurrence, and other pertinent data. Then he will march his men to a place of safety.

When a chauffeur, truck driver, or similarly trusted inmate runs away, it generally can be considered another victory for temptation. But when there is an escape from within the walls, some officer is to blame. With every guard obeying orders implicitly, escape from the institution proper is an impossibility.

For aid in recapturing men who escape from Illinois prisons, there is a system of quickly blocking all adjacent highways by the state police and every officer that can be spared takes part in this blockade. And frequently the employees of one branch of the penitentiary will assist those of another in such emergencies.

In the matter of riots and strikes, it must be noted that there are two kinds; violent and passive. In violent strikes, which are really riots, word must be gotten to the officials with as little loss of time as possible. Then non-participating inmates must be separated from those actively engaged in the disturbance. The officer is expected to bear in mind that complete coöperation between himself and his superiors may result in averting an an extremely dangerous situation. A few men with adequate equipment and concerted action can quell mobs of considerable size, and the officer's part in that concerted action will be to obey promptly and efficiently all orders given by his superiors.

The passive type of strike takes the form of a lack of responsiveness on the part of the inmates to the orders of the officer. Strikes of this nature, if handled promptly, can usually be brought under control with little difficulty.

In the case of unusual weather conditions, such as fog, sudden darkness, or severe storms, the officer is taught always to act in favor of safety. If inmates on the farm detail, for instance, are overtaken by a thundershower of perilous proportions, their officer should at once march them to a place of security. When a fog comes up during the night, however, the action to be taken will be dictated by the warden and his Captains. The inmates will be kept locked in their cells, officers on the walls and the ground patrol will be especially alert and observant, and cellhouse keepers will supervise the making of counts as often as the Captain-in-charge orders. When the warden or the captain feels that the weather has cleared up sufficiently to permit the normal routine of the prison to continue safely, commands will be given to that effect, and the officers will proceed as ordered.

The old and perhaps slightly frayed platitude concerning the relative values of an ounce of prevention and a pound of cure is probably more applicable to a penitentiary than to any other human situation. Institutional life is usually uneventful, but trouble does sometimes arise, trouble which is generally preceded by certain peculiarities in the behavior of that part of the inmate body planning to create it. For instance, during the recreation period the inmates, instead of being harmlessly intent on their various games, may be grouped about the yard, conversing in low tones and gazing furtively about them. There may be no actual disorder, the inmates may seem just as respectful as always — perhaps even more respectful than is customary — but the shouts and laughter which the officer is accustomed to hear may not be in evidence.

The well-trained officer immediately will confer with his fellow guards, and if it is agreed by all that there is something untoward in the air, a report will at once be made to a superior, who will institute an investigation. This investigation may disclose that a hunger strike, a riot, or even a wholesale escape was being planned for the future and, possessing this information, the officials will be able to isolate the source of the dissension and prevent the outbreak.

Such alertness is an indispensable characteristic of the good prison officer. The history of prison riots and strikes indicates plainly that the inmates suffer most, and the prevention of such emergencies will add to the welfare of the men as well as that of the state.

Abnormality on the part of the inmates is a certain sign of impending trouble, abnormality being interpreted as any noticeable deviation from accustomed conduct. Of course, there may arise occasions when an escape is planned by two or three men and subsequently reported to the authorities by another inmate. This information will be acted on without loss of time, even though informers, or "stool-pigeons," are not looked upon with favor by anyone connected with a prison. In the opinion of the inmates a stool-pigeon it not part of the human race and wise officials will not encourage such subterranean activities. Illinois prison officers are trained to discharge their duties without the help of informers, and no branch of the Joliet Penitentiary makes use of the vicious system which causes one inmate to spy on another.

Chapter 17

WHEN IS A LAWBREAKER REFORMED

The recreation period at Stateville! Five playing fields filled with inmates variously occupied while officers stroll around alertly and the tower guards on the walls maintain an unceasing vigil. In the C-House yard, two softball games in progress, with spectators standing three and four deep along the foul lines and calling loudly for base hits or strike-outs, according to their preferences. Ten men in violent action on the volleyball court, and another ten more sedately concerned with the flight of horseshoes. A dozen quartettes dashing about madly in pursuit of handballs, which they propel with varying degrees of skill towards the big wall. Many chess and checker games are played at a long wooden table; activity on the basketball courts, horseshoes, etc., and several hundred non-athletes walking or sitting or standing in large and small groups, discussing topics of the present, the past, and the future.

". . . so I says to her, I says, 'Listen, Toots, you may not be bad down in Peoria, but up here you're just another . . .'"

". . . Herbie was on the junk, see, an' I mean he really had a skinful this night. He just didn't . . ."

What, exactly, is a "reformed" convict? What are his salient characteristics, and how does he differ from his unreformed mates?

Broadly, a reformed convict is one who, after having been released from a penitentiary, does not return. He is an ex-inmate with whom society has declared a truce and who has given no overt cause for a suspension of that truce. He lives within the law.

Of course, an ex-convict may ostensibly be behaving himself while in reality continuing, with more care than before, his criminal comings and goings. He may keep out of trouble, and still steal for a living. However, he will not keep out of trouble for any lengthy period. Modern police methods are making it practically impossible for the thief to remain free indefinitely; sooner or later he will be entrapped in the tentacles of some law enforcement agency.

How, then, may it be ascertained what proportion of inmates renounce felonious ways following their release from a penitentiary? What method is there of obtaining statistical data on the percentage that do reform?

In the case of inmates released on discharge, the method must be largely negative; that is, the information available will be limited to those that do not reform. If a man has served a sentence at a Joliet institution, is discharged from the institution, and then is committed to prison in another state, the warden of the Illinois penitentiary wherein the man was an inmate will be acquainted with the latest imprisonment. This intelligence will will come from the Department of Justice at Washington, where there is maintained a clearing house of case histories and where complete records are kept of every man fingerprinted in the United States and Canada. Of course, occasionally there will be a workhouse or rural jail which does not send to Washington the fingerprints of its prisoners, but these are exceedingly few.

It is through this exchange of information by states that a man who, though he has never before been arrested in a certain section of the country may, on the basis of past record, be declared a habitual criminal and dealt with accordingly.

Nevertheless, the fact remains that no attempt can be made to keep from thievery the man going out of prison on discharge. He will be ignored until again apprehended.

The case is different with an inmate leaving on parole. He is required to keep in constant touch with his parole agent, who in turn advises the Supervision office. His opportunity for criminal endeavor is so materially reduced that in the year 1957 only a small percentage of the men paroled from Illinois institutions were guilty of conduct warranting their return to prison. Furthermore, it is mandatory that the authorities know at all times what the parolee is doing — whether he is working industriously and living in domestic harmony; what forms of recreation he has adopted; who his leisure-hours companions are; in short, what he is doing with himself.

There must be some determinable reason for the disparity between those recidivists who return from parole and those who have left the prison on a discharge. The author feels that the explanation lies in the word "supervision." A parolee, the statement is repeated, *must account for his actions.*

Chapter 18

CRITICISM OF PRISONS

When the subject of penological progress comes up for discussion a comparison usually is made between institutions of yesterday and those of today. It is often implied, if not actually stated, that during the past few decades most penal institutions have sloughed off the skin of unenlightenment and emerged with an entirely new identity.

Such a comparison is of value only to sophists, and such an implication is fundamentally fallacious. It is not any more possible to group all prisons in a common category than it is to demonstrate the parity of all universities, or hotels, or social groups. There is just as much dissimilarity between two prisons as there is between any pair of random selections. In fact, the only point of analogy is that the incarceration of criminals is the prime function.

There are two angles from which a critical estimate of a prison may be made, two standards by which its efficiency may be judged. These are the physical or structural characteristics of the buildings themselves, and the administrative policy followed by the officials.

Concerning the first point, Illinois can offer an almost simultaneous study of a thoroughly modern and a thoroughly antiquated prison, in the Stateville and the Joliet Branches of the penitentiary. Joliet is a relic of Civil War days. And it has not attained old age gracefully. There is nothing mellow about its turrets and its ramparts; rather there is a sort of senile harshness which eats into the soul and depresses the mind. The limited space within the walls, however, did not preclude the erection of shops and factories to replace the outmoded ones. Adequate recreational facilities were extended to the inmates. We once felt there would be little use in undertaking a rebuilding program and that what Joliet needed was not rejuvenation but quick death.

The general atmosphere of the place being what it is, the task of rehabilitation was far more difficult than in a newer institution. A man responds most unreadily to reformative measures when he can find in his surroundings nothing to relieve the enervating drabness which inevitably accompanies a prison. He may be wholly conscious of his need for moral and mental overhauling, but the environment soon produces in him a spiritual apathy which can be counteracted by nothing short of removal to another place of confinement.

Joliet once was reserved principally for proven agitators, incorrigibles, and other definitely unimprovable types. The prison personnel, psychiatric and sociological departments take just as great an interest in the inmates there as they do in those of any other branch, but experience has taught that all that can be done is to watch carefully for a change of spirit in the individual inmate and, having found it, recommend the transfer of the man to the more temperate climate of Stateville.

All of that has been changed. An extensive modernization program carried on in the Joliet unit has converted the antiquated, backward structure into an up-to-date one, with new, well-lighted, roomy and airy cells for almost 1200 inmates.

Stateville is a relatively new prison. It was erected in accordance with modern ideas; it is in most respects, completely up-to-date. Indeed, in comparison with the majority of other penal institutions throughout the country, it is as the aeroplane is to the one-horse shay.

There are five cellhouses at Stateville. One is rectangular, four are of the circular, panopticon variety. Each of the types has its distinct advantages. In the panopticon houses, four circular tiers rise above a circular flag. The doors of the cells, which are entirely of glass, face inside, and each cell has a window facing directly onto some portion of the ground. An octagonal tower rises in the center of the flag, from which an officer can see into all the cells of all the inmates almost at any time. In this type of cellhouse, the ventilation, sanitation, and ease of surveillance are good. However, it is to be remembered that every inmate can see the officer, and he can see only those in front of him.

The rectangular house contains five tiers of cells. These cells are back-to-back and do not have individual windows. Neither is it possible for the keeper to see into all of them at once; his inspection must be made either from the gallery of the tier or from the catwalk which runs around the cellhouse walls.

In the dormitory on the farm, reserved for men in trusty positions, the inmates are housed in rooms accommodating five men each.

The shops and factories are airy and well-lighted; the machinery is as modern as is economically possible. All units of the institution are integrated and connected by tunnels and broad walks. There are underground passages leading from the Administration Building to all strategically important buildings.

However, an institution, like a human being, may appear robust when actually it is in a state of internal deterioration. The health of a prison depends solely upon the officials into whose care it is given. No advantage to anyone can accrue from permitting antedated treatment "on the inside," however modern may be the external appearance.

Inmates of a penitentiary should be neither pampered nor persecuted. There are prisons in which cruelty is accepted as normal; where rehabilitation is merely a vaguely recognizable but unfamiliar term. There are other prisons that still countenance stripes, the ball and chain, contract labor, whipping posts, and like adjuncts of a supposedly discarded system.

On the other hand, there are prisons wherein the inmates are subject only to such restriction as the walls themselves provide. There are institutions that truly may be termed "rest homes."

Such things being so, what is needed is not a comparison of the prison of today with the prison of "yesterday," but an analysis of individual policies of operation at this very minute. The author has devoted considerable time to a study of practical prison management, as opposed to theoretical penology. He found that each and every abuse prevailing in a penal institution is attributable directly to the warden.

It is, of course, not possible to offer herein a separate and individual study of every prison in this country. Nor is it necessary. After all, this book is concerned solely with the institutions of Joliet. Suffice it, then, to say that in Joliet there will be found no prisoners fettered at the ankles, or clothed in stripes, or suspended by the wrists in solitary confinement, or subjected to the cat-o'-nine-tails.

But neither will any inmates be found making their own rules.

Chapter 19

THE IDEAL PRISON

Every penitentiary warden who is sincerely interested in his work has at one time or another indulged in the daydream of constructing the "Erehwon" of penology, the perfect penitentiary. Of course, there would be, if these reveries should magically become reality, a wide divergence in the various conceptions of penal perfection; probably no two of the dream prisons would be the same.

Some may believe that the suggestions which will follow are entirely the product of a fanciful flight, that they have few practical possibilities. The author, however, while admitting their dissimilarity to anything so far attempted, maintains that the system proposed not only would place prison management on a level in consonance with general social advancement, but would also result ultimately in a very considerable reduction in the price which the public pays for combating crime. Nor, in our opinion, are these ideas completely without the support of precedent.

"The old order changeth—." Was it considered possible, in 1900, that man someday would leave the clouds beneath him as he acended on wings? Was it believed possible that the soy bean would play an important part in industrial construction? Did it occur to anyone that the stereopticon could be made to speak? Yet all these things did happen and, happening, altered the entire philosophy of most of the world. Why, then, would it be fantastic to hope that some day this altered philosophy may be extended to include within its liberal limits a truly productive institutional system? The term "rehabilitation and reformation" is gradually attaining a niche of great social significance; people are beginning to think of criminals as, in most cases, curable.

We have, in progressive prisons, abandoned the negative treatment of prisoners, but the disappearance of barbaric forms of degradation does not mean that the positive approach has reached its apex.

Much, much more must be done before we shall have achieved any appreciable amount of self-satisfaction.

No prison should contain more than one thousand inmates with proper classification according to type, etc. Any larger penal population makes it impossible for the warden to perform one of his primary duties, that of becoming personally acquainted with every man in his charge. At present, wardens deal with an unwieldly mass; there is little opportunity for studying individuals. Consequently, in order to insure that none will feel discriminated against, all must be treated exactly alike. There can be made no allowance for psychological differences; and character is relegated to temporary limbo. Practically the only occasions on which any one inmate is able to separate himself from his fellows are those on which he violates a regulation.

Perhaps there are those who will commend this state of affairs, on the grounds that one who has been convicted of a criminal act deserves nothing more, and nothing less, than all others similarly convicted. It may be argued that the psychology of a felon is manifestly anti-social and that his character is best left severely alone, being not an attractive kind.

This attitude descends directly from the days of the whipping post and the stocks; it conflicts sharply with the modern trend. From present indications, the people of many nations are reverting to the thought processes of the Dark Ages; cruelty is again on the march. We must look forever forward, not back, because once we embrace the policy of oppression, of deliberately hurting the helpless, we cease to be the champion of progress.

And who is more helpless than the inmate of a penitentiary?

Returning to the matter of an ideal prison system, there should be, instead of one institution such as Stateville with nearly four thousand inhabitants, four institutions with one-quarter that number each. A classification center, a Diagnostic Depot, would serve as a receiving and distributing agency, as it does now, but with this difference: segregation would be greatly facilitated. Each prison would have only a certain type of men— the incorrigibles would be separated from the improvables, the first-timers from the habituals, etc.

It is easy to see how such a system would benefit all concerned. The man who exhibited a desire to abide by the rules would not be forced to suffer the same discipline as the troublemaker; and, conversely, the agitator would not receive unmerited leniency. The warden would be able personally to observe the actions of every inmate; he could discuss their problems with them and make constructive suggestions. The officers also would play a more important part in the rehabilitatory program; they would have fewer men in their care and, consequently, would know them better. They would submit recommendations to the warden regarding the individual attitudes of the prisoners, and these recommendations together with those made by the warden himself, would be forwarded to the Parole Board, for consideration in disposing of the cases.

This plan would offer a real incentive to the inmates, for by their behavior and work in one institution they could earn either promotion or demotion to another. For instance, if a man in the prison where the most lenience was shown displayed a desire to abuse that leniency, he would be transferred to tougher surroundings Similarly, if an inmate, after a period of disciplining, showed a willingness to coöperate with the authorities, he would be moved up the institutional scale. Thus would be engendered in all who truly desired to benefit by their imprisonment a sincere appreciation of right conduct, and the struggle for reformation would be half won. But it must be remembered that many of the worst criminals are the best prisoners.

Of course, it is realized that behavior within the walls cannot always be taken as the true criterion of character. The really "bad" felon is often the best behaved of inmates. A good prison record would not be able to counteract a thoroughly vicious criminal record. The Parole Board would be obligated to make sure that justice was handed out. However, even if an inmate had little chance for early release, it would be to the advantage of both himself and the prison if he could be persuaded, rather than forced, to conduct himself properly while incarcerated.

A vital contribution of the ideal prison would be providing a complete educational program and work for all inmates, and paying them for their labors. As stated before, the principal cause of crime is a lack of familiarity with work. If the criminal were to put forth honest effort, he sooner or later would fall into the habit. The curse of some penitentiaries, past and present, is that they keep a large proportion of their inmates in idleness, with resultant mental and physical degeneration.

There would, of course, be operated in conjunction with these hypothetical institutions a farm from which would be secured the foodstuffs required for feeding the inmates. Possibly it would be advisable to have several small farms; one or two could be manned exclusively by prisoners who have been declared good parole risks. These farms would represent the ultimate in penal freedom, as the Honor Farm at Stateville now represents. Only men who had demonstrated their trustworthiness would be assigned there, and the supervision would be kept to a minimum.

Each institution would offer religious and educational facilities, and again there would be experienced an increase in efficiency because of the small number of inmates. The various chaplains would have an opportunity to inquire much more intensively into the spiritual needs of the men, and those taking school courses would receive far more personal attention from the teachers

It has been said that county jails constitute a menace to the welfare of society, and in many cases this assertion may unfortunately be substantiated. Too often the officials in charge of the jail permit prisoners to enjoy privileges totally at variance with their best interests. Such prisoners form exaggerated ideas of their own worth, and stringent measures are often necessary to disabuse them, when they enter the penitentiary. When a man has been arrested for a felony, he should be kept in a state-supervised jail until the court has decided upon his punishment — provided, of course, he cannot make bond. If his crime should be deemed deserving of a prison sentence, he would be transported to one of the Diagnostic Depots of the State Penitentiary, as at present; but if his term of servitude should be set at less than a year, he would be confined in a state institution designed for that purpose, rather than in a county jail.

In the matter of jail or penal administration, it must be remembered that fundamentally, the internal conditions depend upon the officials. The author knows of many city and county jails where conditions are all that could be desired, but we also know of some where a great deal of improvement could be made. It undoubtedly would be to the benefit of the community, the country, and the state if an integrated system of jails were instituted, a system under which all prisoners would be treated in accordance with their needs, rather than with their desires. It is certain that many men could be guided back to normal living by intelligent treatment while still in the pre-penitentiary stage of their criminal career, and such treatment should come from authorities at the jails. There are in every city and town chronic offenders who never commit crimes calling for prison sentences, but who nevertheless must be put away periodically.

This sort — dipsomaniacs, petty larceny addicts, and similar civic nuisances — should be confined in an institution for that type, but a greater effort should be made to extend mental and moral therapy to them.

Crime is a social disease; it must be attacked in much the same manner that yellow fever and bubonic plague were attacked. A concentrated and coöperative onslaught will succeed where isolated efforts fail. Society must make up its mind to use all of its collective weapons. But those efforts must be practical to be effective. Theory to a degree is good, but in many cases not workable and very impractical.

Chapter 20

FROM MINOR TO MAJOR LEAGUE CRIME

"The child is father to the man."

Penological problems would be far less complex, society would have a much smaller burden of taxes to bear, and this country would waste a great deal less of its potential productiveness, if juvenile delinquency were eliminated or even reduced substantially. Very few men enter a penitentiary without having previously committed offenses less serious than the one for which they were last sentenced. The large majority of penal inmates started out as juvenile delinquents, and from petty crimes climbed the ladder until they reached the rung that lodged them in prison. If they had been counseled wisely in their early youth, they never would have earned the unpleasant experience of a term in the penitentiary.

How can juvenile delinquency be dealt with more satisfactorily? What changes are necessary in the method of dealing with young offenders? The authors are convinced that if certain revisions were effected in the attitude of society towards the matter, prisons one day would become practically obsolete.

First, the laws pertaining to juveniles are badly in need of overhauling. Now in Illinois, almost any youngster can be sent to St. Charles for almost any sort of an act, criminal or otherwise. If neighbors should happen to take a dislike to a certain boy, they can have him committed to the School, where he will live constantly in an anti-social atmosphere. A new institution was recently erected at Sheridan, Illinois, for segregation of

739

youthful incorrigibles, but building new institutions is not the answer. The attack must be made at the source — the parents of the delinquent. Certainly, no reflection is directed at St. Charles or Sheridan. They are both operated as efficiently as possible, but a reformatory is no place to raise good citizens.

No boy who has been removed from his home and sent to a reform school ever should be returned to that home. His parents have proved their inability to raise him properly, and he should be placed in other surroundings upon his release. At present, the policy is being followed to a certain extent, and it must be admitted that when it is necessary to find a home for a young offender, careful investigation is made into all circumstances But the work is not sufficiently comprehensive, in practice. It is in most cases restricted to those boys whose previous homes are non-existent, or so manifestly unsatisfactory that it would be almost a criminal act to send the boy back there.

The author maintains that no matter what type the previous home may have been no boy who has been taken from there and placed in a state institution should be returned there. A different domestic environment should be found for him so that he may make an entirely fresh start. The expense of maintaining the boy should, of course, be paid by the state, and constant attention should be given to the progress being made in the effort towards social readjustment. He should be placed under the supervision of persons with experience who have good, sound judgment and not all theory.

The next suggestion probably may be ten or twenty years ahead of present beliefs, but the authors are reasonably positive that eventually it will become fact. The reference is to legislation having to do with marriage. Every man and woman seeking a marriage license should be thoroughly examined as to his and her mental and physical health. Efforts are now being made to prevent those suffering from venereal diseases from marrying, but no restriction is placed on those with mental deficiencies. Indeed, it is possible for a man or a woman to marry immediately upon release from an insane asylum; they may produce hopelessly handicapped children. Some standard should be adopted for judging the mental fitness of all citizens who seek to marry and bear children.

It was asserted above that delinquents should be given a different home atmosphere than the one in which they lived prior to being placed directly under the jurisdiction of the state. Such a program could be extended to include many thousands of children not actually considered potential menaces.

In fact, everyone living in those sub-marginal urban districts known popularly as the "slums" should immediately be transferred to other localities and their former habitations razed.

Tenement houses cannot possibly have a legitimate place in a modern civilization; they should be wiped out as a greater threat to society than the plague.

There should be a nation-wide extension of the housing projects which are in some cities providing the less-privileged classes with adequate homes at a reasonable cost.

Well ventilated and sufficiently heated apartment houses should replace the crowded flats which now constitute the residence of many, many thousands of families.

More and better recreational facilities should go along with the new homes. City children have far too little space in which to play. It should not be necessary for them to have their baseball diamonds and hop-scotch courts in the middle of busy thoroughfares, where their lives are constantly imperiled by traffic. Playgrounds should be provided; an effort should be made to take every child into the country for a month each summer. There is nothing quite so salutory as a knowledge of the workings of nature.

Educational and religious training are, of course, essential to the development of productive men and women, and in this connection credit should be given to the many church groups and lay organizations which lend a helping hand to the underprivileged. And by all means, supervision during leisure time and at play is a must.

Governmental aid, in the form of substantial appropriations, should be extended to these groups, for their burden is heavy.

Boys' Town, while unquestionably an exceedingly meritorious attempt to deal with the problems of socially handicapped juveniles, does work with a more or less select class. Its young citizens are hand-picked; they represent the best elements in their stratum. Such discrimination is not possible in large cities. If any are to be helped, all must be helped. And helping them takes money.

If the financial, industrial, and commercial leaders of the country could only comprehend that they actually would save dollars by underwriting a program of slum clearance — they will pay in future years for maintaining penitentiaries to imprison the children who were not allowed to mature normally — juvenile delinquency would be reduced immeasurably in a short time.

Perhaps we Americans will sometime — may it be soon! — realize that the future of our nation lies entirely in the bodies and minds of our children and that by insuring them the natural right to grow up decently in reasonable comfort, we will be laying a secure foundation for our collective prosperity.

Chapter 21

IS DEATH PENALTY EFFECTIVE?

There is no intention to enter into an intensive investigation and analysis of various arguments advanced by proponents and opponents of capital punishment, inasmuch as all there is to say on that subject has long since been said.

The author merely wishes to state that nothing in his experience has shown him that capital punishment is really effective, considering the matter from the point of view of ultimate benefit to the state. True, it does immutably prevent the individual offender from further transgressing the laws of the land, but it also prevents the adoption of any reformative measures. The executed man, or woman, will no longer annoy society with his, or her, malefactions, but neither will society ever profit from whatever constructive skill or abilities the condemned person may possess.

Moreover, there is no evidence to substantiate the assertion that capital punishment reduces materially the number of capital crimes. A small number of states in this country have abolished official executions. And in none of them has murder become more widespread than it was before the abolition. Indeed, in many cases where capital punishment is practiced, the per capita number of homicides is considerably greater than in those states which make no use of the hangman's noose, or the electric switch, or the gas chamber petcock.

The fact is that during the past century there has been, all over the world, a definite tendency away from the death penalty. Something like twenty-five countries have abolished it entirely, and those retaining it have generally specified that murder shall be the only offense for which it may be imposed. In the United States, as one expert observed, the modern movement "is to substitute a permissive death penalty for the mandatory death penalty."

The primary duty of a penitentiary warden is to comply with the orders of the court, and if the court orders the execution of a man or woman, the warden must see to it that the man or woman is executed.

In Illinois, the only crimes punishable by death are murder and kidnaping for ransom. The method of execution is the electric chair, of which there are three in the state, one at the Cook County Jail in Chicago, one at the Joliet Branch of the Penitentiary, and one at the Menard Branch.

When a prisoner under the sentence of death is received by the warden, the first concern is maximum security. This security is best insured if the condemned person is kept segregated — not solitary of the "hole," but merely in an isolated cell, where there can be no contact with any but authorized persons. These persons include the doctor, who will give whatever medical attention is needed; the chaplain, who will provide spiritual support; and such relatives and friends as may be permitted to make periodic visits. The prisoner also has the privilege of writing as many proper letters as he desires.

The usual time of execution is at one minute after midnight. The warden is present at all executions, and certain officials are detailed to specific posts in connection therewith. The warden is responsible also for receiving, searching, and escorting to their proper places official witnesses and those whose connection with the trial of the condemned man made permissible their presence.

The author has been present at many executions. We have seen men march bravely to death; seen them swagger to the chamber, only to collapse at the sight of the chair. Some leave this world cursing an reviling the society with which they could not live at peace; some have made peace with themselves and their God, and meet their end quietly.

But whatever the attitude and the conduct of the condemned, the problem of future prevention of that type of crime remains unsolved, and in some cases at least, absolute justice has not been served.

It would seem that murderers ought to be included in that broad program which now strives to treat criminals in terms of themselves, rather than of their crime. If, instead of the death penalty, or even a determinate number of years, the person who committed a murder were to be sentenced to imprisonment for a period of from one year to life, there would be afforded the opportunity of studying the personality of the offender, the circumstances surrounding the case, the mental and moral adjustment made after incarceration — in short, all factors which enter into the commission of any crime. Under this policy, it would be within the realm of possibility that the prisoner could be rehabilitated and returned to society — no doubt there would be some who never should be released — and the expense of maintenance, in the meanwhile, would be a small price to pay for this achievement.

It does not appear that the theory of Garofalo is much of a force in crime prevention, for people continue to kill each other in spite of the examples made of other killers. Probably the problem of the murderer will have to be included in the general sociological plan for attacking crime at its roots, although murder is peculiar to no particular crime or district.

One thing is patent: The dealth penalty is not of much practical value nor consistent with civilized progress. The sentence in no way is uniform, even though the crimes may be identical.

APPENDICES

Appendix A

RULES AND STATUTES RELATING TO *PAROLE* AND *PARDONS* IN ILLINOIS

* * * * * *

FOREWORD

Pursuant to the power conferred on the Parole and Pardon Board of the Department of Public Safety of the State of Illinois by Section 7 of "An Act to revise the law in relation to the fixing of the punishment and the sentence and commitment of persons convicted of crime or offenses, and providing for a system of parole," (Known as the Sentence and Parole Act), the said Parole and Pardon Board at a meeting of the members held at Springfield on November 11, 1954, adopted the following Revised Rules and Regulations concerning the parole of prisoners from the Illinois State Penitentiary, the State Reformatory for Women and the Illinois State Reformatory at Sheridan, and ordered that they be printed and promulgated as in force and effect on and after January 1, 1955

CIVIL ADMINISTRATIVE CODE*

*Chapter 127, Illinois Revised Statutes, 1951.

Section 5. EXECUTIVE AND ADMINISTRATIVE OFFICERS, BOARDS, AND COMMISSIONS. In addition to the directors of departments, the following executive and administrative officers, boards and commissions, which said officers, boards and commissions in the respective departments, shall hold offices hereby created and designated as follows:

* * *

In the Department of Public Safety.

The Parole and Pardon Board, which shall consist of five persons, one of whom shall be designated by the Governor to be chairman thereof. * * *

Section 55b. PAROLE AND PARDON BOARD — POWERS AND DUTIES — RECORDS. The Parole and Pardon Board in the Department of Public Safety shall exercise and discharge all the rights, powers and duties heretofore vested in the parole board and in the Department of Public Welfare in granting paroles to persons sentenced or committed for crimes or offenses and in the supervision of aftercare of persons so paroled. The action of a majority of all the members of the Parole and Pardon Board shall be the action of said Board. No parole shall be granted except upon the concurrence of a majority of all the members of the Parole and Pardon Board. The action of the Parole and Pardon Board in granting a parole and the action of the Board in denying any such application for parole shall be recited in the records of the Board. * * *

749

PERTINENT SECTIONS OF THE SENTENCE AND PAROLE ACT*

*As Amended in Force July 9, 1951.

An Act to revise the law in relation to the fixing of the punishment and the sentence and commitment of persons convicted of crime or offenses, and providing for a system of parole. Approved June 25, 1917. (Section 801 et seq. Illinois Revised Statutes 1951.)

Be it enacted by the People of the State of Illinois, represented in the General Assembly:

Sentence for Misprision of Treason, Murder, Rape and Kidnapping — Eligibility to Parole. Section 1. In all cases where any person, male or female, over ten years of age, shall be tried by a jury and the jury shall find the defendant guilty, the jury shall also by its verdict fix the punishment, and if the punishment imposed is imprisonment, the jury shall fix the term of such imprisonment; if the case is tried by the court, without a jury, or on a plea of guilty, and the court shall impose imprisonment, the court shall fix a definite term of imprisonment, and the court in each case, shall fix the place of confinement. In every such case of imprisonment, the court shall sentence the defendant to the penitentiary, except as is provided in clauses one and two in section three in this Act, and in such cases the court shall commit as in those clauses provided.

Every person so sentenced shall be held in the appropriate institutions, that is to say, the Illinois State Penitentiary or the State reformatory for women or the Illinois State Reformatory at Sheridan, Illinois, for and during the definite term in said sentence named, subject to the provision for transfer and commitment to the penitentiary, from the Illinois State Reformatory at Sheridan, Illinois contained in clause 1 of section 3 of this Act and subject to parole and subject to be earlier discharged, as in this Act provided, by the Parole and Pardon Board of the Department of Public Safety, and it shall be deemed and taken as a part of every such sentence that all of the provisions for parole and discharge in this Act contained shall be a part of said sentence as fully as though written in it.

Every person sentenced and committed under this section "one" shall, in the discretion of the Parole and Pardon Board, be eligible to parole under rules and regulations adopted therefor by the Parole and Pardon Board, such paroles to be as follows: Persons sentenced for life may be eligible to parole at the end of twenty years; persons not sentenced for life but sentenced for a definite term of years shall not be eligible to parole until he or she shall have served the minimum sentence provided by law for the crime of which he or she was convicted, good time being allowed as provided by law; nor until he or she shall have served at least one-third of the time fixed in said definite sentence. It is expressly provided that the definite sentence provided for in this section "one" shall be applicable only to the crimes enumerated in this section "one" and definite sentences shall not be applicable to any other crime or offense enumerated in this Act; and further, that indeterminate or general sentences shall apply to all other crimes and offenses enumerated in this Act, but not to the crimes or offenses enumerated in this section "one."

Persons Eligible to Parole. *Section 1a.* All persons heretofore and hereafter sentenced and committed under the provisions of "An Act in relation to the punishment of criminals," approved June 23, 1883, as amended, shall be eligible to parole as follows: persons sentenced for life may be eligible to parole at the end of twenty years; a person not sentenced for life but sentenced for a definite term of years shall not be eligible to parole until such person shall have served at least one-third of the time fixed in said definite sentence.

Indeterminate Sentences — Commitment for Recovery of Fine or Costs. Section 2. Except for the crimes enumerated in section one of this Act, the courts of this State, in imposing a sentence to the penitentiary or to the reformatory for women or to any other State institution now or hereafter provided by law for the incarceration, punishment, discipline, training or reformation of persons convicted and sentenced to, or committed to such institutions (not including, however, county jail), shall fix the minimum and maximum limits or duration of imprisonment. The minimum limit fixed by the court may be greater but shall not be less than the minimum term provided by law for the offense and the maximum limit fixed by the court may be less but shall not be greater than the maximum term provided by law therefor.

For the purpose of determining the minimum and maximum limits or duration of imprisonment, the court may, after conviction of the person, consider the evidence, if any, received upon the trial, and the evidence, if any, as to aggravation and mitigation of the offense, received on a plea of guilty, and may also hear and receive evidence as to the moral character, life, family, occupation, and criminal record, if any, of such person so convicted. It shall be deemed and taken as a part of every such sentence as fully as though written therein, that the Parole and Pardon Board, by and with the approval of the Governor in the nature of a release or commutation of sentence or commitment, may terminate the term of such imprisonment or commitment earlier than the maximum fixed by the court, as provided in Section 9.

No court of otherwise competent criminal jurisdiction shall be deprived of jurisdiction to sentence and commit or commit, under this Act, for terms of imprisonment for a crime or offense in this Act enumerated, although such crime or offense may in addition to such imprisonment, be punishable by other or alternative punishment.

No person shall by any court be committed to the penitentiary, to the reformatory for women, or to any other State institution for the recovery of a fine or costs.

Department of Public Safety and Department of Public Welfare to Adopt Rules — Records — Copy of Register. Section 5. The Department of Public Safety and the Department of Public Welfare, with respect to prisoners and wards committed to the respective jurisdiction of such Department, shall adopt such rules concerning prisoners and wards committed to the custody of said department as shall prevent them from returning to criminal courses, best secure their self-support and accomplish their reformation.

Whenever any person shall be received into the Illinois State Penitentiary, the State reformatory for women or other institution for the incarceration, punishment, discipline, training or reformation of prisoners or wards of the State, the Department of Public Safety or the Department of Public Welfare, as the case may be, having custody of such person, shall cause to be entered in a register the date of such admission, the name, nativity, nationality, with such other facts as can be ascertained of parentage, education, occupation and early social influences as seen to indicate the constitutional and acquired defects and tendencies of the prisoner or ward, and based upon these, an estimate of the present condition of the prisoner or ward and the best possible plan of treatment. Each of said departments shall carefully examine each prisoner or ward when received, and shall enter in a register kept by the name, nationality or race, the weight, stature and family history of each prisoner or ward, also a statement of the condition of the heart, lungs and other principal organs, the rate of the pulse and respiration, the measurement of the chest and abdomen, and any existing disease or deformity, or other disability, acquired or inherited; upon the register shall be entered from time to time minutes of observed improvement or deterioration of character and notes as to the method and treatment employed; also, all alterations affecting the standing or situation of such prisoner or ward, and any subsequent facts or personal history which may be brought officially to the knowledge of the department bearing upon the question of parole or final release of the prisoner or ward. Every public officer to whom inquiry may be addressed by either the Department of Public Safety or the Department of Public Welfare concerning any prisoner within the custody of either of said Departments shall give said department all information possessed or accessible to him which may throw light upon the question of the fitness of said prisoner or ward to receive the benefits of parole or to be again placed at liberty.

A complete and accurate copy of the register of the Department of Public Welfare relating to prisoners and wards committed to its custody, together with all additions or amendments thereto which may be made from time to time, shall be transmitted by said Department to the Parole and Pardon Board in the Department of Public Safety.

Official Statement — Filing — Transmitting to Parole and Pardon Board — Department of Public Safety. Section 6. In all cases, whether the sentence be definite or indeterminate, the judge by or before whom any prisoner or ward is convicted or committed, and also the State's attorney of the county in which he or she was convicted or committed shall file an official statement with the clerk of the court to be transmitted to and to thereby furnish the Parole and Pardon Board an official statement of the facts or circumstances constituting the crime or offense whereof the prisoner or ward was convicted or committed, together with all other information accessible to them in regard to the career of the prisoner or ward prior to the time of the commitment for the crime or offense of which he or she was convicted or committed relative to his or her habits, associates, disposition and reputation and any other facts and circumstances which may tend to throw light upon the question as to whether such prisoner or ward is capable again of becoming a law-abiding citizen: Provided, that the official statement herein required of the judge and the State's attorney need not include therein the evidence received after conviction as an aid to the court in fixing the minimum and maximum limits or duration of imprisonment as provided in Sections 2 and 3 of this Act, nor any conclusions or findings of fact resulting from such evidence. The official court reporter, at the dictation of the judge of the court or the State's attorney of the county, shall write the official statements of the judge and State's attorney above referred to at the time of the conviction or commitment of the prisoner or ward. The clerk of the court shall prepare a statement, giving the name and residence of the trial judge and also the names of the jurors and witnesses sworn at the trial and shall attach such statement, together with the official statement of the trial judge and State's attorney and a copy of the judgment, order or record of conviction, to be certified as a mittimus and deliver same, so attached, to the sheriff of the county for transmission to such institution, reformatory or penitentiary, as the case may be, at the time of the delivery of the prisoner or ward to the officers of such institution, reformatory or penitentiary; and the officers of the Department of Public Safety or the Department of Public Welfare, as the case may be, in charge of such institution, reformatory or penitentiary shall report to the proper officer of the Department of Public Welfare the receipt of such prisoner or ward with such other official information as the department may require, within five days after the receipt of such prisoner or ward. A complete and accurate copy of the statement and record so delivered to the sheriff and transmitted by him to the Department of Public Welfare shall be delivered by said Department to the Parole and Pardon Board in the Department of Public Safety.

Rules and Regulations—Employers or Sponsors—Enforcement of Rules and Regulations—Eligibility to Parole—Final Discharge. Section 7. The Parole and Pardon Board shall establish rules and regulations, not inconsistent with this Act, under which prisoners in the Illinois State Penitentiary, in the State reformatory for women and in such other State institutions as are now or may hereafter be provided for the incarceration, punishment, discipline, training or reformation of the prisoners or wards committed thereto, may be allowed to go upon parole outside of the institutional buildings and enclosures, and shall issue paroles in accordance with the provisions of this Act and of such rules and regulations adopted hereunder.

The Parole and Pardon Board may provide in its rules and regulations that arrangements shall be made for honorable and useful employment while on parole when, in its judgment, such employment is desirable or necessary in any particular case. However, no prisoner or ward shall be released from either the penitentiary or the reformatory for women, or such other institution herein in this Act mentioned until the Parole and Pardon Board shall have made arrangements or shall have satisfactory evidence that arrangements have been made for a proper and suitable home free from criminal influence and without expense to the State while upon parole. The prospective employer or sponsor of any prisoner or ward shall not be a person who holds office by election or appointment or any employment whatsoever with the State of Illinois, any county, township, city or village, or any municipal corporation or quasi-municipal corporation in the State of Illinois; nor shall said employer or sponsor be a committeeman of any political party in the State of Illinois.

For the purpose of obtaining satisfactory evidence, the Board or any employee thereof, designated, in writing, by the Board, shall have power to administer an oath to the prospective employer or sponsor of any prisoner or ward and may interrogate him as to any matter relevant to his fitness to assume the responsibility of providing honorable and useful employment or a proper and suitable home, as the case may be, for any such prisoner or ward; but no prospective employer shall be required to travel outside of the county in which he resides to be so examined.

All prisoners and wards so temporarily released upon parole, shall, at all times, until the receipt of their final discharge, be considered in the legal custody of the officers of the Parole and Pardon Board, and shall, during the said time, be considered as remaining under conviction for the crime or offense of which they were convicted and sentenced or committed and subject to be taken at any time within the enclosure or such penitentiary, reformatory and institution herein mentioned. Should any prisoner or ward who is paroled be declared to be a parole violator he shall be given credit for time spent on parole only to the date of the violation as determined by the Parole and Pardon Board at a hearing conducted upon the return of the prisoner or ward to the institution; however, in the discretion of the Parole and Pardon Board the prisoner or ward may be paroled at any time subsequent to his return as a parole violator.

Full power to enforce such rules and regulations and to retake and reimprison any inmate so upon parole is hereby conferred upon the officers and employees of the Parole and Pardon Board. The order or writ certified to by the warden, superintendent or managing head of such penitentiary, reformatory or such other institution above mentioned, with the seal of the institution attached and directed to all sheriffs, coroners, constables, police officers or to any particular persons named in the order or writ shall be sufficient warrant for the officer or other person named therein to authorize the officer or person to arrest and deliver to the proper officer of the penitentiary, reformatory or such other institution the body of the conditionally released or paroled prisoner named in the writ, and all sheriffs, coroners, constables, police officers or other persons named therein shall execute the order or writ the same as criminal processes. In case any prisoner or ward so conditionally released or paroled shall flee beyond the limits of the State, he or she may be returned pursuant to the provisions of laws of this State relating to fugitives.

No prisoner or ward sentenced or committed under Section 2 or 3 of this Act, shall be eligible to parole after his or her commitment in the penitentiary, reformatory for women or State institution in this Act mentioned until he or she shall have served the minimum limit or duration of imprisonment fixed by the court (or, in case the prisoner or ward was sentenced prior to the effective date of this amendatory Act of 1943, until he or she shall have served the minimum term of imprisonment provided by law for such offense) and, in either event, less good time allowed as provided by law. Unless a prisoner or ward is earlier discharged as provided in section 9 of this Act, the term of imprisonment of a prisoner or ward committed hereunder shall terminate at the expiration of the maximum limit or duration of imprisonment fixed by the court (or, if the prisoner or ward has been sentenced or committed prior to the effective date of this amendatory Act of 1943, at the expiration of the maximum term provided by law for the offense for which such prisoner or ward stands convicted), making allowance, in either event, for good time as provided by law.

In all cases of definite sentence provided for in section one of this Act, persons sentenced for life or for a definite term of imprisonment may be paroled in the discretion of the Parole and Pardon Board; persons sentenced for life may be eligible to parole at the end of twenty years; persons not sentenced for life but sentenced for a definite term of years shall not be eligible to parole until he or she shall have served the minimum sentence provided by law, for the crime for which he or she was convicted, good time being allowed as provided by law, not until he or she shall have served at least one-third of the time fixed in the definite sentence. Provided, however, persons heretofore or hereafter sentenced and committed under the provisions of "An Act in relation to the punishment of criminals," approved June 22, 1883, as amended, shall be eligible to parole in the manner and under the conditions prescribed in Section 1a of this Act.

(NOTE: The above section of the statute was amended by two separate bills in the 67th General Assembly. The above explanation of the statute integrates the content of the both amendments.)

May Parole Outside State — Violation of Parole — Further Parole After Violation. Section 7a. The Parole and Pardon Board may parole a non-resident prisoner or ward, or a prisoner or ward whose family, relatives or friends reside outside of this State, to a person, firm or company in some state other than Illinois, to serve his parole.

Such paroled prisoner or ward shall be required to make regular monthly reports in writing to the Board, obey the rules of the Board, obey the laws of such other state, and in all respects keep faithfully his parole agreement until discharged as in this Act provided by the Parole and Pardon Board. Should such prisoner or ward so paroled violate his or her parole agreement, such prisoner or ward shall from the date of such violation be deemed to owe the State of Illinois service for the remainder of his or her maximum sentence, and should such prisoner or ward so violating said parole be returned to this State pursuant to the provisions of "An Act authorizing the Governor to enter into certain reciprocal agreements with other States," approved January 7, 1936, or should such prisoner or ward so violating said parole again at any time return to the State of Illinois, he or she shall be subject to be again arrested or apprehended on the writ or order of the warden, superintendent or managing head of the penitentiary, reformatory or institution from which such prisoner or ward was paroled with full power and authority in the Parole and Pardon Board and its employees and agents and all officers as is provided in other cases to return such parole violator to such penitentiary, reformatory or other institution. The case of such parole violator, when so returned shall be brought before the Parole and Pardon Board for determination of such parole violation, and if the Board shall determine upon hearing, that such prisoner violated his or her parole agreement, he or she shall be detained in said penitentiary, reformatory or other institution to serve the maximum limit or duration or his or her imprisonment fixed by the court (or, if the prisoner was sentenced or committed prior to the effective date of this amendatory Act of 1943, the prisoner shall be detained until the expiration of the maximum term of his or her sentence as provided by law) giving, in either of such events, credit only for time faithfully served in prison and on parole before violation: Provided, however, such returned prisoner or ward may again be paroled or discharged earlier than the termination of such maximum limit or duration of imprisonment or sentence, as the case may be, in the discretion of the Parole and Pardon Board.

Parole and Pardon Board — Powers and Duties as to Parole — Written Statement Submitted to State's Attorney. Section 7b. The Parole and Pardon Board in the Department of Public Safety shall exercise and discharge all the rights, powers and duties heretofore vested in the parole board and in the Department of Public Welfare in granting paroles to persons sentenced or committed for crimes or offenses and in the supervision and aftercare of persons so paroled. The action of a majority of all the members of the Parole and Pardon Board shall be the action of the Parole and Pardon Board. No parole shall be granted except upon the concurrence of a majority of all the members of the Parole and Pardon Board. The action of the Parole and Pardon Board in granting a parole or in denying any such application for parole shall be recited in its records.

In consideration of any application for parole due consideration and weight shall be given to the record of the prisoner's conduct kept by the superintendent or warden.

All sessions of the Parole and Pardon Board shall be open to the public and it shall keep a public record of all persons appearing for or against any application for parole.

Within thirty (30) days after a prisoner is paroled, the Parole and Pardon Board shall submit to the State's Attorney of the county in which the prisoner was sentenced, a written statement which shall include the following:

1. The name of the paroled prisoner and the date of said parole;

2. The name and address of the person to whom paroled.

The statement so submitted and a duplicate thereof shall respectively be placed on file in the office of the State's Attorney to whom submitted and the Department of Public Safety, at Springfield. Both shall be open to public inspection at any time during the business hours of said offices.

Paroled Prisoners Furnished Clothing, Money and Transportation. Section 8. Upon granting parole to any prisoner or ward the Parole and Pardon Board shall provide him or her with suitable clothing, a grant of money up to a maximum of $50 which may be paid to him or her in installments at the discretion of the Board and shall procure transportation for him or her to his or her place of employment. The amount of money granted to each particular case shall be determined upon the basis of need by the Parole and Pardon Board.

(NOTE: The above section of the statute was amended by three separate bills in the 67th General Assembly. The above explanation of the statute integrates the content of all amendments.)

Supervision of Paroled Prisoners — Discharge of Prisoner or Ward. Section 9. The Parole and Pardon Board shall keep in communication, as far as possible, with all prisoners and wards who are on parole from the penitentiary, reformatory for women, or other institution for the incarceration, punishment, discipline, training or reformation, also with the sponsors of such prisoners or wards, and when, in the opinion of the Parole and Pardon Board, any prisoner or ward who has served not less than six months of his or her parole acceptably (the Parole and Pardon Board may require a longer service upon parole) has given such evidence as is deemed reliable and trustworthy that he or she will remain at liberty without violating the law and that his or her final release is not incompatible with the welfare of society; and whenever it shall be made to appear to the satisfaction of the Board that any prisoner or ward has faithfully served his or her term of parole and the Board shall have information that such prisoner or ward can safely be trusted to be at liberty and that his or her final release will not be incompatible with the welfare of society, it shall have power to cause to be entered of record an order discharging such prisoner or ward for or on account of his or her conviction or commitment, which said order when approved by the Governor shall operate as a complete discharge of such prisoner or ward, in the nature of a release or commutation of his or her sentence, to take effect immediately upon delivery of a certified copy thereof to the prisoner or ward, and the clerk of the court in which the prisoner or ward was convicted or committed shall, upon presentation of such certified copy, enter the judgment of such conviction or commitment satisfied and released pursuant to the order.

(NOTE: The above section of the statute was amended by two separate bills in the 67th General Assembly. The above explanation of the statute integrates the content of both amendments.)

RULES AND REGULATIONS

of the

PAROLE AND PARDON BOARD

CONCERNING PAROLES

1. Prisoners in the Illinois State Penitentiary, the State Reformatory for Women and the Illinois State Reformatory at Sheridan serving indeterminate sentences shall be eligible to consideration for parole in accordance with the following statutory provisions:

(A)   When he or she shall have served the minimum limit or duration of imprisonment fixed by the court, or

(B)   In case the prisoner was sentenced prior to July 1, 1943, when he or she shall have served the minimum term of imprisonment provided by law for the crime of which he or she was convicted.

In each case "Good Time" shall be deducted as prescribed by the rule of the Department of Public Safety providing for the diminution of sentences as required by statute, hereinafter referred to as "Good Time," as distinguished from "Merit Time."

(NOTES) — For the rule providing for "Good Time" in diminution of sentences, see Appendix.

2. The Parole and Pardon Board will also recognize time earned under the "Progressive Merit System" established in the Illinois State Penitentiary, the State Reformatory for Women and Illinois State Reformatory at Sheridan, hereinafter referred to as "Merit Time," and "Industrial Credits" requested by the respective wardens (which have been approved by the Board), in determining when a prisoner serving an indeterminate sentence may again be eligible to consideration for parole after his or her case has been continued. In no case shall "Merit Time" earned under the "Progressive Merit System" operate to reduce the minimum or maximum terms of imprisonment.

(NOTE)—For the rule establishing the "Progressive Merit System" and providing for "Industrial Credits," see Appendix.

3. Prisoners sentenced to the Illinois State Penitentiary, the State Reformatory for Women and the Illinois State Reformatory at Sheridan, for the crimes of murder, misprision of treason, rape and kidnapping shall in the discretion of the Parole and Pardon Board be eligible to consideration for parole under the following statutory provisions:

(A)   Persons sentenced for life shall be eligible after the service of the minimum of twenty calendar years provided by law.

(B)   Persons sentenced for a definite term of years

shall be eligible to consideration for parole when two conditions have been satisfied, namely:

1. Such person must have served the minimum sentence provided by law for the particular crime of which he or she was convicted, "Good Time" being allowed.

2. Such person must also have served at least one-third of the time fixed in said definite sentence.

4. For every month a docket shall be prepared at each Division of the Illinois State Penitentiary, the State Reformatory for Women and the Illinois State Reformatory at Sheridan, listing the names of all prisoners in the respective institutions who are eligible to consideration for parole at that time, as determined by these rules and the provisions of the Sentence and Parole Act.

Prisoners serving indeterminate sentences shall have their names placed on the respective dockets as follows:

Prisoners who are completing their minimum periods of imprisonment (as fixed by statute or the court), shall have their names placed on the dockets for the months in which they will have served such minimum periods of imprisonment, less "Good Time."

Prisoners whose cases have heretofore been continued to future dates for consideration shall have their names placed on the dockets the month preceding that in which the continuances expire, after allowing "Merit Time" earned under the "Progressive Merit System" and "Industrial Credits."

Prisoners serving sentences for definite terms of years or for life shall have their names automatically placed on the dockets when eligible to consideration for parole as provided in Rule 3.

The names of prisoners whose cases are continued for a year or less, shall appear on the docket for the month to which the continuance was ordered.

5. Only those prisoners, serving indeterminate sentences, who are in "Grade A," as determined by the wardens of the

respective institutions under the "Progressive Merit System," and shall have been in "Grade A" for three consecutive months, at least ten days prior to the date of the subcommittee sessions at the several institutions, shall be entitled to consideration for parole.

6. (A) Prisoners serving definite and intermediate sentences running concurrently shall not have their names placed on the dockets until they are eligible to consideration for parole under the definite sentence.

(B) A prisoner serving an indeterminate sentence and a sentence for a term of years under the Habitual Criminal Act, the sentences running concurrently, shall have his name placed on the docket when he becomes eligible for parole on the habitual sentence.

(C) A prisoner serving an indeterminate sentence and a life sentence under the Habitual Criminal Act, the terms to run concurrently, shall be eligible to parole when twenty years have been served on the habitual sentence.

7. Subcommittees of the members of the Parole and Pardon Board shall attend the several Divisions of the Illinois State Penitentiary, the State Reformatory for Women and the Illinois State Reformatory at Sheridan each month (except in July and August — the July docket shall be heard in June and the August docket in September), and hear only those prisoners whose names appear on the respective dockets for hearing.

8. On the first day of the respective sessions of the subcommittees and the day immediately following if so designated by the members of the Board, relatives, friends and counsel for the prisoners may attend and be heard in behalf of the prisoners whose names appear on the docket, as well as persons who desire to protest the release of the prisoners.

No subsequent oral arguments will be heard in cases appearing on that particular docket, but attorneys or other persons may submit in writing to the Parole and Pardon Board any brief or statement of fact in behalf of or in opposition to the parole of any inmate whose name appears on the docket.

9. Notice of subcommittee meetings shall be given by the Board to the Trial Judge and State's Attorney of the county in which the respective prisoners whose cases are to be considered were convicted, and to the complaining witnesses.

10. At the conclusion of the sessions of the subcommittees at the respective institutions, they shall make reports of the interviews with the prisoners, and of those who appear in their behalf, if any, and those who appear in protest, if any, and shall prepare summaries giving all available pertinent information concerning the prisoners.

11. The members of the Parole and Pardon Board shall attend in conference in Springfield monthly (except in July and August) and consider the cases of all prisoners whose cases appear on the dockets heard at the preceding subcommittee sessions.

In addition to the reports of the subcommittees, they shall consider pertinent information directly submitted to the Board, and the conduct records of the prisoners kept by the wardens or superintendent.

Oral argument in favor of or in opposition to the parole of a prisoner will not be heard by the members in conference.

12. If the members of the Parole and Pardon Board in conference determine that a prisoner serving an indeterminate term is entitled to parole, they shall enter an order for parole. If they determine that a prisoner is not a fit person to serve his sentence outside the penitentiary, a parole shall be denied, and such further order entered as in the judgment of the members is deemed warranted.

13. When a prisoner serving a sentence for a definite term of years or for life is denied parole by the Parole and Pardon Board, further consideration will not be given until the time designated in the Board order. In the event that a time is not specifically designated, further consideration will not be given until the lapse of one year from the date of the order denying parole.

14. In its consideration of the question of whether a pris-

oner should be paroled, the Parole and Pardon Board shall evaluate all the factors in each case, including the prisoner's conduct record, and grant or deny release on parole in accordance with its judgment.

15. When a prisoner serving an indeterminate sentence is denied parole and his case continued to a future date, the order for the continuance is no assurance that the prisoner will be paroled at the subsequent hearing.

The prisoner will again be interviewed, all factors in his case again considered, and such order entered as is deemed warranted.

If, at any time, prior to the date to which any case has been continued, the Board, upon a hearing, is satisfied that the prisoner should be paroled, its former order may be revoked and a parole authorized.

16. A rehearing will be granted only by the affirmative action of the Board in conference.

After a parole is denied a rehearing may be requested by the inmate. Such request must be made in writing and must set forth new facts and circumstances with reference to the crime for which subject is serving or extraordinary circumstances or facts which have arisen or both, which have not heretofore been considered by the Board and which upon examination would warrant such rehearing.

Oral argument in support of the application will not be permitted.

When a rehearing is granted, the case of such inmate shall be placed on a subsequent docket for hearing.

17. At the close of each conference of the Parole and Pardon Board, the Superintendent of the Parole and Pardon Board shall cause to be sent to the warden of each institution a copy of the order entered in the case of each prisoner in his institution whose case has been heard, to be transmitted to the respective inmates.

18. When an order for the release on parole of a prisoner is entered, it shall not be effective nor shall the prisoner be

released, until the Parole and Pardon Board has made arrangements or shall have satisfactory evidence that arrangements have been made for his or her honorable and useful employment while upon parole in some suitable occupation, and also for a proper and suitable home free from criminal influence and without expense to the State.

19. Before being released on parole each prisoner shall be required to enter into and execute a written agreement with the Parole and Pardon Board, on a form which has been approved by the Board, wherein shall be stipulated the terms and conditions upon which parole has been granted, and containing a promise by the prisoner that he will faithfully observe the rules governing prisoners on parole. After release on parole, each parolee shall monthly make a written report to the Parole Agent assigned to supervise him, giving the information required to be made in the Parole Agreement so long as the prisoner shall be on parole and until a final discharge is issued and delivered to him; provided, that, where parolees are inducted into any branch of the Armed Forces of the United States, supervision of such parolees may be temporarily suspended by the Superintendent of Supervision of Parolees.

20. When prisoners are released on parole they shall be under continuous supervision by the Superintendent of Supervision of Parolees until the expiration of the maximum periods of their sentences; subject, however, to earlier discharge under the following conditions:

(A) Parolees who have not previously been sentenced to a penitentiary or reformatory in Illinois, or elsewhere, shall be eligible to consideration for a final discharge at the end of three years.

(B) Parolees who have had one previous sentence to a penitentiary or reformatory in Illinois, or any other state, or a Federal Penitentiary, shall be eligible to consideration for a final discharge at the end of four years.

(C) Parolees who have had two or more previous sentences to a penitentiary or reformatory, whether in Illinois or elsewhere, shall be eligible to consideration for a final discharge at the end of five years.

Issuance of a discharge at the end of the above periods shall be within the discretion of the Parole and Pardon Board and shall be conditioned upon the favorable recommendation of the Division of Supervision of Parolees based on the parolee's faithful performance of the parole agreement; provided, that, if a parolee at the expiration of six months from the date of his release on parole is serving satisfactorily in the Armed Forces of the United States of America, or in the United States Merchant Marine, he may, in the discretion of the Parole and Pardon Board, be granted a final discharge.

21. When a paroled prisoner is returned to the Illinois State Penitentiary, the State Reformatory for Women or the Illinois State Reformatory at Sheridan upon a warrant issued for a violation of the terms of the Parole Agreement, his or her name shall be placed on the next parole docket prepared in the regular course at the institution where he or she is confined; provided his or her return to the institution is at least ten days prior to the next succeeding meeting of the subcommittee at the institution. Such prisoner shall be heard by the subcommittee of the Parole and Pardon Board which attends the institution, a report shall be made, and the case of the prisoner shall be considered by the Parole and Pardon Board. If the Parole and Pardon Board determines that the prisoner has violated any of the terms and conditions of parole, he or she may be declared a parole violator and the case continued to a future date for further review and consideration. If it is determined that the prisoner has not violated the terms and conditions of parole, the Board shall so declare, and the prisoner shall be ordered to resume parole subject to arrangements for suitable employment and a proper home.

22. When a paroled prisoner is returned to the Illinois State Penitentiary, State Reformatory for Women or the Illinois State Reformatory at Sheridan under a new sentence for a crime committed while on parole, his or her case under the

prior sentence shall be heard by the Parole and Pardon Board and an order entered declaring the prisoner a parole violator on the prior sentence, and the case continued until he or she is eligible to consideration for parole under the new sentence.

23. When a parolee is released on parole he shall be given credit for time served under his sentence only for the period of time on parole during which he has faithfully complied with all the terms and conditions of his parole.

In the event of violation, the determination of credit for time served in faithful compliance shall be in accordance with the statutory provision that the Parole and Pardon Board shall determine the date of violation at a hearing conducted upon the return of the prisoner to the institution.

Upon failure of a paroled prisoner to make reports as required by the Parole Agreement, or in the event he otherwise violates any of the terms or conditions of his parole, he shall be considered in default. If at any time he is returned to the penitentiary and declared a parole violator he shall be given credit only for the time served in prison and on parole before violation.

When a prisoner is returned to the penitentiary upon a warden's warrant for violation of parole he shall be given credit for the time served up to the date of violation as declared by the Parole and Pardon Board and also the time during which he is being held in custody on the warden's warrant until he is again released on parole.

RULES GOVERNING PRISONERS ON PAROLE INCORPO-RATED IN THE PAROLE AGREEMENT EXECUTED BY A PRISONER PRIOR TO RELEASE

1. The prisoner shall proceed at once to his place of employment and report to his employer whose name is given above. If paroled to Cook County, he shall first report to the Chicago Office of the Division of Supervision of Parolees, 160 North LaSalle Street, 16th Floor, for the purpose of registering.

2. Upon reporting to his employer, the prisoner shall immediately fill out and sign an arrival report and mail the same

to the Parole Officer at the Division of the Illinois State Penitentiary of which he was an inmate on the date of his parole. The arrival report must be endorsed by the employer, or a representative of the Division of Supervision of Parolees.

3. The prisoner must not change employment, nor leave employment, nor change his home address, unless granted permission by the State Superintendent of Supervision or his duly authorized agent. In the event of sickness or loss of position, the prisoner shall immediately report the fact to his Parole Agent. The prisoner is confined solely to the jurisdiction of the county to which paroled and must not at any time go beyond its boundry lines unless permission is granted by his Parole Agent. The prisoner shall not leave the State of Illinois without a Parole and Pardon Board order and notice of the same shall be given the prisoner by the Superintendent of Supervision or his duly authorized agent.

In the event the prisoner is granted an out-of-state parole, he shall not leave the State to which he is paroled without an order of the Parole and Pardon Board. Notice of the transfer shall be given by the Parole Officer at the Division of the Illinois State Penitentiary from which the prisoner was paroled.

4. The prisoner must make a written report on the first day of every month and mail or otherwise deliver the same to the Parole Agent who supervises him, until a Final Discharge is granted, unless sooner discharged by expiration of sentence. This report must state the number of days worked and the amount of money he has earned. If he has been idle during any portion of the month, he must state the reason. Out-of-state parolees shall mail their reports to the Parole Officer at the Division of the Illinois State Penitentiary from which the prisoner was paroled.

5. The prisoner will carry out the instructions of his Parole Agent, report as directed, and permit the Parole Agent to visit him at his residence and place of employment. In the event of loss of employment, the prisoner shall make every effort to secure gainful employment and shall coöperate with his Parole

Agent in his Agent's efforts to obtain employment for him.

6. Reports of the prisoner, either verbal or written, made to or submitted to his Parole Agent, which are subsequently found to be false, will be rejected by the Division of Supervision of Parolees and will not be used in crediting paroled time served and, in addition, may be considered a violation of parole.

7. The prisoner must abstain from the use of intoxicating liquors or narcotics in any form. He shall not associate with other prisoners on parole nor any person having a criminal record. He shall not visit improper places of amusement nor disreputable establishments. He must not carry weapons of any description. The prisoner shall not write to nor visit any inmate of any penal or correctional institution. The prisoner shall not own, buy, drive nor ride in an automobile for pleasure or business unless granted permission by his Parole Agent. The prisoner shall not marry without obtaining permission from the State Superintendent of Supervision or his duly authorized agent.

8. The prisoner must respect and obey the laws and conduct himself in all respects as a good citizen. He must not be away from home after 10:30 P.M., unless granted permission by his Parole Agent.

9. While on parole and until the right of franchise has been restored after final discharge, or discharge by expiration of sentence, the prisoner shall not register as a voter and shall not vote in any primary, special or general election inasmuch as his right of franchise was revoked when he was sentenced to the penitentiary.

10. Said prisoner so released under the terms of this parole agreement, shall at all times, until the receipt of his Final Discharge or until he is discharged by expiration of sentence, be considered in the legal custody of the Department of Public Safety, under conviction for the crime or offense for which said prisoner was sentenced, subject to be taken at any time within the enclosure of the Illinois State Penitentiary.

11. The prisoner if paroled or transferred outside the State of Illinois shall obey the laws and abide by the parole

regulations of such receiving state, as well as the state of Illinois, and shall submit to supervision by the parole or probation supervisory authorities of such receiving state.

The Parole and Pardon Board, the Division of Supervision of Parolees of the Department of Public Safety, and the Warden of the Division of the Illinois State Penitentiary of which the prisoner was an inmate, have a lively interest in the subject of this parole. They will counsel and advise him as he may need, and will assist him in any reasonable way to re-establish himself in society.

They will vigorously follow and rearrest him in the event that he willfully violates the conditions of his parole, sparing neither time nor expense in so doing, whether paroled within or without the State, and whether the violation occurs within or beyond the boundaries of the State of Illinois.

Full power to enforce the foregoing rules and regulations and to retake and reimprison any inmate upon parole is conferred upon the Superintendent of Supervision and/or his representatives. It shall be the duty of the Superintendent of Supervision and the Warden of any Division of the Illinois State Penitentiary to enforce these rules in harmony with the provisions of the statutes.

CIVIL ADMINISTRATIVE CODE

(Section 127. Illinois Revised Statutes, 1943)

THE DEPARTMENT OF PUBLIC SAFETY

Section 55a. Powers and Duties of Department of Public Safety.

The Department of Public Safety shall have power:

Section 3. To exercise the rights, powers and duties which have been vested by law in the Department of Public Welfare as the successor of the Board of Pardons.

PARDON ACT
(As Amended and in Force July 1, 1943)

Applications

An Act to regulate the manner of applying for pardons, reprieves and commutations. Approved May 31, 1879. (Chapter 104½, Illinois Revised Statutes, 1943.)

Application for Pardon — How Made. Section 1. Be it enacted by the People of the State of Illinois, represented in the General Assembly: That hereafter all applications for reprieves, commutations and pardons shall be made by petition in writing to the Governor, signed by the party under conviction, or other persons in his behalf, which petition shall contain a brief history of the case and the reasons why such pardon should be granted; and shall also be accompanied by a statement in writing made by the judge and prosecuting attorney of the court in which the conviction was had; stating the opinion of said judge and prosecuting attorney in regard to the same, or satisfactory reasons shall be given to the Governor, why such statements of the judge and prosecuting attorney, or either of them, do not accompany such petition; and it shall be the duty of such judge and prosecuting attorney to give such opinion, whenever such petition shall be presented to them.

Notice. Section 2. Notice of the proposed application shall be given by publication for three weeks prior thereto, in a newspaper published in the county where the conviction was had, a duly certified copy of which notice shall accompany said petition; Provided, the Governor may dispense with publication of notice, when in his judgement justice or humanity requires it.

Board of Pardons

An Act in relation to pardons and the commutation of sentences. Approved June 5, 1897. Title as amended by Act approved June 29, 1943.

Rules and Regulations — Record of Proceedings. Section 4. The Department of Public Safety shall make all such rules and regulations for the orderly conduct of its business, as may be deemed necessary. The Department shall cause proper records to be kept in its office of its acts and proceedings, and shall hear all applications for pardons and for the commutations of sentences in order in which they are filed; but the Department may take up any application out of its regular order, where the exigencies of the case require it.

Petitions for Pardons — Hearing — Notice. Section 5. All petitions and requests for pardons and commutations shall be addressed to the Governor, and, as to form, accompanying statements, publications of notices, etc., shall be governed by the Act of May 31, 1879, entitled, "An Act to regulate the manner of applying for pardons, reprieves and commutations," except that the three weeks' notice provided in that Act to be given shall have reference to the hearing before the Department of Public Safety, and not the Governor; and every such petition or request shall, before its actual presentation to the Governor, be filed and kept in the office of the Department of Public Safety for the preliminary action of the Department.

Meetings of Department of Public Safety or Officer Designated. Section 6. The regular meeting of the Department of Public Safety, or of the office or agency of the Department designated by the Director thereof, shall be held on the second Tuesday of the months of January, April, July and October in each year, and special meetings may be called at any time by the Governor, or the Director of the Department.

Hearing of Applications — Report of Governor. Section 7. The Department of Public Safety shall, upon due public notice, give a full hearing to each application for pardon or commutation filed with it, allowing representation by counsel, if desired, after which it shall, without publicity, make report upon each case to the Governor, accompanying such report with the original petition and all accompanying papers and documents, and in such report shall be embodied the conclusions and recommendations of the Department, with its reasons therefor, briefly stated. The report to the Governor shall be advisory to him in his constitutional action upon the case.

Record to be Kept — Department of Public Safety Not to Act as Court of Review. Section 8. A full record of the report and recommendation made in each case shall be kept in the office of the Department of Public Safety. The Department shall in no case act as a court of review to pass upon the correctness, regularity or legality of the proceedings in the trial court which resulted in conviction, but shall confine itself to a hearing and consideration of those matters only which properly bear upon the propriety of extending clemency of the Governor.

Governor May Hear Application for Reprieve in Case of Death Sentences. Section 9. This Act shall not deprive the Governor of the right to hear any application made directly to him for a reprieve of a death sentence where the exigencies of the case require such reprieve in order to give the Department of Public Safety the time and opportunity to properly investigate the case.

DEPARTMENT OF PUBLIC SAFETY RULES GOVERNING APPLICATIONS FOR PARDON AND COMMUTATION OF SENTENCE

The Department of Public Safety of the State of Illinois, by Joseph D. Bibb, Director, having heretofore designated the Parole and Pardon Board as the agency to hear petitions for pardons, reprieves and commutations of sentence and make reports to the Governor, does hereby adopt and promulgate the following rules and regulations governing petitions for pardon and commutations of sentence.

1. All applications for pardons, reprieves and commutations of sentence shall be made by petition in writing, addressed to the Governor, and conform to the following requirements:

(A) The petition shall be signed by the applicant or other person in his behalf.

(B) If signed by another person, the full address of such person shall be given, and his interest in the applicant stated.

(C) Each petition shall contain a brief history of

the case, a brief biography of the petitioner, setting forth his full and correct name, any aliases he has been convicted under, his age, place of birth, the different places where he has resided, the years of residence in each place, the occupations pursued in each locality, and the reasons why a pardon or commutation of sentence should be granted.

2. Each petition must be accompanied by four copies and shall be filed in the office of the Parole and Pardon Board at Springfield at least twenty days prior to the succeeding regular meeting of the Pardon Board.

3. Pursuant to Statute, each original petition shall be accompanied by a statement in writing made by the Judge and Prosecuting Attorney of the court in which the conviction was had, stating the opinion of the Judge and Prosecuting Attorney in regard to the same, or satisfactory reasons shall be given why such statement of either of them does not accompany the petition. Copies of the petition shall be furnished to the said Trial Judge, Prosecuting Attorney and present State's Attorney in each case if they are available; and proof thereof may be made by a receipt of such official, or affidavit that it was delivered, or a registered receipt of the United States Post Office if sent by registered mail. Such proof of service shall be attached to the original petition.

4. Notice of the hearings on all petitions shall be given by publication, as required by Statute, for three successive weeks prior thereto in a newspaper published in the county where the petitioner was convicted; and a certificate of such publication must accompany the original petition, unless the Governor dispenses with such publication.

5. The published notice shall contain the name of the person convicted, the fact that he is applying for a pardon or commutation of sentence, the date of sentence, the crime of which he was convicted, the nature of the sentence, the court in which he was sentenced, and the date when the petition will be heard by the Pardon Board.

6. A copy of the published notice of the application for

pardon or commutation of sentence shall be given to the present State's Attorney of the county in which the applicant was convicted; and if he is not the State's Attorney who prosecuted the applicant, a copy of the petition shall be served on the Prosecuting State's Attorney. Proof of the service of notice and copy of the petition, as provided for in Rule 3, shall be attached to the original petition.

7. A copy of the published notice of application for pardon or commutation of sentence shall be served on the complaining witness at least twenty days before the date of hearing, and proof of such service (as provided for in Rule 3) shall be attached to the original petition.

If the complaining witness cannot be found upon diligent inquiry, an affidavit setting forth the efforts made to locate the witness shall be attached to the original petition.

8. At the quarterly meetings of the Pardon Board counsel for applicants, as well as others who appear in their behalf and those who appear in opposition, will be heard.

9. At each quarterly meeting as aforesaid, a docket shall be prepared listing all petitions which comply with the Statutes and these Rules, and shall have been filed in apt time. Counsel and those who wish to be heard in favor of or in opposition to the respective petitions on the call of the docket, must register in Room 110 Centennial Building in Springfield. The cases will be called in the order of registration.

10. The Pardon Board shall in no case act as a court of review to pass upon the correctness, regularity or legality of the proceedings in the trial court which resulted in conviction, but shall confine itself to a hearing and consideration of those matters only which properly bear upon the propriety of extending clemency by the Governor.

RULES AND STATUTES GOVERNING RESTORATION OF CITIZENSHIP RIGHTS TO DISCHARGED PROBATIONERS AND DISCHARGED PRISONERS

Loss of Citizenship

Infamous Crimes—Statute Governing Loss of Certain Rights Upon Conviction Thereof (Chapter 38—Illinois Revised Statutes, 1947)

Paragraph 587 — Infamous Crimes

Every person convicted of the crime of murder, rape, kidnapping, willful and corrupt perjury or subornation of perjury, arson, burglary, robbery, sodomy, or other crime against nature, incest, forgery, counterfeiting, bigamy, or larceny, if the punishment for said larceny is by imprisonment in the penitentiary, shall be deemed infamous, and shall forever thereafter be rendered incapable of holding any office of honor, trust or profit, of voting at any election, or serving as a juror, unless he or she is again restored to such rights by the terms of a pardon for the offense or otherwise according to the law.

By the terms of this statute both probationers and prisoners convicted of the crimes set out above are no longer entitled to exercise the rights of a citizen of the State of Illinois relative to the holding of public office, participation in elections, or service as a juror. By law a certificate of citizenship can be conferred by the Governor of the State restoring the right to vote and to serve on juries. The right to hold public office cannot be restored by reason of Article 4, Section 4, of the Constitution.

It is necessary that discharged probationers as well as discharged prisoners secure a formal restoration of their rights as citizens in order to exercise those rights. The statutes and rules relative to restoration of citizenship are set out here in order that everyone entitled to make application for such restoration will be acquainted with the procedure for doing so.

DISCHARGED PROBATIONERS

(Chapter 38 — Illinois Revised Statutes, 1947)

Paragraph 790 — Termination of Probation — Record —
Restoration of Citizenship —
Application to Governor

Upon the termination of the probation period, the probation officer shall report to the court the conduct of the probationer during the period of his probation, and the court may thereupon discharge the probationer from further supervision, or extend the probation period not to exceed six months in cases of a violation of a municipal ordinance, and not to exceed two years in other offenses. When a probationer is discharged upon the expiration of the probation period, or upon its earlier termination by order of the court, entry of the discharge shall be made in the records of the court, and the probationer shall be entitled to a certified copy thereof. At any time after the discharge of a probationer, the Governor, upon the application of the probationer, may grant to him a certificate of restoration to all his rights of citizenship, excepting such rights, as by reason of conviction for infamous crime, or otherwise, are thereafter denied him by the Constitution of this State. The court in which the order of discharge from probation was entered, shall upon request of the Governor, furnish him a statement of the deportment of such person during the probation period, and may make such recommendation to the Governor as it deems proper respecting the restoration of citizenship rights of such person.

RULES AND REGULATIONS
for
DISCHARGED PROBATIONERS
in Applying for
RESTORATION OF CITIZENSHIP RIGHTS

1. A sworn petition in duplicate, addressed to the Governor, must be submitted, and must contain the following information:

   A. A brief history and background of the applicant.

   B. A brief statement of the facts and circumstances of the offense whereof he was convicted or plead guilty.

C. The term of court, the date probation was granted, and the name of the judge granting probation.

D. The date of discharge from probation and the name of the judge entering the discharge order.

E. A recitation relative to petitioner's conduct during the probation period, and a recitation, if true, that at no time had there been a violation of any of the conditions imposed by the court in granting probation.

F. A prayer for the restoration of citizenship rights lost by reason of the conviction and probation.

2. The petition should also contain a statement as to whether the applicant is a native born citizen or whether he has been naturalized, and if so, the date of the naturalization and the court in which the naturalization order was entered.

3. Likewise, attached to and made a part of the petition should be two certified copies of the order of discharge, which may be secured from the clerk of the court.

4. The statement of the discharging judge contemplated by the statute may accompany the petition, but if it does not, the judge will be requested by the Governor to submit such a statement and recommendation.

5. Each petition for restoration of citizenship rights to discharged probationers shall be addressed to the Governor, but should be filed in the office of the Parole and Pardon Board, Armory Building, Springfield, Illinois.

DISCHARGED PRISONERS
(Chapter 108 — Illinois Revised Statutes, 1947)
Paragraph 49 — Certificate of Restoration

The Governor shall have the right to grant any person that has been, now is, or may be hereafter confined in the penitentiary, reformatory or correctional institution, whom he shall deem a proper person to enjoy that privilege, a certificate of restoration to all his rights of citizenship, excepting such privileges as, by reason of conviction for infamous crime, or otherwise, are thereafter denied such person by the constitution of this State, although such person may have been guilty of an infraction of the rules and regulations of the prison, reformatory or correctional institution. The warden or managing officer upon request of the Governor, shall, in cases of application for such restoration, furnish him a statement of the department of such person during his imprisonment, and may at all times make such recommendation to the Governor as he shall deem proper respecting the restoration to citizenship of any such person.

PROCEDURE AND INFORMATION
for
DISCHARGED PRISONERS
in Applying for
RESTORATION OF CITIZENSHIP RIGHTS

1. Request for restoration of citizenship rights should be made in writing to the warden of the institution from which the prisoner has been discharged or paroled.
2. The petition may be informal and should set forth in general why the applicant believes himself worthy of restoration of his citizenship rights.
3. The petition will be forwarded by the warden or managing officer to the Governor, with a recommendation attached.
4. The Governor will, if he deems it advisable, have the record of the applicant checked by the Parole and Pardon Board for his information in acting upon the application.

DEPARTMENT OF PUBLIC SAFETY RULE PROVIDING FOR DIMINUTION OF SENTENCES OF CONVICTS IN THE ILLINOIS STATE PENITENTIARY

Whereas, Section 1 of "An Act in relation to certain rights of persons convicted of crime," approved March 19, 1872 (as subsequently amended), provides that, "The Department of Public Safety is authorized and directed to prescribe reasonable rules and regulations for the diminution of sentences on account of good conduct, of persons heretofore and hereafter convicted of crime, who are confined in the State penal and reformatory institutions;"

The Department of Public Safety, by Joseph D. Bibb, Director, pursuant to the authority of the above Section, hereby orders and prescribes that the rules and regulations for the diminuation of sentences on account of good conduct shall be set forth herein.

Diminution of Sentences

Inmates of the Illinois State Penitentiary serving indeterminate sentences, where the maximum is less than life, and inmates serving sentences for definite terms of years (but not including sentences for life), who have no infractions of the rules and regulations of the penitentiary or laws of the State, and who perform in a faithful manner the duties assigned to them, shall be entitled to the diminution of time from their respective sentences as appears in the following tables, for the respective years of their sentences, and pro rata for any part of a year where the sentence is for more or less than one year.

Inmates Received Prior to February 1, 1952

In the case of inmates received in the Illinois State Penitentiary system to begin service on their sentences prior to February 1, 1952, "good time" shall be computed in accordance with the Statutes of 1872, as provided by the former order of the Department of Public Safety, and in accordance with the following table:

Number of Years of Sentence	Good Time Granted	Total Good Time Made	Time to be Served if Full Time is Made
1st year	1 month	1 month	11 months
2nd "	2 "	3 "	1 year & 9 months
3rd "	3 "	6 "	2 " 6 "
4th "	4 "	10 "	3 " 2 "
5th "	5 "	1 year & 3 months	3 " 9 "
6th "	6 "	1 " 9 "	4 " 3 "
7th "	6 "	2 " 3 "	4 " 9 "
8th "	6 "	2 " 9 "	5 " 3 "
9th "	6 "	3 " 3 "	5 " 9 "
10th "	6 "	3 " 9 "	6 " 3 "
11th "	6 "	4 " 3 "	6 " 9 "
12th "	6 "	4 " 9 "	7 " 3 "
13th "	6 "	5 " 3 "	7 " 9 "
14th "	6 "	5 " 9 "	8 " 3 "
15th "	6 "	6 " 3 "	8 " 9 "
16th "	6 "	6 " 9 "	9 " 3 "
17th "	6 "	7 " 3 "	9 " 9 "

(Continued on following page)

Number of Years of Sentence	Good Time Granted	Total Good Time Made	Time to be Served if Full Time is Made
18th "	6 "	7 " 9 "	10 " 3 "
19th "	6 "	8 " 3 "	10 " 9 "
20th "	6 "	8 " 9 "	11 " 3 "
21st "	6 "	9 " 3 "	11 " 9 "
22nd "	6 "	9 " 9 "	12 " 3 "
23rd "	6 "	10 " 3 "	12 " 9 "
24th "	6 "	10 " 9 "	13 " 3 "
25th "	6 "	11 " 3 "	13 " 9 "

For each additional year 6 months is earned.

Inmates Received After February 1, 1952

In the case of inmates received in the Illinois State Penitentiary system to begin service on their sentences on or after February 1, 1952, "good time" with reference to the minimum time of a sentence to be served before an inmate is eligible for parole consideration shall be computed in accordance with the previous rule and table, but with reference to the maximum of a sentence shall be computed so that in no case shall "total good time made" exceed one-third of the total number of years of sentence, in accordance with the following table:

Number of Years of Sentence	Good time Granted	Total Good Time Made	Time to be Served if Full Time is Made
1st year	1 month	1 month	11 months
2nd "	2 "	3 "	1 year & 9 months
3rd "	3 "	6 "	2 " 6 "
4th "	4 "	10 "	3 " 2 "
5th "	5 "	1 year & 3 months	3 " 9 "
6th "	6 "	1 " 9 "	4 " 3 "
7th "	6 "	2 " 3 "	4 " 9 "
8th "	6 "	2 " 8 "	5 " 4 "
9th "	3 "	3 " 0 "	6 " 0 "
10th "	4 "	3 " 4 "	6 " 8 "
11th "	4 "	3 " 8 "	7 " 4 "
12th "	4 "	4 " 0 "	9 " 0 "
13th "	4 "	4 " 4 "	8 " 8 "
14th "	4 "	4 " 8 "	9 " 4 "
15th "	4 "	5 " 0 "	10 " 0 "
16th "	4 "	5 " 4 "	10 " 8 "
17th "	4 "	5 " 8 "	11 " 4 "
18th "	4 "	6 " 0 "	12 " 0 "
19th "	4 "	6 " 4 "	12 " 8 "
20th "	4 "	6 " 8 "	13 " 4 "
21st "	4 "	7 " 4 " 4	14 " 8 "
22nd "	4 "	7 " 4 "	14 " 8 "
23rd "	4 "	7 " 8 "	15 " 4 "
24th "	4 "	8 " 0 "	16 " 0 "
25th "	4 "	8 " 4 "	16 " 8 "

For each additional year 4 months is earned.

Forfeiture of Good Time

In case any convict who may become entitled to any diminution of this sentence by the provisions aforesaid shall be guilty of violating the prison rules or misconduct, or a violation of any law of the State, he may for the first offense forfeit two days; for the second offense, four days; for the third offense, eight days; for the fourth offense, sixteen days; and in addition thereto, whatever number of days, more than one, that he is in punishment, may be forfeited. For more than four offenses, the Director of the Department of Public Safety, upon the recommendation of the Warden of the Division of the Penitentiary in which the convict is imprisoned, shall have the power, at his discretion, to deprive such convict of any portion or all of the good time that the convict may have earned, or may earn in the future.

Progressive Merit System

A "Progressive Merit System" for the purpose of encouraging and rewarding good conduct and industry in the Divisions of the Illinois State Penitentiary has been adopted by the Department of Public Safety.

Under this system prisoners serving indeterminate sentences who are denied parole and their cases continued to future dates for further consideration may by good conduct and industry earn "Merit Time" and thus advance the dates of review of their cases.

Promotions

Under this system grades five in number and designated as A, B, C, D, and E were established. The rules for promotion from one grade to another are governed by the behavior and industrial efficiency of the prisoner.

On admission the inmate is placed in C, the neutral grade, where "Merit Time" is neither earned nor lost. If his behavior is satisfactory, the inmate is promoted to B in three months' time, and after three months in B, if his behavior remains satisfactory, he is promoted to A.

The inmate must be in A grade at least three months and

have served his minimum sentence, less "Good Time," before he will be eligible to a parole hearing by the Parole and Pardon Board.

In A grade the inmate earns ten days' "Merit Time" per month, and in B grade five days.

A table of the "Merit Time" which may be earned by a prisoner from the period of a continuance under an indeterminate sentence in acceleration of the time when he may again be considered for parole is as follows:

Continuance in Years from Date of Admission	"Merit Time" Award in			Case Reviewed in		
	Years	Months	Days	Years	Months	Days
2	0	6	15	1	5	15
3	0	10	15	2	1	15
4	1	2	15	2	9	15
5	1	6	15	3	5	15
6	1	10	15	4	1	15
7	2	2	15	4	9	15
8	2	6	15	5	5	15
9	2	10	15	6	1	15
10	3	2	15	6	9	15
11	3	6	15	7	5	15
12	3	10	15	8	1	15
13	4	2	15	8	9	15
14	4	6	15	9	5	15
15	4	10	15	10	1	15
16	5	2	15	10	9	15
17	5	6	15	11	5	15
18	5	10	15	12	1	15
19	6	2	15	12	9	15
20	6	6	15	13	5	15

Demotions

For violation of prison rules an inmate may, at the discretion of the Merit Staff, be demoted in grade. For every grade he is demoted, he must remain three months in the grade to which he is demoted.

Examples

Demotion from grade A to grade E, four grades, remains in grade E for twelve months, and is then promoted to grade D, where he remains for three months, and is then promoted to grade C.

Demotion from grade A to grade D, three grades, remains

in grade D for nine months before promotion to grade C.

Demotion from grade B to grade E, three grades, remains in grade E for nine months before being promoted to grade D, where he remains for three months, before being promoted to grade C.

If an inmate is demoted to a grade lower than C, he loses "Merit Time" at the rate of ten days per month in E and five days per month in D. Upon being promoted to C again, he must remain in this grade, before promotion to B, the required three months, plus the time lost in D or E. If this amounts to less than one month, it is counted as an even month. If more than one month, any fraction of a month is ignored. Once inmate is promoted to B after demotion, only the usual three months must elapse before promotion to A.

Example

Demotion to Grade E from grade A.

Dropped four grades, 12 months in grade E, 3 months in grade D.

Loss of 120 days in E.

Loss of 15 days in D.

Total loss of 135 days or 4½ months.

Lost time to be made up: 4½ months in grade C, plus customary 3 months in grade C, or total of 7½ months in grade C.

Promotion to grade B, 3 months in grade B.

Total of 25½ months before an inmate who is demoted from grade A to grade E, can again reach grade A.

Minor violations, unless a number, usually three or more, occurring within a period of a year or less, generally do not call for demotion, solitary punishment for varying lengths of time usually being considered sufficient.

If, however, a series of minor violations occur within a period of a year or less, demotion of one grade may be decreed, or retardation in present grade for thirty, sixty, or ninety days, if inmate is in grade below A.

For single violations of a more serious nature demotion or

retardation may be called for even if inmate has no previous violations.

For flagrant, obviously serious violations inmate may be demoted a number of grades, even as low as D or E.

When an inmate is demoted to either grade D or E, he automatically forfeits all "Merit Time" earned, prior to his demotion.

Advancement to higher grades or demotion to lower grades shall be made by the Merit Staff of the respective divisions of the penitentiary in the exercise of a sound and impartial discretion.

The respective wardens shall cause to be kept accurate records of the conduct of all prisoners, showing advancements and demotions, and such records shall be made available to the Parole and Pardon Board.

Industrial Credits

In addition to "Merit Time" that prisoners may earn under the Progressive Merit System, the wardens of the Divisons of the Illinois State Penitentiary are authorized to award prisoners, who have shown exemplary conduct, special diligence or trustworthiness, credits of not exceeding sixty days' time in diminution of time to be served after continuance of their cases, and thereby accelerate the time for consideration for parole; provided that such credit shall be subject to the approval of the Parole and Pardon Board; and provided further, that where prisoners have shown exceptional bravery or fidelity, the Board may, by an order, approve recommendations of the wardens for ninety days' time for "Industrial Credits."

In no case shall "Merit Time" or "Industrial Credits" operate to reduce the maximum of a prisoner's sentence.

Publisher's Note:

As *Inside The World's Toughest Prison* was going to press, the Illinois General Assembly, in its six month session which ended July 1, 1961, re-codified and modernized the State's criminal laws for the first time since 1870.

We are able only to summarize some far-reaching changes which affect penitentiary inmates; the judiciary and juries, and law enforcement agencies. They follow:

1. All persons confined in a penitentiary shall be eligible for parole at the end of 20 years, regardless of length of sentence.

2. The court shall fix the punishment in all cases of convictions. The only power the jury retains is in capital cases. It may then return a verdict of death. However the court is not obligated to follow such verdict and may sentence to prison instead.

If the jury does not return a verdict of death the court can only sentence to imprisonment.

3. If the jury does return a verdict of death the defendant still has two chances to avoid it:

(a) That the judge may not agree with the jury's verdict.

(b) Even if he does, the defendant has the opportunity to persuade him differently in a pre-sentence hearing.

4. Types of punishment have been changed. The life sentence as such has been eliminated. All sentences in excess of one year shall be for an indeterminate term and to the penitentiary or equivalent institution.

5. The age of infancy was raised from 10 to 13, which means that all juvenile offenders under 13 must be handled by the Family Court.

6. A new law designed to cover fleeing misdemeanants who are endangering the lives of others by such flight permits a peace officer to use force likely to cause death or great bodily harm when he reasonably believes that such force is necessary to prevent an arrest from being defeated by resistance or escape and the person to be arrested " . . . indicates that he will endanger human life or inflict great bodily harm unless arrested without delay."

Appendix B

PENITENTIARY
AND
UNDERWORLD
GLOSSARY

A-1 — Prime; the best; altogether trustworthy.

ACE — Same as A-1.

ACE — One dollar.

ACES — Anyone or anything considered to be the best or most desirable.

AGITATOR — A prison inmate who is continually endeavoring to stir up other inmates to dissatisfaction or cause revolt.

AIR — Loose or misleading talk; idle chatter.

ALLIGATOR BAIT — Poor food, or meal; also slang expression for a colored person (Negro).

ALLEY APPLE — Stone or brick used in street fighting.

ALTAR — A toilet, especially the porcelain bowl.

ANCHOR — To settle down to a steady job.

ANGEL — A male pervert.

ANGEL — Anyone who furnishes money for some extensive crime that requires a great deal of planning and preparation.

ANGLE — To make money by illegitimate means; to fish for a sucker.

ANNIE OAKLEY — A free ticket or pass.

ANOINT — To flog or whip.

AN "X" — An ex-convict.

ANUS BANDIT — A convicted sodomist.

ARTIST — Any skillful crook or confidence man or woman who inspires respect in his or her work by less gifted criminals.

BADGER GAME — A blackmailing scheme, in which the victim is taken to a room or apartment by the woman accomplice and there discovered by the "husband."

BAG YOUR HEAD — Be quiet.

BALDY — A term for an old man, regardless of the hair he may or may not have.

BALE OF HAY — A blonde woman.
BALE OF STRAW — A blonde woman.
BALLOON JUICE — Idle talk.
BALLYHOO — Loud talk; noisy conversation.
BAND HOUSE — Jail or prison (House of Correction, Chicago).
BANG-UP — Excellent or successful; desirable.
BANJO — A shovel.
BANK — Solitary.
BARBERING — Conversation.
BARK — The skin.
BARREL — To drink, especially to drink to excess.
BARRELED — To be drunk.
BARREL HOUSE — Cheap lodging house, speakeasy, or brothel.
BARREL HOUSE DRUNK — Hopelessly intoxicated.
BARREL STIFF — An old, worn-out bum, living in barrel houses.
BAT — A criminal trial. "Go to Bat."
BAT — A prostitute.
BAT — A drinking bout.
BATS — Insane or erratic.
BAT HOUSE — Insane asylum.
BATTER — To solicit or beg alms.
BATTER THE DRAG — To beg on the street.
BATTER THE PRIVATES — To beg from door to door in a residential
    district.
BATTY — Insane; erratic.
BEAGLES — Sausages.
BEAK — The nose.
BEAN — The head.
BEAN TOWN — Boston, Massachusetts.
BEANERY — The inmate dining room.
BEARD JAMMER — One who conducts a disorderly house; a whoremaster.
BEAT — A neighborhood or district controlled by a politician, upon which
    a criminal or criminal gang is supposed to have a monopoly.
BEAT — To evade or escape the consequences.
BEAT THE RAP — The charge was dismissed, or sentence evaded.
BEE — To beg or borrow.
BEEF — A complaint.
BEEF — To complain or inform; to turn State's evidence.
BEEFER — An informant or complainant.
BEEZER — The nose.
BELCH — A protest or complaint.
BELCHER — A complainant or faultfinder.
BELLYACHE — To complain or protest, especially when this is carried on
    over a long period.
BELLYFULL — Enough or more than enough of anything.
BELLY ROBBER — A cook, steward, or other official entrusted with feed-
    ing prisoners.
BENNY — An overcoat.

BENT — Crooked; criminal; outside the law.

BERRIES — "The Berries," anything worthwhile or valuable.

BERRY — One dollar.

BIG HOUSE — A prison or penitentiary.

BIG SHOT — A leading character; one with authority over a number of underlings or henchmen; a gang leader.

BIG SHOT — A penitentiary expression by inmates with reference to inmates assigned to offices, etc. Some inmates in these positions at times assume an attitude of superiority.

BINDLE — Bedding; necessary shaving utensils, etc.

BINDLE STIFF — A tramp or worker carrying his bedding.

BIRD — Anyone not moving in the same circle as the speaker or his gang; an outsider; a newcomer.

BISCUIT — A revolver or pistol.

BISCUIT SHOOTER — A waitress or short order cook.

BIT — A penitentiary sentence.

BITCH — A loose woman.

BLACK BOTTLE — Knock-out drops (chloral hydrate) or poison.

BLACKLIST — To place on the blacklist; to defame or decry.

BLACK MARIA — Police patrol.

BLAST — To shoot; to assassinate.

BLIND — Front end of a baggage or mail car on a passenger train.

BLIND — A legitimate business enterprise used as a cover under which to operate a criminal enterprise.

BLIND — Hopelessly intoxicated.

BLINKY — One with poor eyesight, or completely blind.

BLOCK — The head.

BLOCK — A watch.

BLOKE — A casual name for any individual.

BLOOMER — An error; a failure.

BLOT OUT — To kill.

BLOTTO — Drunk.

BO — Hobo.

BOB — A shoplifter.

BOILED — Intoxicated. usually when incapable of thought or action.

BOILER — An automobile; a camp cook.

BONE HEAD — A dolt or simpleton.

BOOB — An uninitiated person or a thieves' victim.

BOOBY HATCH — A police station.

BOODLE — Petty graft exacted from prisoners by a turnkey or trusty.

BOOGLE — A Negro.

BOOK — A life sentence.

BOOK — Police blotter or other police records.

BOOKED — A charge entered on the police records or "Blotter" when arrested.

BOOKIE — A race-horse bookmaker; one who accepts bets on horses.

BOOKIE JOINT — A place where horse race wagers are taken.

BOOSTER — A shoplifter.

BOOZE FIGHTER — A heavy drinker.
BOUNCER — An employee who ousts disorderly or quarrelsome persons.
BOX — A safe or money box.
BRACE — To ask for money. To address or speak to usually when in search for alms.
BRACELETS — Handcuffs.
BRAINS — Anyone directing a gang.
BRAKIE — A railroad brakeman.
BRASS — Fake jewelry.
BRASS — Nerve.
BRAT — A passive sex pervert.
BREAK — A piece of good fortune or luck.
BREAK — To make an attempt; to escape.
BREEZE — Idle chatter.
BREAK — To ask for or receive leniency for a violation.
BREEZE — To depart.
BRIGHT EYES — A lookout man or woman.
BROAD — A woman or girl.
BRODIE — A fall; leap; failure or unsuccessful attempt.
BROKER — A narcotic peddler.
BROWN — The rectum.
BUCK — A dollar.
BUCK — To oppose; to contend with.
BUCK — A Catholic priest.
BUDDY — A pal or good friend.
BUFFALO — To intimidate or bluff.
BUG — An insane or simple-minded individual.
BUG DOCTOR — A psychiatrist.
BUGGED — To be placed in an insane asylum or psychiatric division of an institution.
BUGGED — A place protected by burglar alarms.
BUG HOUSE — A lunatic asylum.
BUG HOUSE — Crazy; simple-minded or idiotic.
BUG HOUSE SQUARE — Washington Square, Chicago.
BUGGY — An automobile.
BUGGY — Crazy; a stir-bug.
BUGS — Crazy.
BULL — A uniform policeman.
BULL — To deceive; lie to. Something offensive or worthless.
BULL BUSTER — One with a morbid passion for assaulting the police.
BULLETS — Beans.
BULL HORRORS — A morbid fear of the police.
BULL PEN — The cage or pen in a jail in which prisoners are kept, while awaiting trial or transfer to prison.
BULL SIMPLE — Afraid of the police.
BURG — A city, town, or village.
BURN — To electrocute.
BUM — A tramp who does not travel and who will not work.

BUM — Cheap, undesirable, inferior.

BUM — To beg or solicit.

BUM BEEF — An unjust accusation.

BUM DOGS — Sore feet.

BUM FLASH — A false rumor.

BUM FLIPPER — A sore hand.

BUM RAP — An unjust accusation.

BUM TICKER — A bad heart; heart trouble; a bad action of the heart.

BUMP OFF — To kill; a killing.

BUNDLE — Loot or plunder.

BUNDLE OF TIME — A long sentence, or a long Parole Board setting.

BUNK — False.

BUNK — A bed.

BURNER — A cook

BURN UP — To aggrevate; get a person "hot under the collar."

BURR HEAD — A Negro.

BURY — To get a long sentence; or a long Parole Board continuance.

BUSH PAROLE — Escape from prison.

BUST — An error or a bad "Break."

BUST — A drinking bout.

BUST — To strike or hit.

BUST WIDE OPEN — To confess; to tell all you know.

BUTCHER — A prison physician or surgeon.

BUTCHER — To kill.

BUTCHER — A barber.

BUTTONS — A messenger.

BUZZ — Talk or conversation.

BUZZ — To question or converse with.

"C" — Cocaine.

"C" NOTE — A hundred dollar bill, or one hundred dollars.

CABBAGE — Paper money.

CAB JOINT — A brothel to which patrons are driven by taxicab, the drivers usually, or in many instances, receiving, a certain fee or percentage of whatever the patron spends in the "joint."

CANARY — An informer.

C AND A POCKET — A large pouch or pocket in the coat.

CACKLEBERRIES — Eggs.

CACKLER — An egg.

CALL — To force an issue.

CAMERA EYE — A detective or police officer with a good memory for faces.

CAN — A prison or jail.

CAN — A toilet.

CANNON — A pistol or revolver.

CANNON — A pickpocket.

CANUCK — A Canadian.

CARRYING A FLAG — Traveling under an assumed name or alias.

CASE — An observation or spying. To look over the scene of a proposed crime, or to look over the route to be used for a getaway.

CASE A JOINT — Same as "Case."

CASE NOTE — A dollar bill.

CAT HEADS — Biscuits.

CENTURY — One hundred dollars. A hundred-dollar bill.

CENTURY NOTE — A one hundred dollar bill.

CHATTER — Talk, conversation.

CHEATERS — Spectacles, eye-glasses.

CHEATERS — Marked cards or dice.

CHECK OUT — Die; give up or abandon; to leave.

CHEESE EATER — An informer.

CHEW — To talk (like chew the fat).

CHEW THE FAT — To talk aimlessly.

CHI — Chicago.

CHICKEN FEED — Small change; a small amount of money.

CHIN — To talk.

CHINK — A Chinaman.

CHIPPY — A young girl.

CHISLER — A petty thief; a cheap gambler; an intruder.

CHISLE — To intrude.

CHOKER — A collar.

CHOPPER — A machine gun; the operator of such a weapon.

CHOPPERS — The teeth.

CHOW — Food.

CHUCK — Food.

CHUCK HOUSE — An eating house or restaurant.

CINCI — Cincinnati, Ohio.

CINDER BULL — A railroad policeman or detective.

CIRCUS BEES — Body lice.

CIRCUS SQUIRRELS — Body lice.

CLAW — The hand.

CLEAN — Out of funds; penniless; "broke."

CLEAN — To rob.

CLEAN — No evidence.

CLICK — To succeed.

CLICK — Group of persons who band together.

CLINK — A jail.

CLIP — To steal.

CLIP — To strike.

CLIP JOINT — A place where customers do not get their money's worth; or a resort where persons are flimflammed and cheated.

CLOSE YOUR YAP — Shut your mouth.

CLOUT — To steal.

CLOUT — To strike.

COKE — Cocaine.

COKE PARTY — A gathering at which cocaine or some other drug fur-

nishes the stimulation.
COLD — Dead or unconscious.
COLD COCK — To render insensible with a blow from a bottle.
COLD ONE — An empty wallet, money-box or safe.
COLD SLOUGH PROWLER — A thief who specializes in robbing empty houses.
COLLAR — To arrest.
COMEBACK — A retort or reply.
CON — A convict.
CONK — The head.
CONK — To strike on the head.
CONNECT — To meet; enter into an agreement.
CON RACKET — Confidence game.
CONSENT JOB — A theft or arson committed with the consent of the owner or landlord in order to obtain insurance money.
CONTACT — A connection of affiliation made by a criminal to protect himself from arrest or to make crime easy.
COOK UP — To arrange or "frame-up" a situation or plan.
COOK UP — Prepare opium for smooking.
COOLER — A police station, or a punishment cell in prison.
COOLER — A silencer for a pistol, rifle, or a small machine gun.
COON — A Negro.
COOP — A police station.
COOTIES — Body lice.
COP — A policeman.
COP — To steal.
COP — To understand.
COP A JOINT — Sex pervert expression.
COP A PLEA — To plead guilty to a lesser crime than the charged.
COP A SNEAK — To walk away.
COPPED OUT — Plead guilty to a lesser crime.
COPPER — A policeman.
CORNER — Solitary confinement building in prison.
COW — A prostitute.
CRAB — A body louse.
CRAB — To complain or find fault.
CRAB — To spoil an arrangement.
CRACK — Any statement or remark considered in bad taste, ill advised or insulting.
CRACK DOWN — To place close attention to, or to work unusually hard.
CRACKED — Simple-minded.
CRACK A JUG — To open a safe.
CRACKED ICE — Unset diamonds or those removed from settings.
CRAP — Anything regarded as foolish or without value.
CRASH THE GATE — Join a party without invitation.
CRATE — An automobile.
CRAZY AS A BEDBUG — Erratic, especially when given to sudden, aimless moves and actions.

CREEPERS — Felt or rubber-soled shoes.

CRIB — A safe or money box.

CRIB — A gambling dive.

CRIB — A harlot's house or room.

CRIP — A cripple.

CROAK — To die; to kill.

CROAKER — A physician.

CROAKER JOINT — A physician's office.

CRUM — A body louse.

CRUMMY — Verminous; undesirable; inferior or cheap.

CRUSH — To escape from a prison or jail.

CRUSH OUT — To break jail, especially with violence.

CUPID'S ITCH — Any venerial disease.

CURTAINS — Death; the end.

CURVE — A beautiful woman.

CUSH — Money.

CUSHIONS — Comfort; ease; luxury.

CUT — A division of loot.

CUTOR — A prosecuting attorney.

CUTTING UP — Discussing an absentee's actions or morals.

CUTIE — A girl or woman.

CZAR — The warden of a prison.

DAMPER — A cash register or money drawer.

DARB — Unusually skilled or able; excellent.

DAUBER — A painter.

DEAD BANG — Caught in the act.

DEAD ONE — A reformed criminal.

DEN — A hangout, a resort, or a meeting-place.

DEUCE — A two-dollar bill.

DICER — A hat; a fast freight.

DICK — A detective.

DIG — To look into a person's past.

DINERO — Money.

DINGOES — Tramps who refuse to work.

DINGY — Crazy, insane.

DIP — A pickpocket.

DIPPY — Crazy.

DIRT — Money; gossip.

DIRTY — Having money.

DIRTY TOWEL — The inmate barber shop in a prison.

DISH THE DIRT — To serve up scandal or gossip; to explain the details of a projected enterprise.

DITCH — Get rid of; to abandon.

DIPPING THE WICK — Sexual intercourse.

DIVE — Any place of ill repute.

DIVVY — A share, as of loot or funds.

DIVVY — To divide or share.

DOG — The foot.

DOG — Syphillis.

DOG EYE — To inspect or scrutinize.

DOG IT — To stall.

DOGS — Sausages.

DONNEKER — A toilet or washroom.

DOPE — Narcotics.

DOPE — Information.

DOPE — A stupid person.

DOPE FIEND — A drug addict.

DOPE PEDDLER — One who retails narcotics to drug addicts.

DOPEY — Under the influence of a drug.

DOPEY — Slow of thought, simple-minded.

DOPESTER — One who acquires information.

DOPESTER — One who offers information on horse races.

DOUBLE CROSS — A trick on "Frame-up," especially when played upon an associate or partner.

DOUBLE CROSS — To cheat a companion or a friend.

DOUBLE O — An observation or spying.

DOUBLE SAWBUCK — A twenty-dollar bill.

DOUBLE SAWBUCK — A twenty-year prison sentence.

DOUGH — Money.

DOWN THE HATCH — To swallow food or drink.

DRAG — Influence.

DRAG — A street; a railroad line.

DRAG — Loot.

DRAG MAN — Confidence man.

DRESS PARADE — Applied to Negroes who attend the weekly cinema or ball game in a prison.

DRILL — To work; to walk.

DRILL — To shoot.

DRIP — Nonsense; non-essential; useless matter or material; worthless advice.

DRIVE — A thrill.

DROPPER — A paid killer.

DRUM — A safe.

DRUM — A crook's hangout or den.

DUCAT — A dollar.

DUCAT — A ticket.

DUCK — To escape; to run.

DUCK THE NUT — To hide; to drop quietly from sight.

DUGOUT — A heavy eater.

DUKES — The hands.

DUKIE — A sandwich.

DUMMY — A mute.

DUMMY — A pretended feint to gain sympathy; one who is slow of thought or speech.

DUMMY UP — To become silent; cease talking or giving information.

DUMP — A hangout or place of refuge.

DUMP — Any dirty resort.

DUMP — To get rid of; to abandon.

DUST — Money.

DUST — To leave in a hurry.

DUSTER — A box car or freight car thief; a chicken thief.

DUTCH ACT — To commit suicide. In prison, sometimes called: "Frustrating the Parole Board."

DYNO — Liquor.

DYNO — A pick and shovel worker.

EX-CON — An Ex-convict.

EARIE — Listening to another's conversation; eavesdropping.

EASY — Soft-hearted; charitable; easy to influence.

EAT YOUR DUCK — Be on your way; get going.

EM — Morphine.

END — A share or portion.

EYE BALL — Observe; look on; to watch.

EYE OPENER — A drink of liquor; something to waken one.

FADE — To go away; to disappear.

FAG — A homosexual.

FAG — A cigarette.

FAGGOT — A homosexual. Same as "fag."

FAIRY — An effeminate man or boy.

FAIRY STORY — A pitiful or misleading story told in order to gain sympathy or to achieve an end.

FAKER — One who shams or pretends.

FALL — To be tripped up by a misleading or unlikely story.

FALL — To be arrested.

FALL GUY — A scapegoat; one who is made to take the blame for a crime.

FALL MONEY — Money put aside to fight convictions.

FALL TOGS — Clothing especially selected by a criminal or his lawyer to give him a good appearance on trial and thus possibly influence the jury or judge in his favor.

FAN — To search, especially a person or his clothes.

FANNING A SUCKER — Searching a victim's clothing for loot.

FANNY — The buttocks.

FED UP — More than satisfied; had enough.

FEED — Meals.

FENCE — A receiver of stolen goods.

FIDDLE — To conceal.

FILE — A pickpocket.

FIN — Five dollars; a five-dollar bill.

FIN — A five-year sentence, or parole board setting.

FIN — The hand.

FINGER — To betray to the police.

FINIF — A five-dollar bill.

FINK — A questionable person; an informer.

FIREWORKS — Gun play.

FISH — A newly sentenced prisoner.

FISH — Paper money.

FISH GALLERY — Prison gallery in cellhouse where newly arrived prisoners are housed or celled.

FISHING — Attempting to secure anything by dubious means.

FIVE C'S — Five hundred dollars.

FIXER — One who squares a crook's affairs with the police.

FLAG — An alias; a fictitious name.

FLAG — A warning.

FLAG — To accost or detain.

FLASH — A gaudy or well-dressed person.

FLASH — To display or exhibit.

FLASH — A rumor.

FLAT — Penniless.

FLAT BROKE — Penniless.

FLATFOOT — A uniformed policeman.

FLAT DOG — Bologna sausage.

FLAT TIRE — A person unproductive of further income; an impotent man.

FLICKER — A faint or pretended faint.

FLIMFLAM — To cheat or defraud.

FLIP — To board a moving train.

FLIP — Flippant; pert; outspoken.

FLIPPER — A hand.

FLOATER — A migratory worker.

FLOOZIE — A girl or woman.

FLOP — A bed, or a place to sleep.

FLOP — To sleep.

FLOP — To fail.

FLOP HOUSE — A cheap lodging house.

FLUFF — A blonde girl or woman.

FLUKE — Any chance advantage or lucky stroke of fortune.

FLUNKEY — A porter, waiter or servile worker.

FLUTER — A degenerate.

FLY A KITE — To send out an underground letter from prison.

FLYING KITES — Same as above; passing worthless checks.

FLYING LIGHT — Hungry; without food; traveling without any excess impediment.

FLY COP — A detective.

FLY DICK — A detective.

FLYING JIB — A talkative person.

FOG — To shoot.

FOX — To out-think or out-maneuver another.

FRAIL — A woman or girl.

FRAME — A false accusation.

FRAME UP — A false accusation.

FRILL — A girl or woman.

FRISK — Search; especially of the person.

FROLIC — To denominate any lawless activity.
FRONT — A good appearance or a bad appearance. A "Good Front" or a "Bad Front."
FRONT — One who maintains an apparently innocent enterprise as a blind behind which lawless persons may work without fear.
FRUIT — A degenerate.
FRY — To electrocute.
FULL — Intoxicated.
FUNKY — Evil smelling.

"G" — One thousand dollars; a "Grand."
"G" NOTE — A one thousand dollar bill.
"G" MEN — Federal Government operatives.
GAB — Idle talk or chatter.
GAB — The mouth.
GAFF — Punishment; a hard pace.
GAFFER — A boss; foreman, etc.
GAFF WHEEL — A gambling wheel controlled by the foot of the operator.
GAG — Any begging trick, "Ghost story," or other recital.
GAG — A joke or hoax.
GALL — High spirits; courage; impudence.
GAMS — A girl's legs.
GANDER — To look; to spy upon.
GANDY DANCER — A person who walks with a peculiar gait.
GANGSTER — A member of a criminal mob or an individual who knows the workings of the underworld.
GAPPER — A mirror.
GARBAGE — Food.
GARBAGE CAN — An old prostitute.
GARBAGE HOUNDS — "Dugouts" who thrive on felons' fare.
GAS — Talk; idle chatter.
GASH — The mouth.
GASH — A street woman or one willing to ignore her virtue.
GASH HOUND — A man continually seeking women.
GAT — A pistol or revolver.
GATE CRASHER — An extremely unpopular individual; who habitually "butts in" where he is not wanted.
GEE — A glass of liquor.
GEE — Any individual — "guy."
GEEZER — Any man, particularly someone rather queer, out of the ordinary.
GETAWAY — An escape from pursuit or confinement.
GET BY — To earn a bare living.
GET BY — To escape or evade trouble or arrest.
GET TO To bribe.
GET WISE — "Smarten up." To advise or explain to.
GIMICK — A lame person.
GIMPY — Lame, crippled.
GIN — A colored prostitute.

GIN MILL — Any saloon.

GINK — Any man.

GINNED — Intoxicated.

GINNY — An Italian.

GIVEN A PASS — Reprimanded and excused for a violation.

GIVEN A PASS — Not prosecuted for a crime because of information furnished the police concerning other guilty persons and testifying for the State prosecutors thereto.

GIVEN THE AIR — Discharged from the job. Requested to leave, or refusal to have further connections with.

GIVEN THE EAR LOFT — Pass information confidentially.

GLASS ARM — An arm likely to fail under constant strain.

GLASS JAW — A weak or sensitive chin.

GLASS JAW — A coward; one easily defeated.

GLAUM — To take or seize.

GLIM — A light.

GLIM — An eye.

GLIM BOX — A small box containing burned cloth, used for the purpose of lighting cigarettes, etc., by causing a spark created by friction of a small button or washer against a piece of stone to alight in the box, causing the cloth to smolder.

GLIMMER — An eye.

GLOM — To snatch; seize; grab; steal. "Glaum."

GOAT — A scapegoat; one blamed for another's crime or mistake.

GO BY — A slight or "cut."

GOLD BRICK — To shirk or malinger.

GOLDBRICKER — One who shirks or malingers.

GOLD DIGGER — Any woman who gets whatever she can from men without the necessity of making any return.

GOLD DUST — Cocaine.

GONE ON THE ROCKS — Penniless; broke.

GONGER — An opium pipe; an opium addict.

GONOPH or GONOV — A thief; usually allied with pickpockets or cheap pilferers.

GOOD HEAD — One to be trusted.

GOOF — A simpleton; a dupe.

GOOFY — Foolish; simple-minded.

GOPHER — A gangster or other hard character.

GOPHER MEN — Safe-robbers.

GORILLA — A thug or bully.

GOSPEL FOWL — Chicken.

GO TO BAT — To go to trial.

GO TO PRESS — To get to work.

GO TO PRESS — Sexual intercourse.

GO-BETWEEN — An intermediary; a procurer.

GOW — Opium.

GOWED UP — Under the influence of drugs or liquor.

GRAB — To arrest; to seize or lay hold of.

GRAFT — Any criminal activity.

GRAFTER — Anyone living by his wits.

GRAND — One thousand dollars.

GRAPEVINE — Manner in which underworld information is passed to its destination.

GRAVY — An unearned, easily acquired amount of money.

GRAY — A white man.

GREENBACKS — Paper money.

GREASE — To pay for protection.

GREASE — Butter.

GREASER — A Mexican.

GREASE BALL — An Italian.

GREASE JOINT — A dirty restaurant or lunchroom.

GREASY SPOON — The inmate dining room used by inmates assigned to the Farm Detail outside the walls at noon meal.

GREASY SPOON — Same as "Greasy Joint."

GRIPSTER — A chronic inmate complainer.

GROUND PADS — Shoes.

GUFF — Back talk; or any meaningless or misleading talk.

GUM — To spoil; to interfere with; to upset a plan or arrangement.

GUMMED THE WORKS — Spoiled a plan or arrangement.

GUMSHOE — A detective.

GUMSHOE — To spy on or to observe.

GUN — A crook; gunman or thief.

GUN — To spy on or to observe.

GUN MOB — Any "Mob" or "Guns" or thieves.

GUNSEL — A passive male homosexual.

GUT REAMER — A vulgarism best undefined.

GUTS — Bravery or courage.

GUTS — The bowels.

GUY — Any man.

GYP — A confidence game or confidence worker.

GYP — To flimflam, cheat or defraud.

HABIT — The drug habit.

HAM — An inefficient worker.

HAM — To walk.

HAND JIG — Self-abuse.

HANDLE — A name, by which a person is called.

HANG OUT — A resort or place frequented by an individual or gang.

HAPPY DUST — Cocaine.

HARDWARE — Weapons in general; knives, guns, or razors.

HARDWARE — Table silverware.

HARNESS — Shoulder holster.

HARNESS BULL — A uniformed policeman.

HARP — Complain.

HASH HOUSE — A restaurant or eating house.

HASH SLINGER — A waitress.

HAG — An old woman, usually one with a nasty disposition.

HAY BAG — A woman vagrant.

HAY BURNER — A horse.

HAY WIRE — Gone wrong; broken down; inefficient.

HEAT — Police following a crime or series of crimes; trouble.

HEATER — A revolver or pistol.

HEAVY MAN — An armed watcher in a gambling house.

HEEL — Any incompetent or undesirable person.

HEEL — To walk.

HEEL — The end of a loaf of bread.

HEELED — Armed.

HEELED — Provided with money.

HEIFER — A young woman.

HEIFER DEN — A brothel.

HEIST — A hold-up.

HEP — Well informed.

HICK — A farmer.

HICK — One who is ignorant of impending events.

HIDEOUT — A place in which to remain hidden from the police or gang enemies.

HIDEOUT — A criminal gang meeting place.

HIGH — In high spirits; elevated by drink.

HIGH BALL — A "proceed" signal.

HIGH HAT — A slight or "cut."

HIGHJACK — To rob.

HIGHJACKER — A liquor carrier bandit.

HIGH PRESSURE — To force or argue another into a deal; intimidate.

HIGH TAIL — To move swiftly.

HIP — Wise; knowing.

HIT THE BALL — To work hard; to travel swiftly.

HITCH — A prison sentence.

HOCK — To pawn or pledge as security for a loan.

HOLD OUT — To retain more than one's share of loot; to withhold information of value.

HOLE — Solitary.

HOLE UP — To hide away from the law.

HOLLER — The plaint or a victim who "hollers" for assistance; put up a "holler."

HOOD — A hoodlum.

HOOK — A razor.

HOOCH — Liquor.

HOOFER — A dancer.

HOOK — A crook; more especially a pickpocket.

HOOK — To steal.

HOOK SHOP — A house of prostitution.

HOOKER — A drink of liquor.

HOOKER — A harlot.

HOOP — A ring.

HOOP — An automobile tire.

HOOSEGOW — A jail.

HOOSIER — An inefficient worker.

HOP — Opium or narcotics in general.

HOP — A dance.

HOP HEAD — An opium addict; more loosely, any drug addict.

HOP JOINT — A resort where opium is smoked.

HOP MERCHANT — A drug peddler who meets his customers on the street, in doorways, etc.

HOPPED UP — Under the influence of opium or of any narcotics.

HORN IN — To butt in; to intrude.

HORNY — Amative; lewd.

HOT — Alive; lively; amorous; lewd.

HOT — "Wanted" by the police for some crime but lately committed.

HOT — Angry.

HOT CHAIR — The electric chair.

HOT JOINT — A house or store to be robbed while occupied or while business is being conducted.

HOT JOINT — A resort full of customers and lively.

HOT SEAT — The electric chair.

HOT SHORT — A stolen automobile.

HOT SQUAT — The electric chair.

HOT STUFF — Stolen goods.

HOT STUFF — Something remarkably well worth while.

HOT STUFF — A passionate woman.

HOTTER THAN A PISTOL — "Wanted" by the police for a recent crime; public-enemy number one.

HOTTER THAN A PISTOL — A prisoner in a penitentiary who has extremely contraband articles in his possession.

HUMP — The middle of a prison sentence.

HUMP — Sexual intercourse.

HUNCH — An inspiration or premonition.

HUNKY — Any common laborer.

HUNKY — A Lithuanian.

HUSTLER — A grafter.

HUSTLER — A criminal or a street woman.

HUSTLING SHEETS — Selling newspapers.

HYPO — A hypodermic needle.

HYPO — A drug addict, especially one who uses a needle to administer the drug.

ICE — Diamonds.

IN A CRACK — To cause someone to be in a compromising position.

INK SLINGER — A clerk or other office worker.

INFO — Information; advice.

INSIDE — Information or knowledge shared by only a few.

INSIDE — "Inside the walls" in prison.

INSIDE — At Joliet Penitentiary, meaning the Old Prison.

INSIDE — When a convict is taken off an assignment outside the walls and brought back "inside the walls" it is said that he is brought "inside."

INSIDER — One "in the know."

IN THE CLEAR — Above suspicion; free from blame; out of danger.

IN THE KNOW — A person or persons having information or knowledge shared only by a few.

IRISH TURKEY — Corned beef.

IRON MAN — Silver dollar.

JAB — A hypodermic injection.

JACK — Money.

JACK ROLLER — A thief who robs in alleys, especially when the victims are intoxicated.

JAIL HOUSE — A city or county jail.

JAKE — Satisfactory; pleasing; quite correct.

JAM — A difficulty or trouble.

JAMMED UP — In a difficulty or trouble.

JAMOKE — Coffee.

JANE — Woman or girl.

JAVA — Coffee.

JAW FEST — A long talk; conversation.

JAY — Coffee.

JAZZ — Sexual intercourse.

JAZZ — To speed up.

JERK — A disliked individual.

JEW FLAG — A dollar bill; any paper money.

JIGGER MAN — A lookout for other thieves.

JIGGERS — An exclamation of warning.

JIM — To spoil or deface.

JIMMY — A burglar's tool for forcing a door or window.

JERK-SILLY — Applied to an inmate who chronically masturbates.

JIT — A nickel.

JIVE — Small talk; to josh.

JITNEY — A nickel.

JOB — Any criminal enterprise.

JOCKER — An active homosexual.

JOHN — A free spender.

JOHN HANCOCK — A signature.

JOHN LAW — A policeman; sheriff or constable.

JOHNSON — Coffee.

JOINT — Any hangout or gathering place.

JOINT — The male sexual organ.

JOINT — A prospective place of burglary or robbery.

JOLT — A stiff drink.

JOLT — A prison sentence.

JOLT — To strike.

JOY HOUSE — A brothel.

JOY POWDER — Morphine.

JUG — A jail or prison.

JUG — Solitary; to imprison.

JUG — A safe.

JUG HEAD — A stupid person.
JUICE — Nitroglycerine.
JUMP — To depart.
JUMP — To have sexual intercourse.
JUMP — To admonish.
JUMPING JIVE — Jazz music.
JUNGLES — A tramp's camp.
JUNGLE BUZZARD — A tramp or yegg who preys on others of his kind.
JUNK — Anything regarded as worthless.
JUNK — Narcotic drugs.
JUNKER — A drug addict; a dope fiend.
JUNK HEAD — A drug addict.
JUNK PEDDLER — A narcotic peddler, who sells the "stuff" to addicts.
JUST A BREEZE — A prison sentence about completed.

KALE — Money.
KANGAROO COURT — A mock trial in jail.
KAYOE — To achieve unusual success.
KAYOE — O.K., "all right"; a knockout.
KEISTER — A suitcase.
KEISTER — The buttocks.
KELLY — A hat.
KIBITZ — Unwanted, unwelcome advice.
KIBITZER — One who volunteers advice and who endeavors to conduct
    another's affairs.
KICK — An objection.
KICK — To object or oppose.
KICK IN — To contribute or donate, usually under protest.
KICKS — Shoes.
KID — A young person or girl.
KID — A reference to a passive homosexual.
KID SIMPLE — Having a nuerotic passion for boys or one boy.
KIKE — A Jew or any cheap merchant.
KINK — A criminal; one who is not straight.
KIP — A bed or a place to sleep.
KIP — To sleep.
KIP DOUGH — Money for a bed or lodging.
KISSER — The face or mouth.
KISS OFF — A dismissal, usually when the one dismissed has been de-
    frauded or injured in some way.
KITE — A letter.
KNEELING AT THE ALTAR — Committing pederasty.
KNOB HEAD — A stupid individual.
KNOCK — To inform.
KNOCKER — One who informs.
KNOCKER — The principal witness or complainant..
KNOCKDOWN — An introduction.
KNOCK DOWN — An introduction.
KNOCK OFF — An arrest.

KNOCK OFF — To kill.
KNOCK OFF — To cease work.
KNOCK OVER — To raid or to arrest.
KNOWLEDGE BOX — A school house; the brain.
KUTER — A quarter (25¢).
LACE — To punch, beat or manhandle.
LAM — A hasty getaway or escape.
LAM — To assault.
LAMB — A young man.
LAMSTER — A fugitive from justice.
LAMP — To see; to view; to look at.
LAMPS — The eyes.
LAW — Any police authority.
LAY — Sexual intercourse.
LAY LOW — To hide out.
LAYOUT — The full details of a crime.
LAY OUT — To knock down; to render unconscious.
LAY OF THE LAND — The full details of a crime.
LEARY — Suspicious; afraid; dubious.
LEATHER — A wallet or pocket-book.
LEFTY — One minus a left arm or hand. A left-handed person.
LEGIT — Legitimate.
LEG IT — To run.
LETTUCE — Paper money.
LEVEL — Can be trusted. "One who is 'on the level'."
LILLIES — The hands.
LIMEY — An Englishman.
LINE — A persuasive manner of speech, or a winning address.
LINE UP — The daily inspection of newly captured prisoners at police
    headquarters.
LINGO — A language or a variety of speech.
LIT — Intoxicated.
LIVE WIRE — A free spender.
LOCO — Crazy; erratic; unbalanced.
LOCO WEED — Marajuana.
LONER — One.
LONGHANDLED UNDERWEAR — A unionsuit.
LONGHORN — A Texan.
LONGIES — A unionsuit.
LONG ROD — A rifle.
LOOGIN — A newcomer to a gang.
LOOKER — A spy or observer.
LOOKER — An attractive girl or young woman.
LOOKOUT — A member of a gang who watches for the police during a
    robbery or other crime. A "Jigger Man."
LOONY — Crazy; erratic.
LOSE OUT — To be taken off a good assignment in prison for violation
    of the rules.

LOSER — An ex-convict.
LOST — Murdered. Anyone who has been "put on the spot" or disposed of by gang justice.
LOUSE CAGE — A hat.
LOUSY — Disreputable; inferior.
LOUSY — Well supplied with money.
LOW DOWN — The truth; the inside facts; reliable information.
LUG — A stupid person.
LUG — To carry.
LU LU — Anything unusually worthy or desirable.
LUMP — A package of food.
LUNK HEAD — A stupid person.
LUSH — A drunkard.

"M" — Morphine.
MAC — A pander; a lover or associate of lewd women.
MADAME — The woman in charge of a brothel.
MADE IT — Granted a parole.
MAIN DRAG — The main street of a town or city.
MAIN GUY — The boss; one with authority. God.
MAIN STEM — The main street or a town or city.
MAKE — To recognize; to discern; to discover; to accomplish.
MAKINS — Cigarette tobacco and papers.
MAN — A prison guard.
M and C — A mixture of morphine and cocaine.
MARK — An easy mark; a pickpocket's victim.
MARRIED — Handcuffed together.
MARRY — To enter into homosexual relations.
MARRIED — Having unnatural sex relations.
MASH — To pass. "Mash it to me."
MAWK — A slovenly, unclean harlot.
MAX "X" — Maximum "X," the maximum of a prison sentence, as when the Parole Board advises a prisoner he is to serve his sentence in full, less Statutory "Good Time." All of it.
McCOY — Neat; good-looking; unusually excellent or genuine.
MEAL TICKET — A woman supporting a lover or pander; any source of free income.
MEDITATION MANOR — Solitary.
MEIG — A five-cent piece; also, one cent when found in the plural, as "fifty meigs."
MELT — Loot which may be melted down.
MESS MOLL — A woman cook.
MICK — An Irishman.
MILL — A free-for-all fight.
MILL — To ramble aimlessly about.
MINNIE — Minneapolis, Minnesota.
MISSIONARY — A pimp or procurer; a "White Slaver."
MITT — The hand.
MITT — To great or shake hands with.

MOB — A criminal band or gang.

MOB OF CANNONS — A gang of criminals, especially a group of pickpockets.

MOLL — A woman.

MOLL BUZZER — A pickpocket preying on women.

MOLL WORKER — A pickpocket preying on women. Same as "Moll Buzzer."

MONICKER — A name, especially of an individual.

MOOCH — To beg; to stroll about; to walk away from.

MOOCHER — A beggar.

MOONSHINE — Liquor manufactured or sold, or both, outside the law.

MOPE — To walk away; to leave.

MOPE — To dawdle.

MOP MARY — A scrub woman; a charwoman.

MOSS — Hair.

MOUTHPIECE — A lawyer.

MUD — Opium.

MUG — The face; a grimace.

MUG — To photograph a criminal.

MUGGING — Making faces; to give silent warnings behind another's back; or to warn.

MULE — Corn liquor.

MULE SKINNER — A teamster or mule driver.

MUSCLE — To use force or intimidation so as to secure a share in a "racket" or graft, or to force one's way into an enterprise or gang by threat or violence.

MUSCLE MAN — One who "muscles" for himself or in the interest of others.

MUSH — The face.

NAB — To catch; to arrest.

NAGS — Race horses.

NAIL — To catch; to arrest.

NAIL A RATTLER — To board a fast train once it has got under way.

NECK — To stare at or watch closely.

NECK TIE — A hangman's noose.

NEEDLE — A hypodermic needle, or a dose of drug so administered.'

NEEDLE — To treat a soft drink or "near beer" with some form of alcohol, ether, etc., to give it a "kick," making it intoxicating.

NEEDLE BEER — Beer treated as above.

NERVE — Courage; "gall," audacity; "guts."

NEW JOINT — The Stateville Penitentiary at Joliet.

NEXT — Aware of what impends; "wise" to what is going on.

NICK — To steal; to arrest.

NICKEL NURSER — A stingy individual, one who nurses his funds.

NIFTY — Desirable; excellent.

NIGGLE — To have sexual intercourse.

NIP — To open a locked door by means of a small pair of hollow-nosed nippers, which grasp the key from the wrong side of the door, allowing it to be turned in the lock.

NIP — To steal a stud or other piece of jewelry from the person.

NIPPERS — The pliers serving to open a locked door.

NIX — Stop; no; cease; a warning.

NIX OUT — Same as "nix."

NOB — The head.

NOSE BAG — A meal; to eat.

NOTCH HOUSE — House of prostitution.

NOTCH JOINT — House of prostitution.

NUT — An insane or erratic individual.

NUT — The cost of an operation; overhead expense.

NUT HOUSE — An insane asylum. The Psychiatric Division of the Menard Prison.

NUTTY — Crazy; erratic; simple-minded.

OBIE — A country post-office.

OFFICE — A warning or sign of recognition from one to another person.

ON THE ROUTE — To permit other convicts in a penitentiary to read a newspaper or magazine received by a convict, who, when he has finished reading it, places the cell numbers of other convicts in the order he wishes it delivered on the front of the newspaper or magazine and they pass it on as they finish with it.

OILED — Intoxicated.

OIL OF JOY — Any strong drink.

OLD HEAD — Anyone with experience at any particular line of work or crime, or with a thorough knowledge of lie.

OLD LADIES' HOME — A brothel where decorum and the proprieties must be observed.

OLD MAN — Anyone in authority or in a superior position.

ON THE BAN — Deprivation of all entertainment privileges to some inmates of a prison because of violation of prison rules.

ON THE BOOST — Shoplifting.

ON THE BUM — Literally, broken in pocket and spirit.

ON THE CRACK — Out for burglary or other theft.

ON THE CUSHIONS — Any state of comfort, wealth or ease.

ON THE DODGE — Fleeing from justice; avoiding the police.

OLD JOINT — The Old Prison at Joliet.

ON THE ERIE — Listening to other's conversation; eavsdropping.

ON THE FLY — Moving swiftly.

ON THE HOOK — A person not in good standing.

ON THE ROCKS — Literally, standing. Impoverished.

ON THE LAM — Avoiding the police; running at top speed.

ON THE LEGIT — Honest; in earnest; trustworthy.

ON THE MAKE — Doing well; making money; successful.

ON THE MUSCLE — Quarrelsome; overbearing.

ON THE MUSCLE — Same as "Muscle."

ON THE NUT — Out of funds; living on the "nut."

ON THE PLUSH — Any state of comfort, wealth or ease.
ON THE PROWL — Committing burglary or looking for an opportunity to do so.
ON THE Q.T. — "On the quiet"; do a thing when it will not be known.
ON THE RACKET — Crooked; criminal.
ON THE SPOT — Market for assassination; in danger.
OPEN UP — To become confidential.
OUT — An alibi or excuse.
OUTFIT — A group of people or a commercial firm.
OUTFIT — Personal effects.
OUT OF LINE — Unmanageable; hard to control.
OUTSIDE — Out of jail or prison, at liberty. The "outside world" as referred to by those in prison.
OUTSIDE — Not included in an arrangement or plan.
OWNER'S JOB — Same as "Consent Job."
OFF YOUR FEED — Not having an appetite; stomach out of order.

PACK — Carry a gun or other weapon.
PACK — Carry any goods or property.
PACK — A package of cigarettes.
PACK — A homosexual expression.
PAD — A bed.
PADDED — Having loot concealed upon the person.
PALM OIL — Money paid as a bribe for protection against police interference.
PAN — The face.
PAN — To defame or belittle behind a person's back.
PAN-HANDLER — A begger who solicits alms upon the street.
PAPER — A railroad ticket.
PAPER — Bad checks or counterfeit money.
PAPER-HANGER — One who passes bad checks or counterfeit money.
PAPER TIME — The additional time a prisoner received from the Parole Board due to pressure brought to bear by newspapers.
PARALYZED — Intoxicated to a degree but still able to move, even if limited in action and reaction.
PASS — To excuse; excused.
PASSER — One who passes or "shoves" counterfeit money.
PAROLE JITTERS — Nervously awaiting action of the Parole Board.
PAY-OFF — The division of spoils after a robbery; the settlement of accounts; the profitable conclusion of an enterprise.
PEARL DIVER — A dish-washer.
PEARLS — The teeth.
PEDDLER — Seller of narcotics.
PEDIGREE — A criminal's record as held by the police.
PEEPERS — The eyes.
PEG — A leg; artificial or otherwise.
PEG — A one-legged person.
PEG — To watch or spy on a person or place.

PEG HOUSE — A disorderly house or resort where pedaresty is practiced by female impersonators.

PEN — A forger, one who uses a pen.

PEN — A penitentiary.

PENITENTIARY AGENT — A public defender. (A lawyer appointed by the Court.)

PEN MAN — A forger.

PENNYWEIGHT JOB — A jewel robbery.

PEN YEN — Opium.

PERCENTAGE BULL — A policeman who will accept a certain part of the proceeds of a robbery or of the profits in a shady deal in return for his protection ,assistance or indifference.

PETER — A safe.

PETER MAN — A safe-blower.

PETER WORK — Safe robbery.

PHONEY — False; unreal; imitation; valueless.

PHONEYMAN — A peddler of cheap jewelry.

P. I. — A pimp or pander.

PICKINS — Money obtained by begging or by any other dubious means or graft.

PICK-UP — An arrest; a solicitation for immoral purposes; the one who is arrested or solicited.

PICK-UP — To arrest; to solicit for immoral purposes.

PIE — Easy; simple; desirable; pleasant; unusually welcome.

PIE-EYED — Intoxicated.

PIECE — A share or part of the loot or proceeds of a "racket" or crime.

PIECE — A woman or girl who will "listen to reason"; in this sense, as a "piece of tail," or a "piece of skirt."

PIGEON — An informer.

PIGEON JOINT — A store where burglars' tools may be purchased, or a resort specializing in the supply of such instruments.

PIG MEAT — A young boy or girl.

PIKE — A road, street, or railroad.

PILL — Pellet of opium cooked over the nut oil lamp and ready for smoking in the pipe.

PILL — A cigarette.

PILL SHOOTER — A physician.

PIMP — One who lives on the earnings of a streetwalker or prostitute, or who solicits trade for his woman or "meal ticket."

PIMP STICK — A cigarette.

PIN ARTIST — An abortionist.

PINCH — To arrest; to steal or pilfer.

PINEAPPLE — A bomb.

PINEAPPLE — To bomb or dynamite.

PINHEAD — A drug addict; a clerk; a fool or numb-skull.

PINK — In good physical condition.

PIPE — Easy; simple of accomplishment.

PIPE — To look; to spy on; to observe.

PIPE DOWN — Be quiet; cease talking.

PISTOL ROUTE — Death by shooting.

PITCHMAN — A fakir or peddler of novelties or small pieces of merchandise who works in the streets, etc.

PIVOT — To solicit for immoral purposes.

PLANT — A pre-arranged job or crime.

PLANT — A hiding-place for loot.

PLANT — To bury, as loot or a corpse; to arrange a situation.

PLAY — To scheme or gamble on success as in a hold-up or robbery.

PLAY BALL — "To go along"; to help.

PLAY THE DOZENS — To curse one another.

PLUG — To shoot; to work hard.

POGEY — A jail or workhouse.

POKES — A purse or money bag.

POKE — To strike.

POLISH THE MUG — To wash the hands and face.

PONCE — A young man maintained by a woman of means as a lover.

POOCH — A dog or pet.

POOR FISH — Any individual regarded as deficient.

POP OFF — To talk wildly or in a threatening manner; to argue.

PORK — A corpse.

POSSESH — A possession, but generally applied only to "prushun."

POULTICE — A dish of bread and gravy.

POUND THE EAR — To sleep.

POWDER — A drink of liquor.

POWDER — To go away; to pass by, to flee.

POWDER UP — To drink; to become intoxicated.

PRATT — The buttocks.

PRIVATE — A private house; a home.

PROP — A diamond pin or stud.

PROWL — An investigational work; especially one taken for the purpose of planning a robbery or estimating the opportunities for one.

PROWL — To look for information.

PROWL — To burglarize.

PROWLER — A sneak thief.

PRUSHUN — A boy enslaved by an older tramp or "jocker."

PUFF — Powder to be employed in blowing a safe.

PULL — Influence. "Drag."

PULL THE PIN — To quit work; to leave; to go away.

PUNK — Bread.

PUNK — A passive homosexual.

PUNK — Of little account; displeasing; worthless.

PUNK AND GUT — Bread and cheese.

PUSH — A crowd; a gang or clique.

PUSHER — Boss of a working gang, who pushes the work along.

PUSH OVER — Any easy job or a crime easy to commit without fear of detection.

PUSH OVER — A prostitute or any other easily obtained woman.

PUSH OVER — Easily defeated.

PUT THE BLOCKS TO — To have intercourse.

PUT THE BOOTS TO — To kick a person after having been knocked down.

Q — The C. B. & Q. Railroad.

Q.T. — The quiet; on the "Q.T."

QUACK — A prison doctor.

QUAIL — An underage girl; a "chicken-hearted" man.

QUEER — Counterfeit money.

QUEER — Crooked; criminal.

QUEER — An effeminate or degenerate man or boy.

RABBIT FEVER — The effect on some inmates when they are placed on the "Farm" or any outside detail; a temptation to "lam."

RACE — To extort; to run after for money, especially applied to the methods of "pimps" and "gold diggers."

RACKET — Any "graft" or type of criminal activity.

RACKETEER — One who operates a "racket."

RAG — A newspaper.

RAG — A woman.

RAG HEAD — An Oriental, one who wears a turban.

RAG HOUSE — A tent.

RAGS — Clothing.

RAIL — A railroad worker.

RAILROAD BULL — A railroad policeman or detective.

RAKE — A comb.

RAMBLER — A high-class tramp or hobo, one who rides only fast passenger trains.

RAMBLING — Travelling at high speed.

RANK — A poorly handled crime or job of work.

RANK — To inform on a pal.

RANK — Poor, worthless; disagreeable.

RANKED — To be seen or recognized while committing a crime.

RAP — Any sort of betrayel or indiscretion, in the sense a blow has been struck at another, or at his safety.

RAP — An identification, as by a witness to a crime.

RAP — A nod or to greet; to acknowledge a greeting.

RAP — A prison sentence.

RAP PARTNER — An accomplice; associate in a crime.

RAPE HOUND — A sex offender.

RAPE TOOLS — The glans, penis and testes.

RAPPER — The principal witness or complainant in a criminal case.

RAT — One not to be trusted; a "squealer" or "stool."

RAT — To inform or betray.

RAT CRUSHER — A box-car burglar.

RATTLER — A passenger train or fast freight.

RAZOR BACK — A roustabout or circus laborer.

RAWHIDE — To work desperately. To force others to work.

RAWHIDER — A hard worker; a severe taskmaker.

REACH — To bribe; to intimidate or buy off a complainant.

READERS — Marked playing cards.

RECORD — A history of a criminal's career.

RECRUIT — A newly "converted" thief or prostitute.

RED BALL — A fast freight.

RED CROSS — Morphine.

RED EYE — Caught in the act of a crime.

RED EYE — Liquor; an egg, especially when fried.

RED HANDED — Caught in the act of a crime.

RED LEAD — Catsup.

RED ONE — A poor business stand.

RED LIGHT — To do away with.

REEFER — A refrigerator car.

REEFER — A marijuana smoker.

REEFER DEN — A resort where marijuana furnishes the stimulation.

REEFER — A marijuana cigarette.

REEFING — Securing a wallet or pocket-book from the pocket of a victim by working up the lining of the pocket between the fingers until the article is easily reached.

REGULAR — One who conforms to the usages of the underworld.

REGULAR — Trustworthy; reliable.

RELIEVERS — Shoes.

REP. — Reputation.

REPEATER — One continually in trouble; one who has served more than one prison sentence.

RHINO — Money; cash.

RIB — To josh or kid.

RIB UP — A frame-up; an arrangement; a pre-arranged deal.

RIDE — To mistreat or annoy; to bully. usually over a long period of time.

RIDING THE RODS — Riding on the braces beneath a car.

RIGGING — A gamblers' "harness."

RIGHT — Sympathetic; a criminal's friend or associate.

RIGHT GUY — A "Square" dealer.

RIGHTY — A "double" or one who looks enough like another to be taken for him; a disguise.

RINGER — Something or someone introduced into a game of chance or into a shady deal to give an unfair advantage; an accomplice.

RING TAIL — A grouchy individual.

RISE — To stir into action.

RISER — Anything that stirs to action.

ROAD — Railroads and highways.

ROAD STAKE — Money to live on while travelling, or with which to secure transportation.

ROAR — A protest or complaint.

ROCK — A diamond or other precious stone.

ROD — A pistol or revolver.

ROLL — Money.

ROLL — To rob a drunken or sleeping person.
ROOTIN TOOTIN OIL — Sperm.
ROPE — A hangman's noose.
ROOTING — Robbing.
ROSCOE — A pistol or revolver.
ROT GUT — Poor liquor.
ROUNDER — A "good fellow," a free spender.
ROUST — To crowd against a person or push into a crowd to permit the picking of a pocket in the confusion.
ROWDY DOWDY — The hustling and shoving about by a pickpocket mob.
RUBBER CHECK — A worthless check.
RUB OUT — To kill.
RUBE — A farmer; an outsider; a stranger to any circle of life.
RUMBLE — To recognize.
RUMBLE — A recognition or acknowledgement.
RUM DUM — Intoxicated to the point of foolishness.
RUMMY — A drunkard.
RUMMY — Nervously disorganized from drinks or drugs.
RUN AROUND — To avoid or to fail to meet at a pre-arranged point.
RUNNER — A "Trusty" or messenger.
RUST EATER — A track layer or steel worker.
RUSTLE — To secure; ability to locate and acquire by any means.
RUSTLER — One who rustles; a thief.

SAC — Sacramento, California.
SACK — The stomach.
SALES-LADY — A prostitute.
SAN BERDOO — San Bernardino, California.
SAND — Sugar.
SAND — Courage; nerces; "guts."
SAP — A fool or sap-head.
SAP — A policeman's club or billy.
SAP — To beat.
SATCHEL — The buttocks.
SAVVY — To understand; to know; to realize.
SAW-BONES — A physician.
SAW BUCK — A ten-dollar bill.
SAW BUCK — A ten years' sentence.
SCAB — A strike-breaker.
SCISSORS BILL — An outsider to any circle or clique; an inefficient worker.
SCOFF — To eat.
SCOTT JACK — Money for food.
SCORE — The proceeds of a robbery or buglary.
SCRAM — To leave hastily.
SCRAM HEAT — Same as "Rabbit Fever."
SCRAPS THE MUG — To shave.
SCRATCH — Money, especially banknotes.
SCRATCH — To forge.

SCRATCH HOUSE — A cheap lodging house or brothel.

SCRATCH MAN — A forger.

SCREW — A prison guard; a turnkey; or a jailer.

SCREW — Sexual intercourse.

SCREWBALL — A simple-minded person.

SCREWY — A simple-minded person; crazy; insane.

SETTLE — To arrange or "fix."

SETTLED — Imprisoned.

SET-UP — A pre-arranged deal; an "easy" proposition; a likely spot for a robbery.

SEWER HOGS — Ditch diggers.

SHADOW — One who follows or keeps under surveillance.

SHADOW — To follow or trail to observe.

SHAG — A chase or organized pursuit by the police or an irate citizenry.

SHAG — Sexual intercourse.

SHAKE DOWN — To force a contribution.

SHAKEDOWN — A search of a prisoner's person, cell or assignment.

SHARK — A professional in a certain line.

SHARPEN UP — To practice, as at picking pockets, etc.

SHELL — An egg.

SHELL OUT — To contribute or donate, usually under protest.

SHEEPSKIN — A pardon from the Governor or President.

SHEET — The record of a criminal's career as recorded by the Police Dept.

SHEETS — Newspapers.

SHILL — A decoy for a confidence game.

SHINE — A Negro.

SHIV — A knife.

SHIVE — A razor. "Shiv."

SHONNICKER — A Jewish pawnbroker.

SHORT — An automobile.

SHOT — Same as the two definitions for "Big Shot."

SHOVER — One who passes or "shoves" counterfeit money.

SHOVING THE QUEER — Passing counterfeit money, checks or money orders.

SHOW UP — The daily inspection of newly captured prisoners at Police Headquarters.

SHROUD — A suit of clothes.

SIDE KICK — A partner or friend.

SIMPLE — Simple-minded.

SIMP — A simple-minded or foolish person; one easily led.

SING — To complain.

SING — To inform.

SINGLE "O" — One working a lone "game" or racket.

SINKERS — Doughnuts or crullers.

SITTING PRETTY — Contented; happy; well off.

SKELTON SCREW — A master key or key.

SKIN — To cheat or defraud.

SKINS — Paper money.

SKINNING A POKE — Taking the money and other valuables from a stolen wallet.

SKINNER — A mule driver or teamster.

SKIP IT — Forget what was said. "Forget it."

SKIPPER — One in authority; the boss.

SKIRT — A woman.

SKUNK — One not to be trusted.

SKUNK — To cheat or defraud; to inform.

SKYPIECE — A hat.

SKY PILOT — A minister.

SLAM — To strike; to hit.

SLANT-EYE — An Oriental.

SLAP HAPPY — Simple-minded; foolish; said to be caused by chronic masturbation.

SLEIGH RIDE — To cheat by a false story or by sharp practice.

SLEIGH RIDE — A debauch on heroin.

SLICKED UP — Well dressed.

SLICKER — A skillful crook.

SLIDES — Shoes.

SLIP-INS — Vaseline, etc., used by pederasts in committing sodomy.

SLOP — Beer.

SLOP UP — To become intoxicated.

SLOUGH — To strike or assault.

SLOUGHED — Arrested.

SLUG — A bullet.

SLUG — To strike or hit.

SLUGGER — A hired intimidator; thug.

SLUT — A loose girl or woman.

SLUM — Cheap jewelry.

SMACKER — One dollar, especially a silver dollar.

SMARTEN UP — To advise or explain to.

SMARTEN UP — "Get wise."

SMOKE — Cheap liquor.

SMOKE — To shoot.

SMOKE POLE — A pistol or revolver.

SMOKY SEAT — The electric chair.

SMUDGE — A small camp fire.

SMUTS — Obscene pictures or postcards.

SNAG — To commit pederasty.

SNAILS — Cinnamon rolls.

SNAKE — A crooked individual.

SNARK — An informer.

SNEAK — To leave; to stroll away in a casual manner so as to divert suspicion.

SNEAKERS — Slippers.

SNIFFER — A cocaine addict.

SNIFTER — A drink of liquor.

SNIPE — A cigarette stub.

SNIPE SHOOTING — Picking cigarette stubs from the street or sidewalk.

SNIPS — Scissors; wire cutters.

SNITCH — A tale-bearer; a spy; or "stool."

SNITCH — To inform on one's partner or fellows.

SOUTH GATE DISCHARGE — At Stateville prison, when an inmate dies and his body is removed in a pine box through the South Gate.

SPEAR — To obtain.

SPEED BALL — A glass of wine, or more especially when "doped."

SPIEL — A "ghost story"; a speech; a grind.

SPIELER — A "grinder" or ballyhoo man; a fast, able dancer.

SPIKE — To upset a plan or prevent the accomplishment of a design.

SPILL YOUR GUTS — To confess; to break a confidence.

SPLIT — A share of loot.

SPLIT — To divide, as loot.

SPLON — A drug addict.

SPOILED WATER — Lemonade or other "soft" drinks.

SMOKE WAGON — A pistol or revolver.

SPOT — To discover; to place in a pre-arranged locality or spot.

SPOTTER — An employee paid to spy on other workers.

SPOTTER — One looking over the scene of a projected crime for a band of thieves or other criminals.

SPRING — To free from jail or prison.

SPUDS — Potatoes.

SQUARE — To settle for; to arrange; to pay off.

SQUARE — Honest or above board.

SQUARE IT — When a matter has been arranged or "settled."

SQUARE SHOOTER — A fair and square associate or acquaintance.

SQUARE JOHN — Same as "square shooter." An honest citizen.

SQUAWK — A complaint; a cry.

SQUAWK — To inform; to cry out; to complain.

SQUAWKER — A dissatisfied customer; or one who, having been defrauded makes a "squawk or complaint."

SQUEAL — To inform, or to betray a secret. The ultimate crime in the underworld.

SQUEALER — An informer or police spy.

STACH — To hide or conceal, as loot.

STACK — To hide or conceal, as loot.

STAKE — To advance or loan money to another.

STALL — A pickpocket's partner, the man who jostles the victim in order that the "wire" may work to better advantage.

STALL — To delay; to pretend; to fence for time.

STALL — To loaf.

STARVATION RATIONS — Meals, as designated by prison inmates.

STASH — To hide or conceal, as loot.

STEAM UP — To become intoxicated; to become angry.

STEER — An advice or direction.

STEER — To advise or direct.

STEM — A road or street.

STEMMER — One who begs on the street.

STEW — A drunkard.

STEW BUM — A drunkard.

STICK — To remain with; to stand by.

STICK — To defraud or cheat.

STICKER — A knife; a scarf pin.

STICK-UP — A robbery.

STICK-UP MAN — A robber.

STICKS — The country; an outlying district of a city.

STICKS — Matches.

STIFF — A corpse.

STIFF — A conceited man.

STIFF — Dead drunk; stiff as a corpse.

STIFF — A note.

STILTS — Crutches.

STING — To cheat or defraud.

STINGER — The tongue.

STINKER — An onion.

STIR — A prison.

STIR BUG — One who has become slightly simple-minded or actually insane from long confinement.

STONE JOHN — A jail or prison.

STOOL — An informer or sneak.

STOOL — To inform on one's friends or associates in the underworld.

STOOL PIGEON — Same as "Stool."

STOP OVER — A short jail sentence.

STRAIGHT — Honest; reliable; to be trusted.

STREETS — Freedom, the outside world as designated by prisoners in confinement.

STRETCH — A prison sentence.

STRETCH — To hang a person.

STRETCHERS — Shoe laces.

STRIDES — Trousers.

STRING — To mislead or jolly along to a desired end.

STRONG ARM — A hold-up man, one who steals by virtue of his strength.

STRONG ARM — A hired thug or guard.

STRONG ARM — An assault — to beat; to rob by violence.

SUCKER — An easy mark, one who will believe anything he is told.

SUCKER — The victim of a thief or gang.

SUCKING BAMBOO — Smoking opium, the pipe being usually of bamboo.

SUGAR — Money.

SUGAR DADDY — An elderly man supporting or contributing to the support of a "gold digger" or other loose girl or woman.

SUPER. — A superintendent.

SWEAT — To worry.

SWEAT — To give the third degree.

SHUT EYE — Sleep.

SNOOPER — An intruder.

SCALLION SKINNERS — At Stateville prison, those inmates assigned to work in the vegetable room.

SWAP LIES AND SWAT FLIES — What a prison inmate does to pass the time during a sojourn in solitary confinement.

TAIL — One who follows or trails.

TAIL — The buttocks.

TAIL — Sexual intercourse.

TAIL — To follow or shadow.

TAKE — Proceeds of an entertainment or show.

TAKE — To cheat or defraud.

TAKE FOR A RIDE — To take an unwanted or untrustworthy gang member or an enemy for an automobile ride, the purpose being to kill the victim away from the city or in an infrequented street, and left there.

TALENT — Clever crooks.

TAMP UP — To assault or beat.

TANKED — Intoxicated.

TANK UP — To drink to excess.

THE FRONT — At Stateville prison, the Administration Building.

THE SCHOOL — The Pontiac, Illinois Penitentiary, formerly a Reformatory, as referred to by prisoners in the Joliet Penitentiaries.

THIN ONE — A dime.

THIRD RAIL — Strong, cheap liquor.

THROW ONE'S GUTS — To tell everything one knows; to break confidence; to confess.

TICKER — The heart.

TICKER — A watch.

TICKET — A summons given a violator of prison rules to report at Solitary for hearing; or a summons to report to some assignment for varied purposes.

TIN EAR — To eavesdrop; to listen with special care.

TIP — An advice; a bit of information.

TIP OFF — An information or advice.

TIP OFF — To enlighten or warn.

TIP UP — To inform or "squeal."

TOGS — Clothes.

TONGUE — An attorney.

TOOL — An individual used as an instrument to attain an end by another or others.

TOOL — A pickpocket.

TOO TIGHT — Too bad; sorry.

TOP — The head.

TOP — To hang.

TOPS — Sincere; trustworthy.

TORCH — A revolver or pistol.

TORCH — An arsonist.

TORPEDO — A gunman; a bodyguard for a "big shot."

TOUCH — The act of borrowing.

TOUT — One who gives tips on race horses, usually for a fee.

TRAP — A place of concealment.
TRIGGER MAN — An assassin or gunman.
TRIM — To defraud or cheat.
TROUPER — An actor.
TRUSTY — A prisoner allowed special privileges after having been on good behavior.
TUMBLE — A recognition.
TUMBLE — To become aware; to be "wise."
TURN DOWN — To refuse an application or request.
TWIST — A woman, especially one with loose or "twisted" morals.
TYPEWRITER — A machine gun.
TAKE IT EASY — Banal idiom used by inmates upon greeting one another.

UNDER COVER — Hiding.
UNDER COVER — Proceeding with an enterprise in a secret manner.
UNDER COVER MAN — A employer's detective or spotter watching the workers without their knowledge.
UNDERGROUND — Anything done in an underhanded manner. A prison guard, who, for sufficient remuneration will take letters out or bring in contraband for inmates.
UNDERGROUND KITE — A letter sent out of a prison by an inmate in some manner other than that authorized by the rules of the institution.
UNLOAD — To get rid of, as something of doubtful or little value.
UNMUGGED — Not listed on police records; a criminal not as yet identified or "wanted" by the police.
UP AND UP — Successful; doing well; to be trusted.
UPHOLSTERED — Infected with a venereal disease.
UP THE RIVER — Any prison.

V — Five dollars.
V — A five years' prison sentence.
VAG — A vagrant.
VAG — To arrest and sentence as a vagrant. "He was vagged."
VAGINA VANDAL — A convicted rapist.

WAKE-UP — The day of release from prison.
WEED — To take money from one's pocket as a donation to a beggar.
WEED — To take more than one's share of loot.
WEED — Tobacco.
WEEDING A POKE — See "skinning a poke."
WEEPING AND WAITING — Waiting in jail to learn the result of an appeal for a new trial.
WHACK IT — Self-abuse. Masturbation.
WHACK SILLY — A self-abuse victim. Simple-minded; foolish.
WHEEL — Same as "shot" and "Big Shot."
WHEEL — A local dignitary (prison) in convict clothing who will do anything for you — for six packs.
WHIRL — A trial or attempt; a "go" at a crime.
WHITE CROSS — Cocaine.
WHITE MAN — A good fellow; a trusted individual.

WHITE MULE — Corn liquor.

WHITE TOP — At the Joliet prisons, prison officers of the Captain and Lieutenant rank, the top portion of their uniform cap being white.

WHIZ — A fast or unusually capable worker.

WHIZZ COPS — Pickpocket detectives.

WING DING — A farcial method of a prison inmate of impressing authorities that he is mentally deranged, so that he may be placed in Nut Alley (Detention Hospital) where he can scoff the best viands in the joint.

WINGLESS PIGEON — A "bird" of the "stool" variety; an informer.

WINGS — Cocaine.

WINGY — A man with one "wing" or arm.

WIRE — A pickpocket.

WISE — Knowing; aware of what impends; possessed of "inside" information or knowledge shared by but a few.

WISE GUY — A "Smart Aleck" or "know it all."

WOLF — A "Jocker"; an active part male pervert.

WOOD-BUTCHER — A carpenter.

WOODEN MONEY — Counterfeit money.

WOOD HEAD — A woodsman or lumberman.

WOODY — Insane; stupid.

WOP — An Italian.

WORKING PLUG — A laborer or workman.

WORK OVER — To administer the "third degree," or to mistreat a prisoner; to assault.

WORKS — Everything; the end or termination; to kill.

WORKS — A passive part male pervert.

WREN — A young woman or girl.

WRONG — Contrary to the underworld's belief.

WRONG GUY — One not to be trusted.

YAKYDOCK — A concoction made by prison inmates, consisting of the fermented juice of potatoes, raisins, prunes, and containing yeast. (Usually hidden in a big jar or vat, in some hiding place, and left to ferment for two weeks or more.)

YAP — A farmer; newcomer; greenhorn.

YAP — The mouth.

YARD DICK — A railroad detective.

YEGG — A thief.

YELLOW — Cowardly; lacking in nerve.

YEN — Opium or the opium habit.

YEN — A yearning.

YEN SHEE — Opium.

YIP — To cry out; to complain.

ZOO — A prison or jail.

ZOOK — A worn-out old prostitute.

Appendix C

EXAMPLES OF INSTITUTIONAL
FORMS AND RECORDS

Fig. 1. This form is used by the Chief Guard's Office when a bulletin is issued by Warden Ragen. It is signed by the Lieutenants and Captains to show that they have read the bulletin.

Fig. 2. This form is used to list all Exempt items that inmates purchase, such as: watches, shoes, razors, clothing, pipes, pen and pencils and athletic equipment. The date of each purchase is listed, also, the amount.

Fig. 3. This form is used by inmates who are out of grade and those inmates are limited to only the necessities, such as, toilet articles, legal papers, stationery, smoking tobacco. The Officer in charge instructs each clerk as to what articles these inmates may purchase.

Fig. 4. When an inmate buys a Pie (1.15) the clerk issues a ticket of this form to the inmate. The serial number is taken from the face of this ticket and entered on the inmate's trade ticket.

Fig. 5. When an inmate buys chocolate milk, the clerk fills out this form and enters the serial number on the back of the inmate's trade ticket.

Fig. 6. When an inmate purchases Ice Cream he is issued a ticket such as this one. The clerk waiting on the customer enters the serial number of this ticket on back of the inmate's trade slip. Should any descrepancy occur, a quick and accurate check can be made. These tickets are retained by the Commissary after delivery of Ice Cream.

Fig. 7. An inmate is permitted to buy up to seven quarts of milk per week. A ticket of this kind is issued to the inmate for each quart of milk purchased. The serial number of this ticket is entered on back of the inmate's trade slip. As the inmate requests milk to be delivered, he turns this ticket in to the Cell House Commissary man. When delivery is made, the inmate delivering the milk picks up a ticket for each quart delivered. In turn, these are checked against the inmate's trade slips to ascertain the amount of milk sold against the amount delivered.

Fig. 8. When an inmate purchases bonds, his amount of bonds purchased and the balance are carried on this card. The amounts of purchases are given to the clerk by the Officer in charge, and the clerk enters the information on this card.

Fig. 9. This form is used for Weekly Inventory report for the General Kitchen.

Fig. 10. This form used by General Store Stockroom to procure printing orders from Vocational School.

Fig. 11. This form is used to record issues from Basement Stock, items not on hand in Stockroom.

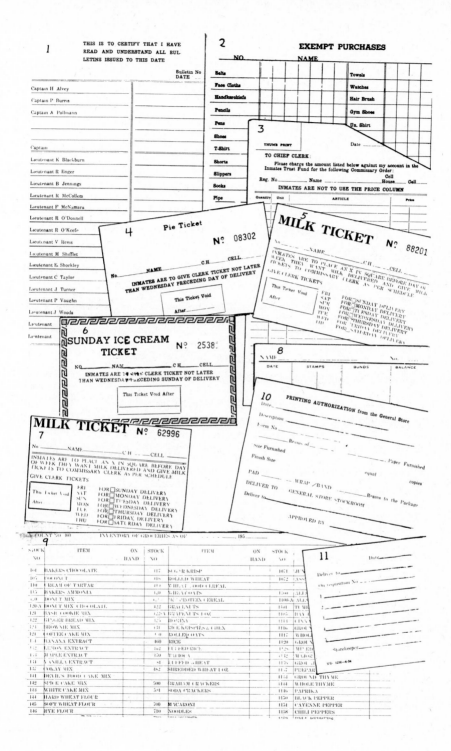

1

THIS IS TO CERTIFY THAT I HAVE
READ AND UNDERSTAND ALL BUL-
LETINS ISSUED TO THIS DATE

Bulletin No
DATE

Captain H Alvey

Captain P Burris

Captain A Pollmann

Captain

Lieutenant K Blackburn

Lieutenant R Enger

Lieutenant B Jennings

Lieutenant R McCollem

Lieutenant F McNamara

Lieutenant R O'Donnell

Lieutenant R O'Keefe

Lieutenant V Revis

Lieutenant M Shifflet

Lieutenant E Shockley

Lieutenant C Taylor

Lieutenant J Turner

Lieutenant P Vaughn

Lieutenant J Woods

Lieutenant

Lieutenant

2 EXEMPT PURCHASES

NO. NAME

Belts		Towels
Face Cloths		Watches
Handkerchiefs		Hair Brush
Pencils		Gym Shoes
Pens		Un. Shirt
Shoes		
T-Shirt		
Shorts		
Slippers		
Socks		
Pipe		

3

THUMB PRINT   Date

TO CHIEF CLERK :
Please charge the amount listed below against my account in the
Inmates Trust Fund for the following Commissary Order:

Reg. No _____ Name _____ Cell House ____ Cell ____

INMATES ARE NOT TO USE THE PRICE COLUMN

| Quantity | Unit | ARTICLE | Price |

4 Pie Ticket   N°. 08302

No ____ NAME ____ C.H. ____ CELL ____
INMATES ARE TO GIVE CLERK TICKET NOT LATER
THAN WEDNESDAY PRECEDING DAY OF DELIVERY

This Ticket Void

After ____

5 MILK TICKET   N°. 88201

No ____ NAME ____ C.H ____ CELL ____
INMATES ARE TO PLACE AN X IN SQUARE BEFORE DAY OF
WEEK THEY WANT MILK DELIVERED AND GIVE MILK
TICKETS TO COMMISSARY CLERK AS PER SCHEDULE
GIVE CLERK TICKETS

This Ticket Void
After ____

FRI   FOR SUNDAY DELIVERY
SAT   FOR MONDAY DELIVERY
SUN   FOR TUESDAY DELIVERY
MON   FOR WEDNESDAY DELIVERY
TUE   FOR THURSDAY DELIVERY
WED   FOR FRIDAY DELIVERY
THU   FOR SATURDAY DELIVERY

6 SUNDAY ICE CREAM TICKET   N°. 2538?

NO ____ NAM ____ C H ____ CELL ____
INMATES ARE TO GIVE CLERK TICKET NOT LATER
THAN WEDNESDAY PRECEDING SUNDAY OF DELIVERY

This Ticket Void After ____

7 MILK TICKET   N°. 62996

No ____ NAME ____ C H ____ CELL ____
INMATES ARE TO PLACE AN X IN SQUARE BEFORE DAY
OF WEEK THEY WANT MILK DELIVERED AND GIVE MILK
TICKETS TO COMMISSARY CLERK AS PER SCHEDULE
GIVE CLERK TICKETS

This Ticket Void
After ____

FRI   FOR □ SUNDAY DELIVERY
SAT   FOR □ MONDAY DELIVERY
SUN   FOR □ TUESDAY DELIVERY
MON   FOR □ WEDNESDAY DELIVERY
TUE   FOR □ THURSDAY DELIVERY
WED   FOR □ FRIDAY DELIVERY
THU   FOR □ SATURDAY DELIVERY

8

NAME ____ No. ____

| DATE | STAMPS | BONDS | BALANCE |

10 PRINTING AUTHORIZATION from the General Store

Date ____
Description ____
Form No ____
Size Furnished ____   Reams of ____
Finish Size ____   Paper Furnished ____
                                        equal
PAD ____ WRAP /BAND ____   copies
DELIVER TO ____
Deliver to ____ GENERAL STORE STOCKROOM ____ Reams to the Package

APPROVED BY ____

9

COUNT NO 860   INVENTORY OF GROCERIES AS OF ____ 195 ____

STOCK NO.	ITEM	ON HAND	STOCK NO	ITEM	ON HAND	STOCK NO.	
101	BAKERS CHOCOLATE		117	SUGAR KRISP		101	
107	COCONUT		118	ROLLED WHEAT		102	
110	CREAM OF TARTAR		119	WHEAT FOOD CEREAL		103	
115	BAKERS AMMONIA		120	WHEAT OATS		100	
120	DONUT MIX		121	2K PROTEIN CEREAL		105	
120-A	DONUT MIX CHOCOLATE		122	BRAZIL NUTS		106	
121	BASIC COOKIE MIX		122-A	BRAZIL NUTS 1 OZ		107	
122	GINGER BREAD MIX		125	HOMINY		111	
123	BROWNIE MIX		131	RICE KRISPIES & CHEX		116	
124	COFFEE CAKE MIX		139	ROLLED OATS		117	
144	BANANA EXTRACT		160	RICE		120	
132	LEMON EXTRACT		162	PUFFED RICE		128	
133	MAPLE EXTRACT		169	TAPIOCA		112	
134	VANILLA EXTRACT		81	PUFFED WHEAT		112	
135	COLA? MIX		482	SHREDDED WHEAT 1 OZ		117	
141	DEVILS FOOD CAKE MIX					113	GROUND THYME
142	SPICE CAKE MIX		500	GRAHAM CRACKERS		114	WHOLE THYME
143	WHITE CAKE MIX		501	SODA CRACKERS		116	PAPRIKA
144	HARD WHEAT FLOUR					1150	BLACK PEPPER
145	SOFT WHEAT FLOUR		700	MACARONI		1151	CAYENNE PEPPER
146	RYE FLOUR		710	NOODLES		1158	CHILI PEPPERS

11

Date ____
Deliver to ____
On requisition No ____
1 ____
2 ____
3 ____
4 ____
Storekeeper ____

VS - 12M—4-54

Fig. 12. This form is used for Weekly Inventory of Shoes.

Fig. 13. This form is used for Weekly Inventory of Clothing Room.

Fig. 14. This form is used for making inventory lists on Tear Gas and Ammunition that is kept in the Armory.

Fig. 15. Armory. This form is used for making a report on the condition of the trip and the bus. This is for transferring inmates from one Institution to another. The one who uses this form is the bus driver.

Fig. 16. Used as pages for gallery books.

Fig. 17. Gate Number One. Used for employees to sign in and out for work.

Fig. 18. Cell House. Record of inspection of vents in cell house.

Fig. 19. Any Officer. Laundry slip that must accompany Officer's laundry to the Institution Laundry.

Fig. 20. Clothing Room. This form is issued to inmate by the Officer in charge of the Clothing Room and inmate must have it to draw clothing from the Clothing Room.

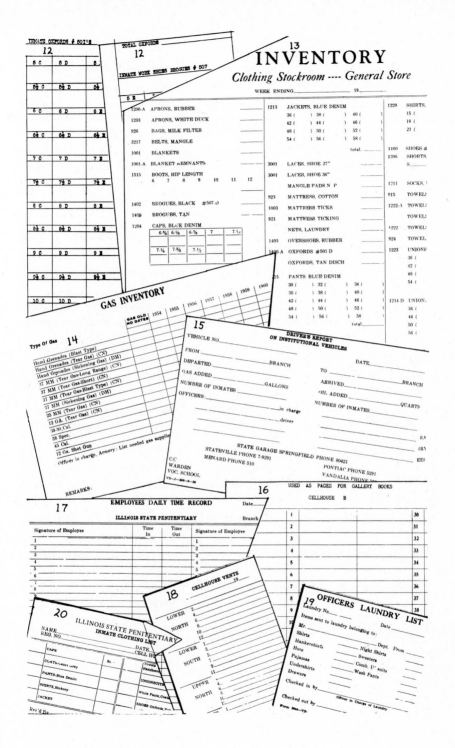

12

INMATE OXFORDS & 501'S

5 C	5 D	5 E
5½ C	5½ D	5½ E
6 C	6 D	6 E
6½ C	6½ D	6½ E
7 C	7 D	7 E
7½ C	7½ D	7½ E
8 C	8 D	8 E
8½ C	8½ D	8½ E
9 C	9 D	9 E
9½ C	9½ D	9½ E
10 C	10 D	

12

TOTAL OXFORDS

INMATE WORK SHOES BROGUES & 507

5 E

1200-A	APRONS, RUBBER	
1203	APRONS, WHITE DUCK	
926	BAGS, MILK FILTER	
3217	BELTS, MANGLE	
1001	BLANKETS	
1001-A	BLANKET REMNANTS	
1515	BOOTS, HIP LENGTH	
	6 7 8 9 10 11 12	
1402	BROGUES, BLACK #507-D	
1409	BROGUES, TAN	
1204	CAPS, BLUE DENIM	

| 6-¾ | 6-⅞ | 6-⅞ | 7 | 7-⅛ |
| 7-¼ | 7-⅜ | 7-½ | | |

13
INVENTORY
Clothing Stockroom ---- General Store

WEEK ENDING_____ 19____

1213	JACKETS, BLUE DENIM		1220	SHIRTS,
	36 ( ) 38 ( ) 40 ( )			15 (
	42 ( ) 44 ( ) 46 ( )			18 (
	48 ( ) 50 ( ) 52 ( )			21 (
	54 ( ) 56 ( ) 58 ( )			
	total_____		1400	SHOES #
			1306	SHORTS,
3001	LACES, SHOE 27"			S_____
3001	LACES, SHOE 36"			
	MANGLE PADS N P		1211	SOCKS,
923	MATTRESS, COTTON		915	TOWELS
1003	MATTRESS TICKS		1222-A	TOWELS
921	MATTRESS TICKING			TOWELS
	NETS, LAUNDRY		1222	TOWELS
1403	OVERSHOES, RUBBER		924	TOWEL
1400-A	OXFORDS #501-D		1223	UNIONS
	OXFORDS, TAN DISCH			36 (
1215	PANTS BLUE DENIM			42 (
	30 ( ) 32 ( ) 34 ( )			48 (
	36 ( ) 38 ( ) 40 ( )			54 (
	42 ( ) 44 ( ) 46 ( )		1214-D	UNION,
	48 ( ) 50 ( ) 52 ( )			36 (
	54 ( ) 56 ( ) 58			44 (
	total_____			50 (
				56 (

GAS INVENTORY

Type Of Gas	14	GAS OLD NO DATES	1954	1955	1956	1957	1958	1959	1960
Hand Grenades (Blast Type) (CN)									
Hand Grenades (Tear Gas) (DM)									
Hand Grenades (Sickening Gas) (CN)									
37 MM (Tear Gas-Long Range) (CN)									
37 MM (Tear Gas-Short) (CN)									
37 MM (Tear Gas-Blast Type) (CN)									
37 MM (Sickening Gas) (DM)									
25 MM (Tear Gas) (CN)									
12 GA. (Tear Gas) (CN)									
30-30 Cal.									
38 Spec.									
45 Cal.									
12 Ga. Shot Gun									
Officer in charge, Armory : List needed gas supplies									

REMARKS:

15

DRIVER'S REPORT
ON INSTITUTIONAL VEHICLES

VEHICLE NO._____

FROM_____

DEPARTED_____ BRANCH_____   DATE_____

GAS ADDED_____ GALLONS   TO_____

NUMBER OF INMATES_____   ARRIVED_____ BRANCH_____

OFFICERS_____   OIL ADDED_____

_____in charge   NUMBER OF INMATES_____ QUARTS

_____driver

STATE GARAGE SPRINGFIELD PHONE 80421
STATEVILLE PHONE 7-9291
MENARD PHONE 510

PONTIAC PHONE 5291
VANDALIA PHONE

C.C
WARDEN
VOC. SCHOOL
VS-J-306-6-58

16   USED AS PAGES FOR GALLERY BOOKS

CELLHOUSE B

17   EMPLOYEES DAILY TIME RECORD   Date_____

ILLINOIS STATE PENITENTIARY   Branch_____

Signature of Employee	Time In	Time Out	Signature of Employee
1			1
2			2
3			3
4			4
5			5
6			6
7			
8			
9			

1		30
2		31
3		32
4		33
5		34
6		35
7		36
8		37
9		38
10		

18   CELLHOUSE VENTS   19__

LOWER NORTH	2 4 6 8 10 12
LOWER SOUTH	3 5 7 9 11
UPPER NORTH	4 8

19   OFFICERS LAUNDRY LIST

Laundry No._____

Mr._____   Date_____

Items sent to laundry belonging to:_____

Shirts	Dept. From_____
Handkerchiefs	
Hose	Night Shirts
Pajamas	Sweaters
Undershirts	Comb. U suits
Drawers	Wash Pants

Checked in by_____

Checked out by_____   Officer in Charge of Laundry

Form 3644-V5

20   ILLINOIS STATE PENITENTIARY
INMATE CLOTHING LIST

NAME_____
REG. NO._____

DATE_____
CELL HO_____

CAPS				
COATS, Levit Grey	Sz.		Towels
PANTS, Blue Denim			Handkers
			UNIONSUITS
SHIRTS, Hickory			White Pants, Chef
JACKET			SHOES Oxfords

Rec'd By_____

Fig. 21. Any Assignment. This slip is used to accompany inmate's laundry to the Institution Laundry.

Fig. 22. Warden's Apartment or Assistant Warden's Apartment. Used to accompany any laundry for either the Warden's Apartment or Assistant Warden's Apartment to the Warden's Laundry.

Fig. 23. Officer in Charge of Transfer to Pontiac or Menard. Used as a receipt to be signed by Officer at either Pontiac or Menard. Re: personal property of inmate.

Fig. 24. Cell House. Record of inmates transferred from one cell house to another. This is a daily record.

Fig. 25. Any Tower. Daily report of equipment in tower. Turned into the Officer in the Armory.

Fig. 26. Any Assignment. Request to Power House Officer for light bulbs.

Fig. 27. Front Gate. Used to pass visitor in and out of the Institution. This pass must be signed by the visitor in the presence of the Officer at the Front Gate before entering the Institution and then must be signed again in the presence of an Officer before the visitor is passed through the Guard Hall on the way out of the Institution. This pass is used for Institution visits not for persons visiting inmates. It is the responsibility of the Officer who checks the signature in the Guard Hall to make certain that the signature is the same as the first one. He then initials same.

Fig. 28. Any Officer or Official of the Institution who is Furnished Their Food by the State of Illinois. Request to storekeeper for foodstuffs.

Fig. 29. Cell House. Used to show assignments of inmates and also designates color of inmate.

Fig. 30. Outside Detail Officer. Record of rail-road car and contents received at the Institution or passing through Sally Port.

Fig. 31. Officer's Kitchen and General Kitchen. Record of daily tool report. Kept in their respective files.

Fig. 32. Isolation. Pass slip for inmate from Isolation to assignment after release from Isolation.

Fig. 33. Power House. Count slip submitted by Officer in charge of Power House at count time, to Chief Guard's Office.

Fig. 34. General Store. Any item received at the General Store is recorded on this type of slip and kept on file in the General Store.

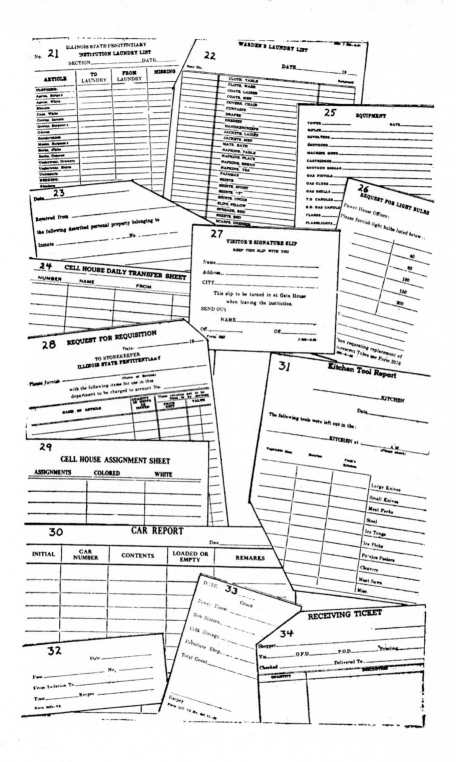

Fig. 35. Any Assignment. Used to report accident. Re: employee
or inmate.

Fig. 36. Personnel Office. Record of employee kept by Personnel Officer.

Fig. 37. Any Assignment. Pass ticket for inmate to and from assignment.
This ticket is signed by the Officer where ticket originates.

Fig. 38. Isolation Officer. Record of inmate doing time in Isolation.
This record is kept at Isolation.

Fig. 39. Cell House. Laundry list of inmate's laundry submitted by cell
house to Laundry.

Fig. 40. Information Desk (J. B.) and Mail Office, Stateville. Used to
show persons who have corresponded with and visited inmate. This record
is sent to the records office and is used by the Parole Board. This form
is used only for inmates who appear on the parole docket.

Fig. 41. Cell House. This form (signed by cell house keeper) accompanies
any piece of clothing sent from cell house to clothing room for repair.

Fig. 42. Outside Detail. Evening count slip prepared and turned into
count desk at Chief Guards' Office by Lieutenant in charge of Outside
Detail.

Fig. 43. Any Assignment. Used for making disciplinary report on inmate,
(violation of rules, etc.).

35

ACCIDENT CAUSE CLASSIFICATION

RESPONSIBILITY FOR ACCIDENT:

A. INJURED PERSON

B. FELLOW WORKER

C. OFFICER IN CHARGE

D. INSTITUTION

ACCIDENT CAUSES

1. OPERATING MACHINERY OR OTHER EQUIPMENT OR WORKING WITHOUT AUTHORITY
2. OPERATING OR WORKING AT UNSAFE SPEED
3. MAKING SAFETY DEVICES INOPERATIVE
4. USING IMPROPER TOOLS OR APPLIANCES
5. FILING OF MATERIALS.
6. MATERIAL HANDLING.
7. ASSUMING HAZARDOUS POSITION OR POSTURE.
8. WORKING ON MOVING OR DANGEROUS EQUIPMENT.
9. DISTRACTION, TEASING, ABUSING, AND STARTLING.
   FAILURE TO USE OR IMPROPER USE OF SAFE ATTIRE OR PROTECTIVE EQUIPMENT IMPROPER SIGNALS.

37
Pass Inmate Number_____
Name_____
To_____

Officer_____

3684-A   J-362—4-59

Date_____

42

OUTSIDE DETAIL EVENING COUNT

Officer _____   Date _____

Farm Detail

24-Hour Detail

Lock Count

Lay In

In

Total Detail Count

FORM 3598—VS—NO 434—9—

38
CELL HOUSE_____

DATE_____

IN   OUT

ISOLATION OFFICER

J-128—3-80

36   TIME SHEET

EMPLOYEES

Name	Entered Service	Occupation	
Resident Address	Street	City	County
Department	Left Service		
Rate	Change in Rate Due		Amount
Reason for Leaving			
Commutation			

19	July	Aug.	Sept.	Oct.	Nov	Dec.	Jan.	Feb.	Mar	Apr	May	June	19	July	Aug	Sept	Oct	Nov	Dec	Jan	Feb	Mar	Apr	May	June
1													1												
2													2												
3													3												
4													4												
5													5												
6													6												
7													7												
8													8												
9													9												

TOTAL SHIRTS **39** PANTS_____   CELL   HOUSE _____   JACKETS_____   MISC. _____   DATE_____

FORM No. 3689—YS

RELIEF	D	E	F	00	01	02	03	04	05	06	07	08	09	10	11	12	13	14	15	16	17	18
												30	31	32	33	34	35	36			

ILLINOIS STATE PENITENTIARY

INMATE REPORT   196_

43
No._____   Date_____
ASSIGNMENT_____
INMATE_____
Is Reported For_____

41
TO THE CLOTHING ROOM
Assignment_____
Reg. No_____   Date_____
Repair_____ Name_____

Officer_____

Form 3610—VS—77 2 80

48   53   **40**   VISITING RECORD—JOLIET PENITENTIARY

No._____   Name_____   Date_____

NAME		RELATIONSHIP

74   75   7_   79

Form 500—VS—Litho

Fig. 44. Laundry. Used to keep record of Officers' shirts and pants received at the laundry.

Fig. 45. Master Mechanic. This form is used by the Master Mechanic authorizing the repair of equipment. The stub is kept on file in the Master Mechanic's file and when the order is returned it is also filed.

Fig. 46. Mail Office. Used when Officer in charge of Mail Office interviews an inmate. Re: putting additional persons on his correspondent and visit list.

Fig. 47. Any Employee in Supervisory Capacity. Used to make a disciplinary report on an employee.

Fig. 48. Chief Guard. Daily count kept in Captain's Office. The count from this sheet is entered into a permanent ledger and it is kept in the Captain's Office.

Fig. 49. Cell House. Used by night Cell House Officer to show gallery count.

Fig. 50. Cell House. Record of daily gallery count.

Fig. 51. Mechanical Store. This card is used as a stock bin card. It designates the number of the particular stock; its description as well as its size and classification. Each bin carries one of these cards for identification of stock purposes.

Fig. 52. General Store and Mechanical Store. Record of stock and location.

Fig. 53. Any Assignment. Record of request to Armory officer for repair of lock.

Fig. 54. Segregation. Record of daily count.

44 — OFFICER'S SHIRT LIST

NUMBER	NAME	PANTS	SHIRTS	BUNDLES

50 — CELLHOUSE COUNT

DATE_____

GALLERY	COUNT	COUNTED BY
1		
2		
3		
4		
5		
6		
7		
8		
FLAG		
TOTAL		

OFFICER IN CHARGE CELLHOUSE

Form 3500—VS—J—397—6—56

45

MASTER MECHANIC'S ORDER NO._____ No. **Illinois State Penitentiary**

45 _____195_____ Master Mechanic's Office_____195____

Make: Repair: Furnish: Make: Repair: Furnish.

For_____ For_____

As per order_____

_____

Return this order promptly to the office when job is completed.
No work is to be done or material furnished without this order.

Master Mechanic

Form 3500-A—VS—34!—5-50

51

ITEM NO. _____   CLASS _____

SUB-CLASS _____   UNIT _____

J-528-8-58

46

Date_____

Inmate's Name _____ NUMBER _____

requests that the following person be added to his approved visiting and correspondence list:

NAME:_____

ADDRESS._____

AGE_____RELATIONSHIP_____OCCUPATION_____

INMATE'S MARITAL STATUS _____

Number of persons on list at present time _____

Number of persons to be removed from list :_____

52

June 30, 19____ Inventory

Location_____

Stock No. _____

Description_____

Classification_____

Number of Units_____

Unit Price_____Total_____

Counted By_____

Checked By_____

Form 504—J—300—5-58

47

DEPARTMENT OF PUBLIC SAFETY
Springfield, Illinois

Date of Violation_____

Name _____

CONSIDER THIS A DISCIPLINARY REPORT FOR VIOLATING THE RULES AND REGULATIONS, AND THE FOLLOWING ACTION HAS BEEN TAKEN. IF IMPROVEMENT IS NOT MADE, FURTHER DISCIPLINARY ACTION WILL BE TAKEN.   Warning _____

Suspended _____ days

Do you realize to be a good custodial officer is a challenge — either you are in command of your assignment and the inmates, or the inmates command you. Apparently you are lacking the ability to handle the assignment given you, or you just don't care. _____

Improper searching of: _____Inmates _____Assignment _____Cell House _____Dormitory,
_____Cellhouse _____Yard _____Line _____Assignment
Improper supervision of inmates assigned to you: _____Dormitory

_____ work.

53 — LOCK REPAIR TICKET

CELLHOUSE:_____   19____

DATE:_____

LOCK REPAIRS ON CELL NO._____

REMARKS:_____

48

Gal. No. C.H. "B"	Gal. No.. "C"	"D"	"E"	"F"	
1.	1.				
2.	2.				Front Line
3.	3.				
4.	4.				Farm Detail
5.	Hall..				
6.	Total				Total
7.					
8.					
9.		TOTAL CELL HOUSE COUNT _____			
10.		TOTAL OUTSIDE CO_____			
Hall.					

54 — SEGREGATION COUNT

DATE_____ 19____

SEG COUNT_____

TRANSIT COUNT_____

HELP COUNT_____

TOTAL COUNT_____

SEG. OFFICER_____

49 — NIGHT GALLERY CHECK
CELLHOUSE

DATE: _____

GAL.	TOG	IN	TOG	IN	TOG	IN	TOG	IN	TOG	IN	TOG	GAL.	IN	TIME
1														
2														
3														
4														
5														
6														

Fig. 55. This form gives the information as to what boilers are operating and which are in reserve or repair. It tells which wells are pumping and the wells in reserve. This is sent to the Warden and Chief Engineer by the officer in charge of the Power House.

Fig. 56. Any Officer or Official Authorized to Issue Special Letters to Inmates. After this form is signed by the issuing officer, it permits inmate to obtain a special letter head from the cell house keeper in charge of the cell house he is assigned to.

Fig. 57. Outside Detail Platform. Record of gasoline used by Institution equipment.

Fig. 58. Cell House. Used to keep a running count by cell house door keeper of inmates in and out of cell house.

Fig. 59. Any Assignment. Record of time inmate leaves assignment and returns to assignment.

Fig. 60. Cell House. Used to show movement of inmates from cell to cell.

Fig. 61. Sally Port. Count sheet showing inmates checked out to Sally Port and back into the Institution.

Fig. 62. All Chaplains. History sheet on Inmate.

Fig. 63. Armory. Record of target shooting of Officers.

Fig. 64. Master Mechanic's Shop. This tool list accompanies inmate to assignment he is to work.

55
OFFICER'S POWERHOUSE REPORT
POWERHOUSE

OLD—NEW—PRISON

DATE _____

BOILER   No.1   No.2   No.3   No.4   No.5   No.6

BOILER FEED PUMPS _____
FIRE PUMPS _____
SOFT WATER SYSTEM _____
CHLORINATOR SYSTEM _____
RESERVOIR (Water in ft.) _____
DEEP WELLS _____
ELECTRICAL EQUIPMENT _____
REMARKS: _____

59
INMATE MOVEMENT CHART

NAME	NO.	DEST.	OUT	IN	NAME	NO.	DEST.

62
CHAPLAIN'S OFFICE RECORD

INMATE RECEIVED—DATE _____

NAME _____ NO _____

AGE _____ NATIONALITY _____

NATIVITY _____

COUNTY _____

CRIME _____

SENTENCE _____

COLOR _____ RELIGION _____

OCCUPATION _____

MARRIED _____ SINGLE _____ DIVORCED _____

PARENTS LIVING: FATHER _____ MOTHER _____

BROTHERS _____ SISTERS _____

EDUCATION _____

DRINK _____

NOTIFY IN CASE OF SICKNESS OR DEATH _____

RECORD _____

DEPENDENTS _____

Form 3592—VS

rm 3712 — 8-1.   **PERMIT FOR SPECIAL LETTER**
56   Date: _____ 19__

INMATE NO _____ NAME _____

Has been granted permission to write one special letter to the following address for the reason indicated:

Name: _____
St. & No. _____
City: _____ State _____
Relationship _____

_____ Death
_____ Sickness
_____ Business
_____ Employment
_____ Parole
_____ Case
_____ Other Reason

57

GASOLINE ISSUED FOR: _____
FROM TANK LOCATED AT: _____ 19__

VEHICLE	MILEAGE READING	GASOLINE No. OF GALS.	OILS No. OF QTS.	RECEIVED BY:

64

TOOL LIST	
Name No.	Date
No.	ITEMS

58

DIVISION	FULL COUNT	IN HOSPITAL	IN ISOLATION	LAY INS	SICK CALL	CHECK COUNT			

60
CELLHOUSE MOVEMENT SHEET
DATE _____

NUMBER	NAME	R	SENTENCE	FROM	CELL	TO	CELL	COUNT	CHECK

CHECKED BY _____
VS No. 80 _____

SOUTH GATE COUNT _____ **61** _____ DATE _____

REG. NO.	NAME	OUT	IN	COUNT CHECK	REG. NO.	NAME	OUT	IN	COUNT CHECK

63   DATE _____

	30-30 RIFLE				PISTOL				
SHIFT	SHOT	HIT	MISS	TOTAL	SHOT	HIT	MISS	TOTAL	GRAND TOTAL
OFFICER									

Fig. 65. Visiting Room. Record kept in visiting room showing time that the Information Desk phoned re: visit, number of inmate, time visitor arrived in visiting room and time visitor left visiting room.

Fig. 66. Master Mechanic. For authorization of purchase. Used for special purchases and in emergency only.

Fig. 67. All Assignments. Used for requisitioning supplies (monthly) from the General Store. This is in quadruplicate and then distributed.

Fig. 68. Cell House. Submitted by cell house keeper to the Captain's Office at count time.

Fig. 69. Guard Hall. Record of telephone message. Re: inmates or employees.

Fig. 70. Assistant Warden and Senior Captain. Record of personal merit of inmate.

Fig. 71. Cell House. Record of any inmates whose last two numbers of their Institutional number are shown on card and are in the cell house.

Fig. 72. Any Assignment. This Gate Pass accompanies any equipment etc., that passes through either Sally Port or Guard Hall.

Fig. 73. Any Assignment. Used when request is made to have inmates detailed to work other than regular hours on an assignment.

Fig. 74. All Assignments. Record of locks etc., submitted to officer in charge of Armory. This is a monthly procedure.

Fig. 75. Clothing Room. Record of clothing issued to inmate.

Fig. 76. Cell House. Record of locked and tried doors in cell house.

INMATES' VISIT RECORD SHEET

65   DATE_____

NUMBER	REC.	IN	OUT

66

OFFICE OF THE
MASTER MECHANIC
ADMINISTRATION BUILDING
STATEVILLE BRANCH

Mr. A. D. Borio
Business Manager
         Date____

Dear Sir:
     Kindly issue an OFD authorizing the purchase
of the following:

FROM:

QUANTITY	UNIT	DESCRIPTION

67

Form 9612 (Gand.)

DATE_____ 19____

REQUISITION TO STOREKEEPER

DELIVER TO____ SECTION____   OBJECT CODE____

SECTION NO. ____   FUNCTIONAL CODE____

		THESE COLUMNS NOT TO BE FILLED IN BY SECTION
QUANT.	UNIT	UNIT PRICE	VALUE

No.____ 70

Color____ Occupation____

Name____   Rec'd____

Crime____

Sentence____

R____

71

CELL REGISTER CARD

| 10 | 11 | 12 | 13 |

72

No.____ Date____ 195__

ILLINOIS STATE PENITENTIARY

GATE PASS

I have this day passed the following through my assignment

TO____

68 **CELL HOUSE COUNT**

COUNTED BY	Gallery	COUNTED BY
	1	
	2	
	3	

69

A telephone message was received____ (Time and Date)

From

REGARDING

73   **SPECIAL DETAIL**

Date____

TO:
THE SENIOR CAPTAIN:
     Subject to your approval I would like to have the following named in
mates assigned to ____, detailed to work at ____:

No.   Name   No.   Name

No.

PURPOSE:

REMARKS:

THEY WILL WORK AS FOLLOWS:
FROM ____ A.M UNTIL ____ A.M.   FROM ____ P.M. UNTIL ____ P.M.
FROM ____ days of the month, TO ____ day of the month inclusive.
NECESSARY COUNTS TO BE MADE AT ____
REQUESTED BY ____ Officer in Charge

____ Captain ____, the Officer so assigned is t

74   **KEY LOCATION CHART**

ASSIGNMENT   RING NO.   TOTAL KEYS   (CHECK)

        YES   NO

ARE ALL LOCKS IN USE WHERE ORIGINALLY ASSIGNED............
ARE ALL RINGS & KEY NUMBERS CORRECTLY AND PLAINLY MARKED..
ARE ALL KEYS CORRECTLY AND PLAINLY NUMBERED......
ANY LOCKS OR KEYS THAT SHOULD BE REPAIRED O
DO YOU HAVE ANY LOCKS OR KEYS NOT PROPERLY
THE ARMORY..

76
CELL HOUSE   DATE____

Gal.   Officer

1	(Locked and Tried By)	
2	''	''
3	''	''
4	''	''
5	''	''
6	''	''
7	''	''

REG. NO.   CRIME: REC.

NAME: 75   SENTENCE: OCC.

ITEM	DATE ISSUED							ASSIGNMENT
C. COATS								
JACKET								
CAPS								
SHOES: POLICE								
SHOES-COMM.								
SOCKS								
TOWELS								
HDKFS.								
UNDERWEAR								
NICK: SHIRTS								
DENIM O'ALL								
STATE SHORTS								

Fig. 77. Cell House. Daily vacancy report turned in by cell house keeper to Captain's Office, showing vacancies on assignments and also designates color of inmates.

Fig. 78. Assistant Warden and Senior Captain (Disciplinarian). History card on inmate showing conduct record, assignments, etc.

Fig. 79. Mail Office and Information Desk. Record of inmates correspondence and visits prepared for Parole Board on inmates appearing on parole docket.

Fig. 80. Power House. Daily record of boilers, etc.

Fig. 81. Cell House. Record of daily vacancies.

Fig. 82. Officer in Charge of Officer's Training School. Summary of information on officer. Re: employment record.

Fig. 83. Inventory Control Office. Record of new equipment issued to assignment.

Fig. 84. Any Assignment. Record showing lock and location on assignment. This is kept at the Armory.

Fig. 85. This is used to transfer Inventory items.

Fig. 86. Cell House. Record of inmates who have celled in a particular cell in cell house.

77 — VACANCY REPORT FOR ____ CELLHOUSE

ASSIGNMENT	WHITE		COLORED		GAL.	TOTAL
	VACANT	ASSIGNED	VACANT	ASSIGNED		
Gen. Kitchen						
Dining Room					1	
E. C. H.					1	
Sick Bay					2	
General Store					2	
Bakery					3	
Vegetable Room					3	
Commisary & Lib.					3	
Hospital Help					3	
Officers Kitchen					3	
Off. Bar						

78

Number _____ Name _____

Color _____ Crime _____ Sentence _____

Received _____ County _____

Occupation _____ Assigned _____

Board Action _____

Criminal History _____

79 — CORRESPONDENCE RECORD

NAME			RELATIONSHIP

OUTGOING

NAME _____ STREET _____ CITY _____ STATE _____

INCOMING

NAME _____ STREET _____ CITY _____ STATE _____ RELATIO

80 — OFFICER'S POWERHOUSE REPORT

POWERHOUSE

OLD—NEW—PRISON

DATE _____

BOILER   No.1   No.2   No.3   No.4   No.5   No.6

BOILER FEED PUMPS _____

FIRE PUMPS _____

SOFT WATER SYSTEM _____

CHLORINATOR SYSTEM _____

RESERVOIR (Water in ft.) _____

DEEP WELLS _____

ELECTRICAL EQUIPMENT _____

REMARKS _____

81 — VACANCY REPORT FOR ____ CELLHOUSE

ASSIGNMENT	WHITE		COLORED		GAL.	TOTAL
	VACANT	ASSIGNED	VACANT	ASSIGNED		
Gen. Kitchen						
Dining Room						
E.C.H.						
Sick Bay						
General Store						
Bakery						
Vegetable Room						
Commisary & Lib.						
Hospital Help						
Officers Kitchen						
Off. Barber Shop						
Asst. Ward. Apt.						
Off. Quarters						
Guard Hall						
Mail Office						
Information Desk						
Officers Comm.						
Off. Tailor Shop						
Night Detail						
Bakery Detail						
Textile						
Barber Shop						
Mattress Shop						
Marble Shop						
Clothing Room						
__ Unit						

82 — ILLINOIS STATE PENITENTIARY, JOLIET, ILLINOIS

Date _____

TO: Mr. Joseph E. Ragen, Warden
Stateville Branch

Dear Sir:

Listed below you will find a summary of information, relative to the employment record of named officer:

OFFICER _____ EMPLOYED _____ LE__

ABILITY _____ COOPERATION _____

EFFICIENCY _____ APPEARANCE _____

ATTENDANCE _____ CONDUCT _____

REMARKS _____

Respectfully yours,

83 — NEW EQUIPMENT ISSUE REPORT

TO: INVENTORY CONTROL OFFICE

FROM: GENERAL STORE STOCK

INVOICE NO. _____

PURCHASE ORDER NO. _____ DATE OF INVOICE _____

PURCHASED FROM _____ REC. REPORT NO. _____

DATE ISSUED _____

ISSUED TO _____ COST _____

ITEM _____

CLASS NO. _____

INVENTORY _____

Hook Nu

84

Make of Key	Ins't No.	Exact location of lock.

85 — ILLINOIS STATE PENITENTIARY

STATEVILLE — JOLIET
INVENTORY CONTROL OFFICE
EQUIPMENT TRANSFER PERMIT

Number _____

_____ 19 ____

FROM _____

TO _____

INVENTORY NO.	DESCRIPTION OF PROPERTY	AMOUNT

86 — PERMANENT CELL RECORD

CELL

NUMBER	NAME	DATE IN	DATE OUT

REC'D BY _____

DATE OF DELIVERY _____

Record of Inmates who have o CELL HOUSE

ORIGINAL

Fig. 87. Mechanical Store. This card is used, here in the office of the Mechanical Store to designate the number of the particular stock, records requisitioned issues; records materials received, shipper's or vender's name, invoice and quarterly number, and records the balance of this particular stock at all times. It is very essential that we use this card as our stock control card.

Fig. 88. Veterans' Service Officer. These forms are used in the Veterans' Service Office as part of the permanent records.

Fig. 89. Cell House C. This form is used for the purpose of the 4-C Outside Detail Break Down Count as following: one copy to Captain Burris, one copy to Captain Alvey and one copy to the South Gate.

Fig. 90. This form is used for the purpose of giving the break down of the Book Bindery line by the cell House "C" Door Clerk.

Fig. 91. Cell House C. This form is used for the purpose of the Vocational School line by the Cell House "C" Door Clerk to give break down of the line.

Fig. 92. Cell House C. This form is used for the purpose of giving the breakdown of the Barber Shop line by the Cell House "C" Door Clerk.

Fig. 93. These forms are used by the Veterans' Service Office in answering requests for information of a military nature for Detail Assignments.

Fig. 94. Inmate's Laundry. This form is used as a daily Record of Tools, Sewing Kits and Needles, checked out to inmates.

Fig. 87. Mechanical Store. This card is used in the office of the Mechanical Store to designate the number of the particular stock, record requisitioned issues; record materials received, shipper's or vender's name, invoice and quarterly number, and balance of this particular stock at all times.

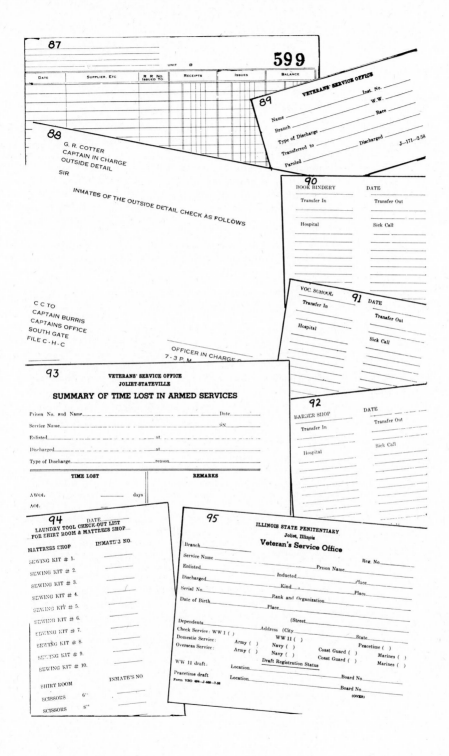

87

DATE	SUPPLIER, ETC	R R No. ISSUED TO	RECEIPTS	ISSUES	BALANCE

UNIT @

599

88

G. R. COTTER
CAPTAIN IN CHARGE
OUTSIDE DETAIL

SIR

INMATES OF THE OUTSIDE DETAIL CHECK AS FOLLOWS

C C TO
CAPTAIN BURRIS
CAPTAINS OFFICE
SOUTH GATE
FILE C - H - C

OFFICER IN CHARGE
7 - 3 P. M.

89

VETERANS' SERVICE OFFICE

Inst. No. ____

W.W. ____

Name ____

Race ____

Branch ____

Type of Discharge ____

Transferred to ____   Discharged ____   J.-171.-2.58

Paroled ____

90

BOOK BINDERY   DATE

Transfer In   Transfer Out

Hospital   Sick Call

91

VOC. SCHOOL   DATE

Transfer In   Transfer Out

Hospital   Sick Call

92

BARBER SHOP   DATE

Transfer In   Transfer Out

Hospital   Sick Call

93

VETERANS' SERVICE OFFICE
JOLIET-STATEVILLE

SUMMARY OF TIME LOST IN ARMED SERVICES

Prison No. and Name____   Date ____

Service Name____   SN ____

Enlisted____   at ____

Discharged____   at ____

Type of Discharge____   reason ____

TIME LOST		REMARKS
AWOL	____ days	
AOL		

94   DATE ____

LAUNDRY TOOL CHECK-OUT LIST
FOR SHIRT ROOM & MATTRESS SHOP

MATTRESS SHOP   INMATE'S NO.

SEWING KIT # 1.

SEWING KIT # 2.

SEWING KIT # 3.

SEWING KIT # 4.

SEWING KIT # 5.

SEWING KIT # 6.

SEWING KIT # 7.

SEWING KIT # 8.

SEWING KIT # 9.

SEWING KIT # 10.

SHIRT ROOM   INMATE'S NO

SCISSORS   6''

SCISSORS   8''

95

ILLINOIS STATE PENITENTIARY
Joliet, Illinois

Veteran's Service Office

Branch ____

Service Name ____   Reg. No. ____

Enlisted____   Inducted____   Prison Name ____

Discharged____   Kind ____   Place ____

Serial No.____   Place ____

Date of Birth____   Rank and Organization ____

Place ____

(Street ____

Dependents ____   Address (City ____

Check Service: WW 1 ( )   State ____

Domestic Service: WW 11 ( )   Peacetime ( )

Overseas Service: Army ( )   Navy ( )   Coast Guard ( )

Army ( )   Navy ( )   Coast Guard ( )   Marines ( )

WW 11 draft: Draft Registration Status   Marines ( )

Peacetime draft   Location ____   Board No. ____

Location ____   Board No. ____

Form VSO 484—J-488—7.58   (OVER)

Fig. 96. This form is used in inventory filing of records.

Fig. 97. These cards are used as part of the permanent record of the Veterans' Service Office for veterans.

Fig. 98. Record Office. This form, printed special at the Vocational School, is used exclusively by the Outside Detail Captain's Office, Stateville. They are used on all correspondence, space permitting, with the Institution Offices and Officials regarding burials, trailer court transactions, receipt and disposition of shipments that do not go inside the walls and general office business.

Fig. 99. This is an inmate's account card. The inmate's name and number are entered at the top of this card. His balance is listed on the first line of this form. Every time an inmate trades, the date is stamped on this card and the money subtracted from his balance.

Fig. 100. This is a regular inmate trade slip. Any inmate who has no denials uses this form on his trade day. They are permitted to trade once a week.

Fig. 101. Power House officer makes this form out each Friday for the Chief Engineer giving him the water level and static level.

Fig. 102. This chart gives information as to the amount of steam used, in pounds of coal used to make up such amount of steam. "Feedwater" pump" shows water pumped into boilers. "Make up Meter" shows amount of well water added to the return to make up the feed water amount. Used by the Power House officer.

Fig. 103. This shows the hours each well is pumped. The total water pumped each day and total consumption and per capita consumption. This report is sent to the Chief Engineer by the officer in charge of the Power House.

Fig. 104. This is the daily coal report used at the Power House to show coal consumed each day. This is sent to the Chief Engineer's Office daily by the Power House officer.

Fig. 105. Power House count slip made out by the Officer in charge of the Power House.

Fig. 106. Library card used in the Grade School library for all Fiction books. The card is used for charging out books to inmates and is then placed in the pending file so that the location of all books is known.

Fig. 107. Request slip for High School book returns.

96

LOCATION

ILLINOIS STATE PENITENTIARY, JOLIET
INVENTORY CONTROL OFFICE
UNIT PROPERTY RECORD

ARTICLE _____

QUANTITY _____
UNIT COST _____
TOTAL COST _____

MAKE AND/OR TRADE NUMBER _____

SERIAL NUMBER (if any) _____

INVENTORY NUMBER _____

PROCURED FROM _____

DATE PURCH   DATE RECD

97

VETERAN'S RECORD

W.W.

Name _____   Place _____

No. _____   Prison Name _____   Place _____

Race _____   Inducted _____   At _____

Enlisted _____   Kind _____   Copy ( )

Discharge _____   Discharged-Orig ( )

Serial No. _____

Rank & Organization _____   Place _____   National Guard ( )

Coast Guard ( )   Others _____

98

SOUTH GATE
OUTSIDE DETAIL
STATEVILLE

CAPTAIN'S OFFICE
FARM DETAIL

99

NAME   REG. NO.

DATE   BAL. FWD.

100

Thumb Print

Date _____ 19 ___

TO CHIEF CLERK:

Please charge the amount listed below against my account in the
Inmates Trust Fund for the following Commissary Order:

Reg No. _____   Name _____   Cell
House _____   Cell _____

INMATES ARE NOT TO USE THE PRICE COLUMN

Quantity	Unit	ARTICLE	a	Price

101

ILLINOIS STATE PENITENTIARY
Stateville Branch

WEEKLY REPORT OF WATER TESTS AT WELLS

Well	Original Air Line Setting of Well	Original Static Reading of Well	CURRENT READING			Change of Water Level From Previous Reading		
			Water Level	Static Level	Pumping Level	NON-PUMPING Up Down	PU	Up
No. 1 CENTER	520'	319'						
No. 2 SOUTH	520'	445'						
No. 3 NORTH	480'	416'						
No. 4 OUTSIDE	520'	330'						

MASTER MECHANIC

VS—4M—5-54

102

Daily Evaporation Report

DATE _____

EVAPORATION LBS

No. 1 Evap. lbs _____   No. 2 Evap. lbs _____

7 _____   7 _____
11 _____   11 _____
3 _____   3 _____
11 _____   11 _____
7 _____   7 _____
3 _____   3 _____
H _____   H _____

No. 3 Evap. lbs   L.   H   No. 4 Evap. lbs   L.
7 _____   7 _____
11 _____   11 _____
3 _____   3 _____
7 _____   7 _____
11 _____   11 _____
3 _____   3 _____
H _____   3 _____

103

DAILY WATER REPORT

_____ hour period ending _____ A.M. _____ 195_

WATER IN RESERVOIR
AT BEGINNING OF DAY _____ GAL.

HOURS ON   WATER PUMPED

NORTH WELL _____ GAL.

CENTER WELL _____ GAL.

SOUTH WELL _____ GAL.

OUTSIDE WELL _____ GAL.

FARM WELL _____ GAL.

TOTAL WATER PUMPED _____

GRAND TOTAL OF WATER
IN RESERVOIR AND
WATER PUMPED _____

WATER IN RESE_

NORTH CHAMBER _____

CENTER CHAMBER _____

SOUTH CHAMBER _____

TOTAL _____

CONSUMPTION _____

PER CAPITA CONSU_

104

NEW PRISON

DAILY COAL REPORT

DATE _____

ON HAND _____

CONSUMED _____

RECEIVED _____

ON HAND BALANCE _____

VS—4M—3-54

105

DATE _____

Count

Power House _____

Sub Station _____

Cold Storage _____

Furniture Shop _____

Total Count _____

106

LIBRARY   FICTION

TITLE _____

AUTHOR _____

NAME	NUMBER	DATE

GRADE SCHOOL

107

Name _____   No. _____   C. H. _____

You are charged with the following book(s) which are to be returned
to the Stateville School's library for the reason(s) checked below:

Name of Book: No:

You are required to return this notice to the school with comment.

☐ You are on next month's discharge list (Paroled).
☐ The above book(s) are needed by the school.
☐ Another inmate wishes temporary use of the book(s) If you wish
   the book(s) returned to you, check this square ☐
☐ You have completed the courses using the book(s).
☐ You have discontinued your studies in the book(s).
☐ You have drawing equipment (tools) that shall be turned in also.
☐ _____ Stateville Schools Library.

Return your Book Permit with the book(s) to clear the records.

Fig. 108. This form is used to report the summary of monthly business to the business office.

Fig. 109. High School Examination Grades Record.

Fig. 110. The Grade School Request for Return of Loaned Books is sent to inmates whose books are overdue. This is one means of obtaining the return of overdue library books.

Fig. 111. The Grade School Book Permit card is used to permit Grade School text and library books to inmates other than inmate students and teachers. Inmates, other than students and teachers, are required to keep this permit in their cells while in possession of Grade School books.

Fig. 112. High School Warning Notice.

Fig. 113. High School Drop Slip.

Fig. 114. Receipt for High School book delivered.

Fig. 115. Receipt for High School books received.

Fig. 116. Receipt for individual's cell. Drawing tools and drawing materials can be permitted in inmate's cell.

Fig. 117. This form is used to report monthly business to the business office.

Fig. 118. Honor Farm. These forms are issued to the following assignments, and they in turn, keep a daily record of the feed that is used to feed the livestock assigned to them. They then turn the card into the Farm Office for a recapitulation of the feed used on the farm at the end of the month.

Fig. 119. High School Library look record.

FORM 3 (VS—5C—9-52) **108** ILLINOIS STATE PENITENTIARY, JOLIET
INVENTORY CONTROL OFFICE

SUMMARY OF CHANGES IN PHYSICAL INVENTORY

During Month of_____ 19____

Note: This form and forms 1 and 2 are to be filed with Business Managers Office within ten (10) days of close of month covered by this report.

CLASSIFICATION		INVENTORY BEGINNING OF MONTH	ADDITIONS (Detail on Form 1)			TOTAL ADDITIONS	DEDUCTIONS (Detail on Form 2)		
NO.	NAME		VOUCHER PURCHASES		TRANSFERS AND ALL OTHER		DISPOSALS AS APPROVED ON "Order to Dispose"	TRANSFERS AND ALL OTHERS	TO DEDU
			Equipment or Permanent Improvements	Other Appropriations					
		(A)	(B)	(C)	(D)	(E)	(F)	(G)	(H)
610	LAND, RIGHTS OF WAY AND EASEMENTS								
611	BUILDINGS								
622	IMPROVEMENT OF BUILDINGS								
631	HIGHWAYS AND WATERWAYS								
632	BRIDGES, VIA								
640	IMPROVEMENT								
650	TUNNELS AND FACILITIES								
	SUB-T								
510	OFFICE FURNITU EQUIPMENT								
521	PASSENGER AUTO								
522	OTHER MOTOR VE								
530	HOUSEHOLD EQUIP FURNISHINGS								
540	MACHINERY, IMPLE MAJOR TOOLS								
550	SCIENTIFIC INSTRUM APPARATUS								
560	LIBRARY BOOKS, MAF INGS AND SPECIM								
570	LIVESTOCK								
580	EQUIPMENT NOT OTHE CLASSIFIED								
	TOTAL								

109 STATEVILLE CORRESPONDENCE SCHOOL

NAME _____

_____ NUMBER _____

ASSIGNMENT_____ High School

The grade on your recent examination in _____

(subject) _____ was _____

Please continue to submit lessons regularly.

110 GRADE SCHOOL C. H.

Name _____ No._____
You are charged with the following book(s) which are to be returned to the Stateville School's library for the reason(s) checked below:
Name of Book:_____ No:

You are required to return this notice to the school with comment. (Paroled).

☐ You are on next month's discharge list.
☐ The above book(s) are needed by the school. If you wish
☐ Another inmate wishes temporary use of the book(s). Check this square ☐
☐ the book(s) returned to you, check this square ☐
☐ You have completed the courses using the book(s).
☐ You have discontinued your studies in the book(s).
☐ You have drawing equipment (tools) that shall be turned in a_____ Stateville Schools Library.
☐ Return your Book Permit with the book(s) to clear the recor_____

111 STATEVILLE SCHOOL BOOK PERMIT

No._____ IS CHARGED WITH THE SCHOOL BOOKS LISTED BELOW. ALL REQUESTS FOR BOOKS AND ALL BOOKS RE TURNED TO THE SCHOOL MUST BE ACCOMPANIED BY THIS PERMIT

| DATE | DUE | CLASS | RETURNED | NUMBER |
| | | | | |

112 CELL HOUSE_____

NAME _____ No._____

We have not received any lessons from you in_____ since_____

Inactivity does not aid you in acquiring an education or in completing this course. Let us hear from you in a form of a lesson or by sending your attempts at the problems, which cause you to be inactive. To remain an active student you must start sending work at the rate of a lesson every ten days.

Return this slip with your next lesson or report on the back side of it the reason for your delay in sending in lessons.

STATEVILLE CORRESPONDENCE SCHOOL

113 INTER-OFFICE NOTICE
STATEVILLE CORRESPONDENCE SCHOOL

(Name)

Has (dropped) (completed) the course in _____ (Number)

(Date)

High School

Note :

UPON RECEIPT, INITIAL AND PASS_____
PARTMENT.

CLERK
LIBRARIAN
INSTRUCTOR

115 SCHOOL'S BOOK RECEIPT

I have received the following books from the School:

High School

Keeper _____
Cellhouse _____

114 KEEPER'S BOOK RECEIPT

I have received the following book from the cell-house keeper:

High School

Name _____
Number _____

116 ILLINOIS STATE PENITENTIARY

Permit No._____

Name _____ Date _____

High School

is permitted to have drawing tools and drawing material in his cell.

THESE ITEMS ARE TO BE RETURNED TO THE SCHOOL UPON COMPLETION OF THE COURSE OR ON PAROLE OR DISCHARGE.

Superintendent of Education

118 DAILY FEED RECORD MONTH_____

AMOUNT ON HAND BEGINING OF MONTH _____

17_____
18_____
19_____

117 ILLINOIS STATE PENITENTIARY, JOLIET
INVENTORY CONTROL OFFICE

DETAIL OF ADDITIONS TO INVENTORY

During Month of_____ 19____

I.C.O. FORM I (VS—1M—9-52)

CLASSIFICATION NUMBER	I.C.R. NUMBER	VOUCHER NUMBER	REFERENCE	AMOUNT	
				DETAIL	TOTAL FOR SUMMARY FORM 3

119 TITLE _____
AUTHOR _____

| NAME | NUMBER | DATE |
| High School | | |

Fig. 120. These forms are used for change of address addressed to the Local Draft Boards for inmates.

Fig. 121. These forms are used for the permanent records of the Veterans' Service Office. For replys to the Local Draft Boards.

Fig. 122. High School Permanent Record.

Fig. 123. High School Report Card.

Fig. 124. High School Long Term Record.

Fig. 125. High School Book Receipt.

Fig. 126. Receipt for supplies sent to High School student.

Fig. 127. Teacher's request for consultation with High School student.

Fig. 128. Work Tag Order. Accompanies lumber requisition (if wood is solid lumber) to cutting room. One card for each item on requisition. Then follows each operational phase that is necessary for item such as: tenoning, mortizing, dadoing, etc. Made out by cost clerk, checked and approved by Mr. G. Early, Drafting Dept. officer.

Fig. 129. This card is used for Inventory purposes only. The card is filled out by stock room clerks and after inventory, it is filed by inventory clerk.

Fig. 130. Bureau of Identification. Identification card. This card is used for temporary workers, such as outside construction workers. Their picture is mounted on reverse side of card.

Fig. 131. Bureau of Identification. Bertillion card, which is mounted on inmate's picture.

120 Request for Change of Address and Information for Selective Service Classification Purposes

SELECTIVE SERVICE DATE

Institution No.

Name ___ Last ___ First ___ Middle ___

New address is ILLINOIS STATE PENITENTIARY, BOX 1112, JOLIET, ILLINOIS

Registered for Selective Service under name of ___

Home address at time of registration ___ AT ___ IN ___

Number and location of Draft Board ___

Selective Service Order ___ Classified ___ Date ___

Place of birth ___

STATEVILLE SCHOOL BOOK PERMIT

INMATE ___ No. ___ IS CHARGED WITH THE SCHOOL BOOKS LISTED BELOW. ALL REQUESTS FOR BOOKS AND ALL BOOKS RETURNED TO THE SCHOOL MUST BE ACCOMPANIED BY THIS PERMIT.

DATE	DUE	CLASS	RETURNED	NUMBER

High School

---

121 ILLINOIS STATE PENITENTIARY

JOLIET

VETERANS' SERVICE OFFICE

These forms are used for the permanent record of the Veterans' Service Office wireless to Local Draft Boards.

Veterans' Service Office

Local Board No.
Selective Service System

Gentlemen:

Thank you for your letter of ___ in which you request information concerning the above-identified registrant.

A search of our records indicates the following:

Paroled ___ Discharged ___

Transferred ___

---

126 STATEVILLE CORRESPONDENCE SCHOOL

Send supplies to

No. ___

Student ___

Assignment ___ eraser

___ pencil ___ envelope

___ tablet ___ pen

___ lesson paper

High School

---

127 STATEVILLE CORRESPONDENCE SCHOOL

Unofficial request for

Student ___ No. ___

Assignment ___ Date ___

for lesson interview on

course ___ type of exam

High School

Remarks ___

Teacher ___

---

128 WORK TAG ORDER

W.O. No. ___ M. S. No. ___

Date ___ Key No. ___

For ___

Item ___

Fin. ___ Style ___

Remarks ___ Quantity ___

---

129 FURNITURE FACTORY

Milled parts for: ___ bin no ___

Item ___ Finish: ___

	RECEIVED	IN	OUT	BALANCED
		/		

---

122 THE STATEVILLE HIGH SCHOOL

PERMANENT RECORD CARD -- NOT TO BE TAKEN FROM SCHOOL

NUMBER ___ NAME ___ LAST ___ FIRST ___ AGE ___ RACE ___

DATE OF ENTERING SCHOOL ___ ASSIGNED GRADE AT ENTRANCE ___ 1 2 3 4

CLASS YR. ___ 1 2 3 4

SUBJECT		
ENGLISH 1	SPANISH 1	
ENGLISH 2	FRENCH 1	
	AM. HISTORY	
	AM. HISTORY	
	CIVICS	

---

123 THE STATEVILLE HIGH SCHOOL

TERM REPORT CARD

Number ___ Name ___

Date Entered ___ Grade Assigned ___ Graduation Date ___ Gen. Av. ___

Subject ___ Grades by the Month ___ Subject ___ Grades by the Month ___

Month	1	2	3	4	5	6	7	8	9	10	11	12	Month	1	2	3	4	5	6	7	8	9	10	11
English													Science											
Literature													Accounting											
Gen. Arith.													French											
Algebra																								

---

124 EDUCATIONAL RECORD

NAME ___ RACE ___ AGE ___ NUMBER ___

DATE ADMITTED ___ OFFENSE ___ SENTENCE ___

STARTED EDUCATION ___ TEST ___ SCORE ___ DATE TESTED ___

REMARKS ___ VIOLATOR ___

DRAWING PERMIT NUMBER ___ OCCUPATION ___

INSTITUTIONAL SCHOOL RECORD

Course	Started	Completed or Dropped	Grade

High School

130

Whose picture appears on the reverse side of this card is employed by

___

at the Illinois State Penitentiary.

Employee's Signature

---

131 ILLINOIS STATE PENITENTIARY JOLIET, ILLINOIS

Name ___ No. ___

Height ___

Weight ___ Alias ___

Comp ___ Rec'd ___

Hair ___ From ___ Age ___

Eyes ___ Crime ___ Race ___

F. P. C. ___ Sentence ___

Ret. ___ Paroled ___ Nat'y ___

Previous Record ___ Final Disc. ___

Scars, Marks, etc. ___

Fig. 132. This card is used for perpetual inventory purposes in both stock rooms.

Fig. 133. This is used for special items only. Made out by cost clerk, checked and approved by the Drafting Department Officer and then sent to the Industrial Officer as a breakdown on what the item will cost.

Fig. 134. This card is used for all Walnut finished stock, sales and pro- production stock control cards.

Fig. 135. This card is used in conjunction with cost sheet when prices on original cost sheet are changed due to fluctuating lumber prices.

Fig. 136. This card is used as complete material break down on upholstery materials and hardware that is used on standard stock items.

Fig. 137. These forms are supplied by the Veterans' Service Office to the Diagnostic Depot and used by them to notify the VSO of the veterans received.

Fig. 138. The Grade School Inmate Student Report Card is issued to the inmate student three times each term. The Inmate Student Report Card is issued to the inmate student to show him how he is progressing in his studies.

Fig. 139. High School Permit to buy.

Fig. 140. High School Lesson Grade Card.

Fig. 141. Power House. Daily chlorine dosage is shown on this chart.

Fig. 142. Bureau of Identification. Alias card. Used for new arrivals, also finger prints of the four fingers of either hand on reverse side of card.

Fig. 143. Cell House. Record of cell partners of inmate.

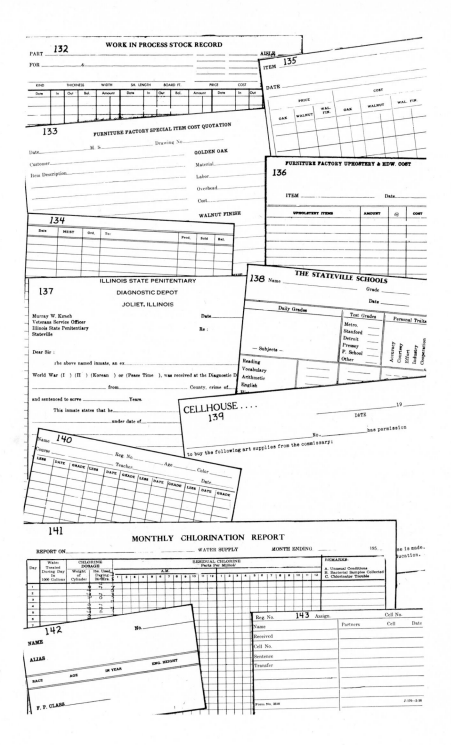

WORK IN PROCESS STOCK RECORD

PART _____ **132**

FOR _____ &. _____

AISLE _____

KIND	THICKNESS	WIDTH	SH. LENGTH	BOARD FT.		PRICE		COST
Date	In	Out	Bal.	Amount	Date	In	Out	Bal.	Amount	Date	In	Out

ITEM **135**

DATE _____

	COST

PRICE			COST
OAK	WALNUT	WAL. FIN.	OAK	WALNUT	WAL. FIN.

133 FURNITURE FACTORY SPECIAL ITEM COST QUOTATION

M. S. _____ Drawing No. _____

Date _____

Customer _____

Item Description _____

GOLDEN OAK

Material _____

Labor _____

Overhead _____

Cost _____

WALNUT FINISH

FURNITURE FACTORY UPHOSTERY & HDW. COST

136

ITEM _____ Date _____

UPHOLSTERY ITEMS	AMOUNT	@	COST

134

Date	MSIST	Ord.	To:	Prod.	Sold	Bal.

137 ILLINOIS STATE PENITENTIARY

DIAGNOSTIC DEPOT

JOLIET, ILLINOIS

Murray W. Kirsch
Veterans Service Officer
Illinois State Penitentiary
Stateville

Date _____

Re : _____

Dear Sir :

the above named inmate, an ex _____

World War (I) (II) (Korean) or (Peace Time), was received at the Diagnostic D _____

_____ from _____ County, crime of _____

and sentenced to serve _____ Years.

This inmate states that he _____

_____ under date of _____

138 Name _____

THE STATEVILLE SCHOOLS

Grade _____

Date _____

Daily Grades	Test Grades	Personal Traits
	Metro.	Accuracy
	Stanford	Courtesy
— Subjects —	Detroit	Effort
	Pressey	Industry
Reading	P. School	Cooperation
Vocabulary	Other	
Arithmetic		
English		

CELLHOUSE . . . .
139

19 _____

DATE _____

No. _____ has permission

to buy the following art supplies from the commissary:

Name **140**

Course _____

Reg. No. _____

Teacher _____ Age _____

Color _____

Date _____

LESS	DATE	GRADE	LESS	DATE	GRADE	LESS	DATE	GRADE	LESS	DATE	GRADE	LESS	DATE	GRADE

141

MONTHLY CHLORINATION REPORT

REPORT ON _____ WATER SUPPLY MONTH ENDING _____ 195 _____

Day	Water Treated During Day In 1000 Gallons	CHLORINE DORAGE		RESIDUAL CHLORINE Parts Per Million		REMARKS:
		Weight of Cylinder	lbs. Used During 24 Hrs.	A.M.		A. Unusual Conditions
				1 2 3 4 5 6 7 8 9 10 11 12	1 2 3 4 5 6 7 8 9 10 11 12	B. Bacterial Samples Collected
						C. Chlorinator Trouble
1						
2						
3						
4						
5						
6						
7						

142

No. _____

NAME _____

ALIAS _____

RACE	AGE	IN YEAR	ENG. HEIGHT

F. P. CLASS _____

Reg. No. **143** Assign. _____ Cell No. _____

	Partners	Cell	Date
Name			
Received			
Cell No.			
Sentence			
Transfer			

Form No. 3516

J-179—2-58

Fig. 144. Power House. This shows the information taken daily from each of the different reports and is made out on the first of each month for the Chief Engineer by the officer in charge of the Power House.

Fig. 145. Honor Farm Dairy. Progressive Sheet.

Fig. 146. Honor Farm Dairy. This sheet is used for a daily production sheet for the individual cow.

Fig. 147. Honor Farm Dairy. This sheet is used when the cow has complications when calving.

Fig. 148. Power House. These charts are made out daily at each well. They show the amount of water pumped, hours not in service and the meter reading. These forms are used by the Power House Officer.

Fig. 149. This card is used for complete parts break down on standard stock items such as furniture factory manufacturers. When a new item is to be contemplated for manufacturing as a stock item, draftsmen draw plans for each part and as a whole, which is then checked and approved. The card is then made out by the cost clerk and draftsman and then checked and approved.

Fig. 150. Cell House. Record of inmates checked in and out of cell house.

Fig. 151. Cell House. Record of cell search.

Fig. 152. Officer in charge of shift at Diagnostic Depot. Record of shift officer at the Diagnostic Depot (daily).

Fig. 153. Any Assignment. After this form is signed by the issuing officer and stamped by the Senior Captain, this serves as a pass for inmate to the designated assignment.

Fig. 154. Honor Farm Dairy. Livestock Count and monthly record of specified groups of milk cows and calves.

Fig. 155. Honor Farm Dairy. This form is used for the purpose of identifying the individual cow.

Fig. 156. The Grade School Term Report Card is maintained as a permanent record of each inmate student's progress. Bi-monthly grades and term test grades are recorded as well as promotions and demotions.

Fig. 157. The Grade School Inmate Supply Card is maintained by the officer who issues student supplies. This record is maintained as a check on wastefulness.

Fig. 158. Grade School Completion Notices are sent to the Record Office for inclusion in the inmates' file upon their successful completion of the Grammar School curriculum.

Fig. 159. The Inmate Student Record Card is a permanent record maintained by the Grade School on all inmate students. It records his arrival, promotion or demotion and his transfer to other assignments. This record is permanently on file at the Grade School for all students past and present.

Fig. 160. Farm Office and Dairy. These forms are used as original copies sent on all letters and receivers sent out of this office.

Fig. 161. Grade School Schedule of Classes forms are issued to the inmate students at the beginning of each term. This form is used to schedule each inmate's subjects for the term.

Fig. 162. Senior Captain. Used for detail change for inmate. Authorized by Senior Captain.

Fig. 163. Senior Captain. Used when inmate is transferred from one branch of the Institution to another. For example: from the Joliet Branch to Stateville.

Fig. 164. Information Desk. This form is filled out and signed by person visiting inmate and is kept in the Information Desk records.

Fig. 165. Information Desk. This form is issued by the Officer of the Information Desk to a person who has visited an inmate and wishes to purchase commissary for inmate. After this is presented to the Officer's Commissary and the order is filled, the form is returned to the Information Desk for permanent filing.

Fig. 166. This form is used to report items made at the "M & M Shops" and that are to be set up on Inventory.

Fig. 167. Monthly High School Report Card.

154
DAIRY DAILY LIVESTOCK COUNT - MONTH OF _____ 19___

Date	Herd-Bulls	Cows in Milk	Dry-Cows	Total Milk-Cows	Heifers over 2 Years	Heifers 1 Year to 2 Years	Heifer Calves	Total Heifer-Calves	Bull-Calves	Total Count	Check	Births	Deaths	
1														
2														
3														
4														
5														
6														
7														
8														

157 Name _____ Paper _____
Pencils _____
No._____
Erasers _____

155

Name _____
Date of Birth _____
Sire _____
Dam _____
Sold to _____
Died _____
Breeder _____
Bought of _____

CALVING RECORD

Sire of Calf	Date Fresh	Name or Number of Calf
		1st.
		2nd.
		3rd.
		4th.
		5th.

162 ILLINOIS STATE PENITENTIARY
_____ 19___ SENTENCE _____

DETAIL CHANGE

Inmate _____ No._____
Assignment _____
Detail

COUNT AT——DAILY _____
SUNDAY & HOLIDAYS _____

156
THE STATEVILLE GRADE SCHOOL
TERM CARD

NUMBER _____ NAME _____ AGE _____
Date of Entering _____ Last _____
Assigned to Grade _____ Date of Graduation _____

SUBJECT	GRADES											
MONTH	1	2	3	4	5	6	1	2	3	4	5	6
Arithmetic												
Civics												
Geography												
Grammar												
History												
Literature												

GRADE ENTRANCE _____
Grade _____
Par. Mean. _____ Par.
Vocabulary _____ Vocal
Read. Aver. _____ Read.
Arith. Reas. _____
Arith. Co. _____

163 ILLINOIS STATE PENITENTIARY — JOLIET
INMATE TRANSFER
_____ 19—.
No._____
Please Transfer _____ To _____
Now at _____
Reason _____
Senior Captain

158 STATEVILLE ELEMENTARY SCHOOL
COMPLETION NOTICE

Date _____

Record Clerk _____

_____ has completed the Elementary

School course and received a Will County Diploma

Superintendent Of Education

164
NAME _____ NO._____
ADDRESS _____
CITY _____ STATE _____
RELATION _____
NAME _____
ADDRESS _____
CITY _____

159
NO._____ NAME _____
ENTERED _____ AGE: _____

GRADE	DATE	TESTED	ASSIGNED TO GRADE
			DISPOSITION

165
RETURN INFORMATION DESK

Pkgs._____ Pints _____
Received _____ Date _____
Permit _____ to purchase
$_____ in merchandise in the Officers' Commissary for
_____ No._____ to be forwarded
to cell _____ in cell house _____ this date only.
Maximum amount $2.00

160
FARM SUPERINTENDENT
ILLINOIS STATE PENITENTIARY
JOLIET, ILLINOIS

166 NEW EQUIPMENT ISSUE REPORT

TO: INVENTORY CONTROL OFFICE
FROM: M. & M. SHOPS, STATEVILLE
ISSUED TO: _____ (NAME OF ASSIGNMENT)
DESCRIPTION OF ITEM: _____

161
STATEVILLE GRADE SCHOOL
SCHEDULE OF CLASSES

PERIOD	I	II	III	IV
MONDAY				
TUESDAY				
WEDNESDAY				

167 THE STATEVILLE HIGH SCHOOL
Name _____ Date _____

Subject	Grade	Subject	Grade
English		Science	
Literature		Accounting	
Bus. Arithmetic		French	
Algebra		Spanish	
Geometry		Typing	
Trigonometry		Art	
Civics		Shorthand	
History		Biology	
Gen'l. Math.		Latin	
General Average		(Over)	

Fig. 168. Honor Farm Dairy. Monthly butter fat production sheet for each individual cow.

Fig. 169. Envelope for High School lesson return.

Fig. 170. This shows the results of the water analysis made daily at the Power House. This is sent to the Chief Engineer weekly.

Fig. 171. This form is used to report monthly business to the business office.

Fig. 172. Yearly Inventory listings of the various assignments.

Fig. 173. Chief Guard's Office. This form is used by the Chief Guard's Office to record the data pertaining to an employee's vacation. The date is listed when the employee is due a vacation, the amount of days due; opposite this is listed the actual date the vacation began, and the number of the days taken. This is done for each vacation.

Fig. 174. Bureau of Identification. Inmate Interview Form. This form is used when interviewing new arrivals at the Diagnostic Depot. This information is used for the fingerprint cards, description sheets, and the Captain's interview sheet.

Fig. 175. High School Lesson Sheet.

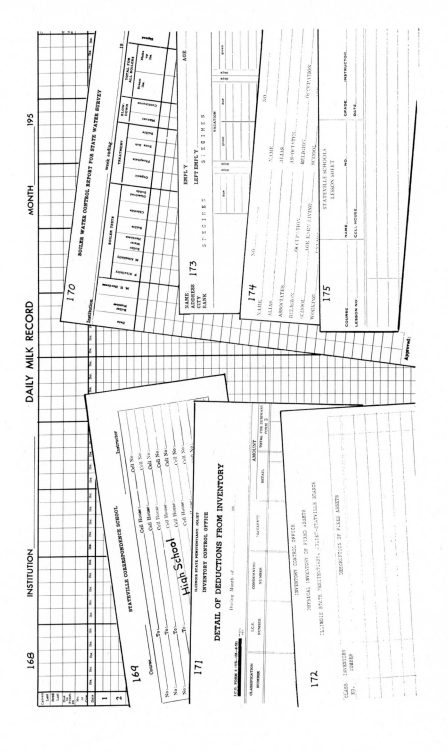

Fig. 176. Bureau of Identification. Inmate Statistical Form. This form is used for statistics covering the inmates received, released and transferred. This form, when completed at the end of the month, is forwarded to the warden.

Fig. 177. Bureau of Identification. Inmate Escape Form. This card is used when inmates escape. It is filled out with the inmate's picture mounted on front of the form and mailed to various law enforcing agencies.

Fig. 178. Bureau of Identification. Inmate Finger Print Card. This card is called the master finger print card which is used as a permanent record. This card is used for all new arrivals.

Fig. 179. Bureau of Identification. Inmate Finger Print Card. This card is used for the criminologist division at the Diagnostic Depot.

Fig. 180. Bureau of Identification. Applicant Finger Print Card. This card is used for all new applicants. Picture of applicant mounted on reverse side and used as a permanent record.

Fig. 181. Bureau of Identification. Inmate disposition release form. This form is used for all discharges and paroles which is signed by the Warden and forward to the Illinois State Bureau at Springfield.

Fig. 182. One-half Sheet Forms: Used for various short forms and letters.

Fig. 183. Bureau of Identification. Applicant finger print report form. This form indicates whether the applicant has any kind of a record at any of the following Bureaus: Chicago and Springfield, or the F. B. I.

Fig. 184. Library card used in the Grade School library for all Non-Fiction books.

Fig. 185. Library card used in the Grade School library for all Text books. The card is used for charging out books to inmates and is then placed in the pending file so that the location of all books is known.

Fig. 186. Grade School Date Due slips are placed in all library books that are loaned to inmates. The date due is stamped in the proper column.

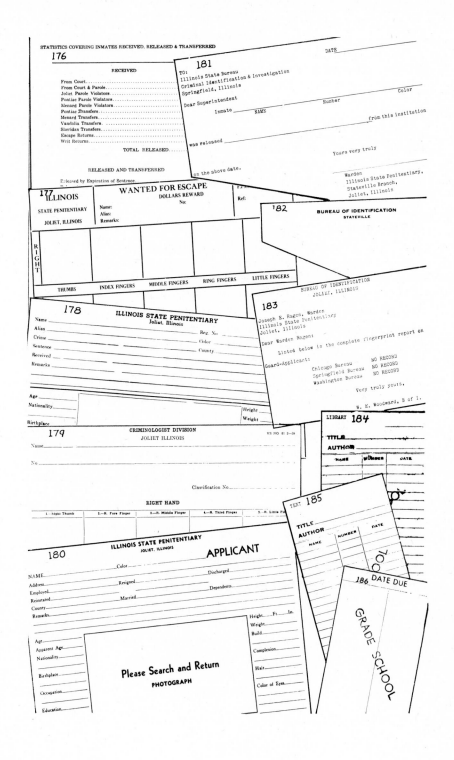

STATISTICS COVERING INMATES RECEIVED, RELEASED & TRANSFERRED

176

DATE _____

RECEIVED

From Court.............................
From Court & Parole...................
Joliet Parole Violators...............
Pontiac Parole Violators..............
Menard Parole Violators...............
Pontiac Transfers.....................
Menard Transfers......................
Vandalia Transfers....................
Sheridan Transfers....................
Escape Returns........................
Writ Returns..........................

TOTAL RELEASED......

RELEASED AND TRANSFERRED

Released by Expiration of Sentence.........

181

TO:
Illinois State Bureau
Criminal Identification & Investigation
Springfield, Illinois

Dear Superintendent

Inmate _____ NAME _____ Number _____ Color _____

_____ from this institution

was released _____

on the above date.

Yours very truly

_____
Warden
Illinois State Penitentiary,
Stateville Branch,
Joliet, Illinois

177 ILLINOIS

STATE PENITENTIARY

JOLIET, ILLINOIS

WANTED FOR ESCAPE
DOLLARS REWARD
No:

Name:
Alias:
Remarks:

Ref:

R I G H T

THUMBS | INDEX FINGERS | MIDDLE FINGERS | RING FINGERS | LITTLE FINGERS

182 BUREAU OF IDENTIFICATION
STATEVILLE

BUREAU OF IDENTIFICATION
JOLIET, ILLINOIS

178 ILLINOIS STATE PENITENTIARY
Joliet, Illinois

Name _____
Alias _____
Crime _____
Sentence _____
Received _____
Remarks _____

Reg. No. _____
Color _____
County _____

Age _____
Nationality _____
Birthplace _____

Height _____
Weight _____

183

Joseph E. Ragen, Warden
Illinois State Penitentiary
Joliet, Illinois

Dear Warden Ragen:

Listed below is the complete fingerprint report on

Guard-Applicant:

Chicago Bureau   NO RECORD
Springfield Bureau   NO RECORD
Washington Bureau   NO RECORD

Very truly yours,

W. E. Woodward, B of I.

179 CRIMINOLOGIST DIVISION
JOLIET ILLINOIS

VS NO 81 2—39

Name _____

No _____

Classification No _____

LIBRARY **184**

TITLE _____
AUTHOR _____

NAME | NUMBER | DATE

RIGHT HAND

1.—Right Thumb	2.—R. Fore Finger	3.—R. Middle Finger	4.—R. Third Finger	5.—R. Little Finger

ILLINOIS STATE PENITENTIARY
JOLIET, ILLINOIS

180 APPLICANT

_____ Color _____

NAME _____
Address _____
Employed _____
Reinstated _____
County _____
Remarks _____

Discharged _____
Resigned _____
Dependents _____
Married _____

Height __Ft.__In.
Weight _____
Build _____

Age _____
Apparent Age _____
Nationality _____

Birthplace _____

Occupation _____

Education _____

Complexion _____

Hair _____

Color of Eyes _____

Please Search and Return
PHOTOGRAPH

TEXT **185**

TITLE _____
AUTHOR _____

NAME | NUMBER | DATE

186 DATE DUE

GRADE SCHOOL

Fig. 187. This card is used for itemizing all standard stock items received into stock rooms and a perpetual unit price on each part is kept up by stock clerk.

Fig. 188. Bureau of Identification. This form is used for all inmates released from the Institution. This is to certify they have been photographed and finger printed and to have been compared with these upon arrival.

Fig. 189. Bureau of Identification. Employee's Record Card. This card is filled out and signed by new applicant. Picture is mounted on front of card.

Fig. 190. Bureau of Identification. Outside construction workers forms. Information is used to fill out finger print cards.

Fig. 191. This letter head used by the Stateville School of Barbering, a barber school licensed by the State of Illinois, for the purpose of inter-institutional correspondence.

Fig. 192. This card used by the Stateville School of Barbering for the purpose of recording the hours spent on each given subject by the student barber. This is required by the Department of Registration and Education.

Fig. 193. This card used by the Stateville School of Barbering for the purpose of recording grades, examination dates, barber license numbers, and general barber records required by the Department of Registration and Education.

Fig. 194. This form used by the Stateville School of Barbering to provide barber information needed by student, apprentice and registered barbers upon their release from this institution.

Fig. 195. Chief Guard's Office. This form is used by the Chief Guard's Office for payroll purposes.

Fig. 196. Information Desk. Used to pass **one** visitor of inmate through the Guard Hall to Visiting Room or where ever the visit is being held. This is signed by the Officer at the Information Desk.

Fig. 197. Information Desk. Used to pass **two** visitors of inmate through the Guard Hall to Visiting Room or where ever the visit is being held. This is signed by the Officer at the Information Desk.

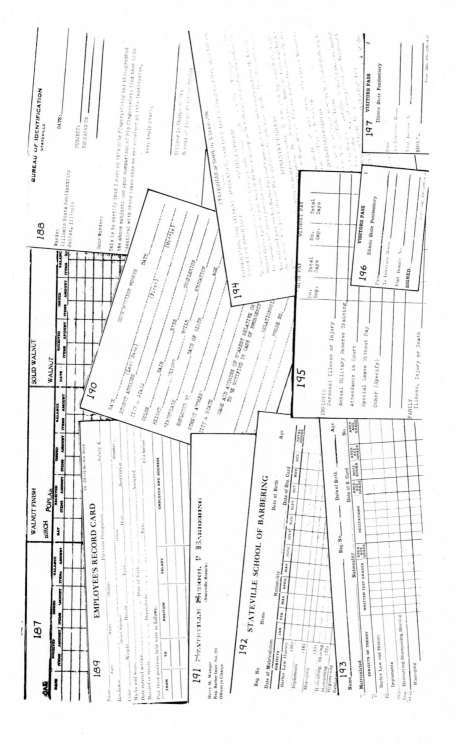

187

QAP	RECEIVED				ISSUED				BALANCE	
SIZE	ITEMS	AMOUNT	ITEMS		DAY	ITEMS	AMOUNT	ITEMS	ITEMS	AMOUNT

WALNUT FINISH   BIRCH   POPLAR   SOLID WALNUT   WALNUT

188

189

EMPLOYEE'S RECORD CARD

Name _____ Present Occupation _____ Salary $ _____
Residence _____ (Street) (Town) (County) (State)
Color _____ Weight _____ Eyes _____ Hair _____ Institution _____
Marks and Scars _____ Height _____ Date of Birth _____ Acquired _____
Date entered service _____ Title _____ Civil Service _____
Married or Single _____ Dependents _____

Past three positions held were as follows:

FROM	TO	POSITION	EMPLOYER AND ADDRESS	SALARY

vs. 2M—12-36—Not Stock

190

CONSUMPTION WORKER   DATE _____

NAME _____ (Last Name) (First) (Middle)
STREET ADDRESS _____
CITY & JAIL _____
COLOR _____ HAIR _____ EYES _____ BUILD _____ COMPLEXION _____
HEIGHT _____ WEIGHT _____ DATE OF BIRTH _____ EDUCATION _____ AGE _____
BIRTHPLACE _____
EMPLOYED BY _____
STREET ADDRESS _____
CITY & STATE _____
NAME AND ADDRESS OF NEAREST RELATIVE OR
TO BE NOTIFIED IN CASE OF EMERGENCY _____ RELATIONSHIP _____
PHONE NO. _____

191

STATEVILLE SCHOOL OF BARBERING
(Stateville Branch)

Harry M. Weniger
Reg. Barber Instr. No. 131
Officer in Charge

192

STATEVILLE SCHOOL OF BARBERING

Reg. No. _____ Name _____ Nationality _____ Date of Birth _____ Age _____
Date of Matriculation _____

SUBJECTS	JAN	FEB	MAR	APRIL	MAY	JUNE	JULY	AUG	SEPT	OCT	NOV	DEC	TOTAL HOURS
Barber Law History (16)													
Implements													
Massaging (16)													
Haircutting (11)													
Shampooing (17)													
High-and ...													

193

Name _____ Reg. No. _____ Date of S. Card _____ Age _____

SUBJECTS OF THEORY	WRITTEN TEST GRADES	AVER. AGE GRADE	RECITATIONS	AVER. AGE GRADE	NOTE BOOKS	AVER. AGE GRADE
Matriculated						
Barber Law and History						
Implements						
Haircutting Shampooing Shaving						
Massaging						

194

STATEVILLE SCHOOL ...

195

	WITHOUT PAY		WITH PAY	
	No. Emp.	Total Days	No. Emp.	Total Days

EMPLOYEE
Personal Illness or Injury
Annual Military Reserve Training
Attendance in Court
Special Leave Without Pay
Other (Specify)

FAMILY
Illness, Injury or Death

196

VISITORS PASS
Illinois State Penitentiary

Pass _____
To Interview Room _____
Visit Inmate No. _____
SIGNED _____

197

VISITORS PASS
Illinois State Penitentiary

_____
In Interview Room _____
Visit Inmate No. _____
SIGN _____

Fig. 198. These forms used by the Stateville School of Barbering for the purpose of instructing student barbers on barber theory, anatomy, skin and scalp diseases, etc.

198 STERILIZATION AND SANITATION

1. Why is it important to practice sanitation and hygiene in
2. What is meant by hygiene?
3. The study of hygiene is divided into how many classes?
4. What is meant by sanitation?
5. What is sterilization?
6. Name four ways in which sterilization may be accompl
7. What is an antiseptic?
8. What is a germicide or disinfectant?
9. What is a deodorant?
10. What is meant by (a) asepsis; (b) sepsis?
11. What is meant by sterile?
12. For what objects may boiling water be used for steri
    should they remain in the boiling water?
    .... that have been boiled be kept ...... —what

198 THE EXCRETORY SYSTEM

1. Name the parts of the excretory system.
2. How is the waste matter discharged?
3. Locate and briefly describe size and function of the kidneys.
4. With what kind of blood are the kidneys supplied?
5. What are glands? Describe their function.
6. Name seven important glands of the body. Briefly describe each.
7. Briefly describe the action of the thyroid glands.

THE RESPIRATORY SYSTEM

1. What is respiration?
2. What is meant by abdominal breathing? Costal breathing?
3. How many openings has the pharynx?
4. Where is the larynx located?
5. Briefly describe the vocal cords.

THE CIRCULATORY SYSTEM
(Vascular & Lymphatic)

1. Define blood.
2. What are these blood vessels called?
3. What is the action of the arteries and can they b
4. What are veins?
5. What are capillaries?
6. What two branches compose the vascular system?
7. What is the function of the blood vascular system
8. What are the functions of the blood?
9. What organ forces the blood through the body?
10. What is the color of the blood in the arteries; in tl
11. What portion of the body is blood?
12. Of what is blood composed?
13. What is plasma; of what is it composed?
14. What is the ....

**198 DIGESTIVE EXCRETORY AND
RESPIRATORY SYSTEMS**

THE DIGESTIVE SYSTEM

1. Of how many elements is the body composed? Name them.
2. What substances are produced by the combination of these elements?
3. What is water (H2O)?
4. What elements form mineral matter, or inorganic salts?
5. Where are the inorganic salts found?
6. What part does iron play in the blood?
7. What are carbohydrates?
8. Of what are fats composed, and in what forms are they known to us?
9. What do proteins contain?
10. Name some of the foods that are rich in various forms of proteins.
11. What other substances are very essential to the body?
12. How are vitamins designated?
13. What are the effects if the diet is defic...... Vitamin A?
14. Where is Vitamin A mainly found?
15. What is the effect if the diet is defic
16. Where is Vitamin B found?
17. What is the effect of the lack of Vital
18. Where is Vitamin C found?
19. What is Vitamin D and what is the eff
    ...... is the process of repair called a?
    .... must under

**198 DEFINITION OF COMMON TERMS
APPLIED TO DISEASE**

What is meant by an epidemic?
What is meant by congenital disease?
What is meant by (a) seasonal disease (b) occupational disease?
What causes (a) parasitic disease (b) pathogenic disease?
What is meant by (a) systemic disease (b) pathogenic disease?
What is a venereal disease?
What is meant by deficiency disease?
What is a disease?
What is a skin disease?
What is meant by (a) acute disease (b) chronic disea...
What is meant by (a) contagious disease (b) infect...

**DISEASES OF THE SEBACE...
(OIL) GLANDS**

Briefly describe comedones blackheads. Where do thi
and how are they removed?
What is seborrhea; what parts are affected and what is
What is a steatoma, and how is it treated?
What are milia, and what is their treatment?
What is acne, and what is the main cause of the diseas
What is asteatosis, and what is the treatment for sam
What is an acne rosacea?
me the common disease of the sebaceous (oil) gl
m.

DISEASES OF ...
cribe hydrosyst...
cribe the sud...

198 PITYRIASIS

What is pityriasis pilaris?
What treatments are recommended for pityriasis steatoides?
What is pityriasis simplex?
Differentiate between pityriasis and seborrhea.
What treatments are recommended for pityriasis capitis?
Name and briefly describe the two types of pityriasis.
Define pityriasis.

DERMATITISIS

Define dermatitis venenata.
What is meant by dermatitis medicamentosa? Give treatment for same.
Briefly describe dermatitis seborrheica.
What is meant by dermatitis?
...ne dermatitis combustionalis.

ECZEMA

**198 NON-CONTAGIOUS AFFECTIONS OF
THE HAIR**

Name three non-contagious affections of the hair that come under the category
of atrophia piloris (atrophy of the hair).
Define monilethrix.
What is fragilitas crinium?
Define canities.
What are the causes of hair losing its color, and what treatments are recom-
What is trichorrhexis nodosa?
What is hypertrichosis, and how is it tr
mended?
How treated?
What is trichoptilosis; how treated?
Name the six non-contagious affection...

PIGMENTATION
Define albinism. Is there any treatment
What is meant by vitiligo? Give tre
Name several types of naevi (nevi).
What is ...... lentigo senilis?
.... an? Give treat
.... tment.
.... h patches, or
......? Give treatm...

HYPER...
(New
......rum and wha

.....ve treatmen

DISEAS...
b) onchon
onychia (
hatrophia
hocrypto...
...ohatrophi
...that may

198 SHEDDING AND REGROWTH OF HAIR

Is the shedding of the hair painful?
What is the present-day barber trying to accomplish?
What is the difference between the animal and the human in regards to
shedding of the hair?
What happens while the old hair is attached to the middle follicle region?
What causes the old hair to fall out?
What may happen after a severe illness?

NAILS

Define the nail bed.
What part of the nail is the free edge?
Describe the nail bod...
What is a nail?

198 THE NERVOUS SYSTEM

1. What is a nerve?
2. What functions do the nerves perform?
3. How many divisions are there to the nervous system?
4. Name and describe each system.
5. What is the principal nerve center?
6. Where is the brain? What protects it?
7. What is the front and upper part of the brain called? The back and lower
   portion called?
8. What portion of the brain...... ...ent of intelligence?
   ....cerebrum?

...... the spinal cord? What are they called?
...? Name them.

......rves?
....us action? Decrease the nervous action?
...... What nerves cause it to turn pale?
...and vaso-constrictor nerves belong?
...hat does it result in?

...nal condition?
...e there? How are they known?
...rves.
...nerve?
...e motor oculi nerve?
...ve?
...chlear nerve?
...al nerve? What kind of nerve is it?
...rigeminal, or trifacial nerve? Name
...
...What does it supply?
...ranch? What does it supply?
...ndibular branch supply? How large
...
...does it supply?
...e? What does it supply?
...nerve?
...? What does it supply?
.... does it supply?

198 HONING AND STROPPING

How is the razor turned in honing?
What is the result to the razor edge when it is passed over the hone?
What is the appearance of the razor edge after honing, when seen through the
magnifying glass?
How is the razor tested after honing?
How is the science of honing acquired?
How is the razor stroked across the hone?
...or tested?
...erfect edge?
...honing?
...the rough or overhoned edge?
...stropping?
...between honing and stropping in stroking the razor?
...a freshly honed razor?
...n shaving with a blunt edge razor?
...the keen edge on the ...
...a coarse edge?

SHAVING

...bbing the lather into the beard?
...r steaming the
...why is the rota
...is shaved first
...wild hair?

...is shaved wit...
...l not be use
...patron ma...
...e to sugges...
...to sugges...

198 BLOOD SUPPLY OF THE FACE AND SCALP

1. Does the hair contain blood vessels?
2. What blood vessels contain the nutriments and oxygen that are necessary
   for the hair?
3. Name and locate the principle arteries that supply the head.
4. Into how many branches do the common carotids divide, and what does each
   supply?
5. Whe...

...id artery change its name?
...ting at the temples?
...il supply?
...eme posterior of the scalp:...
...ed to the ...

198 MUSCLES OF THE MOUTH

Describe the quadratus labii superioris.
What is the insertion, function and nerve supply of this m...?
Name the principle muscles of the mouth.
What is the origin, insertion, function and nerve s... of the caninus
(levator anguli)?
Define levator, anguli.
What is the origin, insertion, function and ner...
...toris (depressor labii inferioris)?
...tion of t'
...m, er
...ne
...ed?
...and nerve
...give to the fa...
...ion and nerve
...inator muscle

198 RAZORS

How is the size of the shears usually gauged, and what sizes are most commonly
used?
Name the various plain grinds. Which is preferable?
What are the two main types of shear grinds, and which type is mostly used?
What types of grinding are there, and which is most widely used?
What important things should be learned about razors?
What is a crocus finish?
Name the different types of shears. Which type is most commonly used?
Name the parts of the razor.
Name the parts of the barber shears.
In what different ways are razors finished?
...... the term "grind" mean?
.... measured, and what width is most commonly used?
.... is not desirable?
.... zor?

198 PERSONAL HYGIENE

1. What is meant by personal hygiene?
2. What are some of the means used for health maintenance?
3. How is the skin used as an index to health?
4. Give four rules regarding poison.
5. What is acne, and briefly describe each?
6. Why is cleanliness essential?
7. Why is it im...
8. Wh...

.... to have pure wat
......ials of mouth hygi...
......given the teeth?
......be kept clean?
......be kept clean?
......bromidrosia, (b) t...
......at the barber be
......cal examinations
......s disease? Name
......vent a barber fr...
......e dressed?

BACTERIOLO...

.......he types of bac...
......anisms?
.... germs and m...
......bacteria in con...
......bacteria are a...

IPPERS
...rs. Which is most popular?
...ppers. Start by giving the ...

198 HAIR TONICS

Should a barber keep a record of hair tonic treatments? Give reasons.
How is a scalp steam given?
What are hair tonics and what are there benefits?
Why should the barber familiarize himself with the different kinds of hair tonic?
What is a scalp steam?
Where does the barber get correct information regarding administering of vari-
ous lotions, tonics and other preparations?

HAIRCUTTING

How should the fingers of the left hand be held in doing finger work on the sides
and back of the head?
Why is it necessary to learn to use hand clippers before the electric clippers?
On which side is the clipper work started?
Name the six styles of haircuts.
Give positions to hold the razor to shave the neck outline on the right side;
on the left side.
What is involved in a neck shave?
Which finger is inserted in the finger grip of the shears?
Of what aid is singeing to the hair? Give reasons.
What is the appearance of the short pomp, in a side view?
What does the art of haircutting imply?
....ing done? ....gainst?

Fig. 199. These forms are used for ordering wood to be used for any item whatsoever, whether a stock item, a special item, or an item that is to be repaired.

Fig. 200. This form is used by the Master Mechanic's Office to request quotations from suppliers.

Fig. 201. This letter head is used in the Master Mechanic's Office for inter-departmental and inter-institutional correspondence.

Fig. 202. This form is used in the various Master Mechanic's Departments for the ordering of parts and equipment used in their operation and on their assignment.

Fig. 203. This form is used by the J. B. Power House and the S. B. Power House and the Farm Colony to report on boiler water and is then transmitted to the State Water Survey Division.

Fig. 204. This form is used in the Master Mechanic's Office in requesting O.F.D. orders from the Business Manager.

Fig. 205. Any Assignment. Request to Master Mechanic's Shop for repair of equipment or request for maintenance needs.

Fig. 206. This letter head is used in the Master Mechanic's Office for inter-departmental and inter-institutional correspondence.

Fig. 207. Lieutenant in Chief Guard's Office. This form is made out at count time.

Fig. 208. This form is used to report purchases made by the inmates' officers benefit funds in order to set items of equipment up on inventory.

Fig. 209. This report is used to notify the Inventory Control Office that new equipment was issued from the "M & M Store" stock.

199

FURNITURE FACTORY
LUMBER REQUISITION
FROM LUMBER YARD

No._____ Date_____

NO. OF PIECES	THICKNESS	WIDTH	LENGTH	BOARD FEET ORDERED	KIND OF WOOD	NO. CUTS PER BRD. TOTAL	TO BE USED FOR			DESCRIPTION	ITEM	BOARD FEET DELIVERED	PRICE
							THICK	WIDTH	LENGTH				

---

204 REQUEST Date_____

To: MASTER MECHANIC'S SHOP

FOR_____ (Department)

PLEASE_____

NO WORK WILL BE DONE
OR MATERIAL FURNISHED
_____ ORDER

Requesting Officer
FORM 312—VS—LITHO

---

206 OFFICE OF THE
MASTER MECHANIC
ADMINISTRATION BUILDING
STATEVILLE BRANCH

---

200 STATE OF ILLINOIS
WILLIAM G. STRATTON, GOVERNOR

DEPARTMENT OF PUBLIC SAFETY
GENERAL OFFICE SPRINGFIELD

REPLY TO
ILLINOIS STATE PENITENTIARY
JOLIET BRANCH
Joseph E. Ragen, Warden
JOLIET

REQUEST FOR QUOTATION

TO:

Reference_____
Date_____

Gentlemen:
We request you to quote us prices on the articles listed below. There will be no deviation should an order be placed on t
Please read carefully the following instructions as there will be no deviation should an order be placed on t
basis of this bid.
1—Prices must be quoted FOB Joliet, Illinois.
2—No Illinois Retailers' Tax is to be included as State purchases are exempt.
3—We reserve the right to increase or decrease quantity by not more than 10% without change in pr
4—No substitution will be accepted without prior approval.
5—If there is an error in the extension price it is understood that the unit price is to prevail.
6—It is understood that your bid does not obligate us in any manner whatsoever.

Very truly yours,

JOSEPH E. RAGEN WARDEN
Illinois State Penitentiary, Joliet

QUANTITY	UNIT	DESCRIPTION OF ARTICLE	UNIT PRICE	EXTENS

207

STATEVILLE COUNT

Min   Pl_____   _____ 19__

Fire Watch	
Guard Hall	
Administration Building	
Gen. Hospital Patients	
Gen. Hospital Help	
Detention Patients	
Detention Help	
Officers' Kitchen	
Officers' Kit. Specials	
Isolation Punishment	
Isolation Help	
Segregation	

---

205 OFFICE OF THE
MASTER MECHANIC
ADMINISTRATION BUILDING
STATEVILLE BRANCH

Mr. A. D. Borio
Business Manager   Date_____

Dear Sir:
    Kindly issue an OFD authorizing the purchase
of the following:

FROM:

QUANTITY	UNIT	DESCRIPTION

---

201 OFFICE OF THE
MASTER MECHANIC
ADMINISTRATION BUILDING
STATVILLE BRANCH

202

MATERIAL REQUEST TO MASTER MECHANIC

DEAR SIR:
WE ARE IN NEED OF THE BELOW LISTED MATERIALS:

PART NAME OR DESCRIPTION	PART NO.	AMOUNT	SIZES	MODEL OR MAKE, SER. NOS., ETC.

---

209 NEW EQUIPMENT ISSUE REPORT

TO: INVENTORY CONTROL OFFICE
FROM: MECHANICAL STORE
INVOICE NO._____
PURCHASE ORDER NO._____ DATE OF INVOICE_____
PURCHASED FROM_____
DATE ISSUED_____
ISSUED TO_____
ITEM_____

---

203 BOILER WATER CONTROL REPORT FOR STATE WATER SURV

Institution_____
_____ week ending_____

Date	Boiler Number	M. U. Hardness	BOILER TESTS							TREATMENT					Bl Da
			P. Alkalinity	M Alkalinity	Boiler Water Hardness	Sodine	Chlorids	Dissolved Solids	Organic	Phosphate	Soda Ash	Sulphite	Manual		

---

208 INMATES AND OFFICERS BENEFIT FUND
NEW EQUIPMENT REPORT

TO: INVENTORY CONTROL OFFICE

FROM: Chief Clerks Office

The follwing item has been purchased through the Inmates or
Officers Benefit Fund as indicated:

INMATES ☐   OFFICERS ☐

P.O.#_____ OFD#_____ ON OPEN ACCOUNT ☐

PURCHASED FROM_____
_____ BANK_____

Fig. 210. Chief Guard's Office. This form is used by the Chief Guard's Office for the purpose of obtaining a confidential rating of an employee. It is used when an employee is on a probationary status, and also when an employee is given a new assignment.

Fig. 211. This form is used to report the receipt of lumber stock for the Master Mechanic and is filled in by whoever is the receiving officer.

Fig. 212. Chief Guard's Office. This form is used by the Chief Guard's Office for the purpose of rating an employee. A copy of this form is kept in the personnel office and used in the event that this institution is used as a job reference by the former employee. This form is used only when a person has left the employment of this institution.

Fig. 213. Daily electric meter readings taken at the sub-station. This is sent to the Chief Engineer by the officer in charge of the Power House.

Fig. 214. This form is used in replying to the **Various** Local Draft Boards' requests for information on the sentences of inmates.

Fig. 215. This form used by the Stateville School of Barbering to notify the Department of Registration and Education, Barber Division when an apprentice barber discontinues his apprenticeship under a registered barber. This information required by the Barber Division under a ruling passed in 1959, in that a registered barber under whom an apprentice barber is serving, must notify the Barber Division as to the date the apprentice serving was discontinued.

Fig. 216. Senior Captain. Inmate's honor pledge signed by any inmate detailed to work in a position of trust. (Especially outside the walls.)

Fig. 217. Bureau of Identification. Inmate Statistical Form. This form is used covering the number of crimes; minimum and maximum number of years and minimum and maximum number of sentences. This form when completed is forwarded to the Warden.

5. A — Officious. Has an overbearing manner.
   B — Very exacting. Sometimes oversteps his auth-
       ority.
   C — Is firm, but fair and just in his dealings.

6. A — Cannot assume responsibility
   B — Tends to follow rather than lead
   C — Is willing and able to accept res

210

7. A — Has an indifferent attitude towards safety and security mea-
       sures. Doesn't think it can happen here.
8. B — Believes inmates are constantly plotting to outwit him or to
       escape. Over emphasizes or exaggerates.
   C — Realizes that inmates have fewer incentives and different
       values than free men. Is alert and cautious.

SECTION 3 — JOB PERFORMANCE

Check the one statement in each of the following groups which you believe most acc
describes this employee's performance.

1. A — Either resents or pays little attention to instructions.
   B — Accepts instructions, but follows them only half-heartedly.
   C — Follows closely directions of supervising officers.

2. A — ... supervision of tools.
   B — ... importance to the security of tools, but sometimes has trou
        ... tools and is able to account for them at all times.
        ... mproper attitude towards supervision of equipment a
        ... supervision to equipment and supplies, but needs mc
        ... ion of equipment and supplies. Makes certain they c
        ... used.
        ... ate counts of ...

211   LUMBER RECEIVED

PURCHASE ORDER NUMBER

FROM   LENGTH

DATE

DESCRIPTION

SIZE

212   ILLINOIS STATE PENITENTIARY
           JOLIET, ILLINOIS

Date

TO: Mr. Joseph E. Ragen, Warden
    Stateville Branch

Dear Sir:

Listed below you will find a summary of information, relative to the employment record of the following
named officer:

EMPLOYED   LEFT

OFFICER   COOPERATION

ABILITY   APPEARANCE

                        CONDUCT

Respectfully yours,

OFFICE OF THE CHIEF ENGINEER

213   DAILY REPORT OF ELECTRIC METER READINGS
           AT THE SUB STATION — STATEVILLE
           FOR MONTH OF _____ 19___

DATE	METER #1 READINGS	DAILY KW HRS. USED	DATE	METER #2 READINGS	DAILY KW HRS. USED
1			1		
2			2		
3					
5					
6					
7					
8					
9					
10					
11					
12					

214   STATE OF ILLINOIS
           WILLIAM G. STRATTON, GOVERNOR

           DEPARTMENT OF PUBLIC SAFETY
           GENERAL OFFICE, SPRINGFIELD

ILLINOIS STATE PENITENTIARY
JOLIET BRANCH
JOSEPH E. RAGEN, WARDEN
JOLIET

Veterans' Service Office

216
ILLINOIS STATE PENITENTIARY

HONOR PLEDGE

I, the undersigned inmate of the Illinois State Penitentiary, _____
Branch, in consideration of being detailed to work in a position of trust and
honor, do promise William G. Stratton, Governor and Joseph E. Ragen, Warden, on my word of honor that I will obey all orders of all officers or employees
of the institution.

I further promise that I will not trade nor traffic while holding this position of honor, neither will I be guilty of any immoral or illegal conduct.

I further promise that I will not escape, or try to escape
every thing in my power to prevent escape of any prison...

I further promise that I will give any information to
that may come to my knowledge of the violation of any ru

I, the undersigned have read the above and thoroughly
do hereby honestly promise to fulfil...

Local Board No.
Selective Service System

Gentlemen:

Thank you for your letter of
in which you request information concerning the above-
identified registrant.

A search...

ILLINOIS STATE PENITENTIARY
JOLIET BRANCH
JOSEPH E. RAGEN, WARDEN
JOLIET

215
STATE OF ILLINOIS
WILLIAM G. STRATTON, GOVERNOR

DEPARTMENT OF PUBLIC SAFETY
GENERAL OFFICE, SPRINGFIELD

217   INMATES RECEIVED UNDER NEW NUMBERS — JANUARY THRU

CRIME CHARGED	NO. OF CRIMES	NO. OF YEARS Min. Max.	AVERAGE SENTENCE Min. Max.
ABORTION			
ACCESSORY AFTER FACT			
AIDING AND ABETTING IN ESCAPE			
ARSON			
ASSAULT WHILE MASKED			
ASSAULT TO COMMIT A FELONY			
BIGAMY			
BRIBERY			
BURGLAR FOUND IN BLDG			
BURGLARY			

Department of Registration and Education
Barber Division
Springfield, Illinois

Gentlemen:

Please be advised that _____, apprentice
_____ has discontinued his service
_____ W Wengar,

Fig. 218. Bureau of Identification. Inmate Description of Prisoner Form. This form is used to take a complete description of each inmate upon arrival at the Diagnostic Depot. This is used as a permanent record. The information from this form is recorded in the Athropometric Book.

Fig. 219. Bureau of Identification. Employee's Identification Card. This form is signed by applicant. Thumb print printed on form. Their picture is mounted and then the form is sent to Warden Ragen for his signature and then returned to employee.

Fig. 220. This form shows where the daily electrical power was used. The report is sent every month to the Chief Engineer by the officer in charge of the Power House.

Fig. 221. This chart shows by the hour, the operation of the Power House. All of the information taken daily is used at the end of the month on the monthly reports sent to the Chief Engineer.

Fig. 222. These forms are used by the Veterans' Service Office as power of attorney to inspect the case files of veterans in the offices of the Veterans Administration.

Fig. 223. These forms are power of attorney forms used by the Veterans' Service Office in applying for military and medical histories from the military services.

Fig. 224. These forms are used for interview sheets by the Veterans' Service Office and requests for information from the Veterans Administration Office in Chicago.

Fig. 225. These forms are used for correspondence by the Veterans' Service Office.

Fig. 226. These forms are used as part of the permanent records of the correspondence of the Veterans' Service Office.

Fig. 227. These forms are used as part of the permanent records of the Veterans' Service Office for both the inmate veteran and employees.

Fig. 228. These forms are used primarily by the Personnel Department (Job Applicants) and by the Veterans' Service Office. They are power of attorney forms.

218

ILLINOIS STATE PENITENTIARY
DESCRIPTION OF PRISONER

FBI #_____
SBI #_____

Name_____
Alias_____
Received_____ County_____
Crime_____ Sentence_____
Race_____ Birthdate_____ A_____
Height_____ Birthplace_____
Weight_____
_____ Occupa_____

220

OFFICE OF THE CHIEF ENGINEER

MONTHLY REPORT OF ELECTRIC METER READINGS, NEW PRISON
FOR PERIOD:

METER NUMBER	LOCATION	CURRENT READING	thru PREVIOUS READING	CONSTANT
14983551	Canning Plant			
16276068	Canning Plant			
14983550	Cold Storage			10
15241001	Cold Storage			0
15718776	Furniture			10
15930243	Furniture			10
16375159	Garment St.			100

219

ILLINOIS STATE PENITENTIARY JOLIET, ILL
EMPLOYEE'S IDENTIFICATION CARD

	Hair	
	Eyes	
	Comp	
	Age	RIGHT THUMB
	Height	
	Weight	

WARDEN

FOLD ON LINE
Name_____
Address_____
City_____ State_____
County_____

221

FEED WATER TEMP.	OUT TEMP.	STEAM PRESS	1 GR. F-BOX	1 RED UPT.	2 GR. F-BOX	2 RED UPT.	3 GR. F-BOX	3 RED UPT.	4 GR. F-BOX	4 RED UPT.	5 GR. F-BOX	5 RED UPT.	6 GR. F-BOX
HOUR													
7													
8													
9													
10													
11													
12N													
1P													
2													

223

This is to request and authorize Murray W. Kirsch,
Veterans' Service Officer of this Institution, to make
copies of my Health and/or Service Record and to send
these copies out of the institution in the prosecution
of whatever claims I may make.

Date_____

222

VETERANS SERVICE OFFICE
ILLINOIS STATE PENITENTIARY
JOLIET, ILLINOIS

REQUEST FOR AND CONSENT TO RELEASE OF INFORMATION
FROM VETERANS ADMINISTRATION RECORDS

VETERANS ADMINISTRATION   name of veteran

to

name and address of individual to whom information is t_____

Veterans' Service Of_____
Illinois State Penitent_____
Box 1112
Joliet, Illinois

ILLINOIS STATE PENITENTIARY
JOLIET BRANCH
JOSEPH E. RAGEN, WARDEN
JOLIET

VETERANS' SERVICE OFFICE

_____ Health and Service
_____, I will furnish it upon

225

STATE OF ILLINOIS
WILLIAM G. STRATTON, GOVERNOR
DEPARTMENT OF PUBLIC SAFETY
GENERAL OFFICE, SPRINGFIELD

Enlisted:_____
Discharg_____
Rank:_____

228

Serial No._____

REQUEST FOR AND CONSENT TO R_____
FROM VETERAN'S R_____

To_____

NAME OF V_____

NAME AND ADDRESS OF ORGANIZATION AGENCY OR INDIVIDUAL T_____

VETERAN'S S_____

VA CLAIM NUM_____

I hereby request and authorize ☐ Army ☐ Navy ☐
☐ Coast Guard ☐ Veterans Administration to release the fol
records identified above, to the organization, agency, or individua
☐ 1. SERVICE RECORD • DATES ETC.
☐ 2. HEALTH RECORD, HOSPITALIZATION ETC.
3. Disciplinary Record
4. Type of Discharge Issued
Reason For Discharge
_____TIONAL INFORMATION DESIRED

224

VETERAN NO._____

INTERVIEW SHEET

VETERAN SERVICE OFFICE
ILLINOIS STATE PENITENTIARY
BOX 1112
JOLIET ILLINOIS

DATE_____ INST_____
NUMBER_____

NAME_____
1 REGARDING_____
2 REGARDING_____

226

VPS NO. _____

ILLINOIS STATE PENITENTIARY
JOLIET, ILL.

NAME_____
SERIAL NO._____   ·Veterans' Service Office

DATE_____ WW_____

227

INST NO_____   _ODY

INTERVIEW REGARDING_____

CASE NO_____
C NO_____

_____ THE INFORMATION IS TO BE ISSUED.

ACTION TAKEN

Fig. 229. Armory. Used by officers taking target practice.

Fig. 230. High School Art Permit to keep in cell.

Fig. 231. Lesson Return Envelope for the Correspondence School.

Fig. 232. Switch Board Operator. 7 - 3. Used to record regular calls made by phone from listed assignments to Operator.

Fig. 233. Captain's Office. Daily count sheet listing inmates on various assignments. Made out and signed by Lieutenant in the Captain's Office at 5:30 A.M., 5:00 P.M. and 8:30 P.M. counts.

Fig. 234. Chief Guard. Daily record of Officers on duty, vacation, etc.

Fig. 235. All Assignments. Record of all tools on assignment. This is taken monthly.

Fig. 236. Information Desk. Used to keep record of all visits to inmate, showing address of visitor, etc.

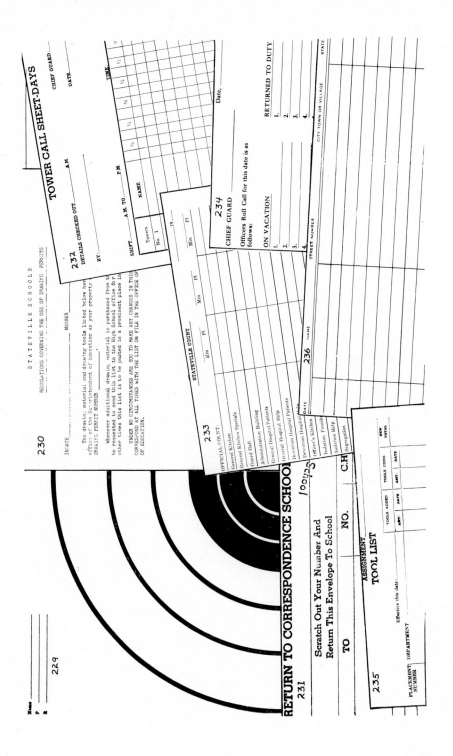

Fig. 237. Cell House. Record of bar rapping in cell house. Taken daily.

Fig. 238. Senior Captain. Letter head used by Senior Captains at the Diagnostic Depot. This is both at the Joliet and Stateville Branches.

Fig. 239. Cell House. Cell House count sheet. This shows the number of men from a cell house at various assignments.

Fig. 240. Switch Board Operator No., 3 to 11 Shift. Record of regular calls made by phone from listed assignments to Operator.

Fig. 241. Interviewing Officer at the Diagnostic Depot. This form is used to list the names of persons inmate desires to be approved as his correspondents and visitors.

Fig. 242. Cell House. Record of movement of inmates from cell to cell.

Fig. 243. Senior Captain. Record of interview of inmate by Senior Captain for a detail. This is kept in the Senior Captain's office.

Fig. 244. General Kitchen. Record of daily cost of meals regarding inmates.

Fig. 245. Form used by interviewing officer at Diagnostic Depot. This examination of prisoner sheet supplies personal history, data of inmate for Classification Board, Senior Captain and Record Office. Reverse side lists inmate's personal property on receipt, authorization for prison officials to censor inmate's mail.

Fig. 246. Short history of inmate, photograph and other pertinent information. If further information is needed, Record Office is consulted. Synopsis of disciplinary record on reverse side.

237

#3590 BAR REPORT

(X) FOR (GOOD)
(O) FOR (REPAIR)

TO THE WARDEN
STATEVILLE

SIR:

Respectfully submitting report of bars, cross-bars, windows, screens, locks and doors

Cell-House_____ This is a Monthly Report of Galleries and Vestib

GALLERY #_____ MONTH OF_____

BARS	1	2	3	4	5	6	7	8	9	10	11	12	13	14	15	16	17	18
BARS																		
X-BARS																		
WINDOWS																		
LOCKS																		
DOORS																		
SCREENS																		

BARS	22	23	24

238

OFFICE OF THE
SENIOR CAPTAIN

239

IN CHARGE_____
COUNT CHECKED ALL AROUND_____
TIME_____
CALL SHEET 3 TO 11 SHIFT_____ DATE_____ P.M.
LIEUT._____

240

TOWERS — OFFICER'S NAME	
No. 3	
No. 5	
No. 6	
No. 9	
No. 10	
No. 11	
No. 12	
No. 14	

General Kitchen
General Kitchen Specials
Guard Hall
Administration Building
General Hospital Patients
Officers Kitchen
Isolation Punishment

241

INMATES' MAILING LIST

No._____ an inmate of the Illinois State Penitentiary, have read my rule book
have been advised by an officer in the school at the Diagnostic Depot of my privileges as an inmate of the Institution,
especially rules covering my visits and correspondents Listed below are my prospective visitors and correspondents.

MARITAL STATUS: Single_____ Married_____ Divorced_____ Separated_____ Common-law_____

WIFE'S NAME_____

CHILDREN_____ AGE_____

ADDRESS_____

FATHER_____ LIVING_____ DECEASED_____

242

CELL MOVEMENT SHEET

DATE	NUMBER	NAME	FROM	CELL

243

Interviewed in Re_____
No._____ Div._____
Married_____ Live_____
Wife's Name_____ Age_____ Live_____
C_____ Age_____ Live_____
H_____ Age_____ Live_____
L_____
D_____ Live_____
B_____ Live_____
E_____ Live_____
N_____ Live_____
Father_____

244

ILLINOIS STATE PENITENTIARY
DAILY MEAL COST
DINING HALL

	BREAKFAST		DINNER	
	PER	COST	PER	COST
	LBS		LBS	

	HEAD
INGREDIENTS	
USED	LOAVES
BREAD	LBS

TOTAL NO. MEALS_____

245

EXAMINATION BLANK

EM: JOHN JOE DOE

Number H 00000 _____ Age 23

- Rec'd Menard 3-5-47 as #00001; Trans. Joliet 1-10-48 as #00000; Trans. Pontiac 7-20-
00001; Trans. Menard 12-19-50 as #00000; Trans. Menard 5-24-51 as 0000
- 0001; Rec'd Menard 3-21-49; Rec'd Joliet 12-19-50 as #00000 _____
Trans. Joliet 7-10-52 as #00000 _____

Name John Doe _____ Alias_____ Color White _____ Age 23

Received November 7, 1952 _____ County Vermilion _____ Sentence 1-20 yrs _____ Mother N.

Crime Auto Larceny _____ Nativity Hoopeston, Ill. _____ Father American _____ Nationality Irish-English

Date of Birth Feb 15, 1929 _____ Father American _____ Alien_____ Mother Died_____

Citizenship American _____ Naturalized_____ Mother Died_____ Number of Children_____

How long in U.S. life _____ Father Died_____

Parents Living single _____ Wife Living_____ Divorced_____ Separated_____

Marital State single _____ Religion_____ Social Security Number 000 0

Parents Living Together yes _____ Associate_____ Disposition_____

Born of Married Parents yes _____ After_____ Asylum_____ urban

Economic Conditions marginal _____ Dependent_____ none

Residence Before 14 Years of Age urban _____ Age Left School 18 _____ Inherit Anything no

Relatives Inmates of Penal Institutions 4 _____ Real Estate no _____ How Long Employed 1 Yr. at $42.00

Occupation_____ Date_____ Ins. Ed. or Drafted_____

246

Number 00000 _____ Color NEGRO _____ Crime Involuntary Manslaughter _____ Name John Doe _____ Age 4

Received June 12, 1959 _____ County COOK _____ Sentence 1-3 Years

Occupation Freight Handler _____ Assigned_____

Criminal History 19A C. H C = Chicago, Ill. (Assault & Batt.) 10 Days_____

Board Action Paroled, effective 6-12-60 _____

Approved 7-17-59; (1) Early & Late Detail (27 OC & WQ (3) Wires In C. Vil. 6 Pu to 6 Pu

Wanted_____

Physical Health Classification (A . . . .

Fig. 247. Front Gate. Record of all persons who enter the Institution on visits or on business. This does not include Institutional group visitors. This record includes the signature of person and other pertinent information. It is the duty and responsibility of the Officer in charge of the Front Gate to witness the signature of the person at the time of entry and to witness the signature when the person is ready to leave, making certain the signature is the same.

Fig. 248. Used when assigning man to trusted assignment.

Fig. 249. This is a "Write-Up" which is used in recommending transfer of an inmate to a trusted assignment. It is approved by five (5) supervising officers. The Record Clerk indicates whether he is wanted by another authority, whether there is an escape record, narcotic, etc., when he meets the board, release or discharge date.

Fig. 250. Letterhead used by Assistant Wardens for Inter-Institutional memoranda and correspondence.

Fig. 251. Form used by Outside Platform. Receipt for supplies and commodities delivered to General Store Receiving Room.

Fig. 252. Detail Count Forms used to keep running count of inmates assigned to Details.

Fig. 253. Letterhead used by Senior Captains for Inter-Institutional memoranda and correspondence.

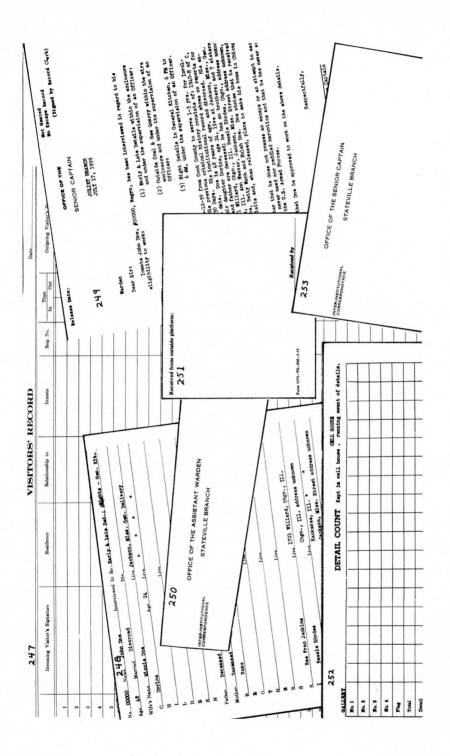

VISITORS' RECORD

Date_____

Not Wanted
No Escape Record (Signed by Record Clerk)

Incoming Visitor's Signature	Residence	Relationship to	Inmate	Reg. No.	Time In	Time Out	Outgoing Visitor's S...
1							
2							
3							
4							
5							

247

OFFICE OF THE
SENIOR CAPTAIN
JOLIET BRANCH
JULY 17, 1959

Release Date:

249

Warden

Dear Sir:

Inmate John Doe, #00000, Negro, has been interviewed in regard to his
eligibility to work:

(1) Early & Late Details within the enclosure
and under the supervision of an Officer:

(2) Outside Coal & New Quarry within the supervision of an
enclosure and under the supervision of an
Officer:

(3) Night Details in General Kitchen, 6 PM to
6 AM, under the supervision of an Officer:

...1-12-59 from Cook County to serve 1-3 yrs. for involuntary... His previous criminal history record shows no report... His ex-
pires... His 18 years of age, of Jackson, Miss., Gen.
90 Days. Is 48 years 24, live at Jackson; and 7 sisters
date. Doe has no brothers; address unknown,
Mr father are deceased Chgo., address unknown,
ll father, Chgo., Miss. Street address received
, Ill. Ann Webb and Eulah Doe, plans to make his home in Chicago
e, Betty Webb when released, plans to make his home
Asks and, when released, that he has never at-

never that he does not possess an escape or an attempt to es-
never used nor peddled narcotics and that he has never at-
the U.S. Armed Forces.

that Doe be approved to work on the above details.

Respectfully,

_____
Captain

Received by _____

253

OFFICE OF THE SENIOR CAPTAIN
STATEVILLE BRANCH

INTER-INSTITUTIONAL
CORRESPONDENCE

Received from outside platform:

251

Form 1571-VE-1M-3-59

OFFICE OF THE ASSISTANT WARDEN
STATEVILLE BRANCH

250

INTER-INSTITUTIONAL
CORRESPONDENCE

No. 00000 Name John Doe   Interviewed in Re-Early & Late Det.; Outside - Gen. Kit.
Married Divorced   Div.   Live Jackson, Miss. Gen. Delivery
Age 48
Wife's Name: Winnie Doe   Age 24   Live.   "   "
C. Darling   Live.
H.   Live.
L.   Live.
D.   Live.
E.   Live.
B.   Live.
Father- Deceased
Mother- Deceased
M. None
R.   Live. 1721 Willard, Chgo., Ill.
O.   "   Chgo., Ill. address unknown
T.   "   Live. Kankakee, Ill. "   "
H.   Live. Jackson, Miss. Street address unknown
R.
8 Bee Fran Jenkins
S. Bessie Rhodes

248

252

DETAIL COUNT Kept in cell house - running count of details.

CELL HOUSE

GALLERY
No. 1
No. 2
No. 3
No. 4
Flag
Total
Detail

Figs. 254-261. Forms used by the two assigning Captains. When inmates are transferred from Diagnostic Depot, they are assigned according to classification reports and aptitude tests. Every effort is made by the captains to place them in assignment they are capable of handling or furthering, whether it be academic, vocational or both. Often, an inmate does not adjust well on one assignment and it is necessary to move him many times before he is finally settled into an assignment where he can get along. These forms are representative of an average inmate's file in the office of the Senior Captain in charge of assignments.

MAY 12, 1959

254

PEOPLE OF THE STATE OF ILLINOIS)
     -vs-)   Indictment No. 00-0000
)
JOHN DOE, age 48 years)   M U R D E R

OFFICIAL STATEMENT OF FACTS

This cause came on to be heard before the Honorable William Kingston, one o[f]
the Judges of the Criminal Court of Cook County, on May 11, 1959, upon the defen[dant's]
plea of guilty to involuntary manslaughter. Judgment was entered on said plea a[nd]
the defendant was sentenced to a minimum term of one (1) year and a maximum term
of three (3) years in the Illinois State Penitentiary.

The facts in this case are briefly as follows: On September 4, 1958, at
approximately 11:00 A.M., the defendant and his common law wife, ...
engaged in a drinking-bout when the[y]

- 2 -

254

In Re: John Doe
      Indictment No. 00-0000

According to our files, the defendant has the following previous criminal
record:

F.B.I. #0000000 - John Doe

D-00000 John Doe - July 3, 1945 30 days H of C A.D.W. Judge Henson
          Offs. Christain, Wilson & Machen, 5th Dist.
E-00000 " Doe - May 31, 1956 La Crosse, Wis. Vag.
          - Sept. 16, 1953 Inv. Off. James & Co....5th Dist.

State's Attorney

BY: _____
     Assistant State's Attorney

ILLINOIS STATE PENITENTIARY JOLIET, ILLINOIS

Name John Doe **254** No. #01234
Height 5-2   Alias None
Weight 150   Rec'd 1-4-60 Age 22-56
Comp. Lt   From Cook Co Race White
Hair Dk brn wvy Crime Armed Robbery
Eyes Brn   Sentence 2-4Yrs Nat'y Ill
F.P.C. 21 W M Paroled
Ret. 21 U IO 14 Final Disc.
Previous Record 1956 Crim Crt, Chgs, Ill 6mss Prob for Armed
Robbery; Disch.
Scars, Marks, etc. I. Tat: Upr arm JOANN on ribben acr heart.
III. Conn eyebrows. Wide face.

254

254

STATE OF ILLINOIS
DEPARTMENT OF PUBLIC SAFETY
DIVISION OF THE CRIMINOLOGIST
Joliet-Diagnostic Depot UNIT

CLASSIFICATION REPORT

NAME: DOE, John   AGE: 48
CRIME: Involuntary Manslaughter

( ) Criminologi[st]
( ) Sup't of Pr[ison]
( ) Sup't of Cor[...]
( ) Warden
( ) Jackets
( ) Date July 1[...]
DISTRIBUTED TO

Admitted: Jul[...]

1-1[...]

OFFENSE:

    John Doe was received from Cook County on June 12, 1959 under [a]
to the Official Statement of Facts, on September 4, 1958 our inmate and his common-law [wife]
had an argument after engaging in a drinking bout. Doe struck his common-la[w wife]
sentence of from 1-3 years for involuntary manslaughter. Acco[rding]
at this time and, on September 11, 1958, she became ill and was taken to the Cook Cou[nty]
Hospital where she remained in a stuporous condition until her death on September 1[...]
A Coroner's Jury found that she had died as the result of a blow ....
his guilt: "It's true that I had this fight wit[h .....]
but she was well and hearty ...

254

CLASSIFICATION REPORT (Continued) DOE E-0000X July 1, 195[9]

- 2 -

Egocentric personality. Problematic prognosis

        Joliet Branch

RECOMMENDATION: A routine work assignment in keeping with the pr[...]
      psychologist's report which indicates it is ver[y ...]
that he will benefit by academic schooling.

_____, Chairman
Classification Board

254 Illinois State Penitentiary
    INMATE REQUEST

General Store   Dec. 10, 1959
  ASSIGNMENT   DATE
To Captain (_____) Sr. Captain _____
Inmate No. 00000
Name John DOE
Wishes to interview you in regards to:

Personal interview re another assignment

                         Keeper

Form 3506—VS—18M—7-53

(RN) John Miller Doe

ILLINOIS STATE PENITENTIARY

254

EXAMINATION BLANK

Name __John Doe__ Alias __Johnny Johns__

Received __6-12-59__ County __Cook__ Color __Negro__

Crime __Involuntary Manslaughter__ Sentence __1-3 yrs__

Date of Birth __4-25-11__ Nativity __Jackson, Miss.__ Father __Miss.__

Citizenship __Amer.__ Father __Amer.__ Nationality __A__

How long in U.S. __Life__ Naturalized _____ Alien _____

Parents Living __Yes__ Father Died _____ Mother Died _____

Married 1930—Jackson, Miss.

Marital state: __Divorced - 1934__ Wife Living __Yes__ Number of Children _____

Parents Living Together __Yes__ Divorced _____ Separated

Born of Married Parents __Yes__ Religion __Baptist__ Social S Number _____

Economic Conditions __Fair__ Associates __Hal Jones- #00000__ Disposition I

Classification Transfer _____ Urban _____ After _____ Urban

254

Captain Stevenson
00000

254 **CHAPLAIN'S OFFICE RECORD**

INMATE RECEIVED—DATE __6-12-59__ No. 00000

NAME __John Doe__ NATIONALITY __Afro-Amer.__

AGE __48__

NATIVITY __Jackson, Miss.__

COUNTY __Cook__

CRIME __Inv. Manslaughter__

SENTENCE __1-3 Yrs.__ RELIGION __Protestant__

COLOR __Negro__

OCCUPATION __Freight Handler__ DIVORCED __1934__

254

STATE OF ILLINOIS
DEPARTMENT OF PUBLIC SAFETY

July 8,

TRANSFER ORDER NO. _____

In accordance with the findings and recommendation of the Classi general direction of the State Criminologist, and pursuant to the p Department of Public Safety, by virtue of "An Act in relation of the tiary, and to repeal certain parts of designated Acts" approved June John Doe _____ an inmate of the I tiary, Joliet Diagnostic Depot NO. __00000__

Group III. Without evidence of mental disord or mental deficiency.
Questionably improvable offender.
Problematic prognosis.

RECOMMENDATION: Joliet Branch

---

254 **GENERAL STORE JOLIET DIVISION**

TO:
Mr. K.D. Colling
Senior Captain-Joliet Branch: Sept

Sir:

Subject to your approval, I should like to have inmate #00000 assigned to the inmate Dining Room, transferred to the Butcher St

Thank you for your time and attention in this regard, I am,

Very truly yours,

cc: File

torekeeper

254

Completed by Officer: __Walter Terry__

CELLHOUSE __"B"__ CELL TRANSFER DATE __March 25,__ 1960 No. 00000

INMATE: __Doe__ TO: Cell __812__

FROM: Cell __809__ No. __00000__

WITH: __Inmate Johns__

REASON: __To assist me in my studies__

__Walter Terry__
Cellhouse Keeper

O.K. __Sherman K. Smith__

AUTHORIZED BY _____
LIEUTENANT __iam B. Robson__

ILLINOIS STATE PENITENTIARY
PHYSICIAN'S EXAMINATION OF INMATE REG. NUMBER 0000

254 DIAGNOSTIC DEPOT

Cook County AGE E __48__ WEIGHT 180 HEI

NAME __John Doe__ COLOR EYES __brown__ DATE OF BIRTH

COLOR __Negro__ COLOR HAIR __black__ OCCUPATION __freight handler__

NATIVITY __Miss.__ EDUCATION __5th Gr.__ CRIME & SENTENCE __Invol. Mansl.__

CHILDREN __two__ RELIGION __Bapt.__ VACCINATION _____

FAMILY DISEASE & HABITS __none__ CRIME IN FAMILY __None__

____ VD DISEASE __None__

SKIN __clear__

GENERAL APPEARANCE __good__ FACIAL EXPRESSION __pleas__ TEMPLE TUBE

MUSCULAR __yes__ USE OF DRUGS __no__ TOBACCO __yes__ LIQU

STATE OF NUTRITION __good__

DEFORMITIES? LOXFEST AND PHYSICAL DEFECTS __none__

KAHN __neg.__ UNDULANT FEVER TEST __LYM HE
chest, fractured left leg 1951 L NP

254

Federal Bureau of Investigation
United States Department of Justice
Washington, D.C.

6-22-59
#00000

The following is a transcript of the complete record appearing in the files of the Fed of Investigation concerning number FBI .285.206.D..., which number should be quoted correspondence, including any disposition submitted.

I.S.P. COPY

Contributor of Fingerprints	Name and Number	Arrested or Received	Charge	Dispositi
PB Chgo Ill	John Doe	6-30-45	A D W	30 das H or
PD La Crosse Wis		1-56		

254
ILLINOIS STATE PENITENTIARY

Sentence __1-3 Yrs.__
7-3-59 19

Transfer __John Doe__ No. 00000

From __Diagnostic Depot (Joliet)__

TO __JOLIET__

Check this _____

Senior Captain

254

EMERGENCY DETAIL.

Hon. Joseph E. Ragen,
Warden

Please Detail __John DOE__ No. 00000

Now at __Diagnostic Depot__ To __JOLIET__

Reason __Classification Completed__

__July 2,__ 19 59

254

ILLINOIS STATE PENITENTIARY

INMATE REPORT

No. __00000__ Date __10-27-59__ 19

ASSIGNMENT __General Store__

INMATE __Doe__

Is Reported For __neglecting to do his assigned work__

Inmate Doe was previously warned and ordered to clean his assignment before leaving the store.
It is most important that an assignment where foodstuffs are stored be kept immaculately clea at all times. This inmate has been warned on different occasions about cleanliness and assignment.
kets, rubbish, n it was called y remark. Be- us warning it lined and

Gaines
Keeper

STATE OF ILLINOIS
DEPARTMENT OF PUBLIC SAFETY

255

March

TRANSFER ORDER NO. _____ 000000

In accordance with and pursuant to the power vested in the Department of Public Safety, in relation to the Illinois State Penitentiary, and to repeal certain parts of designation June 30, 1933, as amended, _____ DOE, JOHN J. _____ an inmate of the Illinois State Penitentiary, No. 00001 _____ is hereby ordered transferred to the Illinois State Penitentiary, _____ Menard

STATE OF ILLINOIS
DEPARTMENT OF PUBLIC SAFETY
DIVISION OF THE CRIMINOLOGIST
MENARD D D UNIT
CLASSIFICATION REPORT

255

Name: DOE, John   Age: 27   Admitted:
Crime: Murder   Sentence:

00001-Menard

OFFENSE & RECORD: This 27 year old white male was admitted on 1-16 under a 99 year sentence for murder. The subject County under the time of arrest, except admits to state that he he no details concerning his offense. He was ever questioned committed in Prosser, Washington on 12-20-56. They were sen Illinois to have plead guilty to grand jury.

STATE OF ILLINOIS
DEPARTMENT OF PUBLIC SAFETY
DIVISION OF THE CRIMINOLOGIST
MENARD D D UNIT
CLASSIFICATION REPORT

255

Name: DOE, John   Age:
Crime: Murder

00001-Menard

at the Ft. Belvoir, Virginia Disciplinary Barracks sometime in late 1 just escaped from the military compound but was returned. On 12-2-5 at the stockade and again attempted to escape. On this occasion he wounded in the right thigh and buttocks. On 1-21-53 subject asked jou in an attempted escape in which they struck a guard subject received those in the sentence for those of offense was an actu worth Disciplinary Barracks he made a failure to adjust there or el purpose, a further transfer to Lend, where he remained until his publicly through there is not now an ext where he remained until his addicts to heroin during his travels about the country prior arε standard all credit present of ener. In addition, subject admits to have.

STATE OF ILLINOIS
DEPARTMENT OF PUBLIC SAFETY
DIVISION OF THE CRIMINOLOGIST
MENARD D D UNIT
CLASSIFICATION REPORT

255

Name: DOE, John   Age:
Crime:

in each month, but tells us he is presently directing his efforts to of permitted letters increased. He also indicates that he will prob his mother once a month.

PERSONALITY: Physically, who appears somewhat older than his height, who describes his present health as of six operations sug. He appears in 1940, and a appendectomy. The gunshot lectomy and several following he developed following only occasionally comb gdition that attempt are at present are at present an explosion during in

sanctioned mode of behavior. His attainment drive to the extent that he has failed to achieve a good circumstances except for one brief flareisde. This is rather the responses of what appears to be a socially undesirous of participating in the social milieu except there was, undoubtedly, the suggestion of non-uniform during a poster-adjustment period, we feel the personality di for by this and there must certainly have been other ri valuing. He tells us he has no friends except his wi way. He denies any prior heterosexual affairs or int night stands." The offense for which he has been sent in societal terms involvement than any of his previous different bases of motivation for it. Subject states but I never saw any reason to say so or show why it, not over an extended period, and committed without any sentence, t e quest in of his future community adjustment in today's interview suggest his best chance of adjus guin at the Stateville Divis on.

CLASSIFICATION: GROUP III. Without psychotics or improvable of tender. Highly inadequate and unstable personality type. Guu

RECOMMENDED PLANS: Stateville Division, Medium sec tarent in an assignment as a plu

---

STATE OF ILLINOIS
DEPARTMENT OF PUBLIC SAFETY
DIVISION OF THE CRIMINOLOGIST
MENARD D D UNIT
CLASSIFICATION REPORT

255

Name: DOE, John   Age: Admitted:
Crime: Sentence:

00001-Menard

Upon leaving school he began a nomadic type existence which took him to Florida, Baltimore, and eventually back to Wemdaysburg, where he was apprenticed himself in t trade to an uncle with whom instructor. Long on 12-28-50 and followig same the age of in t including four basic training stars. In consenting this experience, subject states t ever I did in Korea, where during this experience a earned a number of d credit for it." We was returned to the United States from July 1952 and was o this body guard unit at Ft. Meyer, Virginia but did satisfaction and general u stated above. While in military prison, a series of wekends involved in furth day month seven-two days in isolation, but after transfer in took additional a number of additional oral courses in Kathmatio comp in 1955, he went to a set-up school satisfactory in t but the mother tells us in a letter he was unable to t prepare to have maintained a

---

EXAMINATION BLANK

255

Number _____ 00001

Name	John Doe	Alias	None		Number	00001
Received	1-30-58	County	Marion	Color	White	Age	27
Crime	Murder		Sentence	99 yrs.			
Date of Birth	10-7-30		Nativity	Wemigaburg	Daughter	Pa.	Mother	Pa.
Citizenship	Amer.		Father		Nationality		Scotch-Irish
How long in U.S. Life		Naturalized		Alien			
Parents Living	Mother		Father Died	1949	Mother Died		
Marital State	Married	Wife Living	Yes	Divorced		Number of Children	None
Parents Living Together	Until Father Died			Separated			
Born of Married Parents	Yes		Religion	None		Social Security	Yes
Economic Condition	Fair		Associates	May Dos		Disposition	If-Odegit
Residence before 14 Years of Age	Rural			Alter		Rural & Urban	
Relatives Inmates of Penal Institutions	If-A-type-Odegit			Asylum		None	
			Age Left				

STATE OF ILLINOIS
DEPARTMENT OF PUBLIC SAFETY
DIVISION OF THE CRIMINOLOGIST
MENARD PSYCHIATRIC UNIT

CLASSIFICATION REPORT

Menard # 00001   July 1, 195_

Name: DOE, John   Age: 23   Re—Admitted: 12-19-50 yr
Crime: Auto Larceny   Sentence: 1-20 yr

1. Transfer: RECLASSIFICATION
2. Classification   1. Sattville Division (Segregation Unit) from the Menard Psychi-
3. Recommendations   atric Division.

suicidal patterns as attention-getting mechanisms. Questionably improvable offender.
Doubtful prognosis.

3. This 23-year-old white male last saw the Board of Pardons and Paroles on the ma-
1952 docket, so that previous reclassification was not given.
that he could not use this as a technical chan—
was originally admitted to the ___

STATE OF ILLINOIS
DIVISION OF THE CRIMINOLOGIST
MENARD PSYCHIATRIC UNIT

CLASSIFICATION REPORT

Menard # 00001   Admitted:
Name: DOE, John   Age: Sentence:
Crime:

                          RECLASSIFICATION

1. Transfer:
2. Classification
3. Recommendations

while within the Psychiatric Division he was allowed to work and attend
religious services. While attending church, he w—
while on the pretext of going to the toilet, while already 5 hours af wh—
Under the guise of going to the rest—room he threatened to jump, af—
asked using the rafters, this entire period of the administrative as a—
throughout from the premi—— He used this bargain of his psy—
—— the basis of

RECLASSIFICATION REPORT   12-28-50   DOE

is some sibling rivalry and a feeling, on inmate's part, that the younger c—
have been shown preference by the parents. Although his behavior is permis—
linquent, we do not see a picture of organized criminal attitude inhibi in—

CLASSIFICATION: Group III. Without psychotic o—
tionally improvable offender. Doubtful prognosis. Unstable personality.
Alpha 146). Kahn not reported. Very superior intelli—

RECOMMENDATION: Joliet Division.

helpful to this inmate. Some mechanical trade training ad—

PAROLE VIOLATE
PREVIOUS NUMBER
OODL - PONTIAC

STATE OF ILLINOIS
DEPARTMENT OF PUBLIC SAFETY
DIVISION OF THE CRIMINOLOGIST
JOLIET DIAGNOSTIC UNIT

CLASSIFICATION REPORT

00000
Name: DOE, John   Age: 21
Crime: Larceny of a Motor Vehicle

                          RECLASSIFICATION

BEHAVIOR ON PAROLE: Inmate was original
                             Diagnostic Depot at Joliet.
twenty year sentence for auto larceny. He was paroled Marc—
the Joliet Diagnostic Depot as a parole violator December—
te a farm set-up near Hoopeston, Illinois. He said that, d—
very little work and, after a few days, he obtained employm—
million Malleable Company. He claims he got along alright
being careful to observe the various requirements. However
planned to go to a dance near Cissna Park and, according to
they would furnish the transportation. Later, the three la—
said he did not know the automobile had been stolen until tr—
of town. Inmate said that he was swept into the auto theft,
left his placement and began stealing the automobiles, Inmat—
in Danville and was later called by his agent. He then sto—
have the nerve to go through with it, and, therefore,
so things could be straightened out. Inmate said
into Pennsylvania where he wrecked it. With this vehicle, inm—
selling part of the merchandise and also includ—
said he also maintained ——
and that ——

RECLASSIFICATION REPORT   12-20-50

                                        Inmate was
                                        was made for segregati—
nostic Depot and recommendation was made for segregati—
administratively transferred to Statesville's serious adjustment
though inmate was not involved ar. July 29, 1948, after reporti—
was transferred to Pontiac's Pontially inclined prisoner. Inmate
of annoyances by parent.
stitutional adjustment at Pontiac.

RECLASSIFICATION REPORT   12-28-50

                                        Inmate had
                                        spending a
                                  tention Home, Vermilion County. Committed to St. Charles
to Sheridan after making several attempts to escape and also was repo—
inmate made ——— average ——— activity. He was released in 1945.

REVIEW OF PREVIOUS RECORD:

REVIEW OF SOCIAL FACTORS:
                                        ren born to parents of English-Irish background.
                                        home and by the time he was 12 years old he departed as
                                        vision. Inmate's early home life, al—
                                        by age 13
                                        inmate attended public high school education while
                                        that he also had great commitment, was very irreg—
                                        prior to his—. Following his release
                                        terms of employment. Inmate tells us that he ——
                                        pattern of ——— ———, being careful to observe ——

STATE OF ILLINOIS
DEPARTMENT OF PUBLIC SAFETY
DIVISION OF THE CRIMINOLOGIST
JOLIET DIAGNOSTIC UNIT

CLASSIFICATION REPORT   December 23

                                        Admitted: November 21,
Age: 44   Sentence: 3-4 years

Name: DOE, John
Crime: Burglary

OFFENSE: Officially, on August 18, 1950 John Doe was received from DeKalb County J—
for burglary. Officially, on August 18, 1950 our inmate entered through a window
for hours in a prison into a bakery and ——. When 22, 1949 under questionable circumstan—
according and had broken into Doe pled guilty. He unites from which made machine wo—
2nd floor and Doe pled from West Virginia and to win that he perpetrated Illinois bel—
read on his parent—"I'd come up for about 6 weeks and want to know how I got arre—
days. I'd been drinking along case of a dampf I remember being in the club when I was arre—
I'd been working getting drunk.

                                        The inmate has a long criminal record
                                        in 1934 when he was arrested and the
                                        to obtain police records were ocif.—

CLASSIFICATION REPORT (Continued)   December 2,

                                        FBI # 100000

and trembling dizziness. When I noticed money I got into trouble. My shaking interfer—
with my work; I'd lose a job; and then wander di—dots and get nothing. I have the bum—
that he has been released ——. During the past 4 years, after having lost so many jobs,
corn. He worked as an agricultural ——. Having the Indian siding that work required considera—
ing. Doe tells us he was married in 1944 and that this ——. Doe has work required consideratio—
brief part of the marriage, he has had no primary group relationship sinc—
did when he was about 20 years of ——

ILLINOIS STATE PENITENTIARY

EXAMINATION BLANK

Name: John Doe   Alias: Joe Doe   Number: 44

Received: 11-21-50   County: DeKalb   Color: White   Age: 44

Crime: Burglary   Sentence: 3-4 yr.

Date of Birth: 5-25-14   Nativity: Milwaukee, Wis. Father: Alex.   Mot

Citizenship: Amer.   Father: Amer.   Nationality: German—

How long in U.S.   Life   Naturalized: Alien

Parents Living: No   Father Died: 1919   Mother Died: 1919

Marital State: Sep-1949   Wife Living: Yes   Number of Children.

Parents Living Together: until father died   Divorced   Separated

Born of Married Parents: Yes   Religion Catholic   Social Sec
                                                         Number.

Economic Condition: Fair   Associate: None   Dispositio

Residence Before 14 Years of Age:

Religion

Fig. 262. This form completed at Officers' Training School and submitted to Stateville Payroll Clerk.

Fig. 263. This form completed at Officers' Training School and submitted to Stateville Payroll Clerk.

Fig. 264. This form completed at Officers' Training School and submitted to Chief Guard's Office.

Fig. 265. This form completed at Personnel Office for Personnel Office Payroll Card File.

Fig. 266. Employee's Indentification Card issued by Bureau of Identification.

Fig. 267. This form filled out by applicant at Officers' Training School and sent to the Bureau of Identification.

Figs. 268-270. Emlpoyee's Finger Print Cards used by Bureau of Identification

Fig. 271. Bureau of Identification Employee Form.

Fig. 272. This form completed at and kept in the Chief Guard's Office.

DEPARTMENT OF PUBLIC SAFETY

262

Name _____ Date of Birth _____

    Last   First   Middle

Institution
or Division _____ Employed _____

Have you ever been employed by the State of Illinois, University of
Illinois, or as a teacher in the Public School System?

Yes or No _____

If the answer is _____

FORM W-4 (Rev. Aug. 1954)
U.S. Treasury Department
Internal Revenue Service

EMPLOYEE'S WITHHOLDING EXEMPTION CERTIFICATE — DATE OF BIRTH _____

Name _____
Print
Home Address _____ PAY ROLL CODE _____

263

Social
Security No. _____
    City

HOW TO CLAIM YOUR WITHHOLDING EXEMPTIONS

1. IF SINGLE, and you claim an exemption, write the figure "1"
2. IF MARRIED, one exemption each for husband and wife:
  (a) If you claim both of these exemptions, write the figure "2"
  (b) If you claim one of these exemptions, write the figure "1"
  (c) If you claim neither of these exemptions, write the figure "0"
3. Exemptions for age and blindness:
  (a) If you or your wife will be 65 years of age or older, write the figure "1"
  (b) If you or your wife is blind, write the figure "1"
    and you claim both of these exemptions, write the figure "2"
4. If you claim exemptions for one or more dependents, write the number of such exemptions
5. Add the number of exemptions

I CERTIFY ...

264

        DATE _____

NAME _____
    LAST   FIRST   MIDDLE

TRADE _____

MILITARY SERVICE _____ BRANCH _____

THEATRE OF OPERATIONS _____

    COUNTY _____

265

Name DOE, John   Unit SB

Address 100 West Summer Street, Joliet, Illinois

County Will   Date of Birth 1-1-30

Appointed June 7, 1960   Civil Service Yes

$305.00

ILLINOIS STATE PENITENTIARY JOLIET, ILL

EMPLOYEE'S IDENTIFICATION CARD

Hair	
Eyes	
Comp.	
Age	
Height	
Weight	

RIGHT THUMB

266

WARDEN

FOLD ON LINE

Name _____
Address _____
City _____ State _____
County _____
TITLE _____

PLEASE WRITE PLAINLY

Date _____ FILL IN ALL QUESTIONS

267

STUDENT OFFICERS

NAME _____
    Last _____ (First) _____ (Middle)

Address _____
    (Street Number)

Town _____ County _____

Previous Occupation _____

Color _____ Hair _____ Eyes _____

Height _____ Weight _____ Education _____

Birthplace _____
    (Town) _____ (State)

Married _____ Single _____

LIST BELOW LAST THREE POSITION HELD

STARTED MO. YR.	ENDED MO. YR.	POSITION HELD	SAL.	EMP.

EMPLOYEE OR

APPLICANT   268

Name _____
  (Surname)   (Given name)   (Middle Name)

Address _____

F. P. C. _____

Ref. _____

Date _____ Color _____ Sex _____

RIGHT HAND

1. Thumb	2. Index finger	3. Middle finger	4. Ring finger	5. Little finger

---

Branch of service _____ IF NO MILITARY SERVICE MARK NONE

From _____
  (Month)   (Year) To _____

NAME AND ADDRESS OF NEAREST RELATIVE
TO BE NOTIFIED IN CASE OF EMERGENCY

Name _____
Address _____

269

APPLICANT

LEAVE THIS SPACE BLANK

LEFT HAND

6.	7.	8.	9. Ring finger	10. Little finger

SIGNATURE OF PERSON FINGERPRINTED _____

	LAST NAME	FIRST NAME	MIDDLE NAME	SEX

CONTRIBUTOR AND ADDRESS   COMPANY AND ADDRESS   RACE

WARDEN
STATE PENITENTIARY
JOLIET, ILL.

RESIDENCE OF PERSON FINGERPRINTED _____ HT (IN.) WT

SIGNATURE OF OFFICIAL TAKING FINGERPRINTS _____ DATE OF BIRTH

TYPE OR PRINT ALL REQUESTED DATA _____ NUMBER _____ HAIR EYES

LEAVE THIS SPACE BLANK

270

APPLICANT

ILLINOIS STATE PENITENTIARY
JOLIET, ILLINOIS   *Chgs. card*

NAME _____

CLASSIFICATION _____

Please Search and Return

REF. _____

CLASS _____

REF. _____

RIGHT HAND

1. RIGHT THUMB	2. R. FORE FINGER	3. R. MIDDLE FINGER	4. R. RING FINGER	5. RIGHT LITTLE

(25239—2500—3-51) _____

271

ILLINOIS STATE PENITENTIARY
JOLIET, ILLINOIS

NAME _____ Color _____   # APPLICANT

Address _____

Employed _____ Resigned _____ Discharged _____

Married _____ Dependents _____

Left Service _____
Probation Ends _____
Living in _____ Out _____
Remarks _____ C. S. _____

Height _____ Ft. _____ In.
Weight _____
Build _____

Complexion _____

Hair _____

Color of Eyes _____

and Return
...APH

SICK

272

Name _____
Street _____ LEFT
City _____
County _____
Title _____

Fiscal Year: This form completed at and Kept in Chief Guard's Office

MONTH	1	2	3	4	5	6	7	8	9	10	11	12	13	14	15	1st	16	17	18	19	20	21	22	23	24	25	26	27	28	29	30	31	2nd
JULY																																	
AUG.																																	
SEPT.																																	
OCT.																																	
NOV.																																	
DEC.																																	
JAN.																																	
FEB.																																	
MAR.																																	
APR.																																	
MAY																																	
JUNE																																	

Figs. 273-278. Forms used by Chief Guard relative to employee personnel.

Fig. 279. Personnel record card form is enclosed with this letter to Director Bibb. Carbon copy of letter filed with Director's Correspondence in Personnel Office.

Fig. 280. Employee's Record Card is submitted to the Personnel Office from the Bureau of Identification and the Officers' Training School, and is sent, along with letter, to the Superintendent of Prisons. Copy of this letter is filed in Superintendent of Prisons correspondence. Several names may be listed in one letter.

Fig. 281. This form sent up from Bureau of Identification.

NAME: DOE, John Doe
ADDRESS 1313 Cass Street
CITY Joliet, Will Co., Ill.
RANK Guard; Gd.-Sgt. 2-19-59

EMPL'Y 4-7-58

273

LEFT EMPL'Y

105 Everett Ave.,
ll.

274

due

given

11-11-58

-58

-59

ILLINOIS STATE PENITENTIARY
JOLIET, ILLINOIS

TO: Mr. Joseph E. Ragen, Warden
Stateville Branch

Dear Sir:

Listed below you will find a summary of information, rel
named officer:

OFFICER

ABILITY _____ EMPLOY

EFFICIENCY

EMPLOYEE SERVICE EFFICIENCY REVIEW
Supervisory Rating Form

275

Confidential Rating of:

Employee's Name DOE, John Doe

Assignment 7-3 Shift

Assigned from (date) 1-15-59

INSTRUCTIONS

ATTE

DATE EMPLOYED:

Our system of rating employee performance should be regar
correcting, improving, and in general raising the level of performa
specific shortcomings of an individual are identified, many things
him more effective on the job. The institution has the responsibility
the kind of training which will aid in his development. However, tr
without an accurate and unbiased appraisal of employee performa
ployee training program.

The nature of this institution is such that the safety and securi
dependent one upon the other. Therefore, in justice to yourself and t
obligated to rate all factors on this form with complete candor and t
member that if we have good men working with and for us, our jo
a confidential report and your name will not be used)

276

5 A — Officious. Has an overbearing manner
    B — Very exacting. Sometimes oversteps his auth
    C — Is firm, but fair and just in his dealings

7 A — Has an indifferent attitude towards safety and securi
      sures. Doesn't think it can happen here
    B — Believes inmates are constantly plotting to outwit him
      escape. Over emphasizes or exaggerates
    C — Realizes that inmates have fewer incentives and diff
      values than free men. Is alert and cautious

A — Cannot assum
B — Tends to follo
C — Is willing and

SECTION 3 — JOB PERFORMANCE

Check the one statement in each of the following groups which you be
describes this employee's performance.

1 A — Either resents or pays little attention to instructions.
    B — Accepts instructions, but follows them only half-heartedly.
    C — Follows closely directions of supervising officers.

2 A — Is careless in the supervision of tools.
    B — Attaches proper importance to the
      accounting for them.
    C —

EMPLOYED: 4-7-58   DOE,

277

RANK: Guard; Grd.-Sgt. 2-19-59

DEBIT

DATE: REASON:

4-15-58   Worked overtime at Tailor Shop.
4-16-58   Worked overtime at Tailor Shop.
7-4-58   Holiday, Day Due.
9-18-58   Worked night of Legion Show.
11-9-58   Suspension
11-11-58 Vacation to 11-17-58 inclusive.
11-27-58 Day due for Holiday
25-58   Day due for Holiday
         to 1-8-60 inclusive.   Extension Course.

278

GUARD   Guard-Sergea

TIME SHEET

EMPLOYEES

Name DOE, John Doe   Entered Service 4-7-58

Resident Address 1313 Cass St.   Street Joliet   City

Department   Left Service

Rate   Change in Rate Due

Reason for Leaving

Commutation

1959

	July	Aug.	Sept.	Oct.	Nov.	Dec.	Jan.	Feb.	Mar.	Apr.	May	June	19	
1													1	
2													2	
3													3	
4													4	D'
5													5	
6								D'					6	
7								D'					7	
8								D'					8	
9													9	
10			W'					D					10	

279

STATE OF ILLINOIS
WILLIAM G. STRATTON, GOVERNOR

DEPARTMENT OF PUBLIC SAFETY
GENERAL OFFICE, SPRINGFIELL

Illi
Jo

ILLINOIS STATE PENITENTIA
JOLIET BRANCH
JOSEPH E. RAGEN, WARDEN
JOLIET

June 7, 1960

Re: DOE, John

Mr. Joseph D. Bibb, Director
Department of Public Safety
Armory Building
Springfield, Illinois

Dear Director Bibb:

I am enclosing personnel record card
covering the above named employee who was recently assigne
to duty as a guard at this institution.

Yours very truly,

279

BIRTH
CITIZEN OF
UNITED STATES   PLACE OF BIRTH
NATURALIZED
SEX   SINGLE   MARRIED   WIDOW   AGE AT TIME OF EMPLOYMENT
HEIGHT   WEIGHT   COLOR OF EYES   COLOR OF HAIR   DATE AND PLACE
NUMBER OF CHILDREN   NUMBER AND AGE OF DEPENDENT CHILDREN   COMPLEXION   SEPARATED
OTHER DEPENDENTS
PHYSICAL DEFECTS OR AILMENTS   DRAFT CLASSIFICATION
IN CASE OF EMERGENCY—NOTIFY   NAME
PREVIOUS MILITARY SERVICE   FROM   TO   BRANCH OF SERVICE   ADDRESS
CIVIL SERVICE
EDUCATION   DATE ATTENDED   POSITION
GRAMMAR SCHOOL   FROM   TO

280

STATE OF ILLINOIS
WILLIAM G. STRATTON, GOVERNOR

DEPARTMENT OF PUBLIC SAFETY
GENERAL OFFICE, SPRINGFIELD

ILLINOIS STATE
JOLIET BR
JOSEPH E. RAGE
JOLIE

June 7, 1960

Re: DOE, John

Mr. Joseph D. Bibb, Director
Department of Public Safety
Armory Building
Springfield, Illinois

Att'n: Mr. Gilbert P.
Sup't of Pris

Dear Sir:

I am enclosing Employee's Record Card covering
the above named employee who was recently assigned to du
as a guard at this institution.

It would be appreciated if you would have a memb
of your staff make an investigation on Mr. Doe and forw
a copy of your report to my office.

VS—2M—12-56—Not Stock

281

EMPLOYEE'S RECORD CARD

Name DOE,   John   Previous Occupation Laborer   Salary &
      (Last)   (First) (Middle)   Will
                                  None   (County)
Residence 100 West Summer Street, Joliet, Illinois   Institution State
          (Street Number)   (Town)
Color White Weight 150 Height 5-10 Eyes Brown Hair Brown Assigned 6-7-6
Marks and Scars None   Date of birth 1-1-30 Title Guard Civil Ser
Date entered service 6-7-60
Married or Single Married Dependents 3

Past three positions held were as follows:

FROM	TO	POSITION	SALARY	EMPLOYER AND ADDRESS

Military Service This form sent up from Bureau of Ident.   This space.

Remarks   ions demotions suspensions, etc.

Fig. 282. Second carbon copy of application sent with this letter to Mr. Cavanaugh. Copy of letter for employee's jacket. This type investigation used only when applicant resides in Cook County. No regular inquiry forms sent on Cook County applicants.

Figs. 283-287. This letter along with the attached forms is sent to the Director. Copy of same is sent to Superintendent of Prisons. Copy is retained in employee's personnel jacket.

Fig. 284. This form to be completed in duplicate with an extra (onion skin) copy. Both forms are to be sent to the Director, onion skin copy is retained in employee's personnel jacket.

Fig. 285. Two copies of this form to be completed and sent to the Director.

Fig. 286. This form completed in duplicate. One copy sent to the Director. One copy filed in employee's personnel jacket.

Fig. 287. This form completed in duplicate at Officers' Training School and submitted to Personnel Office. One copy is sent to Director and the other retained for employee's jacket.

Fig. 288. Employee photograph taken at Bureau of Identification.

Fig. 289. Employment Application — Employee.

282

DEPARTMENT OF PUBLIC SAFETY
GENERAL OFFICE, SPRINGFIELD

JOLIET BRANCH
JOSEPH E RAGEN WARDEN
JOLIET

COUNTY_____Will

285

NAME___DOE, John
VOTING ADDRESS___100 West Summer Street, Joliet, Illinois
DATE OF APPOINTMENT_____June 6, 1960
DEPARTMENT___Public Safety___DIVISION___ISP Joliet
POSITION TITLE___Guard_____SALARY___$305.00
NO.☐

June 7, 1960

Re: DOE, John

Mr. Joseph E. Cavanaugh
2857 West 71st Street
First Floor
Chicago 29, Illinois

Dear Mr. Cavanaugh:

    I am enclosing copy of employment
covering the above named guard applicant.

    It would be appreciated if you wou
investigation on Mr. Doe and forward a copy
report to my office.

Yours very
SECOND CARBON

PERSONNEL RECORD
ISP J
(DIVISION OR

286

STATE OF ILLINOIS
DEPARTMENT OF PUBLIC SAFETY
    This form completed in duplicate. One copy sent to the
    One copy filed in employee's personnel jacket.

NAME___DOE, John_____BIRTH DATE___1-1-30
LEGAL ADDRESS___100 West Summer Street, Joliet, Illinois
COUNTY___Will_____WARD_____PRECINCT.
POSITION___Guard_____SALARY $305.00 DATE OF EMPLOYMENT
OFFICE OR HEADQUARTERS WHERE EMPLOYED___Stateville
CIVIL SERVICE___Yes___DATE CERTIFIED___6-7-60___CLASSIFICATION.
    (YES OR NO)
NATIONAL EXTRACTION___American
PREVIOUS OCCUPATION, TRADE OR PROFESSION___Laborer
PREVIOUS STATE EMPLOYMENT___None___(DATE WHEN EMPLOYE
    State of Illinois
    DEPARTMENT OF PERSONNEL
    Springfield, Illinois

282

Full Name_LOE, John -- etc._____Age_____Born Month
    Last___First___Middle

Box or Street Address_____City_____Prev
How long have you lived in this City?_____

Place of Birth_____Social Security No
In case of illness notify?_____Address
Are you a citizen of U. S.?_____Naturalized
How long have you lived in Illinois?_____Race

287

EMPLOYMENT APPLICATION

1. TITLE OF POSITION APPLIED FOR (SEPARATE APPLICATION FOR EACH TITLE)___DATE
2. NAME — LAST___EMPLOYMENT (NOTIFY PERSONNEL DE
    LOCATION
    PREFERENCE
    FIRST___MIDDLE
3. MAILING ADDRESS—NO. AND STREET___CITY___STATE___COUNTY
4. LEGAL ADDRESS (IF SAME AS ABOVE, WRITE "SAME") (ADDRESS FROM WHICH YOU LAST VOTED)___PHONE NO.
5. BIRTHDATE___BIRTHPLACE—CITY & STATE OR COUNTRY___CITIZEN OF U.S.?___IF NATURALIZED,
    OWN PAPERS OR WI
    FOR INSTRUCTIONS
6. HEIGHT___WEIGHT___HAVE YOU ANY PHYSICAL DISABILITY? YES___NO___☐ YES ☐ NO
    DESCRIBE;
7. SEX___MARITAL STATUS
    ☐ MALE ☐ FEMALE___☐ SINGLE ☐ MARRIED ☐ SEPARATED ☐ DIVORCED ☐ WIDOWED___NO. OF DEPE
8. DATE MARRIED___FULL NAME OF HUSBAND OR WIFE___IF WOMAN, GIVE FULL MAIDEN N A
9. IN EMERGENCY, NOTIFY—NAME, ADDRESS AND
10. HOW LONG HAVE YOU LIVE
    IN ILLINOIS, IMMEDIATELY
    TO DATE OF APPLICATION
11. NOW EMPLOYED
    BY STATE OF
    ILLINOIS—GIVE:

283

STATE OF ILLINOIS
WILLIAM G STRATTON GOVERNOR

DEPARTMENT OF PUBLIC SAFETY
GENERAL OFFICE, SPRINGFIELD

June 7, 196

Mr. Joseph D. Bibb, Director
Department of Public Safety
Armory Building
Springfield, Illinois

Dear Director Bibb:

John Doe, Joliet, Will County Illinois, reported at this
institution and was assigned to duty as a guard effec
June 7, 1960, at a salary of

288

JOE DOE
6 14 60

IF EMPLOYED
DATE BUT
EMPLOYED—GIVE
HAS BEEN ARRES

IF "YES"

HAVE

IF "YES" GIVE DETAILS IN WRITING ON ATTACHED SHEET.

NOTIFY OF ANY COMMUNIST, NAZI OR FASCIST ORGANIZATION, GI

—FROM
    TO___FROM
    TO
TY COMPENSATION FROM THE U.S. VETERANS ADMINISTRATION FOR WAR SERVICE CONNECTED
SABILITY

REPORT OF APPOINTMENT OF TEMPORARY AND PERMANENT EMPLOYEES

284

Institution or Division

Date

This form to be completed in du
(onion skin) copy. Both forms
Director, onion skin copy is r
personnel jacket.

To the Director
    Department of Public Safety
    Springfield, Illinois

In accordance with authority granted by you, I have appointed the follow

NEW EMPLOYEES

NAME	POSITION	DATE STARTED	RATE OF PAY
DOE, John	Guard	6-7-60	$305.

289

Full Name_DOE___John___None___Age_30_Born Mouth_January
    Last___First___Middle___Date_Jur
Box or Street Address__100 West Summer St.__City_Joliet__County_Wil
How long have you lived in this City?_30 Years___Previous Addresse
Place of Birth___Joliet, Illinois
In case of illness notify_Mary Doe___Social Security No._000 00 0000
Are you a citizen of U. S.?_Yes___Address__Same Address
How long have you lived in Illinois?_30 Years_Race_White___Date
Color of Eyes_Brown_Color of Hair_Brown___Height_5' 1
Number and Ages of Dependent Children_None___Marital Status_Married_Numb
Any relatives working for the State?_No___Name___Other Depe
Position___Division_I
Have you ever been employed by the State of Illinois?_No_From
Position Held___Department___Date
Were you a member of State Retirement System?_No___Divisi
Do you have

Figs. 290-292. Kuder Employee-Personnel Tests.

Fig. 293. This form completed in duplicate. One copy sent to the Director. One copy filed in employee's personnel jacket.

Fig. 294. Bureau of Identification Finger Print Report Form — Employee Personnel.

Fig. 295. This form completed at Bureau of Identification (if applicant has record) and forwarded to Personnel Office for filing.

Fig. 296. This form signed by applicant and sent to Personnel Office for filing with his personnel jacket.

Fig. 297. This form filled out and signed by applicant in Officers' Training School and sent to Personnel Office for filing in personnel jacket of employee.

Fig. 298. Application Blank — Employees.

Fig. 299. Two copies of this form completed. One sent to retail credit as designated in instruction book, one copy filed in employee's jacket.

NAME _____ _____ _____ AGE ___ SEX ___ GROUP _____ DATE OF TEST _____
Print   Last   First   Initial   M or F

First Revision, Feb.

290

SELF-INTERPRETING
PROFILE SHEET
for the
KUDER PREFERENCE RECORD
VOCATIONAL
Forms, CH, CM

MEN and WOMEN

DIRECTIONS FOR PROFILING

1. Copy the V-Score from the back page of your answer pad in the box at the right.

If your V-Score is 37 or less, there is some reason for doubting the value of your answers, and your other scores may not be very accurate. If your V-Score is 45 or more, you may not have understood the directions, since 44 is the highest possible score. If your score is not be-tween 38 and 44 in...

291

SELF-SCORING
ANSWER PAD
for the
**KUDER
PREFERENCE
RECORD**
FORM CH
Prepared by
G. FREDERIC KUDER

Scores

V. _____
O. _____

292

293

STATE OF ILLINOIS
DEPARTMENT OF PUBLIC SAFETY

START
O →

This form completed
One copy filed in o...

NAME _____ DOE, John
LEGAL ADDRESS _____ 100 West Summer Street, Joliet, Illinois
COUNTY _____ Will
POSITION _____ Guard
OFFICE OR HEADQUARTERS WHERE EMPLOYED _____ Statevi...
CIVIL SERVICE _____ Yes SALARY $305.00 DATE OF E...
(YES OR NO)
WARD _____ DATE CERTIFIED _____ PRECINCT _____
NATIONAL EXTRACTION _____ American MONTH...
PREVIOUS OCCUPATION _____ 6-7-60 CI...
PREVIOUS STATE EMPLOYMENT, TRADE OR PROFESSION _____ None
REFERENCE _____ DEPARTMENT _____ (POSITION) _____ Labor...

294

BUREAU OF IDENTIFICATION
JOLIET, ILLINOIS

Joseph E. Ragen, Warden
Illinois State Penitentiary
Joliet, Illinois

Dear Warden Ragen:

Listed below is the complete fingerprint report on Guard-Applicant.

Chicago Bureau   NO RECORD
Springfield Bureau NO RECORD
Washington Bureau   NO RECORD

Very truly yours,

W. E. Woodward, B of I.

295

Federal Bureau of Investigation
United States Department of Justice
Washington, D. C.

The following is a transcript of the complete record appearing in the files of the Federal Bureau of Investigation concerning number FBI _____, which number should be quoted in future correspondence, including any disposition submitted

I.S.P. COPY

CONTRIBUTOR OF FINGERPRINTS	NAME AND NUMBER	ARRESTED OR RECEIVED	CHARGE	DISP...

ILLINOIS STATE PENITENTIARY

296

NOTICE TO APPLICANT

It is impossible to employ men who have been convicted or served a sentence. Inquiries will be sent to the various bureaus and if there is anything in your past that will show a conviction or sentence it will be impossible to employ you. You are the sole judge of your background, and if you care to report for duty when notified, you may do so pending final reports from the fingerprint bureaus. If the records indicate an arrest or conviction it will be impossible to continue you in the service.

_____ Ragen, Warden

ALL APPLICANTS MUST FILL IN THE BELOW IN HIS OR HER OWN HANDWRIT...

297

Date _____

Name _____ Age _____ Education _____ Height _____

Home Address _____ City _____ State _____

Why are you seeking employment of this type? _____

What kind of work do you think a prison guard does? _____

What do you think is the purpose of a prison? _____

What quali... _____

stitution c... _____

This _____
in _____
of... _____

298

EMPLOYMENT APPLICATION
State of Illinois
DEPARTMENT OF PERSONNEL
Springfield, Illinois

1. TITLE OF POSITION APPLIED FOR (SEPARATE APPLICATION FOR EACH TITLE)

2. NAME – LAST

3. MAILING ADDRESS–NO. AND STREET   EMPLOYMENT (NOTIFY PERSONNEL)   DAT...
                                           LOCATION
4. LEGAL ADDRESS (IF SAME AS ABOVE, WRITE "SAME") (ADDRESS FROM WHICH YOU LAST VOTED)   PREFERENCE   CITY   P.O. ZONE   COUNTY

5. BIRTHDATE   FIRST _____   MID...
6. HEIGHT   WEIGHT   BIRTHPLACE–CITY & STATE OR COUNTRY
7. SEX   HAVE YOU ANY PHYSICAL DISABILITY? YES   CITIZEN OF U.S.?   PHONE NO.
   ☐ MALE ☐ FEMALE   DESCRIBE   NO   ☐ YES ☐ NO
8. DATE MARRIED   MARITAL STATUS   IF NATURALIZED, GIVE
                  ☐ SINGLE ☐ MARRIED ☐ SEPARATED   DATE AND PLACE OR WRITE
9. IN EMERGENCY, NOTIFY–   FULL NAME OF HUSBAND OR WIFE   ☐ DIVORCED   FOR INSTRUCTIONS
   NAME, ADDRESS AND PHONE NO.   ☐ WIDOWED   NO. OF DEPENDED
                                                           IF WOMAN, GIVE FULL NA...

BIRTH DATE

56167

CHARACTER–FINANCIAL INQUIRY   Acct.
Retail Credit Co.

299

CHECK HERE ☐   CHECK HERE ☐   Special Service
If Trade Experience   If Special   Reports Re-
also desired on In-   Report desired   quested
dividual   1½ Basic   on Form
Charge   Report   4511.2
Form (Inspection has
instructions below)

CHECK
TYPE OF
REPORT
DESIRED →

If not checked, regular basic rate report   Date   June 7, 1960   Married?   X
will be made.   (In reporting, quote back)

File No. _____   Full Name _____ DOE, John _____ Age 30 _____ How long? 30 yr

Residence Address _____ 100 West Summer Street, Joliet, Ill. _____ Occupation
(St., City, State
or Prov.)   Unemployed   How long out?

Employer _____   Mo. Notes $ _____
Bus. Address
(St. & City)

Former Address _____   Amt. $ _____

Transaction
Special Information Desired:

(2426) Special attention to habits and character.

Two copies of this form completed. One sent to retail credit, as designated in instruction book, one copy for employee's jacket.

BANK & TRADE
REFERENCES
(Furnish full
service)

IF BLOCK CHECKED FOR 1½ BASIC RATE REPORT INCLUDING TRADE EXPERIENCE:

FULL TIME INSPECTORS: Make street investigation and in addition clear bank and trade references given or develop... Make two personal calls if necessary. Write report...
...personally. Make two personal calls if necessary...
...develop trade and bank experience...

Fig. 300. Employee Retail Credit Check.

Fig. 301. Copies of this form are sent to the authorities in area of applicant's residence, namely: County seat of applicant's county; references listed by applicant; to schools, colleges, etc., listed by applicant; chief of police of applicant's home town; and former employers.

Fig. 302. This form completed at Officers' Training School and forwarded to hospital.

Fig. 302. This form completed in quadruplicate in hospital. One copy sent to personnel for filing in employee's jacket. All medical records sent to personnel office if employee resigns, goes on leave of absence, or is disqualified.

Fig. 303. Employee's Medical Examination Form completed in Institution Hospital. One copy sent to Personnel Department for filing in employee's jacket. All medical records sent to Personnel Office is employee resigns, goes on leave of absence or is disqualified.

Fig. 304. This form used by prison physician relative to obtaining military information regarding applicant.

Fig. 305. This form signed by applicant and filed with personnel jacket and is used to obtain military information when necessary.

300

RETAIL CREDIT COMPANY
SPECIAL PERSONNEL SELECTION
AND SPECIAL SECURITY-PERSONN
SELECTION REPORT

COPY

CAUTION TO CUSTOMER: Under the terms
of our agreement, this report is submitted
with the understanding that it is to be
held in STRICT CONFIDENCE. Under no
condition is information in this report
to be passed on directly or indirectly
to the person reported on.

	File No. or Requestor
Acct. No. 56167	ns

Evansville OFFICE
Former Address
REPORT
FROM   Salem, Ill.   Present or Former Address

6-11-57   10
DOE, John
Lockport, Illinois, R. R. #3
Unemployed

Date of Birth or Age: 5-31-30

1. Number of Years Known: (To you or informants)	1. 15-15-1 records
2. Racial Descent: (Do not answer in areas where laws prohibit).	2. AS
3. Net Worth?	3. $4M
4. Annual Income?	

300

WRITE A PARAGRAPH ON EACH OF THE FOLLOWI

13. EDUCATION: Tell what schools or col and scholastic record if obtainable.
14. TRAITS: Is he honest, ambitious, de training? Does he possess initiativ to get along with others? Popular?
15. FINANCES: What makes up worth? Is h means? Any other property? Any outs Speculate in stock market? Credit at or heavy indebtedness?
16. INTERESTS: How does he spend his leis civic clubs, church or other interest
17. HEALTH-HABITS: Cover past and presen or injury. Complete details on prese or drugs.
18. Citizenship-Loyalty: Native Born? A any organization of a subversive citizen? Foreign Born? If so, name country whe

STATE OF ILLINOIS
WILLIAM G. STRATTON, GOVERNOR
DEPARTMENT OF PUBLIC SAFETY
GENERAL OFFICE, SPRINGFIELD

301

Dear Sir:

Prisons are the concern of every citizen, and tax interest in the proper operation of an institution that confine of offenses against the State. Records indicate that 95% of are someday released. It is our idea to send them out as bett the right type of personnel our task of rehabilitating men is portant, therefore, that we have the background of every empl

Will you please fill out the reverse side of this letter relative to person, and any information you may give us will be treated as confidenti

Very truly your

Copies

302

NAME: (Last name first)_____ County_____

ADDRESS: _____

Married, Single, Divorced, Widower_____

Do you use Alcohol or Drugs_____

Do you, or have you had any venereal disease_____

Have you been to a Doctor during the past two years_____

Do you, or have you had any history of illness or injury_____

Waist Measurements_____

DO NOT WRITE BELOW THIS LINE:

Chest Measurements: IN_____OUT_____Blood Pressure_____

Pulse:_____

Color Hair_____

STATE OF ILLINOIS
WILLIAM G. STRATTON, GOVERNOR
DEPARTMENT OF PUBLIC SAFETY
EMPLOYEE'S MEDICAL EXAMINATION

303

Position or rank_____
Date of examination_____

Employee's Name_____
Examined at_____

HISTORY

1. Sex_____ 2. Age (Nearest birthday)_____
3. Has employee consulted any physician with in the past year? (Details)_____
4. Chronic illness or disability_____

5. Previous surgery & dates_____

6. Use of habit-forming drugs or alcohol_____
7. Date of last vaccination _____
   Typhoid_____Small Pox_____
8. Was immunization innoculation (s) given with t amination - Typhoid_____Small Pox_____

EXAMINATION

Height_____Weight_____
General development_____
HEAD AND NECK:
Hair_____Mouth_____
Teeth_____
Throat_____Thyroid_____

RECTAL:
Hemorrhoids_____
Other conditions_____
EXTREMITIES:
Disabling defects_____
Varicosities_____
Other defects_____

THORAX AND B
Defects_____

LUNGS:
Auscultation_____

HEART:
Murmurs_____
Sounds_____
Blood Press_____
Pulse_____
Was electr_____
ABDOMEN:
Contour_____
Musculatu_____
Hernia_____
Masses_____
Tendernes_____
Scars_____
GENITALIA
Signs of _____
Abnormal_____
REMA_____

I find
above as:

STATE OF ILLINOIS
William G. Stratton, Governor
DEPARTMENT OF PUBLIC SAFETY

304

Re:

To:

The above-named person is being processed for employment by the Departmer
Public Safety. In order to more properly evaluate his background, emplo
record, and physical condition, we would appreciate the following inform

( )   Case summary and diagnosis if possible

( )   Loan of X-Rays

( )   Is subject receiving, or has he received compensation
      for injury or illness while in your facility

We will promptly return your films if the loan of same has been requeste

( )   Any information you may have pertaining to background
      mployment record of subject while in the service

**REQUEST FOR AND CONSENT TO RELEASE OF INFORM
FROM VETERAN'S RECORDS**

305

TO

NAME OF VETERAN (Type or print)_____

ETERAN'S SERIAL NUMBER_____

VA CLAIM NUMBER_____

NAME AND ADDRESS OF ORGANIZATION, AGENCY, OR INDIVIDUAL TO WHOM INFORMATIO
IS TO BE   ELEASED

I hereby request and authorize ☐ Army ☐ Navy ☐ Marines ☐ Air
☐ Coast Guard ☐ Veterans Administration to release the following informat
records identified above, to the organization, agency, or individual named hereon:

☐ 1. SERVICE RECORD * DATES ETC.
☐ 2. HEALTH RECORD, HOSPITALIZATION ETC.
☐ 3. Disciplinary Record
☐ 4. Type of Discharge Issued
☐ 5. Reason For Discharge

ADDITIONAL INFORMATION DESIRED:

PURPOSE FOR WHICH THE INFORMATION IS TO BE ISSUED:

Fig. 306. All disbursements for inmates from the Inmate's Trust Fund Account.

Fig. 307. All debits and credits are recorded on this ledger card which is retained in the Chief Clerk's Office. The duplicate ledger card retained in this Inmates' Commissary are balanced once a month.

Fig. 308. All debits and credits are recorded on this ledger card which is retained in the Inmates' Commissary.

Fig. 309. All Credits to Inmates' Trust Fund account are listed on these sheets and all posting is made from them.

Fig. 310. This form is made at the Inmates' Commissary for the daily trading. All postings in the Chief Clerk's Office are made from this form.

Fig. 311. Inmate properly fills out this form as his request to deduct monies from his trust fund account. They must be signed by the inmate and his signature witnessed by an Officer. Persons must be on their approved writing list. All are approved by Joseph E. Ragen, Warden.

Fig. 312. Every inmate who has personal property held in the Chief Clerk's Office has a ledger sheet. The attached brown envelope has the same information and contains the items. The inmate also receives an institutional receipt for all the contents.

Fig. 313. We have $3,000.00 cash fund used for Inmates' Trust Fund Account which is balanced each day and this form is used.

Fig. 314. Inmates fill out properly for trading at Commissary.

Fig. 315. Used daily to pay off inmates discharged or paroled.

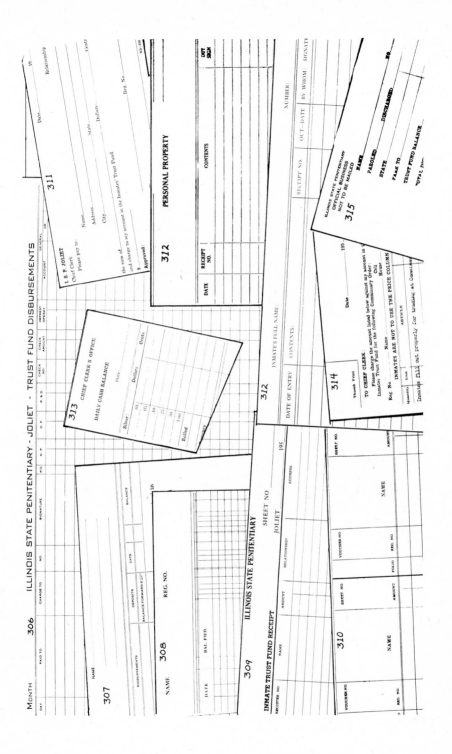

ILLINOIS STATE PENITENTIARY - JOLIET - TRUST FUND DISBURSEMENTS

306

MONTH

DAY	PAID TO	NO	CHARGE TO	SIGNATURE	PIC	N F	O F	P & D	CHECK NO	CHECK AMOUNT	IMPREST OPERAT	ACCOUNT	GENERAL	DR

NAME

307

311

19

Date

Relationship

I S P JOLIET
Chief Clerk
Please pay to

Name

Address

State

City

Dollars Cents

the sum of
and charge to my account in the Inmates' Trust Fund
$
Approved:

Reg. No.

V3-6M

308

REG. NO.

NAME

BAL. FWD.

DISBURSEMENTS DEPOSITS BALANCE FORWARD 3 -

DATE DEPOSITS BALANCE

in

313

CHIEF CLERK'S OFFICE

DAILY CASH BALANCE

Date

	Dollars	Cents
Silver:		
	.05	
	.10	
	.25	
	.50	
	1.00	
Rolled		

312

PERSONAL PROPERTY

DATE	RECEIPT NO.	CONTENTS

312

309 ILLINOIS STATE PENITENTIARY

SHEET NO

JOLIET 195

INMATE'S FULL NAME

DATE OF ENTRY CONTENTS:

RECEIPT NO OUT—DATE BY WHOM SIGNATU NO

OUT SIGN

315

ILLINOIS STATE PENITENTIARY
OFFICIAL BUSINESS
NOT TO BE MAILED

MAIL

PAROLED

STATE DISCHARGED

PASS TO

TRUST FUND BALANCE

TOTAL m

314

195

Date

TO CHIEF CLERK:
Please charge the amount listed below against my account in y
Order. Inmates Trust Fund for the following Commissary Order.
Cell House

Reg. No. Name

INMATES ARE NOT TO USE THE PRICE COLUMN

Quantity	Unit	ARTICLE

Thumb Print

Inmates fill out properly for trading at Commissa

INMATE TRUST FUND RECEIPT

REGISTER NO NAME AMOUNT RELATIONSHIP:

ADDRESS

SHEET NO

310

VOUCHER NO	SHEET NO	VOUCHER NO	REG. NO	NAME	AMOUNT

REG. NO NAME AMOUNT FOLIO

NAME

Fig. 316. Discharged and Paroled inmates signs this form in triplicate as receipt for State Gratuity and fare. Twice monthly they are vouchered to Springfield for replenishment of funds to Inmates' Benefit Fund.

Fig. 317. Inmate fills out form properly as his request to purchase bonds. Officer must witness signature. Bonds are purchased from local bank and placed in the inmate's personal property jacket. An Institutional receipt is given to him. Impossible to send receipt as they are all pre-numbered and audited. Receipt machine used. Duplicate copies — one to inmate, one retained in office.

Fig. 318. This is used to compile the daily disbursements of the Inmates' Trust Ledger.

Fig. 319. Inmate processes this blank as his request to order. All magazines, newspapers, books, court papers, etc., are ordered through the institution from a permitted list. When received they are checked and those not ordered through the institution are returned.

Fig. 320. It is an institutional rule that all newspapers, magazines, musical instruments, court records, etc., must be ordered through the institution. When the order is placed, this card is filled out and when the material is received it is checked with this card. Anything not ordered through the institution is returned to the sender marked not permitted.

316

ILLINOIS STATE PENITENTIARY DIVISION
THE DEPARTMENT OF PUBLIC SAFETY

Joliet, Illinois_____19____

RECEIVED of JOS. E. RAGEN, Warden of the Illinois State Penitentiary, Joliet Branch, Division of The

Department of Public Safety_____DOLLARS

In full for the following items as allowed me as a_____Prisoner

Cash allowed by law . . . . $_____
Transportation to . . . . $_____
TOTAL $_____
_____No._____

WITNESS TO SIGNATURE

317

FORM FOR PURCHASING UNITED STATES SAVINGS BONDS

DATE_____19___

** All information must be printed or typewritten **

I. S. P. JOLIET
Chief Clerk's Office

☐ CO-OWNER   ☐ BENEFICIARY
(Check one of the above.)

Miss   Last Name
Mrs.   Given first name   Initial   City   State
Mr.   Name of Street
          Street No.   AMT. TO BE DEDUCTED_____ Cost

No. BONDS_____DENOMINATION_____ Mat. Value _____No._____

INMATES' FULL NAME_____ First   Initial   Last Name   No._____

INMATES' SIGNATURE_____WITNESS_____ Officer

APPROVED_____ Warden

318

INMATES TRUST FUND

Recapitulation of disbursements for_____19____

	STATEVILLE	JOLIET BR.	IMPREST P & D REPL.	MISC. REPL.	TOTAL	DAILY P & D
Imprest Fund						
Harris Trust						Ch'k Nos. Inc.
Fr. Nat'l Lkpt.						to
Bk:						to
TOTALS						

ORDER BLANK 319

Newspapers—Magazines—Books

Cellhouse_____Register Number_____ Name_____ (Print Name)

Please order and charge to my account :_____

Subscription for { _____ months   Is this a renewal?_____   Price_____
                  { _____ years

Publisher's name and address_____

Answer YES or NO to renewal_____

Signed_____ Keeper_____
        (Inmate)

Fill in completely; give all information possible. If order is for subscription, indicate how many months or years
_____ Send order to Chief Clerk's office on Monday.

320

NAME_____

NO._____

DATE OF ORDER	ORDERED	VENDER	AMOUNT	DATE REC'D	REMARKS
It is an institutional rule	that all newspaper, magazines,				
records, etc. must be ordered	through the institution. W				
card is filled out and when	the material is received it is				
Anything not ordered through	the institution is returned to				

Fig. 321. The face of the jacket is self-explanatory. You will note that notations are made of any escape or attempted escape and of any prison or jail sentence which the inmate may have served previous to his incarceration here. Notation is also made of any connection the inmate may have had with narcotics; also, if he is wanted by other authorities upon his release from here, this information is given on the jacket.

Fig. 322. The violations recorded on the back of this jacket are only those when the inmate is placed in Isolation, not violations when the inmate is denied any privileges such as earphones, movies, ball games or reprimanded and excused.

Fig. 323. This card is kept in cell house to record inmate's cell partners, dates in cell and date of transfer. Earphone numbers and cell numbers are also recorded.

Fig. 324. This card is used in the Senior Captain's office. Offense and nature of violation is recorded on this card. Also, what disciplinary action if any is recorded under column "Disposition."

Fig. 325. After obtaining officer's signature on inmate leaving the Institution on Court Order, this receipt is kept in inmate's jacket.

Fig. 326. Approximately two months prior to the inmate's release by expiration of sentence, this form is prepared in the Record Office and sent to the prison physician who records any illness or disability the inmate might have. It is the general rule to give all inmates $25.00, however, in hardship cases it is quite customary that they receive the maximum, which is $50.00. When processed by the prison physician he in turn returns it to the warden's office and it is later filed in the Record Office jacket.

Fig. 327. When inmates leave the institution by discharge, parole or is returned to court by some type of writ, he is fingerprinted and photographed. Fingerprints are checked with the prints on file in the Bureau of Identification for comparison and to make sure we are releasing the correct inmate.

Fig. 328. This form is sent to the Record Office requesting information. When given to the inmate, he receipts for the papers on the back and it it filed in his jacket in the Record Office.

Fig. 329. Form used by Mail Office to secure signature of inmate for registered, certified, special delivery, etc., mail.

Fig. 330. Form used by Mail Office advising inmate as to whether person is on approved mailing and visiting list.

321   00000

REG. NO. _____

Name John Doe
     Joe Doe
Bureau _____
Associates _____
Rec'd Jol October 20, 1950   Trial Judge Wilberg
Crime Murder   State's Atty. John S.
                              County Cook
Sentence 15 years   Court Term September
Pleaded Verdict   Date of Sentence Sept
Color Negro Age 42 (5/5/08) Hair Ky blk   Case No. 50 - 122
Nationality Negro Build Sl Long Weight 170   Eyes
Nativity La. Religion Baptist Education 8gr   Heig
Married Yes Wife Living Yes Children 2   Fath
Occupation Interior Decorator Left Home 19   Mo
Correspondent Wife, Mrs John Doe, 555 East St   Pa
Smokes Drinks   PREVIOUS CRIMINAL RECORD

1 term S.P. Jackson, Michigan
1 term H of C, Chicago, Ill

322   PROGRESSIVE MERIT SYSTEM
GRADE
E
D
C 10/20/50
B 1/20/51
A 4/20/51

DATE	PUNISHMENT RECORD	STAFF ORDER	DATE	PUNISHMENT RECORD
5/2/51	Gambling with inmates	(7)		
9/24/52	Having contraband coffee in cell	(2)		
5/4/53	Talking back to	(7)		

323 (earphone #)
Reg. No. 00000 Assign V.S. 1161 Cell No.
Name John Doe   Partners   Cell
Received 11/7/50 from D.D.   29777   352B 11/7
Cell No. 352B   30296   358B 11/1
                         30296   363B 12/2
Sentence 15 years   29165 32284 319C 2/26
                         52284 28395 323C 3/15
Transfer 3B2 Shots 11/9/50   25765 10901 202C 4/14
5B Coal 12/22/50   37105   319D 8/3
3C Voc. Sch. 2/26/51   35095
3D Tailor Shop 8/3/55   42021   412C 5/1
                                   (over)

324   Name John Doe
Number 00000   Murder
Color Negro Crime   County
Received 10/20/50   Assigned 3/8/51
Occupation Interior Decorator   3B Tailor 4/0-03 Discharged
Board Action
Criminal History SP Jackson, Mich. as #00000 (Larceny Store) 1933-Disch. Exp. 8/30/36.
H. of C. Chicago, Ill. (ADW Knife) 1948 -10 days

326
Name John Doe
Received from Cook   DATE May 9, 1959
Murder   NUMBER
                          County   10/20/50
being discharged by expiration of sentence on charges of Murder under sentence of 15 years   years
this 19 day of July, 1959, from the Illinois State Penitentiary, Joliet,
Assetd.
I, Joseph E. Hagen, Warden of the above designated Institution, recommend the payment of
to the above-styled inmate, and the reasons for my approval therefore are:

                              Warden
Neg. No recommendation. PRISON PHYSICIAN DATE

BUREAU OF IDENTIFICATION
STATEVILLE
327
                              DATE: February 16, 1954
Warden
Illinois State Penitentiary
Joliet, Illinois   SUBJECT: John Doe # 00000
                    RELEASED ON order of HC AD Testificandum
                    Writ to Cook Co. (2/16/54)

Dear Warden:
This is to certify that I have on this date fingerprinted and photographed
th   of his fingerprints find them to be
id

BUREAU OF IDENTIFICATION
STATEVILLE
327
Warden   DATE: July 19, 1959
Illinois State Penitentiary
Joliet, Illinois   SUBJECT: John Doe #00000
                    RELEASED ON DISCHARGED EXPIRATION OF SENTENCE.
Dear Warden:
This is to certify that I have on thi
the above subject; and upon comparis
Identical with those taken when he wa
(over)

328   Illinois State Penitentiary
       INMATE REQUEST
VOCATIONAL SCHOOL NO. 2   3/8/51
         ASSIGNMENT   DATE
To RECORD OFFICE
Inmate No. 00000
Name John Doe
Wishes to interview you in regards to
A copy of Indictment Papers, Mittimus,
                    /s/   Keeper
13   (over)
Officer /s/   329
Please have the following inmate sign for
  ☐ Registered Mail
  ☐ Certified Mail   Date
  ☒ Legal Documents
  ☐ Special Delivery
From:
                    John Doe # 00000
Return this form to the mail office. (Inmate's Signature)

330
Inmate John Doe   Date
The below named person has, has not, been placed on
your approved Mail and Vist List.

                              Mail Office
The inmate is notified if the visitor has
or has not been approved.

Fig. 331. The information on the front of this card is completed on all new arrivals at the Diagnostic Depot and forwarded to the Record Office at Stateville. On the back of the card you will note the violations of the rules are recorded. In the event the inmate loses Statutory Good Time or is demoted in grade, the reason for the demotion or loss of good time is recorded on this card by the clerk in the Record Office.

Fig. 332. This memorandum card is part of the inmate's Record Office jacket. The information recorded on this card is entered by one of the clerk's in the Record Office.

Fig. 333. Inmate Report Forms: This form is completed by employees who report to the Senior Captain any inmates who violate the institution rules. The disciplinarian who interviews the inmate regarding the report records on this form the disposition taken — whether the denial of earphones for a certain number of days, the denial of movie pictures, ball games or whether reprimanded and excused or whether placed in isolation for any number of days, but in no instance over 21 days.

Discharged: 7/17/59

PROGRESSIVE MERIT SYSTEM
ILLINOIS STATE PENITENTIARY

ASSOCIATE.

331

NO. 00000

COUNTY Cook

NAME JOHN DOE   COLOR Negro   EDUCATION 8th Grade

CRIME Murder   RECEIVED 10/20/50   SENTENCE 15 years.

GRADES		WORK ASSIGNMENT	F.B.I. RECORD	ADDITIONAL INFORMATION
C	10/20/50		SP Jackson Mich. #00000 (Larc Store) 1933 -	
B	1/20/51		Disch Exp: 8/30/36.	
A	4/20/51		H of C Chicago, Ill (ADW) Knife) 1948 - 10 days	

333

ILLINOIS STATE PENITENTIARY

INMATE REPORT

00000   Date 4/15/58   195

ASSIGNMENT 3 D Tailor

INMATE John Doe

Is Reported For concealing at 9:...   ...traband box
with small amount of grease ...
box. He had it inside of ...
ankle when I shook him dow...
room ticket. Said it was ...
beside the point, he als...
out of writing a violat...

den. 15 d...

332

Name John Doe   No. 00000

MEMORANDA

To be used for additional information when inmates Jacket ... have space.

333

ILLINOIS STATE PENITENTIARY

INMATE REPORT

No. 00000   Date 11/3/58   195

ASSIGNMENT 3-D Tailor Shop

INMATE John Doe

Is Reported For Talking in the big dining room ...
after the bell had rang and inmates were going
back to cell house. He was seated on 8 stand
the second supper ...
the above date.

PUNISHMENT RECORD

...d additional punish.
...space is filled. Plus

...is part of the inmate's Record Office
...tion recorded on this card is entered
...in the Record Office.

333

ILLINOIS STATE PENITENTIARY

INMATE REPORT

00000   Date 1/10/58   195

ASSIGNMENT 3 D Tailor

INMATE John Doe

Is Reported For having a machine needle and solder
in his bunk. This afternoon on a shake down
we found this machine needle and this solder
on th... ...tom of the inmates earphone box.

333

ILLINOIS STATE PENITENTIARY

INMATE REPORT

No. 00000   Date 9/8/57   195

ASSIGNMENT 3 D Tailor

INMATE John Doe

Is Reported For contraband in his cell. This afternoon we shook down cell 319 and found this
hot wire hidden in a cadet coat and the
sharpened nail in the desk. This is on one
of three inmates in the cell.

333

ILLINOIS STATE PENITENT...

INMATE REPORT

No. 00000   Date 6/27/56   195

ASSIGNMENT 3 D Tailor

INMATE John Doe

Is Reported For Talking in the waiting r...
barber shop.

333

ILLINOIS STATE PENITENTIARY

INMATE REPORT

No. 00000   Date 5/4/55   195

ASSIGNMENT 3-D Tailor Shop

INMATE John Doe

Is Reported For Disobedience

10 days Isolation

333

ILLINOIS STATE PENITENTIARY

INMATE REPORT

No. 00000   Date 2/2/55   195

ASSIGNMENT 3-C Vocational School

INMATE John Doe

Is Reported For Not working as told

5 days Isolation

333

ILLINOIS STATE PENITENTIARY

INMATE REPORT

No. 00000   Date 12/1/54   19...

ASSIGNMENT 3-C Vocational School

INMATE John Doe

Is Reported For Possessing contraband wire a...
having a razor blade

10 days Isolation

333

ILLINOIS STATE PENITENTIAR...

INMATE REPORT

No. 00000   Date 9/7/54   195

ASSIGNMENT 3-C Vocational School

INMATE John Doe

Is Reported For Talking in barber shop w...
when told to be quiet he told the o...
to mind his own business

2 days Isolation

333

ILLINOIS STATE PENITENTIARY

INMATE REPORT

No. 00000   Date 5/6/53   195

ASSIGNMENT 3-C Vocational School

INMATE John Doe

Is Reported For Talking back to an officer

7 days Isolation

Fig. 334. Inmates write Special Letters to Courts, Attorneys, etc., on this type of letter. The coupon is filed in Inmate's Mail Office Jacket.

Fig. 335. Mail jacket. Maroon colored 4 x 9 filing envelope.

Fig. 336. This is regular letterhead paper issued to each inmate each Sunday in order to write to approved persons on his list.

Fig. 337. Form used for recording receipt of inmate's mail.

Fig. 338. Classification reports are prepared on all new arrivals by a member of the Classification Board and copies are forwarded to the Record Office, Senior Captain and Superintendent of Prisons.

334

Initials of approving Officer: _____

TO

NAME _____

STREET AND NUMBER _____ BOX 1112

CITY _____ STATE _____ 19___ JOLIET, ILLINOIS

TO INSURE PROMPT DELIVERY
PLACE INMATE'S NUMBER ON ALL
MAIL ADDRESSED TO HIM.

334

1 NUMBER _____ DATE _____

2 Censored and approved by: _____

3 NAME _____ LETTER SENT TO FOLLOWING ADDRESS:

4 IF WRITTEN FOR ONE INMATE BY ANOTHER, ENTER NAME NAME _____
   AND NUMBER OF THE ACTUAL WRITER IN SPACE BELOW

5 WRITTEN BY _____ STREET AND NUMBER _____

   CITY _____ STATE _____

6 NUMBER _____ RELATIONSHIP _____

7 INMATE'S NAME AND NUMBER MUST BE SIGNED AT THE BOTTOM DO NOT WRITE BELOW THIS LINE
   OF THIS LETTER AND CORRESPOND WITH THAT ON THIS COUPON.

   DEATH ☐ EMPLOYMENT ☐ OTHER REASON ☐
8 SICKNESS ☐ PAROLE ☐
9 BUSINESS ☐ CASE ☐
10

S P E C I A L

335

336

Relationship of Address _____

For prompt delivery address reply
the same as the heading at right.

Name _____

Street _____

City _____ State _____

Do not write in the space above

Register Number _____

Name of Sender _____ (Written)

Box 1112

Joliet, Illinois

NAME 337 NUMBER

INCOMING MAIL

		1951									
1	Wife Mary L. Doe 5432 East St Chicago Ill	1/3	1/13	4/5	4/5	4/5	4/5	4/5	4/5	4/5	10/15
2	Friend Rev C E Doe Chicago Ill										
3	Friend E Olson Odee Chicago Ill										

... paper issued to
... in order to write to
... list.

φ 00000 Doe, John

CLASSIFICATION REPORT - November 20, 1950   - 2 -

... of Argo and almost one year for the Michael
... occasions; the first time in 1926, with
... born to this union. His most
... in August, 1948. There are
... union, although inmate tells me
... time of this offense, but inmate
Leisure time activities have been
... boards, etc.

... well-built individual who is pleas
... during the interview situation. He
... citation being the functional loss of
... this, but this does not seem to be
... first was purelyan economic crime, and
... in his statements that he definitely
... ment, and that he tried to make it the
... get a true story of the same offense, wit
... inmate does maintain that the trouble was
... explosive temper, but does admit that
... first real serious trouble he has gotten
... of person, who takes an indifferent at
... a full anti-hostic course in Detroit,
... at during his stay in Michael Reese Hospi
... that he was cured

... Without psychosis or intellectual defect.
... improvable offender. Problematic to
... ionality. Dull intelligence by clinical
... Army Alpha, and no further psychometric

... Department.

... should first go to school then home further
... quired.

Wilson M. Menke (Chairman)
Classification Board

338

STATE OF ILLINOIS
DEPARTMENT OF PUBLIC SAFETY
DIVISION OF THE CRIMINOLOGIST

JOLIET DIAGNOSTIC DEPOT ___ UNIT

CLASSIFICATION REPORT

Name JOHN DOE

Crime: Murder

No. 00000 Age 43 Date November 20, 195_ Sentence: 15 yrs.

OFFENSE:

Inmate was found guilty by a jury in Cook County and was sentenced to
serve a 15 year term for murder. According to the State's Attorney's
The deceased had so weapon in his hand, when killed by inmate. Inmate, our inmate stabbed a man during an argument under a "T" structure at 2300 Back 31St.,
a rather lengthy story of the ... inmate leading up to by inmate. Inmate admits his guilt but tells
with his mother-in-law wife at a tavern, and they were separated for a couple of minutes at closing
time, and his wife stabbed to walk down the street. He maintains that he was out
this fellow as they went under the "L". We started to follow me and sought to pull away from
I was and at him for molesting my wife, didn't know what he had in his pocket, and I swung at me.
... One witness testified about the argument over my connectio wife, but he didn't see him
did me. A 'decembered' when I thought was a policeman came across the street, and I stabbed
... had helped in Court if a statement could have been leading to me not badly. I feel I could
... ald for the picion right there. I took the victim was an a jury trial, and At my trouble and if he had been
... ring up the fact that the victim was an a jury trial, and At my impossible for my lawyer to
... and had a very bad record in the neighborhood? It allowed him in the Penitentiary several
... ot that I had even been in trouble, but that was 15 years ago.

PRISON RECORD:

Inmate's previous record includes:
The Penitentiary for breaking into ... in 1928; a 2-8 year sentence in one City, ... room in
... days in the House of Correct ... a share between 1-28-33 and ... in the ... Michigan
... It with a deadly weapon. According to ... inmate ... in 1946 and 3-0-34. Since then Michigan
... by himself in Detroit during the Depression, and the ... sentence was out $12.00 fine for
... was with his mother during the Depression, and the jail sentence in 1946 was for a scrap

AL FACTORS:

This 43 year old ... is the only child born ...
Doris, inmate ... to 5-4-02. Who born to a Negro family is now
... that he has remarried. He stated that he was ... providing an opportunity Anxious a year ...
... was with his mother until it ...
... shared to the ...

Fig. 339. Booklet containing Correspondence and Visiting Regulations for individuals on inmate's visiting and correspondence list.

Fig. 340. This jacket is kept at the Information Desk office until inmate is released and then forwarded to Record Office and inserted in the inmate's jacket.

339

REGULATIONS

INMATES VISITS AND CORRESPONDENCE

JOLIET - STATEVILLE BRANCH

ILLINOIS STATE PENITENTIARY

JOSEPH E. RAGEN

WARDEN

339

A correct method for addressing your envelope is indicated by the sample:

John Doe
250 Clark Street
Elmview, Illinois

Place
Stamp
Here

Mr. James Doe
Box 1112   Joliet, Illinois
Reg. No. 91836

Since it is always possible that in the process of censoring, your letter could become separated from the envelope, you should include the inmate's name and number in the upper part of the first page of your let-

as he may deem improper. All outgoing and incoming mail will be censored. Correspondence should be confined strictly to family matters and must not include criminal or objectional matter.

It is permissible for you to send snapshots, or photographs; but they must not contain nude or suggestive poses. Do not send more than five photographs at one time. The maximum size of permitted photographs is eight by ten inches, and snapshots are preferable. Please do not send pamphlets, newspaper clippings, letters from other persons, etc., unless they contain important news of a member of the immediate family.

Certified checks, postal or express

339

proved visits. It is necessary that you show proper identification and permit a personal search for items of contraband, such as pocket knives, cigarette lighters, pens and pencils, medicine, drugs, etc. Persons carrying a weapon or under the influence of liquor will not be permitted to visit. Ladies must dress in conservative clothing. If their costumes are too provocative, visits will not be permitted.

While in the visiting room, remember that profanity or unusually loud talk are not permitted. If you have young children, keep them under control. Do not let them run and distract others. There are no provisions for serving meals to visitors.

You will find the employees of the prison courteous and cooperative, and we solicit

stances. We sincerely hope that you will accept these rules as a measure of institutional security and not as intentional harrassment. It is our sincere wish that you visit your relative or friend confined here; but we will protect ourselves against the occasional person who would commit a thoughtless or criminal act.

339

...or as a correspondent must accept this ...final.

...uld an inmate later wish to add a ...person to his list, he may make op...on and after proper check, if found ...ble, the person can be added. How...o inmate will be allowed to have an ...ve number or correspondents and

...ate may receive visits once every ...the hours of 8.00 a.m. ...ception of Sun-
...accom-

339

In the event of serious illness or injury, ...eath of an inmate, the person named ...e inmate or his nearest relative will be ...d promptly by telegram ...es via any other media. Unconfirmed ...ed as the work of cranks. The dis...apital is well equipped and staff. ...inmate who becomes ill or injured ...ve proper care.

...DING ESCAPE) III 228, p. 92
...hoever conveys into the penitentiary, ...any jail or other place of confine...g disguise, instrument, tool or weap...g adapted or useful to aid a pris...king his escape, with intent to ...escape of any prisoner ...mitted or detained ...or aids, abets

339

...visit, write or in any way demonstrate in...terest in them.

...ooklet is confined to the general ...s of the prison relating to visits and con...inmates. Special problems and con...may arise from time to time which ...uire additional rules and regula...order for proper controls to be ...ed. When such become necessary, ...to be regarded in the same man...hose set forth in this handbook.

...als of the prison are fully aware of ...d that inmates may derive from ...those sincerely interested in their ...ent. Visits by those with proper in...will abide by the rules and regu...are welcomed in the interest of the ...concerned. You can assist the insti...fficials in the discharge of their du...he inmate and society; while at the

---

The complete visiting schedule is as follows:

STATEVILLE BRANCH
Monday through Friday
  8.00 a.m. to 3.00 p.m. — 2 adults —
  1 hour
Saturdays
  8.00 a.m. to 3.00 p.m. — 1 adult —
  ½ hour
Outside Details
  Saturday only — 8.00 a.m. to 3.00 p.m.

JOLIET BRANC
...day through Friday
...to 3.00 p.m. — 2 adults —

...from any jail, prison, or any lawful deten...tion whether such escape is attempted or ...effected or not or conceals or assist or ...convict after he has escaped, shall upon ...ty as the prisoner whom he aided or abet...ted, except that in case the prisoner is sen...tenced to death, the penalty shall be ...shall be imprisonment for life in such aid ...tentiary. (As amended by act ...6, 1927.

L. 1927, p. 398)

VISITORS
When a ...role

same time, you may save yourself time, expense and many inconveniences by following the directions given herein.

GENERAL
1. Office hours of the institution are from 8.00 a.m. to 3.00 p.m., Mondays through Fridays. If phone calls are considered necessary, they should be made during office hours. Calls at other hours are many times incomplete. More detailed information can be obtained by correspondence. Inquiries relative to inmates must be addressed to the Warden of the prison. Always use the **name and number** of the inmate about whom you are making inquiry.

Phone Numbers   **Address**
Joliet Branch 2-3741   P. O. Box 1112
Stateville   7-3607   Joliet, Illinois

340

RECEIVED	CRIME	AGE	RACE	NUMBER		FAITH	ASSIGNMENT
10/20/50	Murder	42	Negro	00000		Baptist	put in pencil
COUNTY	SENTENCE			NAME			GRADE
Cook	15 years			John Doe			

LAST VISIT

APPROVED VISITORS

1. ~~Mother~~ - Ann Doe
2. Father - Henry Doe
3. Wife - Mary L. Doe
4. Friend - Rev. C. E. Doe
5. Friend - Ellison Doe

DATE OF:

2/7/59	5-3
3/7/59	4-3
4/7/59	5
5/7/59	5-3
6/7/59	5-3
7/7/59	3
8/7/59	4-5

NOT PERMITTED TO VISIT

Brother - Mike Doe - X-Con

340

VISITORS PASS   **1**

Illinois State Penitentiary

Pass *Mary L. Doe*

To Interview Room

Visit Inmate No. *00000*

SIGNED */s/ By Officer in Charge*

Form 3885-VS—18M—12-57

340

John Doe   NO. *00000*

NAME *Mary L. Doe*

ADDRESS *555 East St*

CITY *Chicago*   STATE *Ill*

RELATION *Wife*

NAME _____

ADDRESS _____

CITY _____   STATE _____

RELATION _____

Form 3886A—VS—4M—12-56

Fig. 341. Folder containing pertinent information for use by Parole Board, et al., and filed in inmate's jacket in Record Office.

Fig. 342. This form is prepared under the supervision of the Captain in Charge of the Diagnostic Depot and the information on this form is obtained from an interview with the inmate. Copies are distributed to the Record Office, Senior Captain and Division of Criminologist.

Fig. 343. This form is completed by the Identification Officer and is forwarded to the Record Office to be filed in the inmate's jacket.

Fig. 344. Inmate's Examination Statement.

Fig. 345. Transfer Orders on inmates who are at the Diagnostic Depot are prepared by the Classification Board and forwarded to the Superintendent of Prisons for his signature. The original copy is returned to the Superintendent of Prisons and copies are distributed to two copies to the Diagnostic Depot, one copy to the Record Office and one copy to the Parole and Pardon Board. The date of transfer out of the Diagnostic Depot is recorded on the back of the transfer order by a clerk in the Record Office and the Warden's signature is stamped on each copy prior to the distribution.

Fig. 346. A copy of the arrest record of all men received from court or when received in transfer from another state prison is forwarded to this institution by the Federal Bureau of Investigation, Washington, D. C. It is first sent to our Bureau of Identification where copies of his arrest record is made and furnished to the Senior Captain, Parole and Pardon Board, Division of Criminologist and Sociologist. His arrest record is recorded in the Bureau of Identification and the original is sent to the Record Office where it is filed in the inmate's jacket.

341

00000

BOARD
STATEMENTS

BUR. OF INV. [ ]

TRANSFER ORDER
& CLASSIFICATION [ ]

EXAMINATION SHEETS [ ]

---

342   ILLINOIS STATE PENITENTIARY

EXAMINATION BLANK

Name John Doe .... Alias ... Joe Doe .... Number 00000
Received 10-20-50 .... County ... Cook ... Color .. Negro .. Age .. 42
Crime Murder .... Sentence 15 yrs.
Date of Birth May 5, 1908 Nativity New Iberia La. Father La. Mother La.
Citizenship American .... Father American .... Nationality Afro-American
How Long in U.S. Life .... Naturalized .... Alien
Parents Living Father .... of death Unknown
Living Together No
Married Parents Yes
Conditions Marginal
Before 14 Years of Age
Inmates of Penal Institution
  8th grade
  None
  Interior Decorat...

---

343   PERSONAL PROPERTY

INMATE NO. 0000000   Date 10-20-50

CASH: $2.50   NAME: JOHN DOE

CHECKS: None   COLOR: Negro

MONEY ORDERS: None

Valuables forwarded to
Chief Clerk's Office: None

Contraband Articles:
1 tube toothpaste

EXAMINATION OF PRISONER 344   No. 00000

Name John Doe   Court (term) Sept.

Alias Joe Doe   Received Oct 20 1950   County Cook

                        Crime Murder

Associates None   Sentence 15 yrs.   Court Record
                         Race Negro   Chew No
Religion Baptist   Height 5-9 pl   Drink Yes
                         Weight 170   Smoke Yes
Occupation Int. Decorat Build Sl hvy   Drugs No
  Illt. ☐ H.S. ☐ Yrs. Teeth Getting poor
  Read ☐ Gr.S. ☑ Grd.
  Write ☐ Coll ☐ Yrs.

What age earned own living? 19

Working at time of arrest? yes

If not, how long unemployed?

Average weekly earnings $ 35

Longest period of employment 3 years

Father's name Henry Doe

EYES	NOSE	HAIR	COMPLEX
Dk brn rt eye; left		Ky blk cut	
cataract upr lft eye	short	Fair
sl dkr & turns	Rect	GrEd	Light
outward	Sinuous	Ky	Floc
Off Col	Twisted	Cur	Ruddy
Cata	Crushed	Wavy	Sall
Remarks:	Br. Ridge	Str't	Negro
	Remarks:	Friz	Mex
		Wooly	Remarks:
	3tr	Bald: Temp	Sl dk
		Back	
		Top	

the articles returned to me, con-
...perty I had in my possession upon
State Penitentiary. I understand the
...ad are not permissible and you here
...m as you see fit.

JOHN DOE
Inmate's Signature

---

345   STATE OF ILLINOIS
       DEPARTMENT OF PUBLIC SAFETY

TRANSFER ORDER NO. 000000

In accordance with and pursuant to the power vested in the
Act in relation to the Illinois State Penitentiary, and to repe...
June 30, 1933, as amended,
No. 00000 an inmate of the Illinois State Penitent...
is hereby ordered transferred to the Illinois State Penitentiary.

Administrative Transfer—5-1-44

John Doe

Group III: Without psychosis or
defects. Questionably improvabl...
Problematic to doubtful prognosis.
Recommendation:
  Refer to Classification Report of M...
20, 1950   Stateville Di...

therefore it is ordered that the managing head of the division of said
...ve mentioned prisoner is incarcerated, transfer him from said division, c
...tiary. Joliet-Stateville Division, together with all p...
...and fingerprints, relating to his case; that the managing head of the divi...
...ate him there, until legally released, as though said prisoner had bee...
...is order is issued pursuant to authority given the...

---

346   Federal Bureau of Investigation   11-16-50   4190 fh
                                              J. Edgar Hoover
       United States Department of Justice   Director
40-48 M.B.   Washington, D. C.

The following is a transcript of the complete record appearing in the files of the Federal Bureau of Investigation
concerning number FBI 181 599 which number should be quoted in the future correspondence, including any disposition submitted.

I.S.P. COPY

The following is the record of F.B.I. number 181 599

Contributor of Fingerprints	Name and Number	Arrested or Received	Charge	Disposition
PD, Houston, Texas	John Doe #E-0000	4-27-27	Inv.	rel.
PD, Houston, Texas	Joe Doe #E-0000	10-26-28	burg.	
SF, Jackson, Mich.	John Doe #00000	9-29-33	Larc. (store)	2 to 4 yrs. 8-30-36 disc max.
Co Jail, Chgo. Ill	John Doe #00000	12-27-48	ADW	12-28-48 no M.C.
PD, Chgo.,Ill.	John Doe #D-00000	12-25-48	ADW knife	10 das. HC
Co Jail Chgo.,Ill.	John Doe # 0000000	5-26-50	manslaughter	6-30-50 cha changed to 10-20-50 s Pen. (15 y
	John Doe	10-20-50	Murder	15 yrs.

Figs. 347-352. In envelope: An outline in the procedure in selecting and approving inmates for assignment to the outside detail and then to the farm.

No. 00000 **347** Name John Doe   Interviewed In Re: Outside Detail

Age 29   Married Yes   Div.

Wife's Name Mary Doe   Live 111111 S. ___   Administrative Transfer 4-1-44

C	John	Age 9	Live
H		Age	Live
L		Age	Live
L		Age	Live
D		Age	Live
R		Age	Live
E		Age	Live
N			

Father William Doe   Live 11 ___

Mother Helen Doe   Live ___

B	Frank	
R		
O	Edward	
T		

Not wanted

OFFICE OF THE

SENIOR CAPTAIN

Discharge date
September 18, 1961

Record Clerk

STATE OF ILLINOIS
DEPARTMENT OF PUBLIC SAFETY

350   March 6   19 58

TRANSFER ORDER NO. 000000

in accordance with and pursuant to the power vested in the Department of Public Safety, by virtue of "A ___
Act in relation to the Illinois State Penitentiary, and to repeal certain parts of designated Acts" approv ___
June 30, 1933, as amended, ___   Menard Diagnostic

DOE, JOHN J.   State Penitentiary, Menard Diagnostic
Penitentiary, Menardville.

Never attempted
to escape.

Narcotics
charged from Army
of syphilis

348

Warden Joseph E. Ragen,
Stateville Branch.

Dear Sir:

Re: 100000 - John Doe

Subject was assigned to the outside detail on June 1 ___
He has earned - via seniority - a transfer to the farm.

The record clerk has searched the inmate's file and ___
below any added information or changes in record since hi ___
the outside detail.

We recommend his transfer from the outside detail t ___

Respectfull ___

Senior Cap ___

Approved: ___
Assistant Warden

---

349   Not wanted

OFFICE OF THE

SENIOR CAPTIAN

Discharge date
September 18, 1961

Warden Joseph E. Ragen,
Stateville Branch.

Dear Sir:

John Doe, #00000, white, was interviewed in re ___
transfer to the Outside Detail.

Received on September 19, 1950 to serve a sent ___
3 to 20 years for Robbery. He previously served 1 ___
House of Correction, Chicago, Illinois, and 1 term ___
State Reformatory, while his institutional record c ___
yard denial, 1 show denial, 1 earphone denial, 1 ba ___
and 2 isolation punishments. He is 29 years old; m ___
his wife, Mary, and a son, John, aged 9, live at 11 ___
Ashland Avenue, Chicago, Illinois. His parents, Mr ___
William Doe, live at 11111? South Ashland Avenue, C ___
Three brothers and two sisters live as follows: Fr ___
parents; Edward, 00 Adams Street, Peoria, Illinois; ___
whereabouts unknown; Martha, with parents; Mrs. Margaret Smith,
333333 N. Madison Street, Chicago, Illinois; Mrs. Helen Brown,
Milwaukee, Wisconsin, street address unknown. Receives regular
mail and visits and states he will rejoin his wife upon release.

352

STATE OF ILLINOIS
DEPARTMENT OF PUBLIC SAFETY
DIVISION OF THE CRIMINOLOGIST
MENARD D D   UNIT

CLASSIFICATION REPORT

00001-Menard

Name: DOE, John   Age: 27   A

Crime: Murder   3

OFFENSE & RECORD: This 27 year old white male was admitted on ___
County under a 99 year sentence for murder. ___
provides no details concerning the offense, except to state that ___
May Jo Doe, were arrested in Prosser, Washington and under questio ___
shot a Marine in Marion County, Illinois en 12-22-56. They were ___
to Illinois and en 1-8-58 subject entered a plea of guilty to the ___
cent newspaper accounts indicates subject's wife likewise plead gu ___
thirty year sentence to Dwight. Subject freely admits he is guilt ___
Marine in Marion County in 1956, but insists that the indictment o ___
of fact, namely the date of the crime, the manner of killing, and ___
the victim. According to inmate's account, he and his wife began ___
from San Francisco to Pennsylvania, reaching Illinois the afternoo ___
junction of bypass U.S. 50 and U.S. 50, near O'Fallion, they picke ___
enlisted man who told them he was enroute to some point in Indian ___
free service. Upon hearing of the impending discharge, subject de ___
probably carrying at least $300 and determined to rob him. A few ___
mentioned in conversation that he had noted their license plate nu ___
part of Pennsylvania they were from. At this point subject decide ___
to kill the youth in order to avoid any possibility of later ident ___
subject was driving, but shortly after entering Marion County, he ___
he had three rifles and a shotgun stored in the back seat. Some m ___
believed the Marine had fallen asleep, he selected a Winchester rif ___
one shot into the victim's back. He relates that the surprise of t ___
wife to temporarily lose control of the car and that, although she ___
ly, because the victim was thrashing about, it became necessary fo ___
front of the automobile and subdue him. When the victim was quie t ___
still alive, however. He reports they continued for about thirty minutes drivi ___
fore reaching the village of Luka, they drove about three hundred a ___
highway and dumped the still breathing body in a wooded grove. Su ___
then continued their drive to Pennsylvania, returned to the West Co ___
Idaho and Washington, and were arrested in Prosser, Washington on a ___
violation. Their confessions were apparently obtained after inform ___
police there through the wife's family that they had committed some ___
Previous record: While AWOL from the Army, subject was arrested an ___
years after a dyer act violation in Missouri in October 1952. This ___
and he was returned to military authorities who sentenced him to fi ___

351
(XX) Joe

ILLINOIS STATE PENITENTIARY

attempt escape or

EXAMINATION BLANK

Name   John Doe

Received   3-20-58   Alias   None   Number   0 0 0 0 1

Crime   Murder   County   Marion   Color   White   Age   27

Date of Birth   10-5-30   Sentence   99 yrs.

Citizenship   Amer.   Nativity   Wormleysburg, Pa.   Father   Pa.   Mother   Pa.

How long in U.S   Life   Father   Amer.   Nationality   Scotch-Irish

Parents Living   Mother   Naturalized   Alien

Marital State   Married   Father Died   1949   Mother Died

Parents Living Together   Until Father Died   Wife Living   yes   Number of Children   None

Born of Married Parents   yes   Divorced   Separated

Economic Conditions   Fair   Religion   None   Social Security Number   Unk.

Residence Before 14 Years of Age ___   Associates   May Doe   District ___

Re ___

Figs. 353-355. Completed questionnaires from inmate's correspondence and visiting list.

353

STATE OF ILLINOIS
William G. Stratton, Governor
DEPARTMENT OF PUBLIC SAFETY
General Office, Springfield

ILLINOIS STATE PENITENTIARY
JOLIET BRANCH
Joseph E. Ragen, Warden
JOLIET

Date: _____

ADDITION TO CORRESPONDENCE AND VISITING LIST
Return completed form to Warden Joseph E. Ragen,
Illinois State Penitentiary, Box 1112, Joliet, Illinois

Re: _____ Register No. _____
The above referred inmate was received at this institution on _____ from _____
County to serve _____ years, for the crime of _____

You have
He has requested permission for correspondence and visits. Before this request is approved, we ask that you complete the form on the reverse side of this letter and return same to me as soon as possible

If you do not return the completed form, it will be this inmate.

For your information, he is at present incarcerate inmate maintains a good record, he is permitted one va names are on his approved visiting list will be admitted son is permitted to visit. Members of the inmate's far

Visiting hours are from 8:00 A.M. to 3:00 P.M. on days. Daylight Saving Time as adopted.

Permission is granted the inmate to write one lette care to write, may be received by the inmate. Letters a and the inmate's name and number must appear on yo ible and written in English. All letters must bear name

No articles or merchandise of any kind are perm orders are permissible if properly named and numbered this institution. (Do not send cash.)

Most newspapers and magazines are permitted but otherwise, they will be returned to the sender.

354

STATE OF ILLINOIS
William G. Stratton, Governor
DEPARTMENT OF PUBLIC SAFETY
General Office, Springfield

ILLINOIS STATE PENITENTIARY
JOLIET BRANCH
Joseph E. Ragen, Warden
JOLIET

Date _____

CORRESPONDENCE AND VISITING QUESTIONNAIRE
Return completed form to Warden Joseph E. Ragen,
Illinois State Penitentiary, Box 1112, Joliet, Illinois

Re: _John Doe_ Register No. _0000_
The above referred inmate was received at this institution on _____ from _____
County to serve _____ years, for the crime of _____

He has requested permission to correspond with and receive visits from you. If you desire to do so, we ask that _____ the reverse side of this letter and return same to Warden Joseph E. Ragen, Illinois

ed that you do not wish to correspond or visit with

e Diagnostic Depot, Joliet, where he will remain for at the conclusion of which, he will be transferred to

ys after _____. After that time, if he rteen days However, only two persons whose names e with the exception of Saturday, when only one per- ill be given preference.

days only No visits are permitted on Sundays or Holi-

n week, but as many letters as relatives and friends be addressed to Post Office Box 1112, Joliet, Illinois. ter and your envelope. All correspondence must be leg- dress of writer.

from the outside; however cashiers checks and money may be used to make purchases at the Commissary at

must be ordered by the institution for the inmate.

Very truly yours,

Joseph E. Ragen
WARDEN

355

INMATES' MAILING LIST

I, _John Doe_, No. _00000_, an inmate of the Illinois State Penitentiary have read my rule book and have been advised by an officer in the school at the Diagnostic Depot of my privileges as an inmate of the I.S.P. and especially rules covering my visits and correspondents. Listed below are my prospective visitors and correspondents.

MARITAL STATUS: Single_____ : Married _X_ : Divorced_____ : Separated_____ : Common-law_____

WIFE'S NAME _Mary L. Doe_ ADDRESS _555 East Street Chicago, Illinois_

CHILDREN: _0_ AGE_____

FATHER LIVING_____ DECEASED _X ?_

FATHER'S NAME _____ ADDRESS _Unknown_

MOTHER LIVING_____ DECEASED _X_

MOTHER'S NAME _____ ADDRESS _____

STEP FATHER: _____

STEP MOTHER: _____

BROTHERS: _____

SISTERS: If married, give married name and address.

NON-FAMILY CORRESPONDENTS:

NAME	AGE	ADDRESS	OCCUPATION	RELATIONSHIP	TIME KNOWN
Rev. C. X. Doe		Chicago, Illinois		Friend	
Ellison Odoe		Chicago, Illinois		Friend	

For listing other correspondents use reverse side of sheet. Explain in detail why necessary

Fig. 356. This is a set of court papers received on each new arrival. This includes the Mittimus, Indictment and Statement of Facts. These are all retained in the Record Office jacket.

Civil Department
507 County Bldg.
Telephone FRanklin 2-3000

JOHN S. BOYLE
State's Attorney
of
COOK COUNTY, ILL.

Criminal Branch
26th & California
Telephone BIshop

356

Chicago 8, Illinois
October 2, 1950

PEOPLE OF THE STATE OF ILLINOIS) Indictment No. 50-1223
)
        - vs -   )
)
JOHN DOE, Age 43 years   ) MURDER

OFFICIAL STATEMENT OF FACTS

This matter came on to be heard on July 25, 1950, before the Honorable Wilbert
F. Crowley, one of the Judges of the Criminal Court of Cook County. A plea of not guilty
was entered and a jury trial was had. On September 29, 1950, the jury returned
of guilty and sentenced the defendant to the Illinois State
Fifteen Years.

No. 1

356

356
STATE OF ILLINOIS, }ss.
County of Cook.

PEOPLE OF THE STATE OF ILL

vs.

JOHN DOE

To the Department of Public Safet

In compliance with the

the sentence and commitmen of

system of parole and to repeal

June 25th, 1917) and particula

and for my official statement

vs.

General Number   50-1223

in the indictment

AND attach thereto a copy

a mittimus in the above

The name and res

Wilbert F. Crowley   627

Jurors:
Brightleys Severinghau
Janis Laughlin
Paul Meyer

STATE OF ILLINOIS,)ss.
County of Cook.)

I, Vincent J. Poklacki, Clerk of the Criminal Court of Cook County, in said
County and State, do hereby certify that the above and foregoing documents attached to
the copy of the judgment order or record of conviction, certified as a mittimus, are
respectively:

1. The Official statement of Vincent J. Poklacki, Clerk
   of the Criminal Court of Cook County.

2. The official statement of John S. Boyle, State's
   Attorney of Cook County, and concurred in by
   Wilbert F. Crowley
   Judge of the Criminal Court of Cook County.

3. Copy of Indictment.

in the above entitled cause, and same are hereby
Safety of

---

356 No. — 50-1223

Criminal Court of Cook County

Penitentiary Mittimus

Act of June 30, 1933

The People of the State of Illinois

vs.

John Doe

Term   Fifteen Years

Executed by delivering the body of the within named Defendant to the Department of
Public Safety this   20th
day of   OCTOBER   A.D. 19 50

ELMER MICHAEL WALSH
Sheriff

By   A. KAKIN
Deputy

RECEIVED AT DIAGNOSTIC DEPOT

JOLIET   OCT 20 1950

I. J. No.   56   356
General No.   50-1223
CRIMINAL COURT OF COOK COUNTY
June   Term, A.D. 19 50
The People of the State of Illinois
vs.
John Doe

INDICTMENT FOR
MURDER

A TRUE BILL

JOHN B. DIEZEL
Foreman of the Grand Jury

WITNESSES

JOHN J. SMITH
QUINTILLA PASSMORE
ESTELLE STEWART
WILLIAM LINDSAY

Filed   JUNE 30   19 50
By   Vincent J. Poklacki Clerk
Bail $ No Bail

---

356 G.J. No.
eneral
No.
Criminal Court of Cook County
Term, A.D. 19
The People of the State of Illinois
vs.

INDICTMENT FOR
MURDER

A TRUE BILL

FOREMAN OF THE GRAND JURY
WITNESSES

Filed   19
By   Clerk
Bail $

J. No.   356
eneral No.
CRIMINAL COURT OF COOK COUNTY
Term, A.D. 19
The People of the State of Illinois
vs.

INDICTMENT FOR

A TRUE BILL

Foreman of the Grand Jury
WITNESSES

Filed   19
By   Clerk
Bail $

---

356 G.J. No.
General
No.
Criminal Court of Cook County
Term, A.D. 19
The People of the State of Illinois
vs.

INDICTMENT FOR
MURDER

A TRUE BILL

FOREMAN OF THE GRAND JURY
WITNESSES

ed   19
Clerk
Bail

Fig. 357. Officers who escort inmates who are returned to court on Writ of Habeas Corpus or other court order are supplied at the Record Office with a copy of the prisoner's mittimus, a certification of the mittimus copy and a sheriff's receipt for transfer of custody.

357

UNITED STATES OF AMERICA

STATE OF ILLINOIS } ss. PLEAS, before a BRANCH of the CRIMINAL COURT

COUNTY OF COOK } ss. OF COOK COUNTY, in said County and State, at a term

thereof begun and held at the Criminal Court House in the City of Chicago, in said County, on the

first **Tuesday** being the **fifth** day of **September**_____, in the year of our

Lord one thousand nine hundred and **fifty** and of the Independence of the United

States the one hundred and **seventy fifth**_____

Present: HONORABLE **Wilbert F. Crowley**____

Judge of the **Superior**____Court of Cook County

and Ex-Officio Judge of the Criminal Court of Cook

County.

John S. Boyle, -   , State's Attorney)

Attest **Vincent J. Peklecki,** Clerk   **Elmer Michael Walsh**Sheriff of Cook County

BE IT REMEMBERED, to-wit: On the **twenty second ninth day of September**

in the year last aforesaid, it being the term of Court aforesaid, the following, among other proceedings, were had

and entered of record in said Court which said proceedings are in the words and figures following, to-wit:

THE PEOPLE OF THE STATE OF ILLINOIS,

vs.   INDICTMENT FOR **Murder**____

No. **50-1223**   _____

JOHN DOE   _____

This day come the said People, by   **JOHN S. BOYLE**_____State's Attorney,

and the said Defendant as well in his own proper person as by his Counsel also comes, and now neither the said

Defendant nor his Counsel for him saying anything further why the judgment of the Court should not now be

pronounced against him on the_____**verdict**

of guilty, heretofore rendered to the indictment in this cause.

THEREFORE, it is considered, ordered and adjudged by the Court that the said Defendant_____

John Doe_____is guilty of

in manner and form as charged in the indictment_____

_____**verdict**_____of gui

at hard labor in the Illinois State Penitentiary for s

in manner and form as charged in the indictment _____

whereof he stands convicted and adjudged guilty, for

from and after the delivery of the said De

to the Illinois State Penitentiary, and that the said D

be taken from the bar of the Court to the Common ja

by the Sheriff of Cook County to the Department of Pe

is hereby required and commanded to take the body

John Doe_____and confine him in sa

term of **Fifteen years**

he be thereafter discharged.

IT IS FURTHER ORDERED that the said Defend

issue therefor.

STATE OF ILLINOIS }

COUNTY OF COOK } ss.

I, **Vincent J.**

Cook County, in said County and State, do he

perfect and complete copy of an order entered

of the State of Illinois, versus_____**John Doe**

WITNESS **Vince**

SEAL Seal thereof, at Chica

day of_____**Septe**

To the Sheriff of Cook County to Execute

(SIGNED) _____

357

Sheriff's Receipt   (Prisoner on Writ)

(Or in Transit)

FEBRUARY 16,_____ 19 **54**.

in re : No. **00000**   **JOHN DOE**

A prisoner of the Illinois State Penitentiary, Joliet, Illinois, brought to ____**COOK**

COUNTY, on a writ of :

HABEAS CORPUS AD TESTIFICANDUM

or in transit.

The above named prisoner received into my custody, care and control from Joseph E Ragen, Warden of

the Illinois State Penitentiary, Joliet, Illinois, the purpose of such custody, care and control being safekeeping for

the said Joseph E. Ragen, Warden, and during the period of his stay in my County while on the above stated writ,

or in transit. Subject will be returned to the custody of Joseph E. Ragen, Warden, or his duly authorized represen-

tative upon order of the court.

I also acknowledge receipt of a certified copy of the prisoner's Penitentiary Mittimus, Indictment No

_____**50-1223**

Sheriff _____

County, Illinois

Deputy

Sheriff _____

County, Illinois

---

357   **ILLINOIS STATE PENITENTIARY**

JOLIET

State of Illinois)

) ss

Will County)

I, **James H. Dickson**_____, Record Clerk of the Illinois State Penitentiary at Joliet, Illinois and

Keeper of the Records and Seals of said institution, do hereby certify the within, above, and foregoing to be a true,

perfect and correct copy of a **MITTIMUS No. 50-1223**_____

now on file in my, the said, office in the Case of the People of the State of Illinois, vs_____

_____**JOHN DOE # 00000**_____

In testimony whereof I have hereunto set my hand and affixed the Seal of said institution at Joliet, Illinois, this_____

_____**14th**_____day of_____**February**_____A. D. 195_**4**

Record Clerk of the Illinois State Penitentiary at Joliet, Illinois.

INDEX